BOSE

BOSE

The Untold Story *of*
An Inconvenient Nationalist

CHANDRACHUR GHOSE

PENGUIN
VIKING
An imprint of Penguin Random House

VIKING

USA | Canada | UK | Ireland | Australia
New Zealand | India | South Africa | China | Singapore

Viking is part of the Penguin Random House group of companies
whose addresses can be found at global.penguinrandomhouse.com

Published by Penguin Random House India Pvt. Ltd
4th Floor, Capital Tower 1, MG Road,
Gurugram 122 002, Haryana, India

Penguin
Random House
India

First published in Viking by Penguin Random House India 2022

Copyright © Chandrachur Ghose 2022

All rights reserved

15 14 13 12 11 10

ISBN 9780670096008

Typeset in Adobe Caslon Pro by Manipal Technologies Limited, Manipal
Printed at Replika Press Pvt. Ltd, India

www.penguin.co.in

MIX
Paper from
responsible sources
FSC® C016779

Dedicated to my mother,
to whom I owe everything in life

Contents

1

The Early Years

The boys of the seventh class at the Ravenshaw Collegiate School, in Cuttack, rolled in laughter while the teacher read out an essay written in Bengali. The teacher occasionally paused to savour and comment upon the spelling, grammar and the style, and joined in the laughter. He was reading out an essay written by a boy who recently moved into the school from the very English Protestant European School. Although the boy was new to the school, he was treated with some respect for his knowledge of the English language and his reputation as a good student. Moreover, he came from a well-known family. His father was the first elected chairperson of the city municipality, and also the public prosecutor. The immediate reason for the burst of mirth in the class was the boy's poor knowledge of the Bengali language; that too, being a Bengali himself. It was ironic that learning this language was the reason for the boy changing schools, since the Calcutta University had made it a compulsory study in matriculation, intermediate and degree examinations. The diffident twelve-year-old at the receiving end of the ridicule was mortified, but at the same time made a calm resolve to overcome the shame. By the end of the year, the young boy with a heavy sounding name made good on the promise to himself. Subhas Chandra Bose scored the highest marks in Bengali in the annual examination.

Apart from this minor incident, moving to an Indian school from a European one helped Subhas in many ways. It led him to gradually break out of the shell of a lifestyle dictated by the goal of being a good boy: of being obedient to parents, of being studious, and of following in the footsteps of success laid down by older siblings. In what mattered most, he started making friends who became fellow travellers in the world of the development of an adolescent. The attention he received from teachers and

1

students also aided in overcoming his diffidence and to some extent his inherent shy nature. However, he remained unenthusiastic about games, his physical activities being limited to some gardening and gymnastics at home. 'Subhas couldn't do two things—drawing and drill,' recalled his classmate in the Ravenshaw Collegiate School.[1] Although he had to stop learning Latin after leaving the earlier school, he continued with learning Sanskrit from a pundit at home; and the Sanskrit lessons continued to reinforce the virtues of an obedient good boy. Seven years of being assessed on conduct, deportment, neatness and punctuality at the previous school had also left its mark on his mental make-up.

Belonging to an affluent family with an aristocratic lineage going back several centuries, headed by a self-made man who excelled professionally as a lawyer and made his mark in social and to an extent in political circles, life for Subhas was comfortable, but devoid of luxury. The large establishment comprising five older siblings, cousins, uncles and several attendants, made him feel insignificant, but also inculcated the values of sharing space. Absence of parochialism or religious discrimination in father Janakinath too made a lasting impact. Far from being irreligious, Janakinath was a religious eclectic, influenced by the Brahmo Samaj, as well as the Shakta and Vaishnava schools of Hinduism. Mother Prabhabati, a strong-willed lady in charge of the household, was also of a religious disposition.

Like most other children of that age, there was toying with choosing the right vocation in life, without getting fixated on any one of them, although the Indian Civil Service was referred to by his elders with a sense of awe amongst family circles. What was to be done in life was, therefore, not yet a burning problem. It, however, didn't take long to become one. Soon after settling down in the school, Subhas spotted the headmaster Beni Madhav Das and 'felt what I should now call an irresistible moral appeal in his personality . . . I secretly said to myself that if I wanted an ideal for my life, it should be to emulate him.'[2] Although Subhas adored Beni Madhav, it was from a distance, and he had to wait for two more years to have him as a teacher in his class. Subhas was fourteen, and Beni Madhav impressed upon his mind the moral values which became sort of a foundation for his further mental development. Beni Madhav was transferred from the school within a few months and life for Subhas yet again became a drab routine. According to a classmate, Subhas had a role in Beni Madhav being transferred. On the anniversary of Khudiram Bose's martyrdom, Subhas decided to observe the occasion. It was decided that the students would fast and hold a prayer meeting. When someone complained to the Divisional Commissioner about it, Beni Madhav was questioned about why he had not stopped the students—Beni Madhav replied that he had not felt the need to stop the students.[3]

After an emotional farewell, however, the teacher and the pupil 'started a correspondence . . . which went on for some years'.[4] Through this correspondence, Beni Madhav instilled in Subhas a habit of contemplating on nature. This, Subhas wrote many years later, helped him to concentrate his mind, as well as to appreciate the works of Wordsworth, Kalidas and fall back upon the Mahabharata (which he was studying in the original Sanskrit now) in a new light.

While Beni Madhav's guidance opened new horizons to an inquisitive and sensitive mind, it was not adequate to handle the challenge of negotiating the changes associated with the onset of puberty. Subhas came down hard on himself in dealing with the sexual aspects of development— he considered the sex consciousness 'unnatural and immoral'. His approach was to 'suppress or transcend' this new development. As he recounted later, it was at this stage that he started turning against 'the natural attraction of a worldly life and of worldly pursuits in general', though it is not clear what triggered the disinterest.[5]

It was at this time, grappling with the mental and physical changes, and trying to find something beyond what Beni Madhav's guidance could provide, that Subhas discovered Vivekananda.

I was barely fifteen when Vivekananda entered my life. Then there followed a revolution within and everything was turned upside down.[6]

This discovery helped settle his biggest question, that of the goal of life. *Atmanomoksharthamjagathitaya cha* ('for your own salvation and for the service of humanity'[7]), the motto of the Ramakrishna Mission formulated by Vivekananda, was to be the goal of life. Ramakrishna's teaching of renunciation of lust and wealth for attaining a spiritual life further accentuated Subhas's inner struggle.

Ramakrishna's example of renunciation and purity entailed a battle royal with all the forces of the lower self. And Vivekananda's ideal brought me into conflict with the existing family and social order.

Fortunately for Subhas, he found companions in his obsession with Ramakrishna and Vivekananda, who would discuss the ways of spiritualism over meetings, long walks and excursions. This individual and collective quest for spiritual progress led to a break with his past training of obedience: 'I no longer recited Sanskrit verses inculcating obedience to one's parents; on the contrary, I took to verses which preached defiance.'[8] Despite the apparent defiance, one of his favourite activities was reading out the Ramakrishna *Kathamrita* (the Gospel of Ramakrishna) to his mother.[9] Yogic exercises for concentration and self-mortification were seriously taken recourse to, in order to go beyond the theoretical (all these had to be away from the public gaze). But the realization soon dawned that although these helped in building self-confidence and improving self-control, the famed psychic powers were nowhere in sight. Hence, a search began for a guru, essential for guiding and leading to the goal of salvation.

However, the road to salvation laid down by Vivekananda was not only about practising yoga. No less important was the service of the downtrodden. Serving the poor, as taught by him, was the same as worshipping God. The young group thus started on this route too. They started visiting nearby villages offering their services. Subhas mentioned one instance in which they went and taught in the local school. While they were welcomed in some cases, in others, they were looked upon with suspicion. There was a transition from social service to national service when a visitor came to town with messages not thought about by Subhas or his group till then.

Around the time of Durga Puja (usually held in October) in 1912, Hemanta Kumar Sarkar, a fifteen-year-old boy from Krishnanagar in Bengal, stopped over in Cuttack on his way to Puri. Hemanta, who was about two months older than Subhas, was unwell, and the headmaster of his school—the Krishnanagar Collegiate School—Beni Madhav Das, had asked him to go for a change of place for some time. Beni Madhav was fond of Hemanta, a topper in his class, and sent him to meet Subhas with a letter of introduction; he wrote separately to Subhas asking him to accommodate Hemanta at his place. Hemanta, however, was hesitant to land up at Subhas's house, probably awed by the social status of the Bose family.[10] Coming to know that Hemanta had gone over to stay with another teacher in the town, Subhas was offended and went to meet him there. The two young boys instantly took a liking to each other. The next four days were spent in day-long discussions, often spilling over to late evenings; and thus started a relationship that endured through several emotional crests and troughs, spread over three decades.

Hemanta was already a member of a group led by Suresh Chandra Banerjee, a senior Medical College student in Calcutta. Banerjee and his associates, soaked in the philosophy of Ramakrishna–Vivekananda, aimed to build an ashram where the youth would dedicate their lives to nation building. The path of armed revolution chosen by some of his friends did not appeal to Banerjee.[11] The group had started recruiting students, who in due course, would materialize the goal. The members of the group vowed to remain celibate and dedicate their lives to the country.[12] Subhas was greatly impressed by Hemanta's narrative and became keen to join the group. Soon Banerjee wrote to him, after he heard about him from Hemanta, and this communication went on for many years.[13] The main thrust of Banerjee's letters was on the necessity of *Brahmacharya* (celibacy) and contemplation.[14] After Hemanta's return to Krishnanagar, Subhas wrote his first letter to him, in Bangla, which was stiff in style as if it were a translation of an English letter.[15]

With the passing of time, Subhas's spiritual quest became more serious, and his studies took a back seat, even though the final examinations in the school were approaching. Even gurus who were not religious mendicants or sannyasis seemed to lose their appeal to him. To add to the woes of his parents, Subhas now started going around providing relief to the sick amongst the poor, some of whom had contracted infectious diseases.[16] Beni Madhav's expectation that either Subhas or Hemanta would secure the first position in Calcutta University in the matriculation examination appeared almost impossible to fulfil. Subhas's hankering after a religious life, disobedience of parents and disregard for social norms disturbed Janakinath and Prabhabati enough to make them decide that Subhas should be moved out of Cuttack. Calcutta, a melting pot with a much larger and varied population, was more likely to cure him of his eccentricities, if Subhas could be pulled out of his group in the small town.

Subhas, however, surprised everyone with his results in the matriculation examination in 1913. Proving his brilliance as a student, he stood second in the university, falling short of his former headmaster's expectations by seven marks. He scored 609 out of a total of 700 marks, just behind the top score of 616.[17]

Following in the footsteps of his elder brothers, Subhas took admission for Intermediate Arts in the prestigious Presidency College, with Philosophy as the major subject. This decision was in keeping with his spiritual quest of that time: 'I was going to make a profound study of philosophy so that I could solve the fundamental problems of life.'[18] Fully aware that it was easy to get diverted from one's calling in as big a city as Calcutta with all its charm and lure, Subhas was nevertheless determined to stick to his path. He was going to follow Ramakrishna and Vivekananda in the practical life, as far as possible, and as he mentioned, 'In any case, I was not going in for a worldly career.'[19] Thus, as he stepped into college, Subhas had no long-term worldly ambition.

Subhas was more fortunate than his elder brothers in the matter of accommodation in Calcutta. Unlike his elder brothers Sarat and Satish, who had to stay in the Eden Hindu Hostel, Subhas stayed in the house built by Janakinath in 1909 at 38/2 Elgin Road.[20] Once in Calcutta, he met with Suresh Chandra Banerjee, leader of Hemanta's group, with whom he had been exchanging letters till now. Suresh used to live in a mess in Mirzapur Street[21] near the Calcutta University, which was the meeting place for the members of the group. Banerjee later wrote in his autobiography:

> The very first time I met him, I realised that one day he would be a great man. I shared my perception with others too . . . I used to say, 'Look the lion comes,' when I used to see him coming up to my room.[22]

With Hemanta and others, Subhas often travelled to Daulatpur College in Khulna, a key recruiting ground for the revolutionary groups and frequented by the top revolutionaries of the time, including Jatindranath Mukhopadhyay. In Daulatpur College, Subhas became acquainted with Bhupendra Kumar Datta, who would go on to join the Jugantar group.[23]

His parents' hope of seeing some more discipline in their son's life was, however, completely belied by his aggravating rebellious behaviour:

> At Cuttack, though I had regularly roamed about with my friends, I had never absented myself from home at night. But in Calcutta I would often be absent for days without obtaining permission.[24]

Before Hemanta left Cuttack, Subhas had promised to visit him after the examinations were over. Accordingly, in May 1913, Subhas, along with Suresh and a few others reached Krishnanagar. They took a short trip to Palashi (Plassey)—where the defeat of the last independent ruler of

Bengal, Siraj ud-Daulah, led to the establishment of the British rule in Bengal—and then on to Murshidabad, the capital of Bengal before the British era. Stopping over at Hemanta's relative's house in Behrampore, they walked 6 miles to Murshidabad, reading a history of the city on their way. One can well imagine the heady feeling of freedom among a bunch of teens who had broken away from the restraining gaze of elders in the household. One thing that hurt the sentiments of the young brigade was the indifference of the administration toward the tomb of Siraj ud-Daulah.[25] While Subhas joined Presidency College, Hemanta chose Krishnanagar College to continue with the activities of his group along with his studies.[26]

Subhas's reputation as a good student preceded him amongst student circles in Calcutta, especially due to his high rank in the matriculation examination.[27] One of the students who was greatly impressed by stories he heard about Subhas and waited eagerly to meet him was Dilip Kumar Roy—son of the famous poet, composer and playwright Dwijendra Lal Roy. Dilip, who studied in Calcutta's Metropolitan Institution, had bet on his classmate Khitish Prasad Chattopadhyay to top the matriculation examination; but to his disappointment Kshitish stood seventh in overall ranking.[28]

In college, Subhas spent considerable time on getting involved in the college magazine, the debating club, and setting up a fund for the poor. He became the leader of the First Year Debating Union,[29] the secretary of the college union in 1913–14,[30] and the secretary of the Flood and Famine Relief Committee.[31] Among the professors in the college were stalwarts such as Jagadish Chandra Bose and Prafulla Chandra Ray, and Subhas 'went out of my way to get acquainted with such professors . . . who did not belong to our department but was extremely popular with the students.'[32]

During the first-year vacations, immediately on returning to Cuttack, Subhas joined his friends in going out to localities to nurse people suffering from a cholera outbreak. After missing from home for a week, he was tracked down and brought back.[33]

This burst of varied activities such as 'organising debates, collecting funds for flood and famine relief, representing the students before the authorities, going out on excursions with fellow-students', started changing his outlook too. 'Very slowly I was shedding my introvert tendencies and social service was gaining ground on the individualistic Yoga.'[34] He started volunteering for a south Calcutta-based charity organization *Anath*

Bhandar, which required him to go begging from door to door for money and food, every Sunday. It was not easy for him with the kind of upbringing and family background he had, being overwhelmed by a 'sense of shame' by the act of begging, but that was probably the feeling that he strived to overcome, and so persisted with it. Stark poverty not only disturbed him, but goaded him into questioning the existing 'social system'. Social change was not an immediate possibility, so he started with himself. Most of the days he would give away the money he used to get from home as daily allowance, and would often walk to and from college.[35]

The inclination towards social service was increasing, but its connection with the spiritual side remained strong, and that probably prevented Subhas from being taken over by the political environment. Suresh had already introduced him to Jadugopal Mukherjee, the right-hand man of the then undisputed leader of the Bengal revolutionaries, Jatindranath Mukhopadhyay.[36] He was also acquainted with the secret revolutionary groups, particularly with those in the Eden Hindu Hostel.[37] It was natural that the secret revolutionary circles would try to induct him into their fold, as was usually the practice then, but according to Hemendranath Dasgupta who came to know Subhas from around 1915, the influence of Vivekananda stopped him from getting into politics, and he instead focused on the service of the sick and the poor.[38] Subhas later wrote that 'I often met . . . important men in the terrorist-revolutionary movement . . . But I was never drawn towards them . . . because I was then living in a world of my own and held that the ultimate salvation of our people would come through process of national reconstruction.'[39] At the same time, neither he nor anyone in his group had any clear conception of the shape of the final goal, or the ways to reach there.

So, the spiritual quest continued. During the winter vacation of 1913, the group decided to get down to the reality of living the life of ascetics. Off they went to an empty house in Shantipur on the bank of the Ganga, where they wore saffron clothes, and woke up in the darkness of the early morning to spend hours sitting in the cold river with water up to their necks. Back in Krishnanagar, Subhas and Hemanta started frequently visiting a hathayogi sannyasi of the Udasi Sikh community called Indradas Babaji. Subhas was greatly impressed by the sannyasi, for his 'complete renunciation of worldly desires, his utter indifference to heat, cold, etc., his mental purity and loving temperament'; this, however, did not last long, as Babaji disappeared one fine morning. But before leaving, Babaji had put the duo in touch with another sannyasi in Calcutta called Nanak Sharan Das Babaji.[40]

A more serious hunt for a guru began in the next summer. As the vacations commenced, Hemanta left with a teacher on a tour of northern India, purportedly in search of a spiritual guru. The deal was that if he found a guru, Subhas would join him. However, Subhas, not being able to wait, left soon, without informing anyone at home, joining Hemanta at Haridwar, from where they went to Rishikesh and then to Delhi.[41] To be able to make this trip Subhas borrowed money from a friend, which he later repaid from his scholarship. In Delhi, they parted from the teacher, put on saffron robes and travelled to Mathura, Vrindavan, Agra, Varanasi, Bodh Gaya and Gaya, visiting all the prominent religious and historical places in each city.[42]

Although no guru was to be found, the experience gained from this tour gave the young ones an insight into India. In Mathura they failed to find accommodation in a dharmashala as the authorities feared police harassment on account of providing shelter to two young Bengalis, who could turn out to be revolutionaries. Finally, they were put up in a dark and dirty corner of a building, having almost run out of money. They spent some time with a sannyasi in Mathura learning about various aspects of the different Yogas and other religious scriptures. In Kusum Sarovar, Mathura, where they spent three days while they stayed with Haricharan Das Babaji, the Vaishnav Guru of the Raja of Scindia, they went around interacting with other sannyasis, gathering their views and trying to assimilate as much spiritual knowledge as possible. One of them, a Bengali Vaishnav sadhu, explained to them that the different religions were but different paths leading to the same goal, and advised them to adhere to any one religious path and conduct sadhana accordingly. After they had spent a few days learning the Vaishnav texts from him, he suggested that they go to Varanasi, as he thought that the Vedanta school of philosophy would be more suited to their logical temperament. So off they went to Varanasi, stopping over at Agra on their way. At Varanasi, Swami Brahmananda, who knew Subhas's family well, asked them to stay at the Ramakrishna Sevashram, where they got a first-hand experience of how the Ramakrishna Mission focused on providing relief to the poorest of the poor, alongside their spiritual practices. Swami Brahmananda, however, bluntly told the boys that it was not yet time to take *sannyas*, and therefore they should return home. The nearly two months' tour, which ended with visits to Sarnath, Bodh Gaya and Gaya, ended fruitlessly, the primary aim of obtaining a guru being not met.[43] The goal was not achieved, but the tour gave the young boys a first-hand learning experience, a taste of the society, varying religious groups, and not least, the discrimination on the basis of caste.

The return to the Elgin Road house was emotional, for both Subhas and his parents. Prabhabati cried inconsolably, while Janakinath outwardly put up a stoic attitude but also broke down afterwards:

> She started crying on seeing me and could only say 'You were born to ensure my death.' I kept smiling in my mind. Then I met father; embracing me after I touched his feet, he took me towards his room and broke into tears halfway down. He kept crying for a long time . . . after some time both asked me where I had been. I told them everything frankly . . . they had sent telegrams around and had searched at many places; mother was active, but father passive, somewhat with the attitude of whatever happens will happen. . .[44]

This also led to a discussion on spirituality and the duties of life between father and son[45] which probably helped to bring down the wall between them.

Subhas again travelled to meet Hemanta in Krishnanagar after a few days, but the irregularities of the hectic travel took their toll; he was down with typhoid. Brought back to the Elgin Road house, he remained sick for over two months, and restrictions were placed by his family on his meetings with Hemanta. Even when Subhas personally saw to it that Hemanta was allowed to see him, he was not allowed to stay for long. Subhas decided to defy the elders in the family and keep meeting his friend. He would keep a keen eye on how his letters from Hemanta were opened and read by others in the family, before they were sealed again for him; he picked fights with his brothers; as an act of defiance, he left his friend's letters at prominent places so that others could read and be informed of their intention; and he was even ready to leave home in protest. That, however, did not come to pass. After recovering, he went to Kurseong for convalescence and returned to Calcutta after a month.[46]

The First World War started while Subhas fell ill with typhoid. According to him, as he closely followed the developments, the War put his mind firmly on politics, clearing the earlier vagueness a great deal.

He started thinking more clearly about the goal of India and the role of Indians from a purely political perspective for the first time. The nebulous thoughts of dividing responsibility between the British and the Indians, respectively controlling the defence and civil administration, gave way to a new resolve. Concrete ideas on complete independence and development of military strength, two strands that would occupy much of his later political thoughts, started germinating. He realized that

> If India was to be a modern civilised nation, she would have to pay the price and she would not by any means shirk the physical, the military, problem. Those who worked for the country's emancipation would have to be prepared to take charge of both the civil and military administration. Political freedom was indivisible and meant complete independence of foreign control and tutelage. The war had shown that a nation that did not possess military strength could not hope to preserve its independence.[47]

Back in Calcutta, Subhas continued with his earlier activities during his final year of the Intermediate Arts, but 'inwardly I had changed a great deal'.[48] Suresh Banerjee's group, of which he was a part, kept recruiting new members to strengthen its capability for reaching its goal. While one member was sent to England for further studies (for which Subhas gave up part of his scholarship), yet another accepted a commission in the Indian Medical Service. These were to help the group acquire skills and gain practical experience, as well as to financially strengthen it.

Studies were completely relegated to the background. Yet another distraction at this time was a rift in Banerjee's group. Only sketchy details are available from Subhas's letters to Hemanta during this period, from which it appears that some of the members took exception to his intimacy with and preference for Hemanta. Some of them probably went to the extent of indicating that their relationship had developed into something beyond a friendly emotional attachment. Even Beni Madhav and Banerjee were not pleased with their show of intimacy. His letters from this time clearly show how he was deeply hurt by this development: 'If they think we have polluted a holy relationship then death is the only punishment and we must accept it,' he told one of the seniors in the group. Subhas tried hard to clear the misconceptions amongst the members of the group, with some help from a usually supportive Banerjee and a few other senior members, but at the same time was ready to break away if their attitude did not change. A temporary reconciliation materialized after the examinations were over.[49]

When the results were declared for the Intermediate Examination in 1915, Subhas found himself 'low down in the list'[50], of those who passed in the first division. He was not happy. While planning for a two-month trip to Kurseong towards the end of April with his father, Subhas told Hemanta with some amusement that he felt a strong urge to undertake some serious study now that the examinations were over. The unsatisfactory results were certainly bothering him and that probably led him to set the goal that he would take up the Philosophy Honours course for the undergraduate course and come first in the examinations. He divided his study plan during the Kurseong vacation into four parts:

(1) 'Study of man and man's history.
(2) General study of the Sciences—first principles.
(3) The Problem of truth—the goal of human progress, meaning Philosophy.
(4) The great men of the world.'[51]

A letter to Hemanta from Kurseong in mid-May reveals a depressed mind, deeply pessimistic about his future prospects and the state of his health. This state of mind was probably triggered by his illness, the misunderstanding in the group and the distance from an active life. The tone of his writings, however, changed completely once he was back to Calcutta, and he was again his former confident self, planning for the future.[52]

It is one of his letters during this time which first documents the emotional bond he shared with Sarat. The young mind was a little disappointed by Sarat's shift of priorities after marriage: 'Mejadada used to love me—he got married—I found that love no more. He was preoccupied with other things. I was hurt—used to cry silently.'[53]

Returning to college, he joined the Philosophy Seminar, the first students' society of the college which had started under the name Philosophy Club in 1887. Subhas recorded in the Seminar's register some of the books he was reading during his student days—works of Harriet Martineau in September 1915, Caird's *Philosophy of Religion* in November 1915, and Schlegel's *History of Philosophy* in February 1916 (where he also mentioned that he was writing a paper on the 'Transition from Locke to Kant').[54]

An active, regular lifestyle and concentration on his studies probably helped Subhas crystallize his thoughts about his future, which he spelt out in a letter to Hemanta in August 1915. What is remarkable is that even at this stage, career options did not figure in his thoughts regarding the future; he was still thinking of his future in terms of intellectual development.

> With each passing day, I am realising that there is a *definite mission* of my life, for which I have taken birth, *and I am not to drift in the current of popular opinion.* The way of the world is that people will say good things and bad, but *my sublime self-consciousness consists in this that I am not influenced by them. . . I must move about with the proud self-consciousness of one imbued with an idea.*
>
> Now I can understand that three things are essential to be a true human:
>
> *(1) Embodiment of the past*
> *(2) Product of the present*
> *(3) Prophet of the future*
>
> *(1) I must assimilate the past history in fact all the past civilisation of the world*
> *(2) I must study myself – study the world around me – both India and abroad. For this foreign travels are necessary*
> *(3) I must be the prophet of the future. I must discover the laws of progress— the tendency of both the civilisation and therefrom to settle the future goal and progress of mankind. The philosophy of life will alone help me.*
> *(4) This ideal must be realised through a nation—begin with India.*[55]

However, before he could proceed with his 'grand idea', Subhas was in trouble, and events moved so fast that his student life in college came to an end within a few months. According to Subhas's narrative, one morning in January 1916, while he was studying in the college library, he came to know that some students of his batch were manhandled by Professor Edward Farley Oaten while walking along the corridor adjoining his classroom. Subhas, being a member of the Consultative Committee of the students, took up the matter with the Principal, who believed that the professor really had not manhandled anyone, and in any case, since he belonged to the Indian Educational Service, he could not be compelled to apologize.

This led to a strike by the students on the next day. When the Principal failed to break the impasse, he imposed a fine on the striking students. However, at the end of the second day's strike, Oaten settled the matter amicably with the students' representatives, whom Subhas was leading. Despite the amicable settlement, the Principal refused to budge on the fine he had imposed on the striking students even when the students as well as the teachers requested him to do so. This annoyed the students, but they chose to move on, as all seemed to be well.

It was not to be. Within a month another incident occurred—Oaten manhandled another student. The question before the students was what could be done to put an end to this behaviour.

> Constitutional protests like strikes would simply provoke disciplinary measures and appeals to the Principal would be futile. Some students therefore decided to take the law into their own hands.[56]

Professor Oaten was therefore 'subjected to the argument of force and in the process was beaten black and blue'. Subhas strongly denied allegations that Oaten was assaulted from behind; he wrote:

> It was alleged at the time that the students had attacked Mr O. from behind and thrown him down the stairs. This allegation is entirely false. Mr O. did receive one solitary stroke from behind, but that was of no account. His assailants—those who felled him—were all in front of him and on the same level with him. Being an eye witness myself I can assert this without fear of contradiction.[57]

Being the leader of the students' agitation, Subhas was naturally the primary suspect, along with another student named Ananga Mohan Dam, one of the secretaries of the Philosophy Seminar during 1914–15.[58] The college was closed down by the Bengal Government, and an inquiry committee set up, headed by Ashutosh Mukherjee, former vice chancellor of the Calcutta University. Unhappy over the fact that the Government took the measures without consulting him, the Principal of the college fought with the Member in charge of Education, and was suspended too. However:

> Before power could slip out of his hands the Principal acted. He sent for all those students who were in his black list including myself. To me he

said—or rather snarled—in unforgettable words, 'Bose, you are the most troublesome man in the College. I suspend you.' I said 'Thank you,' and went home. Shankaracharya's Maya lay dead as a door nail.[59]

That Sir Ashutosh Mukherjee headed the inquiry committee was reassuring to Subhas, who believed that Mukherjee wouldn't allow the students to suffer. He weighed various options in a letter to Hemanta:

If the Committee finds that we are not at fault, or gives us benefit of doubt, then we will apply to the Syndicate to reinstate us as students of Presidency College. If not reinstated, we will ask for a transfer. If a transfer is granted, we can easily get admitted to another college; otherwise I will be practically rusticated. Rustications like these usually do not last longer than a year; only in cases of grave offense can the rustication be for life, which means the end of studies.

But I have many advantages. I am known to be a good boy; I am known at least by name amongst the important people. The vast majority of public also believes that I am innocent. Ashubabu [Ashutosh Mukherjee] himself knows about me. The evidence given against me by the clerk is also weak. Therefore there is a high probability that I will be let off as innocent. I believe that I will get at least a transfer. If nothing else works, I can file a law suit.[60]

Within a week, he wrote again to Hemanta, 'I think the Committee's attitude towards us is favourable and I hope even if it does not hold us innocent, it will give us the benefit of doubt.'[61]

However, his hopes were belied and he was rusticated. Very strangely, Hemanta does not give his views on the incident or the punishment. Also very strange was the fact that Subhas never disclosed the details of the events to Dilip—neither then, nor later. Dilip read of the event in the newspaper. He did not like the fact of physical assault, but admired the way Subhas took all responsibility on himself, despite nothing being proved against him. At that time, he thought Subhas could have gone scot-free if he would have admitted publicly that assaulting a professor was morally wrong. Later, he wrote, he came to know that Subhas had actually not assaulted the professor.[62] Even Beni Madhav was enraged at the assault on a teacher; 'I had the occasion to speak to Benibabu once. He severely abused the boys and sympathized with James sahib [the Principal],' Subhas told Hemanta.[63] Suniti Kumar Chattopadhyay, who was around six years senior to Subhas and was teaching in Presidency at that time, also felt the attack to be cowardly, but refused to believe that Subhas was actually one of those who hit Oaten.[64]

The question that has repeatedly come up over the years is whether Subhas really physically assaulted Oaten. In his autobiography Subhas does not even as much hint that he did; 'Some students' had taken the decision, and he was an eyewitness. Instead, he focused on the developments whereby he was penalized for remaining at the forefront of the students' movement and for defending their act.

I was asked a straight question—Whether I considered the assault on Mr O. to be justified. My reply was that though the assault was not justified, the students had acted under great provocation. And then I proceeded to narrate seriatim the misdeeds of the Britishers in Presidency College during the last few years.[65]

'Did you really assault Oaten?' The question was put to Subhas more than two decades later by one of his closest political associates, Narendra Narayan Chakraborty. 'No, it all happened so suddenly that I could not see who dealt the blows,' Subhas replied, adding, 'I think it was Ananga.'[66] Subhas 'was supposed to have been connected with the affair, although I never had any proof of this', Oaten himself recalled while talking about the incident.[67]

Ananga later admitted that it was he along with some other students who had physically assaulted Oaten. Subhas accepted the punishment because he was leading the students' protests, but was not involved in the assault.[68]

As the general political atmosphere heated up, with a Government crackdown on the revolutionaries, Subhas's parents and elder brothers, probably aware of his connections and anxious over the recent developments, wanted him out of Calcutta. So, by end of March 1916 the usual topper was back in Cuttack as a rusticated student. In contrast to the earlier attitude of suspicion and disapproval, his family was supportive this time, which helped in improving his bonds with them. At the same time, Subhas was happy with himself over the way he had conducted himself through the crisis. There was no regret in his mind concerning the consequences of his act of defending his fellow classmates at the cost of his academic career.

With the doors closed by the Calcutta University on chances of proceeding with his education, with no indication of when the ban would be lifted, or whether at all, Subhas brought up with his father the question of being sent abroad. The proposal was however immediately shot down, and thus he was only left with the option to try to open the doors which had been closed on him.

Meanwhile, his relationship with Suresh Banerjee's group reached a breaking point. Although reconciliation was effected a few months earlier, Subhas stayed aloof from the group members. According to him, they did not appreciate his stand regarding the confrontation that had led to his expulsion from college. Subhas neither consulted them over his course of action, nor did he inform them of his leaving Calcutta for Cuttack.

With no end in sight, the only option open to Subhas was to kill time and wait till the atmosphere became more conducive to allow him to take up his studies again. This gave him the opportunity to take up social service with gusto. He joined his friends in the town in nursing people suffering from infectious diseases such as cholera and smallpox, especially those who had no one to take care of them. In cases of death from the diseases, his friends would go to the extent of cremating the dead bodies, following the proper funeral rites. He also gathered local youths and started a youth organization 'with different departments for their physical, intellectual, and moral advancement'.[69] Another activity that he participated in, with a lot of interest, partly to stay away from home, was visits to places of historical and religious significance. His group also revived the practice of *Baroari* puja in 1917.

As 'individualistic Yoga had no longer any attraction', he turned towards the exercise of self-analysis, which consisted of 'throwing a powerful searchlight on your own mind with a view to knowing yourself better'.[70] He was still fighting and exploring ways to control the natural sexual urge and its associated thoughts. This process of self-analysis, he mentioned, was able to provide a partial relief.

About a year later, Subhas returned to Calcutta to try his luck and Ashutosh Mukherjee was petitioned to revoke the rustication orders. While he waited to hear from the University authorities, Subhas tried to join the all-Bengali fighting unit—the 49th Bengal Regiment—permission for whose formation was granted by the Government in August 1916, after lobbying by stalwarts of the day such as Maharaja Bijoy Chand Mahtab of Burdwan, Surendranath Banerjee, Sarala Devi, A.K. Fazlul Haq, S.C.

Sarvadhikari, etc.[71] However, he was rejected due to his poor eyesight, and he was quite dejected over this. That Subhas was keen to join a fighting unit formed with the express aim of aiding the British war efforts could imply two things—either, following his realization at the beginning of the war when he lay sick at Cuttack, he was just keen on gaining military training and skills irrespective of the organizational aim; or, that his political views were not yet fine-tuned to the effect of disassociating himself from initiatives to aid the British Government.

Meanwhile, the prospects of resuming his studies were improving. He was informed that if any college was ready to admit him, the University would not object. He decided to try for admission in the Scottish Church College, as although the Bangabasi College was ready to admit him, it did not have an honours course in Philosophy. The Principal of the college, Dr William Spence Urquhart agreed to take him in if the Principal of the Presidency College did not have any objection. First Sarat and then Subhas met with the new Principal of Presidency College, who was gracious enough to allow him to resume his academic career in another institution. Subhas joined the third year of the Bachelor of Arts course with honours in Philosophy in Scottish Church College in July 1917.

In the new college Subhas focused on his studies; here too he joined the Philosophical Society of the college. After failing to join the 49th Bengalis, he now got an opportunity to join the university unit of the India Defence Forces, for which recruitment was then going on, where poor eyesight was not to be an impediment to gain admission. Here, Subhas got military training, and lived a camp life for four months. He thoroughly enjoyed the musketry practice, the drills, the parades, the route marches and the mock-fight sessions, although there was no active service.[72] 'What a change it was from sitting at the feet of anchorites to obtain knowledge about God, to standing with a rifle on my shoulder taking orders from a British army officer!'[73] he wrote later. The 'double company' also did well and drew appreciation from the Governor on the occasion of Calcutta University's convocation and at the Proclamation Parade on New Year's Day. The privileges that went with being a soldier, albeit for a limited period, such as gaining entry to Fort William and having a superior position vis-à-vis the police and other Government agents, also gave him a sense of empowerment, which was not available to an ordinary Indian citizen.

Subhas was very sensitive to the quality of performance by the recruits. He wrote with much satisfaction about the company's good performance in musketry competitions in which they beat the instructors. He would check with the platoon instructor about his opinion of the recruits as soldiers, and would feel proud when their performances were appreciated by the authorities. Subhas thought that it would have been better if, rather than being terminated at the end of a few months, it had led to actual service.[74]

After the training was over, 1918 seemed to have passed by without any major development. In the BA examination, he missed his target narrowly—he was placed second in the list of merit.

For the master's course, Subhas decided to opt for experimental psychology, as he 'was to some extent disillusioned about philosophy' since 'it did not solve any of the fundamental problems' for him, although 'it developed the critical faculty, provoked scepticism, and fostered intellectual discipline'.[75] Hemanta narrated a funny incident around this time, which indicated Subhas's sort of coming of age:[76]

> One afternoon he came and finding me alone, closed the door of my room. Opening a fat book, he asked me, 'Do you know how child birth takes place? When as a child I had asked my mother, she had told me that the baby comes out through the navel. But it is not so! Look at this picture!' Then he explained the whole process from the text book.

~

One evening, while visiting Calcutta, Janakinath called Subhas and made him an offer, which came like a bolt from the blue to him. Janakinath asked him to make up his mind within twenty-four hours on whether he would like to go to England to study for the Indian Civil Service (ICS). A wish to study abroad was there in his mind, which he had brought up with his father when as a rusticated student he was living in Cuttack; but even then, he had not thought of ever trying for the ICS. This was the chance to fulfil that wish. Therefore, it did not take long for Subhas to make up his mind. 'I took counsel with myself and, within a few hours, made up my mind to go.'[77] He was quite sure that he would not be able to make it through the ICS examinations, as only around eight months would be available to him for preparation; a decision on what was to be done in case of success was kept to be taken in future. So, preparations began in earnest. Asoke Nath Bose, Sarat's eldest son, described the goings-on in the household:

Early in September, 1919, we, the children of the household, were very
much surprised to see uncle Subhas one morning in European costume. It
was indeed a surprise as we had never seen him in European dress before
although we were accustomed to see my father and Dr. Sunil Chandra
Bose and occasionally some of my other uncles wear European dress . . .
Also, we saw uncle being instructed by father in the English manners and
customs, etiquette, etc.[78]

Subhas did not get a chance to meet Hemanta before leaving, but wrote to
him about his decision on 26 August, the day after his talk with Janakinath.
He was more interested in obtaining a degree in England; agreeing to
appear for the ICS examinations was a prerequisite to fulfil his real plan,
otherwise Janakinath would not allow him to travel to England. He was
quite sure that he stood no chance for success in the ICS, and would in all
likelihood take up his studies in London or Cambridge from October next
year.[79]

Banerjee's group opposed Subhas's decision to go abroad for higher
studies as an earlier experiment of sending a group member to acquire skill
had gone sour with the member marrying and settling down in England.

A passport was hurriedly obtained with some help from a relative
who was a highly placed police official. Subhas sailed from Calcutta on
15 September 1919, on the British India Steam Navigation Company's
steamer, City of Calcutta.[80]

2

The World Opens Its Doors
Into Public Life (1920–24)

Subhas reached the port of Tilbury on a wet and cloudy day of 25 October 1919. The arrival was delayed by a week due to an ongoing coal strike in England. Over the next few days, after some initial disappointment, with help from his acquaintances he was admitted to the Fitzwilliam Hall, in which the support he received from the Hall's censor, Mr Reddaway, was crucial as the current term had already begun two weeks earlier. The presence of Dilip, who had reached in June and had obtained a seat in Fitzwilliam Hall, was an additional help.[1] For the help he received from the Indian students in getting admitted, 'Subhas was almost absurdly grateful to all of us', Dilip thought.[2]

Subhas chose to take the Moral Sciences Tripos and applied for the ICS. The subjects that he had to study for the civil service examinations included English composition, Sanskrit, Philosophy, English law, political science, modern European history, English history, economics and geography (including surveys and cartography). Although he found the coursework more interesting, the limited preparation time available for the civil services examinations compelled him to restrict himself only to attending lectures. Generally speaking:

> Outside my lecture hours I had to study as hard as I could. There was no question of any enjoyment for me, besides what I could get from hard work . . . In the way of recreation, I attended the meetings of the Indian Majlis and the Union Society.[3]

Here, for the first time, Subhas was seeing for himself what it was like to live in a free country, and the cultural differences made an impression on his perceptive mind. He felt that the weather made people more enterprising, the intense activity was heartening to him, and he was clearly impressed by the punctuality. Especially unique was the social status accorded to students; he was 'greatly impressed' by the measures of freedom allowed to the students, and the 'general esteem in which they were held by all and sundry'. Students were not looked at with suspicion, as in India, as potential revolutionaries. A student being maltreated by professors was unimaginable. On the contrary, the students had the upper hand—they could 'rag' lecturers. Subhas was fascinated by the Union Society debates, where he found that the 'whole atmosphere was . . . exhilarating'. Even Members of Parliament and the Cabinet were equals with students in these debates.[4]

The meetings at the Indian Majlis, where people openly debated political views, were something new to Subhas, and he took to the discussions with enthusiasm. Within a few weeks of settling down, he was reporting to Hemanta about the meetings of Sarojini Naidu, C.F. Andrews and Bal Gangadhar Tilak at the Majlis.[5] This was probably the first time that he wrote about nationalist politics and politicians in his letters—a noticeable development which demonstrated his increasing consciousness of India's colonial politics. 'We get all news about India here—and there is also a lot of discussion on India. Even one who has never thought of his own country cannot help doing so after coming here,'[6] he wrote to a friend. He kept informing Hemanta about the Indian Majlis. This was also the first time he was socially interacting with women, and was greatly impressed by some of the Indian women there:

> Mrs Roy spoke on 'Rights of the Indian Mother' at last Sunday's meeting at the Majlis . . . when will Indian women take up the position of educators in the Indian society? If they don't rise, India too cannot. The day when Mrs Sarojini Naidu spoke here, I was filled with happiness . . . Then I met Dr Mrigen Mitra's wife in London. Although Dr Mitra is a moderate in politics, Mrs Mitra is an extremist—my happiness knew no bounds . . . Mrs Dhar is also an extremist . . . all this I feel that a country where the ideal of womanhood is so high, cannot be but great . . .[7]

Ideologically, Subhas found Cambridge to be politically conservative, where pacifists and socialists would find it difficult to address public meetings due to opposition from the students. He felt that Indians were extra sensitive about 'self-respect and national honour' especially after the Jallianwala Bagh tragedy, and this was aggravated in finding a 'great deal of sympathy for General Dyer' 'among middle class Englishmen'.[8]

When he was writing in 1937 about his Cambridge years, Subhas was aware that the attitude and outlook towards Indians in England had undergone a change from 1919 and 1920 when the Great War still shaped political mindsets and naturally cast its shadow on the political relations. The racial aspect of the British rule was not something to be forgotten by Subhas; it had rankled him as a student in Calcutta. He chronicled in some detail in his autobiography the verbal and physical assaults that Indians would face on a routine basis:

> Incidents in tram-cars occurred not infrequently. Britishers using these cars would be purposely rude and offensive to Indians in various ways . . . Often hot words would pass between Britishers and myself in the tram-cars . . . British Tommies were worse than civilians in this matter . . . In the railway trains it was sometimes difficult for an Indian to travel with self-respect, unless he was prepared to fight. The railway authorities or the police would not give the Indian passengers any legitimate protection.[9]

He later sarcastically described his reaction to these incidents:

> Whenever I came across such an incident my dreams would suffer a rude shock, and Shankaracharya's Doctrine of Maya would be shaken to its very foundations. It was quite impossible to persuade myself that to be insulted by a foreigner was an illusion that could be ignored.[10]

These incidents evidently left a deep impression on a sensitive adolescent mind, which could explain a somewhat childishly revengeful sentence he wrote to Hemanta, 'I am the happiest when I see a white-skinned person is serving me or cleaning my shoes.'[11] Dilip Kumar Roy, studying for the Tripos in mathematics, took this expression to be a manifestation of what he thought to be an inferiority complex.[12] In the same letter, however, Subhas was frank in the admission that 'There are many faults among these people, but looking at their qualities I bow my head'—clearly he was not miserly in offering praise where it was deserved.[13]

Racism, however, was a real problem, even in the land of democracy, though more subtle compared to the streets of Calcutta. A subterranean current of a feeling of superiority amongst the British lay beneath a 'veneer of *bon-homie*' and as a consequence, the overall cordial relationship between Indian and British students rarely matured into 'real friendship'. For instance, the tennis champion of the year was deprived from representing the university in the inter-university championship since he was an Indian. This was done in a way which was procedurally correct, by retaining captaincy to 'an old blue who had already gone down', but the intent behind the move was not difficult to understand.[14]

A more ridiculous instance of an attempt to provide a respectable cover to racial prejudice through bureaucratic machinations was that of preventing Indian students from joining the University Officers' Training Corps (OTC). The Indian students were informed by the university authorities that the India Office had raised objections when they applied for enlisting in the training corps. Subhas and K.L. Gauba were nominated as the representatives of the Indian students by the Indian Majlis, to take up the matter with the Secretary of State for India, E.S. Montagu. The matter was however delegated to the Under Secretary of State for India, the Earl of Lytton, who on meeting the delegates informed them that it was not the India Office which had raised objections to enlisting by the Indian students, but the War Office. The objections were raised in anticipation of resentment from British students, and on the more practical ground that qualified members of the OTC were entitled to commissions in the British Army. The Earl of Lytton made it clear that the British administration was not prepared for such an eventuality just yet. When the Indian students told the OTC staff that they were ready to give an undertaking that they would not demand commissions in the British Army, they were informed that the real objection had indeed come from the India Office.

Dilip, amongst Subhas's closest friends, is one of the few who has recorded his impressions of the student days. According to him, 'round about us we spotted none who could come anywhere near him in stature or one-pointed ardour', although 'a handful, mostly never-do-wells dubbed him an arrogant prig', or an 'interesting freak'; he beat the crammers at their own game, without ever cramming.[15] Again, 'I cannot remember a single student in England who took life a tithe as seriously as he or strove as assiduously to make himself into a standard-bearer of free India.'[16]

The civil service examinations began in July 1920, around eight months after Subhas arrived in Cambridge, lasting for about a month—a month of agony to him. Apart from their practical short-term objective, Subhas's studies gave him a good theoretical grounding across subjects. The rigorous study of political science, economics, English history and modern European history stood him in good stead subsequently. Modern European history particularly fascinated him, as he delved into the works of Bismarck, Cavour and Metternich. Dilip found him reading Gibbon's volumes on the Roman Empire, and the writings of Garibaldi, Mazzini, Lenin, Kropotkin, etc.[17]

> These original sources, more than anything else, I studied at Cambridge, helped to rouse my political sense and to foster my understanding of the inner currents of international politics.[18]

As if having only eight months to prepare was not enough to hurt the competitive student in him, he failed to complete the Sanskrit paper, as he could not fully copy the translation into English that he had done in the rough pages of his answer book, thus throwing away 'about 150 sure marks'.[19] The overall performance was discouraging enough for him to inform his family that he had no chance of success. At last he had the opportunity to concentrate on the coursework of the Tripos, which he had been neglecting so far. The burden of ICS was out of his way.

In about a month's time, however, he was completely taken by surprise, when one night in September he received a telegram from a friend congratulating him. Next morning he found out that the congratulatory message was for the result of the ICS examinations. He was ranked fourth among the candidates who had taken the exam. Subhas was naturally happy, but at the same time the question which he had shoved to the background on the assumption of its remoteness of likelihood had to be resolved now: What would he do if he succeeded?

Once the examination was over, Subhas had more time to go around places, visit new people and participate in social events. Through Dilip, Subhas became close to a few families in England. He spent some time vacationing at Leigh-on-Sea after the announcement of the ICS results, staying as a paying guest with the Bates, who, according to Dilip, became his lifelong friends. 'Mr B[ates] represents English character at its very best,' he wrote to Sarat from there. More intimate was his relationship with the Dharamvirs, with whom Subhas and Dilip got acquainted in one of the students' meetings. The two spent about a week at their house after the ICS results were announced.[20] Dr Dharamvir was an old friend of Lala Lajpat Rai and a staunch nationalist, who 'almost came to adore' Subhas; his wife was the only 'one English lady he came to conceive a real affection and esteem for . . .' whom Subhas called 'didi'.[21] The two friends also lived with the family of Sarat Kumar Dutta in London a few times—who used to live in the rented outhouse of Mrs Palit, widow of Lokendra Nath Palit, former judge and littérateur. Subhas was greatly affected by Mrs Palit's motherly attitude. She too grew to be fond of him. 'I misunderstood him initially, taking him to be a hater of the British people. At that time I could not imagine that he is indeed so generous and broad-minded,' Mrs Palit would tell Dilip later. A frequent visitor to Mrs Palit was the future movie star Devika Rani who, at this time, was on the threshold of adolescence. Subhas became quite fond of her, but was miffed with her parents for keeping their daughter away from them.[22]

As he was making new friends and widening his social circle, Subhas's political ideas were also taking a clearer shape. There wasn't yet anything close to a cohesive and detailed programme, but an increasingly clearer articulation of the main current of his political thoughts, chiefly in terms of principles rather than parties or personalities, was already noticeable. The two events that altered the course of the nationalist movement—the Rowlatt Act passed by the Imperial Legislative Council in March 1919, and the Jallianwala Bagh massacre of 13 April of the same year—had taken place while Subhas was still in Calcutta, but he had only heard 'vague rumours' of events in Punjab as martial law in that province had prevented the flow of information. Although Subhas's letters during this period do not have his own reaction to the Jallianwala Bagh incident, he reported to Hemanta that the Labour leaders told Jagadish Chandra Bose that 'The country which can tolerate Amritsar massacres deserves it.'[23] Tilak had spoken at a meeting in Cambridge urging Indian students to work for the country rather than join Government service, and demanded Home Rule within fifteen years. Subhas recorded, with some amusement, the reaction of the English students who attended Tilak's lecture expecting 'some hot stuff'—'If these are your extremists, we don't want to hear your moderates.'[24]

India needs mass education and organization of labour to make progress, he wrote to his friend Charu Chandra Ganguly, citing the example of the Western world, especially the Soviet Union. The untouchable caste of India constituted the Labour Party, which according to Vivekananda would bring about India's progress.[25] He proposed concrete measures to Chittaranjan Das, the new leader of Bengal, to transform the Indian National Congress (at least in Bengal) into a modern organization, to turn it into a body that would be capable of administering the country. It needed a permanent office, permanent research staff to study various national problems, and its own intelligence department to collect information. He suggested that the Congress committee should frame its policies on the basis of information generated by the research staff and the intelligence department. He also thought that the Congress should have clear policies on the type of Constitution to be framed after gaining Swaraj, Indian currency and exchange, their attitude towards the princely states, expanding franchise, and 'vagrancy and poor relief' and depressed classes (who in Madras, Subhas thought, had become pro-Government due to the lack of the Congress's efforts). Apart from these, he thought that the Congress should have a propaganda department for publishing booklets in every provincial language on 'each and every question in our national life' and distribute them for free amongst people.

Subhas was keenly following developments at home. By the time he had finished taking the ICS examination, Tilak was dead, the revolutionary movement had been suppressed, and Gandhi had consolidated his leadership in nationalist politics, introducing a new method called satyagraha. The non-violent mass movement of non-cooperation led by Gandhi, along with the leaders of the Khilafat movement, was gaining momentum. From Bengal, Chittaranjan Das had emerged as the most prominent leader, overshadowing extremist leaders of yesteryears such as Bipin Chandra Pal and Surendranath Banerjee. The moderates in Congress had broken away to form a new political party. Responding to Gandhi's call, Chittaranjan had given up his legendary legal practice. India was apparently on the threshold of a potential political upheaval.

Subhas could not but have been influenced by these developments. The clash between the promises held out by a career in the civil service and his ideas of national service which developed over the past decade needed a final and clear solution. Whichever way he chose, he was not prepared to regret it in the future. Apart from his own ideals, there was the family to answer to, especially his ailing parents; Janakinath's main condition to send him abroad was to study for the ICS. Now that Subhas had succeeded, what explanation could he give his father if he chose not to join the 'heaven born service'?

To take a final call he turned to Sarat for advice. The dilemma was definitely there, but the correspondence with friends and family during this time clearly shows that he started the journey towards a final decision with a heavy bias against joining the civil service. All the exchanges that took place between him and his family for the next seven months, till he officially informed the authorities of his decision, was essentially an effort to bring them around to his decision, and to be sure himself that he was doing the right thing. In his letter to Sarat, written a few days after the results were announced, he clearly laid down his case. The letter, written while vacationing at Leigh-on-Sea in Essex, reflects clarity of thought which could have only come after seriously considering all options:

> I have been getting heaps of congratulations on my standing fourth in the competitive examination. But I cannot say that I am delighted at the prospect of entering the ranks of the I.C.S. If I have to join this service I shall do so with as much reluctance as I started my study for the C.S. Examination with . . . Given talents, with a servile spirit one may even aspire to be the Chief Secretary to a provincial Government. But after all is Service to be the be-all and end-all of my life? . . . I think it is hypocrisy to maintain that the highest ideals of one's life are compatible with subordination to the conditions of service which an I.C.S. man has got to accept.
>
>   You will readily understand my mental condition as I stand on the threshold of what the man-in-the-street would call a promising career . . . It solves once for all what is the paramount problem for each of us—the problem of bread and butter . . . But for a man of my temperament who has been feeding on ideas which might be called eccentric—the line of least resistance is not the best line to follow. Life loses half its interest if there is no struggle—if there are no risks to be taken. The uncertainties of life are not appalling to one who has not, at heart, worldly ambitions. Moreover, it is not possible to serve one's country in the best and fullest manner if one is chained to the Civil Service. In short, national and spiritual aspirations are not compatible with obedience to Civil Service conditions.
>
>   . . . I may say without hesitation that if I were given the option—I would be the last man to join the Indian Civil Service.

You may rightly say that, instead of avoiding the service, one should enter its ranks and fight its evils. But even if I do so, my position any day may become so intolerable as to compel me to resign. If such a crisis takes place 5 or 10 years hence, I shall not be in a favourable position to chalk out a new line for myself—whereas today there is yet time for me to qualify for another career.

If one is cynical enough one may say that all this 'spirit' will evaporate as soon as I am safe in the arms of the service. But I am determined not to submit to that sickening influence. I am not going to marry—hence considerations of worldly prudence will not deter me from taking a particular line of action if I believe that to be intrinsically right.

Constituted as I am, I have sincere doubts as to whether I should be a fit man for the Civil Service and I rather think that what little capacity I possess can be better utilised in other directions for my own welfare as well as for the welfare of my country.[26]

To Subhas, the sole criterion for making his decision was the question of whether he would be able to serve the country better by being in the service, or out of it. He had little doubt about the path to choose. He continued his efforts to convince Sarat (and through him Janakinath). He articulated his arguments with greater clarity in successive letters. Sarat argued back, but Subhas had his answers to those arguments. Romesh Chunder Dutt did great work, but could have been more productive by remaining outside the bureaucracy; Aurobindo's example was 'more noble, more inspiring, more lofty, more unselfish, though more thorny'; if Chittaranjan Das could give up his legendary practice and plunge into uncertainty at an advanced age, why could not Subhas do the same? Writing to Sarat on 26 January 1921, he pleaded for his moral support—'. . . The question here involved is one of principle. On principle I cannot accept the idea of being a part of the machinery which has outlived the days of its usefulness . . . I am now at the cross-ways and no compromise is possible.'[27] He had not yet written to Janakinath about his thoughts, but promised Sarat that he would, now, and requested him to put in a few words to persuade their father.

M.C. Chagla, who went on to become the Chief Justice of the Bombay High Court, India's ambassador to the US, high commissioner in the UK and then the education and foreign minister, was a student at Oxford and saw Subhas often. According to Chagla, Subhas often used to visit his friend Sen in Oxford. It is difficult to ascertain which Sen Chagla referred to, because he claimed that this friend went on to become India's Chief Election Commissioner and Secretary of the UN Food and Agricultural Organization (FAO). While Sukumar Sen became the CEC, it was Binay Ranjan Sen who became the Director General of FAO. Both were at Oxford at that time. Chagla claimed that after the ICS results were out, Subhas met Mohammad Ali Jinnah in London, who advised him not to give up the service.[28]

Another person who met Subhas at that time was G.D. Khosla, later the Chief Justice of Punjab High Court, who was also appointed by the Government of India in 1970 to investigate the mysterious disappearance of Subhas. Khosla recalled the only time he met Subhas:

It was the day he had decided to resign from the Indian Civil Service . . . I had come upon him in a street near Parker's Piece, where he was the centre of a group of Indian students, hotly discussing the pros and cons of joining the ICS and working for alien exploiters and tyrants. I said I had come up to Cambridge with the firm intention of preparing for the Civil Service examination, and saw nothing unpatriotic or degrading in keeping out at least one Englishman from the privileged band of 'heaven borns' who tyrannised our countrymen. Bose gave me a withering look of contempt, and continued the exposition of his argument.[29]

The final decision was reached by mid-February. On 16 February, Subhas wrote to Chittaranjan, 'the high priest of the festival of national service in Bengal', asking him 'what work you may be able to give me in this gigantic programme of national service', and telling him at the same time that his reply would equip him better to convince his father and brother.[30] Subhas conveyed his decision to Sarat a week later. On 23 February, he wrote to Sarat, 'I am fully convinced now that I shall be able to serve my country better if I am one of the people than if I am a member of the bureaucracy.'[31] As expected by Subhas, Janakinath opposed his plan, even going to the extent of prophesying that home rule was not more than ten years away, implying that there was a golden opportunity of holding a high position in a free India, but to no avail. For a moment, there was a passing thought to join the service only if to save the amount of money spent on him by his family, so that he could contribute to their well-being. Even that, however, was not strong enough to induce him to reconsider.

With the passage of time, he seemed to be getting impatient to plunge into the national movement. 'If we all stick to our jobs and look after our own interests, I don't think we shall get Home Rule even in 50 years,' he wrote to Sarat a couple of weeks before submitting his resignation. He was not sure of the sustainability of the Gandhian–Khilafat movement; it was certainly in need of young people like him who could sacrifice all for the country. For a youngster yet to test the waters of politics, he showed remarkable confidence in his ability to make an impact, to the extent of cockiness: 'If I were sure that the movement would progress favourably, I could easily have waited. The apprehension of failure or slackening impels me to throw myself into the movement before it is too late to mend matters,' he wrote to Sarat.[32]

Although Subhas was impressed by the Gandhian mass movement and acknowledged its strategic importance, he didn't have much faith in the creed of non-violence. He did not believe that a subjugated country can attain freedom on the basis of a non-violent movement. The British rulers were not worried about non-violent charkha–satyagraha, but were afraid of revolutionaries such as Jatindranath Mukhopadhyay, Kanailal Dutta, Barindra Kumar Ghose, Jadugopal Mukherjee, V.D. Savarkar, Krishna Varma, Madam Cama and Aurobindo, etc. He believed that the nationalist movement owed its strength to the revolutionaries who sacrificed their lives singing 'Vande Mataram'. He told Dilip:

> I have spent some time with the revolutionary circles and can say without hesitation that best examples of humanitarianism, courage and sacrifice in our country are to be found not amongst the famous politicians, but amongst the little known revolutionaries.[33]

As a matter of political strategy, however, his approach was in consonance with Gandhi's, in that the 'best way to end a government is to withdraw from it'.[34] This heightened consciousness made his resolve stronger. As he would tell Sarat, 'My greatest objection to joining the service was based on the fact that I would have to sign the Covenant and thereby own the allegiance of a foreign bureaucracy which I feel rightly or wrongly has no moral right to be there.'[35]

Early in April, Subhas visited some friends at Oxford. No account is available of this visit, but it appears that some intense discussion—'stormy time from the mental point of view', in his own words—took place over his course of action. His subsequent letters to Sarat were unusually strong in tone. Looking at his past, he regretted that he did not admit to the inquiry on the Oaten affair that he was indeed associated with the assault on the professor; that he joined the India Defence Force, which required an oath of allegiance to higher authorities; and that he agreed to take the civil service examination. He would have been 'a better and truer man' if he had acted otherwise. Based on his experience, he was firmly against any sort of compromise with his cherished ideals, since 'compromise is a very unholy thing', and one compromise led to another.[36]

On 22 April, Subhas sent a short and straightforward letter to the Secretary of State, Montagu, stating that he wished for his name to be removed from the list of probationers and stating that he would return the allowance of GBP 100 he had received once his resignation was accepted. An unprecedented act, the resignation naturally caused a flutter. Among those who approached him to ask him to withdraw the resignation were the then permanent Under Secretary of State for India, William Duke (through Subhas's eldest brother Satish), lecturers in Cambridge, and secretary of the Civil Service Board in Cambridge, Mr Roberts. A pleasant surprise, however, came in the form of support from Mr Reddaway, who had earlier helped Subhas from losing a year during his admission to the university.

News about his decision to leave the ICS had already spread and created a sensation amongst the Indian community, much to Subhas's dislike: 'I dislike both sensation and popular applause.'[37] He was worried that due to the sensation created, news of his resignation might reach Janakinath, and he wanted to avoid that by all means. Much to his surprise, and relief, he found support from his mother, who wrote to him that irrespective of his father's position, she preferred the ideal of Gandhi.[38]

It was now time to sail back to the homeland. He had no money and had to borrow GBP 90 from Dilip.

~

Over a thousand delegates gathered at Harish Mukherjee Street in Calcutta to participate in the proceedings of the Bengal Provincial Conference in 1917. As the proceedings began, the sixty-nine-year-old Surendranath Banerjee, extremist Congressman-turned-moderate, stood up to introduce the president of the session with words that would indeed turn out to be prophetic:

If I am permitted to indulge in a bit of prophecy which is my birth-right
by virtue of my Brahmanical position, I will say this that he will within a
measurable distance of time become one of the most prominent leaders
of public opinion in this Province. I trust that his election on the present
occasion will be the royal road to that which is the coveted honour and
distinction of public life in India—its highest honour and distinction viz.,
the Presidentship of the Indian National Congress.[39]

Chittaranjan Das's election as the president of the conference marked
the entry into active politics for him. A unique personality, representing
the best traits of the Bengal renaissance, Das had always been associated
with political activity, but had never become a politician in the true sense.
His political activism began with his involvement in Banerjee's Student
Association during his student days at the Presidency College in the late
1880s. While studying in England, he campaigned for Dadabhai Naoroji's
election to the House of Commons in 1892,[40] making speeches at several
meetings, including one presided by W.E. Gladstone (soon to be the British
Prime Minister for the fourth time).[41] Even as Das struggled to come to
his own in the legal practice, Barindra Kumar Ghose, Aurobindo's brother
and emissary to Bengal from 1901 for the purpose of setting up a radical
political network, established connections with him. In the same year, he also
collaborated with the extremist leader Bipin Chandra Pal in the publication
of *New India*.[42] Das's association with the Ghose brothers continued; he
became a patron of the Anushilan Samiti and was one of the three financiers
of *Bande Mataram*, the newspaper published by Aurobindo and Pal.[43] He
supported the Swadeshi movement, raised funds for the National Council
for Education, and attended the Bengal Provincial Conference of 1906 at
Barisal, drafting the main resolution of the conference.[44] In 1906, when
Tilak organized the Shivaji festival, he along with other Maharashtrian
leaders stayed at Das's house.[45] He gradually built a phenomenal legal career,
overturning insolvency to become one of the wealthiest lawyers, famously
defending Aurobindo Ghose and others in the Alipore bomb case (1908),
as well as many other extremists (including Bhupendra Nath Dutta and
Brahma Bandhab Upadhyay),[46] all without any remuneration, sacrificing his
own financial gains. Along with his fame as a brilliant lawyer, word also
spread about his phenomenal propensity for charity.

For the next few years, as the extremist section of Congress remained
inconspicuous, primarily due to the deportation of key leaders such as

Tilak, Lajpat Rai and Barindra, along with Aurobindo's retirement into a spiritual life, Das kept busy with his legal practice (which continued to flourish) and his literary pursuits. He had already made a name as a poet. From 1915, he started publishing the literary journal *Narayan*. In the same year, he served as the president of the Literary Conference of Bengal, presenting a paper on the 'lyrics of Bengal'.[47] Equally given to music, Das viewed it as an effective means of attaining communal harmony.[48]

Das's active involvement coincided with the re-entry of the extremist leaders such as Tilak into the Congress in 1916, after the acrimonious split between the moderates and the extremists in 1907. As the Home Rule movement gathered momentum, Das too extended his support, which played a crucial role in the selection of Annie Besant as the president of the Calcutta session of the Congress, held in December 1917. Edwin Montagu announced in August that responsible self-government was the goal of British policy in India. Around this time, Das clearly enunciated the framework of his political goal. Although he had defended the Bengal revolutionaries in the courtrooms, he was no Aurobindo Ghose; he did not envisage freedom of India by cutting off ties with the Empire just yet. In one of his speeches during this time, he pointed out:

> . . . first of all, we must get a government which will be autonomous in so far as it will be government by the people and for the people. The different provincial governments are to be connected together by some sort of central government and then again that central government is to be connected up with the different parts of this vast empire. That is the sort of Government for which the time has come for which to make a definite scheme.[49]

When Montagu, during his India tour to gauge expectations for reform measures, met Das towards the end of the year, he was greatly impressed, calling him 'an extremist, but a most sensible fellow'; 'He attracted me enormously', he would write in his diary.[50]

At the Congress session held in Calcutta in December 1917 and presided by Besant, Das vigorously argued for provincial autonomy when he rose to speak in support of the resolution demanding 'the immediate enactment of a Parliamentary Statute providing for the establishment of Responsible Government in India, the full measure to be attained within a time limit to be fixed in the Statute itself at an early date'. To loud cheers, he proclaimed 'the time has come when the British Parliament must make up its mind to transfer the powers from the hands of the Bureaucracy to the people of this country.'[51]

With the beginning of his new political life, two tasks to which Das devoted his energy, apart from agitating for self-government, were to bring about a genuine understanding between the Hindus and the Muslims, and to campaign against the widespread internment, especially under the draconian Defence of India Act. Das acknowledged the dichotomy between the Hindus and the Muslims, but stressed on their common culture as Bengalis. He attributed the estrangement between the two to the different directions followed by the communities—while the Hindus accepted English education and progressed, Muslims refused to accept it and at the same time became divorced from the culture of their ancestors. It was important to build a unity without sacrificing the identity of any community, which would give rise to 'great culture . . . made up of the contact of these two great races', which is the 'ideal of the Indian Nationality'.[52]

He was also exhorting Bengal's political workers to overcome their Bengal-centric outlook. Each province had its own identity but was also connected by a shared cultural and religious past (although not politically united in the modern sense, and still a nation in the making)—both for Hindus and Muslims.

As he denounced the internment of Mohammad Ali and Shaukat Ali, Das also made his position clear on the revolutionaries and their methods. The revolutionary method could not be supported, but the revolutionary way was a result of the repressive measures of the Government—'the cause of this revolutionary movement is nothing but hunger for freedom', and it could not be eradicated unless the youth were allowed to take 'their legitimate part in the government of their country, in shaping the course of their national development'.[53]

When the Montagu–Chelmsford Report was published in July 1918, the more radical faction of the Congress comprising Tilak, Besant and N.C. Kelkar, amongst others, rejected it. Surendranath, along with other moderates such as Dinshaw Wacha, Bhupendranath Basu, Ambika Charan Mazumdar and Chimanlal Setalvad, who had been campaigning for the new scheme, formed the new National Liberal League and broke away from the Congress. By this time Das had been able to capture the Bengal Congress and his rupture with his former mentor Surendranath was complete.[54] Even as the agitation on the proposed reforms was building up, an opportunity to open a new front of attack on the Government emerged when the report of the Sedition Committee, headed by Sidney Arthur Taylor Rowlatt was published on 19 July, eleven days after the publication of the Montagu–Chelmsford Report. The committee proposed legislation of several new measures to curb the Indian revolutionary movement, including enactment of a permanent law in the lines of the draconian Defence of India Act, which was to expire with the World War drawing to an end.[55]

A special session of the Congress, held in Bombay on 29 August, called the proposed scheme 'disappointing and unsatisfactory', and demanded full autonomy for the provinces within six years and a full responsible Government in the whole of British India within fifteen years.[56] Das presented two resolutions—one condemning the recommendations of the Rowlatt Committee, and another on the determination of franchise and constituencies for election to the legislative assemblies.[57]

The annual Congress session in Delhi went further ahead in demanding full provincial autonomy immediately. This shift of stance was so radical that a Home Department report to the British Parliament observed, 'The whole meeting was a triumph for the ultra-Left Wing, and by contrast to their attitude the main body of the old Home Rule Leaguers appeared almost conservative.'[58] Vigorously defending the resolution seeking immediate provincial autonomy, Das took Srinivasa Sastri and other moderates to task for objecting to it.[59]

Subhas had made up his mind to join the political movement that was gathering steam under the leadership of Gandhi, but while his heart was with the movement, his intellect was yet to be satisfied with the finer details regarding the nature and objective of the movement, and the leadership's plans for reaching the goal. Reading about the upheavals from a distance and his discussions with his friends would have definitely made him aware of the broad contours of the movement, which he was now keen to assess first-hand.

It was a happy coincidence that he got Rabindranath Tagore, who was on the same ship returning to India, as the first person who could give him some serious insight. The conversation between a twenty-four-year-old impatient young man and a sixty-year-old poet who had been a leading light of Bengal's Swadeshi movement, and who had recently made known his reservations about Gandhi's programme, if recorded, would have made for interesting reading. The only account available, and that too a summarized one, however, is from Subhas. He gathered that the poet, although not 'hostile' to the non-cooperation programme, would like to see greater emphasis on a constructive programme 'so that ultimately a state within a state could be built up, *entirely* on the co-operation and support of the people'. This view, which he thought was analogous to the constructive aspect of the Sinn Féin movement, was close to Subhas's heart: a theme he would repeatedly return to over the next two decades.[60]

Disembarking in Bombay on 16 July 1921, Subhas got an even better opportunity to gain a deeper understanding of the leader's 'mind and purpose'. Mahatma Gandhi was in Bombay, spreading the message of Swadeshi, meeting various groups and raising funds for the Tilak Swaraj Fund. During the past two years, the young follower of the politics of Aurobindo and the spirituality of Vivekananda had been closely following the emergence of the Mahatma as the most powerful political leader in the country, trying to form an estimate of the creed of non-violent satyagraha in detailed discussion with his friends, especially Dilip. He had been studying the world's revolutionary leaders and their methods and tactics. Could Gandhi be a revolutionary like any of them? Now he had the chance to meet the man in flesh and blood for the first time and find out for himself.

As Subhas, clothed in western dress, walked into Mani Bhavan with its Swadeshi ambience, he could not but apologize. The ever-affable Gandhi, probably amused at the awkwardness of the visitor who was almost three decades younger than him, eased him with a hearty laugh and started responding to his barrage of questions. In his hour-long conversation, Subhas tried to understand what probably puzzled him the most—how was Gandhi going to keep his promise of attaining Swaraj by the end of the year? The man impressed him, but his explanations of the programme and expectations regarding the goal of the movement still left him intellectually dissatisfied:

> There were three points which needed elucidation. Firstly, how were the different activities conducted by the Congress going to culminate in the last state of the campaign, namely, the non-payment of taxes? Secondly, how could mere non-payment of taxes or civil disobedience force the Government to retire from the field and leave us with our freedom? Thirdly, how could the Mahatma promise 'Swaraj' (that is, Home Rule) within one year—as he had been doing ever since the Nagpur Congress? . . . His reply to the first question satisfied me . . . The

Mahatma's replies to the other two questions were not convincing . . .
there was a deplorable lack of clarity in the plan which the Mahatma had
formulated and that he himself did not have a clear idea of the successive
stages of the campaign which would bring India to her cherished goal of
freedom.[61]

Subhas tried, unsuccessfully, to convince himself that he probably did not
understand what Gandhi was trying to explain, or possibly the great man
did not 'want to give out all his secrets prematurely'. From England, he
had offered his services to Chittaranjan Das (now known by the epithet
'Deshbandhu'), and meeting him was the first thing he wanted to do on
his return to Calcutta. Now the Mahatma too advised him to do the same.
Shrugging off the disappointment, Subhas set off for Calcutta, excited at
the prospect of meeting Deshbandhu, who had replied to his letter from
Cambridge laying out the many opportunities to take up national work.
Once in Calcutta, he went back to live with his elder brother Sarat and his
family.

Keeping in with the tradition of the Swadeshi movement and the
subsequent secret revolutionary movements, Bengal was politically charged.
It was the season of sacrifices. A large number of students left schools
and colleges following the call of Das, and many lawyers gave up their
legal practices. While the Congress organization was being built up under
Das's leadership to reach the interiors of the province through district
and local committees, several local movements erupted with rapid pace: a
strike followed by the mass exodus of thousands of labourers from the tea
gardens in Assam; a steamer strike in Tipperah; a strike by workers of the
Assam–Bengal railways and in the tea gardens of Darjeeling and Dooars; a
no-tax campaign Midnapore; as well as numerous hartals. The movements
had also helped Das to recruit his next rung of leaders like Birendranath
Sasmal and J.M. Sengupta. Former revolutionaries, who were released
from prisons through a royal pardon as the new Constitution came into
force, also joined the non-cooperation movement and gradually started
reorganizing themselves even as they started working for mainstream
Congress organizations.

With Deshbandhu away, touring the province, Subhas was happy to
return amidst his old friends. Hemanta had given up his lecturership in
the Calcutta University and joined Das as his private secretary; Prafulla
Ghosh had resigned from a lucrative government job; Kiran Shankar Roy,

who returned before Subhas from England, where he was called to the
bar, had given up his practice; Suresh Banerji along with Prafulla had
started the Abhay Ashram, based on Gandhian ideals; Bhupendra Kumar
Datta, after being released from jail by the Royal pardon of 1919, had
joined Congress after an understanding with Gandhi. Subhas also started
making new acquaintances: Bhupendra introduced him to the well-known
revolutionary of the Jugantar Group, Surendra Mohan Ghose.

Despite the surge in organized anti-British campaigns, all, however,
was not well with the Bengal Congress. Criticism by the Bengal
Gandhians, ever suspicious of Das's acceptance of Gandhian tenets, grew
sharper as Das pushed the limits of the non-cooperation methods set by
Gandhi by encouraging peasant and labour strikes. In June, Shyamsundar
Chakravarti, a former extremist-turned-staunch Gandhian, led the attack
on Das for supporting the steamer and railway strikes in East Bengal, and
another leader, Jitendralal Banerjee, resigned from the provincial Congress
committee in protest. The Marwari community of the city, who supported
the Gandhian faction and were the biggest contributors to the Tilak Swaraj
Fund, accused Das of misappropriating money donated to the fund.[62]

As he waited for Das to return, Subhas encountered the leaders of the
Gandhian faction who tried to influence him too. Influenced to some extent
by the factional squabble, Subhas became ambivalent towards joining the
Congress, but his dilemma soon ended as he met Das for the first time:
'During the course of our conversation I began to feel that here was a man
who knew what he was about . . . By the time our conversation came to an
end my mind was made up. I felt that I had found a leader and I meant to
follow him.' Das clearly had Subhas in mind while he was reorganizing the
Congress in Bengal. The developments in the Bengal Congress, and the
suggestions made by Hemanta and Bhupendra Kumar, helped him assign
a specific role to Subhas.[63]

The National College, under the Board of Education established by Das
and Banerjee to provide education to students who had left Government-
aided schools, was in a chaotic state, with the apprehension expressed by
Gandhi while inaugurating the institution in February about to come true.
He had said, 'If professors and the teachers are found asleep, if they are
overtaken with doubt, if they are overtaken with fear as to the future, God
help the students who come under their charge.'[64] Within a few months,
however, some of the Congress leaders in charge of the administration and
some teachers had almost lost interest with the result that the students too

had started losing hope. At Das's place to meet him for the second time, Subhas found an agitated Sabitri Prasanna Chattopadhyay—a Bengali teacher at the National College and slightly elder to him—confronting Das with the problems plaguing the institution. Das was aware of the problem but his hands were tied by the factional feud. Realizing the need for an intervention, he authorized Subhas, Sabitri Prasanna and Kiran Shankar to take charge of the college, housed in Forbes Mansion at Wellington Square,[65] where the newly opened Congress office was also located, and bring it back on track. Subhas was appointed the principal of the college, Kiran Shankar secretary of the Board of Education, and Sabitri Prasanna the superintendent. New teachers were also recruited to strengthen the faculty. Amongst the famous individuals who frequented the college were the novelist Sarat Chandra Chattopadhyay and poet Satyendranath Dutta.[66]

Subhas's first professional employment was thus an unglamorous task, a far cry from bringing on revolution or creating political upheaval; he had to just ensure that the college ran smoothly and that the students were taught on a regular basis. Besides, he would teach English, geography and philosophy too. However, a teaching job was one thing that was in his mind when he had written to Das from England. With that objective fulfilled, he delved into rebuilding the institution with a meticulous attention to the minutest of details and a rigorous discipline. Apart from teaching, he would remain engaged, often till late into the night, in arranging stationery, cleaning up classrooms, keeping an account of the college's income and expenditure and other administrative work. His dedication to teaching once led Kiran Shankar to joke, 'Subhas is teaching the benches in empty classrooms', when someone came looking for him. This was also the time when he began addressing students' meetings.[67]

In his efforts to improve the standard of the college, Subhas met Tagore for advice, and started acquiring instruments and the furniture required for setting up a good laboratory. The hard work of Subhas and his colleagues notwithstanding, the National College was doomed to be swallowed by the political whirlwind which was lashed upon the province at the end of the year.

Although the National College occupied most of his time during the initial days, politics proper was not late in catching up. Around this time, he registered himself as a primary member of the Congress with the South Calcutta district committee by paying four annas. Within a few weeks of being appointed to the National College, Subhas was put in charge of the Publicity Board of the Bengal Congress by Das. Aiming to streamline the Congress organization for increasing its reach and making its campaigns more effective, Das set up several centralized boards for coordinating various aspects of political activity across the province. The other boards were those for national service, swadeshi, propaganda, repression advisory, education and women's organization. Not everyone was pleased with the appointment of a young, inexperienced Subhas, who was not yet a member of the Bengal Provincial Congress Committee (BPCC), to such an important post. Das however deflected all criticism by asking the members of the executive council to trust his judgement.[68]

Early in September, Subhas got a second opportunity to closely observe Gandhi, who spent a few days in Calcutta during his visit to Assam and Bengal. At the end of July, the All India Congress Committee (AICC) had passed two crucial resolutions—one on boycotting the proposed visit of the Prince of Wales in November, and the other, urging people to achieve a complete boycott of foreign clothes (including stoppage of imports of foreign clothes and yarn) by 30 September, and promoting charkhas and hand-spun yarn at the same time.[69] Gandhi had inaugurated the boycott with a bonfire of foreign clothes at a meeting in Bombay on the last day of July and now wanted to impart momentum to the movement in Bengal.[70] At Gandhi's meetings with Congress workers, Subhas would sit quietly and take extensive notes.[71] It was during these days that he came to personally know the top leaders of the non-cooperation movement, such as Motilal Nehru, Lala Lajpat Rai and Maulana Mohammad Ali.[72]

Bengal had been uneasy about responding to Gandhi's call on taking up charkha at a wide scale, but to the call of boycott of foreign clothes and picketing shops the Congress volunteers responded enthusiastically. Ironically, the unkindest cut came from the traditionally staunch supporters of Gandhi, the Marwari community of Calcutta. They grudgingly agreed not to import foreign cloth only till the end of the year, that too probably in the face of a threat of strike by their Oriya employees.[73] Although many of the ex-revolutionaries had joined the movement, some were still hostile and thus an obstacle to the spread of the movement he was trying to build up. Das was well aware that if he could bring them under the movement, it would achieve a tremendous boost. Thus, not only with the objective of neutralizing their hostility, but to gain their support, he organized a closed-door meeting between these opponents of the non-cooperation movement and Gandhi, in which they agreed not to oppose the movement, and some of them even agreed to join it.[74]

To carry out the programme of boycott, the BPCC in September formed new volunteer corps across districts and subdivisions in the province. In Calcutta, the corps had Subhas along with many ex-detenus as members.[75] He would go around picketing shops selling imported cloth, managing a gradually increasing number of volunteers.[76] It was around this time that Subhas started touring the districts with Das.[77] The movement gathered more steam when, in the first week of November, the AICC authorized the provincial Congress committees to undertake civil disobedience as the date of visit of the Prince of Wales approached. It culminated with a relatively peaceful and complete shutdown of Calcutta on 17 November, 'due largely to the wholehearted co-operation of the Khilafat organisations'.[78] This was in complete contrast to the riots that erupted in Bombay, when the Prince arrived on that day, and raged till 21 November, forcing Gandhi to undertake a fast and cancel his plans for starting a civil disobedience (no-tax campaign) in Bardoli. While Das coordinated the volunteers' overall activities, Subhas plunged into organizing the hartal, and at the same time ensured that people faced the least possible inconveniences. He shuttled between the Howrah and Sealdah stations to escort women and children to their destinations in cars marked 'On National Service'.[79] As the secretary of the Publicity Board, Subhas drafted detailed instructions for the hartal, of which around a million copies were printed in Bengali alone, apart from English and Hindi. Distributed in the interiors of the province, these instructions played a significant role. The extent of personal contact he had established with different groups in the city within a short span, and the respect and loyalty of the volunteers that he commanded, left his colleagues with little doubt about his abilities.[80] This demonstration of organizational prowess doubtlessly escalated his position amongst the Congress workers as an able lieutenant of Das.

Calcutta had been the centre of the politics of agitation since the days of Bengal's partition in 1905. Protest meetings, revolutionary conspiracy, picketing, strikes, riots—the city had seen it all. But a total loss of control with the accompanying takeover of the city by Congress and Khilafat volunteers was unprecedented, and frightened the Government as well as the powerful European business community. Their representative in the legislative council agreed with the nationalist press in announcing that the hartal was a revolution. 'Revolution is what these things mean, and as revolution they must be dealt with,' was the demand of R.M. Watson-Smyth of the Bengal Chamber of Commerce in the council. The Government retaliated on 19 November by declaring the volunteer organizations illegal, banning public meetings and by raiding the Congress and Khilafat offices.[81]

It was tempting to the youth brigade to accept the challenge thrown by the Government in a show of strength. Das, however, was in favour of consulting Gandhi and taking stock of the support on the ground that could be garnered if he chose the route of direct conflict. On his return from a Congress Working Committee (CWC) meeting held in Bombay on 22–23 November, Das, armed with resolutions passed by the AICC and the CWC—authorizing provincial committees to undertake civil disobedience on their own responsibility—and feedback received from district Congress committees, got the BPCC to sanction a civil disobedience movement against Government repression, and was designated a 'dictator' by the committee.[82]

Das ruled out the opposition of the Bengal Gandhian camp, who feared violence would engulf the proposed civil disobedience, but chose a graded response, starting with batches of five volunteers going out from 3 December to hawk khadi and enlist support for another hartal to be held on 24 December, the day the Prince of Wales was scheduled to visit the city. A body comprising six volunteers, two each from the Muslim, Marwari and Bengali communities, were chosen to coordinate the volunteer enlistment, and Subhas, now a member of the BPCC, was appointed to direct this apex body. The response to an appeal for enlisting as volunteers was, however, unsatisfactory. Around 5000 volunteers had signed up, but many of them did not mean to keep their pledge to participate. Even the police did not seem concerned enough to arrest any of the volunteers hawking khadi. The dejected expressions of Subhas during these days invited the epithet of 'our crying captain' from Das. A few initial arrests too failed to create any ripple. Angry and frustrated at the lack of participation of the Bengali students, Das struggled to find a way to make an impact. He decided that someone should lead the batches of volunteers whose arrest should generate some political heat. Subhas offered to lead, but was refused permission by Das as it was his responsibility to maintain the steady flow of volunteers. Instead, on 6 November, Das decided to send his son Chira Ranjan at the head of a batch, who was promptly arrested and severely beaten up by the police. To escalate the pressure, Das sent his wife and sister along with Hemanta the next day to hawk khadi and spread the message of hartal. Das's calculations worked spectacularly, as the arrest of Basanti Devi, his wife, and Urmila Devi, his sister, sparked a tremendous reaction in the whole province and led to a rush for enlisting as volunteers. The reaction was not restricted to the general public but affected the police force too. Overnight the Government issued an order to increase the pay of the constables, and intervened quickly to release the ladies by the night, but the impact desired by Das had already been achieved by then. Jails were overflowing with eager volunteers courting arrest, refusing to leave even when the police were keen to let them go.[83] In a curious contrast, the same night, the Bengal moderates led by Sir B.C. Mitter were busy hosting a dinner for the Viceroy Lord Reading, where they pledged their support to the Government against the non-cooperation movement.[84]

The next day when Basanti Devi went out again, followed by a large number of volunteers, the police were careful enough not to arrest her again.[85] On the same day, in an attempt to defuse the situation, Bengal's Governor, Lord Ronaldshay, met Das and asked him to call off the planned hartal. When Das refused to budge, Ronaldshay warned him that the Government would then take measures to maintain law and order. The message was clear and Das had little doubt that he would be arrested soon— and he was, soon enough. The police arrested him and the secretary of the Bengal Congress Birendranath Sasmal on the afternoon of 10 December from his house, as well as Abul Kalam Azad, then president of the Bengal Provincial Khilafat Committee, separately. The police were on the lookout for Subhas too and hoped to find him in Das's house. On getting to know that the police were looking for him, Subhas called the Lalbazar police station and informed them that he was in the Congress office. He was arrested in the evening and taken to the Presidency jail where Das, Azad and Sasmal were also lodged. The jail was now the 'Swaraj Ashram'.[86] As he was taken away, Das appealed to all Indians to keep the movement alive, while making a barbed reference to the moderate politicians, asking them to consider whether they 'will not stand on the side of India in her conflict with the bureaucracy', and then telling them bluntly, 'if you do not stand by for India, you assuredly stand for the bureaucracy'.[87]

With the Government determined to break the movement, large-scale arrests took place within the next few days.[88] As regular prisons proved inadequate for accommodating prisoners, camp prisons were opened, which too were filled up quickly, a problem that was compounded by the prisoners' refusal to be let free, which led the Government to stop further arrests and instead take recourse to the use of lathis and water cannons on the demonstrators. The army was called in to regain control of the city. As the repression continued, the moderate politicians, who had joined the Government to work on the Montagu–Chelmsford reforms, gradually started registering their protest against the repressive measures under the pressure of public opinion which was clearly building up against them. While some resigned from the legislature, others gave up their titles. When the Viceroy, Lord Reading, arrived in Calcutta a week before the Prince's visit, the members of the Calcutta Bar cancelled a banquet which they had planned to host in his honour, in protest against the arrest of Das.[89]

To give the protests of the moderates a concrete shape, Madan Mohan Malaviya approached Reading with a request to meet a delegation of leaders who wanted to propose a conference between the Government and all sections of the political groups in order to break the current impasse. Reading refused to discuss the possibility of holding a conference unless Gandhi called off the boycott; but if Gandhi did, Reading too promised to reciprocate by withdrawing the proclamation banning volunteer organizations and by releasing the arrested non-cooperators. At the same time, he explained to Malaviya that even if he agreed to hold a conference, it would be only to listen to and discuss various points of view, without committing his Government to any particular course of action. Malaviya immediately wired Gandhi about the move and asked whether he would agree to withdraw the ongoing boycott of the Prince's visit and suspend civil disobedience till the end of the proposed conference, if the Viceroy agreed to the idea. On 18 December, Reading, anxious to avoid any unpleasantness during the Prince's visit to Calcutta, sent an urgent message to Montagu seeking the Cabinet's approval for holding the proposed conference in January 1922. He strongly underscored the need to hold the conference (although he did not reveal this to Malaviya) by adding that 'some such step is inevitable, and particularly here in Bengal'. Quite categorically he stated that 'it would be absurd of Governments to continue to enforce a law which rouses such strong opposition when the immediate object of the proclamation can be attained by agreement making for peace'.[90]

Malaviya took the matter to Das in the Presidency jail, where they discussed the proposals along with Azad. Das's youth brigade, including Subhas, fervidly opposed any agreement to the Viceroy's terms, but the leader argued that this was the only chance to show some results to the people for Gandhi's promise of Swaraj by the end of the year, at a time when the Congress had no other concrete achievement to talk about; even if the proposed conference ended in a failure, the Congress would emerge stronger. This line of argument brought the young hotheads around. On 19 December, Das and Azad sent a telegram to Gandhi, who was sceptical about the intentions of the Government and the utility of the conference, recommending withdrawal of the hartal on the conditions that the conference should discuss all issues raised by the Congress, that the Government should withdraw all repressive measures, and that all non-cooperators would be released unconditionally. Gandhi responded the same day, adding two more conditions for withdrawing the hartal: that the terms, composition and date of the conference should be settled first, and that the Ali brothers, along with others imprisoned for asking Muslims to quit Government service, should be released too. To Malaviya's query he made it clear that he would consider suspending non-cooperation only if he considered the conference a success. At the same time, he warned Jamnadas Dwarkadas that the Viceroy was misleading them. This charge, of course, was not true, as Reading's telegram to Montagu clearly demonstrates his genuine willingness to enter into a dialogue with the different groups of politicians, and he had made it clear at the outset that by agreeing to hold the conference, he was not committing to any specific outcome.[91]

When the British Cabinet deliberated upon Reading's telegram on 20 December, an accommodative Montagu (albeit with some reservations) was strongly overruled by the Foreign Secretary, Lord Curzon, and the Secretary of State for the Colonies, Winston Churchill, as a result of which he was compelled to inform Reading that the British Government was not in favour of holding a conference which they feared would inevitably result in demands for Swaraj. Thus, when Malaviya led the delegation to meet Reading on 21 December, on one hand, no agreement had been reached between the Congress leaders, while on the other, the Cabinet had shot down Reading's proposals. Reading stuck to his point that no negotiation was possible without the withdrawal of the non-cooperation movement. By the time Gandhi's delayed approval reached Malaviya, Reading had left the city. The initiative fizzled out, and the opportunity to force the Government into granting provincial autonomy (which was Das's main objective at this point) was lost. Obtaining provincial autonomy would eventually take thirteen more years. According to Subhas, Das 'was beside himself with anger and disgust', and that the 'Congress rank and file' too felt that Gandhi had 'committed a serious blunder'. As far as Subhas was concerned, as the year went by without the promised Swaraj, Gandhi's 'words floated like dreams before my mind's eye'.[92]

Being given key organizational responsibilities and being sent to prison within six months of his return to Calcutta indicated a promising start for Subhas, but at the threshold of his twenty-fifth birthday, he was too young to have much say in political decision-making. Prison life presented little opportunity for any political engagement, except being a spectator to developments outside or engaging in endless debates inside. But with a plethora of senior leaders and the emerging next rung of leadership in the same jail, life could be anything but dull. If any single theme, available from the accounts of some of the inmates, overshadows all other aspects of worry and anxiety associated with prison life, it is that of turning every small thing into mirth and merriment. Reciting nonsense rhymes, singing parodies, mimicking famous leaders, recreating children's language instructions by introducing concepts of British repression, mock publication of satirical newspapers, and fiercely discussing which post each of them would get after the advent of Swaraj were some of the activities that would keep the young men busy. It could not have been any less amusing to Subhas when he found out that his shaving box was being used by a petty criminal as the place to hide hashish smuggled into the jail. Subhas was, however, noted for the care he showered on his comrades. Sasmal would later write that Subhas 'would take so much care of everybody all the time, that it seemed caring for others was the mission of his life'. The centre of his attention, of course, was Das, who continued to suffer from various ailments throughout the months of imprisonment. But that would not stop him from nursing others such as Hemanta and Sasmal when they fell ill. While Subhas was designated as Das's 'cook', Hemanta became his 'servant', eliciting the remark from Sir Abdur Rahim, the Bengal Government's member-in-charge of jails, 'CR, you are a very expensive prisoner. An ICS is serving you as cook and a University lecturer as your servant.'[93]

Subhas's trial started almost a month after his arrest, and on 7 February he was sentenced to six months of imprisonment with hard labour. A visibly disappointed Subhas's reaction to only six months' sentence was, 'Have I robbed a fowl?' Like others, he too was transferred to Alipore Central Jail after being sentenced.

A disappointing end to the year, however, was not to remain the only disappointment. An even greater shock descended upon Das and his team, as on many others across the country, within two months. Gandhi, appointed as 'the sole Executive Authority of the Congress' vested 'with the full powers of the All India Congress Committee' by the Ahmedabad Congress session in December 1921, decided to resume the no-tax campaign in Bardoli under his guidance, which he had postponed in the wake of the violence in Bombay. Bardoli was to be the 'first unit for mass civil disobedience in order to mark the national revolt against the Government for its consistently criminal refusal to appreciate India's resolve regarding the Khilafat, the Punjab and swaraj', he informed the Viceroy, and gave him seven days to withdraw the repressive policies of the Government.[94] But just as the civil disobedience was about to be started after the Viceroy's rejection of Gandhi's demands, news of carnage by a mob led by Congress volunteers, in Chauri Chaura in the Gorakhpur district of the United Provinces, jolted him. On 5 February, reacting to police atrocities, the mob of a few thousands burnt down the police station, forcing twenty-two policemen to be burnt alive or hacked to death, all while shouting 'Mahatma Gandhi ki jai'. 'I personally can never be party to a movement half violent and half non-violent, even though it may result in the attainment of so-called swaraj,' Gandhi wrote to the working committee members, and asked them to convene and decide whether the civil disobedience should be suspended.[95] The working committee, meeting at Bardoli on 11 and 12 February, suspended the civil disobedience programme 'till the atmosphere is so non-violent as to ensure the non-repetition of popular atrocities . . . or hooliganism'. Till then, all Congress organizations were to focus on constructive activities such as popularizing charkha, manufacturing of hand-spun and hand-woven khaddar, organizing national schools, improving the condition of the depressed classes, promoting communal unity, and organizing temperance campaigns.[96]

Gandhi's decision, though warmly supported by moderate leaders, came in for scathing criticism and opposition from a large section of leaders such as Das, Lajpat Rai, Motilal Nehru and Vithalbhai Patel. While Vallabhbhai Patel and Rajendra Prasad stood by Gandhi, another staunch Gandhi loyalist, Rajagopalachari, was puzzled. But before long, Rajagopalachari and Jawaharlal Nehru, who was disappointed by the suspension of the movement too, reconciled themselves with the decision.[97] Rai and Motilal wrote stinging letters, but their views were overruled by Gandhi on the ground that those in prison were civilly dead and did not have the right to advise those on the outside.[98] In jail, Subhas saw Das 'beside himself with anger and sorrow at the way Mahatma Gandhi was repeatedly bungling'. What he thought at that time is not recorded, but it could not have been much different from Das's view. 'To sound the order of retreat just when public enthusiasm was reaching the boiling-point was nothing short of a national calamity,' he would write later.[99]

With mass civil disobedience suspended, the non-cooperation movement was now dead. While Gandhi made it clear that not only would he reject a Swaraj that came at the cost of violence, but that Congress workers would have to wait till they first attained a state of genuine non-violence, neither Das nor the revolutionaries (who had been supporting the non-cooperation movement in Bengal till now) could have possibly submitted to this diktat. There was, however, a difference in the nature of objections which Das and the revolutionaries had towards Gandhi's philosophy. Non-violence was central to the political programme and philosophy of Das, a vaishnav (followers of Krishna, but non-violent). But for him, what mattered more was securing political power in the hand of Indians, for that alone, he believed, would bring material well-being to millions of Indians. He accepted the constructive programmes suggested by Gandhi, but was not ready to make a fetish of non-violence or the spinning wheel. The case of the revolutionaries was quite different. They had agreed to work with Gandhi by abjuring violence for a year for the attainment of Swaraj. Not only did Swaraj not materialize, but the very movement they were propelling in Bengal had been called off. Both Das and the revolutionaries felt let down.

As Gandhi and his followers, with support from the moderates, chalked out what they thought was the programme for moral regeneration to make the country fit for Swaraj, Das started exploring the alternatives. The path he recommended was that of non-cooperation within legislative councils, in addition to general non-cooperation. The central argument he forwarded was that the ease with which repressive laws could be framed and Congress leaders and volunteers arrested, and peaceful movements suppressed on the basis of the laws, was a clear pointer to the failure of the policy of boycott of legislatures advocated by Gandhi and accepted by the Congress. The participation of the moderates in the Government in fact suggested that the Indians themselves were unhappy with the non-cooperation movement, an argument which Ronaldshay had used against Das. Das's proposition was that

in a revolutionary fight, the points of vantage should not be left in the hands of the enemy. Therefore all elected seats in the legislatures, as also in all public bodies . . . should be captured by Congressmen. Where there was room for doing any solid constructive work, they could do so. But failing that, they could at least keep up a systematic opposition to the members and agents of the Government, and thereby prevent them from doing mischief . . . if the Viceroy or the Governor set aside the decision of any legislature, the Government would stand condemned before the bar of public opinion, both inside India and outside. Lastly, under the existing constitution, a vote against the Ministers or their departments could not be overridden by the Governor of any province, and if the provincial legislature voted down the salaries of Ministers, they would automatically be thrown out of office and the working of the diarchical constitution would have to be suspended.[100]

He floated the idea amongst his colleagues in the prison and vivacious debates followed. Not content with the debates inside the prison, Das decided to take it out to the open political field. Restricted in the confines of the jail, he let the message out through the speech of Basanti Devi, who had been chosen to preside over the Bengal Provincial Conference held in May, at Chittagong. As Das would have expected, the Bengal Gandhians led by Shyam Sundar Chakravarti and Jitendra Lal Banerjee vehemently opposed any deviation from the course laid down by Gandhi. Das took the fight to the Gandhian camp on his release in August.[101]

This was also the time when the communist movement was gathering pace. Nalini Gupta, on a recruitment drive, met Das and his followers in the prison, in the guise of a Muslim businessman, promising huge funds from Russia if they were able to start a revolution in the country. Although Subhas and Hemanta were keen, the plan did not proceed any further as it was shot down by Das at the very outset.[102]

Subhas was released on 4 August, two days before the expiry of his sentence. Reviving the National College, of which he was still the principal, became his first concern. Subhas was welcomed back to the college with much enthusiasm at a reception by the students. Soon, he was drawn into the All Bengal Youngmen's Association (ABYA) formed by the initiative of Prafulla Ghosh. Subhas was selected as the chairperson of the reception committee and Dr Meghnad Saha as the president for the first conference of the association held from 16 to 18 September. He made an impression with his speech which, the *Amrita Bazar Patrika* reported, 'in thought and language, in style and delivery, was worthy of the man from whom it came'.

The association aimed to organize youths over sixteen years of age, across the province, in practical constructive work along the lines recommended by the Congress. A permanent organization of the association was formed after the conference with Dr Saha as the president and Prafulla, Subhas and Moulavi Muazzam Hussain as vice presidents. Another person who eventually got involved with the association was H.S. Suhrawardy.[103]

While Subhas concentrated on organizing students and the youth, and Das stationed himself at Murree in Punjab to recuperate, news came in towards the end of September about large parts of northern Bengal being affected by devastating floods. The BPCC immediately dispatched Subhas and Dr J.M. Dasgupta to organize relief in the flood-affected areas. It was the time for Durga Puja, Bengal's biggest religious festival, and Janakinath was not happy with Subhas staying away from the family puja at their ancestral house in Kodalia. But serving the ones who were suffering is what Subhas considered to be his route to spiritual progress, and that is what he had been doing from childhood. He told his father that serving the poor and the helpless would be his form of worshipping the divine, and then left.[104]

From 3 October, Subhas toured all the areas and made a place called Santahar his base station. A relief committee set up with Dr Prafulla Chandra Ray as its president, which had started collecting food, money and clothes, entrusted Subhas to coordinate the distribution of the material. Assisted by about a thousand Congress volunteers, Subhas took care of the relief programme for over six weeks. In extremely challenging circumstances he got down to work with meticulous planning; the limited resources available had to be utilized with maximum efficiency. He organized the volunteers into separate teams, each with clear responsibilities such as food supply, healthcare, postal distribution, information collection, etc. Maintaining discipline was paramount: volunteers were required to report at a specified time every morning for a drill. Reporting late would invite penalty, from which Subhas would not spare even himself. He would also issue regular bulletins providing information on the situation at the localities and on the identification of those who died from the floods.[105]

Once Das returned to Calcutta, he called back Subhas to assist him in the political campaign that he planned to take up with full force. The poor state of the National College was still bothering him. With the establishment at Forbes Mansion being given up due to the lack of funds to pay rent, he shifted the college to another place, but with the stream of students drying up, and the new political environment requiring his complete involvement, the efforts to rebuild the college had to be given up.[106]

Another task that kept Subhas occupied at this time was publishing the newspaper *Banglar Katha*. Annoyed with continuous criticism of his politics by the *Servant*, the mouthpiece of the Gandhi-loyalist Congressmen in Bengal and published by Shyam Sundar Chakravarti, Das was keen to bring out a newspaper that would explain his position. *Banglar Katha*, which used to be published weekly, with Subhas as its editor, now started to be published daily. By November, Das got the Forward Publishing Company Limited registered, with himself as chairman of the board of directors, Sasmal as managing director and Sarat Chandra Bose as one of the directors.[107]

In the meantime, as Gandhi remained imprisoned, Congress struggled to decide on the course of action. In June 1922, the working committee appointed a committee to tour the country and assess the situation in the provinces in order to decide on the possibility of launching a mass civil disobedience campaign. The report was presented to the working committee when it met in Das's house in November. While three of the six active members of the inquiry committee—C. Rajagopalachari, M.A. Ansari and Kasturi Ranga Iyengar—opposed changing the Congress programme of council boycott, three others—Motilal Nehru, Vithalbhai Patel and Hakim Ajmal Khan—argued in its favour. The working committee meeting also endorsed the view that non-cooperators should contest the next round of elections on the issues of Khilafat, the Punjab atrocities and Swaraj, and try to obtain a majority in the councils. A final decision on this was, however, left to be taken at the annual Congress session of 1922.[108]

Subhas stood solidly behind Das. Speaking at a public meeting on 11 December in College Square, he made clear that at a time when unrest was subdued and there was little chance of relaunching mass satyagraha, it was important to create a new 'crisis' to awaken the masses. He had no doubt in Das's assertion that if they contested the elections, the non-cooperators would easily secure a majority in the councils.[109]

As president of the Congress, Das took his battle to the annual session held in Gaya, a session marked by the absence of Gandhi. This was Subhas's first Congress session, and he went as the secretary of the president. Before leaving for the session, he laboured day and night with Sabitri Prasanna to ensure that Das's speech would be printed on time to be distributed in the session. In a brilliant speech, after touching upon global history and politics, explaining his points of view on nationalism, the desirable form of government under Swaraj, describing the course the non-cooperation movement had taken, and demanding rights for minorities, Das cogently weaved the arguments for his central proposition that entering the legislative councils was essential for neutralizing the British bureaucracy. Although Gandhi was physically absent from the proceedings, debates and discussions on almost all issues were premised upon his thoughts and views as perceived by various shades of opinion. Leading the Gandhians from the front, Rajagopalachari succeeded in garnering majority support to defeat the proposal of entering the councils.

Das was graceful in accepting defeat. Closing the session on 31 December, he remarked:

> . . . although today I differ from the majority of the Congress, I have not given up the hope that a day will come when I shall get the majority on my side (Hear, hear, and cries of 'Deshabandhu ki jai'). I hope we have learnt now to respect each other's opinion with hope, in spite of what appears like a split, and I believe we are really united in more points than we differ (applause).[110]

At the AICC meeting next morning, Das announced that he could not remain president of the organization and be bound to a programme that he did not subscribe to. However, he made clear that 'I am not leaving the Congress in the conviction that I shall be able to convert the minority into a majority at no distant date.' On the same day, he announced the formation of a new party within the Congress and released its manifesto endorsed by over a hundred Congress leaders, including Motilal Nehru, Hakim Ajmal Khan, Vithalbhai Patel, N.C. Kelkar, B.S. Moonje, M.R. Jayakar, and S. Satyamurti. The Congress–Khilafat Swaraj party, with Das as president and Motilal, Sasmal, Vithalbhai and Chowdhri Khaliquzzaman as secretaries, retained the creed of the Congress and set to work out in detail a programme for accelerating the attainment of Swaraj.[111]

Das's efforts to sway public opinion in favour of his programme had to begin at his home ground. At the subjects committee meeting of the Gaya Congress, more Bengali delegates had voted in favour of Rajagopalachari (twenty-five against fifteen). Moreover, the Gandhian 'no-changers' had come to occupy the offices of the provincial Congress during the previous year when Das and his followers had been in jail. While the dedicated and disciplined cadre of the Swaraj party started working to build up organizational support, newspapers such as *Banglar Katha* (edited by Subhas), *Kesari* (edited by Kelkar) and *Swadesmitram* (edited by A. Rangaswami Iyengar, nephew of Kasturi Ranga Iyengar, and later editor of *The Hindu*) started building up public opinion.[112]

Jadugopal has mentioned that Subhas's interaction with the Jugantar group steadily increased, with him becoming a regular visitor to the gathering of Jugantar members at Cherry Press in Bowbazar Street. Jadugopal claimed that it was here, in the company of Bhupendra Kumar Datta, Bhupati Majumdar, Upendranath Bandopadhyay, Amarendranath Chattopadhyay, Surendra Mohan Ghose, Satish Chakrabarty, Jiban Chattopadhyay etc., that Subhas accepted that the revolution needed to involve the four pillars of students, peasants, industrial labourers and armed forces. He had at the same time developed good relations with the Dhaka Anushilan Samiti as well. As his political thoughts crystallized, he accepted non-violence as 'Not creed, but policy'. According to Jadugopal, Subhas was the spiritual product of revolutionary Bengal. He had grown up among revolutionaries.[113] According to him, Subhas moved from the Congress line of Dominion Status to that of complete independence due to his increased interaction with the revolutionaries from this time.[114]

Support for the new party from the Bengal districts was yet to be ascertained. Subhas met Jadugopal Mukherjee in 1923 seeking the support of the revolutionaries[115] with a list of districts favouring and opposing council entry. He estimated that if Jugantar members Surendra Mohan Ghose, Bhupati Majumdar and others were to agree, then the Swarajya proposal would sail through the Bengal Congress. Jadugopal reminded Subhas of the revolutionary and non-revolutionary paths. 'Help Deshbandhu, then I will follow your way,' Subhas told him.[116] Jadugopal played an instrumental role in swaying the opinion in favour of council entry.[117] Many years later, he would write that even at that time he felt Subhas would grow up to be the leader after Das. He was particularly impressed by the fact that Subhas mixed with volunteers as one of them, and not as a leader on a higher pedestal.[118] The growth of the Swarajya party was driven primarily by the Jugantar group.[119] The Bengal revolutionaries agreed to Das's request to abjure violence for at least one year.[120]

By the end of January, Das issued the draft of the Swaraj Scheme for consultation, outlining his vision of a Constitution of India once Swaraj was attained, and by the end of February the party's programme was also published. The ultimate goal of the party was Swaraj, but the immediate goal was attaining Dominion Status. In the meantime, on being released from jail early in January, Moulana Azad took it upon himself to strike a compromise between the Congress and the Swaraj party. After hectic negotiations involving leaders of both the parties, Azad and Jawaharlal Nehru succeeded in striking an uneasy compromise, according to which both parties agreed to suspend campaigning on their respective positions on the council entry issue till 30 April, and to work on their other programmes without interfering with each other. The AICC and the working committee met again towards the end of May to find a common ground between the two parties. At the AICC meeting on 26 May, Subhas cited the Mahatma's writing in *Young India* to make a point that the minority party had a right to follow its own programme as long as it did not use the name of the Congress. He emphasized that the middle class and the tenants of Bengal were keen to send representatives to the council who could prevent harmful legislation such as the Tenancy Bill and the Education Bill.[121]

However, when the AICC passed another compromise resolution to the effect that the Congress workers were not to conduct any propaganda against council entry, leading Gandhi loyalists Rajagopalachari, Vallabhbhai Patel, Rajendra Prasad and Jamnalal Bajaj resigned from the working committee in protest. When efforts by Das and Jawaharlal Nehru failed to persuade them to withdraw the resignations, a new working committee, with M.A. Ansari as president and Jawaharlal and Azad amongst the members, was constituted.[122]

The Swarajists might have believed that the issue was settled, but the resignations were just the initial signs of the fight that the Gandhians were about to put up against them. Soon Rajagopalachari announced that the resolution was not acceptable to him, calling it mischievous and against the Congress constitution. C. Vijayaraghavachariar too issued a similar statement. Das, touring south India at the time, was drawn into an unpleasant debate as he refuted these statements. With a number of provincial Congress committees also declining to abide by the resolution, a meeting of the AICC was convened at Nagpur on 8 July to reconsider the resolution.[123]

When a resolution to hold a special session of the Congress to decide on the issue was unexpectedly moved by T. Prakasam, Subhas rose in protest. He pointed out that no prior notice had been given and that it was unfair to raise this issue again after an understanding had been arrived at in Bombay. He warned that insisting on a special Congress at this juncture would start a revolutionary party in Bengal, damaging the non-violent, non-cooperation programme, and was likely to incite a civil war within the ranks of the Congress. Jawaharlal, however, spoke strongly in support of a special Congress, which he thought was the only way to decide on the question and maintain the party's unity. His views drew support from Rajendra Prasad and Rajagopalachari. Attacking the resolution, Das insisted on deciding on the issue in that session rather than waiting for a special session. But the resolution was carried forward by a narrow margin. Jawaharlal's motion, condemning the defiance of the Bombay resolution by some provincial committees, was opposed by Rajagopalachari and Rajendra Prasad, and was defeated by only two votes, leading to the resignation of the working committee.[124]

When another meeting of the AICC decided to hold the special session in Delhi in September, Das welcomed the decision. Appealing for unity within the Congress he argued that the bureaucracy can be effectively challenged only with the sanction of the people, and creating that sanction through various means should be the goal of the Congress for the next two to three years.[125]

It was important for Das to regain the control of the provincial Congress organization. He toured the province taking along Subhas, attending meetings and trying to sway public opinion in favour of the Swaraj party. In August, his followers managed to elect Maulana Akram Khan as the new president and Bhupati Majumdar as the new secretary of the BPCC. With the former secretary, Prafulla Ghosh, refusing to relinquish office, the result was two Congress committees in Bengal. When the dispute was referred to the AICC, Malaviya ruled in favour of those newly elected.[126]

Rajagopalachari and Vijayraghavachariar did not attend the special congress. Mohammad Ali moved a compromise for suspending all campaigning against entering councils and for increasing the intensity of the constructive programme, and read out a message from Gandhi sent to him 'by some mysterious wireless' which permitted the congress to make changes to his programme if necessary. Although the resolution was passed by an overwhelming majority, Vallabhbhai and Rajendra Prasad made it clear that they were still opposed to the idea of entering the legislature, but would not extend the controversy out of personal regard for Mohammad

Ali, whose loyalty to Gandhi was unsurpassed. Subhas was nominated to two committees—one to devise the appropriate method for encouraging domestic manufacturers and boycott British goods, and another to revise the constitution and the rules of the Congress.[127]

With the way to contesting elections now cleared, the Swaraj party issued a detailed manifesto on 14 October, explaining further its programmes and objectives. The immediate goal of the party was 'speedy attainment of full Dominion Status', since 'before the old order of things can give place to the new the authors of the new order must have an effective control of the old'. The members of the party on entering the Legislative Assembly and the councils would therefore demand the control of the existing machinery from the British Government and British Parliament.[128] The Government, of course, was watching the developments, and the Viceroy reacted soon. At a dinner hosted by Mian Mohammad Shafi, Lord Reading made it clear that the administration would not sit quietly in response to the Congress and the Swarajist programmes, and if the Swarajists went ahead with their programme of wrecking the councils, the Government too would wreck the reforms. There was no question of advancing the reforms till the end of the statutory period of the current constitution, and any progress would depend on how well the existing framework was utilized by the Indians.[129] The threats could not have made any impact on Das. He was well aware of them, and prepared for the battle with the Government.

He had been planning to publish the English language daily, *Forward*, but in September, Monomohan Bhattacharya, who was scheduled to be manager of the newspaper, and Upendra Nath Banerjee, whom Das had planned to appoint as the assistant editor, were arrested along with the BPCC secretary Bhupati Majumdar under Regulation III of 1818. Das therefore appointed Subhas as the new manager, and Satya Ranjan Bakshi as the editor, and the first issue of *Forward* was published on 25 October.[130]

The Swarajya party in Bengal, led by Das and his able lieutenants, attained two significant victories towards the end of the year. Das was finally able to wrest control of the BPCC in December, when he was elected president. Only six orthodox Gandhians or 'no-changers' were elected to the BPCC executive committee out of its sixty members.[131]

Next, in the elections held to the legislative councils and the central assembly, the Swarajya party achieved significant success. In Bengal, the party won 47 seats out of 114 elected seats. The most striking feature was the party's victory in 21 out of 39 seats reserved for Muslims.[132]

Subhas, due to the omission of his name in the electoral roll, could not stand for election to the Bengal Legislature.[133] Das wanted Dilip to join the Swarajya party and stand for elections. Despite his immense respect for Das, Dilip was 'disconcerted' by the idea of joining politics. He went to Subhas with his dilemma; Subhas, though pained by his decision, assured him that he would not be forced to do anything against his will. Subhas understood that his calling lay elsewhere, that he was not made for politics. In that context, Dilip has been scathing in his criticism of the Gandhian spinning philosophy:

> The absurd spinning wheel as a message . . . left me cold and I never could understand how even great men like C.R. Das and Pandit Jawaharlal had been persuaded to flirt with khaddar and rationalise a medieval anachronism into a modern panacea.[134]

Lord Lytton tried to persuade Das to form the Government but Das refused, informing the Governor that the Swarajya party's aim was to 'put an end to the system of diarchy', an aim which could not be fulfilled if he accepted office.[135] He further strengthened the party's position within the council by obtaining the support of nineteen independent members led by his former associate, Byomkesh Chakravarti, whose ambition to become a minister had been shot down by Lytton.[136]

From his early days in politics, Das had been vocal about two critical components of his concept of Swaraj—ensuring the involvement of the people who had been kept out of the ambit of bhadralok politics, and ridding the society of the communal problem. Being involved in the swadeshi movement from its inception, he witnessed how dissension between the Hindus and the Muslims was exploited by the Government of the day. Bengal had seen some of the worst riots in the recent past too. It was, therefore, clear to him that to be able to exert pressure on the Government, it was imperative to bring the two communities together. To this end, he worked out a pact with Muslim leaders, spelling out the opportunities to be provided to the Muslims on achievement of self-government, to help them bridge the gap of backwardness. The 'Bengal Pact' was ratified at a conference of the Swarajist and nationalist councillors on 16 December, and was published two days later with Subhas's signature as the secretary of the BPCC.[137] The pact provided that the Muslims' share of representation in the council would be determined on the basis of their population share, with separate electorates; representation to the local bodies would be on a proportion of sixty to forty for the majority and minority communities in the districts, respectively; till the time of the appointment to Government posts amongst Muslims and non-Muslims reached the proportion of fifty-five to forty-five, Hindus would be recruited to only 20 per cent of those posts. The pact also stipulated that no law would be enacted on a religious matter without the consent of three-fourths of the community affected; that music in procession would not be allowed in front of mosques; that there would be no interference in cow killing for religious sacrifices, and both communities, rather than enacting laws on the issue, should come to an understanding on cow slaughter; that representative committees would be formed in each subdivision comprising equal number of members from each community.[138]

The good show by the Swarajists was, however, not good enough for the Gandhians. The Cocanada Congress, held in the last week of December, reflected a reluctant acknowledgement of the Delhi compromise resolution amidst a clear message from the Gandhians that Gandhi's ways were not to be tinkered with in any manner. Das agreed to Rajagopalachari's compromise resolution which reiterated that the Delhi resolution remained valid, but nonetheless, the Congress continued to subscribe to the principle and policy of triple boycott enunciated by Gandhi. Motilal Nehru's motion to refer the Bengal Pact to the subcommittee of the Congress, which was engaged in drawing up a National Pact, was also defeated, despite support from some leaders such as Rajagopalachari and Sarojini Naidu.[139] The pact was, however, accepted by the Khilafat Conference which was under way in Cocanada.

At the beginning of the session, Jawaharlal Nehru and Pattabhi Sitaramayya issued the report that the committee had been set up for revising the Congress constitution. Subhas was unable to attend the meeting of the committee immediately before the Congress session, but sent the committee his opinion that the goal of the Congress should be changed to attainment of complete independence by all legitimate means. The views of the two authors of the report, Jawaharlal and Sitaramayya, were that although they were in favour of independence, they felt that changing the goal of the Congress would give rise to controversy and consequently 'the case of independence will be injured rather than advanced'. While Vallabhbhai Patel opposed the proposal in the subjects committee meeting, arguing that the situation of the country had not improved since a similar resolution was rejected by Gandhi two years ago, Das pointed out that the term Swaraj expressed the idea more eloquently. The formal resolution to the effect that Swaraj included the idea of complete independence, however, was voted out both in the subjects committee and in the open session.[140]

While Subhas held down the fort in Calcutta, focusing on the publication of *Forward* and other organizational work, Das busied himself in strengthening the party at the national level. The crucial role which *Forward* went on to play can be gauged from its assessment by the bitterest critic and opponent of the Swaraj party—the Governor of Bengal, Lord Lytton. Referring to the publicity campaign of the party, he wrote, 'their official organ *The Forward*—a most excellent newspaper, well printed, well edited and cleverly written—is their most effective weapon.'[141] Das was working to build the strategy the party was to take in the councils and the central assembly, in consultation with leaders such as Motilal, M.R. Jayakar, etc. He looked to build a broad coalition with the independent members in the central assembly, a strategy similar to the one he followed in the Bengal council. The Bengal council was scheduled to start its new session towards the end of January 1924, and the party had also started the preparations for the elections to the Calcutta Corporation scheduled to be held within the next couple of months.

It was in this environment that the issue of revolutionary activities, lying dormant for the past few years, erupted again, with an attempt on the life of the commissioner of police in Calcutta, forcefully marking its return to the mainstream political discourse. In doing so, it also provided an avenue to the Government, on the back foot in the legislatures, to intensify its actions against the Swaraj party on the grounds of its purported encouragement to the revolutionary acts. On 12 January, young Gopinath Saha shot dead Ernest Day, mistaking him to be Charles Tegart, the police commissioner, who had earned the ire of the revolutionary groups. The police immediately swung into action, raiding the BPCC office the next day, and arresting some of the Congress workers.

Saha was hanged on 1 March 1924. On hearing that permission would be given to enter the jail to perform Saha's funeral rites, Subhas and Purna Chandra Das (assistant secretary of the BPCC), accompanied by many college students, went to the Presidency jail early in the morning. However, they were not permitted to enter the jail. When at last he touched Saha's clothes given to his brother by the jail authorities, he was very much moved.[142]

The next big political victory of the Swaraj party came in March 1924, when it won the majority of the seats in the Calcutta Corporation elections. The extent of support commanded by Das amongst the Muslims was evident from the fact that out of fifteen Muslim seats in the Corporation, ten were won by the Swarajists. Das was elected the first mayor of the Corporation and appointed Hussain Shahid Suhrawardy as his deputy, even in the face of opposition from the Hindu communalists. Subhas won his seat unopposed and was given the charge of the municipality administration, being appointed the Corporation's chief executive officer (CEO).

Subhas had demonstrated his organizational and administrative capabilities consistently since the time he took the plunge into politics around three years ago, but he was still a political greenhorn, just twenty-seven years old, and not the automatic choice for the post. Contemporary accounts indicate that Das had initially assured Sasmal that he would be appointed as the chief executive, but had to step back when faced with pressure from his powerful group of supporters in Calcutta to whom an 'outsider' from a small town was not acceptable. Some even raised objections on the ground of Sasmal's caste. They preferred Subhas. An insulted Sasmal left Calcutta, resigning his seat in the council, resulting in the weakening of the party. Das had no option but to give in to this uncouth development in the larger interest of maintaining unity in the party, although it must have been extremely distasteful to him.[143]

There is no reliable account of how Subhas saw these developments, or whether he was exposed only to the outer manifestations of the clash in the form of Sasmal's keenness to be elected, without being aware of the underlying politics. Although unlikely, this appears to be the case from an almost casual recounting of the incident two decades later:

> Though my appointment to this important post at the age of twenty-seven was generally approved in Swarajist circles, it did not fail to cause a certain amount of heart-burning in some circles within the party.[144]

This was not all. While the Government took over a month to approve his appointment, Hemanta too was not happy with Subhas accepting the appointment.

Once these hurdles were out of the way, and he took charge of the Corporation on 16 May, it was time to deliver on the promises. This was an opportunity to show that the Swaraj party could not only block and bring down an administration but was equally efficient, if not better, in constructive work. That was to be demonstrated by overcoming obvious tensions between different factions in the party, balancing unlimited expectations from patronage seekers, and neutralizing the manoeuvres of a hostile, provincial Government.

Das laid down the deliverables in his inaugural speech in the Corporation: free primary education, free medical services to the poor, supply of good-quality food and milk, improvement in supply of filtered and unfiltered water, better sanitation, housing for the poor, development of suburban areas, improved transport facilities and greater efficiency in administration at a cheaper cost. The overarching objective was to be the service of the *daridra narayan*.[145] As the chief executive, it was Subhas's responsibility to deliver on the promises that had been made.

Much was done to symbolize the transition of the Corporation into a Swarajist one. Khadi was taken up as the official uniform, streets and parks were named after Indian icons, swadeshi goods received preferential treatment in case of store purchases, receptions for Government officials were stopped and instead the practice of giving civic receptions to nationalist leaders was initiated.[146] As he was used to doing for any assignment that he took up, Subhas threw his heart and soul into executing the big plans. In order to be able to give his full attention to the work of the Corporation, he gave up the post of editor at *Forward*.

It was impossible to achieve the tall order that had been set for the new municipal administration without discipline, and Subhas led from the front to infuse discipline amongst the workforce. He went on rounds of the city almost every day to personally inspect the work, infused the habit of punctuality amongst the staff and went through the files to clear them, often taking them home after work. Khitish joining as the education officer gave him a shot in the arm in implementing the education programme.

Free primary schools for boys and girls sprang up all over the city, Health Associations, financed by the Municipality, were started in every ward of the city by public-spirited citizens for carrying on health propaganda among the people. Dispensaries were opened by the Municipality in the different districts for giving free medical treatment to the poor . . . Infant clinics were established in different parts of the city and to each clinic was added a milk-kitchen for supplying milk free to the children of the poor.[147]

Life was, however, not only about administration and politics. The friends and their mentor had their share of fun as well. The Indian Book Club, Hemanta's book shop in the College Street market, was a gathering place for the young revolutionaries, where Das too used to stop by occasionally. Subhas, on his way back from the office of *Banglar Katha*, would invariably stop by and make tea for everyone on a stove. Since the use of a stove in the market was not allowed, the market superintendent would regularly scold Hemanta. But because the stove was kept behind the bookshelves, he never actually saw that it was Subhas who used to make the tea. Therefore, he did not think twice before complaining to Subhas regarding the risk of a fire when he was on a round of market inspection as the CEO of the Corporation, much to the amusement of Hemanta and their other friends. Hemanta took this matter to a climax by bringing in the superintendent to his shop on a day when CEO Subhas was making tea and his mentor Das waited to be served. Needless to say, the superintendent did not know which way to look and how to escape from such a situation. Hemanta explained to him that given his very low income from selling books, he had no alternative to using the stove in his shop.[148]

While Subhas restricted himself to municipal affairs, significant changes were taking place in the Congress, and the Swarajists were successfully accosting the Government in the legislative assembly and the councils. Gandhi was released unconditionally on 5 February due to his poor health. However, he did not express any views till the time he held extensive discussions on the issue of council entry, vis-à-vis the non-cooperation programme, with Das and Motilal in mid-May. In a statement issued on 22 May, he expressed his inability to agree with the Swarajists on the council entry question, although it was a settled fact by then. He advised the 'no-changers' to concentrate on the constructive programme and let the Swarajists pursue their programme within the legislature. He assured them that if the Swarajists were able to demonstrate their success he would not hesitate to admit his error, and likewise believed that they too would retrace their steps if they were disillusioned by the path they had taken. In a counterstatement, Das and Motilal argued that if non-cooperation was a 'mental attitude' rather than 'application of a living principle', as asserted by Gandhi, they would not hesitate to sacrifice non-cooperation to 'serve the real interests of the country'. After clarifying the Swarajist programme within the councils and the assembly, they emphasized that they would extend their full support to the constructive programme of the Congress outside the legislative bodies.[149]

Soon, differences on another fundamental issue, which had been simmering under the surface of political activities for some time, came to the fore. The Bengal provincial conference at Serajgunj passed a resolution on 2 June, moved by a former revolutionary Shrish Chandra Chatterjee and supported by Das, praising the patriotism of Gopinath Saha, while simultaneously condemning the act of violence. The conference also deliberated on the Bengal Pact, and Das was able to carry it through, in the face of stiff opposition from his political opponents and some 'reactionary Hindus'. The Gopinath Saha resolution was to have more far-reaching consequences for Bengal, as it was equally repugnant to the official circles as to Gandhi. Declaring that 'I cannot but regard the resolution as a travesty of non-violence', Gandhi argued that Saha's 'knowledge that he ran the risk of being hanged made him brave, but not necessarily patriotic'.[150]

All these issues came up for deliberation at the AICC meeting in Ahmedabad towards the end of June. Amongst the key resolutions moved by Gandhi, the first one related to compulsory spinning by Congress members, lack of which would lead to disqualification from the organization's membership. He, however, had to withdraw the penalty clause in the face of a scathing attack on the political relevance of charkha by Motilal, and general opposition from the AICC members.

The biggest jolt to Gandhi's creed of non-violence came from the Congress members' treatment of his resolution on Gopinath Saha. Moving an amendment to his resolution, which, though not substantially different but more direct in appreciating Saha's ideal of self-sacrifice, Das appealed to the AICC to support the amendment to send a message to the Government which, he alleged, was threatening Congress workers in Bengal with arrest. Das's amendment lost by a margin of eight votes, but the message of this narrow defeat was not lost on the Mahatma. 'We had agreed to employ only non-violent non-co-operation; and yet we spoke exclusively about violence. How can we talk about violence at all in the All-India Congress Committee?' asked a hurt and bitter Gandhi. That seventy members out of the 148 present voted in favour of Das led him to regard the voting on the resolution to be Das's triumph, having a 'deep significance' for him.[151]

One of the factors that influenced the Government's decision to release Gandhi in February was that the Bombay Government did not 'believe that Gandhi, though a danger to peace, can be regarded as a serious menace to British rule in India'. It had hoped that 'Gandhi's first action on release may be to denounce Swarajists for their defection from the pure principle of non-co-operation [sic], and thus considerably reduce their power for harm in Legislatures'. That hope now lay dashed.[152]

After strengthening its position at Ahmedabad, the Swaraj party had escalated the offensive against the Government. In a show of strength, Das and Motilal organized a national conference of the party in Calcutta in mid-August. Within the council, the party under Das's leadership had successfully fought off all efforts of Lytton and the officials to organize members to oppose its programme, especially their efforts to wean away Muslim support to the party by whipping up communal sentiments with the help of the two Muslim ministers—Fazlul Haq and Adbul Karim Ghuznavi—as well as the Executive Councillor Sir Abdur Rahim. Das staved off their attempts to discredit the Bengal Pact, in which he obtained the support of the Khilafatists. In March, the Swarajists had blocked the demands for grants for the payment of salaries to the ministers. On 26 August, when Lytton resubmitted the demand to the council, *Forward* carried an exposé on minister Fazlul Haq, publishing a letter purportedly written by him offering a bribe to a Rai Bahadur in exchange for his vote in support of the demand. Haq's claim that the letter was a forgery was not enough to override the sensation that thoroughly discredited the ministers. The new demand was again defeated by the Swarajists, leading to the resignation of the ministers and suspension of the constitution by Lytton.[153]

Governor Lytton took the Swarajist successes as a personal affront to his desire to play a grand role where he imagined himself to be steering the destiny of the country. He had formed a personal dislike of Das from their first meeting, and everything Swarajist had come to be an anathema to him. Driven to frustration by his failure to isolate the Swarajists, and by being outmanoeuvred by them, he now sought to tame them by channelizing his efforts on another front where his actions would be beyond the reach of constitutional politics the reforms claimed to have instituted.

Shortly after his taking charge as the Commissioner of Calcutta Police in March 1923, Charles Tegart had alerted Lytton about a revival of the revolutionary activities which had been suppressed during the war years. Soon, arrests started to be made under Regulation III of 1818, after the Government linked revolutionary organizations to five murder cases in Calcutta and to preparations of overthrowing the Government by force. After the failed attempt on Tegart by Gopinath Saha, Lytton issued a stern warning while inaugurating the new legislative assembly on 23 January 1924. He made it clear that his Government would not be satisfied with bringing to justice the perpetrators of violence, but would 'employ emergency measures, to strike swiftly and unhesitatingly at the leaders, to stop the poison at its source'.[154]

By June, his complaints had reached a hysterical pitch, especially in view of the perceived threat to Tegart's life. In a letter to the Viceroy describing the situation in Bengal, Lytton laid the blame squarely on Das and Subhas for funding the revolutionaries. 'Subhas Bose the new Chief Executive Officer, of the Corporation is subscribing Rs. 1200 a month of his official salary to the Revolutionaries (sic)', and Das was paying them in exchange for their support to his Bengal Pact. Since the revolutionaries were getting large amounts of money from Das and Subhas, they could focus on their core activities without having to bother about raising resources through robbery. Hence, although the situation was apparently peaceful, the reality was actually more alarming. It was necessary to arrest Subhas, Das and other well-known individuals, but to be able to do that, Lytton needed more powers which could be obtained only by enacting a law in the lines of the Defence of India Regulations which had helped the Government to suppress the revolutionary movement during the war years.[155] Reading appreciated Lytton's position, but expressed doubts about whether such a law would not unite the politicians cutting across different points of view and help spread the revolutionary movement to other parts of India.[156] The British Cabinet too expressed strong views against the use of repressive legislation, and in early August the Secretary of State, Sydney Olivier, told Reading that existing regulations, including Regulation III of 1818, must be fully utilized before contemplating on enacting any new law.[157]

Writing to the Home Department on 10 July, the Chief Secretary of Bengal went a step ahead of Lytton in calling Subhas an active revolutionary: 'The revolutionaries now have active members in high places, including four or five members of the Legislative Council and the Chief Executive Officer of the Calcutta Corporation, besides supporters like C.R. Das and Byomkesh Chakravartti.' The Government of India agreed with the assessment, pointing out the increased influence of the revolutionaries in the political life of Bengal:

> For the first time the revolutionaries can command from a political party public countenance, secret subsidies and executive offices in a great corporation and can contribute in return organised support in election campaigns and at political meetings and votes in a legislature. This may clearly create a situation which it will be our duty to suppress at whatever cost and whatever risk.

The Gopinath Saha resolution of the Serajgunj conference was taken as evidence that the Swaraj party was openly inciting the youth to commit murder. Moreover, revolutionaries were being recruited in the Calcutta Corporation.[158]

Having informers among the revolutionary organizations as well as the Swaraj party was central to the Government's ability to keep up with their plans. The informer was also the reason the Government had not been able to arrest the leaders of Swaraj party and Jugantar, especially Surendra Mohan Ghose, whom the Government believed to be the mastermind behind the assassination plots. The informer was so close to the leaders that any move by the Government to detain them on the basis of information provided by him would have exposed his identity. Therefore, towards the end of August, when it lost its informer, the Government panicked. There was now no way to know what the revolutionaries and the Swarajist leaders were planning. As the only way to prevent any serious incident, the Bengal Government wanted to immediately arrest Subhas and seventeen others under Regulation III. Reading agreed with Lytton's view that these seventeen were 'all active and dangerous revolutionaries' and informed Olivier that he had authorized the Bengal Government to execute the arrest warrants, which had already been issued, when the Government felt that the arrests could not be postponed any more. By around the middle of September, he agreed that an ordinance giving special powers to the Bengal Government would be more effective in dealing with the threat of bomb manufacturing and acquisition of arms from abroad by the revolutionary groups which was intensifying in Bengal. The Bengal Government also thought that Das was losing control of the revolutionaries of the Jugantar party and kept pressing for the Viceroy's approval to carry out the arrests.[159]

A press interview by Das also played into the hands of Lytton, which he used well to buttress his claims of the increasing threat to the Government from the revolutionaries. *The Daily Telegraph* on 2 September quoted Das as saying that 'a much more serious anarchist movement than the authorities realise' exists in Bengal, and if 'the Swarajist movement fails, no repression can possibly cope with the anarchy which is sure to raise its head, and violence and disorder will reign supreme'. Clarifying his personal position, he clearly stated that he stood for constitutional progress and against the growing trend towards anarchy. Taken as a whole, the statement was merely a reiteration of his opinion which he had expressed repeatedly since 1917. But the part of his statement acknowledging the presence of a serious revolutionary movement fit perfectly into the argument that the Government was building.[160]

No arrests, however, took place immediately as an exchange of views on the ordinance proposed by the Bengal Government with the Government of India and the British Cabinet went on till late October. On 22 October, Reading informed Olivier that the Bengal Government had scheduled 25 October to announce the ordinance.[161] It was announced on the midnight of 24 October, and by the early morning of the 25th the arrests were made. Subhas was woken up from sleep early in the morning to be told by the deputy commissioner of police that he was being arrested under Regulation III. Reflecting the preparation that had been going on for their arrests, the warrants for their arrests were signed in July.[162] Massive searches were conducted across Calcutta and other towns in the province, but pouring water on the intelligence on the basis of which Lytton had been fuming for many months, and which ultimately brought the Viceroy and the British Government around to announce the ordinance, the police failed to unearth any of the much touted bomb factories or arms which it had claimed that the revolutionaries were accumulating.[163]

By his admission, the arrest came as a surprise to Subhas, and to others as well. Even as the deputy commissioner drove him to the Alipore Central Jail in his car, no one whom he met on the way could think that he was being taken to jail. The surprise was not due to his ignorance of the Bengal Government's moves, for it was public knowledge that the Government was looking for an opportunity to clamp down on the revolutionary groups, but because he had been away from politics since the time of taking charge of the Corporation. He had resigned from the post of the secretary of the BPCC in April, disassociated from the editorial work in *Forward*, and

'Everyone knew . . . that I was engaged day and night in my municipal duties and had been forced to give up politics altogether.' Hemendranath too, in his biography of Subhas, has pointed out the distance Subhas maintained from the work of the revolutionary groups. 'I can tell for certain, that upto the year 1924, Subhas had not the least concern or connection with anarchical activities of any kind whatsoever.' It was rumoured that his arrest could have been the result of some disgruntled subordinates in the Corporation feeding false information to the Government. The *Forward* published a letter in which an agent of the India Office claimed that Subhas was arrested on the basis of verbal testimony of some people and in fact there was no documentary evidence against him.[164]

A wave of protests followed throughout the country. Das, who was convalescing in Simla, rushed back to Calcutta and called a general meeting of the Calcutta Corporation, rising to Subhas's defence and condemning the arrest:

> As the leader of the Swaraj Party and the mayor of the corporation, why should I be let alone if the chief executive officer was arrested? Subhas is no more a revolutionary than I am . . . If Subhas Chandra Bose is a criminal, I am a criminal.[165]

The Corporation passed a vote of confidence in favour of Subhas, with six European members opposing the motion. Nilratan Sarkar, P.C. Roy, Bepin Pal, Shyam Sundar Charavarti and thirty other leaders from Calcutta issued a call for a nationwide hartal on 1 November. The Indian Association also asked the Government to revoke the ordinance and hold trial of those arrested under existing laws.[166]

Motilal Nehru issued a blistering statement on Reading and Lytton for issuing the ordinance and the arrests:

> My view is that the Government has gone mad—stark mad. . . . The immediate objective [of the Ordinance] is undoubtedly dismemberment of the Swarajya Party which has brought about complete discomfiture of the Government of that province and shown up Lord Lytton as a complete failure . . . I am not well acquainted with many of those who have been arrested but have had the privilege of knowing Mr Subhas Chandra Bose for sometime past and can say with confidence that he is as much connected with secret and revolutionary societies and their

methods as Lord Lytton himself is. He is a gentleman of great culture . . .
He had been present at numerous consultations in which I took part and
it has always been a pleasure to listen to his views.[167]

Gandhi's immediate response was strangely a muted one. In his message
to the UP Political Conference, he regretted that a prompt reply to
the repression was being prevented by lack of Hindu–Muslim unity,
indifference to charkha and khadi and the persistence of untouchability.[168]
To Motilal Nehru, he wrote, 'We must not do anything in haste or anger.
We must therefore bow before the storm,' focusing on attacking the
principle of extraordinary measures by the Government and ask for repeal
of Regulation III. He felt 'deeply hurt and humiliated that we cannot
take up with any degree of effect the Government challenge', but that
was not possible till the Congress was a compact organization and till
Hindu–Muslim unity was achieved and substantial work on khadi and
untouchability was done.[169] Defending Das in *Young India*, he used strong
words of condemnation against the imposition of the ordinance and the
arrests—'a demonstration of barbarism that lies beneath a thin coating of
civilization'—which showed that the spirit behind the Rowlatt Act was
alive. But he was also quick to point out that the conflict between the British
and Indian interests leading to anarchical crime, which in turn resulted in
repressive action, moved in a manner of a vicious cycle. Although non-
violent non-cooperation was the solution to the problem, India had not
shown the patience to try it long or far enough.[170] Within a few days,
however, he expressed regret over his use of strong words, repeating that
Indians have jettisoned peaceful non-cooperation, and Bengal's tragedy
could be averted by communal unity, discarding untouchability and
spinning.[171] Speaking at a reception by the Calcutta Corporation, Gandhi
hoped that Subhas would be released soon and 'resume the services
which, from all accounts I have heard, he was rendering with great ability,
efficiency and integrity.'[172]

While the leading Anglo-Indian newspapers, *The Statesman* and the
Englishman, insinuated that Subhas indeed was the brain behind the
revolutionary conspiracy against which the Government acted, *Bharatbarsha*
asked how Subhas could turn into a dangerous revolutionary so soon after his
appointment as the chief executive was approved by the Governor in April.
Sections of the nationalist press, however, blamed Das for precipitating the
crisis by talking about the threat that the revolutionary organizations posed

to constitutional politics. Magazines such as *Shanibarer Chithi* and *Prabasi* held him as indirectly responsible for the arrest of Subhas and the others.[173]

In Alipore Central Jail, Subhas was glad to find seventeen of his political co-workers. The Government, however, allowed him to continue his work as the chief executive of the Corporation till 2 December. He received official files and met his secretary and the deputy executive officer of the Corporation in the presence of a police and a jail officer. The only family member allowed to meet him was Sarat. From jail, he oversaw the publication of the *Calcutta Municipal Gazette*, the first issue of which was published on 15 November. By the end of November, there was also speculation that the Government would release him, but nothing came of that. Even as he concentrated on his official work, Subhas frequently ran into conflicts with the police officers in the jail. He would not tolerate their impertinence and would often take them to task. On 3 December, he was transferred to the Berhampore jail, cutting off the easy access to him, and taking away the facilities provided to him as he was no more allowed to function as the chief executive. The suspense over a probable release sometime soon remained alive, as the Government did not specify for how long he would remain imprisoned.[174]

Worried about the facilities at the new jail, Sarat sent warm clothes for Subhas. The ever-caring elder brother provided everything that the younger brother needed or asked for. He had filed a defamation suit in the Calcutta High Court against *The Englishman* and *The Catholic Herald* for accusing Subhas of being the revolutionary mastermind. Sarat also informed Das about Subhas's view that the Corporation should appoint someone in his place to officiate as the chief executive officer. Accordingly, Subhas's deputy was appointed to the vacant post for three months, while Subhas was granted leave without pay for that period. In the meantime, both brothers kept up their efforts to obtain a response from the Government regarding the charges against Subhas. By the first week of January, the Government communicated to Subhas its refusal to share a copy of the charges.

Being disassociated from municipal work bothered Subhas, but he kept himself occupied with the study of municipal administration and by making plans for the city to be executed when he was released. For this, he asked Sarat to send him books from the Corporation library. Through whatever little extent his Government-sanctioned limit of writing two letters a week allowed him, he discussed the Corporation schemes for city development with Sarat and other colleagues such as Santosh Basu.

Books, as always, were very important to him, and what probably annoyed him the most was the allowance of a paltry Rs 30 by the Government for procuring books and newspapers for all state prisoners; worse, the prison had no library! To tide him over, Sarat was to ask Subhas's friends Dilip and Ksitish, and other known authors, to send books over to build a collection for the political prisoners. The jail superintendent was also persuaded to arrange for books from the local college library, for which Sarat agreed to bear the cost.[175]

Two days after his twenty-eighth birthday, Subhas was again shifted from the jail. On his way to Calcutta, he was informed that his final destination was the Mandalay prison in Burma. After spending the night at the Lalbazar police station, in a cell infested with mosquitoes and bugs, without decent sanitary arrangements or privacy, Subhas's journey to Mandalay began in the darkness of the morning. The four days' journey by ship, as a high-security prisoner, was as good as it could get under the circumstances, with the Assistant Inspector General of police, Francis J. Lowman, participating freely in discussions on a wide range of topics with Subhas and his fellow prisoners. It was only a day before reaching Rangoon that he got the opportunity to write to Sarat and Janakinath about his relocation. The group of prisoners were taken to Mandalay by train, escorted by a large police force.[176]

The hope of an early release, if any, probably died with this transfer to a land far away from home. Amid the bitter reality of being confined to a cage-like jail built from wooden palisades, leaving the prisoners at the mercy of the weather, the only solace at the beginning was the association of the place with some of the most prominent freedom fighters of yesteryears. Lokmanya Tilak, Ajit Singh and Lajpat Rai too had graced the Mandalay prison. There were still some people who could recount anecdotes about the Lokmanya; the lemon trees planted by him still stood as a silent witness to his suffering.

Family, friends, politics, administration of British India's former capital—all these were now a distant reality. For now, there was little to do for Subhas but to embrace what was handed over to him and make the best out of it.

3

Reorganizing the Inner World (1924–27)

'I shall not let you all be in prison for much long,' Das had told Subhas while visiting his protégé in the Alipore jail, when Subhas expressed his apprehension that 'I shall probably not see you for a long time'.[1] Subhas's prognosis came true. He languished in faraway Burmese prisons for nearly twenty-eight months, without knowing, till the moment of release, for how long he would have to remain incarcerated.

Letters remained the only mode of communication with family and political associates, except for a few visits from family members. These letters written to and by him, along with some partially published notes and journals, provide much clarity to our understanding of the man. The forced leisure imposed for a prolonged period gave him the opportunity to reflect on a wide range of issues which interested him. This he utilized to learn new languages, refresh and update his knowledge of literature, history, and economics, etc., try his hand at poultry farming and not in the least, focus on his spiritual sadhana.

Over half of the letters he exchanged from the prison were with *mejda* Sarat Bose. The exchanges between the two brothers portray the deepening of the fraternal bond, which marked their relationship lifelong, starting from Subhas's Cambridge days—but it is probably not displayed so clearly at any other stage of his life. Sarat comes across as the big brother always reaching out to fulfil his younger brother's needs, constantly worried about his health and exchanging views on politics and administration. Subhas, at the other end, not only depended on his elder brother to take care of matters related to his public and personal life, but also explicitly put his complete faith in Sarat's judgement on various issues. Be it the need for books, clothes, money, or returning documents to people, taking care of his court cases against newspapers, passing decisions at the Corporation or contesting elections, Sarat was there to promptly act on his unceasing requests.

The most striking feature of the letters is an almost complete absence of any discussion on national politics. One of the reasons could have been the paucity of news. Subhas complained to Sarat that very little news from India was being published in the Rangoon dailies. He was not allowed to read the *Forward* and was not at all satisfied with the quality of news being published in papers such as the *Bengalee*.[2] It is also possible that he intentionally avoided commenting on the political scene at home knowing that whatever he wrote would be censored by the British officials. Even an innocuous letter he wrote to N.C. Kelkar eulogizing Tilak was withheld by the authorities who considered it to be politically sensitive. He wrote, 'Writing letters has become a problem to me now and something like a nightmare too. The nightmare is caused by the Sword of Damocles hanging over my head in the shape of Police Censor—whose autocracy easily beats that of the late Tsar.'[3]

Thoughts on the working of the Calcutta Corporation and the improvement of civic amenities in the city occupied a large part of his letters during the entire period of incarceration. The Corporation had given him the opportunity to implement his ideas to transform the city and achieve concrete results, and he preferred this to the verbiage of politics at this stage of life.[4] This probably also led him to explore the possibility of getting elected to the district board of the Twenty-Four Parganas.[5]

Within the short span of six months outside prison which were available to him as the chief executive, Subhas had chalked out programmes for developing the city and improving the quality of life of its inhabitants. Frequent inquiries, pithy observations[6] and detailed notes[7] and suggestions, to the extent that was possible, filled the pages of his letters to Sarat and others associated with the Corporation. To stay up to date on the affairs of the Corporation, he insisted that the Government should allow *The Municipal Gazette* and the minutes of meetings to be sent to him, permission for which was initially denied by the Intelligence Branch (IB) of the Criminal Investigation Department (CID).

Subhas wished that there were serious debates on the various aspects of municipal governance before the ideas matured and were put into action. It was critical to keep abreast of the developments taking place on municipal governance in other countries. In the age of specialized knowledge, it was imperative for the Corporation to convince the Calcutta

University to open a sub-department for teaching municipal governance, under the political science department.[8] At a more specific level, while planning for the city's development, he pointed out that it was important to keep in mind the nature of its future expansion. Certain areas needed to be developed only as residential areas and, therefore, facilities such as storage for pulses and hide should be located away from them to keep the environment healthy.[9] Not happy with the city roads and the working of the Roads Department of the Corporation, he planned to write a note to the committee studying the condition of the city's roads, and ask for a competent person to be sent abroad to learn the latest road construction technologies. There was no uniform rule to make the departments efficient: while it was essential to decentralize the Health Department and delegate responsibilities to health associations in the various municipality wards, the Roads Department should be centralized under a specially trained engineer.[10]

The markets in Calcutta needed better organization, and any expansion of these was bound to be haphazard without a proper vision. He was reading up about food preservation, and suggested that the city should have cold storages for preservation of perishable food items such as fish, meat and fruits in order to keep a steady supply of food by reducing wastage, which would also moderate the increase in food prices. He asked Santosh Kumar Basu to get in touch with the Ministry of Health in England or the London County Council to obtain more information on how this could be done. To understand better the price movements of commodities, their monthly prices in all municipal markets should be compiled so that, if necessary, corrective action could be taken in subsequent years based on an analysis of the price variations and their reasons.

It bothered him that Calcutta was behind Delhi, Bombay and Chittagong in the matter of providing compulsory primary education. 'A department which is responsible for the education of all the indigent boys and girls of Calcutta of school-going age cannot fall short of any other department in the matter of importance.' He was annoyed that in spite of his writing a note to Deputy Mayor Suhrawardy 'he had not stirred his little finger yet', but was later happy with the move of the Corporation to undertake an education survey in the city. It was critical for the education officer to not only take steps to make the compulsory primary education successful, but also to be conversant with educational psychology and kindergarten principles.

The problem of river engineering, urban drainage systems and sewage disposal interested him greatly. He was unhappy that the councillors did not pay enough attention to these problems—'Our engineers know precious little about river and our public men know still less'—and hence he took it on himself to delve into studying these to explore the best possible solutions to Calcutta's problems. He thought that it would be helpful to bring an expert from abroad to obtain insights on Calcutta's drainage problems.

Sometimes detailed, and often brief insights on these and numerous other issues, such as that of street lighting, encouraging home industry development through the Social Service Department, exploring innovative ways to generate revenue, preventing recurrence of diseases such as malaria and smallpox, proper cremation of unclaimed dead bodies, managing stray dogs, etc. filled the pages of his letters.

Although municipal administration was of immediate interest to him, he was at the same time pondering over solutions to the problems of national development, of which he identified those of public health, livelihood of the middle class and agricultural growth as the biggest challenges.[11] Orissa, he thought, needed industrial development since the large-scale migration of its people to other provinces in search of livelihood pointed to the low prospects of agriculture. The incidence of migration disturbed him, which he felt leads to a 'laxity in morals', with the breakdown of the family and habitation in 'insanitary and unusual surroundings in strange places where social checks are practically non-existent'.[12]

He was full of praise for *Sanjibani*, a Bengali weekly, which highlighted the issue of exploitation of destitute women. But he resisted the attempts of some quarters to give a communal colour to the problem since, in many cases, the abductors were found to be Muslims; to him, it was a purely humanitarian crisis where even Hindus were found to be abductors. The critical issue for him was that irrespective of religion, everybody should come forward to the aid of such women.[13]

One wonders what the Government, as each letter passed through the scrutiny of the official censors, thought of these systematic and constructive thoughts flowing from the pen of one whom they considered a dangerous revolutionary.

Notwithstanding Das's assurance of getting Subhas and the other state prisoners out of the prison, it became increasingly clear that there was little he could do. A war of words had ensued after the arrests, between Das and Lytton, with Das accusing the Governor of 'plucking up my *Swarajya* shoots which are the healthiest plants in the garden' and the Governor retorting that 'the reason why I do not accept Mr Das's remedy is because he is not my gardener, and he has no responsibility for the consequences of his advice'—referring to Das's refusal to accept office when offered.[14] The arrests under the ordinance, Lytton insisted, were 'repression of crime, not repression of liberty'.[15]

As the president of the Congress session held in December at Belgaum, Gandhi repeated his condemnation of the arrests, but the session did not take up the matter for discussion or for passing any resolution. Mounting a scathing attack on the cult of violence, the Mahatma pointed out in his presidential speech that the country was forced to eat humble pie as it was not ready for launching a civil disobedience movement. By the end of the Congress session, Das was seriously ill; his health had started deteriorating fast since his imprisonment in 1921. On 7 January 1925, when the Bengal Government sought to introduce the Criminal Law Amendment Act— converting the ordinance into a law to be in operation for five years—Das, carried to the council in a stretcher due to his failing health, led the fight to prevent its introduction. The motion to introduce the bill to continue the provisions of the ordinance for five years was defeated by fifty-seven against sixty-six votes.[16] Governor Lytton had to enact the law through the back door by certifying it, using the overriding powers accorded to him by the Constitution.[17]

~

On 20 June, Gandhi wrote in the *Amrita Bazar Patrika* that 'Calcutta demonstrated yesterday the hold Deshbandhu had on Bengal, nay, India . . . The wires that are pouring in from every part of India emphasize the fact of his all-India popularity.'[18] Gandhi was still in Bengal, touring the province for his constructive programme, and had spent a few days in the first week of June in Darjeeling, watching Das recover. When he reached Khulna from Barisal on the morning of 17 June, he was handed a telegram carrying news for which he was not prepared.

Das had passed away on the evening of 16 June.

Overwhelmed by grief, Gandhi broke down while addressing a meeting in Khulna, unable to speak for a few minutes. To regain composure, he sat down and silently worked the spinning wheel. Motilal received the news while convalescing in the Himalayas, with Jawaharlal by his side:

For a long time father sat still without a word, bowed down with grief.
It was a cruel blow to him, and I had seldom seen him so affected. The
one person who had grown to be a closer and dearer comrade to him than
anyone else had suddenly gone and left him to shoulder the burden alone.
That burden had been growing, and both he and Deshbandhu had grown
aweary of it and of the weakness of their people.[19]

Gandhi and Das's friend-turned-foe, Bipin Chandra Pal, waited at the
Sealdah station among a sea of people. When the train carrying Das's body
reached, Gandhi tried to carry the bier, but being swept off by the crowd,
he himself had to be carried on the shoulders of volunteers. Going by
different accounts, between two to five lakh people were out on the streets
of Calcutta to see Das for the last time.

In Mandalay, Subhas was anxious about the failing health of his
mentor. 'How is CR doing now?' he asked Sarat on 6 June. On the same
day, he had written to Das too. Das had visited Sarat at Kurseong on 1 June,
and on his return journey to Darjeeling the next day was accompanied by
him. The last Subhas heard from Sarat about Das was towards the end of
May, when he was told that Das's health was improving in Darjeeling. The
shock to him when he opened the newspapers published from Rangoon on
18 June, announcing Das's death, can be well-understood. He could hardly
believe his eyes. 'It has been stunning in its effect and I feel dazed. I do not
know how long it will take me to overcome the effect,' he wrote to Sarat.[20]
Sarat had, in fact, rushed a telegram to the superintendent of the jail the
day after Das's death, but it had been withheld by the jail authorities. For
the next two days Subhas neither ate nor spoke with anyone.[21]

Subhas first wrote to Das's son Chira Ranjan (who died less than a
year later), and not to Basanti Devi, unsure of her emotional condition. He
finally wrote to her on 6 July along with eight others, including Satyendra
Chandra Mitra, Bipin Behari Ganguly, Jyotish Chandra Ghose, Jiban Lal
Chattopadhyay, Surendra Mohan Ghose, Satish Chandra Chakraborty
and Harikumar Chakraborty. In a deeply emotional letter to the 'Mother',
describing the devastating effect of Das's departure on the youth of Bengal,
they appealed to her to take up the mantle of leadership.[22] A few days later,
Subhas wrote his own personal letter to her. The feeling of helplessness of
being in prison had never been so 'loathsome'. How could he, who himself
needed to be consoled, console her?[23] Subhas wanted to meet Basanti Devi
and toyed with the idea of requesting the Government for an interview,

but eventually gave up the idea. Six more letters to her, written from the prison, are available, but in his letters to Sarat from then on, his anxious queries about her were a regular feature.

He was not happy with most of the articles published in memory of Das, which he thought were superficial. One article by Sarat Chandra Chattopadhyay published in the monthly *Basumati*, however, touched the depth of his emotions and he wrote him a long letter—one of the few occasions when he opened up his heart, remembering his days with his leader:

> Those who were intimate with him are left with a hidden pain in their hearts. By mentioning some of our unspoken tender feelings, you have not only helped in revealing the truth but also lightened the burden on our minds . . . We, who were around him, have today no words to express our bitter sorrow; neither do we feel like expressing it to others . . . As for myself I can say that I fought with him on innumerable questions. But I knew that however much I might fight, my devotion and loyalty would remain unshaken and that I would never be deprived of his love . . . Sometimes I cannot help feeling that Deshbandhu's countrymen and followers are partly responsible for his premature demise. If they had shared his burden to some extent, it would perhaps not be necessary for him to over-work himself to death. But our ways are such that once we accept somebody as the leader, we burden him so much and expect so much from him that it becomes humanly impossible for him to carry all that burden or fulfil all the expectations. We are content to sit back leaving all political responsibilities in the leader's hands.[24]

Even in mourning he was careful to remind Sarat that all papers of Deshbandhu, including the manuscript of the book he was writing—on the philosophy of Indian nationalism—must be carefully preserved. Subhas was keenly aware of the clash of ideals between Rabindranath and Chittaranjan, and his letters tend to indicate that Subhas's philosophy was more in line with Das's nationalism than with Rabindranath. The efforts of Das's magazine, *Narayan*, to revive Bengal's ancient and national culture, and 'at the same time to expose the hollowness of the shallow internationalism in life and literature of Tagore and his school which did not realize the fundamental truth in nationalism' was 'bound to have a profound influence on Bengali thought' in the future.[25] He was studying the articles published in *Narayan* and asked Sarat to put together all the archival issues of the magazine.

While in prison, Subhas wrote a long essay, at the request of Hemendranath Dasgupta, reminiscing about Das, and also revealing his own views on Bengal's cultural and religious history. Das, he wrote, did not believe in doctrines in any sphere of life, and believed that India's social and political philosophy would evolve naturally out of its cultural heritage and its unique problems. Hence, he could not accept the ideas of struggle between classes or communities and was opposed to Marxian doctrines even though he believed in obtaining Swaraj for the masses. He could lay down his life for his religion, yet Islam did not have a greater friend in India than him. He sought to establish a Hindu–Muslim unity through cultural synthesis.

The versatile genius and colourful life of the Bengalis have stemmed from the blend of Aryan, Dravidian and Mongolian blood, which has made them intellectual and emotional at the same time, and produced a combination of the idealistic, the imitative and the creative. Bengal's uniqueness was evident from the fact that it has evolved a distinct culture of its own despite the influence of the Aryan culture. Thus, it was the land where Buddhism found its last refuge after being driven out from other areas; it was a place where the Arya Samaj movement failed to obtain a foothold despite the movement's popularity in northern India, but the Kali-worshipper Ramakrishna Paramhansa was venerated by thousands of educated Bengalis. Bengal's cultural life, Subhas argued, could be defined by the interplay of three predominant streams—Tantra, Vaishnavism, and Navya-Nyaya and Smriti of Raghunandan. Through the systems of Nyaya and Smriti, Bengal was connected to the Aryavarta (or northern India), while Vaishnavism connected it to southern India, and Tantra showed its links with the races of Tibet, Burma and the Himalayan areas. Das, he believed, represented in concrete form the essence of Bengal's culture and civilization, who never forgot Bengal in his love for India and vice versa.[26]

The most noticeable impact of Das's death was a leadership vacuum. Even in the eyes of his opponents, as much as to his followers, Das was the undisputed leader, albeit criticized, harangued and occasionally challenged. No one came close to him in the ability to control Bengal politics. Now, a successor had to be chosen. Gandhi, who stayed back in Bengal till the end of August, managed to patch up the factional squabbles with the help of Maulana Azad and threw his weight behind J.M. Sengupta for the triple posts of the leader of the Swaraj party in Bengal, President of the Bengal Congress and the Mayor of Calcutta Corporation. Sengupta had, of course, made his place through Congress work and by the brilliant role he played in the council as Das's main lieutenant. But he had none of Das's leadership qualities or resourcefulness to be able to hold the fort and at the same time provide an all-India leadership, to patch together the fissiparous tendencies in the province or create new movements. The divergent groups with whom he would need to strike a balance and create alliances included the 'big five' of the Swaraj party, the former revolutionaries (who obtained a majority in the BPCC by the end of 1925 and formed the Karmi Sangha in 1926),[27] and Sasmal and his followers. The necessity of juggling between these forces weakened his position from the very beginning and compelled him to draw authority more from the central leadership of the Swaraj and Congress parties than from his own mass following. The reality of this situation was not lost on Lytton, a situation that strengthened his argument against further reforms.[28] Sarat was not happy; he felt it was a mistake to put anyone in Das's shoes by allowing him to occupy all three posts. Contrary to evincing an interest in the succession struggle, he had some scathing comments to make. On Sengupta's accession to the post of the mayor of the Corporation, Subhas wrote to Sarat that he was glad about the unanimity among the Indian members of the Corporation while electing Sengupta.[29] As the BPCC became increasingly enmeshed in squabbles with the passage of time, he wrote to another friend, 'Congress politics has now become so unreal that no sincere person can be satisfied with it.'[30]

In fact, he was deeply disappointed by the decline of Bengal's politics into an unmanageably factious state. Bengal had rallied around Das, but with his departure, 'Bengalis again took refuge in their narrow selfish world.' 'Throughout Bengal today, a scramble for power is in progress,' he wrote to a friend. 'Today many workers in Bengal have developed a strong business and trader's mentality. They have started saying: "Give me power—else I shall not work." . . . I had never imagined that I would be witness to such a colossal farce enacted in the name of the country.'[31] He advised Hari Charan Bagchi to focus on social service without being influenced by the current state of politics, 'which is continuously getting so polluted that at least for some time it will not be possible to do much good to the country through politics'.[32] He had no idea that he would have to negotiate the unending feud within the Bengal Congress for the next decade and a half.

The elections for the next council in Bengal were to be held towards the end of 1926. Sarat wanted Subhas to contest from the North Calcutta constituency, but Subhas was not keen. Confined to an indefinite detention, he argued that it would be a waste if he, as an elected Swarajist member, could not be present in the council where the party needed to garner all its resources. He was also not sure if the Congress leadership of Bengal as well as the leaders of the Karmi Sangha wanted him to contest the elections. Moreover, he was worried about imposing an additional burden on Sarat for securing the resources for his election, in terms of money and manpower. Besides these, the fundamental reason that made him reluctant was his disillusionment with the councils: 'I am getting disgusted with the Councils because I find that people who go there do not mean to do any tangible work for the country. It is time for the pendulum to swing back in an anti-Council direction,' he told Sarat. Sarat informed Subhas that the Congress leadership wanted him to contest and the Karmi Sangha welcomed his candidature. Many had already volunteered to organize the electoral campaign for Subhas. As far as non-performance of many of those who were elected in the last elections was concerned, Sarat argued that the solution was to ensure not only the strength of the Swarajist bench, but also the quality of the people elected.[33] The brothers discussed in some detail how to go about enlisting support from various quarters, but soon, Subhas was barred by the Bengal Government from any form of electioneering from inside the jail.

The novel method of campaigning adopted by the Swaraj party in his constituency impressed him very much. Coloured leaflets seeking votes for him were distributed through rockets. The South Australian newspaper, the *Recorder*, reported on 9 November 1926:

> The Swarajists extensively distributed handbills by means of rockets which, on flying up in the air, exploded with an exceptionally loud noise. The handbills, printed on multi-colored papers, urged the electore [*sic*] to 'vote for Subhas Chandra Bose, at present within prison walls'. The Swarajists used this method to approach the women voters whom, on account or the observing of the Purdah, ordinary canvassers were unable to approach.

'Very ingenious indeed! Reminds one of the distribution of leaflets from flying aeroplanes in France & Flanders during the last war,' Subhas wrote to Sarat. The method of campaign was reported in newspapers in Rangoon too!³⁴

He was naturally elated by his victory over J.N. Basu, the Liberal Party leader who had won the same seat in the previous election. 'Though I was confident about the result I did not expect such a big majority. I do not know how to express my feelings of gratitude towards those whose combined efforts have brought about this welcome result,' he wrote to Sarat.³⁵

If his indefinite detention had any positives for Subhas, it was the opportunity to concentrate on doing what his busy public life of three years had severely curtailed. His broken health and persistent illness notwithstanding, he utilized the time in taking up some serious study on a variety of subjects, ranging from sewage management to history, politics, anthropology, philosophy, psychology and religion. Medieval Bengali literature fascinated him and he tried to make up for what he called his 'colossal ignorance of Bengali literature'. Despite being born in Orissa, he had little knowledge of the language; on his request, Gopa Bandhu Das sent him books on Oriya grammar and literature. He wrote to various friends, asking for information on instruments used for measurements in physical anthropology, the latest research on the theory of Dravidian migration, and came across information on early and medieval history of Bengal in Burman records which he wanted to share with the historians Rakhal Das Banerji and Ramesh Chandra Majumdar.

Along with his studies, he turned to a deeper pursuit of the spiritual. Sarat sent him Swami Vivekananda's works containing raja yoga. In the jail, Subhas set up a *thakur ghar* (a separate room or place for worship) for meditation. His interest in spirituality was not unknown to his friends and other associates. From prison too, he exchanged his views with them. Dilip, his companion since his student days, was someone to whom he would write about his thoughts as freely as possible, for he was too sensitive to the fact that the censor in the Government office would read through his letters. He believed that the incarceration—'the solitude and the distance from home'—had benefited him in terms of spiritual and philosophical advancements. 'Problems which to me were unsolved seem to be nearing solution,' he told Dilip.³⁶ To another friend he wrote, 'Thanks to this experience, I have come to know myself far better and my self-confidence has increased manifold.'³⁷

He also shared his views on the secrets of meditation and overcoming lust:

> Meditation has two aims—(1) Destruction of the evil faculties, principally to overcome lust, fear and selfishness, and (2) Manifestation of love, devotion, sacrifice, intellect and such other noble attributes. The best means of conquering lust are to visualise the mother-image in all women, to invest women with that halo and to worship God in the mother-form, such as Durga and Kali. When man contemplates God or Guru in the form of the mother, he learns to see divinity in all women; when he reaches this state he has overcome lust. That is why our forefathers, in order to create an image of Divine Power, thought in terms of the form of woman. In practical life, man becomes pure and clean through the process of contemplating 'mother' in all women . . . Devotion and love render a man selfless . . . The way to conquer fear is to worship Power. The images of Durga, Kali etc. are the expressions of Power . . .[38]

Subhas sought to learn more about different spiritual practices (he asked Gopa Bandhu Das for books on Oriya saints and their methods of sadhana), but in the spiritual realm, what seems to have particularly grasped his attention during this time was Tantra.[39] He had read Shivachandra Vidyarnava's *Tantra Tattva* earlier, but now took great interest in John Woodroffe's works (who translated many Sanskrit scriptures under the pseudonym Arthur Avalon) and asked Sarat whether Woodroffe had any disciple who could continue the work.

Dilip was deeply influenced by Sri Aurobindo and, therefore, in his correspondence with Subhas, who had proclaimed Aurobindo to be his spiritual guru just about four years earlier, to whose mission he had decided to dedicate his life and soul[40] the topic of Aurobindo's renunciation of political life to become a spiritual recluse naturally came up. Ever since Aurobindo had left Bengal, his return to the province had always remained alive, albeit as a dormant expectation. His implicit agreement with Das's political strategy[41] in contrast with that of Gandhi's, could not have been unknown to Subhas. In Subhas's opinion, as a mystic Aurobindo had gone even further than Vivekananda. Spiritualism was in his nature, and he had chosen Aurobindo as his guru, but he was uneasy with the thought of renouncing everything in pursuit of the divine. He explained the reason to Dilip:

I agree with you when you say that one may from time to time—and, on occasion, for a long spell—remain withdrawn in silent contemplation in perfect seclusion. But here there is a danger; the active side of a man might get atrophied if he remained cut off for too long from the tides of life and society. This need not, indeed, apply to a handful of authentic seekers of uncommon genius, but the common run, the majority, ought, I think, to take to action in a spirit of service as the main plank of their *sadhana*. For a variety of reasons our nation has been sliding pauselessly down to the zero line in the sphere of action; so what we badly need today is a double dose of the activist serum, *rajas*.[42]

Music and art, to him, were as much of a manifestation of the spiritual as it was of popular culture. He was keen that the children in the family should take lessons in music, and asked Dilip to flood the countryside with his songs. Someone who did not respond to music, he believed, was not capable of excelling in thought or action. As he told Dilip, 'We want that the experience of *ananda*—sheer causeless delight—should quicken every drop of our blood, because we only create in the fullness of *ananda*.' While serious research in music will have to be, of necessity, confined to the experts, it was important to make the joys of art and music accessible to the 'poorest of the poor', to be 'dispensed as a spiritual pabulum of the masses'. It was critical to revive the traditional folk musical forms such as *jatra*, *kathakata* and *kirtan*, which were existing only as relics of the past. He was fascinated by the *Gambhira* music of Maldah but feared that that too would become extinct if efforts were not made to revitalize it as well as to spread it to other parts of the province. It was imperative to 'restore the connection between art and life'. The way Burma had preserved folk music and dance impressed him. From what he had seen of Burmese life, he surmised that art could permeate every corner of society due to the absence of the caste system.[43]

The spiritual yearning also manifested itself through a longing for everything associated with Bengal. Bengal, in his thoughts, became an organic entity with an eternal message, which he felt he could not have realized were he not away from home so long. The letters which frequently discuss the landscape of Bengal, the literature, history and culture of the Bengalis indicate that, for Subhas, it was almost a rediscovery of Bengal from a new perspective, a Bengal to which he was getting more and more emotionally attached. Being in jail was no reason to be unhappy, he told a friend. Rather, it was a matter of pride to suffer for the 'Mother', a chance to spiritually prepare for the national struggle:

> I feel nervous lest the call of duty should arrive before I am prepared for it. At such moments I wish that I may not be released before I am completely prepared.[44]

There were people who wished him to succeed in that preparation. One of them, a former associate—an elderly Congressman who once belonged to the Gandhian 'no-changer' group and believed to be nearing the end of his life—sent Subhas his blessings: 'Be immortal and as a *Yogasiddha* (one who has attained perfection in yogic practices) person gather strength to put an end to the sorrows of our motherland.'[45]

Although spirituality was primarily directed towards development of the inner self, it had a public face too, especially in the form of religious festivals, which were no less important. Thus, the Bengal detenus organized Durga Puja and Saraswati Puja in the prison and asked the Government to provide for the expenses. Since the Government bore the costs of religious festivals for Christian prisoners in India, the superintendent of the Mandalay jail went ahead and provided all facilities for celebrating Durga Puja in October 1925. However, the Government of Burma refused to bear the expenses. The issue of the Government funding the religious expenditures came up again in February 1926 at the time of Saraswati Puja. Unhappy with the attitude of the Government, the detenus informed the Chief Secretary of Burma that they were commencing a hunger strike from 18 February. Although Subhas was only a co-signatory in the letter, it can be assumed that he contributed and subscribed to the arguments in the letter. In part, the letter said:

> To us orientals, religion is neither a social convention nor an intellectual luxury nor a holiday recreation. It is life itself. Religion is woven into the very texture of our daily and social life and it permeates our whole being— individual and national . . . And it is on this basis that our philosophy of values—social and moral—has been worked out . . . in spite of our misery and degradation, India still lives. She lives because her soul is immortal— her soul is immortal because she believes in religion . . . We still claim the right to worship our God after the fashion of our glorious ancestors, and we shall sooner cease to exist than succumb to the religious domination of the West.

The action or rather the inaction of your Government constitutes an unwarranted interference with our religious rights . . . To an European Christian, a Hindu may be a heathen, his religion may be taboo. And it may not be a moral duty to provide facilities for his worship. But we belong to a religion which not only believes in universal toleration but accepts all religions as true and we consequently maintain that the infringement of religious rights of any community is a violation of God's Law.

. . . The materialistic organization of the west is today sitting like a nightmare on India's bosom. Plassey and Assaye, Lancashire and Leeds, Bentham and JS Mill, have done their best to wean us away from our culture, civilization and past heritage. They have failed. From the ashes of the dead past India is again rising phoenix-like to take her place among the free nations of the world, so that she may deliver her message, the message of the spirit, and thereby fulfil her mission on earth. India lives today because she still has a mission unfulfilled.

India is determined to retain her religious liberty at any sacrifice. Whether needless suffering and avoidable sacrifice should be undergone before our rights are recognized, is for this Govt, to decide.[46]

Instead of dealing with the hunger strike, the Burmese Government, however, promptly took measures to ensure that the news of the hunger strike did not reach the Indian people, intercepting all correspondence from the detenus. But *Forward* published a major scoop when on 21 February it printed not only the news of the hunger strike, but also the joint letter of the detenus. The news naturally created a furore in India, and questions were raised in the assembly as well as the Bengal Council. On being persuaded by leaders such as Lala Lajpat Rai and Tulsi Charan Goswami, who sent them messages urging them to lift the strike, and by Shaukat Ali who visited Subhas and others in prison, the detenus ended the strike on 4 March. The pressure on the Government was aggravated when the *Forward* also published extracts from the report of the Indian Jail Committee of 1919–21, in which an official of the prison department, Lt. Col. Mulvany, admitted that he had been forced by the Inspector General of Prisons of Bengal to send false reports regarding some of the prisoners' health. Under pressure, the Government also sanctioned grants for each prisoner for the religious festivals.[47]

Report on hunger strike by the Bengal political prisoners published in *Forward*.
National Library, Ministry of Culture, Government of India.

Subhas had chosen a life of public service, and wider public issues kept him engaged even in prison. However, a strong undercurrent of attachment to the family, beneath the surface of all other activities, is evident from his letters. While in prison, he began to look for the roots of his family and asked Janakinath whether any book or manuscript on the history of the Bose family existed. Sarat, of course, was the pillar of support, taking up all the burden of his brother's worldly responsibilities, but Subhas was particular about remaining up to date regarding his other siblings and their families too. He worried about their career prospects (if *sejadada* Suresh Bose was progressing well with his plan of setting up factories or if he would like to acquire any; if younger brother Sailesh did not join Suresh, he should take up higher studies in textile manufacture or geology after graduation; nephews Amiya and Asoke should be given lessons in music and drawing). In no sense was Subhas a 'Gandhian', but he was ever vigilant about the spinning activities of his family members. He was immensely pleased to receive a punjabi (the Bengali word for what is known as kurta in Hindi) and dhotis made of homespun cotton from *mejobowdidi* Bivabati, Sarat's wife; he thought Asoke was a very good spinner and inquired why other members of the family were not spinning. Even smaller matters wouldn't escape his attention. He was concerned about his youngest brother, Santosh, having to cycle down to Jadavpur every day because he thought Santosh was 'neither strong nor steady as a rider and Russa Road, though wide, has plenty of wheeled traffic'. He often thought of Sarada, who had looked after him as a child. Sarada, who was very old now, had fallen seriously ill when Subhas went to jail in 1921, and for that reason she was not informed initially about his incarceration in Mandalay. 'Sarada very often pines for you . . . [she] is so anxious for you and she says "let me have the good fortune of seeing Subu before my death,"' wrote elder sister Tarubala.[48]

The letters to *mejobowdidi* Bivabati stand in contrast to the bulk of his other letters, in showing the tender worldly facet of his persona, which largely remained eclipsed by the image that developed in the later years. The letters drew pictures of the routine of prison life, character sketches of the co-prisoners, the Burmese society and told stories of interesting incidents as well as clashes with prison authorities—all steeped in humour. Written in flowing Bengali prose and devoid of all the seriousness with which Subhas is usually associated, the letters brought out the fun the prisoners had in gardening, poultry farming, pastime activities such as swimming and playing tennis and badminton and cooking.[49] It was a remarkable trait that characterized the political prisoners, evident from the writings of Hemanta and Sasma[150] on the period of imprisonment during the non-cooperation movement too; the passion for freedom and the consequent suffering never deprived them of the ability to find humour in the simplest of daily incidents.

The fun and humour notwithstanding, as months passed by, the hope of returning home was soon receding. After the Government informed the detenus in January 1926, after an annual review, that their detention had been extended till January 1927, Subhas wrote to Hari Charan Bagchi, 'I no longer worry about my release. Neither should you. By the grace of God I have mental peace now. I feel I have gathered enough strength to be able to spend my whole life here.'[51] He did put up a brave face and might have even steeled his heart expecting the worst, but the distress arising from the uncertainty of how long he would be kept in exile could not but have pulled down his spirits. While the initial agony of imprisonment had reduced, a sense of resignation had taken over, as he wrote to Basanti Devi in April. How far it was demoralizing is clear from another letter to her written in December:

God alone knows how long I shall have to be in prison . . . When I look at it calmly, I feel that for the present prison life is doing me good.

Of course, my heart refuses to accept it under all circumstances. Not only my own kith and kin, but also Bengal and the whole of India shine in matchless beauty in my dreams. Reality has receded from my life—I am now clinging to my dreams. My soul yearns from time to time for the reality behind my dreams. It is possible for a strong-willed person like myself to suppress such transitory cravings of the heart; but, I have already said that I do not accept *sannyasa* and I have therefore no right not to recognise sorrow.[52]

His health had started deteriorating soon after reaching Mandalay. Finding it difficult to adjust to the local climate, Subhas had applied for the transfer back to Bengal in April 1925, but it was turned down by the Government. There would be occasional rumours too, of his return to Bengal. 'The air was thick with rumours about your coming back,' Sarat wrote in October 1925. Expecting an imminent release, Dilip held back his letter to Subhas written in November 1925 by over a month. The following year, in March, there was again a rumour of the detenus being shifted to Madras.[53] The reality, however, was completely different. The Government was in no mood to let the dangerous men go. In January 1927, the Government informed him that the detention was to continue. 'We had a feast on a small scale to celebrate our continuance in our jobs!' Subhas wrote to Bivabati.[54]

When Ernest Thurtle, a Labour MP, asked the Under Secretary of State for India, Earl Winterton, in March 1926 why Subhas was not being brought to a public trial, the reply was that due to threats to their lives it was not possible to bring the witnesses to the court.[55] A year later, in March 1927, when another Labour MP George Lansbury asked whether it was not possible to expedite Subhas's release in view of the confidence expressed in him by electing him to the Legislative Council, Winterton was dismissive of the argument. His response was, 'If a person in prison has the confidence of this or that organization it is not a reason for a remission of his sentence or for dealing with him in a different way from any other person.'[56]

As the campaign for council elections went on and the results came in, Subhas started having frequent bouts of fever, dyspepsia, constipation and pain in the spine. In November, the Civil Surgeon of Mandalay suspected a case of enteroptosis (an abnormal downward displacement of the intestine) and advised further examination in Rangoon. Subhas was taken to Rangoon in mid-December, but the doctors failed to reach any conclusion after keeping him under observation for two weeks; the state of his health too continued to be the same. In January, Sarat, who was annoyed with the findings of the examination in Rangoon, obtained permission from the Bengal Government as well as from the Inspector General of Prisons of Burma for Subhas's medical examination by his *chotodada* Sunil Chandra Bose (the fifth brother) who was a practising physician. The examination by Sunil and Lt. Col. Kelsall, a senior physician of Burma, took place in Rangoon, where Subhas was taken again in the second week of February 1927. Although they could not find any evidence on which to base their diagnosis, both opined that they would treat this as a case of suspected early tubercle and would put him under the best conditions of climate, food and rest. They pointed out that the condition in the jail was not conducive to his health, which continued to deteriorate further through February and March. In an additional report, Sunil opined that Subhas's illness was 'definitely one of tuberculosis of the lungs' and advised taking an immediate sea voyage and prolonged stay in a sanatorium in Switzerland.

While waiting in Rangoon, an incident involving the superintendent of Rangoon Jail, Major Flowerdew, incensed Subhas to press for transfer to either Mandalay or Insein jail. When one morning he sent a note to the Chief Jailor to ensure before leaving office for breakfast that the newspaper reached him, it drew a sharp response from the superintendent. 'Mr Bose is requested not to give orders to my Chief Jailor', scribbled Flowerdew beneath Subhas's note. Such a comment was unacceptable to Subhas; he found it to be insulting and immediately shot off a letter to the Governor of Burma, informing him of the situation and requesting him to direct Flowerdew to apologize. In his letter, he explained that he had to send the note to the Chief Jailor because the jail officers were negligent about delivering the newspapers that arrived with the mail from Calcutta, and whenever not reminded, they did not hand over the newspapers. Bringing this matter to the attention of the jail authorities had not helped. Therefore, sending reminder notes was the only option open to him, and the practice was working fine until that morning when Flowerdew suddenly woke up to a dislike of Subhas giving orders to the Chief Jailor. With tongue in cheek, he told the Governor that though he was aware that the work for which jail officers were paid by the Government included looking after their comforts, he was not presumptuous enough to think that he could order them around. He also reminded him that 'as an officer he had European subordinates of high education and international reputation some of whom at least draw salaries almost double that drawn by Major Flowerdew'. Being in that position, he knew how to give orders and his note could, under no circumstances, be construed as one. Subhas also wrote to Motilal Nehru and J.M. Sengupta to press the Government for an early transfer. Within a few days, Subhas was moved to Insein prison near Rangoon.

The superintendent of Insein jail, Major Findlay, had also been the superintendent at the Mandalay jail and knew Subhas. Taken aback by the condition of Subhas's health, Findlay wrote a strong note to the Government.[57] The British Government was already facing criticism at home for Subhas's condition. During a debate in the House of Commons towards the end of February, Ernest Thurtle had asked the Government whether it was aware of Subhas's 'dangerous state of health': 'Is it the intention of the Government to murder that man?' was his pointed question.[58]

While this was going on, member of the Governor's Executive Council in Bengal, A.N. Moberly, made a statement in the Bengal Council on 21 March, laying down the conditions for Subhas's release. Acknowledging that Subhas's detention 'has exposed this Government to very severe criticism', he explained that 'if Government have not released him or at any rate relaxed the degree of restraint to which he is subjected, it is because they honestly believe that it would not be safe to do so'. Making it clear that the Government was not ready to bring Subhas back to Bengal, and wanted to control his movements in India, he highlighted the fact that Sunil had specifically recommended a sea voyage and a trip to Switzerland. The Government was prepared to allow Subhas to go to Switzerland if he gave a word of honour that he would proceed from Rangoon to Europe in a ship that should not touch at any port in India, and thereafter he should not attempt to enter India, Burma or Ceylon as long as the Bengal Criminal Law Amendment Act remained in force.[59]

Subhas appreciated the frankness of Moberly's statement but refused to accept the offer. Anil Baran Roy and Satyendra Chandra Mitra advised him to accept it, but he would not listen.[60] In a long letter to Sarat, he articulated not only the reasons for his refusal, but also his political position. He informed Sarat that Sunil made his recommendation of sending him to Switzerland as an impartial physician without taking into account the political consequences, and he was not consulted before submitting the recommendations. He was amused when Moberly said in his statement that he was not seriously ill and certainly not incapacitated and wondered whether he be considered so only when he was past cure and facing certain death. Moreover, there was no certainty that the Bengal Criminal Law Amendment Act would not be extended on a permanent basis after its purported expiry in January 1930; in that case he would be forced to be on permanent exile. He knew how the Government viewed suspects and how the police system worked. Even if he accepted the offer and travelled to Switzerland, he was sure that the British spies would concoct unfavourable reports—'All my caution and even timidity will be put down as shrewdness and cunning and all sorts of sinister activities, of which I shall be the author, will be imagined where there are none.' It was quite possible that as the time for the expiry of the Act drew near, he would be painted as a Bolshevik agent, but his 'political complexion is not so red as some interested and malicious people have led Government to think'. He was at a loss on the Government's intention of banning him from India, Burma and Ceylon:

> When I read that I was required to undertake not to return to India, Burma and Ceylon I rubbed and rubbed my eyes and asked myself—'Am I so dangerous to the existence of British rule in India that a deportation from Bengal is not regarded as an adequate safeguard or is all this but a hoax?' If the former, then from one point of view it is somewhat flattering to a nationalist to be told that he is so much of a nuisance to the bureaucracy . . . I have not done any political work outside Bengal and I have hardly any desire to do so, at least for some years to come—for Bengal is big enough for me and for my ambitions.

Subhas braced himself for the continuation of the incarceration: 'We have yet to suffer a lot, both individually and collectively, before the priceless treasure of freedom can be secure,' but he was at peace with himself and could face, with equanimity, any ordeal that came his way.[61]

His official response to the offer was a charge against the Government: 'The position that I have taken up from the very beginning is that I have been imprisoned illegally without trial and without any justification,' he wrote. 'Lawless laws' such as the Bengal Ordinance and the Bengal Criminal Law Amendment Act, enacted to curtail fundamental rights and liberties, would not be tolerated in any civilized society for even twenty-four hours. The fact that the law had to be brought into force by certification of the Governor and the Viceroy, despite rejection by the council and the assembly, showed that legislatures in the country were nothing but a sham.

Moreover, by not allowing him to attend the council, the Government had encroached on parliamentary privileges and subordinated the legislature to the executive branch, reversing the normal relation between the two organs of a Government.

> To accept the conditions imposed by Government would be tantamount to admitting the validity of the act and it is impossible for me to surrender the position I have taken up. While the fight for constitutional liberty is going on—the honour of our nation is in our keeping and we cannot betray that trust. Much as I value my life—I love honour more and I cannot for the life of me barter away those sacred and inviolable rights which will form the basis of the future body-politic of India.[62]

Sarat met Moberly, who had read Subhas's letter and therefore knew of his position, to explore whether the Government was amenable to modify its offer. Following the discussion, Moberly informed Sarat that the Government would allow Subhas to stay at Almora en route to Europe for three months, on the condition that he gave his word of honour that he would not receive or communicate with anyone except relatives without the permission of the Bengal Government. Furthermore, he would have to undertake not to return to India, Burma or Ceylon without the Bengal Government's permission.[63] These conditions too were unacceptable to Subhas.

On 9 May, Earl Winterton informed the House of Commons that due to the lack of improvement in Subhas's health, he would be transferred to Almora. The new Governor of Bengal, Stanley Jackson, had arranged for a special medical examination for when Subhas passed through Calcutta.[64] On 12 May, Subhas was put on a boat in Rangoon. Sarat was officially informed and he tried to arrange for Subhas to meet with their parents. After three days' travel, the boat was stopped near Calcutta where Francis Lowman, head of the intelligence branch of the police, received Subhas and informed him that he would have to appear before a four-member Medical Board which included Nilratan Sirkar, B.C. Roy, Lt. Col. Sands and Major Hingston, the Governor's physician. The report was wired to the Governor in Darjeeling, and on the morning of 16 May, Subhas was informed that the Governor had ordered his release. The police tried to prevent his release by influencing the Medical Board to issue a report recommending his transfer to Almora, or departure to Switzerland, but the board refused.[65]

Just like the incarceration in October 1924, liberty was unexpectedly imposed on Subhas in May 1927.

But what was different from the report submitted by Sunil Bose and Lt. Col. Kelsall in February that made the Governor order Subhas's release at such short notice? 'Is not the public in India and in this country entitled to ask what this man's health was when the Government of India ordered his release?' asked George Lansbury in the House of Commons on 23 May. 'No, Sir. I do not think they are entitled to inquire in the least,' was the reply of Earl Winterton.[66]

Earl Winterton's diktat, however, was inconsequential in India. Even as the press welcomed the return of Subhas, questions were raised on why he alone was released when there were other detenus who were also suffering. The most scathing criticism came from Gandhi: 'I wish it was possible for me to tender the Government of Bengal congratulations upon the release of Sjt. Subhas Chandra Bose,' he wrote in *Young India*, ten days after Subhas's release. Subhas was released, he wrote, not because of the pressure of public opinion, or because the Government found him to be innocent of a crime about which neither Subhas nor the public knew anything, but because his serious illness caused fear for his life. But then why should the Government be afraid of his death in prison, since it was not the usual practice to release every prisoner who became dangerously ill? And if he had to be released because of his illness, why was he not discharged earlier when signs of tuberculosis were first detected? It was 'cowardly to fling a dying man in the face of his relatives and wash oneself of the guilt of his death', he argued. Gandhi rightly pointed out that this kind of arbitrary action provided no solution to the problem of indefinite detention without trial, but remained silent on the effectiveness of his recommended antidote of constructive programme in the past two and a half years. In a strange way, he feared that the agitation against such detention—an agitation that he had neither suggested nor thought would be effective—would now weaken as Indians would be grateful for Subhas's release. The agitation, according to him, was a high-pitched one only because a powerful person such as Subhas had been imprisoned, and now that it had been weakened, it would leave the other prisoners to continue in their present condition. With the onset of arrests under Regulation III and the Bengal Ordinance, Gandhi had taken the position that the country was forced to eat humble pie since people were not ready to mount a mass movement and, therefore, he neither proposed any counteraction except taking recourse to the spinning wheel, nor a resolution in the annual session of the Congress in Belgaum which he presided over. When Sarat had asked him about a year before for guidance on what could be done to secure the release of the detenus, he had again recommended the spinning wheel as the 'sovereign remedy'.[67] In the absence of an alternative programme from him, his claim now that he would 'rather not have any release at all than have a release on false issues, which merely complicate the main issue and make it more difficult to deal with than before', was, therefore, clearly inconsistent with his stand on the issue. The saving grace of this 'painful affair', according to him, was that Subhas had declined all the humiliating conditions proposed by the Government.[68] Gandhi also sent him a telegram on his release, which was likely to be a congratulatory one wishing him recovery of health.[69]

Sarat, along with his family, had gone to meet Subhas on the Governor's launch, and on receiving the release order, brought him to their Elgin Road house. After another round of examination, Nilratan Sarkar, Bidhan Roy, and Sunil advised complete bed rest, and prohibited him from meeting people for the next few weeks. A total ban on meeting people was impractical for the former CEO of the Corporation; within a few days, the prohibition had to be relaxed.[70] In a statement issued on the next day, Subhas said that it pained him that his comrades were still in jail, and his immediate objective was to recuperate so that he could plunge into work at the earliest.[71] Reports were coming in about people doing puja in their homes for his recovery, while many sent their advice on the type of medical treatment to be followed and religious rituals to be observed. In a message thanking people for their overwhelming show of concern, he said that he would utilize the time of rest to prepare for the work ahead, and prayed that when the time came, they should be able to work together, staying focused on the task at hand.[72]

The debate over the Criminal Law Amendment Act and detention without trial was far from over. On 2 June, during a debate on Indian affairs in the House of Commons, the Labourite, George Lansbury, tore into Earl Winterton over the Conservative Government's position on the detenus and the next round of constitutional reforms. After reading out Subhas's letter to Sarat from 4 April, he said, 'I cannot think that the man who wrote that document . . . is the sort of man the British Empire ought to keep in prison under the conditions that he has been kept there.' His verdict was, 'This is one of those cases, which will be remembered in India for all time, of downright persecution of a really good nationalist.'

That Subhas was 'an outstanding figure among those who are in prison' should not divert attention from the conditions under which they were still imprisoned, he argued. Earl Winterton defended the Government's action in Bengal, the only province where revolutionary crime existed and had existed for a long time, by pointing out that the ordinance was in fact imposed under the erstwhile Secretary of State who had belonged to the Labour party. In the course of his reply, he claimed that Subhas was imprisoned not for any political offence, but 'for having broken the law in regard to revolutionary crime'. He also claimed that Subhas was tried by a judge and that the cases against each detenu had been assessed by two judges. On a more general note, he observed that it was fallacious to believe that a lenient regime led to the decline in extremist action; several revolutionaries released by the general amnesty at the end of the First War, he claimed, had 'returned to their evil course—that of taking or attempting to take or threatening the lives of officials and private individuals'.[73]

Till now, whatever Subhas had written about his arrest and imprisonment was confined to his letters exchanged with Sarat and other associates, which, under the gaze of the official censor, did not amount to much. Now he was free, and for the first time issued a detailed account of what went on behind the scenes, in reaction to Winterton's claims, and sent his views to Lansbury. He made it clear that he was not only speaking for himself, but also on behalf of the detenus who were unable to voice their protest. The crux of his rebuttal was that no detenu, including him, was ever produced before or tried by any judge, nor was he given an opportunity to examine the evidence against him. Police officials went silent when he challenged them to produce genuine documentary evidence against him. He was charged with the crime of importing arms, manufacturing explosives and conspiring to assassinate police officers in collusion with Anil Baran Ray and Satyendra Chandra Mitra, and these allegations were read out to him in the Alipore Central Jail about a month after his arrest. In many cases, people who did not even know each other were accused of colluding to commit revolutionary crimes, and when these linkages were challenged, the police changed the names of the people whom they had accused of collusion. Subhas had declined to present a defence without being presented with the evidence, when the charge had been read out to him for the first time. However, when the allegations were again presented to him in February, he had denied all the charges through a written statement in which he had explained that the charges had been manufactured at the insistence of a senior police officer. Thus, Winterton's claim that he did not defend himself was as untrue as his claim that all detenus were informed about the evidence against them.

Subhas pointed out that in a country of 5 crore humans, only one political murder had taken place in the past five or six years, which was that of the murder of Ernest Day by Gopinath Saha. The murder was almost universally condemned and even Saha himself had expressed regret. That Saha was executed for the crime clearly showed that the existing legal framework was adequate to mete out justice. There was a considerable difference of opinion on whether another murder case—that of the Sankharitola postmaster—was a political one. Apart from the fact that many considered it to be a simple case of dacoity and murder, all the perpetrators had been brought to book. Some of the other murder cases highlighted by the Government in support of the ordinance were even considered by many to be the work of agents provocateurs. As far as risks to the lives of witnesses were concerned, Subhas rubbished Winterton's claim. Witnesses in all the cases considered by the Government to be of revolutionary crime were presented in the courts, and nobody ever heard of any harm coming their way. The punishment meted out to him and other detenus was not really because of any revolutionary activity, but for successfully setting up a powerful organization capable of effectively challenging the Government.

Armed with Subhas's letter, Lansbury confronted Winterton in the Commons on 17 June, by asking him to state the date on which Subhas had been brought before a magistrate or a judge, and the date on which the evidence against him had been presented to Subhas for his examination and contradiction. There was no course left for Winterton other than to apologize for his misstatement. He had to admit that:

> So far as I am aware, Mr. Bose was not produced in person before the Judges who examined his case, nor was the evidence against him submitted to him in detail for examination, and I regret if anything I may have said should have misled the hon. Member on these points.[74]

Subhas was shifted to a bungalow in Shillong in mid-June—the Kelsall Lodge—which Sarat had rented for six months. The change in climate helped, and so did the presence of Janakinath, Prabhabati, and Sarat and Bivabati along with their children from time to time. Sunil and Bidhan

Roy kept him under watch. As he recovered, he returned to his schedule of late-night work, much to the displeasure of his parents, and spent a lot of time playing with the children when they came over during their school vacation. Subhas loved children and they took him to be one of them. Apart from participating in their games, every evening he would teach them swadeshi songs by Rabindranath, Nazrul, Atul Prasad and Rajani Kanta, and Sanskrit stotras. The fun and frolic with the children kept him occupied to such an extent that he was at a loss when they returned to Calcutta with Bivabati at the end of their Puja vacation. This 'pang in my heart' led to some hard thinking and 'self-analysis'. 'People like me must become completely non-attached; otherwise there will be only more and more sorrow in store for them,' he wrote to his *mejobowdidi*. His mind did not waver when he had been woken up and taken to Alipore jail about three years ago, and he had spent the following months away from the country with equanimity. Now, with everyone having left, he had the time for 'a silent communion' with nature.[75]

Two issues which were at the top of his mind at this time were the continued detention of political workers and the disputes within the Bengal Congress. The detentions under the Regulation III and the Criminal Law Amendment Act not only violated all forms of justice, but at the same time prevented workers of proven mettle from rejuvenating the political movement in the province. The factional feuds, on the other hand, were rapidly degenerating the formidable organization that Deshbandhu had built.

He looked forward to attending the proceedings in the Legislative Council, which was scheduled to sit from 23 August to 26 August, and obtained Bidhan Roy's permission to travel to Calcutta.[76] The thought of so many of his associates being in prison was troubling him. 'It is distressing to be released all alone . . . I feel as if a burden is pressing on my mind all the time,' he wrote to Satyendra Chandra Mitra. The news of illness of his prison-mates Trailokyanath Chakraborty, Surendra Mohan Ghose and Bipin Behari Ganguly worried him, but there was nothing he could do immediately.[77] He suggested to Nalini Ranjan Sarkar to organize meetings across Bengal demanding the release of the detenus, and prepared the questions which he wanted to raise in the council.

During the three days of the Legislative Council, he raised a number of questions, and intervened with supplementary questions on the facilities provided to the detenus and on the state of their health. Most of his questions were stonewalled by the Government. A frustrated Subhas on one occasion quipped, 'Will the foundation of the British Empire be shaken if the report regarding the health of the détenus be published?' He continued with the same line of questions on the detenus in the next session of the council which sat in mid-December, and the barbs towards the ministers sharpened when they blocked information.[78]

It was important to raise questions in the council, but without the support of a strong organization, such interventions would hardly have any impact on the Government—and the state of the Bengal Congress was far from what was required to pressurize the Government. 'Today our house is on fire,' Subhas wrote to Basanti Devi.[79] He met Sasmal, Satkaripati Roy and other leaders to bridge the gap between the warring factions. Informing Satyendra Chandra Mitra, who was released from prison in August, about his efforts, he wrote, 'I shall leave no stone unturned in the attempt to compose all differences and unify the different groups.' He asked Mitra to try to bring back Anil Baran from Pondicherry, who had left politics and joined Aurobindo in his spiritual quest after being released from prison. 'His departure was a terrible blow to me, from which I do not think I have recovered yet,' Subhas wrote. From Shillong, he issued an appeal for unity, and in the footsteps of his mentor, started making efforts to mobilize support from small groups within the council.[80]

At the same time, he kept pleading with Basanti Devi to come forward and accept the leadership of the Bengal Congress. The reasons were both personal and political. Losing both her husband and her son within a short span, Basanti Devi had withdrawn into a shell of agony. Subhas believed that being more active in the public arena would at least partly reduce the pain of the loss. The reports of exploitation of helpless women and their general condition also deeply troubled him. In this context, a woman occupying the leadership position also had great symbolic significance for him. In a letter to Basanti Devi, he wrote,

The spiritual quest of Bengal has always been voiced through the cult of the Mother. Be it God or be it motherland—whatever we have worshipped we have done so in the image of the Mother. But alas! Today the menfolk of Bengal have become so impotent and cowardly that they are incapable of preventing the molestation of women that is going on in the districts of Bengal.[81]

Sengupta was the leader chosen by Gandhi, but the feuds showed that the leadership question was far from being settled. To make progress, it was imperative to settle the dispute. Subhas believed that Basanti Devi's acceptance of leadership would help to seal the differences. He told her clearly that 'if you do not accept our leadership there is no one else in Bengal whom we can accept from our heart as the leader'. Appointing someone as the chairman of a meeting did not necessarily transform him into a leader.[82]

The state of Congress leadership in the province was demoralizing:

These are critical days for Bengal. There is a serious dearth of 'wholetime' workers. It will be no exaggeration to say that Mr Sengupta has nearly given up Congress work. Kiron Babu has served me a notice that in October he will pass all the burden on to me and retire. I do not now find much enthusiasm or eagerness on Tulsi Babu's part in national work. You know the Big Five—excepting Tulsi Babu all of them are professional people, so they cannot devote much time to Congress work. At the moment only Bidhan Babu is interested in the work of the BPCC but even he has very little time. The treasury of the Congress is absolutely empty.[83]

This was another reason to bring her back into active politics. The impact of Basanti Devi courting arrest during the non-cooperation movement was not to be forgotten. He sincerely believed that she could work the magic again: 'If the youth consider you to be one of them, if they wish to bestow their leadership on you—what objection can you have to that?'[84] When Basanti Devi remained steadfast in her refusal to step forward, frustrating his efforts, an angry Subhas charged that 'You are the foremost among those who have neglected to do their duty after Deshbandhu's death'. But Basanti Devi was determined to not change her mind.

In a private letter, he could open his heart to his 'Mother' and tell her what he could not speak about publicly. His letter of mid-October to her is revealing. Just before the AICC was to meet in Calcutta, he was telling Basanti Devi that politics happened by accident, and that the road to spirituality was more appealing.

I have been thinking for some time why must it all be my headache, why must I alone carry this unwanted burden to my own spiritual detriment?

Politics is not a suitable field of work for me. It is only by chance that I
have drifted into the whirlpool of politics. Now I can . . . go back to my
chosen field. I have no attachment to the material world, so I chose not to
enter worldly life. I do not see any reason why in the present condition of
the country, I should leave the path of peace, create a new worldly snare
and get myself enmeshed in it.[85]

The dilemma was still alive.

At the national level, the Swarajists, at the behest of Gandhi, had
become the political front of the Congress, while he carried with him his
followers to concentrate solely on the constructive programme. Yet, it was
a house divided on the issue of engagement with the Government through
Legislatures. By early 1925, the alliance in the Legislative Assembly,
between the Swarajists led by Motilal and the independents led by Jinnah,
had broken down. Following an acrimonious debate with Motilal over
whether the party's strategy should be responsive cooperation or complete
obstruction, leaders like Jayakar, Moonje and Kelkar walked out of
the executive council of the Swaraj party and vacated their seats in the
legislatures. The Congress was groping in the dark to find a solution to the
waves of communal riots which had been sweeping through the country over
the past three years. With the Bengal Pact dead for all practical purposes,
the Bengal Swarajists, who were opposed by the conservative Hindus, had
lost their influence over the Muslims. In the 1926 council elections, not
one elected Muslim member was a Swarajist. The Congress advocated
joint electorates but the Muslim League was split on the question.

When the AICC met in Calcutta under these conditions from 28
October to 30 October, the stalwarts were away: Gandhi was touring
south India, Motilal was in London and Jawaharlal was in Brussels
attending the International League against Imperialism. Among the
issues taken up for discussion, religious conversions and observation of
religious rituals and ceremonies, which were causes for many instances of
riots, drew heated exchanges. On the second day of the session, Subhas
rose to defend a resolution proposed by Sengupta, which proposed that
no community in the country should impose its religious views or practice
on another community.[86] Hindus should be free to take processions and
play music before mosques, but the processions should not do anything
deliberately to offend worshippers inside the mosque. Similarly, Muslims
should be free to slaughter cows as long as laws permitted, at any place

except a thoroughfare, temples, or generally at places 'exposed to the gaze of the Hindus'. The resolution asked the CWC to appoint arbitrators who would resolve disputes arising out of these two circumstances, and that this proposal be taken up for confirmation at the annual Congress session at Madras. While Mohammad Ali supported the resolution, T. Prakasam wanted to postpone a decision. He wanted a committee to be appointed to tour the country educating people about this initiative, and subsequently report people's reaction to the Madras Congress. Subhas agreed with Prakasam's suggestion of Congress leaders touring the country to propagate the idea contained in the resolution and also to gauge public opinion, but at the same time was keen that the resolution be adopted. The measures outlined in the proposal should be given a chance. He did not claim it to be a perfect solution, but was hopeful that it would help remove misapprehensions among, and the obstinacies of both, extreme Hindus and Muslims. He was categorical that Hindus of Bengal were not going to lose their heads over communal riots, and would not walk along the path of the Muslim leaders if they adopted a 'frantic attitude'. He expressed the hope that the communal troubles were a passing phase, and in view of the role they had to play in obtaining the country's freedom, he appealed to the Bengali Hindus that they should not give up the nationalistic position they had taken up from the beginning of the freedom movement. Resolving the conflict between the two communities also depended, to some extent, on finding credible leadership in each community which would be acceptable to the other communities in each province. From his discussion with the Hindu extremists, he understood that their chief complaint was that they had not found such trustworthy Muslim leadership. He recommended the name of Maulana Akram Khan as one of the Muslim leaders who would go to any extent to establish communal amity.[87]

Speaking at a public meeting a fortnight later in support of the resolution, Subhas came down harshly on the Hindu conservatives in Bengal. Referring to the Calcutta riots of 1926, he recalled that when 'at the Mandalay jail I read in newspapers that Hindus of Calcutta took out a procession playing music in front of a mosque, protected by the Calcutta police under Sir Charles Tegart, I wished that the ground beneath my feet split open'. Were they not ashamed to take the protection of the Calcutta police which were responsible for the incarceration of so many Congress workers? Were they not ashamed to exhibit such helplessness?[88]

Speaking out in this manner, Subhas was putting himself up against the line taken by the Karmi Sangha and others who had been berating the Bengal Pact. His efforts to bring on board the dissenting leaders and sparring factions showed results; Subhas emerged as the potential unifier and was elected as the president of the BPCC in November 1927. As one of his contemporaries noted, 'Never in the history of Bengal-politics did a leader obtain such ungrudging co-operation from all sides as Subhas did.'[89] Unfortunately, this unity was not to last long.

As he took charge as the president of the BPCC, bridging the gap between the two communities remained a top priority.

Occupying the position held in the recent past by his mentor, Subhas outlined his task with absolute clarity. Apart from uniting the religious communities on a common platform for attaining Swaraj, the Congress organization had to be strengthened immediately. His plan was to revitalize the existing branches, bring back old workers to the Congress fold, and recruit new workers in every district. If the organization was not strong, it was but natural that the Government would continue to treat its demands, including that of release of the detenus, with contempt.[90]

4

Alap (1928–29)

On 2 March 1930, Gandhi informed the Viceroy, Lord Irwin, that he was going to launch a civil disobedience movement by violating the salt law, which he considered 'to be the most iniquitous of all from the poor man's standpoint' and since 'the independence movement is essentially for the poorest in the land, the beginning will be made with this evil'. For the next twelve years, India would not see another mass movement of such scale that followed Gandhi's declaration. Gandhi's actions, in taking back the reins of Congress politics and launching the campaign, were perceived by Subhas as those that 'will stand out for all time as some of the most brilliant achievements of his leadership', and they revealed 'the height to which his statesmanship can ascend in times of crises'.[1]

The story of Subhas Chandra Bose between 1928 and 1930 is essentially the story of his struggle to find the ground beneath his feet in Bengal politics, and expanding his presence beyond Bengal to represent the country's impatient youth and the more aggressive schools of political action. It was also the period when he would be offered a place in the high table of Congress leadership as a test case and removed as someone who was too hot to handle. Yet, in just over these two years, Subhas succeeded in providing the thrust that eventually led to the campaign of 1930, by marshalling the extremist forces of the national movement and repeatedly challenging the Gandhian paradigm.

Three years after his mentor had sought Dominion Status for India, Subhas stood at the rostrum of the Bengal Provincial Conference in Basirhat on 8 April 1928, demanding complete independence: 'This Bengal Provincial Conference declares that complete independence is the goal of India.'

On the previous day, Sengupta, the president of the conference, opened his address with effusive praise of Subhas, in front of an audience that included Basanti Devi, C. Rajagopalacharia, Jamnalal Bajaj and Prafulla Chandra Roy. 'Our hope and enthusiasm has been redoubled by having the noblest son of Bengal', the 'great worker' who was 'snatched away from the love and regard of the whole nation by a cruel power', back in action. 'This time we will surely succeed in the great venture.'[2]

The independence resolution moved by Subhas followed the resolution passed by the Madras Congress in December 1927, which had been proposed by Jawaharlal Nehru. It was the first time that the Congress declared independence as its goal, although only part of the resolution proposed by Jawaharlal was passed by the Congress. In the subjects committee meeting held on 25 December, Jawaharlal had proposed

> This Congress declares the goal of the Indian people to be independence with full control over the defence forces of the country, the financial and economic policy and relations with foreign countries. The Congress demands that this right of the people of India should be forthwith recognised and given effect to, in particular by the complete withdrawal of the alien army of occupation.[3]

Swaraj within the empire meant nothing to Jawaharlal. He felt that it was degrading for India to be within the empire: when India was free she could decide her future alliances. However, in the face of opposition by leaders such as Rajendra Prasad and Vijayaraghavachariar, who called the resolution a silly one which would make the Congress a laughing stock of the world, Nehru agreed to shorten it for the sake of unanimity to 'This Congress declares the goal of the Indian people to be complete national independence.' In the open session, Jawaharlal tried to sound defiant by pointing out that curtailing the resolution did not change its essence and that without control over defence, economy and foreign relations, independence would be a 'travesty and camouflage'. The goal of independence was immediate and not a distant one.

Gandhi attended the opening session and an informal meeting, but not the meetings of the subjects committee due to poor health. The absence of active opposition from him was a possible reason for the resolution to have been accepted without any serious challenge. According to Sitaramayya, Gandhi came to know about the resolution after it was passed in the Subjects Committee.[4] Within three days of the close of the session, however, he started airing his views. In a press interview on 30 December, he claimed that his attitude towards the independence resolution was an open secret; his views on independence had not changed since the previous year when he had opposed a similar resolution.[5] A few days later Gandhi wielded his pen, dripping with sarcasm and derision, against the call for independence. The resolution 'was hastily conceived and thoughtlessly passed', he wrote in *Young India* on 5 January 1928. The following week, he wrote in *Young India*, 'Mere brave speech without action is letting off useless steam.' Swaraj, which was the creed of the Congress, was a higher goal and narrowing the goal to independence was a tragedy. The AICC, which passed such thoughtless resolutions, had 'almost sunk to the level of the schoolboys' debating society'.[6]

At the same time, Gandhi let his disapproval be known to Jawaharlal directly. In a tone that he could well have used for an errant schoolboy, Gandhi wrote to Jawaharlal on 4 January, 'You are going too fast . . . Most of the resolutions you framed and got carried could have been delayed for one year.' Gandhi's criticism irritated Jawaharlal. He issued press statements refuting Gandhi's contention that the resolutions passed in the Congress were hasty, reiterating that complete independence with the severance of British connection was the goal of the Congress.[7]

In his annoyance, he shot off two angry letters, severely criticizing Gandhi's role after the collapse of the non-cooperation movement. Not only did he question Gandhi's political wisdom and action, but stressed on how different they were as individuals. A hurt Gandhi asked him to follow his own path and wanted to publish the correspondence to establish the difference of their worldviews.

Jawaharlal had met Gandhi for the first time at the Lucknow Congress of 1916, when none of them had entered the arena of active politics. Gandhi appeared to him to be 'distant and different and unpolitical' at that time, but his work in Champaran enthused him and he felt that his methods promised success. Gandhi's anti-Rowlatt Bill movement again fired up his imagination and he decided to join Gandhi's Satyagraha Sabha. Motilal, however, not only disagreed with the programme of the Satyagraha Sabha, but was furiously opposed to Jawaharlal's participation, which, he had no doubt, would result in his imprisonment. After long discussions with Motilal, Gandhi himself had to break the deadlock by advising Jawaharlal not to aggravate the conflict. Thereafter, he assisted C.R. Das in the Punjab Inquiry Committee and started working closely with Gandhi as he marched on with his non-cooperation programme. He did not always agree with or comprehend what Gandhi said, but by the time Gandhi established his supremacy in the Congress, Jawaharlal had become an ardent follower.

> . . . we felt that we knew him quite well enough to realise that he was a great and unique man and a glorious leader, and having put our faith in him we gave him an almost blank cheque, for the time being at least. Often we discussed his fads and peculiarities among ourselves and said, half-humorously, that when Swaraj came these fads must not be encouraged.[8]

Under Gandhi's influence, Jawaharlal gave up smoking for five years, tried vegetarianism, and took to reading the Bhagavad Gita.[9] As the non-cooperation movement gathered steam, Jawaharlal, as the General Secretary of the United Provinces Provincial Congress Committee, plunged into mobilizing support for the movement. Soon, as the movement peaked during the visit of the Prince of Wales, he was imprisoned along with Motilal, first for three months and again for about nine months. Gandhi's decision to withdraw the non-cooperation movement after the Chauri Chaura incident generated doubts about Gandhian strategy in his mind, but it was not difficult for Gandhi to convince him of the correctness of his decision. His faith in Gandhi as the leader was stronger than the doubts in his mind.

As Jawaharlal stepped out of jail at the end of January 1923, Gandhi was still imprisoned and Motilal had joined Das to form the Swarajya party. It was a difficult situation for him to find the two men, who dominated his life, on opposing sides. That was probably the reason why, despite his ideological closeness and loyalty to Gandhi, he avoided taking sides. He was neither a pro-changer, nor a no-changer; both methods were honourable to him. Helping to obtain a truce between the two sides was his first major intervention in the affairs of the Congress organization.

Jawaharlal articulated his idea of the country's political goal in his presidential address to the UP provincial conference in October 1923, by forcefully making the case that the Congress creed of Swaraj was equivalent to complete freedom:

> What then is our aim and what should be our means? Our creed is short and simple but it shelters many interpretations. We have made

it abundantly dear that we are fighting for complete freedom. We have not the slightest interest in provincial autonomy of the transfer of subjects in the Government of India. Full internal freedom means that we must control the finances and the army and police . . . But the question has arisen whether we should not define 'Swaraj' in our creed as 'Independence'. Personally, I shall welcome the day when the Congress declares for independence. I am convinced that the only proper and right goal for India is independence. Anything short of it, whether it is styled Dominion rule or a partnership in the British Commonwealth of Nations or by any other name, is derogatory to the dignity of India.[10]

Gandhi was too conscious of Jawaharlal's attachment to his path and personality to be bothered by such utterances. He had complete confidence in his influence over his young disciple. Much to his reluctance, Jawaharlal was compelled to become the General Secretary of the Congress for 1924 by Mohammad Ali, the president for that year. He was not sure about Congress's future policy and hence did not want to take up any executive responsibility, but could not refuse Ali either. Soon, he was spending time with Gandhi at Poona and Juhu, as the leader recuperated after being released from prison on ground of health. While the senior Nehru and Das negotiated the position of the Swaraj party with Gandhi, Jawaharlal maintained a careful distance. He wanted his own doubts about the future programme of the Congress to be cleared by Gandhi. In this he was disappointed: Gandhi refused to lay down a clear, long-term plan.[11]

The reluctant General Secretary was again shocked by Gandhi's insistence at the Ahmedabad AICC meeting in June, to make spinning compulsory for Congress membership, which was strongly opposed by Motilal and Das. Jawaharlal offered to resign but did not press for it. At the end of the year, he agreed to continue as the General Secretary at Gandhi's insistence. In the meantime, he was also elected as the chairman of the Allahabad municipality towards the end of 1923.

Despite his occasional friction with Gandhi, Jawaharlal remained philosophically closer to his views and refused to join his father's party. This did not mean any lack of admiration of the father on the son's part— on the contrary, both he and Motilal were deeply attached to and proud of each other.

Towards the end of 1925, when Subhas remained imprisoned in faraway Burma, while Jawaharlal occupied himself with organizing the

annual Congress session at Kanpur. In March 1926, he sailed for Europe
with his wife, who was ill with tubercular infection, and their eight-year-
old daughter, Indira, for her treatment in Switzerland. The next twenty
months proved to be extremely valuable in expanding his mental horizon
by exposing him directly to the different strands of revolutionary and anti-
imperialist movements and their leaders in Europe, and by providing him
with the space to reflect on his next course of action. Jawaharlal met with
Dhan Gopal Mukherjee, Romain Rolland, Shyamji Krishnavarma, Raja
Mahendra Pratap, Virendranath Chattopadhyay and M.N. Roy among
others. But the two most important events were his representation of the
Indian National Congress at the International Anti-colonial Congress
(IAC) at Brussels in February 1927, where he was nominated to the
presidium of the conference, and a visit to Moscow in November, just
before his return to India.

The IAC was 'a milestone in the development of Nehru's political
thought',[12] where his speeches, statements and resolutions reflected the
influence of socialism. It brought him in contact with intellectual and
political stalwarts such as Henri Barbusse, Fenner Brockway, Roger
Baldwin, Ernst Toller and George Lansbury among others.[13] In the League
Against Imperialism formed by the Brussels Congress, Jawaharlal served
in the executive committee along with Lansbury, Einstein, Rolland and
Mme. Sun Yat Sen.[14] The socialist influence strengthened further when
he visited the Soviet Union at its invitation to attend the tenth anniversary
celebrations of the 1917 revolution.

It was, therefore, of little surprise that under the influence of his
European experience he brought the demand for independence from the
fringe to the main platform of the Congress with renewed vigour, although
the question remains whether he had anticipated Gandhi's reaction—
which he struggled to deal with at present. Whatever the assumption had
been, the reality of Gandhi's challenge after his angry outburst to part ways
with him stared Jawaharlal in the face:

> Whilst you were heroically suppressing yourself for the sake of the nation
> and in the belief that by working with and under me in spite of yourself,
> you would serve the nation and come out scatheless, you were chafing
> under the burden of this unnatural self-suppression. And, while you were
> in that state, you overlooked the very things which appear to you now as
> my serious blemishes . . . I see quite clearly that you must carry on open

warfare against me and my views . . . The differences between you and me appear to me to be so vast and radical that there seems to be no meeting-ground between us . . . I suggest a dignified way of unfurling your banner. Write to me a letter for publication showing your differences. I will print it in *Young India* and write a brief reply.[15]

Jawaharlal's response was a complete surrender. He had expected that Gandhi would allow him to follow a different course where there was a fundamental difference in opinions:

Is any assurance from me necessary that nothing that can ever happen can alter or lessen my deep regard and affection for you? That regard and affection is certainly personal, but it is something more. No one has moved me and inspired me more than you and I can never forget your exceeding kindness to me. There can be no question of our personal relations suffering. But even in the wider sphere am I not your child in politics, though perhaps a truant and errant child?[16]

Jawaharlal was faced with a dilemma. He could not step back from his publicly stated view, which was now a Congress resolution; nor could he push it too hard, fearing a potential falling-out with Gandhi. Within three days, in January 1928, Jawaharlal issued a statement in *The Tribune* clarifying that he saw no difference between the terms Swaraj and 'independence', that the word independence afforded greater clarity regarding India's demand than Swaraj: 'Independence is certainly not a happy word, but it conveys a special political significance which is easily understandable.'[17]

The exchange brought out the fault line in the relationship between the two men, but also set a pattern of revolt and surrender, which would keep repeating in the years to come.

~

Gandhi's public outburst notwithstanding, a number of provinces endorsed the independence resolution. Subhas must have been glad about the Madras Congress adopting Jawaharlal's independence resolution, for it gave him the official sanction of the Congress to press for independence. This was a departure from Das's position, of not restricting the meaning of Swaraj to independence. Subhas had often fought with his mentor on this point, pressing for independence to be the declared goal of the Swarajya party, but had nonetheless agreed to follow his leader. Das was no more, and here Subhas was going along with Nehru's proposition.

Gandhi's shadow was not yet upon him, but the Mahatma was watching the rise of the young rebel keenly. In June 1927, Gandhi had written to Satcowripati Roy, 'I am following him [Subhas] as closely as I can through the papers. If you see him, please tell him that I often think of him.'[18] In his Basirhat speech, Subhas reminded the audience that the call for complete independence had been given by Aurobindo Ghose over two decades ago. The acceptance of independence as the national goal by the Congress implied the country's acceptance of the goal voiced by Bengal two decades ago. Subhas refuted Gandhi's argument by pointing out that it was not the declaration of the demand for independence, but the lack of such a demand until then that had made the Congress the laughing stock of the world. Now that the goal had been declared, India had risen in the world's estimation.[19]

Very soon, however, the dream of a unified movement in Bengal started turning sour, with the initiation of the much talked about Sengupta–Bose rivalry. As a senior colleague, Sengupta was gracious to welcome Subhas back from the prison and make way for him to gradually take the lead in the provincial Congress. Subhas too was careful to give Sengupta his due respect. The origin of this rivalry has been described by an active Congress worker of the time as follows:

> I can also bear testimony to the fact that Subhas used always to see Mr Sen Gupta and take his counsels and nobody could question his best motives and sincerity of purpose. Mr Sen Gupta too pulled on very well with Subhas, until a body of disappointed workers rallied round him and set him up again as a rival leader to Subhas.[20]

Apart from the well-known Anushilan Samiti and the Jugantar groups, Bengal's revolutionary society had a number of smaller groups, sometimes at loggerheads with each other, one of which was the Atmonnati, led by the former revolutionary Bipin Behari Ganguly. When Santosh Mitra, a prominent member of Atmonnati, was heckled at a public reception of Subhas by members of some other party, it was assumed to have been done with the tacit support of Subhas. Some members of the Karmi Sangha too were turning against him.

This manufactured conflict precipitated sometime after the mayoral election of the Calcutta Corporation on 2 April, when Subhas lost to B.K. Basu of the Liberal Party, despite having the support of Sengupta.

He returned to the Corporation through a by-election in March 1928, winning uncontested. It was also the time for the election of the Mayor and Deputy Mayor which were held at the first meeting of the Corporation every year. Since Chittaranjan's death, the mayoral position had been held by Sengupta, but in 1928, a section of the Bengal Congress wanted Subhas as the mayor. It was natural for Subhas to resume the work that he had had to leave unfinished due to his imprisonment, and he agreed. The quality of work done by the Corporation had deteriorated due to factional squabbles which naturally led to lack of discipline and dereliction of duties by officers and workers. As someone living in the city, the state of affairs in the Corporation at this time has been described by Nirad C. Chaudhuri as:

> After that [Chittaranjan's death and Subhas's incarceration] there was no one to check its steady descent into inefficiency and graft. The last had reached such proportions when I went to work for it [in 1934] that the popular name for the Calcutta Corporation was the 'Calcutta Corruption'.[21]

Lack of Swarajist majority in the Corporation from 1927, and an anti-Swarajist coalition, however, led to his defeat with forty-nine votes against thirty-nine in favour. Only one Muslim councillor out of eighteen voted for Subhas.[22] Subhas himself explained later that his defeat was brought about by an opportunistic coalition of Europeans, nominated councillors and a few elected Hindu councillors who entered into a secret pact with the majority of the Muslim councillors in the Corporation. He charged that the pact would benefit only the Muslim councillors individually, and not the community. The Hindu hardliners who were criticizing the Swarajya party for being pro-Muslim, Subhas said, were the ones who had promoted this pact to isolate the party. This kind of alliance was possible, according to him, only because the election to the Corporation had been held immediately after the 1926 Calcutta riots, thus resulting in the election of a number of communal representatives.[23]

Accused of being indifferent to Subhas's candidature, Sengupta defended himself, claiming he had done all he could to support Subhas.[24] A fight broke out after the election, and reportedly Subhas's supporters roughed up those who voted against him.[25] Sengupta's address at the provincial conference five days after the election shows that his relation with Subhas had not soured until then. However, as would be evident very soon, the malaise of group rivalry, which had become dormant temporarily, would return with a vengeance.

Not to give up a chance to mock the Swarajya party, the conservative British newspaper, *The Times*, noted with some glee:

> Since his release from detention Mr. Bose has lost his character as a martyr, and to-night's rejection of his candidature is the first evidence of the disgust at his methods and the most telling defeat which the Swarajists have suffered in Bengal.[26]

The defeat was, without a doubt, a setback for his wish to play a deciding role in shaping the city's municipal affairs, but it was not enough to make a dent in his interest in the subject. Even as he remained out of municipal administration, or merely as a councillor, he was frequently felicitated by other municipalities, with whom he shared his philosophy. At a reception given by the Kushtia municipality at the end of March, for instance, he explained that it was important to capture institutions of local governance not only to improve the administration, but also to prove through these institutions that Indians were ready for 'higher responsibilities and for democracy'.[27] It also opened the avenue for reviving the democratic institutions which had existed in ancient India.[28] To him, capturing the local bodies in an organized manner was the only way to be able to implement a programme. Thus, those who were criticizing the introduction of politics in municipalities were only trying to delude people.[29] Moreover, the local bodies offered real power to serve people, in contrast to being a minister in the council who had no real power. This was the training ground to make people fit for Swaraj.[30] Municipalities, therefore, must strive to improve the state of public health, education, etc.[31]

1928 was the year of the turnaround of the national struggle, which led to Gandhi's comeback and his formally taking up the reins of the Congress. The trigger that galvanized the ongoing Congress movement, after a phase of relative calm, was an announcement by the Viceroy, Lord Irwin, on 8 November 1927 that the British Government had decided to appoint a Statutory Commission headed by John Simon, a former attorney general and home secretary of the British Government, to review the working of the Constitution of 1919 and propose steps for reforms towards a more responsible government. Six more members from the House of Commons and House of Lords were appointed to the Commission (including the future prime minister Clement Richard Attlee), but not a single Indian. A Joint Select Committee of the Central Legislature and committees constituted by the provincial legislatures were asked to submit their views and proposals to the Commission.

Irwin met Gandhi on 2 November to inform him about the announcement. Gandhi told the Viceroy, and later the press, that these matters did not interest him. He surmised that Indians would resent and hence boycott the Commission, but left the matter in the hands of the Congress president. At the same time, he assured the Viceroy that he would not initiate such a movement as he had abdicated the political leadership to the Swarajists.[32] In a statement issued on 10 November, Srinivasa Iyengar, the Congress president, called for a comprehensive boycott of the Commission on the grounds that it had been constituted ignoring the Congress's long-standing demand of a round-table conference or a convention parliament to determine India's Constitution, that Indians could not be party to an inquiry into their fitness for Swaraj, and that Indians were excluded from the Commission. At the same time, he urged the Congress to go ahead with framing India's own Constitution.[33] The AICC had already passed a resolution in May 1927 asking the Congress working committee to draft a 'Swaraj Constitution', which had set the ball rolling.

Discussing the Commission in the House of Lords, Secretary of State Birkenhead repeated his invitation to Indian leaders to frame a Constitution of their own, to suggest which form the reforms should take. The words of Birkenhead were toned down this time, compared to a more direct challenge he had thrown in July 1925, immediately after the death of C.R. Das, when he had said, 'let them produce a Constitution which carries behind it a fair measure of general agreement among the great peoples of India', but the message was not lost to the Indian leaders.[34]

The opposition Labour Party in England, after making much noise in criticizing the Government and the Commission, suddenly changed tack and came out in its favour. Motilal, who was in London at the time, conveyed the disapproval of the Congress to Labour leaders.[35]

The Congress responded by adopting a resolution on 27 December 1927, in its annual session in Madras, to boycott the work of the Commission by organizing mass demonstrations and asking the members of the legislature not to serve on the select committee and to obstruct its functioning. The session also empowered the Congress working committee to draft the Swaraj Constitution for India in consultation with other organizations, and place it before a special convention of leaders from various 'political, labour, commercial and communal' organizations by March 1928.

These resolutions set the agenda for 1928. As the president of the BPCC, Subhas issued a statement welcoming the resolutions, stressing on the work to be done on alleviating communal discord, boycott of the Simon Commission and the framing of the Swaraj Constitution. From the beginning of the year, Subhas plunged into the campaign against the Simon Commission and for the boycott of British goods. Apart from organizing meetings and processions in Calcutta, between January and April he tirelessly moved across the province, addressing meetings in Hooghly, Chinsurah, Bangaon, Basirhat, Bankura, Dacca, Kushtia, Manbhum, Mymensingh, Kishoreganj, Rajsahi, Jalpaiguri and other places.

The Government typically was watching for communal fault lines. The Bengal Government noted that 'there is a split among the Mohamedan leaders over the boycott of the Simon Commission and in Bengal the majority are against the boycott. Among Hindus there is less open opposition to the boycott but no real enthusiasm for it.'[36]

3 February, the day the Commission was scheduled to land in Bombay, was chosen by a conference of all boycotting political parties for observing a hartal, and holding public meetings throughout the country.[37] The Bengal Government noted:

> The Calcutta Corporation has decided by a majority to close its offices, schools, workshops and stores . . . Mr Subhas Chandra Bose has issued a manifesto calling on all sections of the community to cease work on that day, and processions are going round with the same object. He is endeavouring also to put a stop to train, tram and bus traffic . . . One interesting feature of the agitation is that Mr Subhas Chandra Bose has issued a letter to the headmasters and principals of the various schools and colleges in Calcutta asking them to close their institutions on the 3rd in sympathy with the agitation against the Simon Commission.[38]

The day of the Commission's arrival in Bombay could have been the day of the real showdown. The date of arrival in Calcutta was known and the volunteers under Subhas waited for the opportunity. The Government, however, would give out neither the time of arrival nor the route of the Commission's movement through the city. Subhas, Sengupta and Kiran Shankar Roy waited at the Congress office for news on the Commission's arrival, ready with volunteers who would put up the 'Go back Simon' banners along the roads. The Government was extra cautious to avoid any unpleasant incidents. The Commission finally arrived in the city in the dark of a foggy winter night, amidst heavy military protection, giving no more opportunity to the leaders and the volunteers than to shout out a few 'Go back Simon' slogans directed at the darkness. Subhas was quite amused in the way the incident developed.[39]

In the series of meetings he held, Subhas explained the different aspects of the boycott campaign and the larger nationalist movement: for example, just how insulting the setting up of the Commission had been would become clear if seven Indians were sent to England to pass a judgement on whether the British were capable of self-government. He also mentioned that there were two ways to obtain Swaraj—either by an armed uprising, or by means of an economic blockade. Since armed uprising was impossible for an unarmed nation, the latter was the only course open to the country. An effective boycott would lead to the closure of the textile mills in Lancashire, and hundreds of thousands of labourers could be rendered unemployed, leading to a possible civil war. He was not against Britain or its interests, but if they suffered in the process of securing India's rights, nobody could blame India.

The British knew that they could not get involved in a global conflict without the help of India, Subhas argued. Therefore, as another war was impending, the Commission was trying to placate Indians. They were under the impression that if they sent the Commission at a time when the Hindus and the Muslims were busy fighting each other, both communities would queue up for their favours. Establishing a communal harmony was against their interest and therefore the British would never do anything to see that happen, he cautioned. Both communities needed to work together to solve the problems related to food, cloth, health and education. Swaraj could be attainable only through the combined efforts of the two communities.

Everybody should wear Swadeshi clothes as religiously as they observed their rituals, Subhas urged. Swadeshi cloth could be relatively more expensive at the beginning but would get cheaper with increased demand when all Indians started using it. It would allow the poor weavers, who were starving, a means of livelihood.

He was also thinking about the important role that women needed to play in the movement. If women determined that they would not allow the use of British clothes, no man would dare to buy them, Subhas asserted. In view of the poor state of their health, women needed to take better care of their own health and inculcate the habit of physical exercise, was his advice. If women did not walk shoulder to shoulder with men in the struggle for freedom, then all efforts would result in failure.

Bengal had helped the British to establish its rule over India. Now Bengal must atone for its sin by agreeing to sacrifice its comforts for the motherland. The Empire depended on the collaboration of Indians; the day people decided to break free, it would become impossible for a handful of foreigners to rule India.[40]

The intensity of the boycott movement in Bengal was making news. 'We have been reading about the great boycott demonstrations that you have been holding in Calcutta and elsewhere and admiring your energy,' wrote Jawaharlal in March.[41] In mid-April, he led a team to hawk khadi on the streets of Calcutta to celebrate the National Week.[42]

At the same time, Subhas was gradually building his constituency amongst the students and the youth, a process that started during the non-cooperation movement of 1921. In 1922, he had played a leading role in the formation of the All-Bengal Youngmen's Association, under Dr Meghnad Saha.[43] The young firebrand was already an icon for the youth of Bengal, and he regularly addressed student meetings and youth conferences with the objective of organizing them, expressing solidarity with their movements, and urging them to spread the ideal of nationalism. To Subhas, youth and students' organizations were analogous to an army: innumerable organizations needed to be set up across the country, which would function as regiments of an army, and unite under the flag of the Congress.[44]

Swaraj could be obtained within two years, Subhas claimed, if ten thousand youth worked tirelessly to implement the national programme. They would travel to the interiors of the land with Swadeshi goods and build up public opinion to the extent that anyone who used British cloth would be branded as a traitor. Subhas was aware that taking a plunge into politics could mean serious disturbances in their studies, yet he would encourage them to sacrifice their studies in order to attain the larger goal.

In doing that, he would often come in the line of severe criticism from various sections of the society, but would take them head-on, stating clearly why he wanted the students' participation.[45]

His message to the students was not limited to the realm of politics. To him, students could be the greatest agents of social change, and for this, he was repeatedly urging them to break the monotony of routines and embrace an adventure-loving spirit. The British Empire, he told them, was the result of their love for the adventure of the unknown. Social progress would only be possible if they came forward and challenged the age-old social traditions and rituals. The goal of the youth movement was to create new streams in all fields—literature, art, society, state, etc. Indian civilization was still alive since it had been able to survive several cycles of regeneration. It was essential to base the dreams of a bright future on the glory of the country's past. There was no alternative to raising the historical consciousness of the youth, which would make them realize India's civilizational achievements in art, philosophy, religion and social science. Only then would it be possible for them to highlight India's contributions to the world; only then would they understand that the institution of *varnashram*, by which various ethnic groups were assimilated in the society, was now outdated, and that modern times needed a more scientific approach towards national integration. It was upon them to build political democracy on the foundations of social democracy. Social evils such as untouchability had to go. These were high ideals, as he never stopped reminding the youth; to materialize these, they would first need a healthy body.[46]

It is clear from many of his speeches at that time that Subhas was trying to increase the reach of the Congress by working with the labour organizations and trade unions, mobilizing them for the boycott movement as well as by taking up labour issues. The initial approach was to find a common ground between the nationalist and the labour movements, rather than treating trade unionism as a separate strand by itself.[47] The Swarajya party under Chittaranjan, who had presided over the All India Trade Union Congress in 1923 and 1924, had made inroads into several trade unions, but after his death the more radical members led by Hemanta Kumar Sarkar broke away to form the Labour Swarajya Party (LSP), which coincided with the increasing influence of the Communist Party. Under the influence of the communists, the LSP had turned into the Workers' and Peasants' Party of Bengal by 1928—in the lines of a 'labour welfare' and 'mass nationalist' party working for achieving Indian independence, as advocated by the British Communist Party.[48] The year was one of the most volatile in terms of labour unrests across the country[49] marked by those at the Lilooah rail workshop, a strike by the scavengers of the Calcutta Corporation, strikes at some jute mills and at the Budge Budge oil depots, which increased Subhas's involvement with the labour movement.[50]

The first major opportunity to present his political views outside Bengal came in May, when he was invited to preside over the Maharashtra Provincial Congress. The speech is remarkable in that it is one of the few speeches where Subhas provided a clear outline of his political views regarding a wide range of topics. Starting with the cultural and political connections between Bengal and Maharashtra, he elucidated his views on democracy, nationalism, labour movements, and his vision for an independent India.

The British rule was different from the 'avalanche-like attacks of Alexander or Chengiz Khan' as it had 'like an octopus embedded its tentacles into the very heart of our social and cultural life, seeking (though in vain) to denationalise and emasculate our whole race'. To those who proclaimed that Indians had to learn the institution of democracy from the West, his riposte was that 'ignorance and effrontery could not go further': democracy was not a Western, but a human institution and political terminology in Indian languages showed that it was a part of the country's history.

He dwelled at length on the importance of nationalism. He was aware of the criticism by cultural and labour internationalism which construed nationalism as 'narrow, selfish and aggressive'. But Indian nationalism was none of that: it was 'inspired by the highest ideal of the human race'— *Satyam, Shivam, Sundaram* (truth, benevolent and the beautiful). He believed in internationalism as much as anybody else, but the approach to it 'must necessarily be through the gates' of nationalism. 'My conception of Inter-nationalism [sic] is a federation of cultures on one side and a federation of nationalities on the other.'

The Congress had not been able to make much progress in organizing labourers and peasants due to lack of programmes which would appeal to their interests, as much as due to a lack of workers capable of working among them. Until then, Subhas admitted that khadi had been the only programme which had helped to offer 'bread and butter' to the masses, but his observation was that the appeal of khadi declined with the decrease in poverty. He was against the method adopted by the labour and communist parties, which only 'serves the interests of our alien rulers'. 'To introduce fresh cleavage within our ranks by talking openly of class-war and working for it' at the moment was a crime against nationalism. Yet, unless the Congress became more alive to the interests of the masses, it was inevitable that sectional and 'antinational' movements would gain supremacy and class war would erupt before political emancipation. It was, therefore, imperative to build a coalition between labour and nationalism. Social and economic reconstruction should happen only after achieving freedom; but freedom implied the democratization of society— 'let us not become queer mixtures of political democrats and social conservatives'. Privileges based on birth, caste or creed must go, everyone must be given equal opportunities, and women must play a more active role in public life.

His vision was that of an 'Independent Federal Republic' with 'her own flag, her own navy, her own army and her own ambassadors in the Capitals [sic] of the free countries'. The goal had to be freedom, and not colonial self-government or dominion home rule. He would not 'hazard a theory' on the line of economic reconstruction of the new India, which should be based on the light of the country's past and the ongoing experiments in the West. However, he clearly had a socialistic economic model in mind.

He was all for the ongoing efforts to find a solution to the communal problems but thought that resolution of the problem could only be possible by 'discovering a deeper remedy'. The religious communities were too exclusive and they needed 'to be acquainted with the traditions, ideals and history of one another—because cultural intimacy will pave the way towards communal peace and harmony'. Secular and scientific education, which roused economic consciousness, was essential to obliterate fanaticism. India had been 'charged by providence with the mission of solving a world-problem viz., the problem of unifying separate ethnic groups, harmonising different interests and points of view and synthesising different culture', and by solving this problem, it could lead the world.

In the meantime, the opposition to the Government was to be built up: 'it is the psychological basis of the nationalist movement. It is only at uniform, consistent and continuous obstruction that we can keep up an atmosphere of resistance to the bureaucracy and develop that moral stamina, lack of which is one psychological cause of our degradation and slavery.' He expected the ongoing movement to peak in a massive civil disobedience and the Congress committees must be prepared, organized as parallel institutions to the British bureaucracy.[51]

That his brief stint as the CEO of the Calcutta Corporation was well recognized is evident from the reception given by the Poona Municipality at that time:

We may be permitted to refer here very briefly to your interest in any sympathy with the administration of Local Self-Governing institutions. Formerly as the chief officer of Corporation of Calcutta and now as a corporator of the same body, you have been devoting a large portion of your energies, otherwise more widely and intensely engaged in national work, to the service of local Self-Government. It is, indeed, highly worthy of you that you should have left the stamp of your genious [sic] on this civic work as you have raised noble hopes in the minds of the Indian people by your magnanimous sacrifice and service . . .[52]

~

Being occupied with provincial politics prevented Subhas from contributing significantly to one of the most challenging tasks the Congress had taken up during the year—that of drafting a constitution for India.

In accordance with the resolution of the Madras Congress, M.A. Ansari invited the different political groups to an All Parties Conference, which held its first meeting in Delhi on 12 February 1928. Stretching over ten days, the meeting failed to reach any agreement as the Muslim League (the Jinnah faction, following a split in the League in December 1927) and the Hindu Mahasabha took adversarial positions. The next meeting held in Delhi on 8 March had the same result, after which Jinnah withdrew from the discussions and sailed for Britain. The third meeting of the Conference in Bombay, on 19 May, appointed a ten-member committee under Motilal (the Nehru Committee), on Gandhi's suggestion, to draft the constitution before 1 July.[53] Subhas did not take part in the proceedings of the conference, and the conflict between Jinnah and the Hindu Mahasabha were too much to handle for Jawaharlal. As early as February, he was writing to Gandhi that 'I have had enough of this All Parties Conference. After ten days of it the strain was too great for me and I fled to avoid riot and insurrection!'[54] However, when the committee was formed, Jawaharlal worked closely with his father, and Subhas was also appointed as a member.[55]

While Motilal and Tej Bahadur Sapru drafted the report, Jawaharlal assisted his father in preparing the drafts and notes for the report. Unavailability of Subhas's correspondence regarding the Nehru Committee makes it difficult to know his exact contribution, but letters to him from Jawaharlal and Motilal indicate that apart from discussing the contours of the report with other committee members, he helped them with information on Bengal. Motilal's letters also indicate that Subhas could attend the committee's meeting only twice during its consultative phase due to his preoccupation with Bengal politics. In June, he joined the ongoing discussions, at Anand Bhawan in Allahabad, one day before the committee's meetings, spread over seventeen days, came to an end. Subhas was also present in an informal conference after the meeting, attended by Motilal, Tej Bahadur Sapru, Jawaharlal and T.A.K. Sherwani, which decided that the committee would try to issue a unanimous report.[56] He joined the final deliberations of the committee when it reconvened after a two-week break, with many prominent non-members joining at the invitation of Motilal. Motilal reported to Gandhi on 11 July that a tentative unanimity had been arrived at on the report of the committee and the 'members have all gone to their respective homes leaving Jawahar and myself to prepare the report and we are now hard at work on it'.[57]

The key recommendation of the report was Dominion Status for India with no separate communal representation in the legislatures, except in provinces where Muslims were in minority and for non-Muslims in the North-West Frontier Province, based on joint mixed electorate. It also recommended reorganization of the provinces on a linguistic basis.

Motilal submitted the committee's report to the All Parties Conference in Lucknow on 28 August. The sticking point was the report's advocacy for Dominion Status, especially in view of the fact that the Madras Congress had adopted a resolution for complete independence. Jawaharlal led the charge with blistering eloquence, but he would not jeopardize the unanimity reached by the committee on the communal issues on account of his disapproval of the goal of Dominion Status. In the face of criticism for signing the report[58] Subhas clarified that the report acknowledged the right to work for complete independence.[59] To be fair, the Nehru report was clear that the principle of Dominion Status was adopted only as a point of 'maximum agreement':

It does not mean that any individual Congressman, much less the Congress itself, has given up or toned down the goal of complete independence. Those who believe in this goal retain the fullest right to work for it. But the maximum agreement thus reached will, we trust, serve as a satisfactory basis for a constitution which all parties can unite to work without prejudice to the right of any party or individual to go further ahead.[60]

An outcome of this conflict was the formation of the Independence for India League (IfIL). Driven by Jawaharlal, the young radicals formed the League on 30 August as a pressure group within the Congress to carry out propaganda for complete independence. A three-member provisional committee, comprising Subhas, Zakir Hussain (later President of India) and Jawaharlal, was set up to draw up the constitution of the League and the rules of the organization.[61] Jawaharlal resigned and Subhas offered to resign from their posts of Congress General Secretary on the grounds of being founders of the IfIL, but both were told by the CWC that there was no conflict between the work of the League and that of the Congress.[62]

In fact, the incompatibility of his ideas with the older leaders was a reason for Jawaharlal to contemplate resigning from the post of the General Secretary as his desperation grew. However, it was never strong enough to make him adhere to his intentions. As he later observed in his autobiography, 'It was surprising how easy it was to win me over to a withdrawal of my resignation. This happened on many occasions, and as neither party really liked the idea of a break, we clung to every pretext to avoid it.'[63]

In a sense, Jawaharlal was a senior to Subhas in the party and had always remained close to its power centre, in contrast to Subhas who was working his way up. They had differences in political outlook, but both were rising youth icons in the organization and had come together on the same platform—representing 'the left wing element in the country and the Congress', in the words of Jawaharla[164]—with the resolve to fight for complete independence for India as well as to change the old political line of incrementalism. Yet there were worries in the international socialist circles that if their main link in the Congress, Jawaharlal, relinquished his post, the League against Imperialism would lose its voice and would result in Subhas getting more powerful.

Remarkably, the younger brother of Sarojini Naidu and India's permanent revolutionary abroad, Virendranath Chattopadhyay (fondly called 'Chatto'), who had persuaded Jawaharlal to attend the Congress of Oppressed Nationalities in Brussels in February 1927 and a reluctant Motilal to visit Moscow with Jawaharlal later in the year,[65] wrote to him:

> It would be a serious political blunder if you resign your position as the General Secretary of the Congress. The reactionaries among whom must, of course, be included Subhas Bose, will take advantage of the situation created by your retirement in order to make the Congress revert to its old position, abandon the Independence Resolution and sever the connection of the Congress with the League.[66]

This was probably one of the earliest assessments of Subhas by the international socialist camp. Chatto, however, did not explain on what grounds he considered Subhas to be a reactionary. In his tour of Europe, Jawaharlal was intellectually impressed by both Chattopadhyay and M.N. Roy.[67] Probably under the influence of his brief but intense exposure to the European socialist–communist movement, Nehru came to view the Swarajya party as the Right Wing of the Congress.[68]

Subhas issued the manifesto of the Bengal branch of IfIL in October. The Bengal Government noted that 'much interest is taken, especially by the more youthful and revolutionary section of the extreme Hindu party',[69] which was followed by a general meeting of the League in Delhi in the first week of November that elected the office-bearers and issued a draft constitution. S. Srinivasa Iyengar was the president of the organization, while Subhas and Jawaharlal were the secretaries. Amongst the members of the all-India council were Kiran Sankar Roy and Hari Kumar Chakravarti from Bengal, S. Satyamurti from Tamil Nadu and Shankar Lal from Delhi. B.G. Horniman, Jamnadas Mehta and Bhupendranath Datta were among the members of a committee set up to draw up a programme for the League. However, despite the sporadic organizational efforts, the IfIL remained largely on paper. Sengupta, however, was not in favour of the formation of the IfIL. In a November meeting of the AICC in Delhi, he opined, 'independence leagues need not be formed, for the Congress itself is a League for Independence'.[70]

Meanwhile, the preparations for the annual session of the Congress to be held in Calcutta at the end of the year had started. Bengal wanted Motilal as the next president of the Congress. In June, Sengupta wrote to Gandhi asking him to use his influence with the Gujarat Provincial Congress Committee to vote for Motilal. Gandhi was agreeable to the suggestion and asked Motilal for his opinion.[71] Motilal was tentative in his response, telling Gandhi that his 'wearing the crown' would be justified only if the constitution-drafting committee can produce 'something substantial' which he can take to the country.[72] Around mid-July, he provided more concrete views to Gandhi. Calling himself 'more or less a spent force', he argued that Vallabhbhai Patel should become the president, on account of his success in the Bardoli satyagraha. If Patel did not agree, 'under all the circumstances Jawahar would be the next best choice'.[73] This was not the first time he was advocating for the selection of Jawaharlal as the president of Congress. In 1927 too, he had shared with Gandhi his 'idea of putting him [Jawaharlal] in the presidential Chair', but that had nothing to do with the fact that Jawaharlal was his son, he claimed, and Jawaharlal himself had 'emphatically declined the honour'.

> The reason why I recommended Jawahar was that among the younger set
> I believed he was most likely to command the confidence of the majority.
> This has since been proved to be true, as is evident by the fact that he and
> I are being mentioned almost in the same breath.[74]

Vallabhbhai was not keen on becoming the president for the year, Gandhi informed Motilal, and as far as Motilal was concerned, Gandhi thought he should be utilized for something more important. Under the circumstances, Jawaharlal was Gandhi's choice and he would recommend his name to the provincial Congress committees unless Motilal had any objections:

> . . . I thoroughly agree that we should give place to younger men. And
> amongst them, there is no one even equal to Jawahar.[75]

Subhas and Sengupta, in the meantime, were trying their best to convince Gandhi and Motilal for the latter's acceptance. On 17 July, Subhas wired Gandhi: 'Bengal unanimous in favour of Motilalji's presidentship. Kindly recommend him otherwise pray remain neutral.' The emotional connect probably was the most important reason for this insistence. 'Bengal was trying to get back Deshbandhu through Motilal,' observed a prominent leader of the revolutionary group Jugantar, but added caustically that the Bengali youth had failed to read Motilal's intention of having the principle of Dominion Status accepted, for which he needed Gandhi's active intervention.[76]

On the insistence of Subhas and Sengupta, Gandhi finally gave his assent to Motilal becoming the next president. On 23 July, he communicated to Motilal and Subhas his decision that the former should take up the responsibility, 'especially for Bengal's sake'.[77] Settling the discussions, Motilal wired his acceptance to Gandhi ('Humbly bow to your decision') and to Subhas and Sengupta ('Gandhiji decided against me I accept his decision and your order').[78]

The Bengal Congress got Gandhi's assent for the president it asked for, but his unhappiness with its way of planning the annual Congress started early, over the plans for the Congress exhibition that accompanied the annual session. As early as in May, acting on a complaint from Satis Chandra Dasgupta, an ardent Gandhi-devotee and founder of the Khadi Pratishthan of Calcutta and the Sodepur Ashram, he advised Sengupta that the Congress exhibition should be built solely around khadi, excluding all foreign things as well as indigenous mill cloth.[79] 'I hold very strong views about swadeshi. But if they do not commend themselves to Bengal, I must wait till Bengal is converted or I collapse,' he added in another letter.[80] When Subhas sent him the circular regarding the Congress exhibition, Gandhi was emphatic in his decision. He wrote:

> According to the circular you will be free to admit many foreign exhibits and mill-cloth. The only difference between Madras and Calcutta would be that Calcutta will exclude British goods, whereas British machinery was exhibited at the Madras Exhibition. In the circumstances I would personally like to abstain from identifying the All-India Spinners' Association with the Exhibition.[81]

The matter irked Gandhi to the extent that towards the end of September, Gandhi informed Motilal that the disagreements over the Congress exhibition made him inclined to skip the AICC session in Calcutta altogether. He only agreed on the latter's insistence: 'I am coming to Calcutta simply for the sake of Pandit Motilalji,' he made clear in another letter in November.[82] When the news of the possibility of Gandhi not attending the Congress session reached Calcutta, Bidhan Chandra Roy sought clear instructions from him—he went to the extent of assuring Gandhi that he would try and close down the exhibition if necessary. Roy pleaded, 'Please let me know your wishes and I will try and follow them. Only I would request you not to be too unbending.'[83]

Assuring Roy that he would attend the Congress session, Gandhi told him that the exhibition should avoid showcasing even small machinery and Indian mill cloth, but not by giving up on principles or solely to please him. In any case, he promised that he would not speak a word against the exhibition even if it went ahead as planned.[84] Towards the end of November, responding to the anxious queries by Gandhi on the final decision of the reception committee, Roy asked him whether the Spinners' Association would participate if the reception committee barred Indian mill textiles from the exhibition.[85] Gandhi perhaps had expected that the clear articulation of his ideas would result in modifications in the programme of the reception committee. However, disappointment was written large on his telegram to Roy after he saw the advertisement regarding the exhibition. 'There is a clear clash of ideals,' was his final verdict; 'It is surely better therefore to leave me out of account.'[86] He explained his position to Motilal in more detail:

> . . . there is no room in this Exhibition for me or khadi in the real sense . . .
> After all Dr. Bidhan and Subhas represent a definite school of thought.
> Their opinion is entitled to my respect as I expect theirs for my own.[87]

Roy wrote to Gandhi in the first week of December, accusing him of not having dealt fairly with the reception committee and informing him of the committee rescinding its earlier resolutions. This made Gandhi angry. He had shown great patience in accommodating the views of the committee, he told Roy. He was not at all happy with the way the entire episode had moved, but in a show of grace, he hurried to send out telegrams to a number of people announcing that he was lifting the ban on the khadi organizations from participating in the exhibition.[88] To Dasgupta, his main khadi disciple on the ground, he wrote, 'The whole affair is bad. But we must not resist.'[89]

It could not have made Gandhi happy that the Calcutta affairs of the Congress were run by a group of people over whom he had no effective control. Clearly, he reached Calcutta in an unhappy state of mind.

As the year came to an end, Calcutta became an extraordinarily busy city. Almost all political leaders who mattered camped in the city for nearly two weeks.

In addition to the annual Congress session, the conferences held in the city between 18 December and 2 January included those of the Trade Union Congress, the All Parties Conference, the AICC, the All India

Youth Congress, the Muslim League, the All-India Khilafat Conference, the Muslim All Parties Conference, the All India Socialist Youth Congress, the Hindustan Seva Dal, the All India National Social Conference, and the All-India Women's Social Conference.

Early on, it became clear that Dominion Status, being the foundation of the proposed constitution in the Nehru report, was going to face a stiff challenge from the radical section of the Congress. The All Parties Convention gathered on 22 December to discuss the report, a week before the opening of the annual Congress session. On 23 December, when Sengupta moved the resolution that the Swaraj constitution should be based on Dominion Status, Srinivasa Iyengar issued a statement on behalf of IfIL contesting the idea.[90] The statement signed by Subhas, Jawaharlal, Kiran Shankar Roy, Sarat and Iyengar among others was a reiteration of the resolution passed by the AICC meeting of 4 November, which stated that the goal of Congress was complete independence but that it accepted the Nehru report's recommendations on settling communal differences. The signatories would therefore abstain from taking part in the proceedings related to the Dominion Status part of the proposed constitution, but participate on the deliberations relating to the settlement of the communal issues. Even as Sengupta's resolution was passed unanimously by the convention, Jawaharlal pointed out that the AICC would discuss and vote on this matter on 27 December.[91]

Gandhi, though staying away from overt involvement in Congress politics, was well aware of the opposition the Dominion Status clause was to face in the annual session. Therefore, he took it upon himself to move the resolution on the acceptance of the Nehru report at the Subjects Committee meeting, which started on 26 December, three days before the main session. The resolution had barely scraped through the working committee meeting by a majority of six against five votes. It stated that the Congress would adopt the Nehru committee report and would restart non-violent non-cooperation if the British Parliament did not accept the proposed constitution by 31 December 1930. During the intervening period of two years, Congress, the resolution set out, would focus on constructive work such as total prohibition, promotion of khadi, boycott of foreign cloth, encouraging greater involvement of women in national work, removal of untouchability, village reconstruction, etc.[92]

Gandhi unleashed his formidable power of persuasion in an attempt to bring the obstinate youth brigade under his spell. The report was 'an organic whole' which could not be accepted or rejected in parts, he argued. Dominion Status was the heart of the report and attacking it with a view to champion the cause of independence would be a 'grievous blunder'. Taking the contest between Dominion Status and independence, which was a 'much abused' and 'equally a misunderstood word', to the masses would only confuse them. The Madras resolution, he pointed out, was not a declaration of independence but only the setting of independence as the goal, and the current resolution would accelerate the pace of arriving at that goal. Throwing the gauntlet at the votaries of independence, he said that they could well have slept over the goal they had set at the Madras Congress but not over this resolution, which gave only two years to the British Government to accept or reject the proposed constitution. They would have to work out the independence at the end of two years. Being the prime mover in setting up the All Parties Conference, the Congress must faithfully accept the report it had produced.

Not unexpectedly, an amendment to the resolution was moved by Jawaharlal the following day. Similar to the resolution adopted at the AICC meeting in Delhi on 3 November, the resolution was for accepting the recommendations of the Nehru committee report as far as the settlement of communal issues was concerned, but insisted that independence instead of Dominion Status was the goal of the Indian people. In opposing Gandhi's resolution, Jawaharlal did not lose the personal touch: 'It might be considered presumptuous on my part to get up and challenge the resolution moved by Mahatmaji,' but he 'felt it incumbent to do so because of the very teaching I have learnt at his feet.' 'I think from whatever point of view you look at it, either from the standpoint of national honour or from the point of view of expediency, if you accept Dominion Status, it would be an extremely wrong and foolish act,' he told the gathering. If the Congress accepted Dominion Status, it would show the world that it accepts the 'psychology of imperialism'. It was necessary to prepare the country for civil disobedience and non-payment of taxes, and the AICC should fix the date and place for the campaign to begin, or call for a special Congress to determine it.[93]

On the third day of the Subjects Committee meeting, Jawaharlal went missing from the venue as Gandhi introduced a modified version of his resolution. In introducing the new resolution, Gandhi returned the warm compliments of his disciple in more than full measure. What he indulged in was nothing short of building the brand for the person he had chosen as the leader of the next generation. The disciple was unhappy, but was not ready to rebel:

> All the twenty-four hours of the day he [Jawaharlal] simply broods upon the grievances of his countrymen. He is impatient to remove the grinding pauperism of the masses. He is impatient against capitalists who are exploiting the masses in the country, who rule over this country, and exploit and bleed this country in the words used by the late Lord Salisbury. I may tell you frankly that he is not in sympathy even with this resolution which I seek to substitute for the resolution which will be withdrawn if you give permission. He thinks that this resolution itself falls far short of what he wants. He is a high-souled man. He does not want to create unnecessary bitterness of words. He seeks deliverance out of it by putting a self-imposed silence upon himself. Hence you find that, although he is a faithful and diligent Secretary of the Congress, he feels that it is better for him this morning to absent himself than to be a helpless witness to the proceedings with which he is not in agreement.

Gandhi's new resolution proposed that the Congress accept the Nehru report while adhering to the Madras Congress resolution on complete independence, since it was 'a great step in political advance, specially as it represents the largest measure of agreement attained among the important parties in the country'. The time given to the British Parliament for acceptance of the report was reduced from two years to one year. If the proposed Constitution was accepted by 31 December 1929, the Congress would adopt it; otherwise, it would organize a campaign of non-violent non-cooperation. The individuals in the Congress, who wanted to campaign for independence, were at liberty to do so.

Jawaharlal was absent and Srinivasa Iyengar, who had spoken against the original resolution, now stood in its support. But uncomfortable questions, probably unforeseen, were raised by the Bose brothers. The resolution 'introduced an atmosphere of unreality', said Sarat. If the British Parliament accepted the report, then according to the resolution the Congress would also accept it, 'and your goal of independence vanishes', he pointed out.

Just before the resolution was put to vote, Subhas rose to make a statement. But Motilal cut him off only after he had spoken a few sentences, as closure had been applied to all discussion on the resolution. Gandhi's resolution was carried by 118 votes, with 45 voting against it. Delegates from Bengal either voted against the resolution or abstained.

Subhas issued his statement to the press the next day. He did not wish to speak on Gandhi's new resolution, he said, but was pressed by several young friends (the revolutionaries) to clarify his position and to make their views known. He failed to understand why the November AICC resolution on the report, which was the result of a compromise between the two schools of thought, was snubbed by Motilal. Although Gandhi characterized that resolution as self-contradictory, his own resolution was no less contradictory. The consequence of the resolution which would arise if the British Parliament accepted the report, thereby committing the Congress to Dominion Status, was unacceptable. Bengal had expected, Subhas said, that Motilal would stand with the younger school, but that expectation had not been met.

Another shortcoming of the resolution pointed out by him was that instead of organizing the non-cooperation campaign to compel the British Government to accept the demands, it was stipulated as an option only in the event of non-acceptance. Unless a non-cooperation campaign was organized immediately, Subhas emphasized, it was absolutely certain that the British would reject, with contempt, even the demand for Dominion Status.

Subhas came down heavily on the soft and incremental attitude of the older leaders. Recent developments, such as the atrocities in Lahore and Kanpur, the death of Lala Lajpat Rai, and the utterances of the Viceroy, had led the younger generation to expect a bold and defiant leadership from the older leaders, he said. The older leaders, however, failed to rise to the occasion, which indicated that they were not alive to the sentiments of the younger generation, and were not aware of how fast they have advanced in the last few years.

Rather than wasting time and energy over quarrelling, the younger generation would follow its own path, cooperating with the older leaders and working under their guidance as long as their policies and programme were in consonance. It was to be seen if the older leaders were prepared to lead with a fighting programme.

The storm having blown over, Jawaharlal was back at the Subjects Committee meeting. So complete was his agreement with Gandhi's resolution that when S. Satyamurti moved an amendment to Gandhi's second resolution on constructive work for the next year, he opposed the amendment. It was remarkable because Satyamurti repeated the same amendment which Jawaharlal himself had moved against Gandhi's original resolution, demanding that the AICC be instructed to devise a programme to prepare the country for civil disobedience and non-payment of taxes. It sought to create the sanction which both Subhas and Jawaharlal had argued for. The reason for his opposition now was that the part of his amendment, which insisted on the country's goal being complete independence, had not been adopted.

The annual session of the Congress opened on 26 December. In his presidential speech on the first day, Motilal explained his position:

> I am for complete independence—as complete as it can be—but I am not against full dominion status—as full as any dominion possesses it today—provided I get it before it loses all attraction. I am for severance of British connection as it subsists with us today but am not against it as it exists with the Dominions.
>
> What matters to me is that Dominion Status involves a very considerable measure of freedom bordering on complete independence and in any day preferable to complete dependence. I am therefore not against an exchange of our abject dependence with whatever measure of freedom there is in full Dominion Status if such exchange is offered.[94]

He argued by referring to Gandhi's utterances that the country was yet to prove that it was ready for complete independence.

Discussion on the Nehru committee report came up in the open session of the Congress on the last day of the year, the third day of the session. Quite symbolically, as the loudspeakers failed, Jawaharlal took on the role to relay Gandhi's short speech in Hindi, sentence by sentence, to the audience.

Carrying forward his statement on the Nehru report resolution, Subhas was the first to rise to move an amendment which was similar to the November AICC resolution and the one raised in the Subjects Committee meeting by Srinivasa Iyengar. There was, however, one significant difference. Iyengar's resolution had made clear that neither Subhas nor Jawaharlal would participate in the proceedings or move any amendment. Now here was a newcomer into politics, who had just stepped into his thirties, challenging the supreme leader of Indian politics who was nearly double his age, in the open session of the Congress.

Subhas felt that he owed an explanation to his Congress colleagues for this change:

> You are aware that in private conversations and elsewhere I said that I do
> not desire to stand in the way of elder leaders. The reason why I did so
> was that at that time I did not feel prepared to accept the responsibility of
> the consequences of a division in this house in case our amendment was
> accepted. Today I feel prepared to accept the consequences and to face
> the issue till the end if my amendment is accepted.[95]

He drew attention to the increasing strength of the impatient youth. 'I and Pandit Jawaharlal are considered moderates amongst the extremists,' and if the elder leaders were not ready to compromise even with these moderates, he was afraid that 'the breach between the old and the new would be irreparable'. The younger generation loved and revered the leaders but were not ready to follow them blindly any more. He threw the question straight to the leaders—could they lay hands on their breasts and say that there was a reasonable chance for obtaining Dominion Status in twelve months? Then why lower the flag of independence even for those twelve months?

Subhas responded to Gandhi's point, that the Madras Congress resolution was simply a decision to have independence as the country's goal and not a declaration of independence, as follows:

> You can say, what do we gain by this resolution of Independence? I say,
> we develop a new mentality. After all, what is the fundamental cause of
> our political degradation? That is the question of mentality and if you
> want to overcome the slave mentality, you will do so by encouraging our
> countrymen to stand for full and complete independence. I go further
> and say, assuming that we do not follow it up by action, but by preaching
> the gospel honestly and placing the goal of independence before our
> countrymen, we shall bring up a new generation.
>
> But I tell you we are not going to sit down with folded hands.
> I have already said that the younger generation realise their
> responsibility and they are prepared for their task. We shall devise our
> own programme and work it out according to the best of our ability
> so that there is no danger that our resolution will be thrown into the
> waste paper basket.[96]

This time, Jawaharlal stood up to support Subhas's amendment. To demand 'Dominion Status was nothing but to be beggars at the door of the British government', was his point of view.

The attack on the Dominion Status was as direct as it could get. The challenge was up to Gandhi to neutralize it. When he rose to respond, he made it clear that he was speaking primarily to young Bengal. If young Bengal thought that 'a mere Gujarati' did not understand them, then they 'would commit a most serious blunder'. Betraying impatience, he issued a stern warning that if his speech was interrupted at any point, he would walk away and demanded 'perfect silence'.

Gandhi was livid with what he considered a breach of trust, dishonouring a compromise. His resolution was the result of a compromise between the different parties. It was an attempt to accommodate the views of as many parties as possible, and those 'who were supposed to be behind that resolution were honour-bound to support it':

> If you have not got that sense of honour and if after giving a word of honour you are not sure that that should be kept at any cost, then I say that you will not be able to make this nation free.[97]

Questioning the doubt of his opponents that the British Parliament could not be convinced within one year, he asserted that if they helped him and followed the proposed programme, Swaraj would come within one year.[98] It was the second time in the decade that he issued the same promise.

When the counting of votes on the amendment was completed at 1 a.m., Gandhi was found to have just about secured the victory for Dominion Status. 1350 delegates voted against Subhas's amendment, and 973 voted in his favour.

Closing the session, Motilal reassured the audience that the Congress programme was as strong as it could be. His advice was to erase words such as 'Dominion Status' and 'freedom', which were borrowed from foreign language, and work towards 'Swaraj' and 'Azadi'. Special mention was reserved for the two youth icons:

> Subhas, I shall call him not brother but my son (cheers). He has always regarded me as father. To me Subhas and Jawahar are alike, (cheers) I make no difference between them. I see no difference between them. (cheers) Both Subhas and Jawahar have told you in their speeches on the

amendment to Mahatmaji's resolution that in their opinion we old-age men are no good, are not strong enough and are hopelessly behind the times. There is nothing new in this. (laughter). It is common in this world that young always regard aged men as behind times.[99]

Subhas could clearly see that it was Gandhi's intervention which swayed the votes towards the Dominion Status resolution. Most of the delegates who voted in favour of Gandhi's resolution did so not as much for their faith in obtaining Dominion Status, but in honour of Gandhi and Motilal, he told the Associated Press. Had Gandhi not argued in favour of Dominion Status, the story would have been different. The fact that 973 delegates voted for his amendment resolution despite the opposition of senior leaders was indeed a moral victory.[100]

The Calcutta Congress was an anticlimax for Subhas. 'While the country was ready, the leaders were not', and Gandhi, 'unfortunately for his countrymen, did not see light'. Gandhi's 'prestige in the country', Subhas believed, was 'badly shaken by the proceedings of the Calcutta Congress'.[101]

The Calcutta experience could not have been anything but unpleasant to Gandhi either. The Congress exhibition and the strong opposition to the Nehru report were not the only sore points. There were more; the first one being the nature of the volunteer corps organized by Subhas to facilitate the session.

With a target of recruiting four thousand volunteers, Subhas utilized his popularity among the youth and the student community but also reached out to the revolutionary groups for help. Leaders of the revolutionary groups were given the responsibility to organize 'units' which they would command as 'Major' or 'Captain'. Subhas himself would be the 'General Officer Commanding' (GOC). 'When the President-elect Motilal Nehru arrived, every effort was made to receive him with royal honours, backed with a military show', observed a government report. Motilal was driven in a flower-decked chariot drawn by thirty-four horses and ridden by postillions in pink and green, and greeted with a hundred and one rockets.[102]

The procession consisted not only of cyclists, motorcyclists, volunteers with flower petals and national flags, but also military bandsmen, infantry and cavalry under the command of Subhas, 'who in his military costume stood like a General on the board of his car'. Mounted sentries were posted in front of the house where Motilal was put up. The Bengal Government noted that the 'military display and the prominence given to it' by Subhas 'was part of the strong attempt made to commit the All Parties Convention and the Congress to the more extreme views of the Independence League'.[103] The transformation of volunteer dress code from khadi to khaki, with batons and the image of Subhas as the GOC reviewing volunteer troops on horseback, made a deep impact on all. Subhas allegedly wanted the volunteers to carry a dagger or a small sword, but the police predictably refused to allow it.

This overt exhibition of a militant attitude did not go down well with Gandhi. Soon after returning from Calcutta, he derided the show in an article in *Young India*:

> The volunteers dressed in European fashion presented, in my opinion, a sorry spectacle in Calcutta and the expenses incurred was out of keeping with the pauperism of the nation. They were no representatives of rough and rugged businesslike farmers.[104]

What escaped the vigilant eyes of Gandhi was that this was not a one-time show but the beginning of an extremist volunteer movement—the dreaded Bengal Volunteers—which would form the nucleus of the surge in revolutionary activity in the following years.[105]

The Government, however, was worried. When the Director of the Intelligence Bureau reported Subhas's plans for setting up the volunteer corps, the Viceroy wanted to know whether it could be dealt with as an illegal association.

The Viceroy was more worried by the end of the Congress session. He informed the Secretary of State that Jawaharlal and Subhas had 'converted independence from a phrase into a definite movement':

> Motilal Nehru, finding himself in danger of defeat on an issue which would involve his resignation from Presidentship of Congress, invoked the aid of Gandhi, who drafted compromising resolution . . .
>
> Though the supporters of independence profess not to have been satisfied by the result of the Congress meeting, there is no doubt that the Congress was a great triumph for extremism. An ultimatum which everybody knows cannot be complied with has been given to the British Government, and the Congress have decided unanimously that if it is not complied with after the end of December next they will revive non co-operation . . . It may be that Gandhi and Motilal Nehru and

their followers are not anxious to see these developments, but in view of the commitment they have made, they will find it very difficult to avoid participating in them without a complete break with the extremists, which they are reluctant to face . . . Gandhi has since tried to tone down his ultimatum and explains that he would be satisfied if the British Government made some definite, serious and sincere move to meet them within the year, but this does not really get him and those who think with him out of the difficulty into which the desire for compromise with the extremists has got them . . .

. . . We are faced now with a party, at present small in number, but active, who, it would seem, mean to attempt to translate independence into a definite policy, and to organise themselves with a view to attaining their object by force, or at least, to create such widespread unrest in the country that the Government will be intimidated into making sweeping concessions. Youth movements and volunteer organisations are being discussed and supported, and it appears that Jawaharlal Nehru and Subhas Chandra Bose do not mean to stop at words, but are prepared for action.[106]

The second incident that irked Gandhi was a demonstration, by thousands of workers of the railway and mills in the Howrah area, in the Congress arena.[107] The workers' procession occupied the main Congress pandal, demanding that the leaders must listen to and investigate their grievances for redressal. Subsequently, they passed resolutions demanding complete independence in the form of a socialist republic. Some of the participants later alleged that as the chief of the volunteers in charge of security, Subhas tried to stop their entry into the pandal, but relented due to the intervention of the elder leaders such as Motilal.[108]

The incident left Gandhi livid. The demonstration was no more than a show, with no element of reality, he wrote in *Young India*. If indeed it had any real strength 'there was no reason why such a vast mass of people as had gathered there could not wrest power from unwilling hands'. The Congress session was more like a circus, he insinuated, and 'the demonstrators had gone not to demonstrate strength, they had gone as if to a circus as sightseers'.[109]

Probably the only event that went without any conflict was the Hindi Prachar Conference presided by Gandhi. Gandhi was highly appreciative of Subhas's role as chairperson of the reception committee of the conference.

As Subhas read out from a printed speech, Gandhi observed that he read the Devanagari script without any difficulty, and his pronunciation was almost faultless. Gandhi was glad that Subhas 'effectively disposed of the calumny that Bengal was indifferent to Hindi' and promised to be the first one to learn the language.[110]

Gandhi wrote letters and articles about the Congress and other issues during and after the session, but strangely remained silent on something that was unlikely to have avoided his attention. Delivering his address as the chairperson of the reception committee of the All-India Youth Congress a day before the All Parties Convention began, Subhas severely criticized the 'effects and consequences' of the Sabarmati school of thought.

He was not criticizing the fundamental philosophy underlying the ashram's worldview, but the effect of the ashram's propaganda. It was:

> . . . to create a feeling and an impression that modernism is bad, large scale production is an evil, wants should not be increased and the standard of living should not be raised, that we must endeavour to the best of our ability to go back to the days of the bullock-cart and that the soul is so important that physical culture and military training can well be ignored.[111]

The fundamental difference in the worldview between Subhas and Gandhi could hardly be overlooked. He was speaking out against the Gandhian philosophy even before Gandhi had gotten to know him well. In his letters, Gandhi still addressed him as 'My dear friend', in contrast to the first-name basis 'My dear Jawahar' in the letters to Jawaharlal.

Perhaps more significant, from Subhas's personal point of view, was speaking out against the influence of Aurobindo, the man he had considered to be his political guru during his student years:

> The actual effect of the propaganda carried on by the Pondicherry school of thought is to create a feeling and an impression that there is nothing higher or nobler than peaceful contemplation, that Yoga means Pranayama and Dhyana, that while action may be tolerated as good, this particular brand of Yoga is something higher and better.

Subhas' idea of spirituality was different. It was galling to him that the Pondicherry ashram's propaganda:

... has led many a man to forget that spiritual progress under the present day conditions is possible only by ceaseless and unselfish action, that the best way to conquer nature is to fight her and that it is weakness to seek refuge in contemplation when we are hemmed in on all sides by dangers and difficulties.

Philosophical differences apart, there were other reasons which might have driven him to this criticism. After many years of hoping that Aurobindo would return to strengthen, if not to lead, its extremist politics, Bengal had given up on him. On the other hand, the influence of Aurobindo had removed his Swarajist colleague, Anilbaran, from the political scene. Dilip too was resistant to joining politics, being under the heavy influence of Aurobindo. The former centre of revolutionary activities—Chandernagar—had been relegated to the background.

India now needed a philosophy of activism, not the passivism inculcated by these two schools. India could no longer live in an isolated corner of the world; it had to adapt to modern conditions. When India would be free, it would have to fight its modern enemies with modern methods. But there was a need for synthesis in the path of India's development, between its ancient culture and modern science. If the cry of 'back to the Vedas' was to be resisted, so was Europe's 'meaningless craze for fashion and change'.

At one stroke, he angered the followers of Sabarmati and Pondicherry, while the international socialists were already viewing him with suspicion. Now, the two influential camps within the country would see him as an antagonist.

In his own survey of the situation, Subhas identified a few distinct strands in the political landscape at this juncture:

Besides the main current of the Congress movement, three other lines of activity were clearly visible at this time. There was an undercurrent of revolutionary activity with a certain amount of following in northern India, an unrest in the labour world which extended to every part of the country, and an awakening among the middle-class youths which was manifest everywhere.[112]

Over the next eleven years that his political career lasted in India, Subhas strove to weave them into his own political world with varying degrees of success.

Significantly, Subhas left out one strand which was no less important in his scheme of things. The electoral politics of the Swarajya party took up much of his time and energy—not so much the happenings within the legislative council, as the affairs of the Calcutta Corporation.

In August 1928, Subhas along with Sengupta had successfully sponsored a motion to compel the Corporation administration to refuse information sought by the education committee of the Statutory Commission. In December, he moved a motion censuring the mayor for throwing a garden party to the visiting Viceroy, which was defeated again due to a lack of support. If Subhas was finding ways to utilize the Corporation for making a political statement, he was suggesting concrete measures for the city's improvement too. Writing in the *Calcutta Municipal Gazette*, he held the absence of a 'full-fledged' road department in the Corporation responsible for the lack of proper roads; road construction was left to the whims and fancies of the district engineers, and there was no policy for building roads in a planned way to keep up with the growing city. While the major cities around the world constructed their roads in a scientific manner, the Calcutta Corporation did not have a laboratory to determine the nature of road surface required for different types of roads. 'If we want to tackle the question of road-making scientifically, we should classify the roads according to the nature of the traffic . . . Moreover, all the parts of the city should receive equal attention,' he suggested. A roads department headed by a full-time roads engineer, aided by an attached laboratory, was essential. The Bombay Corporation, he noted, was doing better work on this aspect.

Drawing attention to the work of the Nagpur municipality, he also pointed out the immense potential of sewage farming after removal of solid and semi-solid substances from the effluent:

> The Calcutta corporation owns the Dhappa (sic) area. It can also acquire other areas if necessary. If these areas are developed with the help of the sewage which now runs to waste, the Corporation will be able to make a lot of money and, thereby, serve the best interests of the rate payers!

The Calcutta Corporation must 'without delay shake off its inertia and tackle the various municipal problems in a thoroughly up-to-date, business-like and scientific manner', if it wanted to retain its reputation as a premier Corporation in India, was his warning.[113]

His growing involvement with labour movements at this time also led him to engage with the union of the Corporation employees. While he encouraged them to organize themselves for their rights and advised them on the way to take their movement forward, his first advice was regarding their behaviour with the people they served:

> . . . whether you are a clerk or an officer, you are, in either case, a servant of the public, and as long as you act and behave as honourable men and as gentlemen, I think you should be proud of yourself . . . You all know that here are some departments—particularly some departments of the Government—the employees of which do not behave as servants of the public. They behave as masters of the public . . . That is all the more reason why in a body like the Corporation you should conduct yourselves in such a way as to set a standard for all public servants.[114]

With his passion for municipal governance and vision for Calcutta's development, the defeat must have stung him, but the political and social canvas in front of him was much larger than it was in 1924.

The immediate task, as the new year began, was to continue the organization of protests against the Simon Commission. The Commission, which had returned to India the previous October for its second round of consultations, reached Calcutta from Shimla on 12 January. Subhas and Sengupta led several thousand protestors with black flags, shouting 'Simon go back' at the motorcade. But the police force was well prepared to prevent any sort of confrontation. The Howrah railway station, as well as the Howrah Bridge, was cleared of all traffic. Normal traffic was stopped for smooth passage, and a large force held back protestors at key places.[115]

The Central Committee members assisting the Commission accompanied it to Calcutta. Subhas was scathing in his criticism. The participation of some sycophantic Raibahadurs and Khanbahadurs did not make the Commission a success, he told a huge gathering at South Calcutta. If taking the evidence of only these people was the objective of the Commission, it could well have been accomplished in England, without it having to travel to India. The most important indicator that the boycott of the Commission was a success, for him, was that the Commission had not been able to negotiate with those who were fighting for the country's freedom.

The Bengal Government was satisfied that the hartal against the Commission was a failure.[116] Subhas admitted that what was achieved was not nearly enough. The movement needed greater active participation. If Gandhi had failed despite having more people behind him than Lenin had at the time of the overthrow of the Tsarist rule, it was because people did not have the force of sincerity.[117]

Calcutta had presented him a stiff challenge, but as the new year rolled in, it became clear that Gandhi was set to gradually, but surely, stage a comeback to Congress politics. One of the most critical issues for him was cleaning up the Congress organization. 'Without complete overhauling of the Congress, there will be no other work,' he wrote in *Young India*.[118]

Gandhi, heading the foreign cloth boycott committee set up by the working committee after the Calcutta Congress, was ready with a programme for the country. In January 1929 he submitted to the working committee his 'Scheme for Boycott of Foreign Cloth through Khadi'. Under the scheme, Congress volunteers in every village and town across the country were asked to go door to door, selling khadi and collecting foreign cloth in possession of the households, which were to be burnt publicly. Dealers were to be persuaded to stop buying and selling foreign cloth. The scheme was like old wine in a new bottle, but was the only one at the moment which gave Congress a tangible programme around which the organization could be strengthened. It gave the Congress workers something to 'do', whose impact was visible and measurable, and in case of successful implementation would boost their confidence. Despite the rise of the youth brigade in the Congress, the organization still depended on him for a concrete course of action at the national level.

Gandhi himself was convinced that the foreign cloth boycott and promotion of khadi was the only programme worth pursuing at the moment: 'Everything else is simply futile' and the boycott 'will be a thousand times more effective than that of the Simon Commission', he wrote in *Navajivan*.[119]

Leaving behind the disagreements of the annual Congress session, Subhas returned to implement the Congress programmes in Bengal. As a new member of the working committee, Subhas was put in charge of both Bengal and Assam[120] and entrusted with the responsibility, along with Jawaharlal, to prepare a scheme for the organization of volunteers to work amongst urban labourers and for rural reconstruction.[121] As in the previous year, he continued with his mass contact programme, addressing public meetings across the province. In the course of the year, apart from holding regular meetings in Calcutta and the adjoining areas of Hooghly, Howrah and the Twenty-Four Parganas districts, he travelled to Pabna, Rangpur, Mymensingh, Sylhet, Chittagong, Khulna, Jessore, Bakarganj and Rajsahi to strengthen the Congress organizations as well as to garner support for the demand for independence.

The foreign cloth boycott movement in Bengal started with Gandhi leading a Congress meeting at Calcutta's Shraddhananda Park on 4 March to light a bonfire of foreign clothes. Claiming that burning clothes at a public place was illegal, the police arrested him along with Kiran Shankar Roy, the secretary of the BPCC, and almost a hundred others.[122] The police charged with their lathis, dispersed the crowd and put out the fire. The crowd retaliated by throwing stones. Charles Tegart, the police commissioner, allowed Gandhi to proceed with his plan of travelling to Burma the following day, on the undertaking that there would be no burning of clothes at public places in the city. Gandhi appealed for the continuation of the cloth-burning programme at private places. On his return from Burma, he was fined by the Presidency Magistrate for one rupee.

'The fire which the Mahatma has lit will not go out; it will have to burn in every house,' Subhas announced. The response to the call for boycott, however, was not gathering momentum, but he continued to hold public meetings almost daily, to persuade people to throw their foreign clothes away. Subhas tried to motivate the Congress workers by reminding them that the burden of sacrifice always fell on a minority—expecting everyone to join the movement would be a mistake. The likes of Mir Jafar and Umi Chand had always existed in history, and the only way to reduce their growing influence was to continue building public opinion.[123] Within the next few days, he issued a detailed programme for the Bengal Congress to put the boycott plan into action, suggesting the widespread use of publicity materials to generate awareness, formation of volunteer organizations in the districts, establishing museums for display of swadeshi goods, setting up training centres for potential public speakers and centres to sell khadi cloth, and compilation of directories to provide up-to-date information on khadi products.[124] The next Holi must be played not with traditional colours, but with fire. Subhas was particularly keen to engage the students in the move against foreign clothes—he appealed to the schools and colleges to institute awards for students who could collect the maximum number of clothes for burning.[125] He set the target of raising a fund of Rs 2 lakh to keep the campaign going and organizing a thousand volunteers in each district. 1929, he announced, borrowing from the Mahabharata, was the *Udyog Parva* (the preparatory phase)—the final battle of Kurukshetra could not be far away.[126]

The preoccupation with the politics of boycott was definitely Gandhian—Subhas was being a disciplined Congressman. The activism was, however, the manifestation of a deeper urge. He did not have the slightest doubt that the British Government would not accede to the Congress's demand for accepting the Nehru Report. 'Only madness or folly could have led one to hope that the mighty British Government would concede even Dominion Home Rule without a struggle,' he observed.[127] The focus had to be on the immediate future—there was too much to do in too short a time to prepare for that phase of mass struggle. The groundwork that needed to be taken up included (apart from the boycott of foreign cloth)—setting up a swadeshi museum, participating in elections to the local boards, the Calcutta Corporation and the Legislative Council, social activities directed against untouchability, campaigns for reducing jute cultivation in the state and helping the labour movement.

He was already a youth icon in Bengal. His speeches and writings were read and discussed among the more radical section of the students in the province, along with those of Swami Vivekananda, Rabindranath, Dwijendra Lal Roy, Sarat Chandra Chattopadhyay (whose novel *Pather Dabi*, revolving around a revolutionary, became immensely popular after being published in 1926).[128] The first collection of Subhas's published articles and letters written between 1923 and 1927 was published in 1928 as *Taruner Swapno* (The Youth's Dream).

Throughout the year, Subhas went around addressing students' and youth conferences within the province at places such as Pabna, Malikanda, Sylhet, Jessore, Khulna, Hooghly, Rajshahi, Howrah and Midnapore, asking them to organize and prepare.[129] Some of these speeches were compiled in another book in 1930, with the symbolically significant name, *Nutaner Sandhan* (Search for the New).

An insightful account from one of the student organizers of the Midnapore Youth Conference of December 1929 throws light on the organizational aspects of such conferences and the impact they had on the local youth:

Earlier when we had decided to hold the Conference and to invite Subhas
to be its president, the idea was not liked by orthodox Congress leaders of
Midnapore who were staunch followers of Gandhi . . . Subhas arrived in
Midnapore by train on 28 December. A unit of the para-military wing of
the Bengal Volunteers, including myself, under the command of Dinesh
Gupta,[130] welcomed him along with several Congress leaders . . . We took
them in a route march through the town of Midnapore . . . He was then
the idol of the youth of Bengal and had already established his reputation
as a top leader of the Congress . . . He seemed to the youth of Bengal to
be a greater realist than Gandhi or Jawaharlal Nehru, although they had
the highest regard for them. Subhas wanted to know from us the position
and strength of our organization and the attitude of the Midnapore youth
towards him . . .

Subhas came and had gone. His stay in Midnapore was short. But
our objective was more than accomplished by his presence and personal
contact. Above all his presidential address to the people and especially to
the youth of Midnapore created a great stir, a tornado in the somewhat
turbid water of the entire district. It gave substantial food for thought in
short as well as long run. It offered a variety of directions in which the
youth could act.[131]

Contours of a new and distinct line of thought on political action started
becoming visible at this time in Subhas's speeches and organizational
efforts. The new element was seen in his efforts to involve the revolutionary
groups in the maintenance and expansion of the Bengal Volunteers (BV).
The volunteer corps, comprising students and the youth, was probably
placed at the centre of his plans for mass mobilization, envisaged to impart
a more radical touch to the movement and allowing a more organized and
public role to the secretive revolutionary societies.

The Bengal Government was keenly watching the impact of Subhas's
proposal on maintaining a permanent volunteer corps. In June 1929,
it noted that the enthusiasm for the youth movement 'shows no sign
of abating and several new units have been founded recently' in several
districts of Bengal. In Calcutta, the volunteers were conducting route
marches in khaki and were inspected by Subhas.[132] Parades continued in
July with volunteers in uniform 'beginning with arms drill with lathis, and
followed by route marches during which the lathis are left behind'.[133] It was,
however, a challenge to maintain the volunteer corps. The Government

was apprehensive of 'local incidents or other factors' which it believed were necessary to keep up the tempo.[134]

Emissaries were going out from Calcutta to other districts to set up volunteer forces there. P.K. Ray, a member of the BV, has described how Dinesh Gupta recruited a host of youngsters in their late teens in Midnapore such as Pravangshu Pal, Prodyot Bhattacharjee, Bimal Dasgupta and others.[135] Many of these would become active in violent revolutionary acts in the following years.

In fact, many of Subhas's speeches around that time emphasized how the contemporary era was one of mass movement, which followed the swadeshi era of the early twentieth century and the subsequent revolutionary period that roughly coincided with the First World War.[136] There were glimpses of him losing patience with the conventional politics, and this was in line with his own radical politics due to which he was able to influence and draw the youth closer to them. There was no dearth of meetings, conferences and resolutions passed in those, but 'We need to introspect how far we have progressed by simply passing resolutions on independence', he told the district youth conference in Howrah.[137]

In appealing to the youth to organize themselves along a path separate from conventional politics, he cited the thoughts of Lenin and Vivekananda. It probably was Subhas's thoughts too that underscored his efforts at raising the volunteer forces. It was better to get hold of ten able men than a hundred dullards, those who would devote to revolution not only their free evenings but their whole life, as Lenin had advised. So had Vivekananda, who said, 'Give me ten men, I will revolutionise India.' Mere political excitement was ephemeral and would not help in the country's progress. It was important to learn from the bureaucracy on how to stay informed about the country. Only then would it be possible to break out of the hypocrisy going on in the name of religion, society and the State. Only if such groups of self-sacrificing and professional workers could be created would the menace of internecine political conflict be overcome. These workers would go on to be specialists in their chosen field of work and drive mass consciousness.[138]

As an indicator of his increasing all-India stature as a youth leader, Subhas was being invited from other provinces to address student and youth conferences. October saw him presiding over the Punjab Students' Conference at Lahore and addressing public meetings in Delhi and Ludhiana. He presided over the Central Province Youth Conference at Nagpur in November, and the Central Province and Berar Student Conference at Amraoti in December.

He stepped into Punjab as Bengal's representative, recalling the links between the two provinces—the history of Punjab's heroes formed an important part of Bengal's literature; the province touched the inner core of Bengal's emotions by showing affection for Jatindranath Das and other Bengali prisoners. Subhas was reported to have told Dr Mohammed Alam, a Congress leader from Punjab, that the death of Jatin Das brought the two provinces closer and they would march shoulder to shoulder in the fight for freedom.[139] The Punjab Government felt that his speech, 'while studiously avoiding direct incitement, was throughout on a note of sentimentalism well calculated to appeal to the immature minds to which it was addressed, and was as dangerous as a more violent speech'.[140]

These meetings gave Subhas the opportunity to take his ideas—which he had been talking about within Bengal till then—to the other provinces, as much as to establish direct contact with the local organizations. There was to be no compromise with bondage, injustice and inequality; the mission that India had to fulfil was not any esoteric or abstract concept, but an original contribution 'to the culture and civilisation of the world in almost every department of human life'. If the students and youth wanted to serve the Indian National Congress they would have to reach out to the labour movements, peasant movements, women's movements, apart from organizing the students and youths themselves. The need was not that of reform, but of radical recreation of the individual and the collective life. He said that 'False standards, hide-bound customs and age-long restrictions will be pulled down and a new order will gradually come into existence'. It would be based on 'liberty and fraternity':

> Freedom for the whole of society will mean freedom for woman as well as for man—freedom for the depressed classes and not merely for the higher caste—freedom for the young and not merely for the old—in other words, freedom for all sections, for all minorities and for all individuals.[141]

At the same time that he was criticizing conventional partisan politics, he was sharply highlighting the shortcomings of revolutionary action too:

> I don't know if there are still people in this country who think that they can rescue India with the help of two-and-a-half bombs and one-and-

a-half pistol. Liberation of India is not so easy. These can be used for
terrorism but not to create revolution. Terrorism and revolution are not
the same. Terrorism can be carried out by a few people, but revolution
will be possible only when the entire nation awakens . . . Just as revolution
can be carried with arms, it is possible to have it without the help of arms;
it can be a bloody as much as a bloodless revolution . . . I strongly believe
that the era of terrorism is over forever. Our main weapon now is mass
organisation.[142]

He argued that when a few revolutionaries had not been able to free the
country even by sacrificing their lives, it should be understood that until the
people at large desire liberation and organize themselves for that purpose,
Indian cannot become free. The fundamental principle of non-cooperation
was to break free from the clutches of the bureaucracy and organize people
with the aim to completely destroy their cooperation and collaboration on
the basis of which the British Government in India had been established.
The British Empire's Indian collaborators was a theme that he would
repeatedly return to.

There is a remarkable similarity between Subhas's thoughts and
the philosophy propounded by the Hindustan Republican Association
(HRA), in its manifesto written in 1924 by Sachindranath Sanyal. Among
others, the manifesto declared that '. . . the party will never forget that
terrorism is not their object, and they will try incessantly to organise a band
of selfless and devoted workers will (sic) devote their energies towards the
political and social emancipation of the country'.[143] The HRA, according
to Jogesh Chandra Chatterji, a former member of the Anushilan Samiti
and later a Member of Parliament, was formed in 1924 as an offshoot of
the Anushilan Samiti by Sanyal, with the support of the top leaders of the
group such as Trailokyanath Chakraborty, Pratul Chandra Ganguli and
Narendra Mohan Sen. Among the young members of Anushilan who got
associated with Sanyal and the HRA at this time, the 'most remarkable'
was Jatindranath Das.[144] It was natural that the strong link between the
Anushilan Samiti and Subhas also resulted in the permeation of ideas.
Moreover, Chakraborty spent considerable time with Subhas in Mandalay.
Das, the secretary of the South Calcutta Congress Committee, joined the
volunteer corps formed by Subhas and held the rank of Major.[145]

The immediate objective of the HRA was 'to establish a Federated
Republic of the United States of India by an organised and armed

revolution'. As had been argued by Chittaranjan Das, the HRA too reiterated that 'official terrorism is surely to be met by counter terrorism'. It is important not to confound his criticism with condemnation. Like Das, Subhas had immense admiration for the bravery and sacrifice of the revolutionaries who formed a large segment of his support base. It is not possible to trace back the specific influences on his thinking, but the broad components of a strong youth organization, focus on social reconstruction and emphasis on the need to move beyond sporadic violent action appear to be a combination of Das's approach as well as of organizations like the HRA (which had transformed into the Hindustan Socialist Republican Association or HSRA in 1928 by Bhagat Singh and Sukhdev) and the Naujawan Bharat Sabha, which too was formed in 1924 by Ramchandra, Bhagat Singh and others.[146]

The incident that possibly triggered his repeated discussion of this aspect was the bombing of the Central Legislative Assembly. On 8 April, the twenty-one-year-old Bhagat Singh and eighteen-year-old Batukeshwar Dutt created a sensation by exploding bombs in the Central Legislative Assembly, in protest against the two proposed repressive laws, the Public Safety Bill and the Trades Disputes Bill, and the manner in which they were being forced into laws. Both Singh and Dutt stood their ground, shouting slogans and throwing HSRA leaflets that quoted French revolutionary Auguste Vaillant, 'It takes a loud voice to make the deaf hear.'[147] Both were sentenced to transportation for life in June. At the same time, widespread arrests began and Jatindranath Das too, who provided the HSRA with the training to make bombs, was arrested in June.[148]

The initial reaction of the prominent Calcutta newspapers was critical and dismissive, demonstrating the downside of secret society action which faced the risk of derision due to the lack of information. While the *Anandabazar Patrika* called the bombing suspicious and mysterious, and 'an act of childish stupidity' of bursting 'crackers', the *Amrita Bazar Patrika* claimed that 'the perpetrators represent no school of thought in the country', and the *Forward* insinuated that it was a calculated act 'to strengthen the hands of reactionaries in India and England'.[149]

As the trial began, Singh and Dutt started a hunger strike from mid-June, demanding better treatment as political prisoners. Das, along with other prisoners of the 'Lahore Conspiracy Case' as it came to be known, began their hunger strike from 13 July. The strike attracted widespread attention from across the country and leaders took up their cause inside and outside the Central Legislative Assembly. Das succumbed after sixty-three days of fasting, and breathed his last on 13 September.

During the hunger strike, Subhas led a joint procession of the South Calcutta Youth Association and the Naujawan Bharat Sabha (NBS), which had its organization in Calcutta too, on 11 August 1929 to observe Political Sufferers' Day.[150] On Das's death, Subhas gave Rs 600 to bring his body from Lahore to Calcutta[151] and sent telegrams to all intermediate stations to arrange for ice, water and other conveniences for those accompanying the body.[152] A crowd of five lakh awaited Jatin's body at the Howrah station. The Bengal Government was unnerved by the reaction and expected trouble. 'There can be no doubt that the younger part of the *bhadrolok* community is very excited and, nor should the dangers of assassination arising from this excitement be minimised,' the Bengal Government reported to the Viceroy.[153] The Government's fears were not unfounded.

The result of Subhas's groundwork with the volunteer corps and students became immediately obvious. As processions, meetings and 'violent propaganda' erupted in almost every district of the province, the Bengal Government noted with alarm that the 'degeneration of the Congress into an organisation that relies on its existence on inflaming the youthful part of the population has been more marked than ever'. The Intelligence Branch reported that 'the members of various youth and student associations throughout the province have been so mixed up with Congress activities in connection with the death of Jatindranath Das, that it is not possible in the majority of cases to separate youth from the Congress'. New youth associations started coming up in various places in the province through the subsequent months.[154]

However, Subhas's appeal to the youth organizations to forgo sporadic acts of violence in favour of organized action did not go unnoticed by the Government.

Subhas Bose is alarmed by the violent tendencies of the younger revolutionaries and the danger that wild acts may upset his schemes for organised action. More than once lately he has spoken of the need of preparation and the time that must elapse before concerted action can begin.[155]

In all these developments, the revolutionary groups and their leaders continued to have important roles. The fractious tendency too, however, continued to deteriorate, having a disruptive impact not only on Congress politics, but also on student, youth and labour organizations. Multiple factions vying for control of political power coalesced around Subhas and Jatindra Mohan Sengupta.[156] Although Subhas had the broad support of the revolutionaries when he returned in 1927, the temporary unity had started falling apart.

Of the two most well-known revolutionary groups of Bengal, Jugantar extended their support to Subhas while the Anushilan Samiti stood behind Sengupta. The specific reason for this split is not clear, but one commentator has claimed that the machinations of a staunch supporter of Subhas made him appear to be biased towards the former.[157] Although the divided camps behind Subhas and Sengupta were evenly balanced, Subhas became the BPCC president with support of some non-aligned members. When Panchanan Chakraborti confronted him for getting involved in the factional feud, Subhas explained to him that the post of president was not important as such and he was only defending himself against the coalition that wanted to oust him from Bengal politics.[158]

That it was not a hollow justification has been explained by Gopal Lal Sanyal, editor of the nationalist newspaper *Atmashakti*, a confidante of Chittaranjan Das and later of Subhas, but above all, an observer with access to the inner scheming in Bengal Congress. Sanyal pointed out that Subhas convinced a reluctant Sengupta to take up the post of chairperson of the reception committee of the Calcutta Congress, and stepped aside from contesting in the mayoral election of the Calcutta Corporation in 1929, supporting Sengupta instead. As president of the BPCC, Subhas had to devote a significant amount of time to ensure that group fights did not derail the movement.[159] The truce arrived at between the revolutionary groups during the Calcutta Congress dissolved as soon as it was over.

Apart from the Madaripur group of Purna Chandra Das (who was with Subhas in Mandalay jail) and Jugantar, the Daccan Sri Sangha of Anil Roy (which reportedly branched out of places outside Bengal, like United Provinces, Assam, Bihar, Orissa and even Burma) and the Chittagong group of 'Masterda' Surjya Sen were the key forces that threw their weight behind Subhas. 'Major' Satya Gupta, a fiercely loyal supporter of Subhas who had been recruited by Anil Roy in the early 1920s, broke away with a number of members of Sri Sangha and took charge of the Bengal Volunteers, which counted among its members veterans like Hem Chandra Ghosh (from whose secret society, Mukti Sangha, many organizations including Sri Sangha emerged)[160] as well as youngsters like Dinesh Gupta and Binoy Bose. In an organizational shift, an All-Bengal Jugantar Party was formed in 1929 in Barisal, governed by a central council that consisted of leaders from different areas and groups such as Purna Das, Hem Ghosh, Surendra Mohan Ghose, Arun Guha, Bhupendra Kumar Datta and Surjya Sen.[161] In terms of violence, there were clearly two lines of thought. While the senior leadership of Anushilan and Jugantar decided to wait for the right time and appropriate preparation, younger members in the different groups were impatient to undertake immediate 'action'.[162] As seen earlier, Subhas was not against violence, but publicly kept discouraging sporadic acts of a bombing here and a murder there.

It must have irked Sengupta to find that workers of his home district, Chittagong, threw in their lot with Subhas. In 1929, the Chittagong District Congress Committee had Subhas to preside over the annual district Congress conference without informing its president Sengupta.[163] Whatever the trigger, Sengupta continued to escalate the expression of his displeasure with the functioning of the BPCC under Subhas in the course of the year. The conflict aggravated after the council elections in the summer of 1929, as the BPCC elections scheduled in November approached.

In August, Sengupta complained to Jawaharlal about a 'nefarious conspiracy to prevent fresh people from coming to the Congress' out of fear that they will topple those in charge of BPCC and asked if he could do something about it.[164] The conflict became a public spectacle when he started making the same allegations in public meetings too. Kiran Shankar Roy came to Subhas's defence, refuting the allegations. As the feud intensified, the Bengal Government kept the Home Department informed on a routine basis. 'Mr Sengupta seems to have the support of the Anusilan party as well as the less extreme elements in the Congress party, whilst Mr Bose is backed by the Jugantar party and the advocates of early and violent action,' it reported in August.[165]

The Government reports, however, appear exaggerated to a great extent, with their propensity to interpret all actions of Subhas and Sengupta in the light of their rivalry, making them look like frivolous contestants of a club election. Thus, according to the Bengal Government, Subhas and Sengupta were competing with each other to glorify Jatin Das, and Sengupta was trying to outdo Subhas in aggressiveness in his speeches in order to win over more youth to his side.[166]

Subhas gave out his side of the story for the first time in October, requesting Sengupta to stop the bickering as 'in a stiff fight with an unrelenting bureaucracy, we require all our forces to be united and concentrated in one direction'. Despite Sengupta's campaign against him, he had 'purposely refrained so far from saying a word in reply' because he realized 'how unseemly it is for this dispute to be carried on in the press and platform'. But now, he had to respond to some serious charges levelled against him. In a measured tone, the statement presented facts to contradict Sengupta's complaints. Subhas reminded Sengupta that not so long ago, it was Sengupta who had asked for the power to nominate his supporters to the BPCC executive council and it was granted to him. In contrast, the present BPCC had elected members and was far more representative. Factional squabble, Subhas pointed out, became a characteristic of the Bengal Congress when, after Chittaranjan's death, Sengupta was at the helm. In view of the immense harm it had done, it was critical to present a united front then.[167]

Such reasoning was obviously not going to change things, and matters continued to worsen along the expected lines. A few days before the elections, Subhas wrote to Basanti Devi that 'Mr Sengupta and his group are making a desperate effort to drive us out of the BPCC . . . Most probably we shall not lose'.[168] The group that propped up Sengupta was a formidable one that included, apart from the Anushilan Samiti, the Atmonnati party of Bipin Behari Ganguly, the khadi groups and the Anandabazar Patrika group.[169] Yet, Subhas was elected BPCC president again for the year, which was disputed by Sengupta's group.[170]

The dispute reached the working committee, and in December, Motilal sent Pattabhi Sitaramayya to survey the situation. Kiran Shankar Roy represented Subhas in Sitaramayya's inquiry. Subhas, however, was not convinced of a fair assessment and withdrew his representation. He shared his apprehensions with Basanti Devi.

> Sengupta's party tried repeatedly to outmanoeuvre and destroy us but so far
> without success. Our dispute is now in Pandit Motilal's hand. Even though
> we did not do anything unfair in the elections, I somehow apprehend that
> Panditji will support Sengupta and invalidate the elections to BPCC.[171]

Surprisingly, Gandhi chose to stay away from the dispute when requested by a congressman to intervene. He claimed that he had no knowledge that the differences between Subhas and Sengupta had become so serious: 'I share fully your grief over them but I do not know what I can do' and 'I can therefore only satisfy myself with the hope that all will be well'.[172]

The matter came to a head at the AICC meeting in Lahore on 27 December, two days before the annual session was to begin. Motilal had passed an interim order that only the old members of AICC from Bengal would retain their membership of the AICC until the dispute had been fully resolved.

Subhas wrote a hostile letter to Motilal, resigning from his membership of the working committee, describing the decision as 'arbitrary, unconstitutional and unprecedented'. He accused Motilal of acting under the influence of Sengupta and his party, and claimed that by concurring with him, the working committee 'has trampled upon the rights and dignity of the Bengal Committee'. Since the new elected members were not being allowed, Subhas asked for an adjournment of the meeting, a motion that Motilal ruled out of order. Motilal retaliated by saying that Subhas's 'representation of the case was misleading, to say the least of it'. When Subhas insisted that he did not consent to the appointment of Sitaramayya for inquiring into the Bengal Congress affairs, Motilal accused him of not telling the truth. Jawaharlal intervened at this point, insinuating that the findings of the Bengal inquiry were so murky that he would rather not have them discussed publicly. Therefore, he suggested that a formal appeal be made for the AICC to consider the matter afresh. Motilal agreed. Subhas was not happy and walked out along with his supporters.[173]

A compromise was agreed upon the next day through B.C. Roy's mediation, who recommended that instead of proceeding with the appeal for a fresh assessment, the newly elected members of AICC from Bengal be allowed to attend the Subjects Committee meeting. The compromise, however, broke down on the very next day when it was found that the *Tribune* had published Subhas's tirade against Motilal and the working committee. Sengupta threw a fit, withdrawing from the previous day's compromise. Jawaharlal too regretted his agreement to the compromise. Both called it an attack on the honour and integrity of Motilal, who was himself quite livid. Subhas was clearly caught on the wrong foot with his accusations that seemed hasty, and they were construed as personal attacks by both the Nehrus. They appeared to be in no mood to relent. Motilal told the AICC meeting, 'So far as I am personally concerned I cannot make compromise with my honour. If however there is any expression of regret and unqualified withdrawal of all the allegations and imputations I may be satisfied.'

Following a chaotic exchange of words, Subhas clarified that his statement was issued on the 27th, before the compromise had been arrived at, and instead of publishing it on the next day, the *Tribune* did so after a day's delay, when the compromise had been struck. It was an unfortunate case of bad timing by the newspaper. As far as Motilal was concerned, Subhas was in a tight spot and had little choice but to offer an apology. Addressing the AICC, he gave a blow-by-blow account of his events as he saw them and made no secret of his apprehension that he was going to get a raw deal. He returned Motilal's compliment in his closing remarks of the Calcutta Congress by saying, 'He is like my father,' and:

> I may assure him that it has never been my desire to cast any aspersion or insinuation against him. Everybody who knows something about the Swarajya Party knows what my feelings were for the late Deshabandhu and I still entertain such feelings towards Panditji. I appreciate if this unfortunate statement had not been published there would have been no trouble.

Motilal too was not keen to drag the matter any further. True to his previous announcement, he declared, 'So far as I am concerned, I fully and frankly accept the expression of regret.'[174] The BPCC election dispute was settled in 1930 when Motilal visited Calcutta.[175]

The Subhas–Sengupta feud had its repercussion on the student movement too. The All Bengal Students' Association (ABSA) was formed at the All Bengal Students Conference of September 1928, with active support and encouragement from Subhas. While Subhas remained at the background as a guest speaker, he had Jawaharlal preside over the conference. At the forefront of the initiative, the students were penalized because of their activism during the visit of the Simon Commission. Subhas had helped some of them, for instance by arranging a private house for the residents of the Eden Hindu hostel when the Presidency College and the hostel were closed by the college authorities.[176]

Differences soon emerged, with a section of the association confronting the ABSA executive over organizational posts and programmes. The differences aggravated during the All Bengal Students Conference at Mymensingh in September 1929, which led to the formation of the

Bengal Provincial Students Association (BPSA) in December.[177] Broadly speaking, while the ABSA represented the Sengupta camp, the BPSA was seen as supporters of Subhas.

Subhas explained his position with regard to the recent developments in a long and detailed statement issued soon after the formation of the BPSA. Answering the criticisms directed at him, among which the primary ones were that of exploiting the students and meddling in students' affairs, he again laid out his vision for the student and youth movement, asserting that those who were now finding fault with him were nowhere to be seen at the time he played the role of a catalyst in organizing the movement. He squarely blamed the Sengupta camp for misleading some of the ABSA leaders with the aim of discrediting him, but assured the students who had spoken out against him that he had nothing but genuine affection for them. Regretting the undesirable developments, Subhas hoped that they would realize their mistake before long, but regardless he would continue to support the student movement as earlier.[178]

In the face of intensified agitation on various fronts, the Government too stepped up its response in the form of arrests and other repressive measures, which it had started contemplating as soon as the Calcutta Congress had ended. In an action reminiscent of the widespread searches and arrests in Bengal in 1921, thirty-one labour leaders, many of them communists and members of the AICC, were arrested on 20 March on the charge of working with the Communist International in conspiring to 'deprive the King of his sovereignty over British India'.[179] The prosecution of those arrested came to be known as the Meerut conspiracy case. At the Bombay AICC meeting in May, Gandhi moved a resolution condemning the 'wholesale arrests and barbarous treatment' of the arrested leaders, arguing that an efficient resistance can be built up only by the reconstruction of the Congress organization.[180]

Although the Government tried to play up the uncharitable remarks found in the captured documents (Jawaharlal a tepid reformist and Subhas a bourgeois and somewhat ludicrous careerist), both Jawaharlal and Subhas extended their support to the prisoners. Immediately after the arrests, at a protest meeting, Subhas called for raising funds to meet the costs of the legal proceedings as well as to provide financial support to the families of the arrested leaders and to recruit new members in the labour organizations so that that labour movement did not suffer because of the arrests.[181] Jawaharlal, who had come down to Calcutta towards the end of March to look after an ailing Kamala Nehru—who had been admitted to a hospital in the city—stayed with Subhas and consulted the Bengal leaders about the best lawyer to be engaged for representing the prisoners.[182] Subhas visited the prisoners in Meerut several times, the first time being in October when the trial began.[183]

While the junior Nehru, as the president of the All India Trade Union Congress (AITUC), remained involved in coordinating the activities of the defence committees and worked with his international contacts in the labour circles to raise the profile of the case, Subhas did not seem to have devoted much time or effort on this matter. He followed the Congress line of considering the arrests as one of the facets of colonial repression which did not merit an exceptional response. This can be guessed from his reference to the case in his speech at Rangpur, where he remarked that 'such incidents have taken place so many times in the past two decades that there is no novelty in them'. Such repression, he held, would continue till the time the labour movement was able to gather strength. He wondered why the AITUC had not decided to boycott the Whitley Commission. The way forward was not only through the cooperation between the different labour organizations, but also through the collaboration between the labour and the nationalist organizations.[184]

On 24 April, the Calcutta High Court awarded damages of Rs 1,50,000 against *Forward*, edited by Satya Ranjan Bakshi, in a suit brought by the Secretary of State and the East Indian Railway. That was the end of *Forward*, which shut down. However, it reappeared as *New Forward* on 2 May, which too had to close in three days due to an injunction by the High Court. Finally, Subhas brought out *Liberty*, which started publication from 5 May.[185] Bakshi, also the editor of *Banglar Katha*, had already been sentenced to six months of prison earlier in April.[186]

In the middle of the year, Gandhi picked up one of his older concerns, which he had been compelled to bury earlier on by Chittaranjan and Motilal. On 6 June, *Navajivan* carried his views on the issue as follows:

> I do not feel that the country has benefited by people getting into the Councils. If however we must enter the Councils then those elected would do well to use this forum to promote the constructive programme, e.g., khadi, etc. Not to enter the Councils would be wisdom of the first order. But next best would be to join them and then to carry on there the work one would be doing outside. I would advise the readers that they

should forget all about the Councils if they have not set their heart on getting elected themselves or getting someone else elected.[187]

Motilal was not wholeheartedly there yet, but he and Gandhi agreed that 'the real strength of the nation is built up by work outside the present legislatures'. As a part of organizational reconstruction, he strongly recommended that the members of the central and provincial legislatures needed to focus on work outside the legislature too.[188]

Subhas agreed with Motilal in principle, but raised the question of whether resigning from the legislatures would help in achieving Swaraj. The few full-time Congressmen in the council (which included himself) were anyway devoting a greater amount of attention to work outside, but experience showed that those who were not full-timers were unlikely to do so. By withdrawing from the legislatures, however, 'we would practically hand over to the enemy an important field of activity which we had captured after a long struggle'. It would mean 'the virtual extinction of the opposition in the legislatures at a time when that opposition was greatly needed'. Although a member of the provincial council for two consecutive terms, Subhas himself had given little time to legislative work and that strengthened his argument that council membership did not appeal to him. 'If the AICC declared against abstention from the legislatures I would still be prepared to resign if that would satisfy Mahatma Gandhi and Pandit [Motilal] Nehru.' He recommended that a final decision should be taken at the Lahore session at the end of the year.[189]

The proposal faced opposition from Bengal, Bombay, Madras and CP Congress committees, which argued that when several issues critically important to the provinces were to be taken up by the councils, they would not be able to influence the legislation in the desired direction by being absent. In the face of opposition, Gandhi moved a compromise resolution at the Allahabad AICC session on 27 July. His resolution said that the AICC agreed that all Congress members of the legislatures should resign in order to prepare for the campaign of non-violent non-cooperation after 31 December 1929, but in view of the contrary opinions of several Congress members, a final decision was to be held back till the annual Congress session at Lahore.[190]

Subhas seconded Gandhi's resolution, since he considered it to be the one that represented maximum agreement within the working committee. The Swarajist policy, he argued, was to engage the enemy on all fronts until Swaraj was achieved, but on certain occasions it was necessary to suspend the confrontation on one front in order to concentrate on the others. The Swarajists were not enamoured of the legislatures and they could not afford to divide the Congress ranks when the need of the hour was a unified struggle against a foreign bureaucracy. The resolution was carried with an overwhelming majority.[191]

The preparatory movement for the Lahore Congress got a new momentum when on 31 October, the Viceroy, Lord Irwin, on his return from Britain announced that the British Government was going to hold a conference of representatives from British India as well as the Indian states for discussing India's constitutional progress after it had considered the report of the Simon Commission in consultation with the Indian Government. The goal of the British policy, he reiterated, was that 'India should in the fulness of time, take her place in the Empire in equal partnership with the Dominions'. Attainment of Dominion Status was the 'natural issue of Indian constitutional progress'.[192]

Leaders of the major political parties convened at the house of Vithalbhai Patel in Delhi on the next day and issued a manifesto in response to the Viceroy's statement. Over the signatures of Gandhi, Motilal, Madan Mohan Malavya, Tej Bahadur Sapru, B.S. Moonje, Khaliquzzaman, Vallabhbhai Patel, J.M. Sengupta and B.C. Roy, among others, the manifesto appreciated the sincerity of the Viceroy's declaration and offered cooperation to the process of developing a scheme of dominion constitution. The manifesto demanded a policy of conciliation, a general amnesty for political prisoners and predominant representation by the Congress as conditions for extending cooperation. The leaders also expressed the hope that the conference was being organized not to discuss when Dominion Status would be granted to India, but to frame the constitution.[193]

This manifesto was not acceptable to the 'independencewallahs', who refused to sign it. Subhas, along with S. Kitchlew of Lahore and Abdul Bari of Patna, issued a counterstatement that the Viceroy's announcement 'as it stands contains nothing over which we could enthuse'. It was one thing that the viceregal announcement did not specify when Dominion Status would be accorded, but even if it was done before 31 December, they would still demand complete independence. Secondly, the proposed conference was not really a round-table conference—it was not known whether the conference would be confined to the representatives of the British Government on one side and those of Indian nationalists on the other, nor was it made clear if the conclusions arrived at by the conference would be binding on both the parties. Rather than be misled by the 'pious statements' of the Viceroy and the secretary of state, the need of the hour was to prepare for the ensuing struggle.[194]

Subhas was opposed to the leaders' manifesto and stuck to his ground, but he was surprised by Jawaharlal's last minute volte-face. Although Jawaharlal intended to sign the counterstatement along with Subhas, he was won over by Gandhi. The long-winded explanation he provided in his autobiography demonstrated again that the persona of Gandhi, whenever needed, had the power to overshadow his principles:

> And yet the joint manifesto was a bitter pill for some of us. To give up the demand for independence, even in theory and even for a short while was wrong and dangerous; it meant that it was just a tactical affair, something to bargain with, not something which was essential and without which we could never be content. So I hesitated and refused to sign the manifesto (Subhas Bose had definitely refused to sign it), but as was not unusual with me, I allowed myself to be talked into signing. Even so, I came away in great distress, and the very next day I thought of withdrawing from the Congress presidentship, and wrote accordingly to Gandhiji. I do not suppose that I meant this seriously, though I was sufficiently upset. A soothing letter from Gandhiji and three days of reflection calmed me.[195]

'Jawaharlal has now given up independence at the instance of the Mahatma,' an unhappy Subhas wrote to Basanti Devi on his way back to Calcutta.[196]

The hopes of the Congress and Liberal leaders who had signed the manifesto were soon dashed as, in a meeting on 23 December with Gandhi, Motilal, Vithalbhai Patel, Sapru and Jinnah, the Viceroy refused to commit the proposed conference to framing a Dominion constitution. The breakdown came at a critical juncture—barely a week before the Lahore Congress.

The year's dominant choice for presidentship of Congress with maximum votes from the provinces was Gandhi, although Subhas received more votes in Bengal (forty-nine votes against thirty-eight for Gandhi and eighteen for Sengupta).[197] Gandhi, however, refused to accept the post and recommended the name of Jawaharlal, who was not happy in the manner he was chosen but decided to go along with it anyway.[198]

The centrepiece of the Lahore session was the resolution on independence, since the period of one year given to the British Government

for accepting the Nehru report had expired. The main resolution moved by
Gandhi set the overall framework for 1930: the failure of the talks with the
Viceroy meant that participation in the proposed round-table conference
would be pointless, the word 'Swaraj' now meant complete independence,
and in pursuance of that creed all Congress members in central and
provincial legislatures and Government committees should resign their
seats. The AICC was authorized to launch a new civil disobedience
movement.[199]

According to Subhas, the goal was set, but without a clear plan of
how to reach there ('The wheels had been set moving, but we were still in
darkness as to how and when we were to begin,' admitted Jawaharlal).[200] As
he felt that Gandhi's resolution was not adequate to take the country closer
to independence, Subhas moved a counter-resolution that he believed
would not restrict the Congress to mere intention but would demonstrate
that they meant business. He asked the Congress to work towards setting
up a parallel Government in addition to launching the civil disobedience
movement. If the programme was to succeed, boycott could not be limited
to selected areas and must be all-round and complete. For instance, boycott
of councils would be useless if not supported by the boycott of local bodies
and courts too. Moreover, the constructive programme advocated by
Gandhi would not ensure progress towards independence unless specific
grievances of the workers, peasants, depressed classes and the youth were
addressed and they were organized to add force to the civil disobedience
campaign. Subhas specifically appealed to the 'younger generation' to
accept his plan. He appeared confident that if not then and there, they
would come around to see his point of view soon.

Sengupta stood in solid support of Gandhi: 'Do you have in India today
another commander who can lead the country to victory than Gandhi?'[201]

In his response, Gandhi categorically asked the Congress to reject the
counter-resolution of Subhas, who he knew 'was a great worker in Bengal'
and 'was the General Officer Commanding of our force at Calcutta'. He
took a dig at Subhas's claim of representation of the youth and also made
clear that as far as youth were concerned, his preference was Jawaharlal.
Subhas, he said:

> considers me an old man of sixty. It is true that I have grown weak and
> he can physically lift me up if he desires to. But I claim I am still young at
> heart. I can outdo younger men. That is why I claim that notwithstanding

the belief that one becomes senile after sixty, I do not feel so at all. I think even today I can control young people. Supposing today I am offered a horse to ride, I shall gladly accept it—I shall not ride the horse myself but I shall lead it; for holding the reins Jawaharlal Nehru is there . . . It is being alleged that I think too much of Jawaharlal. I do not deny it.[202]

Asking for boycott of the law courts and schools was indeed consistent with the goal of independence, he pointed out, but 'wisdom lies in understanding our limitations'. Subhas's recommendation of working towards setting up a parallel Government drew his special ire. Laced with not-so-subtle sarcasm he asked, 'Do you think you can establish a parallel government when the Congress flag does not fly even in a thousand villages?' The hypothetical question was not entirely fair but had some truth to it.

It is not bravery or wisdom and you cannot establish freedom by merely passing resolutions. We are not declaring independence mind you. In Madras, we declared independence as our goal. Here we go a step further and say it is not a distant goal, but it is our immediate objective towards which we are moving. Mr Subhas Bose however seeks to go a step further. I should like to follow him through and through and bring myself to believe that it is possible today to establish parallel government. That means complete declaration of independence. Have we got our organisations to which to go for adjusting our quarrels and have we national schools? No. What then are we going to do after declaring complete independence? Heaven alone knows.[203]

The country and the Congress were not prepared for the radical proposition of Subhas. Yet, how Gandhi's plans evolved over the next decade and a half in the context of the issue of unpreparedness makes for a fascinating study. Was the country more prepared in 1942 or in 1947?

The final victory was Gandhi's. The Congress voted overwhelmingly in favour of his programme for the next year at the stroke of midnight. He was back at the helm of Congress politics and 'the victory of the Swarajists in 1923 was avenged in 1929'.[204] The AICC 'had been authorised to plan and carry out our campaign', Jawaharlal wrote, 'but all knew that the real decision lay with Gandhiji'.[205]

That the Lahore Congress left Subhas with a lingering bitterness is evident from the strong language he used to recall Gandhi's programme a few years later: 'A more ridiculous state of affairs could not be imagined, but in public affairs, we are sometimes inclined to lose not only our sense of reality but our common sense as well,' he wrote in *The Indian Struggle*. The bitterness was aggravated over the mode of deciding upon the new working committee. Subhas and Srinivasa Iyengar opposed the method of nomination for which two lists were prepared by Motilal Nehru (in consultation with Gandhi) and Jamnalal Bajaj. They demanded an election, and on being refused they walked out.[206] Both were dropped from the new working committee, while Sengupta continued to be on the committee. Subhas had proved to be too much of a troublemaker and Gandhi insisted on a homogenous composition of the working committee.

Subhas and Iyengar formed the Congress Democratic Party in protest, but with his imprisonment in January 1930, the new party remained a non-starter.

5

Crescendo (1930–32)

The Gandhi–Subhas relationship had started on a path of ideological conflict, which kept aggravating. Gandhi was well aware that Subhas would not subscribe to his worldview, and by now it should have been clear to him that Subhas's opposition was not cast in the mould of rebellion followed by submission, as was the case with Jawaharlal. In August 1929, he wrote to Satish Dasgupta in Bengal, 'Subhas babu will never pardon the loin cloth. We must bear with him. He cannot help himself. He believes in himself and his mission. He must work it out as we must ours'.[1] This distant but accommodative stance took a hit in the last few months of 1929.

Two letters Gandhi wrote to Subhas in January 1930 are demonstrative of the dynamics of the relationship between them. The first letter written on 3 January, immediately after the conclusion of the Lahore Congress, was a stern admonition and deserves extensive quotation:

> You are becoming more and more an enigma to me. I want you to live up to the certificate that Deshbandhu once gave me for you. He pictured you to me as a young man of brilliant parts, singleness of purpose, great determination and above pettiness. Your conduct in Calcutta therefore grieved me, but I reconciled myself to its strangeness. But in Lahore you became inscrutable and I smelt petty jealousy. I do not mind stubborn opposition. I personally thrive on it and learn more from opponents than from friends. I therefore always welcome sincere and intelligent opposition. But in Lahore you became an obstructionist. In connection with the Bengal dispute, in your writings to the Press you were offensive and the discourteous, impatient walk-out nearly broke my heart. You should have bravely recognised the necessity and the propriety of your

and other friends' exclusion [from the working committee]. It was not aimed at you, Prakasam or Srinivasa Iyengar. It was meant merely to strengthen the hands of the young President by providing him with a cabinet that would be helpful in carrying forward the national work.

. . . How could you, having no faith in the programme, or Prakasam, with philosophic contempt for the present programme, or Srinivasa Iyengar, with his unfathomable unbelief in Jawaharlal and Pandit Motilalji, forward the nation's work? But all the three could help by becoming sympathetic critics offering sound suggestions along their own lines . . . But I do not want to continue the argument. I simply write this to ask you to retrace your steps and otherwise also prove to me and those whose cooperation you would seek, the truth of the certificate issued by Deshbandhu. I do not want to change your view about anything, but I do want you to change your conduct in enforcing those views.[2]

Unfortunately, Subhas's reply is not available, but it seems to have warmed Gandhi towards him to some extent. Both appear to have been making some effort to not let the gap between them widen further. Gandhi's salutation changed from the earlier 'my dear friend' to 'dear Subhas babu' in his letter on 3 January, and finally to 'dear Subhas' in another week. Referring to his closeness to those working on his khadi programme, he wrote on 11 January:

I would love to have the same contact with you. But I cannot have that privilege as our methods and outlook on life seem to differ. I do not mind these differences, what I mind is bitterness. But do let me have your second letter. I am anxious to come nearer to you. I should be sorry to think or to discover that I do not know young Bengal which I love and adore.[3]

Unfortunately, although both would continue to work from the same platform and have some sort of admiration mixed with grudging accommodation of the other's views, the differences would remain too deep-seated to allow them to come close. In a bizarre behavioural pattern that continued till the end, Subhas contested Gandhi, yet at the same time sought his approval and acknowledgement. Somehow, it eluded him that the closeness of Jawaharlal and Vallabhbhai to Gandhi would not come forth without a show of submission.

The opening gambit in the still unclear programme for civil disobedience was announced by Jawaharlal. 26 January was to be celebrated across the country for the adoption of complete independence as the immediate objective. The working committee issued a strongly worded resolution for the occasion, declaring that 'India must sever the British connection and attain Purna Swaraj or complete independence', and that it was 'a crime against man and God to submit any longer to a rule that has caused this fourfold [economic, political, cultural and spiritual] disaster to our country'.[4]

At the same time, Gandhi kept up an incessant pressure on the Congress leaders to enlist more members and keep the old members active. His insistence on increasing the reach of the Congress would show results before long. In addition, there was opposition from within and without the Congress, on the issue of resignation from the legislatures as well as communal settlement. There was even the demand for adhering to the Delhi leaders' declaration and going ahead with the conference proposed by the British Government. The thoughts of balancing the disparate forces and their expectations occupied his mind at the beginning of the year.[5]

At the end of January, Gandhi offered to the Viceroy Lord Irwin the assurance that he was ready to withdraw the civil disobedience campaign if the Government met his eleven demands that included, among others, total prohibition, halving the land revenue, military expenditure and salaries of higher grade officers, abolition of salt tax, discharge of all political prisoners except those involved in murder cases, and impose protective tariff on imported clothes and abolition. If these demands, which were primarily about policy reforms, were met, the Congress would be ready to attend any proposed conference.[6]

He sent a long letter to Irwin on 2 March, arguing his case in detail and issuing an ultimatum that if the immediate steps mentioned by him were not taken by the Government, he would carry on with his plan of civil disobedience. India must 'evolve force enough to free herself from that embrace of death', the curse that was the British rule. He was convinced that his non-violent campaign was the only way to check the organized violence of the Government and the unorganized but increasing violence emerging as a response in the country. He would begin by breaking the salt laws, as he considered the salt tax 'the most iniquitous of all from the poor man's standpoint' and the independence movement was essentially for the poorest of the land.[7]

On 12 March, Gandhi started his march from Sabarmati ashram to Dandi, a journey of about 242 miles, with seventy-eight of his trusted followers. He broke the salt law by illegally producing salt on 6 April.

Dissensions regarding the 1929 Lahore Congress resolutions had surfaced in Bengal too. Thirty-eight out of forty-seven Swarajist members, including Subhas, resigned from the council. As a result of the communal divide over the resolutions, which the Ali brothers had asked the Muslims to oppose, not a single Muslim member resigned.[8]

Subhas was not happy that the Congress did not agree to go the distance he had wanted it to, but he put all his efforts into implementing the programme they had agreed upon. 'Differences of opinion inside the Congress are inevitable', he told a gathering at Calcutta's Harish Park, 'but once a decision over any measure is arrived at, it must be obeyed and carried out by one and all.' Repeatedly referring to the Irish nationalist movement, he explained that although very few people supported it at that time, the Irish nationalists went ahead with their proclamation of independence because they realized that 'the nation could not be roused unless such an ideal was placed before it'. Subhas also felt that in addition to taking up civil disobedience programmes, a component of propaganda 'for infusing the idea of independence' was equally important. 'Britain is a past master in the art of propaganda', he told his audience, and explained to them how it was used as a weapon against Germany in the First World War. He also added that Russia was 'carrying on this art very effectively' at that time.[9]

As the president of the Bengal Provincial Congress Committee, Subhas also chalked out a programme for the villages. Each village Congress committee was to set up a national militia to take over the functions of police and chowkidars; convince villagers to bring their disputes to the local Congress committees instead of going to the law courts; and encourage indigenous industry besides boycotting foreign goods to make the villages economically self-sufficient.[10] Subhas 'and his supporters are endeavouring to make the most of the agitation that is going on in Bandabilla Union Board in Jessore district against the raising of local taxation under the Village Self-Government Act', noted the Bengal Government.[11]

However, before he could take up the campaign properly or celebrate the Independence Day on 26 January, he was awarded rigorous imprisonment for one year by the Alipore Court on his thirty-third birthday, along with fifteen others, for leading the procession on 11 August 1929.[12] 'My congratulations to Subhas and other friends', Gandhi wired Nalini Ranjan

Sarkar.[13] Subhas resigned from the Calcutta Corporation, because he felt that he would be doing injustice to his constituency by holding on to the seat despite not being able to attend to its affairs.[14]

Sengupta was seriously ill, and a few days after hoisting the Congress flag on the Corporation building on 26 January, he left for Singapore on the advice of his physicians. Shortly after his return, he was arrested in mid-March by the Burmese police, on the charge of giving seditious speeches in Rangoon on his way back from Singapore. Barely a week after his return from Rangoon in early April, he was arrested in Calcutta for reading a proscribed book in a public meeting.[15] Thus, as the countrywide movement gathered momentum, the two most important leaders of the most troublesome province were away from the scenes of action. The Bengal Government appeared to be relieved, and noted that 'Things have been very quiet in Bengal' in February, with the absence of Subhas and Sengupta 'having brought about a temporary cessation of political activities'.[16]

The factional rivalry in the Bengal Congress further dampened the possibilities of escalating the mood of the civil disobedience campaign as the date of Gandhi's salt march came closer. While Sengupta backed the All Bengal Civil Disobedience Council with the Gandhian Satish Dasgupta as president, the BPCC formed an All Bengal Council of Disobedience. For the two rival factions, the elections to the Calcutta Corporation scheduled in the middle of March became a more important issue than organizing for the civil disobedience campaign.[17] With a Congress majority in the Corporation, Sengupta was elected mayor although he was in prison, and Santosh Kumar Basu, who was close to the Bose brothers, became the deputy mayor. Not selecting a Muslim as a deputy mayor, however, drew severe criticism from Fazlul Haq, who accused the Swarajya party of violating Chittaranjan Das's legacy.[18] The only development that continued to bother the Government was the steady growth of the youth organizations in different parts of Bengal.

There was practically nothing Subhas could have done under the circumstances. As one of his Congress co-workers described:

He was again in a serene atmosphere, mixing with friends, doing service to workers, thinking, reading and spending time in meditation in a secluded corner conveniently partitioned by him in his cell with a *parda* (sheet).[19]

The 'serene atmosphere' received a rude jolt on the morning of 22 April 1930, when news spread that the political prisoners in the Alipore Central Jail had been assaulted and that Subhas and Sengupta had been seriously injured. According to one version of the incident, which was based on the accounts of a number of eyewitnesses, the assault on Subhas led to him falling down and losing consciousness. The Government put the blame on the prisoners, claiming that 'Subhas was pushed over by the crowd of prisoners in his yard as they were forced back by the warder staff after trying to rush the gate and fell down striking the back of his head, resulting in a slight concussion of the brain'. Rumours quickly spread that Subhas and Sengupta were no more, and thousands gathered outside the gate of the prison. The situation became so grave that the Government had to issue two communiqués to contradict the rumours. The prisoners, however, squarely blamed Superintendent Major Som Dutt for the assault.[20]

Ill treatment of the political prisoners by the jail staff, often leading to physical clashes, was an issue that troubled Subhas. He had a run-in with the jail authorities a number of times in the Burmese prisons and in Calcutta too, so he took up the cudgel for the prisoners. Along with Kiran Shankar Roy, Purna Chandra Das and a few others, he started a hunger strike from 25 July 1930, after his letters to the Government had had no effect. The hunger strike broke down his health and he had to be confined to bed. The strike was withdrawn eventually, when some of the grievances were redressed.[21]

While the non-violent civil disobedience movement continued, a stunning and daring act by the revolutionaries of Chittagong not only shook the Government, but also imbued a new spirit among all the other revolutionary groups in the province.

On the night between 18 and 19 April, a group of revolutionaries under the leadership of Surjya Sen attacked the Chittagong armoury, seizing many arms and supplies, but missed out on the ammunitions for the arms. 'The Chittagong revolutionaries had done what had never been attempted before—what must have seemed to be an unrealisable dream', reported the special superintendent of Bengal's intelligence branch of the Criminal Investigation Department.[22]

While twelve revolutionaries became martyrs in an armed confrontation with the police and the military forces at the Jalalabad Hill, many were arrested soon thereafter. Surjya Sen evaded arrest till February 1933, but was then captured, tried, convicted and executed in January the following year. What the Government had feared about rapid and consistent organization of the youth had finally come true. In fact, one of the leaders of the group called it the 'Chittagong youth rebellion'.[23] During the search of the Congress office at Chittagong, the police recovered a printed speech of Subhas from the All-India Youth Congress in 1928.[24]

It is difficult to find a direct involvement of Subhas with the uprising, especially in view of the decision of the revolutionaries to not involve him in the operations. However, the secret meeting between him and Surjya Sen points to the possibility that he might have been aware of their intention to do something. Ananta Singh, one of the leaders of the uprising, has mentioned that during the Chittagong district Congress conference in May 1929, Subhas had a secret meeting with him, Ganesh Ghosh and Tripura Sen to discuss the youth and volunteer organizations. According to Singh, Subhas gave a tacit approval for the preparation of youth rebellion under the cover of non-violent programmes. The masterminds of the operation— Surjya Sen, Ananta Singh, Loknath Bal, Ambika Chakrabarti and Nirmal Sen, were all staunch supporters of Subhas.[25]

A further pointer to the possibility was Sarat's defence of Ananta Singh and others during the trial. Ananta claimed that Sarat had also given them money and explosives to help them plan a jailbreak.[26]

Subhas's reaction to the Chittagong uprising is not known but, predictably, Gandhi was not happy. On 4 May, after expressions of an initial disapproval, he condemned the incident in the strongest terms in *Navjivan*, calling it *goondaism* and thought that the revolutionaries were akin to *mavalis*:

> You may break the salt law, but that by itself will not get you swaraj. It will no doubt bring about repeal of the law. But if you want swaraj you will have to die for it—of course not in the way they died at Chittagong. That way swaraj would take four months when it could be won in four days. And I do not know when it will be actually won. But what shall we call this beating of innocent workers at night? Is it *goonda raj*? It looks as if it was. There is nothing but *goondaism* in all the accounts that reach me. The *mavalis* are after all ignorant men, and we may endure their methods, but how can we tolerate this goonda rule?[27]

The Government responded by bringing back the Bengal Criminal Law Amendment Act, which gave unfettered powers to the Government for arrest and detention and had expired in March 1930 through an ordinance. The absence of Swarajist legislators made it easy for the Government to pass the new Bengal Criminal Law Amendment Bill 1930 on 21 August.[28]

Neither the civil disobedience campaign nor the Chittagong uprising was enough to inspire unity among the factions in the Bengal Congress, which manifested again during the mayoral election. The seat of the mayor had fallen vacant as Sengupta could not take the oath of office due to his incarceration. The Congress Municipal Association put forward Subhas's name as the mayoral candidate, which was opposed by the followers of Sengupta. A meeting convened on 5 August had to be adjourned due to pandemonium. The next meeting on 7 August had the same fate after three names were proposed for filling the vacant post—that of Subhas, Sengupta and Prince Golam Hossain Shah. Sengupta's name, however, was withdrawn, but his group extended support to Shah. Finally, Subhas was elected as an alderman on 18 August and as mayor on 22 August for the remaining period of 1930–31, although he continued to be in jail.[29]

Subhas and Sengupta were released on the night of 23 September. The next day, Subhas went to the Corporation office shortly after 4 p.m., accompanied by Santosh Kumar Basu, to take oath of office. Following the routine felicitations by corporators and employees, Subhas outlined his thoughts after eight months of imprisonment. Subhas recalled the philosophy of Chittaranjan and his municipal governance schemes for serving the poor, describing it as the basis of socialism. In its entirety, however, Deshbandhu's approach could be termed as a synthesis of socialism and fascism, Subhas claimed. This was probably the first time he publicly spoke about fascism.

He chalked out the programme that he intended to take up during his tenure. Roads, education and housing were to receive particular attention, especially as the city was expanding. Interests of all communities were to receive fair and impartial treatment. Subhas said that his approach to appointments for Muslims would be the same as what it was when he was the CEO in 1924, but it was not possible to promise how far he could implement that policy in the current scenario.[30]

Some changes, both symbolic and realistic, in the Corporation were immediately visible. The cushioned chair in the mayor's room was replaced by a simple office chair, attendance in all the departments became more regular, all complaints from the citizens to the mayor were forwarded to the concerned departments for reporting to the mayor and administrative reports that were due were rushed to completion.

Gandhi was in jail, as he had been arrested on 4 May, but it was now time to pick up the thread where Subhas had to leave it upon his arrest. Responding in a light tone to what must have been a request from Subhas to not suffix the 'Babu' to his name, Gandhi wrote from the Yervada Jail towards the end of October:

> I bow to the mayoral order and drop the offending 'Babu'. As the apers write and know more about my health than I know, where was the use of my saying anything? I am really keeping well. If I was ill there would be details to give. Please remember me to our brother and your parents when you write to them. I had the pleasure of meeting them when I was in Cuttack. Of course I remember our nice letter of January.[31]

The Calcutta Corporation passed a resolution on 13 November by overwhelming majority, condemning the Round Table Conference (RTC) that began in London on that day. As the mayor, Subhas rejected the objections that questioned the relevance of the Conference to the affairs of the Corporation, referring to multiple precedence.

Subhas elucidated his own point of view a week later in a discussion with the British left-wing journalist and member of the Independent Labour Party, H.N. Brailsford. Brailsford asked Subhas if he would still oppose the RTC if Dominion Status was granted to India immediately. Answering in the affirmative, Subhas explained the three reasons behind his stand. Firstly, he said that Britain would retain the economic supremacy over India which would continue to drain the country's resources and keep it poor. Secondly, he could not see any political benefits of India becoming a dominion. Thirdly, Indians would continue to suffer psychologically from a sense of inferiority, and that would prevent their all-round development.

Brailsford found it difficult to understand the last reason. How could Indians feel inferior even if they were living in a dominion? Subhas explained that to be able to understand this point, one had to remember the very long period for which India had remained under the domination of foreign powers. The present education system established by the foreign rulers also reinforced the sense of inferiority. Complete freedom was the only way to unshackle the minds of Indians.

India was likely to obtain Dominion Status within the next few years, but insistence on complete independence was clearly going to prolong the struggle with the British Government, Brailsford thought. It might even lead to bloody confrontation and give an opportunity to the British conservatives to regain their influence. Moreover, the difference between Dominion Status and independence was not so great as to make this suffering worth it.

Agreeing with Brailsford that the struggle was indeed going to be prolonged, Subhas disagreed on the necessity of it to be violent. At least theoretically, he argued, a government could be paralysed by boycotts and strikes. He gave the example of Soviet Russia. The Russian revolution became violent only when the counter-revolutionary forces tried to topple the Soviet Republic. If the British Government was ready to grant Dominion Status, then why had it been so reluctant to accede to the demand for independence, he asked Brailsford in reply.[32]

Chittagong had lit a fire that kept spreading. 'The terrorist groups continue to be active and information shows that they are busy making plans for actions such as that at Chittagong and also for the murder of police officers,' noted the Bengal Government in May.[33] The police and intelligence agencies kept a keen eye on the revolutionary groups and the key leaders. The biggest challenge for the revolutionaries was to operate despite such vigilance. In fact, the Chittagong operation had set an example of a successful operation that had been able to beat the police informers and leakage of secret information. The reports of this period sent by the Bengal Government to the Home Department are replete with incidents of organized violence and collection of bombs and arms across districts. 'There is real intention behind the talk,' the Government concluded.[34] Revolutionary activity was reaching its peak.

On 29 August, members of the Bengal Volunteers (BV) in Dacca assassinated Lowman, the inspector general of police, and wounded Hodson, the superintendent of police. On 8 December, another unimaginable raid took place in the heart of Calcutta, when three members of Sri Sangha who had joined the Bengal Volunteers—Benoy Bose, Dinesh Gupta and Badal Gupta—walked into the Writer's Building, the symbol of British rule in Bengal, and shot dead Lt Col. N.S. Simpson, the inspector general of prisons, and also shot J.W. Nelson, legal remembrancer, in the leg. Following the shooting and killing, the trio took refuge in Nelson's room. When the police eventually entered the room, they found Badal sitting on a chair dead, having consumed poison, and the Benoy and Dinesh lying with bullet wounds in the head and throat.[35]

The boys were known to Subhas and they belonged to an organization that had close connections with him. However, as the mayor of Calcutta, he had to now take a public stand. This situation was not too different from what Chittaranjan had faced in 1924 with regard to Gopinath Saha. Chittaranjan had genuine affection for the young revolutionaries, but temperamentally he was not in favour of political violence. Subhas's position was much more nuanced. As a matter of principle, he was not averse to violence, but had repeatedly cautioned against the futility of sporadic acts of violence. His idea was to prepare the youth organizations for a large-scale and organized operation.

A few days after the incident, C.C. Biswas moved a resolution in the Calcutta Corporation condemning the attack ('dastardly outrage') on the Writers' Building, which drew wide support across party and community lines. Subhas supported the resolution, but instead of mouthing platitudes, went into the deeper reasons for such incidents which, he said, were 'a confession of the temporary failure of the programme and also the temporary failure of Congress leaders' to influence the entire youth of the country.

> It will not do simply to brand as misguided the youths who are responsible for these incidents. The fact stares us in the face that India today wants freedom and wants freedom very soon. The fact also stares us in the face that there are people in this country, whatever their number may be, who want freedom not merely by following the Congress programme, but, if need be, they want freedom at any price and by any means.

The occasion also gave him the opportunity to prove his point of view that the Congress programme was not radical enough to engage the younger generations:

> . . . why is it that in spite of the best efforts of the Congress leaders and in spite of the best efforts of Congress workers all over the country, beginning from Mahatma Gandhi down to the ordinary village worker, we have so far failed to influence the minds and the judgment of the entire younger generation in this country? We have failed, because, so far, the Congress programme has not achieved freedom for India. I firmly believe

that we shall achieve freedom in the long run, but until we can prove by
our success that the Congress programme is the only programme that the
country should adopt and follow, I don't see how it is possible to convert
cent per cent of the population to the cult of non-violence.

If the failure of the Congress programme was one reason for intensifying
revolutionary violence, no less was the role of government repression,
which was crushing all freedom by a rule through ordinances.[36]

The conflicts and the complaints about the education system
notwithstanding, Subhas never lost sight of the central theme of the
Bengal renaissance. He took it up again while speaking on behalf of
the former students at the centenary celebration of the Scottish Church
College, a function that was attended by a plethora of political and
intellectual stalwarts of the day, such as Hasan Suhrawardy, Najimuddin,
C.F. Andrews, Heramba Chandra Maitra, Haridas Bhattacharya, and
Radha Krishnan. Introduced by the Principal, Dr Urquhart, as 'One of the
most famous students of the college', Subhas remembered emperor Asoka
sending out India's message of Dharma to the world, and many centuries
later, how 'when missionaries of an Oriental Religion brought from the
West, along with the message of Christ, the message of Intellectual
Emancipation, an Era of Renaissance dawned on our ancient land, a spirit
of enquiry permeated our intellect and vitalised our minds'. The expanse of
his intellectual landscape could never contract, because 'we are the children
of that Revolution in the realm of thought'.[37]

As the mayor, Subhas attended cultural events too, meeting with
littérateurs of the city and inaugurating a cinema hall. Led by the famous
poet, Jatindra Mohan Bagchi, a group of writers met Subhas at his home
to discuss modern Bengali literature, with a special focus on the youth and
the freedom movement. Greeted with cheers of 'Vande Mataram!', Subhas
also walked into the operator's room on 19 December 1930 to inaugurate
the Chitra cinema hall on Cornwallis Street, which had a capacity of 800,
alongside Birendranath Sircar, the man who had built the theatre and
would go on to become one of India's most well-known film producers
under the banner of New Theatres. The first movie to be shown at the
theatre was *Srikanta*, based on Sarat Chandra Chattopadhyay's famous
novel of the same name.

Subhas did not regularly watch movies, but he had watched a number of
Indian movies on several occasions. He thought, 'Most often the films are

useless, even harmful', but the 'cinema habit, the cinema taste have come to stay'. The question for Subhas was how to make cinemas useful, both from the perspective of content and the national economy. He referred to how the cinemas were being used for educational purposes in Russia. He argued that the cinemas must be encouraged to become a national industry, since it had immense potential. According to him, the Board of Censors needed to be one 'which understands our taste and has imaginative sympathy for our aspirations and needs', to facilitate the growth of the film industry.[38]

Encouraging the setting up of indigenous educational institutions, he told the students of the recently established Calcutta Engineering College that to be successful, it was necessary for such institutions to 'impart education and training which will enable the students to earn their livelihood and fulfil their ambition'.[39] In December, Subhas set up the Bengal Swadeshi League with the aim to coordinate among businessmen, industrialists, economists and Congress workers for the promotion of Swadeshi goods.[40]

It was also a time of bereavement. On 30 December 1930, Subhas lost his younger brother, Santosh Chandra Bose, who was only twenty-five years old.

Apart from discharging his duties as Calcutta's mayor, Subhas toured the districts attending civic receptions and addressing public meetings. In December and January, he visited Pabna, Dinajpur, Kusthea, Jamshedpur and Berhampore. The civil disobedience movement had waned in the face of massive arrests and his core constituencies—the youth and student organizations—were busy planning 'action' and consequently under severe police surveillance. The Bengal Government noted with some relief that 'his speeches were distinctly moderate' in tone during this period.[41] Yet, the Government would never stop being wary of him and he was arrested again soon enough.

On his way from Berhampore to Maldah in north Bengal on 18 January 1931, when the train stopped midway at Amnura (now in Bangladesh), the superintendent of police came into his compartment and served a notice, from the district magistrate of Maldah, barring him from entering the district. The administration feared that his entry into the district would 'likely be attended with unlawful demonstrations, meetings, picketing and other activities of the civil disobedience movement, which may cause obstruction, annoyance and injury to other persons and disturbance of the public tranquillity'. 'Either obey the order and leave the district as a free man or disobey the order and leave it as a prisoner,' the superintendent told Subhas. 'I accept the latter alternative,' was Subhas's response.[42]

In an impromptu trial organized in the first-class waiting room of the railway station, Subhas was awarded a seven days' simple imprisonment, and taken to Rajshahi Jail. Fearing public backlash among swelling crowds protesting his arrest, Subhas was shifted out in the middle of the night, reaching Calcutta the next morning to be lodged in the Alipore Central Jail. He was released on 24 January.

The Independence Day was to be celebrated two days later, on 26 January, but the Calcutta Police served a notice to Subhas prohibiting him from taking part in any meeting or procession. Subhas, of course, would not ever give in to such a diktat. On the 26th, he led a procession from the central municipal office towards the Maidan, where he was scheduled to hoist the national flag and address a public meeting. Just as the procession was about to reach the Maidan, mounted police and sergeants came charging with lathis. Subhas and those accompanying him were at the receiving end of a severe assault. He received several blows on his head and body, and was subsequently arrested. The Corporation immediately held a meeting and issued a strong condemnation. The Corporation offices and affiliated schools and other institutions remained closed in protest on the following day. Calcutta observed a hartal and the Calcutta Stock Exchange too remained officially closed.[43]

Just a day before, the Viceroy had issued an order releasing Gandhi (who had been arrested on 4 May 1930), along with other members of the Congress working committee who had been imprisoned during the civil disobedience movement, unconditionally, and withdrew the directive declaring the working committee an unlawful association. Thus, on the same day as the Congress leaders walked out of jail, Subhas was thrown inside, sentenced to six months of rigorous imprisonment.

While Subhas was in jail, an initiative to arrive at a settlement between the Government and the Congress was launched by M.R. Jayakar and Tej Bahadur Sapru in July 1930, who shuttled between Motilal and Jawaharlal lodged in the Naini Jail and Gandhi in the Yervada Jail. The Nehrus and the AICC general secretary Syed Mahmud were allowed by the Viceroy to travel by a special train to Yervada Jail in August where they, along with Gandhi, Vallabhbhai Patel, Jairamdas Doulatram and Sarojini Naidu conferred with Jayakar and Sapru for three days. The talks, however, failed to reach any agreement, as the Congress leaders insisted on the recognition of India's right to secede at will from the British Empire and claim complete control of defence and economy by a national government, before agreeing to withdraw civil disobedience. In addition, the leaders stipulated that all political prisoners other than those convicted for violence should be released, properties confiscated should be restored, all viceregal ordinances should be repealed and fines and securities taken from convicted satyagrahis should be refunded before Congress could consider the question of joining the round-table conference.[44]

In his closing remarks at the first round-table conference on 19 January 1931, the British prime minister, Ramsay MacDonald, declared that responsibility for the Government of India should be placed upon central and provincial legislatures with adequate safeguards during a period of transition, that the central government should be an all-India federation of both Indian states and British India in a bicameral legislature, and with a legislature so constituted, the British Government would be prepared to recognize the principle of responsibility of the executive to the legislature. Defence and External Affairs, however, would still be the reserve of the governor general and he would continue to have emergency powers to maintain law and order and interests of the minorities. MacDonald appealed to 'those engaged at present in civil disobedience' to 'take their part in the cooperative work that lay ahead'.[45] In response, a meeting of the interim working committee of the Congress held in Allahabad on 21 January and presided over by Rajendra Prasad resolved that the Congress was not prepared to recognize the round-table conference and that the announcement made by MacDonald was too vague to justify any change in the Congress' policy. Before they could publish the resolution, the working committee received a cable from Sapru and Srinivasa Sastri, who were about to leave England for India after the conclusion of the conference, requesting the working committee not to publish the resolution until it had heard them—a meeting that finally took place on 13 February in Allahabad, a week after the demise of Motilal Nehru. It was in response to the prime minister's appeal that the Viceroy announced the release of the Congress working committee members so that they could discuss his statement.[46] On 6 February, twenty-six Indian delegates to the round-table conference issued a statement immediately on arriving in India, expressing hope that the Congress and other parties would come forward to work on the outlines agreed upon at the conference.[47]

In view of the efforts to create an atmosphere of conciliation, the Government of India asked Bengal to consider if the government counsel could ask for only three or four days of imprisonment for Subhas. The Bengal Government refused the suggestion: his deliberate defiance of the Government's order and the manner of confronting the police could have led to a serious situation. When thirty-five members of the Central Assembly wrote to the Viceroy deprecating the police action and arrest of Subhas in Calcutta and cautioning that the incident was likely to defeat the objective of creation of an atmosphere of goodwill[48] the Viceroy's office again suggested an unconditional release of Subhas. The Bengal Government was, however, unrelenting and blunt. Subhas was not a member of the working committee and therefore not covered by the Viceroy's statement. 'It would be a grave mistake to advertise Subhash (sic) by giving him exceptional treatment,' the Bengal Government informed the Government of India on 31 January.[49] He was finally released on 8 March, once Gandhi had reached an agreement with Irwin.[50]

Persuaded by the trader associations, Ghanshyamdas Birla, the Liberal leaders, nationalist Muslim leaders and Viceroy Irwin's statements, Gandhi reached out to him seeking an interview.[51] Thus, the Gandhi–Irwin talks began on 17 February, leading to an agreement called the Gandhi–Irwin Pact, which was published as a Gazette Notification on 5 March. The civil disobedience movement was discontinued on the condition of reciprocal action to be taken by the Government in line with the Congress' demands. It was agreed that the Congress would participate in the next round of discussion on constitutional progress, which would be based on the three key points of federation, Indian responsibility and reservations or safeguards in India's interests on matters related to defence, external affairs, position of minorities, financial credit of India and discharge of obligations. The broad points of the settlement included the following:

(i)   The boycott of British commodities would be discontinued. The Government would not object to propaganda or persuasion directed at encouragement of Indian industries as long as they did not interfere with freedom of action of individuals or create law and order disturbances.
(ii) Picketing was allowed as long as it was not coercive or intimidating.
(iii) Gandhi would not press the demand for a public inquiry against cases of police atrocities.

(iv) Ordinances promulgated to deal with the civil disobedience movement would be repealed (except Ordinance No. 1 of 1931 which was issued to deal with revolutionary activities).

(v) Those who were imprisoned for participation in the movement would be released and pending prosecutions would be withdrawn unless they were involved in violent offences. Only fines imposed and security forfeited but not yet realized would be remitted.

(vi) Additional police deployed in connection with the civil disobedience movement would be withdrawn at the discretion of the local governments.

(vii) Moveable properties seized in connection with the movement or for realization of dues would be returned only if still in the possession of the government.

(viii) Land and other immovable properties forfeited or attached for realization of land revenue or other dues would be returned unless the district collector believed that it would not be possible to recover the dues in reasonable time. District officers would hold prompt inquiries where the government believed realization of dues were not in accordance with the law.

(ix) A liberal policy would be followed for cases of reappointment of government servants and village officials who had resigned and their applications would be considered on merit by local governments if the posts had not been filled permanently since their resignation.

(x) No substantial modification would be made in the salt laws but certain poorer classes would be allowed to manufacture salt for domestic consumption and also to sell within their village of residence.

(xi) Although Gandhi thought that not returning immovable properties forfeited and sold to third parties was unlawful and unjust, the government did not agree with his contention.[52]

At the early stage of the negotiations, the possibility of Subhas getting involved arose but it did not materialize. According to Irwin's version, when he asked Gandhi about the desirability of having a more formal discussion by involving some others like Sastri, Sapru, Jayakar, Malaviya, Ansari and non-official European and Muslim members of the Assembly, Gandhi appeared open to the idea but said that in such a scenario he would like to have one or two of his own, like Jawaharlal, Vallabhbhai and Sengupta. He also might have liked to have Subhas but he was in prison. According to Gandhi's version, the Viceroy objected as Subhas was not a member of the working committee, but Gandhi argued that 'he is my opponent and will denounce me, still, if he wants to attend, we must give him a chance to do so'.[53]

Subhas viewed the pact with some degree of hostility. He could see that to the general populace it appeared as a victory of the Congress, but the youth organizations and especially the political prisoners of Bengal were unhappy. Yet, he also realized that there was nothing he or anybody else could do to bring about any change. Vallabhbhai Patel, 'than whom a stauncher follower of the Mahatma it was difficult to find', was going to preside over the upcoming Karachi Congress. Apart from the members of the working committee whose support Gandhi had already secured, leaders of the right wing in the Congress and 'all the monied interests also desired to see the armistice followed up by a permanent peace, so that they could settle down to business peacefully'.[54]

The opponents of the pact, on the other hand, were a divided and scattered house, Subhas noted. Many of them were still in prison and some had left the radical camp. Srinivasa Iyengar, his comrade in the Independence for India League and the abortive Congress Democratic Party, for instance, had retired from politics due to shabby treatment from the Gandhian camp. Mohammed Alam of Lahore had become a supporter of Gandhi. The left wing, according to Subhas, had two options: either to put up an insignificant opposition at Karachi or refrain from dividing the Congress while still disapproving of the pact. Moreover, merely opposing the pact was not enough; the alternative was to commence the movement again. In such a scenario, Subhas had 'no doubt that the response in men and money would be disappointing'. In short, if the opposition to the pact failed, it would be an exercise in futility, and if it succeeded in toppling the agreement but failed to build up a more vigorous national movement, then too it would be futile. He decided to have a talk with Gandhi before choosing his path.[55]

In Bengal, the Government noted that Sengupta 'is supporting the Irwin–Gandhi pact, while his rival Subhas Bose is biding his time until he is strong enough to wreck it'.[56]

Like Subhas, Jawaharlal too came to a grudging acceptance of the reality of the pact, but his reasons were a bit different, as was his position. Unlike Subhas, who was still an outsider to the Congress inner circle and a consistent rebel, Jawaharlal had already reached the top, his name taken in the same breath with Gandhi and Motilal. After Motilal's recent death he had, by his own admission, moved closer to Gandhi.

After discussing with Gandhi every step of the negotiation as it evolved over three weeks, Jawaharlal claimed that the constitutional clause in the final draft of the agreement gave him 'a tremendous shock' and that he was 'wholly unprepared for it'. Like Subhas, he too looked for ways to negotiate a settled fact that he could not agree with:

> There was nothing more to be said. The thing had been done, our leader had committed himself; and even if we disagreed with him, what could we do? Throw him over? Break from him? Announce our disagreement? That might bring some personal satisfaction to an individual, but it made no difference to the final decision . . . I was perfectly willing, as were our other colleagues, to suspend civil disobedience and to come to a temporary settlement with the Government. It was not an easy matter for any of us to send our comrades back to gaol, or to be instrumental in keeping many thousands in prison who where already there. Prison is not a pleasant place to spend our days . . . Besides, three weeks or more of conversations between Gandhiji and Lord Irwin had led the country to expect that a settlement was coming, and a final break would have been a disappointment. So all of us in the Working Committee were decidedly in favour of a provisional settlement . . . provided that thereby we did not surrender any vital position.
>
> I lay and pondered on that March night and in my heart there was a great emptiness as of something precious gone, almost beyond recall.[57]

As the Nagpur Express reached the Victoria Terminus in Bombay on the morning of 16 March, Subhas found large crowds waiting for him on the platform, shouting 'Vande Mataram!' and 'Subhas Bose ki jai!' Local Congress leaders, workers of the youth leagues and common citizens had gathered to get a glimpse of him. The volunteers at the Congress House gave him a guard of honour.[58]

Subhas met Gandhi at night, their meeting lasting from 10 p.m. till 2.30 a.m. the next day:

> After criticising the Pact, the point that I urged was that we would be prepared to support him as long as he stood for independence—but the

moment he gave up that stand, we would consider it our duty to fight him.[59]

Gandhi assured him that he would ask the Karachi Congress for a very specific mandate for the Congress delegation to the next round-table conference that would be fully consistent with the Lahore declaration of independence, and that he would exert all his influence to secure the release of those prisoners who had not been covered by his pact with Irwin.

Travelling with Gandhi from Bombay to Delhi by train, Subhas got a first-hand view of how popular Gandhi was across the country—not that he had had any illusions about the influence of Gandhi, but he could see then that Gandhi's popularity at that time surpassed even that of 1921.

As soon as they reached Delhi on 19 March 1931, news arrived that the Government had decided to execute Bhagat Singh, Sukhdev and Rajguru. Gandhi faced intense pressure to try and save the lives of the three revolutionaries, and according to Subhas, he did try his very best. Taking a lesson from the history of Irish nationalism, Subhas suggested that if necessary, Gandhi should 'break with the Viceroy on the question, because the execution was against the spirit, if not the letter', of the pact. He recalled how the strong position taken by the Sinn Féin Party during the armistice with the British Government had succeeded in securing the release of an Irish political prisoner sentenced to death. Subhas felt, however, that Gandhi was not ready to identify himself with the revolutionaries, and it 'naturally made a great difference when the Viceroy realised that the Mahatma would not break on that question'.[60]

In Delhi, Subhas again spoke on behalf of those still imprisoned, particularly in Bengal, United Provinces and Punjab. In Bengal alone, about 800 political prisoners had not been released and 450 detenus were still incarcerated without trial. He argued that the public opinion in Bengal could not be reconciled to the terms of the pact unless all the prisoners were released—if not immediately, then at least before the round-table conference.[61]

Speaking at a public meeting in the Azad Maidan on 20 March, Subhas said:

We demand with one voice and one will that the death sentences on Bhagat Singh and his comrades be at once commuted. Bhagat Singh is today not a person but a symbol. He symbolizes the spirit of the revolt which is abroad in the country. We may condemn his methods, but we cannot ignore his selflessness . . .[62]

The police had managed to obtain prior information that Subhas was going to speak about the trio's execution and apprehending trouble, H.W. Emerson, the chief secretary to the Government of India, approached Gandhi to restrain Subhas. Gandhi replied that he had taken every precaution possible and hoped that nothing untoward would take place. He wrote to Emerson, 'I suggest that there should be no display of police force and no interference at the meeting. Irritation is undoubtedly there. It would be better to allow it to find vent through meetings, etc.'[63]

When Subhas had presided over the Punjab Students' Conference in 1929, he had read out a message from Bhagat Singh. On the same day, 19 October, Subhas had arrived at the courtroom to watch the proceedings of the trio's trial, accompanied by Dr and Mrs Dharamvir and Baba Gurdit Singh of the Komagata Maru fame. Subhas had wanted to interview the accused in the courtroom, but had been denied permission. The Rai Bahadur magistrate had inquired if they had come to witness a tamasha. However, as soon as Subhas and his companions had entered the courtroom, the accused had stood up in the dock and raised the slogans 'Long Live Revolution', 'Long Live Proletariat' and 'Down, down with imperialism'. Subhas had acknowledged the greetings with folded hands.[64]

The plenary session of the Congress was scheduled to be held on 29 March 1931 in Karachi. Subhas was invited to preside over the Naujawan Bharat Sabha conference to be held on 27 March. On 24 March, when he was on his way from Calcutta to Karachi, Subhas learnt of the execution of Bhagat Singh, Sukhdev and Rajguru.

Emotions ran high, particularly among the youth organizations, and much of their ire was directed at Gandhi, who they believed did not do enough to have the executions annulled by putting pressure on the Viceroy. A number of days before the Congress conference was to begin, Karachi became a centre of numerous meetings featuring extremist speeches, with posters put up all around the town and revolutionary pamphlets distributed by the workers of the Naujawan Bharat Sabha and the Kirti Kisan Party.[65]

When Gandhi alighted from the train in this surcharged atmosphere at the wayside Malir station, about 12 miles from Karachi on 25 March, he faced hostile demonstrations from the members of the Naujawan Bharat Sabha waving black flags and shouting 'Down with Gandhi', 'Gandhi is no longer our leader', 'Gandhi is a betrayer' and 'Bhagat Singh ki jai'. The workers of the Naujawan Bharat Sabha were reportedly joined by some members of the 'Red shirts' or Khudai Khidmatgar and volunteers from Bombay. 'The scene was a nasty shock to both Mr Gandhi and his followers', reported a special correspondent of *The Times*.[66] Gandhi 'came close to actual physical injury on more than one occasion', reported the director of the Intelligence Bureau.[67] The incident actually had the opposite effect than was expected, in that it weakened the position of the extremist opponents of Gandhi. Abdul Ghaffar Khan, for instance, immediately distanced his Khudai Khidmatgar from the hostile demonstrators, and announced his support for Gandhi.

Jawaharlal's observation that the Karachi Congress 'was an even greater personal triumph for Gandhiji than any previous Congress had been' summed up the situation accurately.[68] The triumph was more remarkable as Gandhi was able to overcome the initial emotional hostility towards him which had created a significant amount of uncertainty regarding the prospects of his success. *The Times* had a curious representation of Subhas and Jawaharlal's positions vis-à-vis Gandhi a few days before the Congress session:

> It is freely admitted that it [Gandhi's victory] may not be won without a struggle. There is the sullen revolt among the Nau Jawan Bharat Sabha . . . There is the infinitely more important opposition from the Moslem sector. There are one or two men, like Mr Bose, ready to challenge his [Gandhi's] leadership for their own personal ends. There is the uncertain attitude of the retiring president, Pandit Jawaharlal Nehru . . .
>
> A shrewd if somewhat cynical student of the situation suggests that Pandit Nehru is sitting back to see whether Mr Bose's young men are capable of pulling the chestnuts out of the fire. If there is a reasonable prospect of a substantial following, the president of the Youth League (Jawaharlal was president of Nau Jawan Bharat Sabha for the preceding year) will probably resume his place at its head. On the other hand, if Mr Gandhi wins the day no one is more likely to be quicker or more zealous in swearing undying allegiance to the Mahatma.[69]

In his presidential speech to the Naujawan Bharat Sabha conference, Subhas spoke both about Bhagat Singh and the Gandhi–Irwin pact. Bhagat Singh had become a 'symbol of the spirit of revolt which has taken possession of the country from one end to the other', and Subhas was afraid that 'India may have to lose many more sons before she can hope to be free'. The pact was 'exceedingly unsatisfactory and highly disappointing', but he did not 'for one moment question the patriotism of those who are responsible for the truce terms'. The pact, however, was an accomplished fact and, therefore, rather than weakening the Congress through unnecessary conflicts, which would strengthen the Government as a result, he suggested taking up a positive programme.

A radical programme was especially necessary because of the fundamental weaknesses in the Congress' policy and programme, which were marred by 'a great deal of vagueness and mental reservation in the minds of the leaders'. He did not believe that such a programme could win freedom for India. 'Their programme is not based on radicalism, but on adjustments—adjustments between landlord and tenant, between capitalist and wage-earner, and between men and women,' Subhas explained.

The new programme should aim at organizing peasants and workers on the basis of a socialistic programme, organizing youths into volunteer corps with strict discipline, abolition of the caste system and eradication of social and religious superstitions of all kinds, organizing the women of the country to work under the new programme, boycott of British goods and creation of new literature to propagate this line of thought.[70] Several Red Shirts too attended the conference.

The Times correspondent claimed that in a private conversation soon after the conference, Jawaharlal 'took pains to dissociate himself from Mr Bose's sentiments, declaring that he had decided to follow Mr Gandhi unconditionally'.[71]

As he had already decided, Subhas did not voice his opposition in the Congress session, where three main resolutions—disapproving violence but admiring Bhagat Singh, Sukhdev and Rajguru; authorizing the Gandhi–Irwin pact and appointing Gandhi as the Congress representative in the next round-table conference; and proposing the economic principles and fundamental rights to be incorporated in the future constitution of India—were passed quite smoothly. Subhas presented his assessment to the subjects committee, informing the members that the left wing of the party will not divide the house by opposing the pact. His additional concern was that if there was rebellion in the ranks of the party after the pact was agreed upon, it would dent the credibility of the Congress in future negotiations.[72]

In accordance with the assurance that Gandhi gave Subhas in their Bombay meeting, the Congress passed a resolution demanding the release of all political prisoners and detenus not covered by the pact. The resolution of the Gandhi–Irwin pact also emphasized that the Congress goal of complete independence remained intact.[73]

As the Congress session came to an end, there was still no place for Subhas in the new working committee, where Sengupta continued to hold his position. The Karachi Congress had undoubtedly been 'Gandhi's Congress'. 'He has come victorious out of all encounters, and his will has prevailed against all opposition', the Intelligence Bureau noted.[74] Subhas later recalled:

> I travelled with him for some days and was able to observe the unprecedented crowds that greeted him everywhere. I wonder if such a spontaneous ovation was ever given to a leader anywhere else. He stood out before the people not merely as a Mahatma but as the hero of a political fight.[75]

Remaining quiet at the Karachi Congress was a deliberate strategy, which was not relevant once the session was over. Subhas's speech on 8 April, at a meeting of the Central Sikh League in Amritsar, which had become extremely volatile after the execution of Bhagat Singh and his comrades with demonstrations on a scale 'as had never before been witnessed',[76] became a cause for concern for the Government. The thrust of his speech was directed against the communalization of Sikh sentiments. Subhas argued against communal representation at the round-table conference, because 'we all are Indians', and 'India can never be free unless we all unite together and fight for justice shoulder to shoulder'. He also said that 'Our Sikh brethren' should not think that 'their equal rights with other major communities will at any time be ignored'. Giving the example of how Bhagat Singh had sacrificed his life for the country's freedom, he appealed that the 'Sikh community has to produce thousands of Bhagat Singh for the country'. After some deliberation, however, the Government decided not to proceed with any legal action as it was doubtful if a court would convict Subhas just on the basis of one sentence.[77]

It was now time to return to Calcutta where, apart from some real political work, the factional squabbles awaited him. The thought must have been weighing on his mind, which made him issue a statement from

Delhi hoping that 'disputes in Bengal will end once for all' after the 'happy termination of the Karachi Congress'. He was stating the obvious when he said that 'political life and activity are not possible in a province unless the prestige, solidarity and discipline of the Provincial Congress Committee are maintained', but it was not possible to foresee that it was not going to happen as long as he would remain in public life, or even after that. He regretted that his opponents had approached the working committee to appoint a referee for supervising the next BPCC elections, as if Bengal could handle its own affairs.[78]

Subhas issued another appeal to all Congress workers a couple of days later, on reaching Calcutta, to recognize the BPCC as the 'supreme political organisation' in the province. He accused Sengupta of going back on his promises and revolting against the BPCC, of which the latest instance was the last mayoral election. The situation at that time compelled him to take up the post of the mayor, albeit reluctantly, 'in the interests of the discipline and solidarity of the Congress organisation in Bengal', but now, in changed circumstances, he was glad to recommend Bidhan Chandra Roy as the next mayor.[79] Roy was elected the new mayor of the Calcutta Corporation with Muhammad Abdur Razzak as the deputy mayor.

Contesting the BPCC in the municipal elections, a rival organization Provincial Congress Sangha and a parallel Municipal Association were set up, on the basis of the allegation that Subhas had rebelled against the AICC and that his followers did not adhere to non-violence. Meetings often ended in scuffles and hurling of chairs.[80]

Through April and May, Subhas focused his efforts on resolving factional fights in different districts. For the Government, the contest between the two groups was a source of mirth, which is reflected in a letter of a 'non-official supporter of Government' from the Barisal district, which the Bengal Government showcased to the Government of India. The writer described the pathetic state of affairs in the districts:

We are heartily enjoying the present political atmosphere of Pirojpur. I mean by this the Congress camp and the bungling in the matter of election. One party announcing by the beat of drum that the meeting of the Congress will be held today, another announcing that the meeting will not be held, one party abusing the other in filthy language, and almost coming to blows. This fact should be an eye opener to the public at large. The Congress people have no real power in their hands.[81]

With matters continuing to worsen among charges and countercharges, the working committee, after discussions with Subhas and Sengupta, appointed Madhavrao S. Aney in early June as the sole arbiter to settle the dispute relating to the BPCC elections. The elections were allowed to take place as scheduled even as Aney looked into the complaints and made his decision.[82]

The political situation, however, had taken a new turn by the time Aney arrived in Bengal in September. On 16 September, a confrontation between the sentries and the detenus at the Hijli detention camp (which is now part of the Indian Institute of Technology, Kharagpur) led to firing on the unarmed detenus, killing two of them—Santosh Mitra and Tarakeshwar Sen—and injuring many. Bengal erupted in angry protests. Frustrated by the factional squabbles which he had failed to bring to an end to despite his sincere efforts, Subhas took the Hijli incident as the definite sign for him to take a drastic step as a new approach towards the elusive unity. Accordingly, two days after the incident, he announced his resignation from the post of the BPCC president and alderman of the Calcutta Corporation.

As the chief organizer of the Congress in the province, he could not have spoken publicly about all the murky and undignified details underlying the pitiable state of disunity in the Bengal Congress. Therefore, Subhas could only give the broad outlines of the problem and how he, as the Congress chief of the province, had tried to deal with it. According to his assessment, there were three ways to end the disputes. Firstly, to deal firmly with all those who had violated the constitution and the rules of the national and the provincial Congress, and had resorted to indiscipline; secondly, to work out a compromise between the different groups to ensure cooperation in all Congress activities; and thirdly, one group standing down completely in order to make place for the other party.

The first two methods failed because 'there was in Bengal a group of Congressmen who were determined to flout the Provincial Congress Committee on every possible occasion', but also because the Congress working committee was unable to discipline such Congressmen.

He had hoped that after Motilal Nehru intervened the dispute would end, but it was not to be. The divisive mentality showed up again during the municipal elections of 1930 and in the formation of the civil disobedience committee. The opposition continued even after the Gandhi–Irwin pact and manifested in the formation of rival Congress committees in the districts, the Provincial Congress Sangha as the rival organization to the

BPCC, a rival flood relief committee and a rival Congress Municipal Association. Subhas was emphatic that the 'oppositionists' were responsible for the disunity, but it had to be admitted too that those in charge of the organization, which included himself, had failed to secure the cooperation of all the groups. This state of affairs undoubtedly had a disastrous effect, particularly in the current situation where lakhs of people were suffering from flood and famine and from government repression. Subhas said, 'I have no doubt that I am interpreting the mind of Bengal correctly when I say that Bengal today demands an end of the present dissensions even if the most drastic measures be necessary.'[83]

Those who were close to him were aware that he had been considering taking recourse to the third option for a long time, to resign from the post of BPCC president and Alderman of the Calcutta Corporation. Subhas announced his resignation on 18 September:

> The conviction has daily strengthened in my mind that no useful purpose can be served by retaining office, if the cooperation of all sections of Congressmen is not secured. Retention of office today is no longer a help but is a positive hindrance to national service . . . I appeal to all that is great and noble in my fellow congressmen in Bengal and earnestly implore them to rise to the occasion and once for all put an end to the present dissensions. I can assure them that I am a stern disciplinarian myself and I bear no ill-will against anybody. I shall be content to work in the capacity of an ordinary humble Congressman and whoever may occupy the presidential chair will be able to commandeer my services. If Bengal can be saved as a result of my self-effacement I shall be happy to pay that price and I shall fee more than amply rewarded if my countrymen will in exchange give me a corner in their hearts.[84]

On the same day, Subhas and Sengupta went to Kharagpur to survey the situation, accompanied by some Congress colleagues. Although they were not allowed to visit the detention camp, they managed to talk to those admitted in the Kharagpur railway hospital. The new height of Government repression had a deep impact on him:

> I have come back from Kharagpur pained and humiliated to an indescribable degree. Our comrades in jail are being killed and shot at like cats and dogs. In these circumstances should we still fight and quarrel?[85]

Both the jail authorities and the Government refused permission to meet the detenus on hunger strike again when he visited Hijli towards the end of the month.

He accused the Government of violating the spirit and the terms of the truce. The ongoing repression is a sure sign that 'Power is slipping out of the unjust authority', as they 'see the awakening of the masses on all sides and sense the end of their days', Subhas argued. He knew that Bengal would not bow down to the policy of repression and 'when the emotionalism that lay hidden in Bengalees (sic) would be released it would carry everything before them and it would conquer'. Bengalis, he said, were never liked by the British, and more brutal repression akin to that unleashed by the Black and Tans during the Irish war of independence was only to be expected.

> Bengalees (sic) were an eyesore to Englishmen for their independent spirit and hankering after absolute freedom. For the last thirty years Bengal had strived and suffered for it and that was why they were so eager to crush them. Before power was finally given up there would be reproduction in Bengal of what the Black and Tans did in Ireland. That would be the acid test of the patriotism of Bengal and prove if Bengal was prepared to pay the price for complete independence . . . If my countrymen are prepared to pay that price, let them ask for complete independence. Otherwise, let them bend down before their masters and accept what crumbs are offered them and entertain the delusion that was independence.

Yet, the truth that could not be ignored was that the 'Britisher owed his position in this country to the divisions and differences among the people'. It was now time 'when the individual should merge himself in the national', as Bengalis 'so richly endowed by nature failed so often because of their inability to do so'.[86]

Sengupta responded to Subhas's gesture by making an effort from his side too to reach out for a settlement. Kiran Shankar Roy and Sarat Bose, representing Subhas, met Sengupta and Nishit Sen, one of his loyalists, to work out the settlement, mediated by Tulsi Charan Goswami. An agreement was reached that all complaints would be withdrawn, fresh BPCC elections would be held in next January or February and an Election Disputes Board would be set up, with three representatives from each side and M.S. Aney as the chief arbitrator. Nirmal Chandra Chandra was to become the interim president of the BPCC till the next elections, with twenty-four more members in the new executive committee with equal representation from both sides.[87]

Sengupta's supporters were not all so forthcoming, demonstrating the fact that there was always the likelihood of groups gathered behind particular leaders to play out their own little game. Noticing this tendency on the part of the newspaper *Advance*, which was considered to be Sengupta's mouthpiece, Jawaharlal reacted sharply in a letter to Vallabhbhai Patel.

> The Advance seems to be continuing to write offensively against Subhas and the BPCC. Its comment on Subhas's resignation was in the worst of taste. I am afraid Sengupta and his party are putting themselves entirely in the wrong.[88]

Subhas was not quite happy with what he felt was Patel's indifference towards Bengal. No visible move was forthcoming from the Congress president after the Hijli incident or the administration's complicity in the communal targeting of the Hindus in Chittagong by the local Muslim population after a police inspector, Ahsanullah, had been assassinated in early September. Jawaharlal too felt that Patel's visit to Calcutta 'in the near future' was 'very desirable', and advised that the next working committee meeting should be held there. He also asked Patel to write to the Viceroy, endorsing the demand of the detenus for an independent inquiry.[89] Patel wrote to the chief secretary to the Government of India on 26 September and to the Viceroy's office three days later.[90] He drew Jawaharlal's attention to Subhas's statement where he 'made a general attack on the working committee for neglecting Bengal since 18 months and a special attack on me for not fixing an All-India Hijli Day'. Complaining about not being informed by either Subhas or the BPCC, Patel stressed on the fact that he had already spoken publicly on two or three occasions and had written to the Viceroy too. There was nothing more he could do and believed that it was not fair to criticize the Government publicly since they had already set up an inquiry.[91] Subhas was clearly expecting much more interest and activity from the Congress president. Clarifying that he had resigned from the BPCC on the day of the incident and that he was under the impression that Patel would have been informed by the working committee members from Bengal, Subhas wondered, with tongue in cheek, if Patel had not seen the newspapers which, in all parts of the country, carried the news about Hijli.[92]

The new BPCC too was not functioning at an optimal pace. Subhas expressed displeasure that a boycott resolution adopted at the annual provincial conference in Berhampore attended by Rajendra Prasad, K.F. Nariman and M.S. Aney in early December was still not confirmed by the BPCC and sent up to the working committee even eleven days after the meeting.[93] Patel had already sensed in October that all was not as well as it appeared to be, and wrote to Jawaharlal on 14 October: 'From the conversation I had with Sengupta [in Bombay] I found that the settlement between him and Subhas is only in name and they have already started attacks against each other'.[94]

Subhas's conflicts with the Government continued. In the middle of October, he was stopped from attending the Bengal Jute Workers Conference at Jagatdal (in the North Twenty-Four Parganas adjacent to Calcutta) and detained in a police station for thirty-one hours without food or water for a large part of it, and not allowed to meet any visitor.[95] He was again stopped from entering Dacca in early November and was detained at Narayanganj when the steamer carrying him and his companions reached the jetty. Although he was not arrested, he was forcibly moved out of Narayanganj by a team led by the acting superintendent of police.[96] Next day, when he attempted to enter Dacca by train, he was first stopped and asked to go back and, on his refusal, arrested at Tejgaon station, about 4 miles from Dacca. Subhas also refused the bail offered to him on the condition that he would return on the next date of hearing. Subsequently, he was moved to the Dacca Central Jail, but released soon.[97]

The treatment meted out to Subhas, which betrayed a certain paranoia on the part of the Government and the local authorities, justified his bitterness in stating that 'in this unfortunate country we do not possess any right in the matter of our personal freedom', being 'entirely at the mercy of local officials'.[98]

The reason for Subhas's trip to Dacca was to hold a Congress inquiry into the police atrocities on the public of Dacca as a result of the assassination of the district magistrate, Durno, on 28 October. In a public meeting at the Albert Hall in Calcutta on 5 November, it was decided that Subhas, along with Hemendra Nath Dasgupta and J.C. Gupta, would conduct an inquiry into the government-sponsored violence.[99] Repressive measures continued in Dacca, and on 20 December, after conducting searches in fifty-three houses and the boarding house attached to the Deepali Girls' High School, the police arrested the headmistress of the school, Leelabati

Nag, and Renuka Sen, a student of the Dacca University, as well as sixteen young men, who were mostly students.

In another instance of revolutionary action, the district magistrate of Tipperah, C.G.B. Stevens, was shot dead by Santi Ghosh and Suniti Choudhury, two students of the local girls' high school.[100]

Subhas travelled to Maharashtra towards the end of December. He presided over the Maharashtra Youth Conference held at the Shivaji Mandir in Poona on 22 and 23 December, where he analysed the reasons for the failure of the round-table conference, and hoped that the Congress would take the radical youth into its folds. He recommended that as soon as Gandhi returned from the talks, he should issue an ultimatum to the Government, which had already ended the truce as was evident by their actions.[101]

Subhas was presented with an address by the Naujawan Bharat Sabha on 24 December, 'wrapped up in silver sheets shaped to represent a pistol'. The next day, he visited Satara and Karad and Sholapur on 26 December. The Government of Bombay noted that at Satara, Subhas 'made a rabid speech' and speaking to an audience of 15,000 in Sholapur, 'he definitely assumed a renewal of the "struggle" and urged preparations for it'.[102]

But it was not Subhas alone who engaged in this. As the failure of the negotiations became final with the end of the round-table conference, attitudes hardened on both sides. On the eve of Gandhi's return from the round-table conference, most Congress leaders were preparing for a resumption of the movement that had been suspended to facilitate the talks. U.P. was preparing for an immediate launching of a no-rent campaign in the districts. Patel declared that 'the coming fight would be the last'. The Government had already started hitting back. Abdul Ghaffar Khan and his brother Dr Khan Sahib were arrested on 25 December. Jawaharlal and T.A.K. Sherwani, on their way from Allahabad to receive Gandhi, were arrested the next day. Bengal was already reeling under widespread searches, arrests and ban on organizations. Following Bengal, ordinances bestowing emergency powers to the provincial governments were declared in UP and the North-West Frontier Province. The stage was set for a confrontation.

S.S. Pilsna, the ship carrying Gandhi, docked in the Ballard Pier at 8 a.m. on 28 December, welcomed by Kasturba Gandhi, the members of the working committee and Congress volunteers, and jeered by followers of Bhimrao Ambedkar who showed him black flags. 'Never was a king or a victorious general given a warmer welcome,' according to Subhas.[103] Speaking at a 'monster meeting' at Azad Maidan in the evening, Gandhi told the crowd that 'If a fight becomes inevitable I invite you to be ready for it. However, I will not give up attempts to save the nation from the fiery ordeal, but if there is no single ray of hope I will not flinch from inviting you to undergo any amount of suffering.' To a journalist he said, 'the question of Bengal must be isolated and considered separately, as the situation there is entirely different'.[104]

Gandhi had sailed for London from Bombay on 29 August amidst hope and apprehension. Subhas was not in favour of the Gandhi–Irwin pact but had held back his opposition for tactical reasons. He explained the thought process behind his conviction, that Gandhi would not succeed based on the developments after the Karachi Congress, a few years later in *The Indian Struggle*.

After Gandhi emerged with complete victory from the Karachi Congress, the question that Subhas toyed with in his mind was how Gandhi was going to use his unique position from there onwards. He believed that the working committee's decision to send Gandhi alone to the round-table conference where 'all kinds of non-descripts, flunkeys and self-appointed leaders arrayed against him like a phalanx' was a wrong one. However, he understood the predicament. According to him, sending more people with him would not be of any greater help as his blind followers would not question him and he would not heed the advice of those who were not his orthodox followers.

The second factor that, according to Subhas, weakened Gandhi's negotiating power, was his position on the communal question. He not only announced that his attendance of the conference was conditional on his success in solving the communal question before he went there, but initially gave the communal Muslim leaders a leeway to try and twist the arm of the Congress into agreeing with their agenda. This situation changed only when, under pressure from the nationalist Muslim leaders, Gandhi had to declare that separate communal electorates were unacceptable to him.

The third strand that convinced Subhas about the failure of the round-table conference was information received from a 'reliable source' by some Congress leaders including himself that the British Government was going to adopt the tactics of ensnaring Gandhi with relatively minor issues at the very outset in order to create differences between the

Indian delegates. That would prevent them from combining against the Government on the major issues. Although Gandhi was informed, the British succeeded in their plan by making the problem of the minorities the biggest issue of all.

Subhas had some genuine admiration for Irwin and believed that though he was a well-wisher of India, 'he could not do more for India . . . due to the reactionary forces that were working against him both in India and in England'. The official attitude towards India hardened with the arrival of the next Viceroy, Lord Willingdon, in April 1931.[105]

The Congress working committee met from 29 December 1931 to 1 January 1932 to deliberate on the next course of action. The committee asked the Government to institute a public inquiry on the events leading to the imposition of the repressive ordinances, and offered cooperation if the ordinances were eased and allowed the Congress the freedom to pursue the goal of complete independence, while the administration of the country carried on in consultation with representatives till the time independence was attained. Gandhi had sent a telegram to Willingdon on 29 December, expressing surprise at the promulgation of the ordinances, widespread arrests and the incidents of shootings, asking him whether the 'friendly relations are closed or whether you expect me still to see you' to chalk out the next steps. The Viceroy was open to meeting Gandhi, but not to discussing the measures taken in Bengal, UP and the NWFP. He found the working committee's setting of conditions deplorable, and could hardly believe that Gandhi expected him to open talks under the threat of resuming civil disobedience. He warned that Gandhi and the Congress would be held responsible for the consequences of their action, 'to meet which the government will take all necessary measures'.[106] The die had been cast.

The Government moved in swiftly. On 3 January 1932, Subhas was arrested under Regulation III of 1818 at Kalyan, on his way back to Calcutta from Bombay, and taken to Seoni Jail in the Central Provinces (CP). Immediately before leaving for Calcutta, Subhas spoke his mind in a statement that thanked Willingdon for coming to 'our rescue by cutting the Gordian Knot' when the working committee was prepared for further negotiation. He reminded people of the warning he had issued about the Gandhi–Irwin pact—that the time for truce had not arrived yet. Now he stood vindicated, but the danger still lurked around. He feared that there might be another proposal for a pact from the Government after some time, but that had to be prevented, for independence was the sole objective and the path to it 'will not tolerate fresh pacts and negotiations'.[107]

On 4 January, Gandhi and Patel were arrested from Bombay, Rajendra Prasad from Patna, and Jawaharlal was sentenced to two years' imprisonment. The working committee was declared an unlawful organization, and four new ordinances were promulgated. The next few weeks saw sweeping arrests, declaration of hundreds of organizations as unlawful, imposition of ordinances in the provinces and widespread police raids. J.M. Sengupta was arrested on 20 January as soon as he returned from his tour of Europe, and Sarat Bose was arrested on 4 February.[108]

A protest meeting was held in the Town Hall in Nagpur on 3 January, as Subhas was being taken to the Seoni jail through the city. Calcutta observed a hartal.[109] Arrested in Dhanbad, Sarat too was brought to the same jail. Subhas's health started showing signs of trouble soon. A patient of chronic constipation, Subhas lost thirty-one pounds (nearly fourteen kg) by the end of May.[110] The civil surgeon diagnosed that he was suffering from sciatica and dyspepsia, suggestive of gall bladder inflammation. Subhas continued to complain of pain in the abdomen and lost more weight. On 30 May, the CP Government transferred him to Jubbulpore for an X-ray examination. For further examination, Subhas was again transferred to Madras in early July, while Sarat was kept back in Jubbulpore. On 17 August, the Madras Government informed the Home Department that Subhas was diagnosed with 'general fibrosis of the lungs—tuberculosis' and recommended transferring him to a general hospital or preferably to a sanatorium at the earliest.[111]

After examining Subhas towards the end of August in Madras, Dr Nilratan Sarkar, Dr Bidhan Roy and Government physicians unanimously reported that the 'patient has tuberculosis of lungs of fibrotic type and has some abdominal trouble, possibly chronic appendicitis'. The doctors recommended that he should be moved to a cooler and drier place and be provided with a diet suitable for Bengalis. They were clear in their opinion that continuing with a restricted life in the jail would aggravate his condition, and he could be completely cured if sent to Switzerland for treatment. In case that was not possible, he was to be immediately moved to the Bhowali sanatorium in Nainital.[112] Subhas left Madras for the King Edward VII Sanatorium in Bhowali on 8 October.[113]

The superintendent of the sanatorium informed the UP Government in the first week of November that there had been no improvement in

Subhas's condition. He was eating better, but had not gained any weight, which remained around 63 kg. At the end of the month, the superintendent reminded the Government that Subhas was not responding to the treatment in the sanatorium.[114]

Pressure was being brought upon the Bengal Government too. On 25 November, Syama Prasad Mookerjee brought in an adjournment motion in the Bengal Council to discuss the critical state of health of Subhas and Sengupta, which was supported by all Hindu as well as Muslim legislators. The legislators demanded that they should either be released or be allowed their choice of place of custody and doctors by whom they wanted to be treated. The Bengal Government agreed to have Subhas examined by a medical board comprising the superintendent, the civil surgeon of Nainital and, on Subhas's request, his brother Dr Sunil Bose along with Dr Nilratan Sarkar.[115]

On 7 December, the chief secretary of UP informed the Home Department that according to the medical board, there had been no improvement in his health in the past seven weeks. The UP Government recommended moving Subhas to Calcutta Medical College for further surgical diagnosis followed by a transfer to Europe for treatment. The Bengal Government, however, refused his entry into Bengal on the ground that it would increase subversive activities in the province.[116]

With the Bhowali sanatorium scheduled for winter closure in the middle of December, Subhas was shifted to the Balrampur hospital in Lucknow on 18 December. By the middle of January 1933, the Government of India had agreed to allow Subhas to travel to Europe for treatment, but stipulated that he would be granted a passport only for France and Switzerland, as the required treatment facilities were available there. Subhas asked the Government to allow him to visit Calcutta, Cuttack or Puri to meet his parents before leaving for Europe, and that his passport be extended to Austria, Germany, Denmark and England. The Bihar and Orissa Government agreed to lodge him in either Bhagalpur or Gaya Central Jail to facilitate the meeting, but it turned out that his parents were too ill to travel and the idea was dropped. The UP Government issued him passport number 7230-C, dated 13 February and valid for France, Switzerland, Italy and Austria. He was not allowed to travel to Germany or the United Kingdom. The Government of India allowed him to visit Germany only towards the end of July 1933.[117]

Arriving in Bombay on the morning of 23 February, Subhas was immediately taken aboard the S.S. Gange.[118]

There was not much scope for involvement in the matters of the world outside. Therefore, as during his stay in the Burmese prisons, Subhas delved inwards. Reading books and meditating formed a large part of his routine. He requisitioned books from the Imperial Library in Calcutta, and when the CID started examining the requested books, it became the subject of a question in the Central Legislative Assembly.[119] Writing political letters was out of question and, therefore, most of his letters to friends and colleagues dealt with personal updates, but to those close to him he would write about his spiritual and philosophical ruminations. Although his health pulled him down, he claimed that his 'brain think more clearly and without haze' during ailments. From Seoni Jail, he wrote to a friend:

> I have always believed in the Divine purpose underlying our human destiny and I am sure my stay at Seoni will not be fruitless . . . I have no doubt that I shall come out a better man, a purer man and a nobler man— one who is ready to give himself up entirely to the service of the Great cause without any thought or sense of self whatsoever. To transcend self is the highest Sadhana and self-immolation is the highest test of our fitness for service. To annihilate self is at once so simple and so difficult to achieve. If I can succeed in this final struggle with myself, I shall win life's battle and then shall I be able to act as a chastened instrument of the Divine purpose.[120]

He read more of Aurobindo's works to catch up with his latest writings.

Away from home, Subhas missed Bengal: 'I long at times for the scenery which one can see only in Bengal—the ocean-like rivers and the smiling fields of wavy corn,' he wrote in another letter. He had visited the interior of Maharashtra, but felt that 'the picture was not complete without the poetic scenery of Bengal'.[121]

As he was about to leave his motherland, Subhas pleaded for unity in Bengal in his parting message:

> One of the dreams that have inspired me and given a purpose to my life is that of a great and undivided Bengal devoted to the service of India and of humanity—a Bengal that is above all sects and groups and is home alike of the Moslems, the Hindu, the Christian and the Buddhist . . . No sacrifice is too dear—no suffering too great—if we are to fulfill this

mission . . . Therefore I say with all the sincerity that I can command, 'Forget your petty quarrels, sink your personal differences—strive to make Bengal united and great—so that in her greatness may be our highest happiness and glory. After all, who dies if Bengal lives; who lives if Bengal dies?[122]

6

The Unstoppable Outcast (1933–37)

'It was a cloudy and somewhat chilly morning on the 6th March in the year 1933 in Venice when I went to the docks to receive my uncle,' reminisced Asoke Nath Bose, Sarat's eldest son, who was then studying at the Technical University of Munich. Meeting Subhas after a year and a half, Asoke saw the 'physical wreck of a man of thirty-six years', who was otherwise 'of robust health and iron constitution'. Subhas had already received a welcoming telegram from the Hindusthan Association of Italy, an organization of Indians in Italy, the previous day, when his steamer had touched upon the Brindisi port.[1] Under instructions from the Italian Government, the Llyod Triestino officials made special arrangements for Subhas's disembarkation in Venice.[2]

On being informed by his parents about Subhas's trip, Asoke had already arranged for Subhas's overnight stay in Venice at the Royale Danielli hotel and also in Vienna, where they proceeded the next day. Journalists from major Italian newspapers and journals arrived at the Royal Danielli to meet Subhas. Although the team of physicians who had examined Subhas in India had recommended going to France or Switzerland, Subhas had chosen Vienna based on the recommendation of his own medical advisers.

Subhas told the journalists that the primary objective of his journey to Europe was to get medical treatment, but he would continue to work for India's independence. This being his first proper visit to continental Europe, he was yet to develop direct access to or acquaintance with any influential figures. Before leaving India Subhas had requested Gandhi and Tagore for letters of introduction. While Gandhi refused, Tagore wrote in a half-hearted manner that was of no use.[3]

Asoke had made arrangements for Subhas's stay at the Hotel Meissl und Schaden for the first few days in Vienna. He received a warm welcome from the Indian community there, especially the Indian students, and as the news of his arrival became known, journalists thronged the hotel.

Soon after his arrival, Subhas got himself examined by leading specialists, and on their recommendation, was admitted in the Sanatorium Fuerth, where he received an X-ray and clinical examination. The problem appeared to be restricted to the abdomen, as the specialists informed him that they had not found any symptoms in his respiratory system.

While undergoing treatment, Subhas was visited by the well-known Austrian cultural historian and writer, René Fülöp-Miller, and his wife. Among the books for which René Fülöp-Miller was known was *Lenin and Gandhi*, first published in 1927. The couple visited Subhas regularly, inquiring about his health, and they helped him find ground in Austria through their vast network in literary and political circles. Another influential couple with whom his friendship grew at this time was the Vetters. Naomi C. Vetter and her husband (who was a high state official and president of two theatres)[4] also helped Subhas connect with leading figures in Austria's social and political circles.

Asoke left Vienna for Munich after staying with Subhas for two weeks. He continued to visit his uncle on holidays and even otherwise when necessary, apart from staying in touch regularly through letters. With Asoke gone, Subhas focused on developing contacts, finding channels to publicize his views and learning the German language.

Gradually he started interacting with the political parties and administrative institutions. The parade of the *Heimwehr* (home guard), the Austrian nationalist paramilitary group, which he was invited to watch, impressed him.

Just over a month before Subhas arrived in Europe, Hitler had climbed to power as the new chancellor of Germany, and fresh elections after the Reichstag fire of February 1933, in which the Nazi party emerged as the single largest party in Germany, had taken place the day before Subhas set his foot on European soil. As the criticism against Nazi oppression started gaining more intensity, Subhas saw in it an opportunity to pitch the story of British atrocities in India to the European audience. He asked Asoke to inquire in Munich if he could use his contacts to have his letter to the editor published in the Nazi newspaper *Völkischer Beobachter*. Subhas sent the letter written in Germany, arguing that although the British press and politicians were vocal about Nazi oppression, they remain silent about repression in India. The letter, however, was not published, which Asoke guessed was due to the pro-British attitude of the Nazi party.

On 4 April, the *Manchester Guardian* published Subhas's letter to the editor which highlighted how the Government of India had imprisoned a large number of citizens without trial, and out of which only a minority were paid any family allowance. Even those who were provided with a family allowance got an abysmally small amount. As a result, a large number of families were thrown into destitution when their breadwinners were kept in jails for an indefinite period of time. He detailed out his argument with the example of Sarat and himself. He suggested some questions which interested Members of Parliament could put to the Government to verify the genuineness of his information.[5] 'Widespread interest has been taken in Mr Subhas Chandra Bose's letter,' the newspaper commented. The Calcutta correspondent reported a response from Bengal that was casual and Subhas had no difficulty in trouncing it. His letters appeared to have had the desired impact, as the newspaper reported that one Labour Party MP was planning to put Subhas's questions to the Secretary of State in the Parliament.[6]

Municipal administration being a subject that he was deeply interested in, Subhas was happy to receive an invitation from the mayor of Vienna. Meeting him on 10 May, Subhas presented him with some copies of the Calcutta Municipal Gazette. He was keen to study the municipal administration of Vienna, for which the mayor assured to provide all help. Under socialist administration for the past twelve years, Vienna had made considerable progress in education, medical relief and social welfare work, but the aspect that impressed him the most was that 2,00,000 persons were provided with housing, and the administration managed to do this only through tax revenues, without incurring any loan. With some local friends, Subhas went around to see for himself the work done by the municipality. He wrote in detail about what he saw to Santosh Kumar Basu, now the mayor of Calcutta, and held the opinion that their city would greatly benefit if the Viennese experience could be utilized by the Calcutta Corporation. He was even willing to write a book if the Corporation was interested.[7]

Early in May, Subhas was discharged from the sanatorium. He was feeling better, although not completely cured. The abdominal pain persisted but was not as severe as before. He took up a room in the Hotel de France in Schottenring, one of the main thoroughfares in the city. The hotel became his principal residence in Vienna until 1936, except for a few months in 1935.

Subhas was keen to visit Germany, but the passport issued to him barred him from going there. Now, armed with the recommendation of his physicians that treatment at Bad Wildbad in the Black Forest, in Germany, would be beneficial for him, he requested the India Office to remove the restriction. In view of the medical reasons, the India Office agreed in May to endorse his passport for Germany.

Although busy with building up public opinion on India's freedom, Subhas kept a vigilant eye on what was happening at home and often discussed developments with his friends. While he was in Indian jails, the communal question became the burning issue in the second half of the year. The British prime minister, Ramsay MacDonald, announced his Government's own formula for the settlement of the communal question in India on 16 August 1932, as Indian representatives at the round-table conference had failed to reach an agreement among themselves. The so-called 'Communal Award' extended separate electorates to the 'depressed classes', in addition to the Muslims, Indian-Christians, Anglo-Indians and Europeans. According to the 'award', a certain number of seats in the provincial legislatures were reserved for the depressed classes which would be filled up on the basis of a separate electorate. Members of the depressed classes were also eligible for contesting from general constituencies. Demanding the withdrawal of separate electorates for the depressed classes, Gandhi commenced a 'fast unto death', arguing that such a provision would divide the Hindu society. The fast ended in six days when, after brisk negotiations, the Hindu leaders came to an agreement with B.R. Ambedkar, the leader of the depressed classes, that separate electorates would be done away with. Along with some other points of agreement, this came to be known as the Poona Pact.[8]

Both Subhas and Jawaharlal felt that Gandhi's fast relegated the freedom movement to the background. 'It served to side-track the political movement at a time when all possible attention should have been devoted to it', was Subhas's thought. He was not so much against the principle of Gandhi's action as against his continuous absorption in the issue. Subhas felt that Gandhi could have done better by delegating the anti-untouchability campaign to others rather than lead it himself. Gandhi's actions, he thought, had shown a lack of foresight at the second round-table conference, by refusing Ambedkar's proposal to him for reserving seats for the depressed classes in the legislature on the basis of a common electorate. 'There is no doubt that if a settlement had then been made with Dr Ambedkar, the terms would have been much better than the terms of the Poona Pact,' Subhas wrote later.[9] 'I felt annoyed with him for choosing a side issue for his final sacrifice . . . Would not the larger issues fade into the background, for the time being at least?' Jawaharlal questioned.[10] The developments were, however, not able to dampen the revolutionary spirit in Bengal, where violent attacks on Government servants continued in response to Government repression.

The British Government published its proposals for India's future constitution on the basis of the round-table conferences as a White Paper just as Subhas reached Vienna. There was no sign of India becoming a dominion, let alone gain independence. The autocratic and arbitrary powers of the Viceroy, the governors of the provinces and the British Government were to continue with some cosmetic changes. 'In these circumstances, nobody who is anybody in India will be found to bless the new constitution', wrote Subhas.

Things took a more drastic turn when Gandhi announced his intention to undertake a fast for twenty-one days from 8 May as part of his anti-untouchability campaign. He had been imprisoned in February for six months, and planned to carry out his fast, which was not aimed against anyone, but as a 'heart-prayer for purification of self and associates', inside the prison. Concerned about his health and also realizing that it was not at the receiving end of the fast this time, the Government released Gandhi on 8 May. Immediately on his release, Gandhi recommended to the Congress president to suspend the civil disobedience campaign for six weeks, and appealed to the Government to withdraw all ordinances and release civil disobedience prisoners. The Viceroy, Lord Willingdon, refused to entertain any such request.

Following a rebuff by the Viceroy to Gandhi's request for an interview for the second time, the Congress decided in July, at Gandhi's instance, to give up mass civil disobedience and substitute it with individual civil disobedience, and disband all Congress organizations. Gandhi was quickly arrested on 1 August and awarded a one-year prison term. However, he was released unconditionally after three weeks, when he commenced another fast in protest against the Government not providing him with facilities to continue his Harijan work. Since he was released before completing his prison term, Gandhi announced that he would not take up any aggressive civil disobedience campaign till August 1934.

Subhas found it difficult to cope with Gandhi's decision to suspend civil disobedience. With him at this time happened to be Vithalbhai Patel, the former president of the Legislative Assembly and elder brother of Vallabhbhai Patel, but more importantly for Subhas, a close associate of Chittaranjan Das. Vithalbhai had reached Vienna to recuperate under medical care in early May, on his way back to India from political tours in the US and Ireland. Although they belonged to different schools of politics, Vithalbhai and Subhas quickly struck a warm and intimate relationship.

Reacting to Gandhi's actions, they issued a strongly worded statement that claimed that 'as a political leader Mahatma Gandhi has failed'. It was time to reorganize the Congress based on new principles and new methods, which required a new leadership. It would be necessary to create a new party if the Congress failed to make these changes. Rather than abandoning non-cooperation, the need of the hour was to make it more militant and wage it on all fronts.[11]

Journalist Alfred Tyrnauer, who was present at the time of the drafting of the statement, later described what he saw—a description that gives an insight into the minds of the two men, separated by nearly a quarter century in age.

> After a cordial welcome, Patel explained, 'we are about to issue a joint declaration against the passive resistance policy of Gandhi. We are both of the opinion that India has arrived at a stage of revolution, where a more active policy is called for. There is but a little difficulty for the wording to be smoothed out. My young friend, Bose, believes that an attack must be sharp like a dagger, whereas I hold that one should not be careless in one's own house'. Bose interrupted, 'Gandhi is an old useless piece of furniture. He has done good service in his time, but he is an obstacle now.'
>
> 'Maybe he is,' agreed Patel reluctantly, 'as an active politician. But his name is of great and permanent value. We must take that into consideration.'[12]

The article, which was published first in *The Saturday Evening Post* was reprinted in the *Bombay Chronicle* weekly on 23 July 1944. It could not have made either Gandhi or his followers happy.

Sometime later, Subhas asked Satyendra Nath Majumdar, the editor of *Anandabazar Patrika*, 'How long will you follow Mahatma Gandhi blindly?' When Majumdar denied doing anything like that, Subhas retorted, 'But I ask, what will be the opinion of anybody reading the Ananda Bazaar daily?'[13]

It is not difficult to understand the feeling of helplessness that Subhas must have been experiencing, compelled to stay so far away from home indefinitely. The only course open to him was to present his point of view to the European audience and try to garner support, so that he would have some support behind him whenever he returned to India.

A good opportunity presented itself when Indians in London elected him the president of the third Indian Political Conference to be held on 10 and 11 June. There was no question of the Government allowing him to travel to England and therefore, he sent his speech to the organizers to be read out at the conference. It was one of his speeches where he articulated his views most comprehensively, analysing the past decade, explaining the current situation and reasons for failure, and presenting his plan for the next phase of struggle. There is an added significance to this speech in that it helps one understand his thought process, since it came at a time when he was discrediting the Gandhian programme.

The analogy he drew to explain the contemporary situation was not surprisingly that of a military offensive:

> The position of the British Government in India today in relation to the Indian National Congress can be compared to a well-armed and well-equipped fortress standing in the midst of territory which has suddenly become hostile . . . The objective of the Indian National Congress is to get possession of the fortress now occupied by the British Government. Towards this end the Congress has succeeded in winning over the sympathy and support of the population living round about and near the fortress. This is the first stage of the campaign from the Indian side. For the next stage of the campaign, either or both of the following steps can be taken:
>
> (1) A complete economic blockade of the fortress, which will starve into submission the army occupying the fortress.
> (2) An attempt to capture the fortress by force of arms.

He observed that 'In India no attempt has been made to storm the enemy's citadel by force of arms', probably giving a hint, for the first time, that the thought of doing something that had never been done before was present in his consideration, even if the idea was still nebulous. The immediate task was to 'launch another fight on a bigger and more intensive scale' which would need 'intellectual and practical preparation', which 'must be scientific and must rest on objective foundations'. The responsibility would be on a new party of determined men and women who could visualize and plan out in detail the 'method of action beginning from today and right up to the conquest of power'. But obtaining freedom was not the end. The party must be prepared with 'a programme for the new state when it comes into existence in India'. He was emphatic that 'nothing can be left to chance':

Let this party be called the Samyavadi Sangh. It will be a centralised and well-disciplined All-India Party—working amongst every section of the community. This party will have its representatives working in the Indian National Congress, in the All-India Trade Union Congress, in the Peasants' organisations, in the women's organisations, in the youth organisations, in the student organisations, in the depressed classes' organisations, and if necessary in the interests of the great cause, in the sectarian or communal organisations as well.[14]

The plan for the new party and its programme was no doubt attractive at an abstract level, but the key practical question that remained unanswered was how to create that party and under whose leadership—the question was all the more relevant as Subhas himself still did not have a dedicated constituency or mass-based disciplined support. As a result, his experience in managing the Bengal Provincial Congress Committee (BPCC) and coordinating among the revolutionary groups had not been a happy one. If he had any thoughts on that, he did not divulge them.

He, however, was acutely aware of his position. As he had written to a friend soon after reaching Vienna:

Where I have taken my stand today, I am alone, friendless. When I look around I feel as if, there is all round me an endless desert of solitude. I am walking along that vast expanse, like a lonely traveller singling only that song: 'If nobody hearkens to your call, march ahead alone.' But this loneliness is not for all time . . . If you have to create men, if you have to build up and organisation stronger than steel, in that case it is absolutely essential to start from the state of utter loneliness.[15]

Fearing that copies of the speech would reach India and especially newspaper editors, the Government of India banned it under the Sea Customs Act on 17 June. The deliberations within the Government before deciding on the ban shows the extent of their annoyance and irritation with Subhas. 'Safe in a foreign country, he obviously wishes to advertise himself as the Lenin of the coming Indian revolution and with this purpose he had had the temerity publicly to condemn Gandhi', the director of the Intelligence Bureau noted derisively. Answering the question about whether to allow the publication and highlight Subhas's advocacy of armed revolution to discredit him, or 'to stamp on him and his new organisation with both feet', the secretary to the Home Department responded, 'It is better to stamp on Subhas and his infant organisation at this and every other opportunity.'[16]

The party, of course, had not yet been established, but Subhas appears to have given some serious thought and effort towards the formation of the Samyavadi Sangha. Eight months after the conference, he wrote to a friend, 'My principal task will be to organise the Samyavadi Sangha and preach the principles of Samyavad. The party that will emerge out of this, will liberate the country.'[17]

In Vienna, Subhas was introduced to Otto Faltis, an Austrian entrepreneur who was then the managing director of the Austrian Eskont Association.[18] With Faltis, he drew up a plan for facilitating a deeper contact between the two countries. On the whole, he found Faltis 'gentlemanly and reliable', but for the plan to be successful he had to be sure. He therefore asked for advice from the Vetters.[19] The planned organization was established in the first week of May 1934 as the Indian-Central European Society, of which Faltis became the managing vice president. Faltis's article providing the details of the initiative was published in the February 1936 issue of *The Modern Review*.[20]

The first city that Subhas visited after arriving in Vienna was Prague, towards the end of June, organized by the Government of Czechoslovakia, where he was welcomed by Edvard Benes, the country's foreign minister.[21] Subhas also met the mayor and was shown around the water works, sewage works and gas works. He was fascinated on seeing an incinerator that would produce electricity by burning municipal waste.[22]

From Prague, he reached Warsaw on 10 July to spend another week there. In Warsaw too, Subhas studied the working of the municipality and was shown around by English-speaking officers specially deputed by the mayor. The large-scale engineering works for water supply (which utilized the river Vistula that flowed through the city, like the river Hooghly through Calcutta), electricity, gas, the transport system, and the municipal bakery with the capacity to produce bread for half the population of the city, all owned and controlled by the municipality, thoroughly impressed him. As on previous occasions, he shared his experience in detail with Santosh Basu, the mayor of his home town. The learning element was there, but as Subhas interacted with the municipal authorities in the great cities of Europe, he also extracted assurances from them that when Calcutta called, they would extend their hand of cooperation and guidance.

The Oriental Institute of Warsaw organized a well-attended reception for Subhas before he left the city. Subhas was touched by the cordiality he received, but above all, the lesson that was closest to his heart was 'to see how people who had been held down for centuries could rise to the occasion and fulfil their civic responsibilities with the greatest ability the moment they were called upon to do so'. Was there any reason to believe that Indians would not be up to the task if the opportunity arose?[23]

His plan to travel to Moscow from Warsaw failed to materialize as the Soviet Government refused him a visa. Instead, he went to Berlin on 17 July. By a curious coincidence, the refusal of the Soviet Government, compelling him to go to Berlin, would be re-enacted in less than a decade's time. In Berlin, Subhas's movements were restricted for a couple of weeks as his health deteriorated.

From Berlin, Subhas travelled to Franzensbad in Czechoslovakia during the last week of August 1933, where Vithalbhai was being treated, and from there both of them travelled to Geneva to attend a conference on India on 19 September. Subhas stayed back to take care of Vithalbhai who was being treated in a clinic at Gland, near Geneva, as his heart condition aggravated. He too was admitted to the same clinic for some time, as his abdominal pain worsened. Here, for the first time, he met Nathalal Parikh who had come down to explore the possibility of taking Vithalbhai to India if the doctors permitted. Nathalal was struck by Subhas's appearance and his passion for India's freedom at the first meeting. His impression was confirmed by what Vithalbhai told him lying on his sickbed.

> I don't think I am going to last long now but I do want you to do one thing and that is to look after Subhas . . . In him I see service and sacrifice incarnate . . . Even at this early age he has all the merits of a great leader

and his statesmanship and diplomacy are something which I have not seen in any other young man in India.[24]

Subhas attended to Vithalbhai diligently till his death on 22 October 1933, and worked with the Indian students to arrange for sending Vithalbhai's body back to India and saw the old man off from Marseilles.

Just before his death, Vithalbhai drew up his will through which he earmarked a part of his assets for Subhas, to be spent on the 'political uplift of India and preferably for publicity work on behalf of India's cause in other countries'. Although Subhas informed some of his close friends about this, he issued a public statement nearly a year later, pledging to spend the amount transparently and strictly according to the wish of the departed leader.[25]

When Asoke travelled to India in July 1934, Subhas asked him to inquire with the two executioners of the will, Gordhanbhai Patel and Purushottam Patel, when they planned to apply for probate of the will. Although they were courteous with him, both refused to commit to any specific time. Asoke estimated the value of the assets bequeathed to Subhas to be Rs 1 lakh.[26]

Next, he visited Nice and spent over a month taking a course on water cure, before proceeding to Rome to attend the Indian students' conference on 22 December. The Italian Government under Mussolini reached out to the Indian student community in Europe, not only inviting them to attend the conference but providing free travel within the country and making arrangements for their lodging. In contrast to the Nazi attitude of not annoying the British, Mussolini was vocal about his favourable disposition to the Indian freedom movement.

The Italian Government invited Subhas to attend the inauguration of the Oriental Institute in Rome by Mussolini on 21 December. Subhas was put up at the Excelsior, the best hotel in Rome. The inauguration of the institute was followed by a congress of Oriental Students in Europe, which was addressed by Mussolini. Subhas liked Mussolini's speech in which he talked about friendly relations with Asia.[27] His own speech at the congress got good press in Italy; the reports were accompanied with brief stories on his life. The press coverage made Subhas a known face. According to Asoke, Subhas would be recognized and besieged by groups of admirers not only in Rome but in other cities too. The congress also helped Subhas forge contacts with the Arab world through the leader of the Arab students' delegation, El Jabri, a Syrian living in Switzerland, who, apart from having long discussions with Subhas, put him in touch with Arab leaders then living in exile in Italy and Switzerland.

Subhas also addressed the third meeting of the Indian Students' Convention, supporting the suggestion to move the office of the Federation of Indian Students in Europe from London to Vienna.[28] Among the students in Europe, one who became quite close to Subhas was Amiya Nath Sarkar (a nephew of the famous historian, Jadunath Sarkar).

In Rome, Subhas met with the top brass of the Italian Government, including Mussolini and Count Ciano. It was only helpful that Gino Scarpa, who had worked as Consul General of Italy in Calcutta, was now in the Foreign Office. Subhas had several meetings with Scarpa in Rome.[29]

Returning to Geneva, Subhas stayed there till the third week of March 1934 when he left for Munich, spending a day in Zurich on the way, and on to Berlin where he spent a couple of weeks in April. In Berlin, he met the mayor of the city, went out surveying the works of the municipality and reported his impressions in detail to Santosh Kumar Basu as he did the case of other cities he visited.[30] One of the members of the National Socialist Party whom Subhas met in Munich was Karl Haushofer, then the professor of World Politics at the University of Munich and a member of the Deutsche Akademie. Apart from having served in the Imperial German Army, Haushofer had been a tutor to the Japanese emperor on military strategy and politics.[31]

On the invitation of Professor Lesny, a Czech Indologist who had spent some time in Santiniketan, Subhas visited Prague towards the end of March 1934 on the occasion of the inauguration of the Indian Society, from where he proceeded to Berlin via Budapest, before returning to Vienna towards the end of April.

A visit to Rome from Vienna was next on his schedule. It was a crucial visit as he met Mussolini on three consecutive days.[32]

Thereafter, Subhas went on a tour of Budapest, Bucharest, Istanbul, Sofia, Belgrade and Zagreb, following which he returned to Vienna around mid-June, where he took up a flat in Peter Jordan Strasse in the 19th Postal District. From Vienna, Subhas informed Asoke that he would stay there till the end of August for a short-wave diathermy at the Cottage Sanatorium, but more importantly that he had been approached by a London publisher to write about his political experience.

When Asoke arrived at Vienna on 12 July, to spend a week there before his return to India for his vacation, he found Subhas had already started working on the manuscript of *The Indian Struggle, 1920–1934*. He had also hired the services of an Austrian lady, Emilie Schenkl, to help him in taking dictation and typing the manuscript. Asoke also found a young Indian, Mahamaya Prasad Sinha, staying with Subhas. Sinha, who would go on to become the first non-Congress chief minister of Bihar from March 1967 to January 1968, had been sent by Rajendra Prasad for treatment of a serious disease of the throat.

Subhas spent September and October in Karlsbad, famous for its hot springs, and returned to Vienna in the first week of November 1934.

Politics in India, in the meantime, continued to change its course, and took a new turn. As the civil disobedience movement fizzled out, a group of forty leaders, including M.A. Ansari, B.C. Roy, Madan Mohan Malavya, S. Satyamurti, Bhulabhai Desai, K.F. Nariman and K.M. Munshi met in Delhi on 31 March 1934 to discuss the current state of the Congress and its future course of action. The leaders' conference proposed a revival of the Swarajya party and its participation in the next elections to the Legislative Assembly with the aim of having the repressive laws repealed, and to have the proposals in the White Paper replaced by the proposals presented by Gandhi at the second round-table conference. After meeting Ansari, Roy and Desai in Patna, Gandhi gave his approval to the proposal on 8 April.[33]

At the same time in a separate statement, Gandhi announced the suspension of 'civil resistance for swaraj', taking the sole authority for any decision on the matter.[34] The Government of India responded by lifting the ban on Congress organizations, except in Bengal and the North-West Frontier Province, and by announcing a general policy of releasing civil disobedience prisoners.[35]

Another conference at Ranchi, held in May, led to the formation of the Swarajya party, which resolved to contest the Assembly elections on the issues of rejection of the White Paper and the summoning of a constituent assembly. The new Swarajya party decided to be under the 'control and guidance of the Congress in all broad issues of the national policy'. Although it rejected the White Paper, the conference felt that a consideration of the acceptance or rejection of the Communal Award was premature at this stage. From Bengal, B.C. Roy and Tulsi Goswami stood in favour of this approach along with leaders from other provinces.

A few days later, the AICC appointed Ansari and Malavya to set up a parliamentary board to 'run and control' elections to the Assembly on behalf of the Congress. Meeting in June, the working committee endorsed the rejection of the White Paper, but on the issue of the Communal Award, it decided that since the Congress claimed to represent all the communities of India equally, 'therefore, in view of the division of opinion, can neither accept nor reject the communal award'. It was an issue that had to be dealt with the constituent assembly once it was formed, rather than before its formation.[36]

The Bengali-Hindus were at the receiving end of the seat readjustments in the provincial legislature as a result of the Communal Award. Although the Award suggested at least ten seats in the Bengal legislature for the depressed classes, it did not stipulate a separate electorate for them as it did for the other provinces. However, it changed the composition of the legislature drastically by allotting eighty seats to the general category (of which at least ten would be occupied by the depressed class members), and 119 to the Muslims; this was in contrast to the existing forty-six seats for the Hindus and thirty-nine for the Muslims. Thus, although accounting for 44 per cent of the province's population, the Hindus were given representation in 28 per cent of the seats, while the Muslims got representation in 47.6 per cent of the seats with a population share of 54 per cent. Increasing the number of seats reserved for the depressed classes to thirty under the Poona Pact meant that the seat share of the general caste Hindus sunk to 20 per cent. The Europeans, with a negligible population share, were allotted a 10 per cent seat share.[37]

Naturally, this caused great resentment among the Bengali-Hindus, which Subhas thought was a 'just grievance'.[38] While *Liberty*, the newspaper representing Subhas-loyalists, opined that the Award would render the Hindus 'politically impotent, and the reaction of this process on the cultural, economic and political life of the province will be disastrous', the mouthpiece of the Sengupta faction, *Advance*, wrote that 'the award has sacrificed the province to the Moslem and European communities and has left no real autonomy to the children of the soil'.[39] At the same time as admitting to the harm done to Bengali-Hindus, Subhas's objections to the Award was more nuanced. As he argued in *The Indian Struggle*, he saw it as an instrument to further divide the Indian society in order to neutralize the meagre concessions proposed in the White Paper:

In trying to divide the people, attempt has been naturally been made to placate those elements—the Moslems, for instance—who according to the official estimate are likely to be more pro-British than the others.[40]

The dynamics of the Big Five also underwent a change following the civil disobedience movement. In the absence of Subhas, Sarat and Sengupta, B.C. Roy established himself as the mainstay of the Gandhian high command in Bengal, joined by Kiran Shankar Roy and Nalini Ranjan Sarkar. Without any mass base, the sole source of power in the Congress remained in the proximity to Gandhi, especially for B.C. Roy.[41]

The dispute in the Calcutta Corporation too continued in the absence of Subhas and Sengupta, and the mayoral election of 1934 became a bizarre phenomenon. In April 1934, A.K. Fazlul Huq became the first Muslim mayor of the city, by defeating Nalini Ranjan Sarkar. While Huq was supported by the Muslim councillors and the Sengupta faction (although Sengupta was dead), Sarkar received the support of the so-called Bose group (although neither of the Boses were present) and the Europeans in the Corporation.[42]

Subhas reacted strongly to these developments in a letter to Satyendra Chandra Majumdar:

I have no faith in the Working Committee dominated by the satellites of Mahatma Gandhi. I have even less faith in the Parliamentary Board, the prominent members of which shirked their duty when the country was passing through a crisis in 1932–33. I have no sympathy, whatsoever, for those erstwhile colleagues of mine who have dragged in Mahatma Gandhi once again into the politics of Bengal to strengthen their own position. Last but not the least, I am ashamed to have anything to do with a party that sets up Sj. Nalini Sarkar as the Mayor of Calcutta on the strength of European support.

I cannot accept—nor can I understand—this attitude of 'don't accept, don't reject' towards the Communal Award. The party of Dr BC Roy has done incalculable disservice to Bengal by supporting Mahatma Gandhi on this question. Bengal should have been quite united on this question.[43]

Subhas decided to receive surgical treatment in November, as all other treatment until then had failed to give him permanent relief. However, on receiving the news that Janakinath had suffered a heart attack in October, he decided to wait for further intimation before settling on a date. He received a cable from Prabhabati on 26 November, informing him that Janakinath was in critical condition and that he should fly back home immediately. By then, he had completed writing the book, and the publisher, Wishart Ltd., had sent it back to him for the final proofreading. Subhas proofread his book through the night, before taking a flight from Vienna to Rome on 29 November 1934.[44]

As night-flying planes had not been introduced yet, Subhas had to spend the night at Rome, and took the Royal Dutch (KLM) flight from there the next day. Reaching Karachi on 2 December, Subhas received the news that his father had passed away on the same day. As soon as the flight from Karachi landed at Dum Dum airport on 4 December, Subhas was handed over a home-internment order. He was to remain at his house at 38/2 Elgin Road during the entire mourning period.

When the mourning period was over, Subhas returned to Europe, landing at Naples on 30 January 1935. His health had deteriorated during his stay at home, and he had finally decided to undergo surgery in Vienna.

The Indian Struggle had been published in December 1934, copies of which were arranged to be delivered to him in Naples by Pulin Behari Seal. Subhas also travelled to Rome, on his way to Vienna, to meet Mussolini and gift him a copy personally.

Subhas was satisfied with quality of printing of the book, and happy with the positive reviews the book received. He wondered whether it could be reviewed by the Nazi newspaper *Völkischer Beobachter* or the Munich newspaper *Münchner Neueste Nachrichten*.[45] The book, however, was immediately banned in India. The Secretary of State for India, Samuel Hoare, informed the British Parliament that he had read the book, and that it was banned as 'it tended generally to encourage methods of terrorism or direct action'.[46] In spite of the effort expended by his friends in Germany, a plan for publishing a German translation failed to materialize.

The most important appreciation, however, came from Romain Rolland, the French littérateur and thinker who had been awarded the Nobel Prize for Literature in 1915. Rolland wrote in a letter dated 22 February 1935:

It is an indispensable work for the history of the Indian Movement. In it you show the best qualities of the historian: lucidity and high equity of mind. Rarely it happens that a man of action as you are is apt to judge without party spirit.[47]

In Rome, Subhas had a long meeting with Maxim Litvinoff, Commissar of Foreign Affairs of the Soviet Union, at the Russian Embassy. He was also invited to have tea with the ex-King of Afghanistan, Amanullah, along with his former foreign minister.[48] From Rome, Subhas travelled to Geneva for a memorial service for Vithalbhai Patel, and met Romain Rolland on 3 April before returning to Vienna.

Subhas's account of his meeting with Rolland was published in the September 1935 issue of *The Modern Review*. He was much delighted to find a realist in Rolland, with some of his thoughts being close enough to Subhas's own. Rolland explained that his fundamental principles were internationalism, justice for the exploited workers, freedom for all suppressed nationalities and equal rights for women as well as men. On the debate between non-violence vs violence, Rolland held that 'non-violence cannot be the central pivot of our entire social activity. It can be one of its means—one of its proposed forms, still subject to experiment.'[49]

Finally, on 24 April 1935, Subhas went through the surgical operation to remove his gall bladder, which had a big stone inside, at Rudolfinerhaus, a private clinic in Vienna. While recovering from the operation, he toyed with the idea of writing more books. At that moment, he had two ideas: one was a history of the Indian nationalist movement, and another one 'dealing with the future course of Indian politics which will embody my ideas as well'. Unfortunately, none of these books materialized. Apart from other factors, the biggest stumbling block was money. The advance paid by Wishart helped him tide through for some time, and also enabled him to employ a secretary, but the situation was no longer sustainable. 'It is impossible for me to live in Europe now without work,' he wrote to Asoke on 28 May 1935. He still depended on his friends back home, but 'I have not yet heard from friends in India as to how long they will be able to go on remitting money to me'.[50]

Around this time Subhas received the news that Kamala Nehru, Jawaharlal's wife, accompanied by daughter Indira Nehru and Dr Atal would be arriving in Vienna in the first week of June for medical treatment. He made arrangements to ensure that Kamala would receive prompt medical care on her arrival, and asked Amiya Nath Sarkar and other students in Vienna to receive her at the railway station. After personally ensuring all arrangements needed for Kamala's treatment in Vienna, Subhas left for Karlsbad on 15 June and Kamala for Berlin, both travelling in the same train till Prague.[51]

When Asoke went to Karlsbad to spend some time with Subhas, he found that Subhas's health had improved, but he had not completely recovered. Asoke described a typical day in Subhas's life in Karlsbad at this time as follows:

> He started his day with a course of drinking the medicinal water at the famous hot springs of Karlsbad followed by a walk after which he would have his breakfast. After breakfast he sat down to writing and attending to his correspondence. Fraulein Emilie Schenkl, who had acted as his Secretary in the previous year while he wrote Indian Struggle 1930-34 had been asked to come over to Karlsbad to assist him again and she arrived a few days after uncle had settled down there. After lunch and a little rest, uncle resumed his dictation. Occasionally, we went out on short excursions to the beautiful countryside around Karlsbad. In the afternoon, uncle had to go to the hot springs once again and in the evening before and after dinner, he used to devote himself to studies and preparation of notes for work for the next day . . . Lest we should feel life drab and monotonous, uncle asked me to go out and also take Fraulein Schenkl out occasionally, if she was free, to places of entertainment or for sight-seeing.[52]

Early in September, on receiving news that Kamala Nehru's health had suffered a setback, Subhas left for Badenweiler where she was convalescing. On being released from prison, Jawaharlal flew in on 8 September. Subhas drove up to Basel to meet Jawaharlal. Both stayed at the same boarding house. Subhas left after staying there for about ten days, when Kamala started showing signs of recovery, and went to Badgastein, which was famous for its medicinal waters.[53]

By October 1935, Subhas had started thinking about going back to India. He wrote to Naomi Vetter on 1 October that he would like to attend the next Congress session in 1936, but was not sure how the Government would treat him. If the Government arrested him and sent him to prison straightaway, he would have to think seriously about whether he should go.[54] Despite his earlier meeting with Litvinoff, the Soviet Government refused to grant a visa to Subhas in November.

After visiting Prague (where he again met Edvard Benes, now President of Czechoslovakia), Berlin (where he met leading members of the German Government), Cologne (where he met a number of industrialists), Brussels, Antwerp and Paris, Subhas travelled to Dublin in early February 1936. Since he believed that his passport did not allow him to enter the United Kingdom, he had to reach Ireland via France. The President of the Irish Free State, Eamon de Valera, extended a warm welcome to Subhas. Other than de Valera, Subhas was received by other ministers of the Government and prominent leaders. At Dublin, Subhas addressed a big public meeting which was attended by Maud Gonne McBride, the famous Irish republican revolutionary, suffragette and actress. Although Subhas was not allowed to enter England, there was no such bar for Jawaharlal, who paid a visit to England at that time.[55]

Subhas had already made his plans for the next few weeks. He planned to stay in Dublin for ten to twelve days, followed by a week in Paris, another week in Geneva and then about three weeks in Badgastein again. The plans had to be altered as Subhas rushed to Lausanne to be with the critically ill Kamala, Jawaharlal and Indira. Kamala Nehru's condition deteriorated and she passed away on 28 February 1936.

As the new year set in, Subhas longed to return to India. He wrote to Santosh Kumar Basu:

I want to return, and as soon as possible. There is no pleasure in living abroad when one's whole heart is elsewhere. I admit that one can do useful work abroad and I have not been idle either. But doing any effective work requires some money and plenty of moral support from home. I have neither. There is an obvious limit to what one can achieve single-handedly and without financial resources.[56]

Back in Badgastein, Subhas received a letter from the British Consul in Vienna, communicating a message from the Secretary of State for Foreign Affairs, suggesting that he should not return to India. If he did, he would not be a free man any more. With the hope of stirring some British debate, he also wrote to the *Manchester Guardian* about the Secretary of State's warning, which was published on 23 March:

My last imprisonment was bad enough, legally and ethically. But the proposed imprisonment in the event of my return to India now beats all records. May I ask if this is how British law is going to be administered in India and if this is a foretaste of the expanded liberty which the new Constitution will usher in?'[57]

On the same day, the home secretary to the Government of India informed the Legislative Assembly that 'the return of Mr Bose to India as a free man would be a menace not only to Bengal but to the whole of India'. Reading out a long list of acts which the Government considered subversive, he disclosed that 'When Mr Bose was arrested in 1932 it was not because of civil disobedience but because he was closely associated with terrorism'.[58]

The political situation of the India to which he was going to return to was vastly different from what he had last seen as a free man in 1932.

Dissatisfied with the Congress's 'can neither accept nor reject the Communal Award' policy, a new party—the Congress Nationalist Party—had come into being in August 1934 at a conference in Calcutta. Rabindranath Tagore sent his wishes to the conference, which was presided over by P.C. Ray, and expressed his opposition to the Communal Award. Led by Madan Mohan Malaviya and M.S. Aney, the party drew leaders like Akhil Chandra Dutta, Jamnadas Mehta, N.C. Kelkar, and Santosh Kumar Basu (ex-mayor of Calcutta).[59] The majority of the Bengal district Congress committees expressed their opposition to the Congress policy, and all the seven seats in the Bengal legislature, for which elections were held in October, were won by the Congress Nationalist Party.[60]

Another party that had come into existence in 1934 was the Congress Socialist Party. A conference of socialists at Patna in May 1934 decided to organize the socialists with the Congress into a party.[61] Designed to work as a pressure group within the Congress, the party's leadership included Narendra Dev, Jayaprakash Narayan, Yusuf Meherali, Minoo Masani, Asoka Mehta and Sampurnanand.

In September, Gandhi announced his retirement from active Congress politics due to fundamental differences in outlook and declared in October that 'My interest in the Congress organization will henceforth be confined to watching from a distance, enforcement of principles for which the Congress stands'. The annual session of the Congress at Bombay, which was held in October 1934, reluctantly accepted his decision after reiterating 'its confidence in the leadership of Mahatma Gandhi' and requesting him to reconsider the decision.[62]

The Bengal Government continued to clamp down on revolutionary activities ruthlessly. An estimate provided by the Government in July 1935 showed over 2500 detenus in the state, more than half of them held in detention camps, while some were in jail and home internment. In addition, 229 from the province were imprisoned in the Andamans.[63]

India now had a new constitution as the Government of India Act 1935 came into force from August 1935, and neither Dominion Status nor independence was anywhere in sight. The Act was condemned by virtually all shades of political opinion in India for introducing little real progress from the previous constitution of 1919. The significant changes that were introduced were at the provincial level, replacing diarchy with responsible government and expanding the electorate from the existing 65 lakhs to about 3 crores. The governors, however, retained several discretionary powers and could take over the administration of a province indefinitely.[64]

However much he differentiated his brand of politics from the Congress top brass, at least for some time to come, there was no other avenue open to Subhas than working with and within the Congress. Yet, if he was going to negotiate a change and see the more radical section dominate the future programme of the Congress, he was going to need an ally. At the national level, no one was better or more influential than Nehru. They had their obvious differences, but he was the closest to Subhas in terms of ideological inclinations. As he had written to a friend, Jawaharlal's ideas were in line with his, but the heart was with Gandhi. In fact, the crux of his criticism of Nehru, as articulated in *The Indian Struggle* was:

> With a popularity only second to that of the Mahatma, with unbounded prestige among his countrymen, with a clear brain possessing the finest ideas, with an up-to-date knowledge of modern world movements—that he should be found wanting in the essential quality of leadership, namely the capacity to make decisions and face unpopularity if need be, was a great disappointment.[65]

They had worked together from 1928 and often taken a stand against Gandhian positions a number of times. Evidently, Jawaharlal's surrender to Gandhi's persuasion despite disagreements was a source of frustration to Subhas. The time they spent together in the recent months might also have brought him closer to Jawaharlal. From Badgastein, Subhas tried to persuade him, the next president of the Congress, in a heartfelt appeal:

Among the front-rank leaders of today—you are the only one to whom we can look up to for leading the Congress in a progressive direction. Moreover, your position is unique and I think that even Mahatma Gandhi will be more accommodating towards you than towards anybody else. I earnestly hope that you will fully utilise the strength of your public position in making decisions. Please do not consider your position to be weaker than it really is. Gandhiji will never take a stand which will alienate you.

As I was suggesting in our last talk, your immediate task will be a twofold one—1) to prevent office acceptance by all possible means and 2) to enlarge and broaden the composition of the Cabinet. If you can do that, you will save the Congress from demoralisation and bring it out of a rut.[66]

His efforts to connect with Jawaharlal at a personal and emotional level are evident from his letter asking for advice from the latter on whether returning to India and being arrested would serve any public purpose:

My inclination at the moment as you can very well imagine from your reactions—is to defy the warning and go home . . . My only excuse for troubling you on such a matter is that I can think of no one else in whom I could have greater confidence. The time is so short that I cannot ask advice from a number of people.[67]

Jawaharlal cabled Subhas, advising him to postpone the departure 'pending further developments'. He was angry with the threat of arrest:

It [the government warning] had come as a shock to us all and I was so angry and upset that I spent a bad night . . . It is sad that you will not be present at the Lucknow Congress. I was so looking forward to it.[68]

Talking to the press in Geneva in March 1936, Subhas said 'that both on personal as well as on public grounds I should give him as much cooperation and support as is possible'.[69] It was a clear signal that Jawaharlal would find an ally in Subhas if he ever needed to go against the old guard. It is another story that the signalling failed to have the results Subhas desired.

Subhas was acutely conscious, even a tad touchy probably, of his image as a national leader, as an Irish journalist realized when introducing him to a friend as 'the well-known Bengal leader'. 'Why do you call me a Bengal leader? I am not provincial,' pat came the reply. The journalist admitted, 'He has always struck me as an Indian patriot first and Bengali patriot last'.[70]

Two days before starting his journey, Subhas wrote to Romain Rolland for his concern and his advice to postpone his return: 'I fully appreciate your feelings on this matter . . . but that is a price which enslaved people always had and always will have to pay in this world.'[71]

Subhas set sail for home from Marseilles on 27 March 1936, on the Lloyd Triestino boat, the *S.S. Conte Verde*, which arrived in Bombay at 5.30 a.m. on 8 April. A crowd had already gathered to welcome him back, among which the Bombay police counted workers of the Congress, Congress Socialist Party and also communists, but no front ranking Congress leader as they were away at the Congress session in Lucknow. He was greeted by shouts of 'Inquilab Zindabad!', 'Vande Mataram!' and 'Subhas Chandra Bose ki Jai!'

When somebody from the crowd shouted for a message, Subhas shouted back, 'Azadi Ka Jhanda Uncha Rakho' (Keep the flag of freedom flying high). A CSP member snuck into the steamer by the gangway meant for coolies, garlanded Subhas and handed over a note which said, 'The All India Congress Socialist Party accords a hearty welcome to Mr Subhas Chandra Bose on his arrival in India'.[72]

As soon as he landed, Subhas was arrested under Regulation III of 1818, whisked away to the Arthur Road prison and later to the Yervada Central Jail. The annual session of the Congress meeting in Lucknow, with Jawaharlal as the president, passed a resolution which stated that the arrest was 'a further and significant proof of how British Imperialism continues to use its full apparatus of repression to prevent normal political and personal life in India'. Despite being imprisoned, Subhas was inducted back into the working committee after eight years.[73] 'Is Mr Bose's treatment consistent with English standards of fair play at all? Or is it the sort of thing which ought to happen only among those unenlightened foreigners?' the *Manchester Guardian* threw the stinging question in its editorial.[74] Questions were raised in the House of Commons and in the Legislative Assembly. In fact, an adjournment motion moved by a Congress member of the Assembly was passed in April, criticizing Subhas's arrest.[75] In protest of his arrest, Jawaharlal announced that 10 May 1936 was to be observed as All-India Subhas Day.

Large processions taken out by the Congress and labour parties through different parts of Calcutta converged at the base of the Ochterloney monument. The main resolution at the meeting presided over by Akhil Chandra Dutta, the deputy president of the Legislative Assembly, was condemning the arrest, which was moved by Professor Atul Sen of Dacca.[76]

Both the central and Bengal Governments faced some concerns about Subhas's arrest. They were concerned about the widespread criticism over the treatment of Subhas, but were also in a dilemma about having to get his case re-examined by the courts, as required under law. Moreover, there was the medical opinion of Dr Demel, the surgeon who had operated on Subhas, that if he was kept in prison for long, there were high chances of the relapse of his health problems. Caught in a tricky situation, the Government decided to transfer him to Sarat's house in Kurseong and keep him under home detention.[77] He was moved to Sarat's house at Gidda Pahar in Kurseong in the third week of May. This time, the detainment was more relaxed as he was allowed short walks and occasional visits by family members and others when approved by the police.

In Kurseong too, Subhas's health kept giving him trouble. In September he asked the Government to allow examination by either B.C. Roy or Nil Ratan Sircar. After answering V.V. Giri's adjournment motion in the Legislative Assembly asking for a discussion on Subhas's health, the Government found that five more questions have been submitted for answer and discussion in the Assembly. The Bengal Government had him examined by Nil Ratan Sircar and J.C. Drummond, who recommended conducting further pathological tests in Calcutta if these were not available in Darjeeling. As his health again started deteriorating, Subhas was shifted to the Calcutta Medical College on 17 December. He was finally released unconditionally on 17 March 1937, as both the central and the Bengal Governments felt that the risks associated with his release were considerably low.[78]

On 6 April, Subhas made his first public appearance at a meeting held at the Shraddhananda Park in observance of All-Bengal Subhas Day. He was still too weak to plunge into active politics and decided to recuperate fully before he did so. Taking up an invitation from Dr N.R. Dharamvir and his wife, whom he had known from his student days in England, Subhas reached Dalhousie on 12 May, stopping at Allahabad and Lahore for a few days.

The next five months at Dalhousie were spent convalescing, reading and writing. Subhas asked Asoke, who was now in Calcutta, to ensure that the Calcutta newspapers were regularly delivered to him. He specifically wanted *Amrita Bazar Patrika, Anandabazar Patrika, Advance, Keshari* (Bengali daily), *Lokmanya* (Hindi daily), *Azad, Mohammadi,* and *Basumati.* In addition, he was a subscriber of the Foreign Policy Association, *Foreign Affairs, International Affairs,* and *New Statesman.* To help him in writing, from time to time he asked Asoke to send him reference books and to cull out information from back issues of newspapers.[79] About his present reading habits, he wrote to a friend:

> My interest in philosophy is there—but I have little time for it. To some extent I have kept up my contact with Psychology. I do a lot of political study—I mean study of political philosophy and international politics. Besides this, I try to be 'sabjanta' [know-all] to a certain extent, because a public man must have general grasp of all problems.[80]

National and international politics kept him occupied, but the Calcutta Corporation never left his thoughts. He wrote to the former mayor, Santosh Kumar Basu, that he was worried about the affairs of the Corporation and asked, 'Can you let me have your opinion as to what should be done to cleanse the Aegean Stables (sic)?'[81] To an employee of the Corporation, he lamented about his lack of influence in the internal politics of the Corporation, otherwise 'many things would not have happened which have actually happened during the last few years'. Nepotism had made such inroads during the previous years 'that it makes me hang my head down in shame'. The sad state of affairs in the Corporation was only a reflection of the 'moral inertia that has got hold of our men.' Subhas stated that 'I can only tell you this that if I have anything to do with Bengal Politics—the Augean Stables of the Calcutta Corporation will have to be swept clean', or else the Congress party would have to lose their influence over it.[82] He had made some noticeable impact as the mayor, but it was for too short a time. Unfortunately, the story of the Corporation politics was going to be murkier in the next few years.

He returned to Calcutta in early October and moved to Kurseong again for a couple of weeks, although Gandhi had advised him against it for health reasons. 'I have told S(ubhas) he must not go to Calcutta or take up active duty before he is thoroughly fit. Gandhi wrote to Amrit

Kaur in September: 'Even when he is, he can't replace J(awahar) who has unconsumable energy and single mindedness.'[83]

Subhas was yet to make his comeback to full-fledged politics, while Sarat had taken the plunge after his release from detention on 26 July 1935. Sarat was appointed to head the Congress parliamentary board in Bengal, jointly with B.C. Roy, and also became the acting president of the BPCC. Roy had made some initial effort to let Bengal Congressmen oppose the Communal Award, but retreated to follow the official Congress line after being rebuked by Jawaharlal and Gandhi. Sarat, on the other hand, quickly demonstrated that he was not going to back down so easily. He insisted that the Congress policy was making its position weak in Bengal and complained that the working committee had turned a deaf ear to BPCC's arguments. Although Subhas was away, he was in constant touch, supporting and sometimes guiding Sarat's position.

Admitting that Congress was aware of how hard Bengal had been hit by the Award, Jawaharlal tried to explain to Sarat that it had to be dealt with at the national and not provincial level. The BPCC in response let Jawaharlal know that the predominant opinion in Bengal was that the province was made a pawn in the scheme of national politics, and that Bengal's problems could not be made subservient to national politics. Further, the migration of leaders and workers to the Nationalist Congress Party due to this policy was harming the Congress prospects.

Towards the end of August, the election manifesto issued by the AICC clarified that since the Congress had rejected the new Government of India Act in its entirety, it automatically translated to a rejection of the Communal Award. At the same time, it also opposed any one-sided agitation against the Award as that would lead to a situation of conflict which only strengthened the Government's case. The differences between the BPCC and the AICC, however, continued until Jawaharlal visited Calcutta on 8 November 1936 and worked out a compromise, which allowed for organizational agitation against the Communal Award as a part of the new constitution.[84]

In the elections to the provincial legislatures held in the beginning of 1937, the Congress obtained a majority in Madras, UP, CP, Bihar and Orissa, and emerged as the single largest party in Bengal, Bombay, Assam and NWFP. In the remaining two provinces, Punjab and Sind, it was in the minority. In Bengal, the Congress won in forty-three out of the forty-eight general category seats and six out of the thirty seats reserved for scheduled castes (it contested in seventeen seats), but did not contest any of the seats for Muslims. Including the five seats that the party won in the labour constituencies, its tally stood at fifty-four seats out of the total 250. It had secured approximately 25 per cent of the total votes cast, and 22 per cent of the seats.[85]

A churn was going on in the province's Muslim politics too. At the initiative of the Nawab of Dacca, Habibullah, some influential Muslim leaders like the Nawab of Jalpaiguri, Musharraf Hossain, Huseyn Shahid Suhrawardy and Hassan Ispahani, formed the United Muslim Party (UMP). The other party that was in contrast to this largely urban-centred party was the Krishak Praja Party (KPP) of Fazlul Huq, with a strong rural agrarian base whose main plank was abolition of zamindari and other economic issues. With Huq refusing to join hands with the UMP, the latter invited Jinnah to try again and consolidate Muslim political organization in Bengal. Jinnah succeeded in setting up the Bengal Provincial Muslim League, absorbing the UMP in the process, but failed to win over Huq or his KPP.[86] In the 1937 elections, the maximum number of Muslim seats— forty-three—were won by independent candidates, with the Muslim League securing thirty-nine seats and the KPP securing thirty-six seats.[87]

With a sympathetic Bengal Congress being the single largest party and the Muslim League having contested against it, the KPP favoured a coalition with the Congress. Negotiations, which began in early February, broke down as the Congress could not reach a decision on office acceptance till the third week of March. In addition, there were also disagreements on policy priorities, particularly on the release of political prisoners. Reportedly, Huq's insistence of including Nalini Ranjan Sarkar as a minister was another point of rupture with the Congress. Even when the Congress decided in favour of office acceptance, it was restricted only to the provinces where the Congress had a majority. The working committee stipulated that Congressmen accepting office in provinces where it had failed to get majority were liable to disciplinary action.[88]

As a result, KPP and the Muslim League formed a coalition Government, with the former having three ministers (Huq becoming the chief minister) and the latter having four (which included Nazimuddin, Suhrawardy, Musharraf Hossain and Habibullah). Shrish Chandra Nandi and B.P. Singha Roy from the landholders constituencies, Nalini Ranjan Sarkar from the commerce constituencies, and P. Deb Raikat and M.B. Mullick from among the scheduled caste members also became ministers.

Subhas had to return to Calcutta before long as the AICC and the working committee were scheduled to meet in Calcutta. He had been nominated again for the new working committee appointed at the Faizpur Congress in December 1936, with Sarat substituting for him due to his absence. Subhas wrote to Gandhi with a special request to attend, and Sarat invited him to be his guest.

The AICC met at the Wellington Square while the working committee meetings were held in Sarat Bose's house at 1 Woodburn Park. The meeting of the working committee that ended on 1 November decided that the next year's annual session would be held in February at Haripura, and that nominations for electing the next president would be accepted till January 1938.[89] On the same day, Gandhi wrote to Vallabhbhai:

> I have observed that Subhas is not at all dependable. However, there is nobody but he who can be the President.[90]

There is no clarity as to how Subhas's name came up for the post of the president and how it was finalized. J.B. Kripalani, the Congress general secretary at the time, had vaguely mentioned that Subhas's 'name was being mentioned as the likely president of the forthcoming session of the Congress', without specifying by whom. Kripalani, however, claimed in his memoirs that Subhas himself lobbied with Gandhi for his appointment:

> . . . he approached Gandhiji to solicit his support. Gandhiji told him that he must first think of his health before he thought of anything else. In any case, as he had not been in touch with the affairs of the country for a long time, it would be better for him to wait a year before assuming the responsibility of presidentship. Subhas, however, said that he had been in touch with national affairs and he would soon recover from his ailments. Gandhiji did not argue the matter further, assuring him of his support, whereupon all the other candidates withdrew their nominations and Subhas was elected Congress president unopposed.[91]

Kripalani's account does not quite fit with the available timeline. Subhas had written to Mrs Woods from Dalhousie on 9 September 1937 (but surprisingly not to Emilie Schenkl, although he wrote to her on the same day) that 'I shall probably be elected the President of the Indian National Congress early next year'.[92] Before reaching Dalhousie, Subhas had met

Gandhi in Allahabad in April, when it was too early to even consider the question of the next presidentship. The next time he met Gandhi was in his home in October. More importantly, not only does it go completely against the grain of Subhas's character to have gone to Gandhi requesting for the presidentship of the Congress, but it is incomprehensible why, if he wanted to become the president, he would not discuss it with Jawaharlal as the two were probably the closest they had been at that time.

Quite possibly, Gandhi informed Subhas too that he was going to be the next president of the Congress. Subhas was still too weak and needed to recover fully before taking over the responsibility, which was undoubtedly going to put a lot of strain on his health. In an article published in the *Hindusthan Standard* on 5 December, he wrote, 'I felt that I would benefit more from a month's stay and treatment in a place like Badgastein than I would from a 3 to 4 months' stay at a hill station in India'. Accordingly, he left for Europe on 18 November 1937 by a KLM plane. After landing in Naples, Subhas went to Badgastein again to continue his treatment.[93]

Before boarding the plane, he confided in Asoke that he was going to utilize the time in Europe in writing an autobiography. Asoke was asked to take the help of friends Kali Charan Ghosh and Gopal Lal Sanyal to collect relevant materials and send it to him. For as long as he continued to write, Subhas kept asking Asoke to collect family information from the elders and other relevant materials as well. He had already asked Emilie to wait for him at Badgastein.[94]

Subhas could get about ten days for writing, in which he completed ten chapters, but the manuscript remained unfinished as he left for England when the Secretary of State agreed to his proposal for allowing entry into the country. He was still not aware that the British Government could not stop him legally from entering the country.[95] A reception committee was set up in London, with V.K. Krishna Menon as chairman and Feroze Gandhi as one of the joint secretaries.[96] Announcing his first visit after 1921, the *Manchester Guardian* reported, 'His name is mentioned as the successor to Mr Nehru as president of the Indian National Congress this year.'[97]

Subhas arrived at Dover on 10 January, where he was received by nephew Amiya Bose, and they travelled together to London. Arriving on 10 January at the Victoria station, he was received by 'hundreds of Indians and many English friends'. At a reception at the Dorchester hotel later in the evening, which was attended by a large number of journalists, 'English people who met him for the first time were impressed alike by his pleasant, quiet manner and the decisiveness with which he discussed Indian affairs.' In his interactions, Subhas briefly explained the challenges faced by the Congress ministries in the provinces as well as their achievements, the communal situation and the Congress's opposition to the federation proposed in the new constitution.[98]

In England, Subhas met the former Viceroy Irwin (now Lord Halifax, and leader of the Conservatives in the House of Lords), the former governor of Bengal Ronaldshay (now Lord Zetland and Secretary of State for India), Clement Attlee (leader of the Labour Party), and prominent leader of the Labour Party, George Lansbury (who chaired a public reception for Subhas at the Conway Hall, attended by Reginald Sorensen and Arthur Greenwood, Labour MPs). The British historian, Basil Mathews, wrote to Jawaharlal informing him that Subhas had made a deep impression on him through his interviews on Halifax and Zetland, as a result of which they had no delusions regarding Congress's opposition to Federation.[99]

Regarding his speech at the Conway Hall, the Indian Political Intelligence (IPI) noted:

> This was a clever speech, delivered very quietly and unemotionally: the points were made effectively without any display of rhetoric and were calculated to appeal equally to the Indian and English portions of this particular audience . . . He was subtly bitter all through the speech and very openly so when he attacked the Labour Party' just after Greenwood had delivered his most fulsome message from the Council. In fact the wincing of the three Labour Party officials on the platform was almost audible. He gave the impression that, as a man of breeding and education who had attained eminence in his own country, he was only too painfully aware of the mediocrity of the personalities and speeches of those surrounding him on the platform, who, such as they were, represented the best amongst his sympathisers in this country. On the other hand, he appeared genuinely pleased by the very rousing reception given him by the many Indian students present.[100]

He also met Eamon de Valera who happened to be visiting London at that time.[101] In addition, he met Harold Laski, J.B.S. Haldane, Ivor Jennings and Stafford Cripps, and communist leaders Rajani Palme Dutt and Harry Politt. Following a series of private and public meetings, on 16 and 17

January, he visited Cambridge and Oxford. In Oxford he met G.D.H. Cole and Gilbert Murray. According to some press reports, he had a midnight meeting with Bertrand Russell too.[102] Subhas's visit to England came to an end on 19 January, when he flew out of Croydon to Prague.

It was at this time that the formal announcement of Subhas being the next Congress president was made. He returned to India a day after his forty-first birthday. This time, however, he did not return as a prisoner, but as the *Rashtrapati*. That might have been the perception of the others in the Congress, but for Gandhi, Subhas was just putting on Jawaharlal's clothes for the time being. The telegram he received from Gandhi on his return to India read:

> Welcome home. God give you strength to bear the weight of Jawaharlal's mantle.[103]

7

Rashtrapati (1938)

Shri Charaneshu Ma (Revered mother)!
    Will you not come to Haripura? If you do I shall be very happy . . .
The man at whose feet I learnt politics is not with us today. How happy
he would be if he was with us.[1]

Writing these lines to Basanti Devi must have made Subhas emotional.
In some ways, he was fulfilling Deshbandhu's prophecy, and the only
Bengali to become Rashtrapati after Deshbandhu. The setting too was
similar, only with a few differences. Gandhi had grown into the role of a
permanent super-president and was none too friendly. Motilal's son was
there as a support, but mostly as a mediator between him and Gandhi.
Chakravarti Vijayaraghavachariar, president of the 1920 Nagpur Congress
where he had fiercely criticized Deshbandhu's council entry programme,
sent a message: 'Long time ago I had told you that you will become the
president of the Congress . . . Although your innate humility will stop
you, yet you can comfortably repeat that famous quote of Napoleon—Paris
stands more in need of me than I do of Paris.'[2]

No one knew better than Jawaharlal what was in store for Subhas.
'Subhas Bose has to face an extraordinarily difficult situation than any I
had to face,' he wrote to V.K. Krishna Menon.[3]

Friends and admirers poured in as he reached Calcutta, but Subhas
had to hit the ground running. He addressed a large public meeting
attended by a crowd of 30,000 at the Shraddhananda Park on the occasion
of Independence Day, presided over a memorial meeting for the novelist
Sarat Chandra Chattopadhyay who had passed away a week ago, and then
left Calcutta to attend the Bengal Provincial Conference which was to be
held at Bishnupur on 29 and 30 January. Also present at the conference

was M.N. Roy, who had returned to politics in his home province after about a quarter of a century. The Conference authorized Subhas to form an executive of the Bengal Provincial Congress Committee (BPCC) in consultation with the different groups and their leaders, with the aim of bringing an end to the disagreements among them. He was also authorized to reorganize the Congress Municipal Association for better management of the party's role in the Calcutta Corporation.[4]

বিষ্ণুপুর ট্রেনে শ্রীযুক্ত সুভাষচন্দ্র

Subhas arrives at Bishnupur to attend the Bengal Provincial Conference. *Jugantar*, Vol. 1 (2 February 1938), British Library, EAP262/1/2/89.

In the first week of February, he made a quick trip to Gandhi's ashram in Sevagram.

On 11 February 1938, the youngest president of the Congress left for Haripura from Calcutta, accompanied by his tutor (who had been giving him Hindi and Urdu lessons), and his nephew Asoke, travelling in a reserved second-class compartment of the Bombay mail. Thousands of Congress workers, the party's top leaders, editors of newspapers and members of the Bose family gave him a warm send-off. The Howrah district Congress committee decorated the compartment with a large national flag. The two gentlemen were accompanying Subhas to help him draft letters and take notes of his interactions in their respective languages of proficiency. Asoke's additional responsibility was to take care of Subhas's personal needs.[5]

While travelling by train, Subhas replied to a letter from a member of the Indian Civil Service, who had written to inform him about his resignation from the service and his desire to join the Congress. 'I shall look forward eagerly to meeting you when you are out of the service . . . I shall welcome you into the Congress with all my heart,' Subhas wrote to a young Hari Vishnu Kamath.[6]

ওয়ার্ধায় শ্রীযুক্ত সুভাচন্দ্র বসুর গর্দ্দনা

The Rashtrapati welcomed at Wardha station.
Jugantar, Vol. 1 (8 February 1938), British Library, EAP262/1/2/94.

Large crowds gathered at the stations where the train stopped and Subhas had to speak a few words on his arrival. After taking a short break at the house of a local Congress member in Dadar on 13 February, the president's team boarded a special train. Subhas was received by the chairperson of the reception committee at Udhna and taken to the Bardoli Swaraj Ashram, where Vallabhbhai and Jairamdas Daulatram had been waiting from him. A huge procession took him next to Haripura, from where Subhas was carried in an eighty-year-old chariot belonging to the Bansda royal family, drawn by fifty-one bullocks, to Vithalnagar, about two and a half miles away.[7]

The venue of the Congress session, named Vithal Nagar after the late Vithalbhai's memory, had been meticulously prepared for the occasion. A temporary, two-lane motorable road was constructed to connect the venue with the Navsari, the site was provided with electricity connection, and a large number of temporary huts and community dining halls, where the best vegetarian Gujarati food was to be served, were constructed. Two large huts were given to the president; Jawaharlal stayed in the hut just opposite and the one beside his was occupied by Sarojini Naidu and her daughter Padmaja. A large fleet of brand-new V8 cars were placed at the disposal of the reception committee by the Ford Motor Company, of which two were reserved for the president and his contingent.[8]

Unveiling an eight-foot tall bust of Vithalbhai, Subhas recalled his first meeting with him at the 1922 Gaya Congress, and told the gathered audience about the last days they spent together. Although he had come to be acquainted with Vithalbhai for the work of the Swarajya party, it was only during the last six months of his life that Subhas got to know him intimately.[9]

This huge show, which cost about Rs 7.5 lakh, annoyed Gandhi. 'There are many things here that I liked, but it lacks the spirit of Khadi', he said while at the Khadi and Village Industries exhibition at the Congress venue. He had suggested that the cost of arrangements to hold a village session should not exceed Rs 5000. Presence of cars and electricity was incongruent with the ideal of khadi:

> Rural-mindedness and electrical illuminations go ill together. No have motor cars and motor lorries any place there . . . they brought me to Haripura in a car. They would not allow me to walk. They would not even take me in a bullock cart. That was reserved for Subhas Babu . . . Here there are petrol and oil engines, and water-pipes, stoves and electricity, most of the modern city-dwellers' amenities, including the tooth-paste and the tooth-brush and scented hair oils. The villager is or should be unspoilt by these things.[10]

More than 2,00,000 people gathered to watch the proceedings of the open session. While the leaders arrived in a procession with Subhas at the head, Gandhi was brought to the dais in a car and was helped by Subhas to climb up the steps of the podium. As a choir of Bengali boys and girls sent specially by the BPCC at Subhas's suggestion, and trained by Sarala Devi and Indira Devi, sang 'Vande Mataram', everybody stood in silence. Bankim Chandra's 'Vande Mataram' was followed by the singing of Rabindranath's 'Jana Gana Mana'. The crowd cheered as Subhas's mother took her seat in the women's enclosure. In his opening speech, the chairperson of the reception committee, Darbar Gopaldas Desai, pointed out that all the Congress sessions held in Gujarat had Bengalis as the president: Surendra Nath Banerjee in 1902, Rash Bihari Ghosh in 1907 and Chittaranjan Das in 1921, although due to his incarceration the session had been presided over by Hakim Ajmal Khan. Subhas delivered his speech initially in Hindi but later spoke in English.[11]

Subhas's speech at Haripura was a study in contrast with his speech at the Indian Political Conference five years ago. Whereas on the previous occasion, he had spoken as a revolutionary spoiling for a good fight to liberate India, at Haripura he spoke as a statesman. Devoid of enunciation of abstract political principles and thoughts, his speech was nothing short of a blueprint for the present and the future development of India to progress on the road to independence. It laid down specific action points covering a wide range of topics, calling for radical reforms in many areas. In elaborate detail, Subhas painted the future as he saw it. *The Manchester Guardian* called it the 'President's Socialist Speech'.[12]

The speech started with a bird's eye view of human history, enunciating the principle behind the rise and fall of empires. Empires collapsed after reaching the zenith of prosperity, and the fate of the British Empire could not be any different. Although certain features made it stronger than the historical ones, it would break down unless it transformed itself not only into a federation of free countries, but also only if Great Britain became a socialist state that stopped feeding on enslaved nations abroad. Subhas quoted Lenin to explain his point.

Geopolitically, the empire was facing strain from all ends—Ireland in the West to India in the East. Countries outside the empire such as Italy, Japan and Soviet Russia, 'whose very existence strikes terror into the heart of the ruling classes in every imperialist state', only added to the pressure. 'How long can the British empire withstand the cumulative effect of this pressure and strain?' he asked. In terms of military technology, the emergence of air power had subdued the importance of naval power based on which Britain had expanded its empire.

British rule in India, as elsewhere, thrived on the policy of 'divide and rule', Subhas argued. The new constitution of 1935 followed the same policy in a new form—India was one, the division between British India and the Indian states being an artificial one. Towards building a united India, the Congress had already adopted a policy to prevent exploitation of any group by another. National reconstruction on socialistic lines in free India meant 'have-nots' would benefit at the expense of 'haves'. Congress was for a policy of 'live and let live—a policy of complete non-interference in matters of conscience, religion and culture as well as of cultural autonomy for the different linguistic areas'. The day was not far off when the social and religious disabilities of the depressed classes would be a thing of the past.

The path to national emancipation, whose ultimate stage was severance of the British connection, would be that of non-violent non-cooperation, including civil disobedience. Office acceptance should not lead to a mindset of constitutionalism. There was every possibility that the issue of federation would trigger the next round of civil disobedience.

Subhas emphasized that India had no enmity towards the British people. Having won freedom, there was 'no reason why we should not enter into the most cordial relations' with them. In a free India, it was important to ensure the continuity of the Congress, because only an organization that won freedom for the country could ensure its reconstruction. Towards this goal, the first task of the national Government would be to set up a commission for drawing up a comprehensive plan for reconstruction. The free country, Subhas outlined, would be a multi-party democratic one, with a strong central Government, ensuring local and cultural autonomy at the same time. It would be essential to have a common language which ideally should be a mixture of Hindu and Urdu 'as is spoken in daily life in large portions of the country' and a common script, 'that would bring us into line with the rest of the world'. Subhas recommended the adoption of the Roman script. Then there was the need for framing an appropriate foreign policy.

Population growth needed to be checked, poverty eradicated through measures like land reforms (including abolition of landlordism), liquidation of agricultural indebtedness, increasing crop yield and extension of the cooperative system. To ensure India's growth, large-scale industrial development under state-control, along with cottage industry, would be indispensable. Implementing these plans would require a large amount of investments, which would be raised through internal or external loans.

Until that happened, the current Congress ministries in the provinces should change the character and composition of bureaucracy, whose outlook and mentality in most cases were neither Indian nor national. These ministries should introduce uniform policy for reconstruction in the spheres of education, health, prohibition, prison reform, irrigation, industry, land reform, workers' welfare.

Subhas dealt with the drawbacks of the new constitution at length, and also spoke about the relationship between the Congress and other parties and platforms in his long speech. It was nothing short of a blueprint for the march towards freedom and national reconstruction thereafter.

Subhas ended the speech with wishing a long life to Gandhi, who was needed 'to keep our struggle free from bitterness and hatred', and 'for the cause of humanity' because the fight for freedom 'was not for the cause of India alone, but of humanity as well'. India freed meant humanity saved.[13] Subhas's genuine respect and admiration for Gandhi was never in question, but from now on the ideological distance would only go on increasing. There was enough material in his speech to reinforce his perception that 'Subhas is not at all dependable'.

Yet, despite the thrust on a socialist programme, Subhas's working committee was weaker than the previous year in terms of the presence of leftists. Narendra Dev and Achyut Patwardhan, who were members in both 1936 and 1937, and Jayaprakash Narayan, who was a member in 1936, were not present in 1938. Only Subhas and Jawaharlal remained in the working committee to push the socialist programme. Subhas had Harekrushna Mahtab, a Congress leader from Orissa, inducted into the committee.[14]

At the close of the Haripura session, glowing tributes were paid to Subhas by Govind Ballabh Pant, Sarojini Naidu and Vallabhbhai. It would have been impossible to imagine that in just about a year they would be playing a different role.

On his way back from Haripura, Subhas arrived in Bombay on 24 February. After a tumultuous reception at the Dadar and Victoria stations in the morning where Jawaharlal, B.G. Kher, the Bombay premier, K.M. Munshi, Morarji Desai and Yusuf Meherali were present, he was taken in a procession to the Bombay Congress office, with crowds thronging on both sides of the road. Bombay Talkies, the film studio of Himanshu Rai and Devika Rani, employed six movie cameras to capture the scenes of his welcome. Over 2 lakh people gathered at Azad Maidan to hear him speak in the evening. However, both this meeting and a subsequent one in Dadar had to be cancelled on account of the failure of the sound system.[15] After spending the next few days in Bombay, Subhas started homewards after stopping over at Wardha and Nagpur. By one estimate, in the few days he spent in Bombay, he addressed twenty-five public meetings and was received by fifteen institutions and associations.[16]

Over 1 lakh people welcomed Subhas at the Howrah station on 10 March. The immediate issues which he had to address were the release of political prisoners, improving the state of affairs at the Calcutta Corporation and to bring an end to the factional squabbles that showed no signs of receding. 'Give me time and your cooperation. If I get these from you, I will be able to change the face of political life in Bengal in five years,' he urged in one of his public meetings.[17] It was, however, easier said than done. He was well aware of the problems, but immediately got a taste of what he was dealing with, when, within a few days, thirty members of the Congress Municipal Association resigned, objecting to the power given to Subhas by the last provincial conference to reform the Association.[18] He was not yet the Hercules to clean what he had, a few months ago, referred to as the Augean stables of the Corporation.

Addressing a public meeting organized by the Scheduled Caste League to felicitate him, Subhas appealed to them to dispel their mistrust and join the ranks of the Congress so that they could influence the policymaking in the party. It was due to this mistrust of the scheduled castes and Muslims towards the Congress, which he said was completely unjustified, that they were staying away from the party without a valid reason. Condemning the caste system, he declared that the goal of the Congress was to break the society free from all forms of bondages. Subhas's appeal appeared to have worked, as the organizers of the meeting announced that they were all going to join the Congress.[19]

Gandhi arrived on 15 March to negotiate with the Bengal Government on the release of the prisoners. He stayed at Sarat's Woodburn Park house this time too. The working committee met in Subhas's Elgin Road house from 1 April, when a foreign affairs subcommittee was set up comprising Subhas, Jawaharlal and J.B. Kripalani, the Congress general secretary, to monitor the international situation and advise the working committee and also to clarify Congress's stand on international issues to foreign countries.[20]

In mid-April, Subhas outlined the Bengal Congress programme for the next year, asking the Congress workers in the state to spread out to villages and recruit more people into the organization. He set the goal for the workers to transform Congress to become the representative of all classes and communities in the province.[21] Speaking at a reception given by the students of the Scottish Church College, Subhas recalled his days at the institution. He strongly emphasized the critical need for communal unity and reminded the students that there would always be some powers who would try to divide them by various means. He urged them to become more adventurous, giving them the example of how a few adventurous Englishmen had succeeded in establishing the British Empire in India. Bengali students, he said, also needed to develop a culture of physical development, without which moral and intellectual development would remain incomplete.[22]

Moving out of Calcutta, he visited the Surma Valley where he urged the Congress workers to help improve the lot of the labourers in the tea gardens, and the Midnapore district to revive the Congress organizations.[23] His visit to the Midnapore district 'has stimulated a revival of Congress activities there', as he ensured the absorption of released detenus and internees to the local Congress organizations, as the Government noted.[24]

In May, he travelled to Bombay to preside over the first conference of the premiers of the seven provinces where Congress had formed ministries. The conference of the premiers convened by Subhas was really an effort to translate his ideas expounded in the presidential speech at Haripura into action. Several ministers accompanied the premiers from the provinces for the conference held from 12 to 14 May. It provided an effective platform to the administrators of the provinces to exchange their experiences and develop a mechanism to cooperate on various issues such as civil liberties, agricultural policy, industrial reconstruction, education, rural development and finances. Following this conference, the UP Government decided to hold a similar one to examine new sources of revenue for constructive purposes, and the Bombay Government for jail reforms and labour issues.[25]

Afterwards, he travelled to Poona, where he was taken in a procession through the city and given a reception by the Poona city and suburban municipalities. On 23 May, he returned to Bombay: 'Mr Bose received an enthusiastic welcome when he arrived on the morning of the 10th,' the Bombay Government reported. In the evening, Subhas was accorded a civic reception by the Bombay Municipal Corporation. A tea party given in his honour by the sheriff followed the mayor's address of welcome.[26]

The occasion gave a welcome break to Subhas, to turn, for a few hours, from his entanglement in national and provincial politics, to his favourite subject of municipal administration. He spoke at length about what he had learnt from the municipalities in the great cities of Europe, especially the housing programme sponsored by the municipality of Vienna, entirely from its own tax revenue. It was unfortunate, he said, that although entertainment in India was taxed, the municipalities did not benefit from that taxation. He lauded the Bombay municipality for implementing adult franchise and for its initiative in primary education.

'Civic progress all over the world is moving in the direction of what may be called Municipal Socialism,' consciously or unconsciously, Subhas told the gathering. Municipalities were no more restricted to functions like providing drinking water, roads and lighting. Modern municipalities were taking over much broader responsibilities such as providing education, looking after the health of the people, tackling infant mortality, maternity etc. With the passage of time, it was becoming difficult to draw a boundary for a municipality's ever-expanding responsibilities. He gave the example of a municipal bank operated by the Birmingham municipality. Municipal Socialism, in a broad sense, was 'nothing else but a collective effort for the service of the entire community'. There was an increasing consensus among political thinkers that local self-government was the 'real school of democracy'. It was equally important to remember that India had a rich history of local governance, of which cities like Mohenjo-Daro and Pataliputra were bright examples.[27]

Around the same time, the Labour Subcommittee appointed by the working committee that included Jawaharlal, Jayaprakash, and Masani among others, also met in Bombay to review the measures taken by the provincial Congress Governments and discuss measures to introduce some amount of uniformity in their labour policies.[28]

Following up on the suggestion made at the premiers' conference, that the working committee should appoint an experts' committee to advise the Congress Ministries on the problems of industrial reconstruction, development of power resources and power supply, the working committee authorized Subhas to convene a conference of the Ministers of Industries and seek a report on the existing industries in the provinces and the need and possibilities of new ones. Accordingly, Subhas convened the conference in Delhi in October, which was also attended by G.D. Birla, M. Visvesvaraya and Lala Sankar Lal Basal, among others.[29] Speaking at the conference, Subhas made it clear that although greater efficiency in agriculture was a necessity, it was not enough to solve the problems of poverty and unemployment. It was imperative to increase industrial production considerably and to divert a large proportion of village population to industrial occupation.

> India is still in the pre-industrial state of evolution. No industrial advancement is possible until we pass through the throes of an industrial revolution. If the industrial revolution is an evil, it is a necessary evil. We can only try our best to mitigate the ills that have attended its advent in other countries. Furthermore, we have to determine whether this revolution will be a comparatively gradual one, as in Great Britain, or a forced march as in Soviet Russia. I am afraid that it has to be a forced march in this country.[30]

Although heavy industries formed the backbone of the national economy, it was difficult to make rapid progress in that field without capturing power at the Centre and having full control over fiscal policy. For the time being, the focus, therefore, needed to be on medium and cottage industries. Indian businessmen could easily work towards developing medium industry with the help of the provincial governments. Thus, although Subhas had highlighted the need for state-owned industries in his Haripura speech, there was ample room for private enterprise in his scheme of things, albeit driven by the Government. As far as cottage industries were concerned, he did not see any conflict between them and large-scale industries.

It was important, at the same time, to develop skill and knowledge base. Hence, he emphasized on developing technical education and technical research, and proposed the formation of a national research council.

Subhas suggested that the conference should consider undertaking proper economic surveys in the provinces, develop a mechanism for coordination between cottage and large-scale industries, look at advisability of having regional distribution of industries, make provisions for technical education and appointing an expert committee to give further advice.

Ironically, this strong advocacy for rapid industrialization came from Subhas on 2 October, Gandhi's birthday. The intensity of the advocacy is significant, especially in view of Gandhi's opinion. In the *Harijan* of 23 July, Gandhi wrote:

> It [khadi] It is the only real insurance against famine and unemployment. Even if India were to be industrialized overnight, much of the unemployment would remain . . .If pestilence, poverty and blood-shed are to be avoided, there is no remedy but khadi and other village industries.[31]

Thus, Subhas's plan to direct the provincial governments to move towards progressive and uniform policy measures had made a good start. He took up the most important component, of the vision he had laid out at the beginning of his term, at the end of the year, when he inaugurated the first meeting of the National Planning Committee on 17 December.

Elaborating on his views on the need for industrialization, in an interaction with Meghnad Saha earlier in the year, Subhas had put it in a mild manner that 'all Congressmen do not hold the same view on this question [need for large-scale industries]'. Without a doubt, he was referring to the pushback from the old guard that valued the simplicities of village life more. Being aware of that, Saha had framed his question appropriately: 'May I enquire whether the India of the future is going to revive the philosophy of village life, of the bullock-cart—thereby perpetuating servitude, or is she going to be a modern industrialised nation, having developed all her natural resources, will solve the problems of poverty, ignorance and defence and will take an honoured place in the comity of nations and begin a new cycle in civilisation?'[32]

The pushback had started and Subhas acknowledged it in his opening remarks at the National Planning Committee meeting, devoting a larger part of his speech in an attempt to assuage the feelings:

> During the last few weeks, I have noticed an apprehension in certain quarters as to the possible effects of our efforts to industrial planning on the movement that has been going on since 1921 for the production of Khadi and the promotion of cottage industries . . . It may be remembered that at Delhi I made it perfectly clear in my opening speech that there was no inherent conflict between cottage industries and large-scale industries . . . Not only that. In the National Planning Commission we have reserved a seat for a representative of the All-India Village Industries Association . . . Everybody knows or should know that even in the most

industrially advanced countries in Europe and Asia, e.g., Germany and Japan, there are plenty of cottage industries which are in flourishing condition. Why then should we have any apprehension with regard to our own country[33]

Subhas asked the Planning Committee to focus and first tackle specific problems relating to the 'mother industries, i.e., industries which make the other industries run successfully', such as power, metals, heavy chemicals, machinery and tools, and the communications industry. At the same time, the committee would have to solve the problem of finding adequate capital and credit, without which no plan would succeed.

Alongside the work of national reconstruction, Subhas had to take care of the political agenda that he had set up for himself and the Congress. In some of the issues in the political agenda, he had to follow the lead of Gandhi and the working committee. This was particularly true for the efforts to find a settlement for the communal question.

In the follow up of the Congress's poor show in Muslim constituencies in the 1937 elections, Jawaharlal had launched a Muslim mass-contact programme with the aim of enrolling more Muslims in the Congress. Despite a promising start, the initiative fizzled out due to lack of organizational capabilities. The programme also did not receive much attention from Subhas. The programme was criticized by the Muslim League, leading to a prolonged war of words between Jinnah and the Congress leaders, particularly Jawaharlal. With this controversy in the background, the talks between the Muslim League and the Congress, on members of the former joining the Congress in forming governments in UP and Bombay, also broke down.[34]

In spite of the setbacks, Jawaharlal and Jinnah again started corresponding, which lasted from January to April 1938, without producing any result. This was followed by a meeting between Gandhi and Jinnah on 28 April. Jinnah, however, made it clear that any settlement was possible only if the Congress acknowledged the Muslim League as 'the one authoritative and representative organisation of Musalmans in India' and that the Congress represented only Hindus. Since Subhas was the Congress president at the time, Gandhi asked him to meet with Jinnah and take the discussions forward.[35]

During his Bombay visit in May, Subhas and Jinnah met on the 12th and the 14th. As the talks started, expressing hope, Gandhi wrote to Amrit

Kaur, 'S(ubhas) is very patient. He is a good listener. He may succeed where others might have failed. I would like him to succeed.'[36]

The talks and correspondence between Subhas and Jinnah too failed to make any progress as the Muslim League continued to refuse to proceed further unless it was accepted as the authoritative and representative organization of India's Muslims, a position that the working committee would not agree with.[37]

In June, Subhas himself had to face the reaction of the Muslim League to the Congress outreach programme, when he visited the districts of Chittagong, Noakhali and Tipperah from 4 to 18 June. He found that hostile campaigns were being carried on by the Muslim League against his tour. Not only were leaflets distributed containing what he called 'false and malicious allegations', black flags were shown at places, and a crowd of League workers started throwing bricks at one of his processions through Brahmanberia. Subhas and fourteen others were injured. Some of the leaflets claimed that the Congress was trying to establish a Hindu Raj, enslaving nine crore Muslims, and that life, property, religion and honour of the Muslims were in grave danger in the Congress-administered provinces. It was also alleged that the Congress had prevented the introduction of the Bengal Tenancy Act Amendment Bill in the Bengal Legislative Assembly.

Far from feeling threatened by his programme, Subhas explained in a statement issued to the press that Muslims attended his meetings and processions in large numbers, and that was what made the Muslim League workers 'ferocious'. He threw a challenge to the League leaders to prove their allegations and explained that Congress was opposing the Huq ministry in Bengal not because there were six Muslim ministers, 'but because the government was worthless':

> If there were eleven worthy, patriotic Muslim Ministers, the Congress would not raise its little finger by way of opposition. Likewise, if there were eleven worthless Hindus as Ministers, the Congress would continue its relentless opposition to the Hindu Ministry.[38]

Subhas had to deal with two instances of ministerial crisis during his presidentship of the Congress, first in the Central Provinces (CP) and later in Assam.

When differences among the ministers in the CP led to the resignation of four ministers from the Congress Government led by N.B. Khare, the working committee tasked Vallabhbhai, the chairperson of the Congress parliamentary subcommittee, to resolve the crisis in consultation with the Congress members in the CP Assembly. Although an agreement was reached and the crisis diffused, before long, complaints reached Vallabhbhai about Khare not complying with his end of the bargain. Khare, however, assured him that he would not do anything to precipitate another crisis. Yet, Khare submitted his resignation to the Governor on 20 July along with two of his ministerial colleagues, but when three other Congress ministers refused to resign, they were dismissed by the Governor. Khare immediately proceeded to form another ministry with new ministers.[39]

At a meeting with the parliamentary subcommittee, also attended by Subhas, where Khare, along with the new and old ministers, was summoned, the committee found that Khare had initiated back-channel communications with the Governor with the intention of resigning and subsequently forming a new Cabinet. The working committee asked Khare to step down and let the Congress members of the Assembly elect a new leader. While agreeing to the suggestion, Khare at the same time insisted to be one of the candidates for the election, despite Subhas's advice otherwise. The matter thereafter reached Gandhi, whom Khare met with Subhas and some other members of the working committee, and he was asked to issue a statement admitting his error of judgement. Khare, however, refused to issue the statement that he had drafted with some points added by Gandhi. At a subsequent meeting of the Congress legislators in Wardha, Subhas, presiding over the parliamentary subcommittee, oversaw the election of Ravi Shankar Shukla as a new leader of the Congress party in the CP Assembly.

Matters, however, refused to die down. Khare issued a lengthy pamphlet called 'My Defence', in which we claimed that he was wronged by the Congress working committee, accusing Vallabhbhai of acting on the basis of personal grudge ('Sardar Patel has come to be regarded as a terror . . . No one likes to offend him for fear of his iron hand falling on him some day or other')[40] and later describing the points added by Gandhi in the final draft statement his 'political death warrant'. The Congress president, in his view was 'a puppet in the hands of Mahatma Gandhi'.[41]

Subhas responded by issuing a detailed statement on14 September, which was thirty-two printed pages long, laying down, blow-by-blow, all the incidents that led to the crisis and defending the working committee.[42]

On 22 October, the working committee disqualified Khare from being a Congress member for two years.[43]

On 13 September, an opportunity emerged for the Congress legislative party in Assam, when the Government led by premier Mohammad Saadullah resigned, alleging some of the members had crossed over to the opposition. Saadullah resigned even before the Assembly could take up a non-confidence motion moved by the deputy leader of the Congress, Arun Kumar Chanda. Although the Congress was the single largest party in the Assembly, it did not have the required strength to form the Government on its own. As a result, when the Governor asked Gopinath Bordoloi, the leader of the Congress in the legislature, to form the Government, he agreed but sought time to put together a coalition. Soon, it turned out that although Saadullah had submitted his resignation, it still had not been accepted by the Governor, and efforts were on to form a new Government under Saadullah.

At the instance of the working committee, Maulana Azad rushed to Shillong, followed shortly by Subhas, who was then in Calcutta. Early on the morning of 16 September, Subhas left for Sylhet, where he was received by over 10,000 Congress workers and local leaders. From Sylhet, he reached Shillong in style, in the car of a local businessman who was a supporter, followed by the leaders of the area in twenty-five cars. Once in Shillong, he held meetings with the leaders of the different parties in the Assembly, while Azad met Saadullah and later on other legislators. A difference of opinion, however, arose between Subhas and Azad. While Subhas insisted on the necessity of Bordoloi forming a coalition Government, Azad objected. The legislators of the Congress party also expressed their keenness to form the Government. The matter was finally settled after consulting Gandhi and Vallabhbhai, both of whom gave their support to Subhas's strategy.[44]

Subhas's account is available from a letter that he wrote to Gandhi on 21 December 1938:

> There is a fundamental difference between Moulana Sahib and myself on the point at issue [formation of coalition ministry]. This became manifest when we were confronted with the ministerial crisis in Assam. I can perhaps now claim that I was right and Moulana Sahib was wrong. But if Sardar Patel had not providentially come to my rescue, Moulana Sahib would never have given in at Shillong and perhaps you would not

have supported my view-point against that of Moulana Sahib when the Working Committee met at Delhi. In that case there would not have been a Coalition ministry in Assam.[45]

After hectic negotiations, Bordoloi informed the Governor on the next day that he would be forming the next government with eight ministers, submitting the names of five Hindu ministers. It was decided that the three Muslim ministers to be inducted in the Cabinet would be selected after discussing their readiness to accept the Congress programme.[46] After much behind-the-scenes activity, Bordoloi finally took the oath of office on 20 September, scuttling the efforts by the European legislators and a section of the Muslim legislators to topple the coalition even before it was in office. Subhas stayed back in Shillong to guide and oversee the entire process until the new ministry was sworn in.[47]

Subhas received a warm reception in Shillong from the students and Brother J.I. O'Leary, the Irish Principal of the St. Edmund's College, who claimed to be a friend of De Valera and pledged his support to the development of India according to his instructions.

In July, Subhas got entangled in a controversy on the issue of acceptance of the federal scheme of the new constitution. From the very beginning, Subhas had made his opposition to the part of the Government of India Act 1935 that dealt with the scheme of federation quite clear. He had warned against a drift towards constitutionalism and had gone as far as to predict that the next round of civil disobedience would be on the issue of opposing federation. On 8 July, a journalist from the United Press showed Subhas a press report quoting Frederick Whyte, a British Liberal politician who had been the first president of the Central Legislative Assembly, claiming that from his discussion with an influential member of the working committee then in London, he had understood that the Congress would eventually accept the federal scheme. The member of the working committee who was being referred to was Bhulabhai Desai. Subhas reacted sharply.[48]

In a press statement, he refused to believe that 'any influential Congress leader has been negotiating with the British Government with a view to arriving at a compromise behind the back of the Congress', but instead of stopping at that, went on to issue a strongly worded warning: 'Personally I think that any weakness shown by the Congress or any section thereof during the fateful hour in India's history will amount to treachery of the first magnitude to the cause of India's freedom', and in such an eventuality, it would be his duty to step down from the office of Congress president to continue the struggle against the federal scheme, he said.[49]

Subhas's statement drew an equally sharp counter-reaction from the deputy leader of Congress in the Central Legislative Assembly, S. Satyamurti. He argued that Subhas should have waited for the full statements to come from Whyte and Desai and taken up the matter with the latter in the next meeting of the working committee. Drawing a comparison of how Jawaharlal had accepted the working committee's decision on office acceptance despite his own opposition, Satyamurti said that threatening resignation was akin to being undisciplined and undemocratic, and unbecoming of the Congress president. He reminded Subhas that no individual, not even the president, was greater than the organization they belonged to. Following the admonition on principles, Satyamurti too went ahead to enumerate the conditions under which he would agree with the federation, one of them being an assurance for complete Indianization of the army in the next twenty-five years.

The Bengal branch of the Congress Socialist Party, Minoo Masani and K.F. Nariman, however, came out strongly in support of Subhas and asked Desai to clarify his stand.[50]

On 15 July, Subhas issued another statement, expressing his disinterest in participating in a press controversy. His previous statement was 'nothing more than a forceful reiteration of the Congress view on Federation', which he had issued because 'reports had reached me of efforts being made by the British Government to enlist the sympathy and support of Congressmen in favour of the Federal Scheme'. If he had used strong language, 'it was partly because I feel strongly on the question'. Reactions to his statement showed, he said, that all of it was not a rumour; that indeed there were Congressmen who were in favour of an amended scheme[51]

> I hope and trust and pray that all attempts on the part of Congressmen to whittle down our national demand will cease once for all. Let us not reduce ourselves to the level of parliamentary busybodies by offering Delhi and Whitehall amendments of the unwanted Federal Scheme.[52]

Soon, M.N. Roy too came out in support of Subhas. While Jawaharlal declined to get drawn into the controversy, Vallabhbhai and Gandhi maintained silence.

Having watched the developments silently so far, Desai now wrote directly to Subhas. He claimed that during his meetings with several British politicians during his England tour, he had never said anything that could be construed as being agreeable to a compromise on the federal scheme. Subhas brought an end to the public controversy by releasing parts of Desai's letter.[53] To clear the air, the AICC also passed a resolution during its meeting in the last week of September. It reiterated its resolution condemning the federal scheme that was passed in Haripura 'as doubt has been expressed in certain quarters as to the attitude of the Congress on the question of Federation'.[54]

The controversy was buried, but undoubtedly, Subhas's strong and hasty reaction could not have gone down well with the Gandhian leadership.

Yet another controversy that spilled over to Subhas, although he was not directly involved in it, was a public spat between Sarat and the editor of the *Amrita Bazar Patrika*, Tushar Kanti Ghosh.

During a debate on 15 August in the Bengal Legislative Assembly regarding the Government's proposal to create a publicity department and allocate funds to it, Sarat opposed the proposal, accusing the Government of using funds to influence newspaper reporting. In the course of his speech, he read out from a letter, written by a high official of the Bengal Government to another in July 1933, claiming that Ghosh supported the Government's policy of detaining the more extremist among the political prisoners for a longer period. He threw the rhetorical question of how the editor of a newspaper that claimed to be nationalist could make such a comment to a British official in secret.[55]

With his reputation at stake, Ghosh struck back, bitterly attacking Sarat in the columns of *Amrita Bazar Patrika*, with support provided by *Jugantar* and other district newspapers not well-disposed to the Bose brothers, insinuating that an old incident was being deliberately misinterpreted at the behest of their rival, *Anandabazar Patrika*, whose editor, Suresh Chandra Majumdar, was close to both Sarat and Subhas. After another round of attack in a meeting at the University Institute Hall on 2 September, Sarat brought it up in a BPCC meeting as a resolution condemning Ghosh and his paper. However, an amendment moved by the communist leader Bankim Mukherjee, recommending that the matter be referred to the Congress working committee, was passed in the meeting. Thus, the controversy was set to blow up on a much wider scale.

It was, however, diffused by the intervention of Subhas at this stage. Despite his scathing attack on Sarat, Ghosh was aware of being in a weak spot. As a compromise, Sarat withdrew the amended resolution of the BPCC and Ghosh tendered an apology to Sarat for the personal attack in his newspaper, promised to support all Congress organizations and not to give space to any Government publicity other than speeches and published official documents.[56] With a fairly well-known reputation of being a critic of Subhas and Sarat, Ghosh backed down for the moment, but would spring back with greater force when the opportunity presented itself a year later.

The year also saw massive student unrest in Calcutta, around a conflict between the students and authorities of the St Xavier's College. The trouble started on 30 August with disagreements over the text of memoranda prepared by some students on the occasion of the Rector's Day celebrations in the college, which led to a peaceful demonstration by the students, demanding to be heard. However, a police force was soon summoned by the college authorities, which charged the students with lathis and water hoses. The police also arrested several of the students. The students went on strike, and the college was closed down indefinitely. Processions, meetings and sympathetic strikes took place in other colleges across the state. When the students approached Subhas for guidance, he declined to interfere as two of his nephews (Arabinda Bose and Kalyan Bose, sons of his elder brother Suresh) were leading the strikes and asked them to take guidance from Syama Prasad Mookerjee.

The college authorities agreed to open the college and allow the students back on the condition that Kalyan and Arabinda would have to leave the college. The parents of the students were also told to withdraw their children if they were not satisfied with the methods of the college. Subhas now issued a stern message, who was on his way to Shillong to resolve the Assam ministerial crisis, that the college was still around only because of the weakness of the current Bengal Government. He cautioned the college authorities that their bureaucratic methods were not acceptable, and that if educational institutions could not adapt to the national awakening that was taking place, then he would request them to return to their own country. The new India would not miss them. The college and the students soon reached an agreement, after three weeks of agitation. Kalyan and Arabinda, however, had to leave the college as a part of the compromise.[57]

The job of the president of the Congress was extremely taxing, and through the year Subhas shuttled from one part of the country to another, dealing with the demands of organizational work, framing policies, leading various groups and committees, and negotiating with politicians and pressure groups. Fortunately, he sailed through most of the year with only short bouts of illnesses. In fact, Gandhi wrote to Amrit Kaur in June 1938 that:

Subhas is in Wardha. He is looking a picture of health. All he needed was the work of the type he loves. He has got it and he is happy.[58]

Yet, the stress had begun to affect his health, and from October onwards, instances of illness became more frequent, compelling him on occasions to skip a working committee meeting or postpone planned provincial tours. As the year came to an end, Subhas remained restricted in Wardha by a particularly nasty bout of fever and respiratory problems, and was allowed by the civil surgeon to leave for Bardoli via Bombay under special arrangements on 8 January 1939, to attend a working committee meeting.

Subhas continued his tours around the country when not attending AICC or working committee meetings, or chairing meetings of the new institutions he had already helped to set up or was going to set up. Through these tours, he aimed to build up support for the Congress and sensitize the people about Congress plans and programmes, as well as stay in touch with the provincial Congress committees. On the completion of the Industry Ministers conference, Subhas travelled to Wardha, Amraoti and Nagpur to speak at several public meetings and receptions.[59] Analysing the international situation in Wardha, Subhas said that although a war had been avoided for the time being by England and France giving in to Hitler's demands, the possibility of a war in the near future was very much alive if these two countries refused to agree with Hitler's colonial ambitions. He felt that Hitler would have backed down if these two countries had remained firm instead of surrendering meekly.[60]

On his return to Calcutta on 20 October, Subhas told pressmen that talks with the Huq Government, regarding the release of over 200 political prisoners still in jail, which had been led by Gandhi, had failed. It was now widely felt that the campaign for their release, which had been suspended at the beginning of the talks, needed to be resumed.[61] Subhas left for a week's tour of the north-eastern region on 26 October, travelling to

Gauhati (where he interacted with students at the Henry Cotton College and the Earle Law College), Dhubri, Gauripur, Rangpur and Rajshahi (where a group of communal Muslim students tried to break up his meeting convened by the students of the Rajshahi College).

Once Subhas returned to Calcutta, the BPCC decided to start a movement demanding the release of political prisoners with a 46-member committee set up to direct the campaign.[62] He launched the campaign formally at a large public rally in Shraddhananda Park on 12 November.[63] Khwaja Nazimuddin, minister in charge of the Home Department in the Bengal Government, in turn, accused Subhas of exploiting the 'terrorist' prisoners' issue to bring down the Government, drawing a sharp rebuttal from Barindra Kumar Ghosh, who was one of the pioneers of revolutionary movements in Bengal.[64]

After spending two weeks in Bengal, Subhas left for a tour of north and north-west India starting with Lucknow, on the evening of 18 November. Apart from meeting several groups and addressing several meetings in Lucknow, he visited the political prisoners in Lucknow jail, accompanied by C.B. Gupta, Sachindra Nath Sanyal, Jogesh Chatterji and others. Subhas reached Lahore on 23 November by Punjab Mail, welcomed by over 1000 people at the station. Sikander Hyat Khan, the Punjab premier, made a public appeal to all political organizations opposed to the Congress to not hold any demonstration against Subhas. In Lahore too, he met the political prisoners in Lahore Central Jail.

While Subhas was in Lahore, the Hindu Mahasabha president, V.D. Savarkar, issued a statement disparaging the Congress's claim to represent all Indians. Referring to Subhas's statement, that in a future round-table conference no party other than Congress should represent India, Savarkar argued that only the Mahasabha could claim to truly represent Hindus. Although the Congress had most of the Hindu seats in the last elections, it did not contest the elections representing solely Hindu interests.[65]

From Lahore, Subhas travelled to Batala, Campbellpur (Attock), Jalandhar, Hoshiarpur, Rohtak, Hisar, Ludhiana, Bhagwanpur, Rawalpindi, Amritsar (addressing a public meeting at Jallianwalla Bagh) and Ambala, received by huge crowds at all the places. From Punjab, Subhas travelled to Sind, reaching Karachi on 3 December. He travelled to the interiors of Sind, including Mirpur Khas, Sukkur, Shikarpur, Larkana and Jacobabad. Wherever Subhas went, he was received by massive enthusiastic crowds. At several places, shops and schools were closed down to welcome him.

A visit to the Lucknow Jail.
Jugantar, Vol. 2, Issue 58 (30 November 1938), British Library, EAP262/1/2/336.

At Karachi, he addressed a large gathering of about 10,000 persons and also received a civic address from the Karachi Municipal Corporation.[66] Completing his three-day tour of Sind, Subhas started towards Calcutta on 6 December, making a short stop at Jodhpur.

As he reached Calcutta, news arrived that the coalition ministry in Assam had defeated a no-confidence motion in the Assembly. Subhas sent a congratulatory message to Bordoloi. Talking to reporters, Subhas expressed happiness that his decision in favour of forming a coalition stood vindicated. The success was important to build his case for dislodging the Huq ministry in Bengal to replace it with a coalition led by the Congress.

Among his public engagements in Calcutta was the inauguration of the Sriniketan cottage industry showroom on 8 December in the presence of Rabindranath and his son Rathindranath. Marked by personal warmth, Subhas reminisced how he was at a loss when told about rural reconstruction by the poet during a visit some twenty-four years ago, at a time when the two dominant ideals in front of him were those of Ramakrishna–Vivekananda and the Bengal revolutionaries. The poet urged Subhas, as well as other political leaders, to take forward his work after he was no more.[67]

On 10 December, Subhas left for Wardha to attend the meeting of the working committee. He and Sarat took up the matter of government formation in Bengal with Gandhi, reportedly telling him that the time was ripe for forming a Congress coalition Government.[68] The Fazlul Huq Government had survived a no-confidence motion moved by the Congress legislative party by a narrow margin in August, but only with the support of the European members of Assembly. Those who voted against the Huq Government included its former supporters too.[69] Clearly, Subhas and Sarat saw the opportunity for Congress to step in to replace a Government which they held to be communal and unstable.[70] The induction of two new ministers by Huq without consulting his Cabinet had given rise to further dissension in his party. In fact, during his East Bengal tour in October and Punjab tour in November–December, Subhas repeatedly predicted that the Huq ministry was going to fall very soon, and claimed that if Congress decided to form the Government at that time, it would appoint a Muslim premier to prove wrong those who called the party a Hindu party. However, on reaching Bombay to inaugurate the National Planning Committee, Subhas was shocked to receive a letter from Gandhi, hand delivered by Ghanshyam Das Birla. Dictating the letter in front of Abul Kalam Azad, Nalini Ranjan Sarkar and Birla, Gandhi informed Subhas, 'I am more than ever convinced that that we should not aim at ousting the [Huq] Ministry.'[71] Birla had travelled to Wardha to report to Gandhi his views about the Bengal Government, and was joined by Sarkar, closest friend-turned-bitter-foe of the Boses and Huq's finance minister, the next day.

The letter 'came as a profound shock to me', Subhas replied. Stating that after his and Sarat's detailed discussion at Wardha with Gandhi, he was under the impression that they had agreed to the formation of a coalition ministry in Bengal. He accused Gandhi of changing his opinion under the influence Azad, Sarkar and Birla, and he appeared to rely more on their views than on him and Sarat, who were responsible for running the Congress organization in Bengal. According to Subhas, Gandhi's change in opinion gave rise to a crisis. About the Huq ministry, he wrote

... it is imperative in the national interest that we should pull down the Huq Ministry as early as possible. The longer this reactionary Ministry remains in office, the more communal will the atmosphere of Bengal become and the weaker will the Congress grow, vis-à-vis the Muslim League.

He was at a loss as to why Sarkar, the finance minister in the Huq Government, had changed his mind, as he had personally communicated to Subhas about his intention to resign. He could see that Sarkar was using Gandhi's influence to justify his remaining in office.

What surprised Subhas about Gandhi's decision was that he 'did not feel it necessary to even consult me before you arrived at a decision on such a serious matter'. Clearly, Gandhi's volte-face annoyed him more because, as is evident from his letter, Subhas had already formulated a strategy regarding Bengal which he had explained to Gandhi.

He pointed out that forming a coalition ministry was within the realm of possibility in Bengal, Punjab and Sind, and if implemented it would bring all the eleven provinces under Congress administration, strengthening the party's claim of representing the people of British India, and even the absence of a settlement of the Muslim League would not remain a serious handicap. While working towards that goal, immediate measures should be taken 'to satisfy reasonable Muslims that we are anxious to understand their complaints and to remedy them as far as humanly possible'. If these could be accomplished before the next Congress session at Tripuri, the Congress would be in a position to demand Purna Swaraj and ask the British Government for a definite reply within a specified period. If the Government rejected the demand, then a satyagraha campaign should be launched. In their situation, the British Government could not afford a major struggle to go on in India. Therefore, 'a Satyagraha campaign on a big scale in 1939 will inevitably lead to a Peace Conference between the Congress and the British Government as a stepping stone to our victory', Subhas explained. At the same time, 'a widespread awakening among the States' subjects will weaken the support from the princes on which the British government rely on a great extent'.

Subhas informed Gandhi that he was ready to take up the responsibility of bringing in the coalition governments in those three provinces. He made it clear that 'I feel so strongly on this point that a contrary policy appears to me to be suicidal', and consequently, if Gandhi did not agree to his

[ঘোষাইহাটে বাংলার রাজবন্দীদের সাহায্য বদে অনুষ্ঠিত চলচ্চিত্র অভিনয়ের পূর্বে ওয়েংগাল, গবিন প্যাটেল এবং বোসাইহাটে মন্ত্রবর্গ। প্রভৃতির দর্শনাগের কর্তৃন সতালণ্ডে জীবুক সুভাসচন্দ্র বহু]

Subhas, Jawaharlal and other Congress leaders watching a movie organized
to raise funds for political prisoners in Bengal.
Jugantar, Vol. 2, Issue 79 (24 December 1938, British Library, EAP262/1/2/357.

proposed plan, 'I shall beg you to permit me to relieve myself of my present responsibilities at an early date for I cannot be a party to a policy which I sincerely believe to be harmful to the national interest.'[72]

Gandhi's response is not available, but clearly he would not have liked to have an ultimatum thrown at him. And that would have certainly helped reinforce his decision regarding the choice of the next president of the Congress.

The nationalist press and several political parties had already started discussing the next Congress presidency. By mid-October, it was clear that a substantial amount of support for Subhas's second term as the Congress president was building up. The *National Front*, the mouthpiece of the leftist parties, and the *Hitavada* of Nagpur, a newspaper founded by Gopal Krishna Gokhale, extended their support to Subhas's re-election.[73] The nationalist Muslim leadership in Bengal, led by Humayun Kabir and others, claimed that there was no one other than Subhas who could carry along with him both the left and the right wings of the Congress. More importantly, from the perspective of Bengal, which had become the hotbed of communal conflict, they argued that it was critical for Subhas to be allowed to continue with his programme of economic and social reconstruction so that the communal problem could be amicably resolved. Support also came in from the Gujarat Congress Socialists.[74] During his visit at the end of October, Shillong's district youth association and the district Congress Socialist Party too announced their support.[75] The Leftist leaders in Bengal, such as Muzaffar Ahmed, Somnath Lahiri, Bimal Prativa Debi, Suresh Banerjee, Sibnath Banerjee, Deben Sen and Bankim Mukherjee issued an appeal in the first week of November to all Congress organizations in the country to re-elect Subhas[76] and the Congress committees in Assam and Orissa too declared their support.[77] Despite his disagreements with Subhas on some organizational matters, the veteran scientist and entrepreneur P.C. Ray sent an appeal to Gandhi in support of Subhas.[78] Rabindranath Tagore too sent his recommendation for Subhas to Gandhi. Praising his efforts to promote industrialization in India, *Marhatta* too recommended Subhas's re-election.[79] The All-India Students' Conference held in Calcutta on the first two days of 1939 passed a resolution demanding the re-election of Subhas as the Congress president.[80] Apart from these, appeals were issued by several district Congress committees and leaders in Bengal.

As early as in October, Gandhi wrote to Manibehn Patel, Vallabhbhai's daughter, that 'there is bound to be some difficulty this time in electing the

President'. To Tagore, he wrote towards the end of November that he did not favour Subhas's re-election. 'I have replied saying my personal opinion was that he [Subhas] needed to be free from the Presidential work, if he was to rid Bengal of corruption', Gandhi reported to Jawaharlal about his reply to Tagore. At the time of the working committee meeting in Wardha in the second week of December, he had a two-hour discussion on the issue with Azad and Jawaharlal. According to Kripalani, after the meeting of the working committee on 16 December, Gandhiji, Azad, Vallabhbhai, Jawaharlal and he met informally and discussed the question of the next president. 'It was known at the time that Subhas sought a second term of office, but we were unanimous that Maulana should be the president', he recalled.[81]

The press had somehow already gotten a whiff of what was going on. The *Jugantar* asked on 15 December: 'No hope for Subhas's re-election?' It reported that despite the expression of support for Subhas from various quarters, the 'high command' was not impressed and wanted Azad to become the next president.[82]

By the end of December, Gandhi had made up his mind. On 21 December he wrote to Jawaharlal, 'Maulana Saheb does not want the crown of thorns. If you want to try again please do. If you won't or he won't listen, Pattabhi [Sitaramayya] seems to be the only choice.'[83]

Gandhi's letter makes it clear that his objection was not towards having a leftist president, but with Subhas, increasingly proving his point made a year ago to Vallabhbhai. A leftist president was acceptable if he was dependable, which Subhas was not.

Despite the noise around him, it appears that Subhas had not made up his mind till the third week of December. Speaking in Bombay, he said that once he was relieved of the duty of the Congress president, it would be possible for him to move a resolution at the next plenary session at Tripuri for paralysing the administration if the British Government did not respond to the Congress's demand of complete independence.[84]

An ill Subhas presided over the working committee meeting at Bardoli from 11 to 14 January. Although contemporary press reports and the *Indian Annual Register* mentioned Subhas's presence at the meeting, Kripalani strangely claimed that when the matter of election of the next president was discussed, Subhas was absent. According to Kripalani,

Four names had been proposed for the presidentship of the next Congress: Subhas, Maulana, Sardar, and Pattabhi. Maulana was unwilling to be a party to the contest, but was, however, persuaded by Gandhiji and some of us not to withdraw his candidature, and yielded to our pressure. As soon as he consented to stand, Sardar withdrew his nomination, leaving only three candidates in the field. Having consented at Bardoli, Maulana left for Bombay. A couple of days later he wrote back to Gandhiji that he did not want to contest the election, and also announced his withdrawal in the press. While withdrawing his name he said he was doing so in favour of Pattabhi.[85]

When Vallabhbhai and some others publicly referred to this discussion, Subhas responded that he was not aware that the question of presidentship of the Congress had ever been discussed by the working committee.[86] The working committee deliberating on an issue and arriving at a decision by keeping the president in the dark was, however, a reflection of not only the manner in which the Gandhian leadership functioned, but also of the fact that Subhas was still considered an outsider.

Just before leaving Bombay for Calcutta, Subhas issued a statement covering three broad points. Firstly, he criticized the drift towards constitutionalism among the Congress's right wing. The acceptance of office had undoubtedly enhanced the Congress's prestige, but at the same time accentuated the 'weaker elements in the national character', with many joining the organization in the hope of enjoying the fruits without the need for further struggle. Secondly, he asked the left wing to cooperate with the right wing to the extent that was possible, to achieve the goal of Purna Swaraj, but rued the lack of leftist unity over petty differences. 'Those who believe in Leftism would do well to consider what steps they could take to organise and discipline all radical elements in the Congress on the basis of a clear-cut programme', he said. Subhas took a jibe at those Congressmen, without naming anyone, who he believed were trying to 'whittle down the Congress resolution of uncompromising hostility to Federation.' As far as the federal scheme was concerned, Subhas believed that the question was no more of how to fight the scheme, but what to do if the scheme was silently dropped or postponed sine die.[87] There was still no word from him on contesting the presidential election.

Subhas reached Calcutta on the morning of 16 January. On the same day, Kripalani publicly announced the candidacy of Subhas, Azad and Sitaramayya. 29 January was fixed as the date when delegates from the provinces would vote to elect the next president.[88]

A group of labour leaders from Bengal, who had earlier rooted for Subhas as the next Congress president, including Bankim Mukherjee, Sibnath Banerjee, Deben Sen, Somnath Lahiri and Muzaffar Ahmed, issued another statement reiterating their support for Subhas and opposing Azad's nomination, calling it a communal approach. They questioned whether Azad's election would, in any way, help to bridge the gap with non-Congress Muslims or Congress's Muslim outreach programme, especially when a number of nationalist Muslim leaders had already expressed their support for Subhas. The real reason for nominating Azad, they claimed, was to institute someone at the helm who could be easily influenced to accept the federal scheme with minor tweaking.[89]

The issue of the election turned into a war of words, with Azad declaring on 20 January that he was stepping away from the contest in favour of Sitaramayya, a Gandhian loyalist from Andhra Pradesh. On his way to Santiniketan on Rabindranath's invitation, Subhas issued a statement the next day on the issue, explaining for the first time why he had not withdrawn from the contest, and asking for an election based on a definite programme, as he found that the delegates from a number of provinces had already nominated him. He made it clear that in 'discussing this question all false sense of modesty will have to be put aside for the issue is not a personal one'.

The progressive sharpening of the anti-imperialist struggle in India has given birth to new ideas, ideologies, problems and programmes. People are consequently veering round to the opinion that as in other free countries the Presidential election in India should be fought on the basis of definite problems and programmes so that the contest may help the clarification of issues and give a clear indication of the working of the public mind. An election contest in these circumstances may not be an undesirable thing . . . In view of the increasing international tension and the prospective fight over Federation the new year will be a momentous one in our national history. Owing to this and other reasons, if my services in office are demanded by the majority of the delegates with what justification can I withdraw from the contest . . . If, however, as a result of the appeal made by eminent leaders like Maulana Azad the majority of the delegates vote against my re-election I shall loyally abide by their verdict and shall continue to serve the Congress and the country as an ordinary soldier . . .[90]

Subhas's statement found support from thirty Muslim leaders of the Bengal Congress, and from newspapers like *Jugantar*.

Welcoming Subhas in the famous Amra Kunja on 21 January, Rabindranath said:

> In my mind I have accepted you as the leader of the nation. I have decided that I will speak about it to the people. I don't know other provinces and my words will not have the same force there, but I know Bengal and Bengalis. Bengal today is in dire situation and that is why you will have to respond if I call upon you.[91]

The response came from the Gandhian group—Vallabhbhai, Rajendra Prasad, Jairamdas Doulatram, J.B. Kripalani, Jamnalal Bajaj, Shankarrao Deo and Bhulabhai Desai—on 24 January, asking Subhas to step down in favour of Sitaramayya, and telling him that ideologies, policies and programmes were not relevant to the election of the president. In the view of these seven members of the working committee, the post of the president was largely ornamental like that of a 'Constitutional Monarch', since the 'Congress policy and programmes are not determined by its successive Presidents'. The claim was not wrong in the context of Congress tradition, but Subhas had time and again taken a strong stand on issues, even threatening to resign if required, demonstrating that he was not going to act according to the expectations of the Gandhi group when matters of principle were concerned.

Both Subhas and Sarat questioned the fairness of members of the working committee taking sides in the presidential election.[92]

'We do not see, from the democratic point of view, the necessity and propriety of the seven Working Committee members' statement issued from Bardoli on the 24th January last, though party tactics may have necessitated its issue,' commented *The Modern Review*. Referring to Azad's statement, the magazine wrote, '. . . members of the Congress Working Committee, of whom the Maulana is one, are not ordinary members. They are colleagues of the President and his nominees. For any one of them to practically oppose the re-election of the present incumbent, knowing that he is a candidate, does not seem to us proper'. The *Jugantar*, which was in principle against a contest, commented, 'simply put, the statement of the seven working committee members imply that their wish must be construed as the wish of the nation and whoever they choose must be accepted by all as the Congress president. This mentality is not only deplorable, but viewed from the democratic perspective is as dangerous as fascism'.

Subhas contested the statement of the seven members in his statement issued on 25 January:

> If the President is to be elected by the delegates and not be nominated by influential members of the Working Committee, will Sardar Patel and other leaders withdraw their whip and leave it to the delegates to vote as they like? . . . Otherwise why not end the elective system and have the President nominated by the Working Committee.
>
> It is news to me that there is a rule that the same person should not be re-elected President except under exceptional circumstances. If one traces the history of the Congress one will find that in several cases the same person has been elected more than once. I am also surprised at the remark that Presidential elections have hitherto been unanimous. I remember to have voted for one candidate in preference to another on several occasions. It is only in recent years that the election has been unanimous.
>
> . . . The position of the President today is no longer analogous to that of the Chairman of a meeting. The President is the Prime Minister or the President of the United States of America who nominates his own Cabinet.[93]

Subhas then proceeded to lay some serious charges against his colleagues:

> . . . the questions of policy and programme are not irrelevant and they would have been raised long ago in connection with the election of the Congress President had it not been for the fact that after the Congress of 1934, a leftist has been elected as President every time with the support of both the right and left-wings. The departure from this practice this year and the attempt to set up a rightist candidate for the office of the President is not without significance. It is widely believed that there is a prospect of a compromise on the Federal scheme between the right-wing of the Congress and the British Government during the coming year. Consequently the right-wing do not want a leftist President who may be a thorn in the way of a compromise and may put obstacles in the path of negotiations. One has only to move about among the public and enter into a discussion with them in order to realise how widespread this belief

is. It is imperative, in the circumstances, to have a President who will be an anti-federationist to the core of his heart.[94]

In other words, Subhas made it clear that he trusted none of the Gandhian core group members, not even Jawaharlal. He stated emphatically that he was ready to step away from the contest even at this late hour 'if a genuine anti-federationist, like Achary Narendra Deo for instance, be accepted as the President for the coming year'. This was not to go down well at all with the old guard.

Sitaramayya issued a statement on the same day, declaring proudly that 'I am an ardent devotee of the cult of Gandhism is a fact fairly well-known in the country'. Refuting Subhas's accusation, he stated that 'there is no attempt on the part of any member of the Working Committee to enter into a compromise with the British on the question of Federation'. He would not withdraw from the contest 'because I must not resist the will of valued colleagues'.

In his statement issued on the same day, Vallabhbhai admitted that the issue of presidentship was discussed informally between the members of the working committee on multiple occasions during the Bardoli working committee meetings, 'not by design but by accident' and it was decided that 'it was unnecessary to re-elect Mr Subhas Bose'. The Sardar, however, neither explained why the decision was not communicated to Subhas, who also happened to be at the same place and had been presiding over meetings, nor why the members felt that it was unnecessary to re-elect Subhas.

Statements followed from Jawaharlal on 26 and from Rajendra Prasad on 27 January. While Jawaharlal was not against a contest and did not agree that the post of the president was ornamental, he refuted Subhas on the issue of Federation, claiming that 'it seems to be monstrous for any Congressman to think in terms of compromising on Federation'. Jawaharlal clarified that he did not want Subhas to stand for the election for the same reason that he himself did not agree to be nominated—'I felt that his and my capacity for effective work would be lessened by holding this office at this stage'—and he had communicated it to Subhas. Rajendra Prasad criticized Subhas for being vague about his own programme while accusing other working committee members for their 'imaginary views.'

This was followed by two more statements from Subhas, on 27 and 28 January, where he not only repeated his charge that although 'the

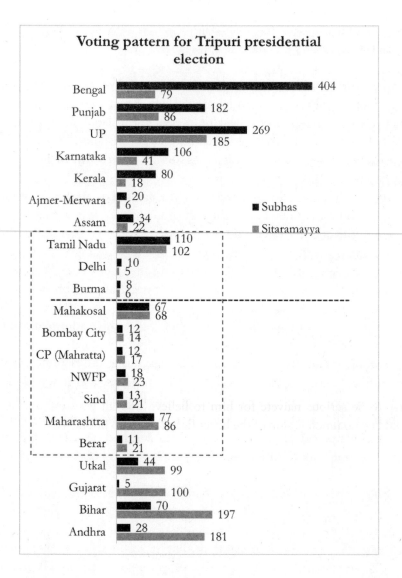

Voting pattern for Tripuri presidential election

Region	Subhas	Sitaramayya
Bengal	404	79
Punjab	182	86
UP	269	185
Karnataka	106	41
Kerala	80	18
Ajmer-Merwara	20	6
Assam	34	22
Tamil Nadu	110	102
Delhi	10	5
Burma	8	6
Mahakosal	67	68
Bombay City	12	14
CP (Mahratta)	12	17
NWFP	18	23
Sind	13	21
Maharashtra	77	86
Berar	11	21
Utkal	44	99
Gujarat	5	100
Bihar	70	197
Andhra	28	181

Congress resolution on Federation is one of uncompromising hostility, the fact remains that some influential Congress leaders have been advocating conditional acceptance of the Federal scheme in private and public', but went further to allege that it is 'generally believed that the prospective list of Ministers for the Federal Cabinet has already been drawn up'. He asked why some important members of the working committee were so much against him 'though there was a general desire in the Congress ranks for my re-election'. Subhas wondered, 'Do they object to me because I would not be a tool in their hands? Or do they object to me because of my ideas and principles?'[95]

At this juncture, Minoo Masani, Yusuf Meherali, Rafi Ahmed Kidwai, Swami Sahajananda, Sardul Singh Caveeshar and Jayaprakash Narayan too declared their support for Subhas. Although he was not a member of Congress any more, N.B. Khare issued a statement soliciting support for Subhas.[96]

When the ballots were counted, it emerged that 1580 delegates had voted for Subhas and 1377 for Sitaramayya. While Subhas obtained majority in ten out of twenty-one provincial committees, with Bengal, Punjab, UP and Karnataka voting heavily for him, Sitaramayya won large victories in Odisha, Gujarat, Bihar and Andhra. Voting in ten provincial committees was settled by a difference of ten votes or less.

As the news of his victory came in, Subhas issued a statement asserting that the elections had created no division in the Congress and that the organization stood united as before. Since the contest was not a personal one, there was no ill-feeling between any individual, he claimed. It was not the time to celebrate, but to accept the great responsibility with deep humility.[97]

With nearly two decades of Congress experience behind him, it would have to be serious naivete for him to believe that all was well and there would be no repercussion of the bitter fight fought so publicly and resulting in the humiliation of his combined opponents.

8

Cul-de-sac (1939–40)

While the war of statements and counterstatements was raging on in the public domain, one man held his silence, only to speak after the dust seemed to have settled. But that was just the calm before the storm. The battle lines had been drawn. Whether Subhas realized it or not, his opponents were biding their time to come at him with the full force of satya and ahimsa, waiting for the signal.[1]

There was never any doubt that Subhas had a great regard for Gandhi the man, and for the role he had played in transforming the character of India's struggle for freedom. Politically and mentally, however, their differences were too big to be bridged. Subhas had started opposing Gandhi's policies and strategies very publicly even when he was a greenhorn in the Congress, which reached the highest pitch in his 1933 joint statement with Vithalbhai Patel against Gandhi. With his larger-than-life stature, Gandhi could afford to (and he did) play down Subhas's dissenting voice as long as he wished. The occasional periods of truce and bonhomie, with 1937 and 1938 being the best period, however, did not alter Gandhi's fundamental attitude towards Subhas. He was still 'not at all dependable'. And now he had thrown a direct challenge not only to Gandhi's policies, but to his indisputable grip over Congress leadership.

Gandhi's statement issued on 31 January was a mix of the grace and strictness of a mentor, but laced with biting sarcasm and a hint of a challenge. It set the tone for what Subhas was about to face very soon:

Shri Subhas Bose has achieved a decisive victory over his opponent, Dr. Pattabhi Sitaramayya. I must confess that from the very beginning I was decidedly against his re-election for reasons into which I need not go. I do not subscribe to his facts or the arguments in his manifestos. I think that his references to his colleagues were unjustified and unworthy. Nevertheless, I am glad of his victory. And since I was instrumental in inducing Dr. Pattabhi not to withdraw his name as a candidate when Maulana Saheb withdrew, the defeat is more mine than his. I am nothing if I do not represent definite principles and policy. Therefore, it is plain to me that the delegates do not approve of the principles and policy for which I stand.

. . . Subhas Babu, instead of being President on the sufferance of those whom he calls rightists, is now President elected in a contested election. This enables him to choose a homogeneous Cabinet and enforce his programme without let or hindrance.

. . . My writings in the *Harijan* have shown that the Congress is fast becoming a corrupt organization in the sense that its registers contain a very large number of bogus members. I have been suggesting for the past many months the overhauling of these registers. I have no doubt that many of the delegates who have been elected on the strength of these bogus voters would be unseated on scrutiny . . .

. . . After all Subhas Babu is not an enemy of his country. He has suffered for it. In his opinion his is the most forward and boldest policy and programme. The minority can only wish it all success. If they cannot keep pace with it, they must come out of the Congress. If they can, they will add strength to the majority.

The minority may not obstruct on any account. They must abstain when they cannot co-operate. I must remind all Congressmen that those who, being Congress-minded, remain outside it by design, represent it most. Those, therefore, who feel uncomfortable in being in the Congress may come out, not in a spirit of ill will, but with the deliberate purpose of rendering more effective service.[2]

The popular Bengali monthly *Masik Basumati* asked caustically, 'When Mahatma Gandhi is not even a four anna member of the Congress, why is he so perturbed by the victory of Subhas?'[3] *Bharatbarsha* argued that the people had not known that by voting against Sitaramayya they were in fact voting against Gandhi. But even if they had known, there was no reason for Gandhi to be so upset with the results of a democratic exercise.[4]

Avoiding any signs of bitterness, Subhas responded that his victory was not a reflection of the country's attitude towards Gandhi, but of the two issues of federation and the right of the delegates to make their

choice regarding the next president freely, which he had placed before the
electorate. Now that the results were out, there was 'neither reason nor
justification for a split within the ranks of the Congress'. He said that 'I
shall try till the last to avert a split whenever any such likelihood appears
before us'.

Subhas assured that there was not going to be any 'violent break with
the past in the Parliamentary or the extra-Parliamentary sphere'. Although
he had had his share of disagreements with Gandhi, he said, he yielded
'to none in my respect for his personality'. His statement ended with what
read like a desperate plea to gain back Gandhi's favour:

> I do not know what sort of opinion Mahatmaji has of me. But whatever
> his view may be, it will always be my aim and object to try and win his
> confidence for the simple reason that it will be a tragic thing for me if
> I succeed in winning the confidence of other people but fail to win the
> confidence of India's greatest man.[5]

On the occasion of the district Congress conference presided over by Kiran
Sankar Roy, Maldah accorded a grand reception to Subhas on 1 February.
Having received a message from Jawaharlal, who was visiting Bengal at that
time, Subhas went to Santiniketan to meet him on the next day. Subhas
also met Rabindranath briefly.[6] He barely had any time to rest, arriving at
Jharia the next day to address a meeting of the coal mine workers. Then, on
4 February, he travelled to Jalpaiguri to attend the annual Bengal Provincial
Conference.

The main resolution adopted by the conference, which was expected to
be placed before the Tripuri session, reflected the tone of the Bengal Congress
led by the Bose brothers. The resolution was moved by Narendra Narayan
Chakrabarty and supported by Bankim Mukherjee and Leela Nag. It read:

> This Conference recommends to the Tripuri Session of the Indian
> National Congress the following resolution for its adoption:
> . . . We have reached a stage in our history when it is not enough
> merely to declare our rejection of the Government of India Act, 1935.
> It is time for the Indian people to demand in the most unmistakable
> manner a constitution of their own making.
> To this end the Congress calls upon the British Government to
> concede the principle of self-determination to India and recognise in its

entirety the constitution based on self-determination which the Congress will submit in accordance with the popular will. This constitution shall be embodied in a treaty between India and Great Britain which will define the future relations before the two countries. The treaty will be drawn up by representatives of the Congress and the British Government and shall be ratified by the Congress on the one side and the British Parliament on the other. In the event, however, of negotiations between representatives of the Congress and British Government breaking down, the Congress will be free to take such measures as it considers desirable with a view to making India's demand for self-determination irresistible.

A period of six months should be fixed within which the British Government would be expected to give a categorical reply to India's national demand. In the event of the reply being unsatisfactory and inadequate, or no reply being received at all, the Congress will take such steps or resort to such sanction as it considers necessary in order to enforce the national demand. In the meantime, during this period of six months, all Congress organisations in the country will be called upon to take necessary steps in Parliamentary and extra-Parliamentary spheres for preparing the Indian people for the coming struggle.[7]

Bengal was prepared to issue an ultimatum, and the Gandhians were not going to like it.

Several leaders who had supported Subhas's re-election, like Satyapal, Sardul Singh Caveeshar, Jayaprakash Narayan, Lala Shankar Lal, Ajoy Ghosh and Srinivas Iyengar came to Calcutta to discuss and develop a common programme on 7 February, convened by Subhas at Sarat's house. M.N. Roy and Narendra Deo were supposed to join the meeting, but they were unable to attend it.[8] It came to light a couple of weeks later, from a letter written by Vishwambhar Dayal Tripathi to Congress organizations in the United Provinces (UP), that the two-day informal meeting of the leaders convened by Subhas at Sarat's house on 7 and 8 February, had agreed on a programme to give the British Government an ultimatum to withdraw the federal scheme and announce the formation of a constituent assembly for drawing up the constitution of a free India within six months.[9]

Immediately thereafter, Subhas left to inaugurate a political conference in Gaya. Down with fever again, Subhas continued his deliberations on the programme for the upcoming Congress session, before travelling to Anand

Bhawan in Allahabad as Jawaharlal's guest, on 13 February. The next day, he was on his way to Wardha to meet Gandhi. Subhas informed the press that the details of the discussion could not be divulged until the meeting of the working committee scheduled on 22 February.[10]

In the middle of this, the Home Secretary announced in the Central Legislative Assembly on 14 February that the Government had decided to lift the ban on *The Indian Struggle*.[11]

Rumours, in the meantime, had started flying that the Gandhian working committee members were ready to resign from it. Gandhi, in fact, had already informed Subhas on 5 February that:

> So far as I can judge, the old colleagues whom you consider as rightists will not serve on your cabinet. You can have their resignation now, if that would be more convenient for you. Their presence would be unfair to you and to them. You should be left free to frame your own programme . . .[12]

Cartoon in *Jugantar* by Kafi Khan (Pratul Chandra Lahiri): Subhas standing outside the Congress working committee office thinking, 'Where have all the members gone?' *Jugantar*, Vol. 2, Issue 114 (5 February 1939), British Library, EAP262-1-2-391.

Subhas reached Calcutta on 17 February, running high temperatures, and over the next few days, his condition continued to deteriorate. His elder brother Sunil diagnosed him with bronchopneumonia in his left lung, and recommended complete rest till he recovered.[13]

On the other side, Vallabhbhai, Bhulabhai, Rajendra Prasad and Kripalani discussed their possible course of action with Gandhi at Sevagram on 20 February. Reportedly, three possibilities were discussed. The first was to resign en masse in the next meeting of the working committee on 22 February, by refusing to take responsibility for the programme proposed by Subhas; the second option was to table a no-confidence motion in the All India Congress Committee (AICC) meeting; and the third was to vote against the proposals presented by Subhas at the AICC meeting. The dominant view was to resign en bloc at the working committee meeting, but they resolved to wait until the meeting before taking any final decision.[14]

The wait was over soon. Thirteen out of the fourteen members of the working committee, that is, all except Sarat, sent their resignations to Subhas on 21 February.

The account of the events leading to the resignations, as available from Kripalani on one hand and Subhas himself on the other, throws some light on how both sides were thinking—and it does not reflect well on the Gandhian group.

Decades later Kripalani recalled:

I, as general secretary, called a meeting of the Working Committee at Wardha on 9 February 1939. It was a routine meeting, always held to prepare the draft resolutions that were to be placed before the session. This was necessary to save time at the session, which is usually held for two or three days. Subhas did not attend this meeting due to ill health.

He, however, wired to say that no meeting of the Working Committee should be held in his absence and that it should meet at Tripuri. In this, Subhas forgot that it was usual for the Working Committee to meet even if the president was for any reason prevented from attending it. This prohibition against meeting to transact routine business was considered by the members assembled at Wardha as a vote of no-confidence in them. Consequently, twelve members of the Working Committee tendered their resignation . . .[15]

One will need to speculate whether Kripalani's memory played truant with him or if he deliberately chose to ignore the actual sequence of events, but his account is far from accurate. As was widely anticipated at the time and as Gandhi's letter to Subhas made it clear, the question of resignation by the Gandhian group (also mockingly called 'Vallabhachari'—followers of Vallabhbhai—by a section of the Bengali press) was a settled issue and just a matter of time. Secondly, it was an oversimplification to claim that the working committee was planning to meet only for routine business.

As Subhas's account shows, there was no question of the other working committee members feeling slighted by him asking for the meeting to be postponed. Subhas wrote soon after the Tripuri Congress:

> Doctors began to give me repeated warnings that it was impossible to go to Wardha. If I gave up all thought of the Working Committee and concentrated my mind on getting well, I might be able to go to the Tripuri Congress—otherwise, even Tripuri might have to be dropped. But all these warnings were like speaking to a deaf person. My preparations went on despite medical advice, and, thanks to friends, I had an aeroplane ready to take me to Nagpur on or about the 22nd February.
>
> On the 21st, I slowly began to realise that the doctors were right and that it was quite impossible to go to Wardha either by train or by plane. I informed Mahatma Gandhi and Sardar Patel by wire to that effect and suggested postponement of the Working Committee meeting till the Tripuri Congress. At that time I had not the faintest idea that the twelve (of thirteen) members of the Working Committee would resign almost immediately.
>
> Much fuss has been made by interested parties over the above two telegrams and it has been alleged that I did not permit the Working Committee to transact even routine business. Such an allegation is altogether unfounded. In the first place, there was nothing in the telegrams to indicate that I did not want the Working Committee to go through routine business . . . In the second place, in my telegram to Sardar Patel, after giving my view regarding postponement, I requested him to ascertain the views of other members ad wire same to me. The reply to my telegrams was the resignation of twelve members of the Working Committee. If these members had desired to frame the resolutions for the Tripuri Congress in my absence, I would certainly not have stood in their way . . . My only anxiety was to have such draft resolutions for the Congress prepared by the Working Committee as all the members would agree to—otherwise there was this danger that when the 'official' draft resolutions came up before the Subjects

Committee, members of the Working Committee would be found arrayed on different sides.

. . . The following telegram was sent by me to Sardar Patel on the February 21st:

Sardar Patel, Wardha
KINDLY SEE MY TELEGRAM TO MAHATMAJI. REGRETFULLY FEEL WORKING COMMITTEE MUST BE POSTPONED TILL CONGRESS. PLEASE CONSULT COLLEAGUES AND WIRE OPINION—SUBHAS.[16]

Cartoon in *Jugantar* by Kafi Khan (Pratul Chandra Lahiri) showing Subhas being offered all sorts of medication and religious remedies to help him recover from his 'strange illness'. *Jugantar*, Vol. 2, Issue 169 (9 April 1939), British Library, EAP262-1-2-450.

Kripalani, however, gave out the real reasons for the old guard's opposition to Subhas, and not surprisingly, the statements issued by Subhas on the issue of federation and the left–right divide, which were apparently insulting to them, was not the most important one:

[Differences with Subhas] had nothing to do with the desire of any member of the Working Committee to accept federation, as Subhas tried to make out. It was also not a question of 'right' or 'left' . . .

It was known that Subhas's views on two important matters went against those held by the majority of members of the Working Committee and Gandhiji. These were not clearly spelt out by Subhas during his first term of office . . .

The two matters about which there were differences were: the first, relating to giving the British government an ultimatum to quit India within a specified period on pain of resumption of the Civil Disobedience Movement on the widest possible scale; the second point of difference was about the role the Congress should play in the freedom movements then underway in the Indian states. . . .[17]

. . . Under these circumstances, had he formed a composite Working Committee as he desired, he would have placed before it the two propositions enunciated in his presidential address at Tripuri. In that case, those who differed from them would have had to resign, or alternatively, he himself would have had to do so, creating an ugly situation. It was, therefore, better for those who differed from him to oppose his election and later to refuse to join his proposed composite Working Committee.[18]

Kripalani argued that Subhas was 'too optimistic about the ultimatum'. More importantly, Gandhi, who was the sole authority on initiating civil disobedience, did not feel that India was non-violent enough to launch another movement: the Congress had no control over those who believed in violence. According to Kripalani, it was not possible for the Congress to agitate for democratic self-government in the Indian states when British India itself was not free. Doing so would give the British a chance to portray the struggle as a conflict between two sections of Indians, as they exaggerated the divide between different communities.

Apart from these two reasons, there was another one 'which could not for obvious reason be mentioned at that time'. It was the use of violence in the struggle for independence. 'The discerning could see something of it', wrote Kripalani, in Subhas's utterances, which was proved true by his later actions. Letting Subhas preside over the Congress was, thus, too much of a risk for too many reasons.[19]

What could Subhas have done? Not much, as it turned out—he was restrained by the forces of the circumstances and probably by his failure to read his opponents fully.

Coincidental as the timing might appear, Gordhanbhai Patel, the sole surviving executor of Vithalbhai's will, that bequeathed the balance amount of his assets, after disposal of the gifts specified by Vithalbhai to Subhas, decided to legally challenge Subhas's right to the assigned amount on 20 January 1939. Vallabhbhai was the moving force behind this challenge, although Gordhanbhai remained at the front. When Vallabhbhai had seen the will for the first time, Gordhanbhai recollected in his memoirs, he 'wanted me to ascertain why all the three men who attested Vithalbhai's signature were men who hailed from Bengal and why two of them were merely students, in spite of the fact that eminent persons like Bhulabhai Desai, Walchand Hirachand, Ambalal Sarabhai and others who were particularly friendly with Vithalbhai, were present at the time in Switzerland, round about Geneva'.[20] The insinuation was unmistakable. Complex legal arguments were woven to contest the clause in Vithalbhai's will that bequeathed assets to Subhas, resulting in a long-drawn legal battle.

This was the first time after Chittaranjan Das that Gandhi's position and policies were facing a challenge from Bengal. Das had challenged the Gandhian leadership, and through his political skills, wrested a victory out of many defeats. But that is where the similarity ends. The differences of the circumstances, which are clear, actually help to understand the differences between the political skills of Das and Subhas. Whereas Chittaranjan approached the Congress with a clear alternative to Gandhi's own and worked to garner support for his programme, Subhas did not put any clearly articulated programme on the table relating to federation or ultimatum. In fact, he could not or did not provide any evidence that the Gandhian wing of the Congress was moving towards a compromise on the federal scheme. His allegations were based entirely on perception and rumours, whereas all the working committee members had, in reality, committed to the Congress's stand against federation. The issue was complex, and if there were subtle movements which Subhas interpreted as signals for a compromise, he failed to build up a concrete case. Yet, so strong was this perception among the left wing that they believed that Subhas could ride on it to his victory.

The second difference was that of the strategy adopted by Chittaranjan in carrying the fight to the finish without caring for what Gandhi, or his followers who controlled the Congress, would think of him. By contrast, at a moment when Subhas had practically gotten the mandate to put together a working committee of his own choice, he spent all his time and energy on placating Gandhi and his followers in the working committee, rather than constructing an alternative. Although on the surface it might appear as if Subhas lacked his mentor's tact and resourcefulness to drive home the victory that he had won, it was not the whole picture.

Chittaranjan had succeeded in consolidating the support of important national and regional leaders like Motilal Nehru, Vithalbhai Patel, Mukhtar Ahmad Ansari, Hakim Ajmal Khan, B.S. Moonje, M.R. Jayakar, N.C. Kelkar, A. Rangaswami Iyengar, S. Satyamurti and Rafi Ahmed Kidwai, among others, in the form of the Swarajya party. By contrast, although Subhas obtained the support of the majority of the AICC delegates, a number of key regional leaders, the Congress Socialist Party (CSP) and other left organizations, the support was not consolidated in the form of an organized body which could step in to replace the old guard. Yet, the support for him failed to translate into support for his programme. Significantly, the executive council of the CSP—the most well-organized forces among these—resolved on 20 February that although the party had supported Subhas as the most suitable candidate, it did not see him as the representative of the leftists and also did not want Congress to be divided into opposing factions.[21] The *National Front*, the mouthpiece of the Communist Party, also argued for the necessity of coordination between the left and the right wings to ensure unity.[22]

That the CSP was not entirely wrong in their assessment is evident from the views expressed by Padma Kant Malaviya, grandnephew of Madan Mohan Malaviya and editor and publisher of the well-known Hindi journal *Abhyudaya*. 'I myself voted for Mr Bose not because I am a socialist but to signify my opposition to the present method of administration of the High Command', Malaviya told reporters. At the same time, he warned that Subhas should not oppose or discard Gandhism as the Congress creed.[23] The support for Subhas was fractured, comprising disparate elements, and he had the unenviable task of organizing it on a common platform, which was all but impossible.

Moreover, the man whom Subhas would have liked most to have beside him—Jawaharlal Nehru—chose to remain with Gandhi although he professed neutrality, just as he had done at the time his father had gone over to the Swarajya party. In fact, his letter to Subhas, written separately from the other twelve members of the working committee, was so vague that there was confusion over whether he had resigned or not.

The rivalry between the leading newspapers in Bengal too was shaping the situation for Subhas to some extent. The stringent criticism of Gandhian politics and organizations by the *Anandabazar Patrika* and the *Hindusthan Standard* in support of Subhas produced a strong reaction from the old rivals and staunchly Gandhian *Amrita Bazar Patrika* and *Jugantar*, introducing, in the process, a gradual shift to being more critical towards Subhas. Writing in support of Subhas was one thing, but being too critical of Gandhi's leadership was not acceptable. This trend was only to strengthen over time.

The Tripuri session was scheduled to be inaugurated on 10 March, but after examining Subhas on 27 February, Dr Nilratan Sarkar found him affected by bronchopneumonia and clearly stated that any activity during this time could seriously damage his health.[24] Subhas's secretary requested the reception committee of the Tripuri session for a postponement, but as a significant amount of effort and money had already been invested, it was a request that understandably could not be accommodated.

Cartoon in *Jugantar* by Kafi Khan (Pratul Chandra Lahiri): Holi celebrations. Subhas telling the working committee members, 'You cannot run away, I will colour you all in red.' *Jugantar*, Vol. 2, Issue 138 (5 March 1939), British Library, EAP262-1-2-415.

From 3 March, Gandhi began a fast unto death, in protest against the Thakore of the princely state of Rajkot. The Thakore had reneged on an agreement he had reached with Vallabhbhai to appoint a committee of ten state subjects, out of which seven of them were to be recommended

by Vallabhbhai, for drawing up a scheme of reforms in the state giving
more power to the people. Subhas sent a wire to Gandhi, praying for his
success and good health, and appealed for a countrywide observance of
All India Rajkot Day on 5 March.[25] Gandhi broke his fast unto death on
7 March, as the Viceroy appointed the Chief Justice of India, Maurice
Gwyer, to find out whether the Thakore had violated his agreement with
Vallabhbhai.[26]

Accompanied by his mother, his brother Sunil and his wife and their
daughter Ila, and his secretaries, Subhas left for Tripuri by the Bombay
Mail on 5 March, despite his precarious state of health, ignoring all advice
from his physicians. A number of delegates from Bengal also travelled in
the same train. Reaching Jubbulpore the next day, Subhas was carried
out of the train in a stretcher and taken to the Congress venue in an
ambulance.

Azad presided over the AICC meeting on 7 March as Subhas was too
unwell to attend. Hectic consultations went on at the venue to determine
the course of action over the next few days. While the twelve resigning
members of the working committee closeted themselves for hours (with
Rajagopalachari present at the deliberations), some of them went and met
Subhas too.

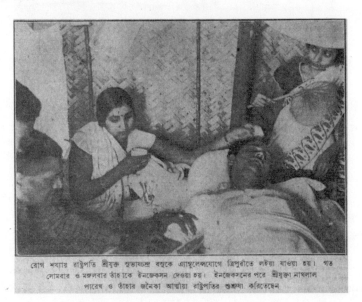

রোগ শয্যায় রাষ্ট্রপতি শ্রীযুক্ত সুভাষচন্দ্র বসুকে অ্যাম্বুলেন্সযোগে ত্রিপুরীতে লইয়া যাওয়া হয়। গত
সোমবার ও মঙ্গলবার তাঁহাকে ইনজেকসন দেওয়া হয়। ইনজেকসনের পরে শ্রীযুক্ত নাথালাল
পারেখ ও তাঁহার জনৈক আত্মীয়া রাষ্ট্রপতির শুশ্রূষা করিতেছেন

Subhas being taken to Tripuri in an ambulance under the care of Nathalal Parikh.
Jugantar, Vol. 2, Issue 142 (10 March 1939), British Library, EAP262-1-2-419.

At the Tripuri Congress.
Jugantar, Vol. 2, Issue 143 (11 March 1939), British Library, EAP262-1-2-420.

When the session began the next day afternoon, Subhas was brought in a stretcher, accompanied by physicians. The scene was symbolically significant as, instead of being on the podium with the president, the former members of the working committee sat below with the delegates, leaving Subhas alone on the stage. It was only when Subhas requested them to take their seat beside him, the members, led by Vallabhbhai, climbed on to the stage.

The non-violent assault began almost immediately, with a delegate challenging the power of the president to accept the resignations of working committee members. Sarat's explanation of the Congress constitution, however, led to the rejection of the question raised.

Next, Govind Vallabh Pant gave a notice for moving a resolution supported by 160 members. The proposed resolution, inter alia, said:

The [All India Congress] Committee declares its firm adherence to the fundamental policies of the Congress which have governed its programme in the past years under the guidance of Mahatma Gandhi and is definitely of opinion that there should be no break in these policies and that they should continue to govern the Congress programme in future. The Committee express its confidence in the work of the Working Committee which functioned during the last year and deplores that any aspersions should have been cast against any of its members.

In view of the critical situation that may develop during the coming
year and in view of the fact that Mahatma Gandhi alone can lead the
Congress and the country to victory during such crisis, the Committee
regards it as imperative that the Congress Executive should command his
implicit confidence and request the President to nominate the Working
Committee in accordance with the wishes of Gandhiji.

Pant's proposed resolution started a heated debate. Subhas explained that
there was nothing in the Congress constitution or past practice which allowed
him to place such a resolution before the AICC, but he was open to hear
others' opinions. Pant argued that there were no technical grounds on which
he could rule out the resolution supported by the majority of the AICC
delegates present, but it was opposed by Sarat and Nariman. After hearing
both sides of the arguments, Subhas ruled that although the AICC could not
take up such a resolution, it would be discussed by the subject committee.[27]

At the following subject committee meeting, Subhas pointed out that
in order for it to be discussed at the AICC meeting, the notice for the
resolution should have been submitted by 28 February. Yet, given the
unusual circumstances and the gravity of the issues raised, he decided to let
the proposal be discussed at the subject committee meeting the next day so
that the members would get the time to mull over it.[28]

By then, it became known that Gandhi would not attend the Tripuri
session at all. As in the Gaya session of 1922, in Gandhi's absence, his
lieutenants took up the cudgels. Just like in 1922, Rajagopalachari, who
had much to do with the idea of the Pant resolution, led the charge.[29]
Addressing a gathering at the Congress exhibition pandal on the morning
of 9 March, Rajagopalachari initiated a direct attack on the elected
president, pitching him against Gandhi:

At present there are two boats floating on the river. One is an old boat
but a big boat, which is piloted by Mahatma Gandhi. There is another
man who has a new boat—attractively painted and be flagged—who calls
to you to get into his boat.

Mahatma Gandhi is a tried boatman who can safely transport you. If
you get into the new boat—which I know is leaky—all of us will go down
and the river Nerbudda is indeed very deep.

The new boatman says: "If you don't get into my boat, then at least
tie my boat to yours." This is also impossible. We cannot tie up a leaky
boat to a good boat exposing ourselves to the peril of going down.

We have only one leader and that is Mahatma Gandhi. We must abide by him, because what he says he means. He is the only safe man in whose boat we should get. He is a seasoned and tried man. To our knowledge for 35 years now we have tried him to our satisfaction.

I ask you not to be misled by tall talk and got into the leaky boat, or do not think: We shall get into the new boat for a while and then again get back into the old boat.

You may not survive to get back to the old boat, for, as I said, the new boat is leaky. Believe in Mahatma Gandhi. We may, perhaps, be able to swim separately, but if we join together we may all go down.[30]

Cartoon in *Jugantar* by Kafi Khan (Pratul Chandra Lahiri) depicting Rajagopalachari screaming 'leave me' as he is pulled from Gandhi's to Subhas's boat. *Jugantar*, Vol. 2, Issue 144 (12 March 1939), British Library, EAP262-1-2-421.

The heated debate on the Pant resolution continued at the subject committee meeting on the next day. At the outset, Subhas clarified that unlike what had been mentioned in the proposed resolution, he had never cast aspersions on any working committee member. The strongest defence in favour of Subhas came from M.N. Roy, Nariman, Sardul Singh Caveeshar and Niharendu Dutta Majumdar. In his caustic speech, Nariman said that it was a matter of shame for a democratic organization that through the resolution, an attempt was being made to tie the hands of an elected president only to make way for one person who was not even a member of the Congress. Starting with the slogan of 'Long Live Democracy', Dutta Majumdar demanded the withdrawal of the resolution. The most vocal support for Pant's resolution came from S. Satyamurti, once a pro-changer and Chittaranjan's comrade in the Swarajya party. 'I ask you delegates to place your hands on your hearts and say whether you are not sorry for the aspersions. Speaking for myself, I should have demanded an apology', he said.[31]

A meeting of the All-India Kisan Committee under Swami Sahajananda Saraswati, attended by N.G. Ranga, Indulal Yagnik and others, however, adopted a resolution welcoming the re-election of Subhas.

As the day came to an end, Subhas had still not gotten the opportunity to write his speech.

The Congress session opened on 10 March with a portrait of Subhas carried in a chariot drawn by fifty-two elephants. The speciality of the procession of the year was that portraits of all former Congress presidents were carried by the elephants.[32]

However, the assault on Subhas continued. Even the speech of the chairman of the reception committee was not devoid of snide remarks. In what was practically an ode to Gandhi, Seth Govind Das, chairperson of the reception committee, observed:

At this juncture, what we need most is solid patriotism, political sagacity and sound leadership. What a pity that at this very critical hour in our history signs of internal strife should manifest themselves! We have begun to think of changing horses in the mid-stream!

To-day we have assembled here under peculiar circumstances. Mahatma Gandhi has declared the election of this year's President as his own defeat . . . I make bold to say that the issue before us is quite simple. A struggle against Federation is a foregone conclusion. What remains for decision is the time and manner of initiating the campaign. I hope that the fight will be a non-violent one. Mahatma Gandhi is the Acharya of non-violence and knows best the technique of non-violent struggle. It is, therefore, naturally expected that it should be left to the good old teacher to decide when and how the next fight should be started.

Like a tried General several times he asked us to march forward, and when necessary he slowed down our pace, and at times cried halt. Under his guidance we have not stumbled yet, and there is no reason why we should deviate from the path so far followed by us.[33]

Running high temperatures, Subhas was forced to stay away from both the subject committee meeting as well as the open session, which were both presided over by Azad. Closing his speech in reply to the amendments proposed to his resolution in the subject committee, Pant clarified that it did not, in any way, imply a lack of confidence in the elected president. The resolution was carried with a few words altered. The thirteen members of the now-defunct working committee abstained from voting.

Sarat read out Subhas's presidential speech, which was the shortest in Congress's history. Along expected lines, Subhas presented his arguments for giving an ultimatum to the British and for the direct involvement of the Congress in guiding the popular movements in the Indian states. He reiterated the importance of working together with the anti-imperialist organizations such as the Kisan movement and the trade union movement, and ended with an appeal to Gandhi:

Friends, to-day the atmosphere within the Congress is clouded and dissensions have appeared. Many of our friends are consequently feeling depressed and dispirited. But I am incorrigible optimist. The cloud that you see to-day is a passing one. I have faith in the patriotism of my countrymen. I am sure that, before long, we shall be able to tide over the present difficulties and restore unity within our ranks.

A somewhat similar situation had arisen at the time of the Gaya Congress in 1923 and thereafter, when Deshbandhu Das and Pandit Motilal Nehru of hallowed memory started the Sawraj Party. May the spirit of my late Guru, of the revered Motilal and of the other great sons of India inspire us in the present crisis, and Mahatma Gandhi, who is still with us, guide and assist our nation and help the Congress out of the present tangle—this is my earnest prayer. Vande Mataram.[34]

The civil surgeon of Jubbulpore, and the Bombay Government's minister in charge of public health, were rushed in as Subhas's health deteriorated sharply the next day. Although both strongly recommended him to shift to the Victoria hospital in Jubbulpore as they found his right lung to be affected by bronchopneumonia, Subhas refused to leave Tripuri.

The Pant resolution was passed in the open session on the last day of the Congress, that is, 12 March, amidst tremendous ruckus. On the previous day, M.S. Aney had moved another resolution, suggesting not to take up Pant's resolution at the open session due to the condition of Subhas's health, but to discuss it in the AICC at some future date. Pant himself supported Aney so that Subhas could be immediately moved to the hospital. When Azad put it to vote, Aney's motion was carried by a clear majority, but the Bengal delegates voted against it, demanding the withdrawal of Pant's resolution instead. Chaos followed, with a number of delegates from Bengal, the United Provinces (UP) and Punjab disrupting the proceedings, taking out their ire especially against Jawaharlal, who tried to explain the reason behind Aney's proposal, until Sarat intervened to calm them down. In view of this reaction, Aney withdrew his resolution.[35] At the open session, when Nariman again proposed to defer the debate and vote on the Pant resolution, Pant himself opposed it.[36]

The *Jugantar* of 17 March published a letter from an anonymous person who claimed to have been an eye witness to the unruly scenes and identified the delegates from Bengal who were allegedly at the forefront. The letter writer named Ashrafuddin Chowdhury, Anil Roy, Satya Ranjan Bakshi, Suresh Chandra Majumdar, Satya Gupta and Panchanan Chakrabarti among others. Ashrafuddin Chowdhury wrote back, denying the claim.[37]

Although the CSP had opposed the resolution at the subject committee meeting, it took a neutral position with respect to it at the open session. Minoo Masani recalled the thorough process within the CSP that led to its taking this neutral stand, in his memoirs:

At Tripuri, before we could take our stand, we had a series of talks with Subhas Babu and with Nehru. Subhas, who was a down-to-earth politician, clearly wanted his own Cabinet and his friends, who would include the Congress Socialist Party, to be in a majority in the Working Committee. He wanted us to cooperate.

Jawaharlal Nehru, on the other hand, said nothing to contribute or advise. He was as vague as ever. When faced with a difficult choice, he would be non-aligned! Subhas Babu was quite cynical towards such an attitude and told us that Nehru was an opportunist who thought about his own position first and then about everything else.

The resolution of the Gandhians, placed before the session by Govind Ballabh Pant, put the Congress Socialist Party squarely on the spot. If the Congress Socialist party voted with Subhas Babu and the communists, it was likely that the Gandhian resolution would be defeated, in which case the Gandhians would be driven out of the Congress which would then, for all practical purposes, be controlled by Subhas Babu and the communists. So far as I was concerned, this was an unthinkable proposition and many of my colleagues shared my view. On the other hand, if we supported the Gandhians, Subhas Bose would be thrown out of the Presidentship. Jayaprakash was not prepared for this, nor did he want to antagonise Subhas Bose and the communists, because he believed in the concept of the 'Left Bloc of progressive forces.'[38]

After the Tripuri session, Jayaprakash issued a statement explaining the reasons behind the CSP's neutral stand. He believed that if the CSP had voted against the Pant resolution, Gandhi and his followers would have been driven out of the Congress, causing incalculable harm to the national struggle. While it was imperative for the working committee to have Gandhi's trust, the party, at the same time, did not believe that Gandhi alone could lead the country to independence. Opposing the resolution would also have strengthened the supporters of Subhas had who created the commotion, thus endangering the unity of Congress. Sarat's opposition to the resolution on national demand too contributed to the decision to remain neutral.[39]

All the resolutions from the left camp attempting to dilute the Pant resolution were squarely defeated. With the Pant resolution passed, Subhas now had to choose a working committee in accordance with Gandhi's wishes. The CSP's decision to remain neutral in the voting, however, did not go down well with all its members, and a number of them from Bengal, UP and Punjab resigned from the party in protest.[40]

A bitter war of words also ensued during the discussion on the resolution on 'National Demand' drafted by Jawaharlal and moved by Jayaprakash: The Congress resolve to achieve independence for the nation and to have a constitution framed for Free India through a constituent assembly elected by the people on the basis of adult franchise and without any interference by a foreign authority.

'This resolution contains nothing but words, ineffective words, which do not lay down any plan of action, words which do not give our people any lead', Sarat burst forth in protest. Picking on the focus of the socialists on unity, Sarat asked:

> Do you want to postpone the struggle till all the people are united? If that is what the resolution means, it will be more honest to say, 'Let us abandon our fight.' If we do not adopt a firm line of action, we shall be betraying our people and will be accused of betraying the cause of the country.[41]

Taking strong exception to Sarat's words and his opposition to the resolution after it was passed by the subject committee, Jawaharlal made it clear that he was opposed to the idea of an ultimatum. According to him, believing that freedom could be won by the use of bombastic phrases was nothing but self-deception, and throwing an ultimatum would give the British a chance to prepare themselves against the struggle. Jayaprakash complained that Sarat's opposition to the resolution was like a stab from the back. The resolution was passed with an overwhelming majority.

The Congress also adopted the resolution on Indian states, reiterating the position taken in Haripura, but added a vague clause that in view of the strengthening people's movement in the states, the working committee may allow a relaxation, or even a complete removal, of the restraints placed on Congress participation according to the situation.[42]

The Tripuri session thus ended with restricting Subhas's scope of action to Gandhi's wishes, and with both his action points either being turned down or diluted. If the Tripuri Congress showed Subhas anything at all, it was that he had miles to go before catching up with the organizational skills of the Gandhian wing.

The huge crowd which waited, along with the mayor A.K.M. Zakariah and Tulsi Goswami, for the arrival of the Bombay Mail at the Howrah railway station on the morning of 14 March, was disappointed to find that Subhas had alighted at Dhanbad. From Dhanbad, he was taken in an ambulance to Jamadoba colliery to spend a few weeks at his brother Sudhir's place. On the same day, the Bombay High Court ruled that Subhas legally had no claim on the amount assigned to him in Vithalbhai's will.[43]

While Subhas recuperated at Jamadoba, pressure began mounting as there had been no progress on appointing the new working committee. Subhas issued a press statement on 25 March, explaining that after the adoption of the Pant resolution, he could no more appoint the working committee without consulting Gandhi, which had not been possible under the circumstances due to his own illness and Gandhi's preoccupation with the Rajkot matter.

On the same day, he started communicating with Gandhi by wire and post to decide on the next course of action. Subhas asked Gandhi whether he would prefer a homogeneous working committee or a committee with members representing different groups. If the working committee had to be homogeneous in Gandhi's opinion, then obviously it would not be possible for Subhas and Vallabhbhai to be on it together. If different groups had to be represented, Subhas recommended that for the ideal distribution, seven members each were to be nominated by him and Vallabhbhai. In addition, Subhas pointed out, if he had to function effectively, he would want someone of his choice in the position of the Congress general secretary in place of Kripalani.

Then he brought up the complications arising out of Pant's resolution with relation to the Congress Constitution:

> Article XV of the Congress Constitution confers certain powers on the President in the matter of appointing the Working Committee and that article in the constitution . . . At the same time, Pandit Pant's resolution lays down that the Working Committee is to be constituted by me in accordance with your wishes. What is the net result? Do I count at all? Are you to draw up the full list of the members of the Working Committee according to your free choice and will, and I am merely to announce your decision? The effect of this would be to nullify Article XV of the Congress Constitution without amending it.
>
> In this connection I must state that the above clause in Pandit Pant's resolution is clearly unconstitutional and ultra vires. In fact, Pandit Pant's resolution itself was out of order, having been received too late. I would have been within my rights in ruling out of order Pantji's entire resolution . . . But I am temperamentally too democratic to attach importance to technical or constitutional points. Further, I felt that it would be too unmanly to take shelter behind the Constitution at a time when I felt that there was the possibility of an adverse vote.[44]

Gandhi still appeared to be indifferent about the Pant resolution and its repercussions. Nearly two weeks after the resolution was moved for the first time, he wrote to Sarat, 'Do you know that I have no official notice of the resolution? I have not even seen the full text.'[45]

Gandhi responded on 30 March that he was against a composite working committee when there were fundamental differences in views of the members. He would not give a straight answer on the implication of the Pant resolution, and left the ball in Subhas's court. He wrote, 'Since you think that Pant's resolution was out of order and the clause relating to the Working Committee is clearly unconstitutional and ultra vires, our course is absolutely clear. Your choice of the Committee should be unfettered.'[46]

The correspondence between Subhas and Gandhi continued till the AICC session. Sometimes the letters touched upon the points of grievances and other details regarding the presidential election and the Tripuri session, but more importantly, about their differences in outlook and political programme. Subhas was not happy about Gandhi's obsessing with corruption in the Congress and the 'bogey of violence' which alarmed him. 'Though I am at one with you in your determination to root out corruption within the Congress, I do not think that taking India as a whole, there is more corruption today than before and so far as violence is concerned, I feel sure there is far less of it to-day than before,' he wrote to Gandhi. He also wrote that 'The international situation, as well as our own position at home, convinced me nearly 8 months ago that the time had come for us to force the issue of Purna Swaraj', and 'we should lose no time in placing our National Demand before the British Government in the form of an ultimatum'. That the idea of an ultimatum was not appealing to Gandhi or to Jawaharlal was intriguing to Subhas, especially because 'in all your public life, you have given any number of ultimatums to the authorities and have advanced the public cause thereby'. Even in Rajkot, he had done the same thing. Subhas said that 'I am so confident and so optimistic on this point that I feel that if we take courage in both hands and go ahead, we shall have Swaraj inside of 18 months'. He also added that:

I feel so strongly on this point that I am prepared to make any sacrifice in this connection. If you take up the struggle, I shall most gladly help you to the best of my ability. If you feel that the Congress will be able to fight better with another President, I shall gladly step aside. If you feel that the Congress will be able to fight more effectively with a Working Committee of your choice, I shall gladly fall in line with your wishes. All

that I want is that you and the Congress should in this critical hour stand up and resume the struggle for Swaraj. If self-effacement will further the national cause, I assure you most solemnly that I am prepared to efface myself completely. I think I love my country sufficiently to be able to do this.

Gandhi would not agree. He responded with 'I smell violence in the air I breathe. But the violence has put on a subtle form', such as in 'our mutual distrust' and the 'widening gulf between Hindus and Mussalmans'. Therefore, under these circumstances, Gandhi wrote that 'I see no atmosphere for non-violent mass action,' because an 'ultimatum without effective sanction is worse than useless'. He added that 'I have the firm belief that the Congress as it is today cannot deliver the goods, cannot offer civil disobedience worth the name'.

Subhas also made known his disapproval of Gandhi's handling of the Rajkot affairs. His aim was to have Congress provide the lead to the agitation in the states in a coordinated manner so that the freedom struggle in the true sense would become a national movement. Subhas wrote:

You risked your precious and valuable life for Rajkot and while fighting for the Rajkot people you suspended the struggle in all other States. Why should you do so? There are six hundred odd States in India and among them Rajkot is a tiny one. It would not be exaggeration to call the Rajkot struggle a flea-bite. Why should we not fight simultaneously all over the country and have a comprehensive plan for the purpose?

In conclusion, I may say that many people like myself cannot enthuse over the terms of the Rajkot settlement. We, as well as the Nationalist Press, have called it a great victory—but how much have we gained? Sir Maurice Gwyer is neither our man nor is he an independent agent. He is a Government man. What point is there in making him the umpire? We are hoping that his verdict will be in our favour. But supposing he declares against us, what will be our position?

Gandhi waffled, as he had no clear answer to Subhas's questions. 'I feel that it has great national importance', was all he could say. On the acceptance of Gwyer's appointment, Gandhi's defence was that by 'accepting the Viceroy's nominee as Judge, I fancy I have shown both wisdom and grace and what is more important I have increased the Viceregal responsibility in

the matter', but he had no answer about the course of action to be adopted
if Gwyer's verdict was unfavourable.

In the face of a barrage of penetrating questions from Subhas, Gandhi
finally gave up, explaining everything away by the difference in outlook
between the two:

> Do you not see that we two honestly see the same thing differently and
> even draw opposite conclusions? How can we meet on the political
> platform? Let us agree to differ there and let us meet on the social,
> moral and municipal platforms. I cannot add the economic, for we have
> discovered our differences on that platform also.
>
> My conviction is that working along our lines in our own way we
> shall serve the country better than by the different groups seeking to work
> a common policy and common programme forced out of irreconcilable
> elements.

Avoiding Subhas's repeated and numerous questions on how he interpreted
the Pant resolution and what he would want Subhas to do, Gandhi finally
gave his verdict, which was no better than his vagueness on the other issue.
He would not accept the responsibility imposed on him by the resolution,
nor would he publicly defy it, asking his followers who forced it to step back.
Worse, he wanted Subhas to take the onus of interpreting and executing it:

> Pandit Pant's resolution I cannot interpret. The more I study it, the more
> I dislike it. The framers meant well. But it does not answer the present
> difficulty. You should, therefore give it your own interpretation and act
> accordingly without the slightest hesitation.
>
> I cannot, and will not, impose a Cabinet on you. You must not have
> one imposed on you, nor can I guarantee approval by AICC of your
> Cabinet, and policy.

Instead of clarifying his own position in the context of the Pant resolution,
he threw a challenge to Subhas:

> Irrespective of Pandit Pant's resolution and in view of diametrically
> opposite views held by two schools of thought, you should forthwith form
> your own cabinet fully representing your policy. You should frame and
> publish your policy and programme and submit the same to AICC. If you

secure majority you should be enabled to carry out policy unhampered. If you do not secure majority, you should resign and invite AICC to elect new president.[47]

Gandhi was thus asking Subhas to form his own working committee and take sanction from the AICC. He himself would not abide by the Pant resolution.

While trying to gain clarity from Gandhi on his views, Subhas also corresponded with Jawaharlal, debating and discussing the developments of the last few months as well as his personal attitude. Even if the conduct of the other Gandhian leaders had been hurtful, he was not too bothered by it. As he wrote to Gandhi:

I am, temperamentally, not a vindictive person and I do not nurse grievances. In a way, I have mentality of a boxer—that is, to shake hands smilingly when the boxing-bout is over and take the result in a sporting spirit.[48]

Jawaharlal's case was different, especially due to the closeness they seemed to have developed during the past three years. When he returned to India in October 1938, after a six-month European tour, Subhas wrote to him, asking him to take up the chairmanship of the planning committee: 'You cannot imagine how I have missed you all these months.'[49] Less than six months later he was writing to a nephew:

Nobody has done more harm to me personally and to our cause in this crisis than Pandit Nehru. If he had been with us—we would have had a majority. Even his neutrality would have probably given us a majority. But he was with the Old Guard at Tripuri. His open propaganda against me has done me more harm than the activities of the 12 stalwarts. What a pity.[50]

Subhas was not off the mark. On 22 February, Jawaharlal had written to V.K. Krishna Menon:

Subhas has gone off the rails and has been behaving badly in many ways. His principal supporters are very irresponsible and unreliable people and it is quite impossible for me to join this motley group with whose viewpoints on national and international politics I do not agree. Yet if I happened to join his Committee, all the burden would fall on me. I would be coming in continuous conflict with his policies, such as they are. Apart from principles and policies, Subhas's methods of work are difficult to put up with. He has paralysed the AICC office and passes orders over its head in all manner of election matters and local disputes— these orders being flagrantly partial and against our rules or procedure. The Working Committee, which was to have met here, could not meet because he was unable to attend owing to illness and he directed us not to transact even routine business.[51]

After they met at Santiniketan, Jawaharlal wrote a long letter seeking clarification from Subhas on his programme and providing a critique of his tenure as the Congress president. 'Before I can determine on my own course of action I must have some notion of what you want the Congress to be. I am entirely at sea about this', Jawaharlal wrote on 4 February. He criticized the use of the terms 'leftist' and 'rightist' by Subhas. He thought that considering Gandhi and his followers in the working committee to be rightists and anyone who opposed them to be leftists 'seems to me an entirely wrong description'.

Jawaharlal rightly pointed out that on the point of federation, 'without first fully discussing a matter with your colleagues it was hardly fair to accuse them en bloc of back-sliding', as a result of which 'most people thought that your colleagues of the WC were the guilty parties'. He complained that although he had sent long notes on 'what our attitude towards Federation should be' and asked for directions, Subhas had not even acknowledged the receipt of the notes. This, he wrote, was a missed opportunity to discuss the matter thoroughly in the working committee:

Unfortunately in this and other matters you have adopted an entirely passive attitude in the WC although sometimes you have given expression to your views outside. In effect you have functioned more as a speaker than as a directing president.

The AICC office had greatly deteriorated due to neglect by Subhas, Jawaharlal alleged, as a result of which 'many office matters get hung up indefinitely'. He criticized Subhas for not articulating his 'definite views' about, or intervening enough on, a number of issues ranging from the states question, the Hindu–Muslim question, about the kisans and the agrarian situation in the states, the workers, and laws passed by the Government such as the Trades Disputes Bill. Moreover, he wrote that 'Your desire to have a coalition Ministry in Bengal seems hardly to fit in with your protest against a drift towards constitutionalism'. Jawaharlal claimed that he was not clear about Subhas's ideas on foreign policy either. His suggestion, under the circumstances, was well-meaning, even if somewhat impractical:

> I suggest to you therefore to examine the position in all its implications, to consider the various problems referred to above, and to write a detailed note on them. This need not be published but it should be shown to those whom you invite to cooperate with you. Such a note will become the basis for discussion and this discussion will help us in finding a way out of the present impasse. Talks are not good enough, they are vague and often misleading and we have had enough of vagueness already.

The criticisms listed by Jawaharlal had some elements of truth, but much of it was sweeping generalizations and some exaggeration. Subhas had been writing on a variety of topics, particularly since his days of exile in Europe, with substantial clarity and depth. His speeches at numerous conferences (as at the Indian Political Conference in London), at the Congress sessions and other statements issued from time to time made his position on the political topics of the day abundantly clear. His weak point lay in the lack of sufficient involvement in agrarian and labour organizations and their relevant issues or specific legislations, but he could hardly be accused of a lack of clarity on the wide range of issues mentioned by Jawaharlal.

Subhas acknowledged Jawaharlal's criticism, but did not respond in detail, as preparing for the Tripuri session was the immediate priority. He stopped with 'While I am fully conscious of them ['my shortcomings'], I may say that there is another side to the story'.

The detailed response came about a month and a half later, in a letter running into twenty-seven typed sheets. Not only did it contain Subhas's response to each of Jawaharlal's charges, but was 'an indictment of my conduct and an investigation into my failings' as Jawaharlal himself put it.

Subhas began his letter of 28 March with 'I find that for some time past you have developed tremendous dislike for me'. He continued:

> I say this because I find that you take up enthusiastically every possible point against me; what could be said in my favour you ignore. What my

political opponents urge against me you concede, while you are almost
blind to what could be said against them.

   . . . Why you should have developed this strong dislike for me
remains a mystery to me . . . I have looked upon you as politically an elder
brother and leader and have sought your advice . . .

Point by point from the justifiability of his standing for re-election, to
canvassing for votes and the conduct of the working committee members,
Subhas provided detailed and sharp, albeit bitter rebuttals on the position
taken by Jawaharlal on several occasions. Jawaharlal acted like an advocate
for the other Gandhian leaders, Subhas wrote with biting sarcasm, who 'is
usually more eloquent than his client'. He also wrote:

You have charged me further with not clarifying my policy in national and
international affairs. I think I have a policy, whether that policy be right
or wrong. In my short presidential speech at Tripuri I gave an indication
of it in the most unequivocal terms . . . I think I gave a clear indication of
my ideas even before Tripuri . . . May I now ask what your policy is? In
a recent letter, you have referred to the resolution on National Demand
passed by the Tripuri Congress and you seem to think much of it. I am
sorry that such a beautifully vague resolution, containing pious platitudes,
does not appeal to me . . .

   To sum up, I fail to understand what policy you have with regard to
our internal politics. I remember to have read in one of your statements
that in your view, Rajkot and Jaipur would overshadow every other
political issue. I was astounded to read such a remark from such an
eminent leader as yourself. How any other issue could eclipse the main
issue of Swaraj passes my comprehension . . . If we follow the present
piecemeal, tinkering and nibbling policy, suspending the popular struggle
in every other state, it will take us 250 years to obtain civil liberty and
responsible government in the states. And after that we shall think of
our Swaraj!

   In international affairs, your policy is perhaps even more nebulous . . .
Foreign policy is a realistic affair to be determined largely from the point of
view of a nation's self-interest . . . Now, what is your foreign policy, pray?
Frothy sentiments and pious platitudes do not make foreign policy . . .

   For some time past I have been urging on everybody concerned,
including Mahatma Gandhi and yourself, that we must utilise the

international situation to India's advantage and, to that end, present the British Government with our National Demand in the form of an ultimatum; but I could make no impression on you or on Mahatmaji . . . Today when you must find fault with me for not appointing the Working Committee forthwith, despite the shackles of the Tripuri resolution, the international situation suddenly assumes exaggerated importance in your eyes. What has happened today in Europe, may I ask, which is unexpected? Did not every student of international politics know that there would be a crisis in Europe in Spring? Did I not refer to it again and again when I pressed for an ultimatum to the British Government?

He had some strong words for Jawaharlal's accusation against him for not intervening in the Trades Disputes Bill:

. . . you have latterly developed the art of making accusations, sometimes publicly without even caring to ascertain facts, where I am concerned. If you desire to know what I did in this connection the best thing would be to ask Sardar Patel himself. The only thing that I did not do was to break with him on this issue . . . And now, coming to yourself, may I ask what you did to prevent the enactment of this Bill? When you returned to Bombay, there was still time for you to act and I believe you were approached by a number of Trade Unionists to whom you gave some hopes. You were in a much better position than myself, because you can always influence Gandhiji much more than I can. If you had exerted yourself, you might have succeeded where I had failed. Did you do so?

Regarding Jawaharlal's emphasis on himself being an aloof, non-partisan and neutral person, Subhas wondered how someone who called himself a full-blooded socialist 'can be an individualist as you regard yourself, beats me. The one is the anti-thesis of the other'.

Jawaharlal's comments on the efforts to bring in a Congress coalition in power in Bengal had ticked off Subhas:

As a doctrinaire politician you have decided once for all that a Coalition Ministry is a Rightist move. Will you kindly do one thing before expressing a final verdict on this question? Will you tour the province of Assam for a fortnight and then come and tell me if the present Coalition Ministry has been a progressive or a reactionary institution? What is the use of your sitting in Allahabad and uttering words of wisdom which have no relation to reality?. . . If you scrap the policy of office acceptance for the whole country, I shall welcome it . . . But if the Congress Party accepts office in seven provinces, it is imperative that there should be coalition ministries in the rest . . .

Regarding Bengal, I am afraid you know practically nothing. During two years of your presidentship you never cared to tour the province . . . Have you ever cared to know what has happened to the province ever since the Huq Ministry came into office? If you did, then you would not talk like a doctrinaire politician . . . But while I say all this I must add that the proposal of a Coalition Ministry arises because the active struggle for Purna Swaraj has been suspended. Resume this struggle tomorrow and all talk of a Coalition Ministry will vanish into thin air.

Jawaharlal welcomed Subhas's frankness but the detailed and passionately argued long letter was clearly a bit overwhelming for him. He responded, 'To endeavour to deal with all these matters properly one would have to write a book, or something like it'. Jawaharlal's lengthy response tried to explain some of the charges against him listed by Subhas in a softened tone, but on the whole, the defence lacked the force of clarity and conviction, which characterized Subhas's lengthy indictment.

One important insight that Jawaharlal's letter provided was his reasons for opposing Subhas's re-election, reasons that he could not have stated publicly:

I was against your standing for election for two major reasons: it meant under the circumstances a break with Gandhiji and I did not want this to take place. (Why this should have necessarily happened I need not go into. I felt that it would happen.) It would mean also, I though a setback for the real Left. The Left was not strong enough to shoulder the burden by itself and when a real contest came in the Congress, it would lose and then there would be a reaction against it. I though it probable that you would win the election as against Pattabhi, but I doubted very much whether you could carry the Congress with you in a clear contest with what is called Gandhism. Even if by chance you secured a majority in the Congress, this would not represent a strong enough backing in the country without Gandhiji and effective work, and even more so preparation for a struggle would be very difficult. There were so many disruptive tendencies already existing in the country and instead of controlling them, we would add to them. And this meant weakening our national movement just when strength was necessary.

The high emotions associated with the charges and countercharges, however, cooled down eventually, and Subhas invited Jawaharlal to come and meet him at Dhanbad, even if for a few hours. Jawaharlal already had a number of engagements and was in a dilemma: 'I cannot say no to you, specially as the question in issue is so important'.[52] Ultimately, Jawaharlal visited Subhas on 19 April.

Emotions, however, were running high in Bengal. A huge crowd attended a public meeting on 17 March at the Shradhananda Park in Calcutta, chaired by Tulsi Goswami, condemning the Pant resolution and the conduct of the right-wing leaders. Among the speakers were Hemanta Kumar Basu, Narendra Narayan Chakrabarti, Ashrafuddin Ahmad Chowdhury and Hemaprabha Majumdar.[53] The critical tone of the speeches directed particularly at Gandhi, Jawaharlal and provincial leaders like Prafulla Ghosh, however, did not go down well at all. Kiran Shankar Roy issued a statement the next day, holding the speeches responsible for creating an atmosphere of tension in the province, and appealed to the people to refrain from commenting on the Pant resolution till Subhas had had a meeting with Gandhi.[54] This started off another round of wrangling in the press with Subhas-loyalists, such as Barada Prasanna Pain (a member of the Bengal Legislative Assembly and chairperson of Howrah municipality) taking strong exception to Roy's statement.

Subhas himself had to intervene to diffuse the escalating tension in Bengal. He issued a statement to cancel the meetings which were to be held in the districts on 4 April, at the behest of the Bengal Provincial Congress Committee (BPCC) secretary, who wished to wait until his recovery. He made it clear that the BPCC directive was issued without consulting him, and he thought that it would be indecent to organize such meetings on behalf of the Congress organizations since he was the president of both the AICC and the BPCC.[55] He also strongly warned against any attempt to turn the ongoing crisis, which was a national issue, into a matter of provincial conflict.[56]

There was not, however, full support for Subhas in Bengal. Those in the camp of the high command had started organizing themselves too. Leaders like Kiran Shankar Roy and Suresh Chandra Das, Subhas's friends-turned-foes, started issuing statements to the press and circulating confidential letters to Congress leaders in the districts, dropping not-so-subtle hints that during the year-long presidentship of the BPCC and AICC, Subhas had not been able to keep his promises or meet expectations, with regard to interventions in the Assembly, strengthening the organization in Bengal or improving the situation in the Calcutta Corporation.[57] Later, Roy picked a fight, alleging irregularities in the appointment of members in the BPCC executive council and the election tribunal. He accused Subhas of filling the majority of these committees with people loyal to him, at the cost of his opponents.[58]

To keep the matter of provincial pride aside, however, was easier said than done. Deeply concerned with the state of affairs, Rabindranath pleaded with Gandhi, 'At the last Congress session some rude hands have deeply hurt Bengal with ungracious persistence. Please apply without delay balm to the wound with your own kind hands and prevent it from festering.' Gandhi's response was to the point: 'I have made certain suggestions to Subhas. I see no other way out of the impasse.'[59]

The political equations within the Congress were also undergoing significant changes, particularly with the Congress Socialists taking a more adversarial position against Subhas. Late in March, after his meeting with Gandhi, Jayaprakash Narayan was quoted in the press, claiming that the CSP would not join the next working committee. Achyut Patwardhan explained that the party was conscious of its limitations and, therefore, would not contribute to destroying the unity of the Congress by going against Gandhi.[60]

As Subhas arrived at Howrah station on the evening of 21 April by the Toofan Express, a crowd of 20,000 gathered at the station, along with prominent leaders of the province, to welcome him back. At a public meeting organized to accord him a reception the next day at Shraddhananda Park, he informed a massive crowd of the present political situation. Although the dissenting voices were trying their best to embarrass him by questioning his effectiveness as a leader, organizationally there was no challenge to him yet. On 24 April, Subhas was re-elected as the president of the BPCC unanimously, and the Calcutta Municipal Association vested in him the authority to select the candidates for the posts of mayor and deputy mayor of the Corporation in the upcoming elections. The followers of B.C. Roy and Prafulla Ghosh, however, stayed away from the BPCC meeting.[61]

Gandhi arrived in Calcutta on 27 April, along with Jawaharlal, Sarojini Naidu, Bhulabhai Desai, Kripalani, Rajendra Prasad and other leaders, received by Subhas and a sea of people at the Howrah station. This time, he stayed at the Sodepur Khadi Ashram, but Jawaharlal was Sarat's guest again. Finally, the long-awaited Gandhi–Subhas meeting took place in the presence of Jawaharlal. Over two days, hectic parleys continued among the leaders to break the stalemate, but it did not produce any results.

The AICC met at Wellington Square in Calcutta on 29 April. A corps of 500 volunteers, divided into ten teams, was set up under the command of Hemanta Basu to facilitate the movement of the leaders and the three-day session.

Gandhi made his final position clear in a letter to Subhas written on that day. Subhas read it out after rising to speak. The Pant resolution tied Subhas's hands to form the new working committee according to Gandhi's wishes, but Gandhi would not suggest any names:

> You have asked me to give you in terms of Pant's resolution the names for the Working Committee. As I have told you in my letters and my telegrams, I feel myself utterly incompetent to do so . . . Knowing your own views, knowing how you and most of the members differ in fundamentals, it seems to me that if I gave you names, it would be an imposition on you . . . Such being the case you are free to choose your own committee . . .[62]

This was the end of the road as far as negotiations on the formation of the working committee were concerned. In his brief speech, Subhas announced his resignation.

Gandhi wanted Subhas to leave out the members who had resigned, in forming the new working committee, which Subhas could not do as he would not be able to fulfil the condition of the Pant resolution—that the committee should enjoy Gandhi's implicit confidence. Moreover, Gandhi was not agreeable to Subhas's conviction that the committee should be composite in nature rather than homogeneous. At the same time, Gandhi himself would not take the responsibility of nominating the working committee. As the last step, his efforts to reach an agreement with the prominent members of the previous working committee also failed to reach a settlement.[63]

Cartoon in *Jugantar* by Kafi Khan (Pratul Chandra Lahiri): National Medical
Emergency—the last attempt at Calcutta. Subhas being prescribed Congress working
committee-brand quinine, with all fifteen pills to be consumed together.
Jugantar, Vol. 2, Issue 188 (30 April 1939), British Library, EAP262-1-2-471.

Jawaharlal made one last attempt to resolve the impasse. He moved a
resolution, supported by Rafi Ahmed Kidwai and Jayaprakash Narayan,
requesting Subhas to withdraw his resignation and appoint the previous
year's working committee. With two members of the committee slated to
retire due to health reasons, the vacancy could be filled up by Subhas in
consultation with his colleagues.

As the AICC reconvened the next day, Jawaharlal started by seeking
a definite reply from Subhas regarding his proposal, but specified that he
did not want a debate on it. On the face of it, the proposition looked
like a reasonable way out, yet Subhas found it 'in effect identical with the
suggestion made informally by Mahatma Gandhi and others . . .' which
he was unable to accept. Since Subhas did not clearly state his objections,
his response implied a sense that the working committee suggested by
Jawaharlal was going to be a continuation of 'a close preserve of a group of
individuals' that did not fit with his idea of greater representation of other
groups. He was ready to reconsider his resignation, but that would depend
on the view adopted by the AICC.

Yet, there was nothing in Jawaharlal's proposal that suggested a
homogenous working committee. Why would Subhas assume that it
indicated one? The reason for his not accepting Jawaharlal's proposition

became clear when he divulged the story of the behind-the-scenes negotiations that took place over the two days before the AICC session, at a public meeting at Hazra Park in Calcutta on 6 May. In summary, it was this:

> After Gandhi advised Subhas to reach out to the leaders opposed to his re-election for exploring the possibility of a settlement, Subhas had the first interaction at Sodepur with Rajendra Prasad to whom he proposed inducting four new members in the 15-member working committee. This would ensure that the Gandhian leaders had the majority and at the same time would have fresh faces too. After initial discussion, they moved to Azad's house. Expressing their inability to accept the four names proposed by Subhas, Azad and Prasad suggested four alternative names for the committee and Jawaharlal as the new AICC secretary. Subhas agreed to their proposal. However, when the Gandhian group and Subhas went back to Sodepur to finalise the decision, the former changed their position, insisting on re-appointing the old working committee. Apparently, the reason for this insistence, which had Gandhi's support, was to maintain the prestige of the old working committee members. Subhas was told that two new members could be inducted on the retirement of two serving members, but the leaders refused to accept Subhas's nomination for those two vacancies. They also turned down his request to appoint two secretaries to the AICC, one each to operate from Allahabad and Calcutta. Thus, the end situation was that to remain president, Subhas had no choice than to re-appoint the entire working committee of the previous year and wouldn't even have the freedom to appoint two new members to fill the vacancies, although the Congress constitution clearly empowered the president to do so. To Subhas the question was, if the former members of the working committee had already taken such an inflexible attitude even before appointment of the new committee, how could they publicly state that they would cooperate with him? It was at this juncture that he firmed up his decision to resign and rejected Jawaharlal's proposition, which was nothing but a repetition of what was proposed to Subhas behind the scenes.[64]

Sarojini Naidu, who was chairing the session after Subhas's resignation, as well as Jawaharlal found his answer too vague, and not wanting a debate on the topic, Jawaharlal withdrew his resolution. Naidu thereafter asked the AICC to elect a new president, as Subhas had refused to withdraw his resignation. When Niharendu Dutta Majumdar moved a resolution again, requesting Subhas to withdraw his resignation, Subhas himself asked Majumdar to withdraw it. Nariman and Lakshmi Kanta Maitra protested the acceptance of the president's resignation without referring the question to the AICC, and the election of a new president with undue haste in the absence of the full AICC, but their motions were turned down by Naidu. M.N. Roy walked out when his request to raise a point of order was also turned down. A resolution moved by Choithram Gidwani and seconded by Mohan Lal Saxena, to elect Rajendra Prasad, was then put to vote and carried.[65]

The new working committee appointed on 1 May, the final day of the session, was the same as the previous year, but with both Subhas and Jawaharlal refusing to serve on the committee, their places were taken up B.C. Roy and Prafulla Ghosh, two Gandhi-camp followers from Bengal. The working committee was now truly homogeneous, as desired by Gandhi.[66]

Cartoon in *Jugantar* by Kafi Khan (Pratul Chandra Lahiri) depicting Kripalani and Patel resisting attempts by Forward Bloc, Communists, Radical Congress League and the Socialist Party to take control of the Congress cart.
Jugantar, Vol. 2, Issue 195 (7 May 1939), British Library, EAP262-1-2-479.

Nearly 15,000 people thronged the venue on 3 May, at the public reception in Shraddhananda Park organized to felicitate Subhas. The extent of the support that was behind Subhas at this moment was evident from the wide array of individuals who organized the meeting. Among the organizers were ex-mayor Santosh Kumar Basu, mayor Nishith Chandra Sen, veteran journalist and editor of *The Modern Review*, Ramananda Chattapadhayay, president of the Sikh Sabha Harjindar Singh, president of Bengal Akali Dal Kehar Singh, editor of *Desh Darpan* Niranjan Singh Talib and a host of other notable political personalities like Suresh Chandra Banerjee, Tulsi Goswami, Humayun Kabir, Sibnath Banerjee, Kumar Bishwanath Roy, Lakshmi Kanta Maitra, Mohini Devi, Bimal Prativa Devi, Hemaprabha Majumdar, Bankim Mukherjee, Abdul Mansur Ahmed, and Rajendra Deb. Also present were Purna Das, Ashrafuddin Chowdhury, Sardul Singh Caveeshar, Swami Govindananda, Narendra Narayan Chakrabarti, Barada Prasanna Pain and Kalipada Mukherjee.[67]

Subhas had lost to the intrigue to which he was clearly no match, but he had won the hearts of Bengal. Rabindranath sent a message of admiration that was read out in the meeting:

> The dignity and forbearance which you have shown in the midst of a most aggravating situation has won my admiration and confidence in your leadership. The same perfect decorum has still to be maintained by Bengal for the sake of her own self-respect and thereby to help to turn your apparent defeat into a permanent victory.[68]

Before the Tripuri Congress elections, Subhas had criticized the lack of coordinated effort on the part of the leftists. At the meeting of 3 May, Subhas announced the formation of a new platform within the Congress for bringing together all progressive and anti-imperialist elements, which he named the Forward Bloc. He traced the sequence of events that led to the formation of the Bloc and explained his views about its role.

At the Haripura session, he had found that instead of gaining strength, the leftists had become weaker compared to the previous year. This, Subhas claimed, was due to the weakness in their policies and programmes. Although there were three leftist formations in the Congress at that time— the CSP, the radical left-wing and the Royists (followers of M.N. Roy)— in addition to those led by Vallabhbhai, Rajendra Prasad, Azad and others, the anti-imperialist and progressive workers in these groups were not united. The efforts that began at that time to form a leftist party to bring all these political workers together gained momentum at the September 1938

AICC meeting, where a draft manifesto was drawn up. The initiative, however, fizzled out due to the lack of interest of the CSP leaders.

The efforts to organize the leftists received a new lease of life at the informal meeting of the Congress extremists and the leftists held in Calcutta in February 1939, which was again opposed by some prominent CSP leaders. At another informal meeting during the Tripuri Congress, it was decided that instead of being named 'The Left Party', the group would be given another name, and a draft programme too was drawn up, regarding which it was agreed that the final decision would be taken at the next AICC meeting. At another meeting, held a few days before in Calcutta, they decided to form a bloc within the Congress to bring together progressive workers of various groups, agreeing upon a common minimum programme. There was another important change for Subhas. During the earlier initiatives, he had decided to extend his support to the planned organization from the outside, without joining it. However, during the previous meeting in Calcutta, he agreed to join and organize it.

The Forward Bloc was to be for the leftists within the Congress what the Gandhi Seva Sangh was for the Gandhian bloc, an institution that the leftists sorely lacked.[69]

At that moment, there was no specific plan for the Forward Bloc. All it had was a sketchy programme, a loose agreement between a few leaders and an overall positive response from the public and the nationalist press, but it was far from being a closely organized effort to challenge the official programme of the Congress. At the same time, although it was toned down, the question of whether this was a move to declare a revolt and disintegrate the Congress from the grievance of being wronged still hung around. The key challenge in front of Subhas, therefore, was to organize the left and progressive forces quickly and put in place a definite programme. Rajagopalachari, Sitaramayya, Rajendra Prasad and Vallabhbhai had already started running the Bloc through press statements. In Bengal, the staunch Gandhian, Satish Dasgupta, started publishing a series of articles defending Gandhi's role in the whole Tripuri fiasco. Subhas knew he would not get much time before the now stray criticisms of the Gandhian leaders turned into a concentrated downpour, heavy enough to kill the initiative before it could germinate. Naturally, he had to start from Bengal and then move out to other provinces.

Public meetings continued to be organized one after the other to felicitate Subhas. Another civic reception was organized in the city on

6 May by the citizens of South Calcutta. Among the conveners of this meeting were Syama Prasad Mookerjee, Sarala Devi Chaudhurani, Tulsi Goswami, Niranjan Singh Talib, Niharendu Dutta Majumdar, and A.K.M. Zakariah. Awarding the title of *Rashtra Gaurav* (pride of the nation) to Subhas, the speakers in the meeting demanded that Prafulla Ghosh and B.C. Roy resign from the working committee.[70] This was followed by a meeting at Howrah on 8 May, under the chairmanship of Barada Prasanna Pain, where Subhas explained his vision of developing the Forward Bloc as the meeting ground for all leftist and progressive groups.[71] On 11 May, he was felicitated in Shantipur. Even when Subhas could not be present, public meetings continued to be held in the district centres to declare support to the local Congress workers for the Forward Bloc.

It was announced around this time that monies raised by the Subhas Congress Fund would be utilised for constructing a permanent building for Bengal Congress, for which Tagore had agreed to lay the foundation stone.[72]

In the middle of May, Subhas travelled to the UP to address the provincial youth conference held in Unnao, under the chairmanship of Batukeshwar Dutt who, welcoming the formation of the Forward Bloc, urged Subhas to bring all leftists on one platform.[73] Speaking in Hindustani, Subhas elucidated the ideas behind the formation of the Forward Bloc and made an observation regarding the Muslim League, which would explain his attitude towards that organization in the near future. He held that an internal change in the Muslim League had started showing since the party become a mass political organization and the more people joined it, the more anti-imperialist and progressive it would become. The party would transition from being a communal organization into a nationalist one. The growth of a leftist faction within the party was inevitable, Subhas felt, and he predicted that the leftist faction of the Muslim League would definitely come to work together with the leftist group within the Congress.[74] He also addressed a number of well-attended public meetings at Unnao and Kanpur.

'I do not approve of the formation of the Forward Bloc. I, therefore, do not attach much importance to it', declared Jawaharlal in Kanpur, a few days after Subhas went there to garner support.[75] In a more cogently argued piece published in the *National Herald* on 27–28 May, Jawaharlal articulated his views on the Forward Bloc. He had already started seeing the bogey of fascism in the new organization which was yet to take a concrete form:

In Calcutta I did not agree with all the suggestions that Subhas Babu had put forward, but I was convinced that he was earnestly striving for a united functioning of the Congress, accepting the Tripuri decisions. I saw no reason why there should be any difficulty in bringing this about, but opposition, which seemed to me wholly unjustified, came and led to his resignation. Perhaps that resignation was inevitable under the circumstances, and yet I regretted it deeply, for it led to a deepening of the fissures that separated individuals and groups in the Congress.

... Subhas Babu's step in forming a Forward Bloc is an understandable corollary to what has happened, yet it is not necessarily a desirable one, for there are obvious dangers involved in it. It is, so far as is known at present, a negative grouping, an anti-bloc, whose sole binding cement is dislike of, or opposition to, the individuals or groups that control the Congress today. There is no positive policy based on definite principles, except a desire to ginger them up generally. There is no restriction which might keep out elements which, politically or otherwise, are undesirable. The doors of the Bloc are wide open, and it is evident enough that a very miscellaneous company are likely to find shelter in it . . .

. . . in a new organization or grouping without this tradition and checks and without any clear principles and ideology, such adventurist and opportunist elements will find full play, and might even, under cover of fine phrases, play a dominating role in it. It is quite possible that fascist and communal elements might also enter its folds and seek to exploit it to further their animus against the Congress and its anti-fascist policy. How will Subhas Babu deal with this situation when it arises? We must remember that fascism grew in Europe under cover of radical slogans and popular phrases.[76]

M.N. Roy's League of Radical Congressmen, though supportive of the Forward Bloc initiative, insisted on a clear attitude toward Gandhi and his followers. In a manifesto issued from Calcutta in late May, the League argued that the approach to treat Gandhi and his staunch followers separately by declaring allegiance to Gandhi, and at the same time, trying to eradicate the influence of his followers in the Congress, was a wrong one. Gandhism was the source of the policy and the programme of his followers. Therefore, if the Congress had to be freed of constitutionalism and the autocratic mentality of a few Gandhian leaders, it was imperative to break free of Gandhism, which had helped the Congress to make progress initially, but had now become an impediment to further growth. The League was a little concerned at the lack of ideological clarity of the Bloc.[77] This clamour for a break with the past worried Jawaharlal.

Cartoon in *Jugantar* by Kafi Khan (Pratul Chandra Lahiri): M.N. Roy asking Subhas, who is shown as a priest carrying an idol of Gandhi and wearing a *namabali* with Forward Bloc and 'Mahatmaji ki jai' written on it, to leave the path of Gandhism. *Jugantar*, Vol. 2, Issue 219 (4 June 1939), British Library, EAP262-1-2-503.

While N.G. Ranga welcomed the move to unify the leftists, Jayaprakash Narayan declared that the CSP would not join the Forward Bloc as it had no programme of its own other than opposing the Congress high command.[78] In mid-June, Narayan issued a joint statement with communist leader P.C. Joshi, condemning the formation of a new party within the Congress, which they held would be antithetical to the Congress's unity.[79] Joshi argued in an article published in the *National Front* that there was no need for an alternative leadership. Similarly, while Soli Batliwala and Swami Sahajananda Saraswati extended their support, prominent Congress leader from the UP, Mohan Lal Saxena, was critical of Subhas's initiative.[80] Active support also came from C.E. Gibbon, the Anglo-Indian leader, and Niharendu Dutta Majumdar, general secretary of the Labour Party, Bombay's Nariman and Ruikar, and Andhra's M. Annapurniah.[81]

Immediately on his return from Kanpur, Subhas presided over a political conference held in Tarakeshwar on 19 May and on 22 May, and after addressing a public meeting at Baidyabati, travelled to preside over the Bogra district political conference on the same day. The hectic schedule, which began immediately after he had barely recovered from his prolonged illness, started taking a toll on his health. Towards the end of May, he was again down with influenza and was advised bed rest for a few days by the physicians.[82] As soon as he felt a little better, Subhas was on his way to Himaitpur to speak at the Pabna district political conference chaired by Hem Chandra Ghosh on 4 June. Huge crowds greeted him on his way when he stopped at Munsiganj and Narayanganj. About 50,000 people gathered at the Dacca railway station to welcome him on his way back from the conference.[83]

The politics of the Calcutta Corporation, however, retained its place in Subhas's overall political horizon, despite his preoccupation with the consolidation of the Forward Bloc and influencing national politics. Both in 1938 and in 1939 he had been given untrammelled power by the BPCC to conduct the affairs of the Congress Municipal Association with the aims of bringing back discipline and reducing corruption. Yet, his interventions were often contested, both within some Calcutta Congress circles and among non-Congress members, particularly where it involved appointments. One such controversy erupted in May, with some corporators revolting against the appointments in the Corporation's standing committees, pitching B.C. Roy against Subhas and forming a rival organization to the Congress Municipal Organization.[84] Similar dissensions arose among applicants in the districts who failed to receive Congress nomination for the legislative assembly or other elected bodies. A more active and wider press coverage, however, also played a role in amplifying the dissensions.

Despite the Corporation affairs becoming a distraction from his national activities, rather than letting it off, Subhas, apparently inexplicably, tended to get involved deeper into its politics. It was not possible for him to devote the time and effort required to what he had described as cleaning the Augean stables, but on the contrary, did much harm in the form of discontent amongst corporators and opportunity-seekers and also the conflict it generated with other leaders. Nirad C. Chaudhuri took an uncharitable but not wholly inaccurate view of Subhas's involvement with the Corporation:

When Subhas Bose came back to the Calcutta Corporation after his release from detention, he became more and more a prisoner in the hands of the hard-boiled and worldly upper middle-class of Calcutta, to whom civic welfare meant the welfare of their class. Still, Bose could never shed his infatuation for this Delilah. He showed his man-of-action's bias in preferring practical power in the Corporation to ideological power in the Congress Working Committee, and until he left India to find salutary release from it, the Calcutta Corporation remained a millstone round his neck.[85]

Subhas could never give up the efforts to give practical shape to his vision of municipal governance which was enriched by his minute observations during the European exile. Tragically, he refused to accept the reality that the factionalism and the vested interest-driven politics in the Corporation were not allowing him to even come close to the implementation of his vision. In Chaudhuri's assessment, the main reason for Subhas's obsession with the Corporation was his knowledge of revolutions in Europe:

Subhas learnt from the history of French and Russian revolutions that political revolutions are driven by city dwellers and labourers, not by rural population—either they follow in the footsteps or they oppose the revolution. Subhas thought it wouldn't be possible for him to bring in a radical change if he didn't have the lakhs of proletariat on his side. This showed his revolutionary mindset.[86]

After his return from Dacca, Subhas spent less than a week in Calcutta, where he addressed a number of public meetings, before he left for Lahore to attend the Radical Youth Conference on 16 and 17 June. Before travelling, Subhas took the first step of organizing the Bloc by appointing Satya Ranjan Bakshi as the secretary of the provincial Forward Bloc, and opening an office at 49L Dharmatala Street.[87] The permission of the Chief Presidency Magistrate was also obtained for publishing *Forward Bloc* as the mouthpiece of the organization with Subhas as its editor.[88]

At Lahore Subhas was received by Dr Dharamavir and his wife, Sardul Singh Caveeshar, Sohan Singh Joshi, Dr Satyapal, Lala Dunichand and Lala Shyamlal and given a guard of honour by the volunteers. At Lahore and then in Attock, Peshawar and Rawalpindi, he addressed a number of meetings. Large crowds gathered on both sides, and women and children showered petals as his procession passed through the streets of Peshawar.[89]

The CSP at this time suffered a split, with Minoo Masani, Achyut Patwardhan, Asoka Mehta and Ram Manohar Lohia resigning from all executive positions in the party due to differences with Jayaprakash and his supporters, primarily over the question of 'communist infiltration of the party'.[90] There were differences over the question of Subhas's re-election too. It turned out that although Jayaprakash was being publicly critical, or at best, being ambivalent about the Forward Bloc, the others were much more opposed to it than him. As Masani wrote in his letter to Jayaprakash:

> Some of us felt far from enthusiastic about it ['Subhas Babu's decision to stand for re-election with the encouragement and support of the communists']. We foresaw, though perhaps dimly, the implications of this clash. But we had not then the guts to come out openly against the move, and if we had, the bulk of our membership would have denounced us as traitors to the mystic 'left'.
>
> At Tripuri again, we found ourselves I the toils of this idea of holding with the rest of the 'left'. You will remember that from the very outset, Achyut, Asoka, Lohia and I pleaded in the Party's executive for supporting Pant's resolution in the Subjects Committee, even if our amendments were rejected. But the majority of the committee decided otherwise. It was only a combination of circumstances that induced that majority to come round on the final vote in the plenary session to the attitude of neutrality.[91]

H.V. Kamath, the secretary of the National Planning Committee announced that he had to resign from the committee as objections were raised by Jawaharlal to his statements issued during the Congress presidential election and his joining the Forward Bloc.[92] According to Jawaharlal, it was improper for the secretary of the committee to get involved in political controversy, which was likely to be a distraction to the work of the committee. Therefore, he advised Kamath to choose either the committee's work or political work.[93] Arguing that he was not informed about any such condition when he was appointed, Kamath chose to resign.

Reaching Bombay on 21 June to attend the AICC meeting, Subhas spoke at length to reporters, focusing specially on the question of unity in the Congress as a result of the Bloc's formation.[94] The first conference of the All-India Forward Bloc began the next day, with Subhas presiding and Nariman as chairperson of the reception committee. Subhas held discussions with several leftist leaders, including Jayaprakash Narayan, N.G. Ranga, Bhupendra Nath Sanyal, Swami Govindananda and Sibnath Banerjee, to work out the modalities of how the left parties could work together without giving up their own identities.[95] They decided to form a Left Consolidation Committee, comprising members from the Forward Bloc and other leftist organizations who had not joined the Bloc, to frame a programme to bring together all leftists on a common platform. The Conference also framed a constitution for the Forward Bloc. Noticing the similarity between the programme of the Bloc and the Congress, the Bengali newspaper *Jugantar* mockingly stated, 'The Forward Bloc appears to be a Congress Improvement Trust; the city will remain the same, but Vallabhbhai's house will be demolished to widen Nariman's street.'[96]

The working committee of the Forward Bloc was announced on 3 July. Subhas was the president, Sardul Singh Caveeshar the vice president, Lala Shankar Lal the general secretary, H.V. Kamath the organizing secretary and Nathalal Parikh the treasurer. Bishwambar Dayal Tripathi and K.F. Nariman too were appointed secretaries. The other members were Akbar Shah (Frontier Province), Dr Satyapal (Punjab), R.S. Ruiker (CP), Niharendu Dutta Majumdar (Bengal), Seth Damodar Swarup (UP), Abdul Rahman (Kerala), and Indulal Yagnik (Gujarat).

Before leaving Bombay for a three-day tour of the Central Provinces, Subhas met B.R. Ambedkar and M.A. Jinnah to find out about the possibility of cooperation between them and the Forward Bloc. In the Central Provinces (CP), he continued with his mass contact programme, visiting places such as Jubbulpore, Khandwa, Itarsi, Harda and Gadarwara, speaking at about a dozen public meetings.[97]

Two resolutions passed by a decisive majority at the AICC, despite strong opposition from the leftists, became the starting point of a new phase of confrontation between Subhas and the Gandhian leadership. While one of the resolutions stipulated that Congress ministries in the provinces could function without interference from the provincial Congress committees and any difference between them would be resolved by the Parliamentary Subcommittee, the other prohibited Congress workers to undertake satyagraha without the permission of the provincial Congress committee. The latter resolution, moved by Vallabhbhai, received the strongest criticism

Subhas meets M.S. Aney in Bombay.
Advance, 1 July 1939, National Library, Government of India.

FORWARD BLOC:—preparing the Constitutional programme on Thursday evening at Nathalal Parek place. Photo shows:—SJ. S. Bose in the centre along with Mr. Jaiprakash Narain, Mr.
Meherally in the left along with Lala Shankeralal. Prof. Ranga & others snapped in the meeting.

Discussing the programme of the Forward Bloc and a broader Leftist platform with
Yousuf Meherally, Jayaprakash Narayan, Lala Shankarlal and N.G. Ranga at Nathalal
Parikh's house in Bombay.
Advance, 4 July 1939, National Library, Government of India.

from Sahajananda Saraswati, who argued that the intervening time between a decision to commence a campaign and obtaining permission for it could make it pointless. Subhas issued an appeal to observe 9 July as an all-India protest day in opposition to both these resolutions. Rajendra Prasad urged Subhas not to go ahead with the protest, pointing out that if subordinate committees or individual leaders started disregarding resolutions adopted democratically at the AICC after much deliberation, then all discipline in the organization would disintegrate. Prasad also instructed the Congress committees and workers not to participate in the protest meetings.[98]

Subhas, however, refused to cancel the programme, claiming it to be in line with the democratic traditions of the Congress. The Left Consolidation Committee (LCC) criticized Rajendra Prasad for attempting to stifle their constitutionally permitted democratic process of converting public opinion in their favour. The Congress president's stricture implied that once a decision had been made at the AICC, there should be no effort to change it, as a statement issued by the LCC asserted. On the contrary, as the statement pointed out, it was the committee's duty to make people aware of the drawbacks of the resolutions.[99] The BPCC executive also adopted a resolution on 9 July against the AICC resolutions, followed by organizing a public meeting along with the Left Consolidation Committee at the Albert Hall. The mood of the meeting can be gauged from the remark of the revolutionary leader Purna Chandra Das, who said that while Hitler and Mussolini hanged their opponents, the Congress high command strangled their opponents with the help of khadi ropes.[100] 'In spite of the ban, however, a great many protest meetings were held all over the country, attended by numerous Congressmen and others', observed *The Modern Review*.[101]

The protest programme was opposed by Jawaharlal too. Two days before the scheduled protests he issued a statement, but in a manner which Subhas had criticized in one of his letters a few weeks before: 'When a crisis comes, you often do not succeed in making up your mind one way or the other—with the result that to the public you appear as if you are riding two horses.'[102] In his statement, Jawaharlal said:

> . . . Is this the way to a united front, of which so much is talked, or a continuation of the struggle of the masses? It is a challenge to the Congress organization which we have built up with so much love and labour and sacrifice, and it can only lead to disruption if persisted in.

Of course, many people who are said to be of the right have acted wrongly often enough, and in a narrow spirit of faction. They have attempted to hold back or suppress advanced elements in our ranks. It may be that the resolutions objected to might be utilised for this purpose. But the action suggested gives the final justification for these resolutions and weakens the argument . . . The two resolutions of the AICC that have been criticized are logical enough as they read, and any organisation which thinks in terms of united and coordinated action might well adopt them. But it is equally true that they might be used for party purposes, and therein lies the danger. Because of this it was my intention, if I had got a chance at the AICC meeting, to speak against the resolution relating to satyagraha.

But the question now is not of the merits of the resolutions, but of the very basic discipline of the Congress and of our allegiance to its constitution. We break that discipline and throw off that allegiance at our peril. I cannot congratulate the Left Consolidation Committee on their first appearance in public in the shape of their statement. This augurs ill for their future.[103]

The next statement he issued on 13 July, however, was more stinging, and in it, Jawaharlal directly criticized Subhas:

I totally disapprove of Mr. Subhas Bose's action in carrying on a campaign against the A.I.C.C. while holding the presidentship of the Bengal Provincial Congress Committee. I would have had no grievance against Mr. Bose had he resigned the Bengal presidentship and then carried on his agitation.

. . . I do not agree with Mr. Bose that the Congress President's view of the requirements of discipline interfere with the basic principles and traditions of democracy. Democracy does not mean licence for one to do anything he likes. The Congress is a democratic body with a certain definite creed and objective. It cannot allow its members to carry on an agitation which injures the cause of the furtherance of its creed.[104]

From Bombay, Subhas travelled to Pune, Hubli and Dharwad, and then proceeded to Gujarat, where he addressed numerous public meetings, including ones at Godhra, Ahmedabad, Surat, Broach and Baroda. 'At all the places visited by him Mr Bose met with a good reception, notably from the Muhammadan public . . . The student element was particularly enthusiastic in welcoming Mr Bose', noted the Bombay Government's confidential report to the Government of India.[105]

Another issue regarding which Subhas had a conflict with the Gandhian leadership was a policy matter that characterized one of the core Gandhian values. While organizing the campaign against the AICC resolutions, he questioned the viability of the prohibition policy that was going to be implemented by the Bombay Government from 1 August, banning the sale of liquor and other intoxicants in Bombay city and its suburbs. In a statement issued on 10 July, Subhas highlighted the problems with the 'methods' adopted by the policy, calling it 'neither scientific nor conducive to the end they have in view', while supporting the moral imperative behind it. He stressed on the adverse impact on the public exchequer and particularly the Parsi community, which had long been associated with the liquor trade. The Parsi community had already started agitating against the ban. Among other things, Subhas said:

The defects in the Prohibition Scheme are more than one . . . Illicit distillation will increase and there will be a rush of men to the wet zone every evening and particularly during every week-end.

Prohibition is a measure of social reform and no social reform can be successfully brought about without winning . . . the goodwill of the people . . . The fact that consistent opposition is being offered by some influential sections of the community shows that the Government have not yet been able to carry with them the approval and goodwill of the people in general.

Mahatma Gandhi did the right thing when he opined that prohibition should not be forced on Europeans in India because they did not believe in it and it would amount to coercion to force it on them. The same principle of non-violence should be applied to Asiatics and Indian people as well both in theory and in practice . . .

Now turning to the economic side of the question, I may say that it is difficult to approve of a method which involves the sudden imposition of an additional tax over a crore of rupees on Bombay alone in order to make good the loss of excise revenue. With millions of half-filled stomachs, with hundreds of thousands dying every year of preventable diseases and with 92 percent of our people still unable to read or write. I consider it no part of statesmanship to raise additional money by heavy taxation, not one rupee of which would go towards the better fulfilment of stomachs or saving human lives or making our people more literate. I am, therefore, inclined to think that the introduction of prohibition by stages is the more appropriate and scientific method. This would not involve heavy taxation for financing prohibition, would save a portion of the taxable capacity of the people for future requirements and would not involve a sudden change in our national economy.

. . . The Parsis are a small but influential community. Who does not know of the many beneficial institutions and activities which have been brought into existence and conducted by them? The overwhelming majority of the community have been opposing this policy and as a minority community the Parsis are entitled to be heard. I understand that the Parsis are apprehensive that the sudden launching of immediate and total prohibition in Bombay will throw into the streets a large number of families and would prejudicially affect the income of the charity trusts many of which are for the benefit not of Parsis alone but of the Indian community in general.

Besides the Parsis, the Muslims of Bombay are also affected by the programme. While they are not opposed to prohibition on principle, they have objection to the 10 percent property tax, which is required for financing prohibition. It is urged on their behalf that the 10 percent property tax subjects them to exorbitant taxation as compared with their population and they resent being taxed in order to force non-Muslims to abstain from drink.

The effect of prohibition on our general economy is of greater consequence than even its effect on the Parsis or Muslim community. To give a small instance, a large number of hotels and restaurants will be badly hit and may have to close down. Not only will their owners suffer loss but the employees will also be thrown out of employment. It is not impossible that migration from the prohibited area to outside places may take place and the importance of the port of Bombay may also be affected. The fact is that while piecemeal introduction of partial prohibition is possible, piecemeal introduction of total prohibition is next to impossible . . .[106]

The twin cardinal offences of defying the AICC and criticizing a core Gandhian programme expectedly created a flutter and hardened the stance of the Gandhian high command. Subhas had to be disciplined and Vallabhbhai became the key mover in that initiative. On 11 July, Vallabhbhai advised Rajendra Prasad:

> I think in the matter of demonstration of the 9th July instruction should be issued to all the Provinces except Bengal for taking disciplinary action against all the office-bearers and Congress organisations who have violated your instructions. But in the case of Bengal you may write a letter to Subhas expressing your regret about his attitude and intimating to him that the question about his attitude and that of his Provincial Congress Committee will be placed before the WC for consideration. He has gone one step further and attacked the Bombay Government prohibition policy also.[107]

The next day, he again wrote to Prasad, suggesting that a meeting of the working committee should be scheduled in the first week of August, as soon as Gandhi and Jawaharlal were available. He was in a hurry:

> I am, however, strongly of opinion that a prompt and clear indication of our attitude is necessary to prevent the rot. In August when we meet we can take no action against him [Subhas], unless we finish the preliminaries beforehand. I would therefore suggest that a notice asking Subhas Babu to explain about his conduct in organising a countrywide agitation and a revolt against the decisions of the AICC which he as the President of the Bengal Provincial Congress Committee is bound to respect and execute . . . Any weakness on our part at this stage is bound to spread indiscipline and weaken our organisation. You must have seen Subhas Babu's statement on the prohibition policy of the Bombay Government. He has done worse than what our enemies could do.[108]

Gandhi, who was in Abbottabad at the time, reacted on 13 July 'with pain and sorrow'. He was aware of Subhas's views as they had discussed it in Bombay, but 'was unprepared for his public statement' against the 'greatest moral reform in the Congress programme'. Because of his position as a former president of the Congress and the serving president of the BPCC, Subhas's statement, Gandhi held, 'is calculated to discredit the Bombay Ministry in a manner the avowed opponents of prohibition could never hope to do'. He criticized the previous governments for paying lip service to prohibition without having the courage to implement the programme, unwilling to forgo the easy revenue from a 'tainted source'. Gandhi went on to give Subhas a lesson in Gandhian economics:

> Subhas Babu has played a most dangerous game by mixing up the communal question with such a purely moral reform as prohibition. It is as much the concern of a Muslim or a Parsi or a Christian as of a Hindu to look after his less fortunate countryman who happens to be a labourer and falls a victim to drink. The Bombay property-owners will pay one crore rupees as additional tax not because they are Parsis or Muslims but because they are property owners. It is altogether misleading to suggest that the tax-payer, himself a non-drinker, will pay the tax for saving the drunkard. He will pay the tax for the education of his children whereas hitherto the drinker has been made by him to pay for that education.
>
> ... Many of them [Parsis] will be weaned from a trade which corrupts the morals of their countrymen less fortunately placed than they. They will themselves be weaned from the drink habit. However mild it may be for them, I know, from having lived in intimate contact with them, that the drink does leave an indelible mark on them. Thirdly, monied men amongst them will have paid for the long-delayed reform.[109]

Apart from Gandhi, three ministers of the Bombay Government, A.B. Latthe, K.M. Munshi and Dr M.D. Gilder also contradicted Subhas through their press statements. Faced with all-round criticism, Subhas issued a second statement on 14 July, where he reiterated that he completely supported the idea of prohibition and his comments were offered as constructive criticism to ensure that the Bombay Government's policy did not result in unnecessary hardship for anyone. If the experimental initiative failed due to certain lacunae, he was afraid that those who were supporting the programme enthusiastically would move away from it.[110]

If Gandhi's statement was firm yet explanatory in tone, Jawaharlal's comment was brief and more measured. He said, 'I must also regret Mr Bose's criticism of the Bombay Government's prohibition programme. His statement on the eve of the launching of the programme seems to be undesirable and unhappy'. By contrast, however, Vallabhbhai's anger was palpable in his statement published in the *Hindustan Times* on 17 July. He accused Subhas of acting at the behest of the Parsis and Muslims and doing a volte-face, first by wishing success to the Prohibition Propaganda

Board of the Bombay Government in March 1939 when the details of the programme were being discussed, and then by criticizing it:

> I was prepared for many things from Mr Subhas Bose. Even his revolt against the Congress and his attempt to disrupt the national institution did not surprise me, as he had already threatened 'civil war' in his correspondence with Gandhiji. But I must confess to a feeling of amazement at the attitude he has thought fit to adopt towards the prohibition scheme of the Bombay Government . . . Subhas Babu has chosen on the present occasion to join the ranks of enemies of the Congress and to add the weight of his personality to the numerous attacks, fair and otherwise, which have been dealt at the Ministry . . .
>
> An unseemly aspect of Mr Subhas Bose's conduct is that the President of a Provincial Congress Committee should have taken the trouble to travel one thousand miles and launch an attack on a Congress Ministry in another province . . .
>
> . . . The resolution directing the enforcement of total prohibition in three years, it is true, was not passed when Mr Bose was President. It was passed before he was elected President. But surely he is bound by it . . .
>
> . . . Why did he not seek an explanation from anyone of the Ministers? . . . Can there be a greater betrayal of the Congress than to argue the brief of the opposition at a time when the Congress Ministry is straining all its resources and fighting with its back to the wall in executing the orders issued by the Working Committee when he was the President of the Congress?
>
> In this connection I am surprised to find that important passages of Mr Bose's first statement on prohibition are clever paraphrases of a memorandum submitted to Gandhiji by two leading Parsi organisers of the anti-prohibition campaign . . . It shows whence Subhas Babu derived his inspiration for the cruel attack on the Bombay Ministry. It is an irony of the fate that the Rashtrapati of a few months ago, who is still a congressman and President of a Provincial Congress Committee and claims to save the Congress from the so-called reformist mentality, has openly allied himself with avowed enemies of the Congress in an unholy conspiracy against the faithful servants of the Congress . . .
>
> The most dangerous part played by Subhas Babu is the adoption of the communal cry raised by the Working Committee of the Muslim League at its last meeting in Bombay. It is significant that soon after

this meeting Subhas Babu had an interview with Mr Jinnah and it is still now significant that he went straight from Mr Jinnah to Gandhiji and communicated 'my views to Mahatmaji'. And when Gandhiji advised him to consult the Ministers, who had studied the question for months, he chose not to do so.

. . . I cannot let his opportunity pass without expressing my surprise at the opposition of Subhas Babu to the taxation proposals of the Bombay Government. The property tax is avowedly intended to shift the burden of taxation from the shoulders of the poor to those of the rich. One would have expected the leader of the Forward Bloc to have congratulated the Ministry which conceived such a genuinely socialistic step. Instead this doyen of radicals pleads the cause of the wealthy property-holders who are asked to part with a small portion of their unearned income. There is neither science nor principle in Mr Bose's criticism; it is just another kick at the Congress.[111]

The fortnightly report from J.M. Sladen, secretary of the Home Department of the Bombay Government, was along the lines of accusations made by Vallabhbhai, but was more explicit in charging that Subhas had acted with the motive of gaining financial favours:

It is understood that Mr Bose's statement was prompted by his desire to extract donations, especially from the Parsi community, for meeting the expenses of the Forward Bloc. About Rs 25,000 are reported to have been collected so far by the organisers of the Bloc, out of which Rs 12,000 are said to have been contributed by two well-known Parsi gentlemen.[112]

The Parsis kept up the pressure on the Government, with a prayer meeting held under the auspices of the Parsi Federal Council deciding to socially boycott M.D. Gilder, the excise minister.[113] The opposition to Subhas's statement, however, was not restricted only to the Gandhian leaders. The communist leader, Gangadhar Adhikari, also issued a statement, asking Subhas to withdraw his statement and support the Bombay Government's initiative.[114]

The rumour mill was put to work to discredit Subhas. The Punjab Government noted:

Subhash (sic) Chandra Bose has, however, lost much support in the Punjab through his attack on the Bombay prohibition scheme. He has been accused of having been bribed by the Parsis and several attacks have been made on him in the press by people who used to support him warmly.[115]

A wave of intolerance was sweeping away the Congress authorities, Subhas retorted. He accused that they were driven by blind rage at the slightest criticism, and that they deployed their entire propaganda machinery to terrorize ordinary Congress workers into silence. Subhas held that the mere fact that the top leaders of the Congress and the Bombay Government had to react with such bitterness showed that his criticism was not without some truth in it. Responding to the allegation of his volte-face, Subhas clarified that he had sent his good wishes to all Congress governments in the provinces, but that did not mean that he was in agreement with the methods they were trying to adopt.[116]

Bengal's Gandhians were not to be left behind in the race to discipline Subhas. Receiving from Vallabhbhai a copy of his correspondence with Rajendra Prasad, the new working committee member from Bengal, Prafulla Ghosh, wrote to Prasad on 18 July:

> I entirely approve of what Sardar says. You should also ask for the names of the BPCC Executive members who voted for the [anti-AICC] resolution. There are many among them who are office-bearers of Congress Committees . . . In fact Subhas's position has suffered on account of this and for his statement re the prohibition policy of the Bombay Government.[117]

Subhas departed for Calcutta, from Bombay, on 23 July. The day before he left Bombay, M.N. Roy reportedly warned Subhas that he would lose his personal influence in the country if he was expelled from the Congress. Subhas told Roy that on the contrary, his influence would only increase, and he hinted at setting up a parallel institution.[118] Unable to agree with the Left Consolidation Committee's programme, M.N. Roy had earlier announced his party's withdrawal from the committee.[119]

The political atmosphere of Bengal was charged up with two issues as Subhas returned to Calcutta after more than a month—the Bengal Government's attitude towards political prisoners and the Bengal Congress wrangle.

The Fazlul Huq Government, in response to demands from the Sarat Bose-led Congress members in the Assembly, had set up a committee

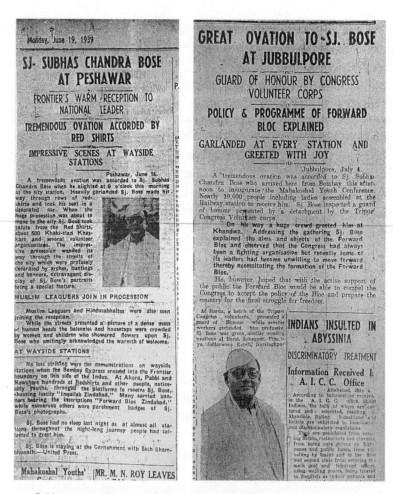

Subhas received a wave of support during his tours across the country.
Advance, 19 June and 5 July 1939, National Library, Government of India.

in December 1938, to look into the modalities of release of the political prisoners still in prison. Sarat himself, from the Legislative Assembly, and Lalit Chandra Das from the Legislative Council, agreed to serve on the committee as representatives of the Congress, on Gandhi's advice. According to Sarat, although 112 prisoners were initially released on the recommendation of the committee, the Government soon hardened its stance towards the remaining prisoners and started disregarding the committee's recommendations. In protest, both Congress representatives resigned from the committee.

Sarat asked Gandhi for his advice. He wrote to Gandhi on 31 May, 'What I am apprehensive of is that the prisoners may commence a hunger strike. If they do so, the situation will become extremely complicated. At the same time, I do not know what hopes I can hold out to them'. Gandhi opined that the prisoners should not take the route of hunger strike, and suggested to the Bengal Government to accommodate Sarat's point of view by taking him back on the committee.[120]

With all efforts and negotiations failing to secure their release, the political prisoners at the Dum Dum and Alipore Central Jails went on a hunger strike from 7 July, demanding unconditional release. The memory of Jatin Das was still fresh in mind, and the prisoners gained wide support across the province. Gandhi, however, objected strongly to the prisoners' hunger strike, writing to the secretary of the political prisoners' release subcommittee of the BPCC, that he considered the hunger strike 'bad and inadvisable'. On receiving letters from Bina Das, Kalyani Bhattacharya, Kamala Dasgupta, Mira Duttagupta and others requesting him to intervene and even participate in the hunger strike, Gandhi told reporters:

Some women are inundating me with wires and letters about the hunger-striking prisoners in Bengal. One telegram peremptorily asks me to discharge my responsibility by myself joining the hunger-strike. Another lays the whole burden on my shoulders of leading the agitation on the ground that the prisoners had suspended their hunger-strike on my assurance . . . I have no doubt that the hunger-strike is wrong. No person should free himself from prison by refusing to take food . . . Therefore, I implore those who are organizing public opinion to persuade the hunger-strikers to give up the hunger-strike, and not to mislead the public by expecting me to do the impossible . . . At the same time I would urge the Bengal Government to put an end to this particular agitation by releasing the prisoners although, as I have admitted, the prisoners have put themselves in the wrong by resorting to hunger-strike.[121]

Asking Rajendra Prasad to follow Gandhi's advice, Vallabhbhai strangely put the political prisoners (including those convicted in revolutionary uprisings such as the Chittagong armoury raid) at par with ordinary prisoners. The hunger strike had become more of a problem of governance for him and of morality for Gandhi. He wrote:

So long as they are on hunger-strike for securing their release we can organise no agitation in support of their release as it would be a wrong and a dangerous precedent to set up . . . We cannot be a party to any act of coercion against the Government of Bengal for compelling it to do a thing which they may reasonably claim to be unfair.[122]

The home minister, Nazimuddin, claimed that the committee appointed by the Government had assessed the case for release of all but twenty political prisoners, and based on its recommendation, 146 prisoners had been released and the case for forty-eight prisoners were being considered. He, however, ruled out the possibility of the Government succumbing to the pressure of hunger strike by the prisoners.[123]

The whole of Bengal was agitating, with innumerable petitions, public meetings and processions organized across districts. Students of many schools and colleges also declared a strike. Although, as suggested by Vallabhbhai, the Gandhian Congress avoided any talk of agitation, the public sentiment was too strong to remain passive. The Gandhian leaders, therefore, focused primarily on negotiations with the prisoners and the Government, and on issuing statements. While Rajendra Prasad issued a statement requesting the prisoners to withdraw their hunger strike and asking Congress workers to strengthen the movement for securing their release, Dr B.C. Roy carried on parleys with the unflinching Bengal Government, pressing for their release.

As the agitation led by the BPCC continued to gather momentum in Bengal, speaking to reporters in Gujarat's Umreth on 21 July, Subhas suggested that the issue of political prisoners' release should be taken up at an all-India level by the working committee, and announced that, led by the Left Consolidation Committee, 30 July would be observed across the country as political prisoners' day. Based on his earlier interactions with the prisoners, he knew that the prisoners had chosen the path of hunger strike after due consideration, and mere appeals for its withdrawal would not produce any results.[124]

Subhas met the prisoners on 27 July at both the prisons. He did not think it would be proper to ask them to withdraw the hunger strike till the time there was a definite assurance regarding their release. The prisoners themselves were of the opinion that such requests from the leaders would indirectly strengthen the Government. Responding to the fear reportedly expressed by Nazimuddin, that other political formations might step in to form the Government if the Huq Government went on a collision course with the Governor on this issue, Subhas assured that the Congress would support the Government in every possible way and not try to form a government themselves.

The emphasis on negotiations and the lack of agitational approach from the Gandhian leadership, combined with the intensifying public sentiment in Bengal made Subhas take up a more confrontational attitude. He issued an appeal to raise Rs 10,000, and organize 10,000 volunteers within a week to be prepared for launching a satyagraha. Although he was disappointed at the lack of support from the Congress ministries in the other provinces, Subhas was confident of gaining popular support from those provinces. At the same time, he stressed that Bengal should be able to solve its own problems. He clarified that he would launch the satyagraha only after hearing directly from the Government about its plan.

Rajendra Prasad and Mahadev Desai arrived in Calcutta and had long meetings with the prisoners and the leaders of Bengal Congress. Desai carried a message from Gandhi, asking the prisoners to give up their hunger strike. The hunger strikers clearly told Prasad that they had no plan to relent unless their demand for unconditional release was met by the Government, while Nazimuddin told him that the Government would not take any decisions unless the hunger strike was withdrawn. Unable to break the stalemate, Prasad left the city with an assurance to place the issue in front of the next working committee meeting.[125]

Gandhi's response to the message from the prisoners, sent to him through Mahadev Desai, surprised even some staunch Gandhians. 'We are pained and disappointed on reading his statement', wrote *Jugantar*. The crux of his statement, that he and the Congress were held back from doing anything meaningful only because of the prisoners' hunger strike, sounded insensitive:

> I am sorry that I can fix no date for their release nor give any other undertaking. I would if I had the power. The only power I have is to plead their cause with all the force at my command. But they give me no chance whatever by continuing their hunger-strike. In so far as it was intended to rouse public attention it has served its purpose. Any prolongation of the fast will now defeat that purpose. There are many who would work actively for their release if the strike is given up. I do feel very strongly that this fast is not justified. The strikers are giving a

bad lead to those who are similarly situated. Such hunger-strikers, if they
are largely copied, will break all discipline to pieces and make orderly
government impossible. The prisoners' cause is essentially just, but they
are weakening it by their persistence. I would ask them to live and listen
to the advice of one who claims to be an expert in fasting and who claims
also to know the science of political prisonership. Let them not hamper
one whom they consider to be their best advocate. I make bold to say that
had the fates not been against them and me, they would certainly have
been discharged before 13th April last. But I do not propose to going
to the past. Suffice it to add that their refusal to give up the strike will
embarrass the Working Committee in whatever effort it might wish to
make to secure their release.[126]

Unwilling to start a public debate with Gandhi, Subhas stopped by
expressing his displeasure at such a statement, which he believed would not
only strengthen the hands of the Bengal Government, but demoralize the
political prisoners. It fell on Dr B.C. Roy, as one of the working committee
members from Bengal, to come forward in Gandhi's defence.

The crisis was finally resolved when the prisoners agreed to withdraw
from their hunger strike for two months, on 3 August, at the mediation
of Subhas and Sarat, who held a series of talks with the prisoners and
the Bengal Government. The Bengal Government remained unrelenting,
making no concessions and argued that the prisoners had begun their fast
without waiting for the Government's final decision on the basis of the
recommendations of the advisory committee. Even as Bengal home minister
Nazimuddin stated that the Government had not agreed to any time limit,
Subhas insisted that if the Government's decision was unsatisfactory at the
end of two months, the prisoners would resume their hunger strike and the
BPCC would commence a movement. The intervening two months would
also give the BPCC adequate time to prepare for a movement.[127]

Gandhi reacted with, 'I congratulate Shri Subhas Babu on having
succeeded in persuading the hunger-strikers to suspend their fast even
for two months and on having undertaken to move the BPCC to take
the necessary action for the release of the prisoners', Gandhi reacted.[128]
The Congress working committee, however, continued to press its
'strong conviction that it is wrong on the part of the prisoners, political
or otherwise, to resort to hunger strike for their release' because then
'orderly government will become impossible'.[129] Just how rankled Gandhi

Political prisoners give up their hunger strike.
Advance, 4 August 1939, National Library, Government of India.

himself was with the hunger strike by the prisoners became evident when he proposed that undertaking hunger strikes should be placed under the control of the working committee.

> Hunger-strike has positively become a plague. On the slightest pretext some people want to resort to hunger-strikes. It is well, therefore, that the Working Committee has condemned the practice in unequivocal terms . . .
>
> It is also worthy of consideration whether a rule should not be passed by the Working Committee making a public and political hunger-strike without permission a breach of discipline . . . Hunger-strike has . . . become such a nuisance that it will be as well for the Working Committee to adopt measures to check it before it assumes dangerous proportions.[130]

The fault line between the AICC and the BPCC was bound to widen over the protest meetings on 9 July, and talks about the Congress leadership disciplining Subhas were doing rounds. In anticipation, those in support of Subhas started preparing to consolidate their organizational strength. A week before Subhas's return to Calcutta, his followers who constituted the majority of the BPCC, led by Sarat Bose, submitted a requisition notice to the BPCC Secretary for convening a meeting to reconstitute its executive council. Among those who signed the notice were Pratul Chandra Ganguly, Bankim Mukherjee, Satya Bakshi, Suresh Chandra Majumdar, Makhanlal Sen, Amarendra Nath Chatterjee, Somnath Lahiri, Bipin Behari Ganguly, Hema Prabha Majumdar, Deben Sen, Hemanta Basu, Sibnath Banerjee, Harendra Natha Ghosh, Bimal Pratibha Devi and Satya Gupta.[131]

As Ashrafuddin Ahmad Chowdhury, the BPCC secretary, scheduled the meeting on 26 July, the Gandhian group led by Kiran Shankar Roy complained to Rajendra Prasad about the constitutional validity of the move, who, in turn, asked Chowdhury to send him all the documents for verification. The opposition party also issued a public statement contesting Chowdhury's decision and calling into question the intentions behind the desire to reconstitute the executive council. With Roy, Arun Chandra Guha, Atulya Ghosh, Bhupati Majumdar, Bijoy Singh Nahar, Harikumar Chakraborty, Prafulla Sen, Suresh Chandra Das, and Surendra Mohan Ghose among the prominent signatories, the statement accused Subhas of trying to fill three-fourths of the council with his followers in order to be able to appoint only his chosen members in the provincial election tribunal. They also alleged that the notice for the meeting had not been served in the proper manner.[132]

All these allegations were stoutly refuted by Bankim Mukherjee at the meeting, where he pointed out that Subhas had already commanded the loyalty of three-fourths members, and that the opposition party was given greater representation compared to other provinces where the Gandhians were in majority. In the newly elected executive council of 149 members, the strength of the Gandhian group declined from thirty-seven to thirteen.[133]

At the same time, a public spat erupted between Sarat Bose and Dr B.C. Roy, as Sarat approached the BPCC on behalf of the Congress Municipal Association to take disciplinary action against the latter and a few others for opposing the Association in the Calcutta Corporation.[134] In a split in the Association that ensued, Roy's followers succeeded in occupying the department-related standing committees in the Corporation.[135] Roy himself issued a lengthy statement blaming the Bose brothers for the corruption and mismanagement in the Corporation while concentrating excessive power in their own hands.[136]

With the prisoners' hunger-strike crisis resolved for the time being, Subhas left for a tour of Orissa to organize the Forward Bloc there. Massive crowds gathered along with provincial leaders such as Nilkantha Das and

Bhagirathi Mishra to receive him in Cuttack on 5 August, and Subhas was taken on elephant through the main roads of the city, which had been decorated to welcome him.[137] In Cuttack, he addressed the students of the Ravenshaw College, the Orissa Youth Conference and the Cuttack Municipality. He was received by Biswanath Das, the premier of Orissa, and a reception was also organized by Harekrushna Mahtab, wherein reportedly both tried to dissuade Subhas from going on to a collision course with the Congress.[138] After addressing more meetings in Berhampur and Balasore, Subhas returned to Calcutta on 11 August, early in the morning, where the big news awaited him.

'Is that all?' a nonchalant Subhas asked the representative of the Associated Press, when he was informed about the decision of the working committee, disqualifying him as president of the BPCC and barring him from being a member of any elective Congress committee for three years from August 1939.[139] 'The Working Committee has come to the painful conclusion that it will fail in its duty if it condones the deliberate and flagrant breach of discipline by Subhas Babu', and hence the punishment 'for his grave act of indiscipline'. The working committee hoped 'that Shri Subhas Babu will see the error of his ways and loyally submit to this disciplinary action'.[140] Decisions to bar leaders like K.F. Nariman, Sheel Bhadra Yajee, Swami Sahajananda Saraswati and many others by the provincial Congress committees followed soon.

Rajendra Prasad also declared the latest election of the BPCC executive council null and void on the ground that proper notice had not been given to the members, thus reappointing the old council, and invalidated the appointment of the election tribunal by the new council.

The verdict did not come as a surprise to Subhas. He had been referring to the possibility of him being expelled from the Congress during his public meetings of the past few weeks. In his formal reaction, Subhas stated:

I welcome the decision of the Working Committee virtually expelling me from the Congress for three years. This decision is the logical consequence of the process of 'Right-consolidation' which has been going on for the last few years . . . The sentence meted out to me may have come as a shock to the vast majority of our countrymen, but not to me. It has appeared as a. perfectly logical development in the struggle between Constitutionalism and Mass Struggle and as an inevitable phase in our political evolution. Consequently, I do not find within myself the

"IS THAT ALL!"

Sj. Subhas Bose Reacts To Disciplinary Action

Calcutta, Friday.

"Is that all!" queried Sj. Subhas Chandra Bose, when the decision of the Working Committee disqualifying him from Presidentship of the B. P. C C and from being a member of any elective Congress body was conveyed to him by the 'Associated Press.'

Sj. Bose seemed to have received the news in an unconcerned manner and when asked for his comment remarked that he was much too busy at the moment with the planning of the Congress House, the foundation stone of which will be held in Calcutta on the 19th by Dr Rabindra Nath Tagore.

Subhas's reaction to the disciplinary action taken against him.
Advance, 11 August 1939, National Library, Government of India.

slightest trace of bitterness or anger. I am only sorry that the Working Committee did not realise that this sort of action should hurt them more than it should hurt me.

. . . What does it matter if I am victimised today? I shall cling to the Congress with even greater devotion than before and shall go on serving the Congress and the country as a servant of the nation. I appeal to my: countrymen to come and join the Congress in their millions and to enlist as members of the Forward Bloc. Only by doing so shall we be able to convert the rank and file in the Congress to our point of view, secure a reversal of the present policy of Constitutionalism and Reformism and

Gandhi's statement that he drafted the Congress resolution
taking disciplinary action against Subhas.
Advance, 24 August 1939, National Library, Government of India.

resume the national struggle for Independence with the united strength
of the Indian people.[141]

The decision of the working committee was defended by Gandhi, who was
the author of the resolution:

Subhas Babu had invited action. He had gallantly suggested that if any
action was to be taken it should be taken against him as the prime mover.
In my opinion the action taken by the Working Committee was the

mildest possible. There was no desire to be vindictive. Surely the word vindictiveness loses all force and meaning when the position of Subhas Babu is considered. He knew that he could not be hurt by the Working Committee. His popularity had put him above being affected by any action that the Working Committee might take. He had pitted himself against the Working Committee, if not the Congress organisation. The members of the Working Committee, therefore, had to perform their duty and leave the Congressmen and the public to judge between themselves and Subhas Babu.[142]

The working committee of the Forward Bloc met in Calcutta on 12 August and adopted resolutions: (a) to commence an all-India satyagraha if the Bengal political prisoners were not released at the end of two months, (b) condemning despatch of Indian troops abroad without the consent of the Indian people and the tendency of some provincial ministries to cooperate in war preparations, (c) asking Congress members of the Central Legislative Assembly to resign in protest of sending Indian troops abroad instead of merely abstaining from attending the next Assembly session, (d) to take necessary steps to raise a well-trained and disciplined All-India Volunteer Corps, (e) to launch a campaign for boycott of foreign cloth and British goods and (f) to make the States' peoples' organizations an integral part of the Congress as 'India is one and indivisible and the struggle for freedom in British India is indissolubly linked up with the struggle in the States'.[143]

The Bloc's working committee also held a meeting with leftist leaders including Jayaprakash Narayan, Ram Manohar Lohia, Ajoy Ghosh and Sahajananda Saraswati, who met at Subhas's Elgin Road house on 15 August, and decided to observe National Struggle Week from 31 August to 6 September. Each day of the week was marked for a different issue, such as the release of political prisoners, demands of farmers and labourers, federation, boycott of British goods, states' movements, etc.[144]

The Bloc and Left Consolidation Committee, however, continued to draw criticism from both the right and some sections of the left. While S. Satyamurti accused the Forward Bloc to be helping the enemies of the Congress and the country, Ram Manohar Lohia accused the committee's programme as being antithetical to the national movement.[145]

While striving to bring together the leftist parties for a common programme, Subhas now escalated the tempo of his offensive against the

Congress working committee. Even Gandhi, whom he had left out of his criticism until then, was not to be spared. Speaking at a public rally in Calcutta on 16 August, he levelled the charge against the Congress leadership that they would not hesitate to compromise with the British imperialists to remain in the seat of power. He cited how Hitler, Stalin and Chiang Kai-shek trampled over their co-workers to establish their supremacy, drawing a parallel with the Congress high command. There was a time when he believed that Gandhi was above all partisanship, but no more. Subhas held Gandhi responsible for the unpleasant circumstances at the Calcutta AICC meet. According to his analysis, the rapid increase in Congress membership and growth in political awareness among the masses made Gandhi and his followers worried that they would lose their grip over the Congress. As a result, they were reaching out to vested interests and the British imperialists to safeguard their position, and were making all efforts to curb a mass movement.[146]

Amidst all the struggle, one development that would have brought Subhas some satisfaction was a firm step towards fulfilling one of his wishes in the development of Calcutta. At the time of his visit to the great European cities in Italy, Germany and Austria, Subhas had discussed their architectural marvel with the then mayor, Santosh Kumar Basu. Now, due to his efforts, a beginning was made for the construction of a city hall dedicated to the nation, with the foundation laid by Rabindranath Tagore, who named it Mahajati Sadan (House of the Nation). Virtually all of Calcutta's public personalities gathered on 19 August to witness the function, except for the leaders of the Gandhian group in the Bengal Congress.

Located near the junction of the Chittaranjan Avenue and Harrison Road (now M.G. Road), the Mahajati Sadan, planned to be the largest building in the city, would be a three-storeyed one with a hall having a capacity of 2500 people, a theatre, offices, provision for accommodation of workers, volunteers and distinguished guests visiting the city, a library and a gymnasium. Out of the project's total budget of Rs 3 lakh, only Rs 32,000 had been raised (of which Rs 10,000 was donated by P.R. Das) and a few firms had promised supply of materials worth Rs 50,000. The remaining amount needed to be raised to complete the project. The Calcutta Municipal Corporation leased out the land at an annual fee of Re 1.[147]

Tagore spoke effusively about the uniqueness of Bengal, 'India's first home for cultivation of national freedom':

Bengal led India in welcoming European culture to her heart. Living currents flowed from overseas stirring her with new freedom. From age-long hibernation, Bengal's intellectual mind awoke to full splendour . . . Where life's call is vital, living centres must respond. Bengal did so even though the call of the new Age came from distant shores. In that lies Bengal's pride, and her true identity . . . in those critical days again, when, our leaders were banished behind jail-bars it was our youth in Bengal who led unhesitatingly in flinging themselves in the face of dire calamity—no other part of India can claim a parallel to this . . . Hundreds of youthful lives in Bengal have burnt themselves out during long terms of imprisonment; Bengali lights are dim, we know, for this reason; and yet we know that the soil in which they were born will give birth again to heroic sons who will not waste their manhood in destructive work but harness it to national reconstruction.

To-day in this great Hall of India we shall lay the foundation of Bengal's prowess, but our strength will not lie in arrogant nationalism, suspicious of friend and foe. We shall invoke Bengal's magnanimous heart of hospitality in which our humanity has found liberation; we shall seek freedom in many sided cooperation. Valour and beauty, resolute work and creative imagination, devotion to truth as well as self-dedication in public service—may these unite in benediction to our land . . . We welcome here the renascent soul of Bengal which has taken solemn initiation from History to dedicate its wealth of intellect and learning at India's shrine . . . We shall come nearer to our united nationalism, never yielding to the egoistic vanity of isolation which hurts our inherent humanity. High over all contentious politics let us keep the banner of truth flying and pray.

> Make them true, O Lord,
> Bengal's vows, Bengal's hopes,
> Bengal's work, Bengal's language,
> Let them be true.
> Bengal's heart, Bengal's mind,
> Brothers and sisters in Bengal's home.
> Let them be one, O Lord, make them one.

And to this prayer let this be added: May Bengal's arm give strength to the arm of India, Bengal's voice give truth to India's message; may

Bengal, in service of freedom for India, never make itself ineffective by betraying the cause of unity.

For Subhas, it was 'the beginning of the fulfilment of a long-cherished dream':

> Those who for years have toiled and suffered—laboured and sacrificed—so that India may be free, have long wished for an abode to provide shelter and protection for their activities and to serve as a visible symbol of their hopes and ideals—dreams and aspirations . . . From this soil sprang the movement that was at once the Reformation and the Renaissance of modern India. It was a movement which knew no provincial boundaries and which transcended the national frontier of India as well . . . To-day our people dream not only of a free India, but also of an Indian State founded on the principles of justice and equality and of a new social and political order which will embody all that we hold noble and sacred.[148]

The plan for the Mahajati Sadan, however, was not set to be realized smoothly. The first volley of sceptical questions was fired by the khadi warrior, Satish Chandra Dasgupta, ever too wary of Subhas's increasing influence. Expressing the doubt that the project was being treated as Subhas's personal one, he demanded that all legal powers be vested in a trust that should be set up by the Congress.[149]

Subhas had, in the meantime, started publishing a weekly, also named *Forward Bloc*, which made its first appearance on 5 August. Apart from his own commentary in the form of signed editorials, the weekly presented analyses of national and international political developments from a left-nationalist perspective, and among the prominent contributors were Humayun Kabir, Gopal Halder, Sudhi Prodhan, Somnath Lahiri, Jyotish Chandra Ghose, Atindra Nath Bose, Sahajananda Saraswati, Hirendra Nath Mukerjee, Sardul Singh Caveeshar, Buddhadeva Bose, Narahari Kaviraj, Benoy Kumar Sarkar, Bhupendra Kishore Rakshit-Roy, Sachin Sen, H.V. Kamath, Muzaffar Ahmad, Nirad C. Chaudhuri, Manmatha Nath Gupta and A.C.N. Nambiar.

The resolutions adopted by the executive council of the BPCC, which met on 25 August, were a veritable challenge to the working committee. Expectedly, the council reposed its trust on the leadership of Subhas, and in view of the widespread unrest caused by the disciplinary action against him, asked the working committee to reconsider its decision. The inadequate notice period which was cited as the ground for nullifying the election of the new council was an inconsequential technicality. That council expressed surprise at the Congress president taking such a step, knowing well that in view of the number of complainants being so few, the results of a reconvened meeting would not be any different. It reminded the president that despite the Pant resolution being ultra vires, Subhas had allowed it to be moved only because a large number of delegates were in its favour. In any case, the council insisted, there was no violation of rules in issuing the notice for the meeting to elect the new council.

The executive council went further in questioning the validity of the Congress working committee, as a new president (Prasad) was selected even before accepting the resignation of the outgoing president (Subhas). Since the new president was not elected by the AICC delegates, the council expressed doubts about whether the working committee commanded the confidence of the majority of AICC members. The council opined that disciplinary actions taken against AICC members should be put on hold, and a tribunal should be appointed by consensus or by three-fourths majority of the AICC to decide on the matter.

Unless these steps were taken by the working committee, the council warned, public dissatisfaction with the decisions would aggravate, and the council would be compelled to defy the working committee in order to act according to public opinion. It was, however, not taking such a drastic step immediately because it was keen to exhaust all options to arrive at a resolution.

Till the time the working committee arrived at a final decision, the council proposed to keep the post of the BPCC president vacant and take all decisions in consultation with Subhas.[150] The resolutions of the executive council were approved by a majority of 213 against 138 votes, at a general meeting of the BPCC. Chaotic scenes followed with tempers running high. Kiran Shankar Roy and Prafulla Chandra Ghosh claimed that they and some others of the opposition had been assaulted by the supporters of Subhas.[151]

On the night of 25 August, Subhas left for a three-day tour of Bihar. As at other places, he was welcomed by a swelling crowd, taken through cities in decorated processions and large public meetings organized at Patna, Muzaffarpur, Khagaul, Arrah, Bihta, Danapur and Bankipur. The enthusiastic reception at all the places that he went did, however, produce a reaction. Chanting the name of Gandhi, a small section of the crowd started pelting stones and hurling shoes at the podium when Subhas was speaking at a public meeting at Bankipur, chaired by Jayaprakash Narayan. Swami Sahajananda Saraswati received injuries, and in the commotion that followed, over twenty people were seriously injured. Rebuking the miscreants, Rajendra Prasad issued an apology the next day.[152]

An important change that was taking place at this time was the shuffling within the ranks of the former revolutionary groups and Subhas's relation with them. While many among them had gone on to become communists, some others kept their distance from the communist movement and reorganized on the basis of affiliation to the Marxist philosophy. Another section, organizationally weakened and suffering from a sort of crisis of ideology and programme, struggled to make themselves relevant to the changed circumstances.

Some members of the *Jugantar* group, which constituted the main plank of support for Subhas from the late 1920s, now spoke out publicly against him. On 25 August, eleven former revolutionaries, including Surendra Mohan Ghose, Bhupendra Kumar Datta, Harikumar Chakraborty, Jibanlal Chatterjee, Bhupati Majumdar and Arun Chandra Guha issued a charter of grievances, which was but an example of the confused state of mind, stemming from a crisis of ideology, among a section of former revolutionaries struggling to remain relevant by invoking their past actions:

> It was only their support that had made Subhas the leader of Bengal, a support that was given to him because his opponents were in favour of dominion status. Subhas was reluctant to move the resolution against dominion status at the Calcutta Congress of 1928 but was compelled to do so due to the pressure put on him by the revolutionaries. Soon, he expressed his unwillingness to be guided by the revolutionary programme chalked out by them. Later developments showed that Subhas was not a revolutionary. It had been easy for him to pose as one only due to the suffering he had to undergo because of his connections with revolutionaries. Although Subhas had moved away from their group as a result of which they had lost faith in him, they extended their support to Subhas during the re-election contest as they saw an opportunity for setting up a revolutionary leadership in the Congress. However, he failed to consult them and ignored their advice while taking important decisions. Making their fears come true, he failed to

nominate a working committee comprising only leftists. Alternatively, if he had resigned at the right time, the entire leftist leadership would have extended their support to him in order to replace the current Congress leadership which is clearly moving towards striking a compromise with British imperialism. Instead of grabbing the opportunity to establish a revolutionary leadership, Subhas kept playing to keep his presidentship secure. The signatories were of the opinion that no revolutionary could work along with the present working committee members and therefore the committee needed to be substituted in entirety. They were not ready to accept even a composite working committee. It was unfortunate that Subhas was being misled by anti-Congress forces. The Forward Bloc neither had a revolutionary programme nor any concrete plan to oppose federation. Instead of bringing more people under the banner of the Congress, it was in effect breaking it up. The majority commanded by Subhas in BPCC was working to obliterate the minority opposition and following the suicidal policy of creating a distance between Bengal and the rest of India. Those who intended to divide the Congress into leftist and rightist camps would turn out to be puppets in the hands of the imperialists. The Congress would undoubtedly be stronger if led by leftists but the way the campaign was being directed now would only strengthen the hands of the imperialists. The force of revolutionary struggle was being used only to grab power. The leftists who are helping to break up the Congress constitute the left-wing of the Indian fascists. Like the European fascists they are smothering the voice of the minority and luring the farmers and labourers with false promises. These fascists go by the name of socialists and communists and spread the falsehood that the real revolutionaries have no mass support base. The signatories declared that they would work to strengthen the Congress and convert it into a mass revolutionary organisation. They would do everything possible to remove from power the Congress constitutionalist leadership before commencing the struggle against imperialism, but would always remain within the Congress. However, they felt that to wage a campaign against opportunists who were trying to create divisions within the Congress it was necessary to work along with the Gandhians and constitutionalists. The struggle would give rise to a united revolutionary leadership once the opportunists were defeated.[153]

~

Completing the Bihar tour, Subhas was on his way to Madras on 1 September, after addressing the Midnapore district conference of leftist political workers at Kharagpur. Taking note of the arrangements made to welcome him, the president of the Andhra Pradesh PCC, Pattabhi Sitaramayya, and the Tamil Nadu PCC, O.P. Ramasamy Reddiyar, issued a warning that no Congress member or Congress committee should participate in his programmes. The Madras Corporation also decided, by twenty-one votes to seventeen, to not present an address to Subhas.

By the time Subhas boarded the train, the German forces had invaded Poland, and the world war had begun. The programme for the national struggle week had also begun in full earnest in Calcutta and the suburbs.[154] The restrictive measures announced by Sitaramayya were, however, futile. Many Congress workers resigned from their posts to join the swelling crowd that welcomed Subhas wherever he went. Alighting at Samalkot, Subhas travelled to Cocanada, where he was given a guard of honour by the local volunteer force. After inaugurating the Andhra Provincial Students' Conference and addressing two more meetings where, apart from talking about the current political scenario, he expressed his support for a separate Andhra province, Subhas left for Madras, attending more meetings on the way at Ramachandrapuram and Mandapeta.[155]

On 3 September, Subhas was 'addressing a mammoth meeting on the sea-beach in Madras where about two hundred thousand people were present . . . when somebody from the audience put an evening paper into his hand. He looked and read that Britain was at war with Germany'.[156] The next morning, a telegram from Vallabhbhai arrived, inviting him to attend an emergency meeting of the Congress working committee at Wardha. Accepting the invitation, Subhas put his South India tour on hold for the moment. 'Let [the] past be buried; let all of us rise as one man', Subhas appealed in a public meeting soon after. He also added, 'Let Mahatma Gandhi as the mentor of the Congress lead the country forward towards independence. The victory will be ours if we are prepared to die so that India may live.' The huge crowds that gathered to hear Subhas, remarked Ramnath Goenka in another meeting organized by the North Indian Association, 'bore testimony to the great regard in which he was held by the people'.[157]

The attitudes of the various political groups and leaders became clear within the next few days, but if there was any sliver of unity visible, it was just the opposite of Subhas's own position.

A group of notable individuals from Bengal, including Rabindranath, Acharya P.C. Ray, Manmathanath Mukherjee, Nilratan Sircar, Ramananda Chatterjee, B.C. Chatterjee and Syama Prasad Mookerjee issued a statement on 8 September, declaring that India 'must stand by Britain and resist the disastrous policy of domination by force'. Not only did the statement claim that 'No Indian would desire even in his own country's interest that England should lose the battle for freedom she is fighting today', but it also let loose the bogey of Nazi domination. If England lost, 'the realisation of Indian independence will be retarded' and 'India will then start a new chapter of slavery under fresh alien domination'. In exchange for India's support, 'England should not miss this great opportunity for establishing ever-lasting friendship with India by restoring self-rule to her'.[158]

The National Liberal Federation of India argued in favour of 'ungrudging and unconditional' support to Britain, and appealed the British Government at the same time to create 'psychological conditions in the country' to ensure 'complete cooperation' on the part of the Indian people. The Hindu Mahasabha saw 'ample room for cooperation between India and England', because defending India from any military attack was of common concern to the British Government as well as Indians themselves, but to make that cooperation 'effective', the Mahasabha urged the introduction of a responsible government at the centre and revision of the Communal Award, among other measures from the Government.[159] Speaking at the Barisal conference of the Mahasabha, B.C. Chatterjee announced unconditional support for England and its allies, pointing out that for Indians, it was a moment to choose between domination by England or by Germany.[160]

Another meeting of 'representative citizens of Calcutta', comprising the Nawab of Murshidabad, P.C. Ray, Justice Charu Chandra Biswas, B.P. Sinha Ray, Tulsi Goswami, Nilratan Sircar and J.N. Basu among others, announced wholehearted cooperation with the Government in the defence of the country and in 'resisting the menace of Hitlerism'. The meeting asked the Government to form at least two regiments in the army, composed entirely of Bengalis, in consideration of the past military services rendered by the Bengalis to the cause of the Empire.[161]

The Secretary of State for India observed in a memorandum to the British Cabinet that the 'outbreak of war was followed by manifestations from Indian Rulers great and small of their loyalty to the King Emperor and their willingness to place all their resources at the disposal of His Majesty's Government'.[162]

Meeting Viceroy Linlithgow in Simla on 4 September, Gandhi 'became disconsolate' and 'broke down' as he visualized the possible destruction of the British Parliament and the Westminster Abbey. His sympathies were with England and France, Gandhi informed the Viceroy.[163] Talking to the press in Rangoon on 8 September, on his way back from China, Jawaharlal made it clear that 'we are not out to bargain. We do not approach the problem with a view to taking advantage of Britain's difficulties'.[164]

The working committee started discussing the war situation in Jamnalal Bajaj's house at Wardha on 8 September. Apart from Subhas, Jayaprakash Narayan, Narendra Deo and M.S. Aney too were present on invitation. K.F. Nariman, Nathalal Parekh and Sardul Singh Caveeshar also arrived to meet with Subhas and discuss the Forward Bloc's strategy. Over 200 Forward Bloc workers descended outside Bajaj's house, shouting 'Subhas Babu ki jai', and demanding that the Congress should not choose the path of compromise.[165]

জনতা পরিবেষ্টিত সুভাষচন্দ্র : কংগ্রেস ওয়ার্কিং কমিটির বৈঠকে যোগদানের নিমিত্ত বিশেষভাবে নিমন্ত্রিত হইয়া ওয়ার্ধায় পদার্পণ করিলে তাঁহাকে এই বিপুল সংবর্ধনা জ্ঞাপন করা হয়

Subhas arrives at Wardh to join the working committee meeting as a special invitee. *Jugantar*, Vol. 2, Issue 309 (14 September 1939), British Library, EAP262-1-2-589.

After deliberating for four days, the working committee asked the British Government:

> . . . to declare in unequivocal terms what their war aims are in regard to democracy and imperialism and . . . in particular, how these aims are going to apply to India and to be given effect to in the present . . . A clear declaration about the future, pledging the Government to the ending of Imperialism and Fascism alike, will be welcomed by the people of all countries, but it is far more important to give immediate effect to it, to the largest possible extent, for only this will convince the people that the declaration is meant to be honoured. The real test of any declaration is its application in the present, for it is the present that will govern action today and give shape to the future.[166]

Jawaharlal was back in the working committee, being nominated as a member by Rajendra Prasad, and the resolution was drafted by him. Although Gandhi was 'sorry' to find himself arguing alone that 'whatever support was to be given to the British should be given unconditionally', he accepted the reality that the nation had not yet imbibed the non-violent spirit to take such a position. In such a situation, the working committee's resolution was the next best thing, and he could not stop admiring Jawaharlal's craft. 'The author of the statement is an artist', he opined, and said:

> Though he cannot be surpassed in his implacable opposition to imperialism in any shape or form, he is a friend of the English people. Indeed he is more English than Indian in his thoughts and make-up. He is often more at home with Englishmen than with his own countrymen . . . Though, therefore, he is an ardent nationalist his nationalism is enriched by his fine internationalism. Hence the statement is a manifesto addressed not only to his own countrymen, not only to the British Government and the British people, but it is addressed also to the nations of the world including those that are exploited like India. He has compelled India, through the Working Committee, to think not merely of her own freedom, but of the freedom of all the exploited nations of the world.[167]

Gandhi had made his views clear a few weeks before when he placed non-violence above the country's independence. He said in a press statement, 'I cannot emphasise my belief more forcibly than by saying that I personally would not purchase my own country's freedom by violence even if such a thing were a possibility'.[168] For now, internationalism and world peace worked well as substitutes for ahimsa. In any case, even if the British Government acquiesced to the Congress' demands, all that the party could offer was its moral support for 'Congress has no soldiers to offer', and 'fights not with violent but with non-violent means'. What was not clear, however, was how the concept of non-violence fit into the practical requirement of men and material for war, which the British Government had been utilizing, regardless of the consent of the Congress. The picture Jawaharlal painted in an article published in the *National Herald* a few days later was also far away from the model of Gandhian non-violence:

> A war policy for a nation must inevitably first take into consideration the defence of that country . . . The army will have to be considered a national army and not a mercenary force owing allegiance to someone else. It is on this national basis that recruitment should take place, so that our soldiers should not merely be cannon-fodder, but fighters for their country and for freedom. In addition to this it will be necessary to have a large-scale organisation for civil defence on a militia basis. All this can only be done by a popular government.
>
> Even more important is the development of industries to supply war and other needs. Industries must develop on a vast scale in India during war time.[169]

A conflict over the prioritization of national defence vis-à-vis non-violence, dormant for the time being, was bound to stare in the face of the Congress leaders sooner than later.

Apart from the war, the working committee also deliberated on the Bengal Congress deadlock. Surendra Mohan Ghose, Hari Kumar Chakravarty, Bhupendra Kumar Datta, Satin Sen, Manoranjan Gupta and Kiran Shankar Roy arrived at Wardha to give their input to the working committee, and also to tell Gandhi that they were waiting for his lead in the current situation.[170] Satya Ranjan Bakshi and Ashrafuddin Chowdhury presented the BPCC side of the story. Deciding that it would not modify its earlier decisions, the committee asked the BPCC to elect a new president, stating on record its displeasure about the 'tone and temper' of the BPCC resolutions as well as their contents, which were 'objectionable in the extreme'. Citing the inability of the BPCC to appoint an election tribunal that would be acceptable to all groups in the Bengal Congress, the committee took it upon itself to appoint a three-member tribunal consisting of Satish Chandra Dasgupta, Kshitish Prasad Chattapadhyay and Priya Ranjan Sen.[171] By the end of the month, the BPCC informed Kripalani that the decision was unacceptable to them as the tribunal appointed by the working committee had the support of just over a fourth of the BPCC members, whereas according to the AICC norms, it must have the backing of at least three-fourths of the members.[172]

Following a meeting with Gandhi that lasted for an hour and a half, Subhas resumed his tour of the provinces. Instead of returning to the southern provinces, Subhas planned to travel to Agra, Lucknow, Allahabad and Banaras in UP after holding a number of public meetings in Nagpur, Amaravati, Akola, Khamgaon, Malkapur and Bombay. However, due to a sudden illness, he had to postpone the plan. He left Bombay on 28 September to reach Calcutta on 1 October, stopping over at Allahabad for a day, where Jawaharlal hosted him in Anand Bhawan.[173]

The public speeches of Subhas at this time show that he was, for that moment, going along with the Congress resolution. He was too much of a practical politician to believe that the British would accede to the Congress demands without a struggle, but chose to wait for the Government's move and the reaction from the Congress. The working committee of the Forward Bloc, which met at Wardha on 17 September, regretted that despite an unambiguous policy enunciated in the resolution on foreign policy and war danger adopted at the Haripura Congress, which clearly stated that 'in the event of an attempt being made to involve India in a war, this will be resisted', the Congress working committee was hesitant to take an emphatic stand.[174] The Congress Socialist Party and the Kisan Sabha, under the leadership of Swami Sahajananda Saraswati, however, announced their complete allegiance going ahead to the decisions taken by the Congress working committee.[175]

The conflict between Subhas and Jawaharlal in the public space continued. When the latter termed Forward Bloc an evil in the course of a speech in Lucknow, Subhas issued a strongly worded retort. 'I do not know what his conception of good and evil is, nor do I know why he has been pleased to call the Forward Bloc an evil,' Subhas said. He added, 'In any case Forward Bloc is a lesser evil than that brand of internationalism which floats in the air and leads us nowhere,'[176] The Lucknow Students' Conference, taking place at the same time, passed a resolution on 23 September, reiterating their confidence in Subhas and declaring that the disciplinary action against him and other Leftists was a serious blow to the unity of national forces.[177]

After a short visit to Gauhati to set up the Forward Bloc office, Subhas left Kolkata on 7 October to preside over an Anti-Imperialist Conference in Nagpur, which was also attended by Sardul Singh Caveeshar, Swami Sahajananda Saraswati, Lala Shankar Lal Basal, H.V. Kamath, N.G. Ranga, R.S. Ruikar, B.T. Ranadive and Ashrafuddin Ahmad Chowdhury. Before leaving Calcutta, he issued a signed appeal for generous public contribution for the Mahajati Sadan, whose construction had started. Subhas was taken to the conference venue in a procession, riding an elephant. Rejecting any possibility of a compromise, he demanded that India should be given complete independence, and only after that would it decide its attitude towards the war. In the event of independence not being granted, he asked Indians to resort to satyagraha.[178]

The British and the Indian Governments had, in the meantime, started preparing to respond to the reactions of the different political groups. They were not unhappy with the support pouring in from various quarters, but were sensitive to the concomitant expectations too. Writing to the Secretary of State for India on 28 September, the Viceroy noted, 'Public opinion here is now quite clearly . . . worked up to a pitch of expectation of a declaration of some sort as regards the constitutional position and our aims in war.'[179]

Leading up to the declaration made on 17 October, the Viceroy met fifty-two people, including Rajendra Prasad, Jawaharlal, Vallabhbhai, Gandhi, Jinnah, Savarkar and others. Reaching Delhi on the morning of 10 October to meet the Viceroy, Subhas was welcomed by the leaders and workers of the provincial and district Congress committees, Majlis-e-Ahrar, the Student Federation, Kisan Sabha and the socialists amidst a guard of honour by Sikh volunteers with open swords. Apart from his meeting with the Viceroy, Subhas discussed the political situation in Bengal and the communal question with Fazlul Huq and Jinnah at the latter's house, met Mufti Kifayatullah, the president of the Jamiat Ulama-e-Hind, and addressed a public meeting at the Gandhi maidan. 'Don't wait for any [favourable] declaration from the British government', he told the audience gathered to hear him.[180]

Cartoons in *Jugantar* by Kafi Khan (Pratul Chandra Lahiri) showing general expectation of a settlement from the talks between Viceroy Linlithgow and Indian leaders and Linlithgow welcoming Indian leaders to his 'Viceroy Stores' offering last chance to a concession. *Jugantar*, Vol. 3, Issues 19 and 26 (8 and 15 October 1939), British Library, EAP262-1-2-620 and EAP262-1-2-620.

The Viceroy's declaration addressed three main points, including those posed by the Congress resolution, but as cautioned by Subhas, there was nothing new in it. Firstly, the British Government had not yet defined, with any precision, its war objectives, partly because it was too early to do so. The objectives were bound to change with the developing war situation, but at that moment, the general aim was to resist aggression and build a better international system. Secondly, as far as future constitutional aim was concerned, the Viceroy confirmed that the goal, as stated in the preamble to the Government of India Act 1919, which was 'progressive realisation of responsible government in British India as an integral part of the empire', and which again was interpreted by Lord Irwin in 1929 as 'the natural issue of India's progress as there contemplated is the attainment of Dominion Status', remained unchanged. The British Government would have been 'very willing' to start consultations at the end of the war with representatives of the different communities and parties and princes to modify the Government of India Act of 1935 'in the light of Indian views'.

Thirdly, the Government of India would have set up a consultative group, comprising representatives of all major political parties in British India and of the Indian princes, presided over by the Governor General, 'which would have as its object the association of public opinion in India with the conduct of the war and with questions relating to war activities'.[181]

'The Congress asked for bread and it has got a stone', was Gandhi's reaction.[182] Bitterly criticizing the Viceroy's declaration, the Congress working committee announced that under the circumstances, giving any support to Britain 'would amount to an endorsement of the imperialist policy which the Congress has always sought to end'. The Congress ministries in the provinces were instructed to resign and all Congress committees and congress workers were asked to be prepared for a possible resistance movement, which had to be purged of all violence, with 'perfect discipline'.[183]

Despite the ominous-sounding resolution, Gandhi clarified that 'further action will wholly depend upon Britain's handling of the crisis' and that 'Congress has left the door open to Britain to mend the mistake'.[184] There was no possibility of a large-scale civil resistance unless Congressmen showed perfect adherence to non-violence and truth, and even then 'there need be none unless we are goaded into it by the authorities'. He explained that 'Though the British Government have grievously disappointed the Congress hope, my hope, I do not seek any gain from their embarrassment'.[185]

Cartoons in *Jugantar* by Kafi Khan (Pratul Chandra Lahiri) showing Gandhi's futile effort to hug and unresponsive Viceroy.
Jugantar, Vol. 3, Issue 40 (29 October 1939), British Library, EAP262-1-2-634.

Following his meeting with the Viceroy, Subhas reached Lucknow on 12 October for an informal conference with the leftist leaders, including

Jayaprakash Narayan, P.C. Joshi and Sahajananda Saraswati. Speaking at a public meeting in the Ganga Prasad Memorial Hall presided over by Chandra Bhan Gupta, Subhas expressed his sympathies for Poland. The Congress, he felt, had lost an opportunity by not pressing for the national demand at the very outset of the war.[186] Returning to Calcutta on 16 October, he announced the nomination of Sheel Bhadra Yajee of Patna and S.G. Patwardhan of Amaravati to the Forward Bloc working committee.[187]

It was a mystery to him, Subhas told reporters, as to why the Congress was yet to implement the war resolution adopted in Haripura. Calling the Congress attitude a dithering one, he cautioned that if the Haripura resolution was not put into action, he would not be obligated to follow the decisions of the working committee or the AICC. He disagreed with the idea that India should wait to hear from the Viceroy's House or the Whitehall in order to decide the next course of action.[188] Claiming that the viceregal declaration proved his prognosis correct, he hoped that those who were expecting the dawn of a new era would join hands with him.[189]

Subhas welcomed the decision of the working committee asking the provincial ministries to resign, but warned that stopping only at the resignation would not achieve much. Reacting to Gandhi's call for unity and discipline, he pointed out that there was no clarity over the Congress programme, and he would commit himself to such unity and discipline only if the programme was progressive enough.[190] As noted by the Bengal Government's report on the political situation in the province:

> Mr Subhas Bose welcomed the decision but insisted that this must be only a prelude to concerted action intended to create the greatest possible embarrassment to Government. Mr. Bose is understood to be insistent that the resignation of Congress Ministries must be only a preliminary to aggressive efforts against the British Government, the creation of a constitutional deadlock in all Congress Provinces and activities directed to fomenting industrial and agrarian unrest, initiating a boycott of British goods, carrying on propaganda against recruitment and assistance in the war and mobilising the Muslim masses on a political and economic programme.[191]

At the same time, he also issued a sharp critique against Fazlul Huq's remarks on the working committee's response to the viceregal announcement, in which Huq accused the committee of ignoring the problems of the minorities and behaving like a spoilt child. Bengal's Hindus could present a far bigger list of complaints against Huq's Government, Subhas said, than Huq could against the Congress ministries in the other provinces. Any civilized person would be shocked to hear the speeches being made by Huq's henchmen in the districts of Bengal, he said in his statement.[192]

Not wanting to escalate the conflict over his removal from the post of the Bengal Congress president under the circumstances, the executive council of the BPCC elected Rajendra Dev as the new BPCC chief on Subhas's suggestion. The council, however, made it clear that Dev would discharge his duties only in consultation with Subhas.[193]

However much Subhas sought clarity on the Congress programme and a more aggressive policy, it was not about to come as Gandhi, now officially in charge of guiding the working committee, held on to his position. In the *Harijan* of 4 November, he reiterated:

> I hold the opinion strongly that whilst by their own action the British Government have made it impossible for the Congress to cooperate with them in the prosecution of the war, the Congress must not embarrass them in its prosecution. I do not desire anarchy in the country. Independence will never come through it.[194]

Meeting at Allahabad from 19 to 23 November, the Congress working committee raised the demand for a constituent assembly to decide the future constitution of India, making it clear at the same time that the organization was not considering any precipitate action. It would 'continue to explore the means of arriving at an honourable settlement, even though the British Government has banged the door in the face of the Congress', the working committee resolved.[195] The same tenor was maintained at the working committee meeting held from 18 to 22 December.

The working committee, at the same time, continued its efforts to strengthen its control over the BPCC. Acting on the basis of complaints received about possible violation of rules in managing funds, the working committee sought audit reports from 1937 onwards, the year when Sarat Bose had taken charge of the Bengal Congress. Auditors appointed by the AICC were asked to inspect all financial documents in the custody of the BPCC and Sarat Bose, as the leader of the Congress party in the Bengal

Legislative Assembly too was accused of violating rules in managing
funds raised from the Congress members of the legislature. Rejecting the
BPCC's objections on the election tribunal nominated by the committee
for the province, the working committee instructed that full cooperation to
the tribunal should be given by the BPCC.[196]

Syama Prasad Mookerjee noted the source of the complaint in his
diary entry of 28 January 1939, finding it difficult to believe:

> Had a talk with Dr [BC] Roy about the election of Subhas as President
> of the Congress. He made the astounding statement that there have been
> serious financial irregularities on Subhas's part. Monies received as purses
> presented to the President have mostly been appropriated by himself—
> while according to previous practice seventy-five per cent should have
> gone to the Provincial Congress funds and twenty-five per cent to the
> Central Fund. I wonder if this is a true accusation.[197]

By the end of December, the working committee noted that the conflict
between the election tribunal and the BPCC continued, resulting in the
resignation of the members of the tribunal. With the BPCC elections at
hand, the working committee appointed an ad hoc committee of eight
members, with Azad as the chairman. Highlighting the irregularities
in maintaining books and dealings in cash at the BPCC, the working
committee issued instructions to strictly follow the rules related to
managing funds.[198] The auditors' report was, however, hotly contested
by Ashrafuddin Ahmad Chowdhury, the BPCC secretary. The auditors
'had conclusions made for them before they started their work, and made
their remarks most often on a distortion of facts or on a slender basis of
facts', Chowdhury contended.[199] The BPCC also protested against the
appointment of the ad hoc committee in its meeting of 6 January 1940,
asking the working committee not to foist an unwanted committee on
the Bengal Congress. While the meeting was attended by 253 out of 544
members, about 140 members of the BPCC with declared allegiance to the
Gandhian Congress refused to take part in it.[200]

The altercation with the Congress working committee over finances
continued in the public space between Rajendra Prasad on one side and
Chowdhury and Sarat on the other. Subhas entered the debate towards
the end of January. In a statement issued on 19 January, Subhas explained
that the BPCC had been living hand to mouth for the last eighteen years,

and it was only in 1939, under his presidentship, that it had surplus funds. This was made possible by organizing the AICC meeting in April 1939 and by amending the BPCC constitution, whereby a part of the four anna membership fee was stipulated for the organization's funds.

The controversy was nothing but a result of the vindictive politics by the working committee, Subhas argued. Since Kiran Sankar Roy's group, which organized the previous AICC meeting in April 1937, was able to generate a very small amount of surplus, the present BPCC's success in generating a large amount of surplus funds had become an eyesore to the Khadi–Roy group. The attempt by the working committee to find faults with the BPCC was:

> inspired by two motives—firstly, to find out if the funds of the BPCC and the Bengal Parliamentary Fund have been utilised for the Forward Bloc; and secondly, to find some plea to take action against the present BPCC, which is not blindly subservient to the present leadership in the Congress and which has a clear left majority.

Subhas accused Rajendra Prasad of partiality by not holding an audit for the Bihar provincial Congress committee, against which there were serious charges of financial irregularities over several years:

> I know that there is deep resentment In Bengal against the high-handed and unjust action of the Working Committee but I assure them that the action of the Working Committee is not against Bengal as such, but against all those, who refuse to offer blind homage to Wardha, no matter to which province they belong.[201]

The arguments continued. As far as the matter of irregularities related to BPCC accounts, both sides had something to say on their behalf. Certain laxities on the part of the BPCC were undeniable, despite its criticism of the methodology adopted by and manner of functioning of the auditors, and it would have been better if Subhas, notwithstanding his reputation for financial integrity, had acknowledged the fact and then worked upon rectifying the lapses. Yet, the working committee's overall attitude towards the BPCC, its focus on Bengal to the exclusion of provinces such as Bihar to which the Congress president belonged, reeked of vindictiveness that drove the Bose brothers to take them to a fight.

A subcommittee appointed by BPCC president Rajen Deb, and comprising Harendra Nath Ghosh, Niharendu Dutta Majumdar, Bankim Mukherjee and Satya Bakshi, that went into scrutinizing the report of the auditors again pointed out several problems in the way the audit had been conducted.[202]

While the conflict between the working committee and the BPCC went on, Subhas continued with his tours to garner support. His popularity continued to be on the rise. As he arrived at Delhi on the first day of 1940 to address the All-India Students' Conference, the press reported his reception:

> An enthusiastic reception was accorded to Sj. Subhas Chandra Bose on his arrival at Delhi this evening to preside over the All-India Students' Federation Conference. A big crowd was inside the platform while a bigger one was waiting outside for his arrival. As soon as Sj Bose alighted, he was profusely garlanded by Miss Renu Roy, Lala Shankarlal, President, Delhi Provincial Congress Committee and others on behalf of the Students' Federation, the Delhi Provincial Congress Committee, the Delhi District Congress and other organisations. Sj Bose was then taken in a mile-long procession led by a hundred Khaksars and Ahrars through the main streets of the city. Houses and bazars were decorated and were flying National Flags. After two hours, the procession terminated at Gandhi grounds where a big pandal for the Federation Conference was built.[203]

Addressing the students, Subhas pointed out that as far as the question of constituent assembly was concerned, a real assembly was one which was convened by a national Government after transference of power, in contrast to an assembly formed under the aegis of an imperialist government and elected on the basis of separate electorate, which would surely end in disaster. In explaining the Congress's unwillingness to launch a struggle, he launched a bitter attack on the leadership:

> But why are they thus shirking a struggle? . . . I presume that they are afraid that once a nation-wide campaign is launched, the control and the leadership of the nationalist movement will pass out of their hands . . . Hence the endeavour to purge the Congress of the Leftists. Hence the vendetta against the Bengal Provincial Congress Committee. And hence

the elaborate efforts that have been made for some time past to resist 'mass invasion' of the Congress through increased membership and to convert the Congress into a close preserve of the Rightists.[204]

Financial contribution towards the Congress Subhas Fund for the construction of the Mahajati Sadan was still much below expectation. To focus on a fundraising drive, Subhas announced that 7–14 January would be observed as the Mahajati Sadan Week.[205] In the face of strong opposition, however, the Calcutta Corporation awarded a grant of Rs 1 lakh Rupees for the construction of the Sadan, through a special meeting convened on 30 January.[206] The move was opposed by B.C. Roy on the grounds that the lease of land for ninety-nine years for a nominal rent of Re 1, and the grant of Rs 1 lakh was awarded to Subhas as an individual and not to a trust or institution. He alleged that even after the grant of lease, there had been no attempt on Subhas's part to form a trust or to take leading citizens into confidence.[207]

N.C. Mitra, a member of the Mahajati Sadan committee gave the antecedents refuting Roy's charges. Mitra said that soon after Subhas's release, an informal conference of leading citizens of Calcutta in April 1937 decided to raise a Subhas Congress Fund for Rs 1 lakh. The objectives of the fund included constructing a building to accommodate the headquarters of Bengal Congress. A working committee of sixty-four members to regulate the fundraising and overseeing the implementation of the plan was set up that included leaders such as B.C. Roy, Abul Kalam Azad, Prafulla Chandra Ghosh and Prabhudayal Himmatsingka. Although numerous meetings of the committee were held, Roy did not attend any of them despite being sent notices regularly. The committee decided in its meeting of 9 February 1938 to approach the Corporation for acquiring the required piece of land. The application for lease was filed by Subhas as an individual, and not as the president of the Congress, since the working committee of the fund decided that the proposed building, apart from being the Bengal Congress headquarters, would also have other uses for the city of Calcutta. The terms of the lease awarded by the Corporation clearly stipulated that on the completion of the building, it would have to be handed over to a board of trustees. The ratepayers in the city were not asked to make any contribution towards the construction of the Sadan, and the grant from the Corporation was sought only in proportion to the facilities which were to be provided for use by general citizens.[208]

The matter, however, soon reached the High Court with a few ratepayers and a couple of councillors obtaining an interim injunction on the grant of money by the Corporation, on 7 February 1940.[209]

Continuing his whirlwind tour of the country, Subhas arrived at Ellore on 9 January, accompanied by M. Annapurnayya, the president of the Andhra Forward Bloc. Carried into the town by a chariot drawn by fifty-two bullocks, Subhas presided over the political sufferers' conference and then left for Madras, where he was met by N.G. Ranga and Srinivasa Iyengar.[210]

The Congress working committee had modified the Independence Pledge during its December 1939 meeting to include a clause on charkha and khadi. The clause asked Congressmen to pledge that they would spin regularly, and use nothing but khadi and the products of village handicrafts for their personal requirements.[211] Subhas felt that 'to convert spinning into a method of political struggle is an altogether mistaken policy'. He pointed out that when India had lost its freedom, 'Indian people knew nothing except hand-spun and hand-woven cloth'. He preferred the pledge of 1930, and allowed Forward Bloc members to organize separate meetings and demonstrations without the spinning clause.[212] A few days later, he asked Forward Bloc workers to modify the 1930 pledge too by deleting the last line which called upon people to carry out the instructions of the Congress. 'One does not know today whether the Congress under Mahatmaji's leadership will ultimately drift. Consequently, it would be dangerous to pledge one's support in advance to the Congress or its executive', Subhas explained.[213]

About the wrangle in the Bengal Congress, he commented, 'There were no differences among Bengal Congressmen as long as I was President. The present differences have been artificially engineered and fostered since the day I resigned.' One of the objectives of this strategy was to prevent Bengal from sending a strong contingent of Leftists to the next annual Congress session.[214]

Before leaving Madras for Bombay on 12 January, Subhas issued a statement on the attitude of the Gandhian Congress towards the Forward Bloc. 'My own belief that by honest hard work we shall be able to convert the majority in the Congress to our point of view has been considerably shaken of late', he said, claiming that 'Rightists are determined to maintain their present ascendency by hook or by crook.' This situation, he said, gave rise to the question whether the Forward Bloc should continue within the Congress.[215]

Addressing a public meeting at Chowpatty in Bombay the next day, Subhas issued an ultimatum to the Congress leadership:

> The ultimatum is that unless you shed yourselves of the reformist mentality and forsake the path of bankrupt constitutionalism of the Liberals quickly enough, the Leftists would assert themselves. They would declare their own leadership and prosecute the struggle for freedom. This would be done by us within the Congress if possible or without the Congress if necessary. The communal question is a fib. It would disappear when the masses appear in the fighting field. The masses would appear only if they are properly lead.[216]

'Some are very impatient', Vallabhbhai observed while speaking at the fourth Berar Provincial Political Conference on 15 January. He pointed out that the Forward Bloc had been threatening to do something for the past few months, but had done nothing by that point.[217] Gandhi responded after some time that Subhas was 'as much reformist and liberal as I am. Only I with my age know it, and he in his youth is blind to the good that is in him.' Gandhi also said:

> Let my correspondents rest assured that, in spite of our different outlooks, and in spite on the Congress ban on him, when he leads in a non-violent battle they will find me following him, as I shall find him following me, if I overtake him.[218]

Subhas reached Patna from Bombay on 14 January. Addressing a public meeting, he said that after the war 'the present order is going to change and the new order which will evolve will mean independence for every country and liberty for every individual'. He also added, 'Imperialism will be given a decent burial', sounding overtly optimistic.[219]

In view of the conflicts within the Bengal Congress, M.N. Roy offered his advice to Subhas. The conflict between the BPCC and the working committee had reached a stage where a split was inevitable, he wrote in a letter to Subhas, but:

> . . . when that inevitable parting of ways take place, it should be an All-India event. It should not be precipitated on a provincial scale. It would be wiser for the BPCC not to be provoked into a revolt which is bound to be

misunderstood as an outburst of provincialism. The Working Committee
has successfully manoeuvred the shift the conflict on a basis of technical
issues which cannot be expected to arouse any protest in other parts of the
country. There is a danger of isolation. That danger must be avoided if
Bengal is to be the spearhead of a revolt against the reactionary ideology
and compromising politics of the present Congress leadership.

Roy argued that opposing the elections to be held by the ad hoc committee
would result in two provincial Congress committees, with the present BPCC
no longer being a party of the AICC. Delegates to the next Congress would be
chosen from the officially recognized committee, putting the current BPCC at
a disadvantage. Roy urged Subhas to participate in the elections because 'with
your popularity cannot possibly substantially change the present relation of
forces', and 'the election will give you the opportunity to counter the Working
Committee by raising serious political issues'. In such a scenario, 'there cannot
be any doubt about the choice of the majority of Bengal Congressmen'.

Even if the present BPCC failed to obtain a majority in the elections
due to election manoeuvres of the working committee, Roy insisted,
the position would not be any worse than that what would be created
by boycotting the elections. Rather, 'with a powerful minority of honest
and determined fighters conscious of their revolutionary purpose', a
'solid foundation for the creation of a left wing will be laid'. For this to
happen, Roy explained with prescience, it was important to ask Bengal
Congressmen to vote on the nature of the Gandhian leadership:

> The rank and file must be told clearly that there will be no struggle so long
> as the Congress remains under the present leadership; that the present
> leaders of the Congress are bound by certain principles which preclude
> any revolutionary struggle; that Gandhism has superseded nationalism;
> that the present leadership is determined to come to some agreement with
> Imperialism; that the ideal of complete independence has been thrown
> overboard in favour of Dominion Status within the British Empire; and
> that the future of the Congress depends on the ability of the rank and file
> to realise their responsibility and assert their will.[220]

Gandhi responded to Subhas's campaign through an article published in
Harijan on 20 January, in which he came clear that he was not 'spoiling for
a fight', but 'trying to avoid it':

Whatever may be true of the members of the Working Committee, I wholly endorse Subhas Babu's charge that I am eager to have a compromise with Britain if it can be had with honour. Indeed satyagraha demands it. Therefore I am in no hurry. And yet if the time came and if I had no follower, I should be able to put up a single-handed fight. But I have not lost faith in Britain.

It has been suggested to me by a Congressman wielding great influence that as soon as I declare civil resistance I would find a staggering response this time. The whole labour world and the kisans in many parts of India will, he assures me, declare a simultaneous strike. I told him that, if that happened, I should be most embarrassed and all my plan would be upset. I must confess that I have no positive plan in front of me. Let me say that God will send me the plan when He gives the word as He has done before now. He has been my unfailing Guide and has sustained me throughout my stormy life. This, however, I know that no plan that I may put before the country will admit of unregulated and sporadic strikes, because that must lead to violence and therefore automatic suspension of the non-violent struggle. It would amount to my dismissal.[221]

'I am still prepared to follow Gandhiji as a humble soldier. When he launches a struggle, he will find me following him amongst his countless soldiers. That is what I want and only this much is demanded by the Forward Bloc', Subhas replied.[222]

On 17 January, Subhas left for a tour of the UP, starting with Banaras, where he addressed public meetings and also a conference of the students of the Banaras Hindu University. He travelled to Meerut, Agra, Lucknow and Shikohabad before returning to Calcutta on 27 January.

Divisions within the leftist camp also continued. Jayaprakash Narayan was not happy with Subhas's programme. 'Mr Bose's recent activities and statements have caused me great distress and I should like to make it clear that he is not justified in associating all leftists with his views', Narayan said in a statement issued on 21 January. The 'ill-conceived leftist offensive' would drive away the overwhelming number of Congressmen who did not fall in the conventional category of leftism but were eager for a struggle. Narayan suggested that Subhas should, 'instead of rallying leftists for a holy war upon the rightists', focus on raising a volunteer corps of 50,000 and fight against the suppression of civil liberties in Bengal.[223]

Both the working committee and the BPCC hardened their stance when Rajendra Prasad announced on 29 January that due to no changes in the attitude of the BPCC and its executive council, the organizational elections would be conducted by the ad hoc committee.[224] In response, the BPCC again deplored the 'foisting on Bengal the unwanted ad hoc committee', calling upon district, subdivisional and primary Congress committees not to cooperate with it and hold protest meetings.[225] After addressing a public rally at Shraddhananda Park on 30 January, Subhas again left for a tour of Bihar from 1 to 14 February.

On 11 February at Hazaribagh, Subhas, accompanied by Shankar Lal, Sheel Bhadra Yajee and Swami Sahajananda Saraswati announced that the leftists would organize a conference at Ramgarh alongside the main annual Congress session.[226] The idea was opposed by Jayaprakash Narayan, who claimed that the Congress session itself being an anti-compromise conference, the one proposed by Subhas would only disrupt Congress's work.[227] In a joint statement, Narayan and Narendra Dev claimed that the draft resolution prepared by the Congress working committee for the Ramgarh session marked a 'turning point' and a 'distinct break with the policy of stalemate'. The statement said, inter alia:

> We hope that . . . those who in the name of Leftism have of late been trying to disrupt the Congress and lower its prestige, will realise now that the time has come when we must put our house in order and repair the breaches that have been made in the national front. Their sole justification for all their actions has been that the Congress would not fight any more and that the Working Committee was soon to enter into a pact with Imperialism. These deductions, as we have often endeavoured to show at some risk of misunderstanding, were based on a false leading of the Congress policy and perhaps certain amount of wishful thinking . . . The greatest responsibility in this connection lies with Mr Subhas Chandra Bose, who we hope, will rise to the occasion.[228]

Maulana Abul Kalam Azad was elected the new president of the Congress, dealing an overwhelming defeat to his contender M.N. Roy, obtaining 1854 votes against 183 votes. Roy accused the Forward Bloc of betrayal for not supporting his candidature.[229]

Chaos broke out when Vallabhbhai arrived at the Howrah railway station to attend a conference in Malikanda. A group of about forty youths held a black flag demonstration and threw the flagstaff at him when Vallabhbhai was getting into his car. Luckily, he emerged unhurt.[230] Attempts to greet Gandhi with black flags were also made the next day when he arrived at the Sealdah station along with Kasturba Gandhi. A group of demonstrators with black flags and anti-Gandhi placards also attacked his public meeting at Malikanda, injuring several persons.[231] When leaving Calcutta, a shoe was hurled at Gandhi at the Lilooah station, which hit Mahadev Desai instead. Desai carried the shoe away with him.[232] Sarat issued an apology, pointing out that the shoe was thrown by two Congress members from Serampore.[233]

Towards the end of February, Subhas became embroiled in a controversy with the press. On 21 February, the *Amrita Bazar Patrika* published a statement issued by the editors of the *Amrita Bazar Patrika*, *Hindusthan Standard*, *Bharat*, *Advance*, *Matribhumi* and *Jugantar*, which decried a warning issued by Subhas at a recent public meeting against 'so-called nationalist' newspapers for 'publishing half-truths and untruths'. Agitated public response in the meeting insisted on the boycott of such newspapers. Calling it a fascist technique, the statement asked him 'to desist from the crude and dangerous tactics'.[234]

Both instances of unruly mob behaviour and complaints of being assaulted by supporters of Subhas continued to find increasing space in the pages of the *Amrita Bazar Patrika* and those who had taken up the campaign of press freedom against him. A former councillor in the Corporation accused that he had been beaten up for opposing Subhas during a public rally on 23 February at Deshapriya Park.[235] Dhirendra Nath Sen, editor of the *Hindusthan Standard*, alleged that he had been removed from his post after issuing the joint statement against Subhas.[236] A meeting presided over by Sen, where M.N. Roy was the key speaker on 6 March, was marked by noisy demonstrations with a few people rushing on to the rostrum.[237] Roy argued in his speech that the only difference between the Gandhian leadership and Subhas was that while the former talked in terms of persuasion, the latter talked constantly about a grim struggle ahead without caring to explain when the struggle was to be launched. He claimed that 'having for a long period monopolised the Press and platform in Bengal, the group headed by Sj Subhas Chandra Bose does not want that monopoly to be broken in the least'.[238]

Led by its editor Tushar Kanti Ghosh, the *Amrita Bazar Patrika* went on an overdrive, soon to be joined by M.N. Roy, Jawaharlal, Rajendra

Prasad and other Congress leaders. The conflict continued to intensify through March. On 1 March, the working committee of the Bengal Provincial Students Federation (BPSF) passed a resolution declaring that the organization 'cannot be party to any agitation against any particular newspaper'.[239] On 9 March, in an editorial named 'Our Fascists', the *Patrika* charged that the Bengal Congress led by Subhas:

> had been so intoxicated with consciousness of power that it had completely forgotten that the methods adopted by it were Fascist, only it had no 'storm troopers' and organisation to give effect to its decision by force. It did not occur to it that Bengal or for the matter of that India would not fight British Imperialism to establish Fascism even of the Swadeshi brand.[240]

The act of nominating Satish Chandra Bose, Subhas's eldest brother, for the upcoming Calcutta Corporation elections, was also questioned. 'The spectacle of power converging within a family is hardly edifying', commented the *Amrita Bazar Patrika* editorial of 10 March.[241]

The BPCC–Congress working committee conflict came to a head when, in its meeting on 29 February, the working committee annulled the BPCC's decision to disaffiliate the district Congress committees of Mymensingh, Hugli and Jessore for cooperating with the ad hoc committee. Observing that the resolution of the BPCC 'coming as it does after a series of acts of defiance of the Working Committee, leaves no room for any further condonation of their indiscipline', the committee asked the BPCC to show cause as to why it should not be disaffiliated. The BPCC and its executive council were suspended until final orders were passed by the Congress president.[242] The BPCC would 'continue to function as before, regardless of any ukase that may emanate from Wardha, Patna or Allahabad', was Subhas's response.[243]

The election of delegates to the Ramgarh Congress, however, showed that the working committee had achieved a sort of victory over the BPCC, with the ad hoc committee succeeding in ensuring the election of 402 delegates out of the stipulated 544. Only ninety-five seats could not be filled up due to non-cooperation, and another forty-seven due to the paucity of members.[244]

On 2 March, Subhas left Calcutta for another tour of the UP, addressing meetings in places like Jhansi, Mathura and Dehra Dun.

Meeting on 12 March in the midst of heavy rains and stormy winds that hampered the construction of pandals, seventy members of the reception committee of the Anti-Compromise Conference elected Swami Sahajananda Saraswati as its chairperson and Subhas as the president of the conference. While the subjects committee for the conference was scheduled to meet on 18 March, the open session was scheduled for 19 and 20 March.[245] Subhas visited Ramgarh on the 16th to supervise the arrangements, leaving for Calcutta on the same evening, and returned on 18 March.

The newly elected BPCC rescinded the direction issued by the former committee controlled by Subhas, of boycotting newspapers, and the new members were 'entertained at a tea party' by Tushar Kanti Ghosh, the editor of the *Amrita Bazar Patrika*.[246] 'The *Amrita Bazar Patrika* has long been lying in wait for an opportunity to catch him at a disadvantage: his attempt to start a boycott against this paper having failed, its tone is becoming more and more openly hostile to him', the Governor of Bengal, J.A. Herbert reported to the Viceroy on 20 March.[247]

In a major political development, the BPCC and the Hindu Mahasabha announced on 28 February that they would contest the upcoming Corporation elections jointly. Syama Prasad later gave his version of how things came to pass:

Subhas and I had a talk one day about the political situation in Bengal. One evening Sarat Bose and we two had a long discussion. I asked them to take up the Hindu cause in Bengal so as to render it unnecessary for us to organise a separate political body. They expressed their inability to do so—first because they thought it might still further rouse Muslims, and secondly, because they themselves being well-known 'Non-Communal Congressites' could not openly do what I asked them to do.

Later on when we started organising ourselves, Subhas once warned me in a friendly spirit, adding significantly, that if we proceeded to create a rival political body in Bengal he would see to it (by force if need be) that it was broken before it was really born . . .

. . . Due to the attack on Hindu rights, we wanted a strong Hindu Sabha party in the Corporation. We were prepared to work with Subhas and run elections jointly, provided we also worked as a team in the Corporation later on. Subhas agreed to this when he found that our strength was not entirely negligible. A selection board was formed,

Subhas, Sarat Bose and Rajendra Ch. Dev representing Subhas's Congress, and SN Banerjee, Sanat Kumar Roychaudhuri and myself representing the Hindu Sabha.[248]

The arrangement, however, fell through after both parties announced their first list of candidates on 4 March. On 7 March, it was announced by both parties jointly that the alliance had come to an end.[249] According to Syama Prasad, the arrangement came to an end 'due to Subhas's attitude', as he insisted on retaining one of his candidates over disapproval by the Mahasabha and asked the Mahasabha to leave out one of their nominated candidates. Mookerjee claimed that the alliance ended because Subhas had not agreed to his proposal that both candidates should have been either retained or dropped.[250]

Subhas presented a rather weak defence of his party's alliance and the subsequent break with the Hindu Mahasabha a few weeks later while campaigning for the Corporation elections. He had tried to come to a settlement with the Hindu Mahasabha, in the background of the recent Calcutta Municipal Corporation Act that, for the first time, stipulated separate electorates, since the Congress was 'always anxious to avoid conflict with other parties'. The pact, however, failed because the Mahasabha could not choose candidates who were acceptable to the Congress. Thereafter, he launched a stringent criticism of the Mahasabha, and asked why the party entered politics and was interested in contesting elections, since there was no question of Hindu interest in the Corporation. For all the years that the Corporation had been in the hands of the Congress, he said, there never was a complaint of crushing Hindu interests. Calling the Mahasabha reactionary, he accused the party of taking a compromising stand on the questions of federation and war, although it followed a policy of non-cooperation with British imperialism. He also felt that Mahasabha leaders were making too much of some instances of stone throwing, and such incidents were a part of public life.[251]

The relations with the Mahasabha reached a low when, on 15 March, Subhas's supporters broke up a meeting of Syama Prasad Mookerjee and hurled stones that hit his head. It was 'The Plague of Fascism', asserted the lead editorial of the *Amrita Bazar Patrika* in its 17 March issue, and called the citizens of Calcutta to defeat 'the candidates of the Fascist Party' in the upcoming Corporation elections.[252] At another meeting the next day, when Mookerjee spoke at a public rally in Calcutta about the breakdown in the Congress–Mahasabha alliance and blamed Subhas for the 'mud-slinging' taking place, there were further disruptions. Mookerjee told the miscreants shouting 'Subhas Bose ki jai' that if Subhas was not really behind them, they were sullying his image. On the other hand, if Subhas really was behind them, then he would ask Subhas to come to the rostrum and point out what was wrong, rather than sending hired goons.[253]

Before long, the pages of the newspapers became the place of charges and countercharges, with attacks on Subhas getting more prominence in the newspapers that had already turned against him. The division amongst the newspapers has been described by Mookerjee as:

We had the *Amrita Bazar Patrika* and *Jugantar* with us entirely . . . *Bharat*, a Bengali daily, powerfully and ably edited and controlled by Makhan Sen was hundred percent anti-Subhas and supported us. The *Hindusthan Standard* and *Anandabazar Patrika*, wielding great influence as they did, were controlled by Subhas and Sarat Bose.[254]

On 18 March, the day Subhas arrived at Ramgarh for the Anti-Compromise Conference, he and the conference received severe lampooning in the editorial of the *Amrita Bazar Patrika*:

For some time past the whole country has been entertained with all sorts of stories about a few weak-kneed Congress leaders who have entered into a conspiracy among themselves to betray the Congress cause and arrive at a compromise with British imperialists. These wicked intriguers, we have been asked in all seriousness to believe, are dancing attendance on British Viceroy and sending secret emissaries to other high personages to secure the privilege of acting as the sole agents of British imperialism in India, in return for which they will gladly wind up the Congress business and put a quietus to the nationalist movement. When such wickedness prevails in high places, it is surely time for an Avatar to appear on the scene to destroy the wicked and stir up the dying embers of nationalism into a glorious flame. And if reports are to be believed' the Avatar has actually appeared on the scene, though he has not yet declared himself as such. But he has made no secret of his mission, and with the help of his faithful followers has undertaken to put to rout the wicked compromise-wallahs at Ramgarh and hit them right, left, and centre. At the Anti-Compromise Conference the clarion-call will go forth, and the

Faithful throughout the land will be summoned to listen, tremble and obey. Honestly speaking, we had almost prepared ourselves to listen to something terrible—some declaration of war and an order to march by the General-Officer-Commanding. But it appears after all that nothing epoch-making is going to happen.[255]

The main resolution on India and the war crisis passed at the Ramgarh Congress, which commenced on 19 March, reiterated that the Congress would not help Britain's war effort with men, money or material. Nothing short of complete independence was acceptable and only a Constituent Assembly elected on the basis of adult franchise would shape India's constitution and determine the country's relation with other countries. Only the Constituent Assembly would be able to solve the problems related to minorities and the Indian states on a permanent basis. The natural step after the resignation of the Congress ministries was civil disobedience, which could be launched by Gandhi alone, when he would be satisfied that Congressmen were strictly observing discipline and implementing the Congress's constructive programme.[256] Gandhi told the gathered Congressmen, 'I feel you are not prepared.' He explained, 'I may also join you in applauding the speakers who have demanded immediate launching of civil disobedience', but 'your general finds that you are not ready, that you are not real soldiers and that if we proceed on the lines suggested by you, we are bound to be defeated'.[257]

In his presidential address at the Anti-Compromise Conference, Subhas urged that the country 'eagerly awaits a clear and unequivocal declaration from the Congress Working Committee that the door has finally been banged on all talks of a compromise with Imperialism'. He declared that 'The age of Imperialism is drawing to a close and the era of freedom, democracy and socialism looms ahead of us'. Since the working committee of the Congress would not give the call for a national struggle, it was not up to others to do so. Subhas proposed to set up a 'permanent machinery' for 'waging an uncompromising war with Imperialism'. The conference passed a resolution to set up an All-India Council of Action with a view to launching and directing the national struggle. The conference also passed resolutions condemning the Government for its repressive policies, congratulating the Majlis-i-Ahrar for implementing the war resolution of the Haripura Congress and acknowledging the problems of the farms as the most important internal problem of India.[258]

The conference opened with the singing of 'Sare Jaha Se Achha' by Mohammad Iqbal and closed with the singing of 'Vande Mataram'.

On his return to Calcutta, Subhas plunged into the campaign for the Corporation elections. The official BPCC, in the meantime, had decided not to take part in the elections, giving ammunition to the Mahasabha's criticism of Subhas. Since the official BPCC dissociated itself from the elections, it appeared that Subhas, like some merchants, was using the trademark of another firm, which the Mahasabha ridiculed.[259]

In the results of the election declared on 29 March, the Bose group won twenty-one seats and the Mahasabha won fifteen out of forty-seven general seats. The Muslim League won eighteen out of twenty-two seats reserved for Muslims.[260] It was clear that neither the Bose Congress nor the Hindu Mahasabha would be able to garner a majority of seats on their own. The Muslim League victory in the reserved Muslim seats would give it the decisive power. On the day of the election (28 March 1940), the *Amrita Bazar Patrika* warned the voters that Jinnah would prefer an alliance with Subhas's group, not only because he wanted to wreck the Congress but also because both the Bose brothers and their followers were Muslim-appeasers. In mid-April Subhas arrived at an agreement with the Muslim League for administering the Calcutta Corporation. 'Hindus Betrayed: Bose Group's Surrender Pact with Muslim League', screamed the headline of the *Amrita Bazar Patrika* on 19 April, mincing no words, accusing that 'Hindus' Civic Rights Bartered for Getting Sj. Subhas Bose Elected as Alderman'.[261] It was a 'Great Betrayal', the paper's editorial declared the next day.

Abdur Rahman Siddiqui, a member of the Muslim League working committee, became the new Mayor of Calcutta, and Phanindra Nath Brahma of the Bose group was elected the Deputy Mayor.

The *Amrita Bazar Patrika*'s editorial of 26 April raised the paper's attack on Subhas a notch further:

> . . . he is nothing more or less than a renegade Congressman who has betrayed the national cause and surrendered to rabid communalists for the sake of a trumpery honour. He may continue to deceive the public for some time more with words that so far as he is concerned have ceased to have any meaning; but future generations will remember him as the lost leader who sold himself for a mess of pottage.[262]

For the Congress, Subhas was not any more a part of their programme or plans. Rather, a reorganized official provincial Congress would have its task cut out in reducing his mass influence. The new BPCC executive was appointed on 21 April, with Surendra Mohan Ghose as the president and Arun Chandra Guha as the secretary. Two of Subhas's close colleagues of his former years were now the face of the opposition. However, his supporters in Bengal were not to take things lying down. Congress meetings were disrupted at various places and speakers were beaten up on occasions. The clash had reached its pinnacle. The newly formed BPCC too carried on the attack on Subhas. 'The strength of an organisation is being sought to be replaced by the strength of a personality supposed to be imbued with wonderful powers,' read a statement issued by former revolutionaries Manoranjan Gupta, Bhupendra Kumar Datta (editor of *Forward* newspaper) and Suresh Chandra Das on 27 April.[263] While Nalini Ranjan Sarkar was not to be left behind, Muzaffar Ahmed and Somnath Lahiri of the Communist Party too joined the party soon to call out Subhas's 'Bluff of a struggle'.[264] C.E. Gibbon, the Anglo-Indian leader who had extended his support to Subhas at the time of the formation of the Forward Bloc, also joined in criticizing him for the alliance with the Muslim League.[265]

With only the *Anandabazar Patrika* and the *Hindusthan Standard* among the newspapers, and his trusted band of Forward Bloc supporters, standing firmly behind him, Subhas fought back the attacks, drawing large crowds in his meetings. The attacks on him continued to grow increasingly virulent. On 1 May the *Amrita Bazar Patrika* alleged that Subhas and Sarat had secretly met the Bengal Premier A.K. Fazlul Huq, promising to make him the uncrowned king not only of Bengal but of the whole of India:

> Secret pourparler sat dinner table between the Bose brothers and the Bengal Premier at the house of a mutual friend to get their nominees into the Cabinet is one of the latest moves of Mr Subhas Chandra Bose to usher in a 'new era in the sphere of Bengal politics'.[266]

Subhas denied the contents of the story published by the *Patrika*, but claimed that if an alliance with Huq fructified, the people of Bengal would bless him, hoping that it would materialize.[267] He issued a statement inviting Tushar Kanti Ghosh to come to a meeting scheduled at the Deshbandhu Park on 2 May and frame his charges against Subhas. Ghosh responded by calling the invitation a trap to harass him in public and alleged that a group of rowdies under the leadership of two of Subhas's followers—Hemanta Basu and Narendra Narayan Chakrabarti—raided the *Patrika* office.[268]

The source of the story on the Bose brothers' secret meeting became clear when the *Patrika* published the accounts of the meeting by A.K.M. Zakariah, an alderman in the Corporation and host of the meeting, and that of Subhas side by side. While Subhas claimed that he and Sarat had met Huq casually and without any previous plan, Zakariah claimed that the meeting was organized at the behest of Subhas.[269]

Fazlul Huq spoke out in mid-June, when in a statement issued from Simla he clarified:

> . . . if I feel that a settlement with the Congress is in the best interests of Mussalmans, I shall make the settlement without taking a plebiscite of Bengal Mussalmans, for, I know what place I occupy in their hearts . . . India must not miss the bus, and I am willing to use all my influence to bring about unity and create a united front. I believe in action and not in words, and my pact with the Bose brothers should demonstrate that Bengal can still lead India in politics.[270]

Attacks by Subhas's supporters on the meetings of both the Hindu Mahasabha and the Congress continued. N.C. Chatterjee and Nepal Roy, two Mahasabha leaders, were injured by attacks on a meeting held on 8 May.[271]

Completely cornered now, Subhas's position was very different from the vision for Bengal's politics he had had six years ago:

> Bengal politics is now corrupt. Relentless sacrifice will make Bengal's atmosphere once again clean and clear. The task is extremely difficult, but not impossible. Believe me, a wonderful change will come about in Bengal within two years. Selfish quarrels of the present will not pollute Bengal's air for very long.[272]

The role of the newspapers could not have surprised him much though. From faraway Vienna, Subhas had complained to the editor of the *Anandabazar Patrika*:

> I can say for myself that except for a few months in 1927 and 1928 I did not ever receive much support. And during the twelve or thirteen years

of my public life, the manner in which I have been tormented by the
nationalist press of Bengal, is something which I have not experienced
even at the hands of the British. British persecution has not lowered me
but raised me in the estimation of my countrymen—on the other hand
persecution by the nationalist press has lowered me in the eyes of my
countrymen.[273]

Towards the end of May, Subhas travelled to Dhaka to attend a special session
of the Bengal Provincial Conference that commenced on 25 May, stopping
at Narayanganj and Madaripur to meet party workers and address meetings.

Upon returning from the East Bengal tour, Subhas announced a new
phase of movement on 2 June, targeted at the removal of all symbols of
slavery from the province, for which he chose the Holwell monument to
begin with. Subhas expressed hope that the Bengal Government would
concede to his demand without delay, and declared that in the event of his
demand going unheeded, he would launch a struggle. He claimed to have
received assurances from the districts that a large number of people would
join the struggle.[274] The monument, as he explained later, was 'not merely
an unwarranted stain on the memory of the Nawab [Sirajuddowla]', but
had 'stood in the heart of Calcutta for the last 150 years or more as the
symbol of our slavery and humiliation'.[275]

Organizationally, the Forward Bloc weakened with leading members of
its working committee, including Vishwambhar Dayal Tripathi, Senapati
Bapat, H.V. Kamath, M. Annapurniah, Sheel Bhadra Yajee, Jatashankar
Shukla, Ashrafuddin Ahmad Chowdhury and Satya Ranjan Bakshi being
in prison by the middle of the year. By early June, the official BPCC had
disaffiliated seven district Congress committees, including those of Dhaka,
Howrah, Faridpur, Maldah and three Calcutta districts for aligning with
the Bose Congress.[276]

Subhas travelled to Nagpur to preside over the second annual
conference of the All-India Forward Bloc on 18 June. In his presidential
address, Subhas deliberated on the achievements of the past year and the
task ahead. The four main achievements that he listed out were successfully
resisting the drift towards constitutionalism within the Congress leading
to the resignation of the ministries, frustrating the Government's attempts
to secure Congress's cooperation in the prosecution of the war, succeeding
in the creation of an atmosphere of struggle, and launching the struggle at
Ramgarh. Subhas pointed out that the struggle was launched in Bengal in

January 1940, even prior to Ramgarh, on the issue of civil liberties which had been consistently violated by the ordinances promulgated by the Government. As a result, he claimed, 'we have restored in large measure the status quo which existed prior to September 1939'. The next task was to demand an immediate transfer of power to the Indian people through a Provisional National Government. 'No constitutional difficulties can be put forward by the British Government with a view to resisting this demand, because legislation for the purpose can be put through Parliament in twenty-four hours,' Subhas emphasized. He pointed out that the provisional Government would convene a Constituent Assembly once things settled down in India and abroad.[277]

'All power to the Indian people' was the new slogan given by Subhas while elucidating his demand for a provisional national Government.[278]

In a curious development, the Congress working committee announced on 21 June that it was 'unable to go the full length with Gandhiji' on the question on non-violence and decided to adopt two different approaches for national struggle and national defence. The committee resolved that:

> While the Working Committee hold that the Congress must continue to adhere strictly to the principle of non-violence in their struggle for independence, the Committee cannot ignore the present imperfections and failings in this respect of the human elements they have to deal with and the possible dangers in a period of transition and dynamic change until the Congress has acquired non-violent control over the people in adequate measure and the people have imbibed sufficiently the lesson of organised non-violence.
>
> The Committee have deliberated over the problem that has thus arisen and have come to the conclusion that they are unable to go to the full length with Gandhiji but they recognise that he should be free to pursue his great ideal in his own way and therefore absolve him from responsibility for programme and activities in India in regard to internal and external disorder . . . The committee wish to make it clear that the methods and basic policy of non-violence in the national struggle for freedom continue with full force and are not affected in the least by the inability to extend it to the region of national defence.[279]

The Governor of Bengal, Herbert, kept a keen eye on the developments. His fortnightly reports to the Viceroy apart from his own opinion on the developments, provide an inside view of the ongoing efforts to corner Subhas. He was not happy that the pact with the Muslim League would help Subhas 'to keep his fingers on some of the resources of the Corporation'. He noted that some sections of the Muslims were happy to have Subhas as an asset who could be used to create divisions in the 'Hindu and Congress circles', but he was not convinced that they would succeed. Some of them also seemed to think that they would be able to leverage Subhas as he would be devoid of friends if the Muslim League deserted him. 'I cannot help thinking, however, that they have taken a risk in trying to outwit so clever and slippery an opponent,' the Governor recorded in his report of 22 April. In his report of 7 May, he noted that 'He who sups with Subhas needs a long spoon, and even if the matter [Bose-League Pact] stopped at Municipal affairs only I would not be too confident of the Muslims getting the better of the deal'. The Governor's report of 7 June shows that Tushar Kanti Ghosh was conspiring on how to corner Subhas further. The Governor wrote that Ghosh, 'in an interview I have just given him, confirmed the impression that so long as Subhas could be denied Press publicity he would weaken his position day by day'. Intrigues were on in the Muslim League too. Khwaja Nazimuddin, the home minister of Bengal, 'has hinted strongly that he himself is getting "fed up" with Subhas and that if he could secure a resolution of full support of war from the Moslem League he would then "pick up" Subhas and complete his political effacement', Herbert noted.[280]

Thus, by the middle of the year, Subhas's position was somewhat like that of Abhimanyu, surrounded from all sides by the official Congress, the Hindu Mahasabha, the Socialists, the Royists, the Communists, the Muslim League and a hostile press. Subhas, however, was no Abhimanyu.

Back in Calcutta, Subhas announced his intention to commence the movement for the removal of the Holwell monument from 3 July, a day that he wanted to be observed as Sirajuddowla Day, 'in honour of the last independent king of Bengal'. He planned to lead a march of the first batch of volunteers on that day.[281] Things, however, were destined to turn out very differently.

On 2 July, Subhas met Tagore during the day.[282] As he was engaged in a post-lunch discussion with B.C. Chatterjee and preparing for a meeting that he had called at 3 p.m., V.B. Janvrin, the deputy commissioner of police, arrived at 38/2 Elgin Road, accompanied by two constables shortly after 2 p.m., and informed Subhas that he was being arrested under Section

129 of the Defence of India Rules (DI Rules). Section 129 permitted the arrest of a person without a warrant, and detention in custody for up to fifteen days without the order of the provincial Government. Subhas was taken to the Presidency jail.[283]

The Mayor, A.R. Siddiqui, questioning the Government's decision, said that the 'effects may very well prove to be the reverse of what the advisers of the Government may have thought they would be'. Siddiqui said that 'His sudden and unexpected arrest came as an unpleasant surprise'. The Corporation was adjourned on 4 July, until the 10th, on the motion moved by M.A.H. Ispahani and seconded by N.C. Chatterjee. Siddiqui was effusive in praising Subhas:

> Mr. Bose's removal has come to me and the Muslim members of the Corporation as a shock. In co-operation with him we had started on a new path fully determined to remove the grievances of all sections of the rate-payers so far as it lay in our power and bring about a healthier atmosphere in the administration of the affairs of the Corporation. Our hopes and aspirations were not altogether mislaid . . . He and his colleagues had extended the hand of friendship to us and we had grasped it with cordiality. Signs were visible that things had begun to move and the administrative machinery had begun to respond to new forces. Expenditure is being curtailed and collections have increased, not by thousands but by lakhs per week and we had hardly got into the stride yet. The disappearance even for a short while of the man who was one of the strongest pillars of the new edifice we had chosen to erect jointly is a handicap the significance of which cannot be ignored.[284]

The adjournment motion in the Bengal Legislative Assembly, moved by Santosh Kumar Basu was, however, defeated by 78 to 119 votes. Calling Subhas 'one of the most loveable personalities in Bengal politics', premier Huq told the Assembly that Subhas's satyagraha came in the way of the removal of the Holwell monument. Urging the withdrawal of the satyagraha, Huq said that if the Government failed to take action within a reasonable period of time, then the satyagraha could be restarted. However, when Sarat asked Huq to clarify what he meant, he did not provide any answers.[285]

Fazlul Huq announced in the Legislative Assembly on 23 July that the Government had 'decided to take immediate steps for the removal of the

Holwell monument', but Subhas continued to languish in jail.[286] Towards
the end of August, he was charged with Section 26 of the DI Rules which
allowed indefinite detention without trial. With no sign of being released,
and with a new case instituted against him for delivering three speeches
and writing an article in the *Forward Bloc*, in addition to the one under
the DI Rules for which he was in prison, Subhas decided to undertake a
voluntary fast at the end of October to protest against the Government's
refusal to withdraw the order of detention. Accordingly, he informed
the Superintendent of the Presidency Jail of his decision through a letter
written on 30 October, the day of Kali Puja. Clearly laying the charge of
being communal against the Government, he wrote that it was known to
him that even if his fast became a fast unto death, it would not bother the
Government because he was not a Muslim. With reference to his decision
to undertake the fast, Subhas wrote:

> The only other point to consider is as to whether the remedy suggested is
> not worse than the disease and I have taken long days and nights to ponder
> over it. My answer to the question is that life under existing conditions
> is hardly worth living. In this mortal world, everything perishes except
> principles. These principles can lively only when the individuals do not
> hesitate to die for them. When individuals perish for a sacred principle,
> that principle does not die—but incarnates itself in other individuals.
> And it is through vicarious suffering alone that a cause can flourish and
> prosper.[287]

In the meantime, Subhas was elected to the Central Legislative Assembly
from the Dhaka constituency on 29 October.[288] He wrote to the president
of the Central Legislative Assembly requesting him to 'kindly take steps
so that I may be able to attend the session commencing in the first week
of November, 1940 at New Delhi.'[289] The Government of India, however,
clarified that the arrest and detention of Subhas was undertaken by the
Bengal Government.[290]

On 26 November, he wrote a letter addressed to the Governor, the
chief minister and the council of ministers of the Bengal Government. He
requested them to preserve the letter for posterity as it contained 'a message
for my countrymen and is therefore my political testament'. He found the
Government's vindictiveness towards him inexplicable. Reiterating that
life under existing conditions was intolerable for him, he wrote:

To purchase one's continued existence by compromising with illegality and injustice goes against my grain. I would throw up life itself, rather than pay this price. Government are determined to hold me in prison by brute force. I say in reply: 'Release me or I shall refuse to live—and it is for me to decide wither I choose to live or die.'

. . . To the Government of the day I say, 'Cry halt to your mad drive along the path of communalism and injustice. There is yet time to retrace your steps. Do not use a boomerang which will soon recoil on you . . .'[291]

Subhas announced that he was going to commence his fast on 29 November, and issued a strong warning against trying to forcibly feed him.

On 5 December, the Superintendent of the Presidency Jail stepped into Subhas's cell and informed him that 'I have orders to send you home. The Ambulance is ready'.[292]

A politically cornered Subhas, now handicapped by the detention by the Government, seemed to have very few options ahead of him. A prolonged jail term appeared almost certain. The future looked bleak.

Yet, the next five years saw Subhas reinvent himself and prove his mettle in a way that probably no one could have imagined. Subhas 'Babu' transformed into 'Netaji'. As it happened, those who had tried to push him into submission formed the ruling and the opposition power blocs after Independence, and many among them would have no qualms in exploiting the image of 'Netaji' and his army of liberation for their political prospects.

9

The Phoenix Rises

On to Germany and Japan (1941–45)

'Sj. Subhas Bose Missing: Mysterious Disappearance From Home Detected on Sunday', announced the headlines on page 5 of the *Amrita Bazar Patrika*, on Tuesday, 28 January 1941:

> Under circumstance of great mystery and dramatic import Sj. Subhas Chandra Bose has disappeared from this Elgin Road residence, which, according to the members of his house, was discovered on Sunday afternoon . . . It is now gathered from the inmates of his house that for the last few days he had not been seeing anybody. Shut up in his room away from the view of anybody he had been performing religious practices . . . Later in the day the Special Branch police searched the house of Sj. Bose for three hours, the room occupied by Sj. Bose being subjected to minute search.[1]

It was only over nine months later that the Government of India would officially inform the Council of State that Subhas had 'gone over to the enemy'. When Yuveraj Dutta Singh[h2] asked on 10 November 1941 whether the Government had any information on the whereabouts of Subhas, E. Conran Smith, the home secretary, replied:

> It has been common talk in certain quarters in this country for some time that Sj. Subhas Chandra Bose is either in Rome or in Berlin and has entered into a pact with the Axis powers to assist by fifth column methods any German invasion of India. Leaflets to this effect have made their appearance in this country and leave no doubt that he has gone over to the enemy.

Conran Smith informed the Council that the source of this information was 'certain leaflets which have made appearance in this country'. He read out extracts from a couple them. While one of them claimed, 'A pact has been signed at a conference in Berlin. The revolutionary Subhas Bose was also present', another read, 'He is now in a European country and is maintaining close contact with his revolutionary party in India. He has already issued a statement signed by his own hand. He is busy with certain foreign powers.'[3]

The secretary of state for India, Leopold S. Amery, was more forthright, though not honest. On 27 November 1941, he repeated in the House of Commons the information provided to the Council of State adding, 'I have no definite information.'[4]

Unknown to everyone except very few in his family and a few of his political associates, Subhas had left home on the night between 16 and 17 January 1941, and travelled to Peshawar by train in the guise of a Muslim insurance agent. With the help of the members of the Kirti Kisan Party and a member of the Forward Bloc working committee from the North-West Frontier Province (NWFP), Subhas then moved to Kabul and crossed over to Russian territory on 18 March. He travelled to Moscow with a passport issued by the Italian legation in Kabul, under the assumed name Orlando Mazzotta, by car and train. Leaving Moscow by train, Subhas reached Berlin on 2 April 1941.[5]

The preliminary impression of the German Foreign Office was that Subhas had gone to Germany for broadcasting propaganda. One of the key persons to meet him after being welcomed by the high officials of the protocol department, therefore, was Hans Queling of the broadcasting department.[6]

Without wasting any time, Subhas met Ernst Woermann, the director of the political department in the German Foreign Ministry, the very next day to discuss his plan. Having arrived only the previous day, Subhas could describe the main elements of his plan in brief:

> . . . he wants to set up an Indian government in Germany, visualizing as a model the Polish, etc., governments in exile. To form his government, he expects certain promises from the Axis Powers, which he wants to formulate in detail. Besides propaganda actions the program furthermore includes the instigation of uprisings in India. As a final objective he has in mind the entry by the Axis Powers into India, in regard to which he

cited the following figures: The Anglo-Indian Army consisted of only 300,000 men, of which at most 70,000 were Englishmen. The major portion of the Indian elements was willing to defect at any time. An army of 100,000 men with modern equipment would be adequate to free India from English rule.[7]

Woermann, obviously non-committal at this stage, suggested that once Subhas had put down his ideas in the form of a detailed document, he should be received by the Foreign Minister, Joachim von Ribbentrop.

Subhas submitted his first detailed plan on 9 April, titled 'Plan for cooperation between the Axis Powers and India'. He argued that despite facing numerous defeats, England had not relaxed its political and economic grip on India, and if it survived the war, its policy would be to restore its power by exploiting India's rich resources. The British Empire was the greatest obstacle not only to India's attainment of freedom but also to human progress. With the hostility of Indians towards Britain, they could help by providing material assistance in achieving the common aim of the Axis powers and India, that is, the destruction of the British Empire.

He proposed a comprehensive plan for implementation in four geographical areas: Europe, Afghanistan, the independent tribal area between Afghanistan and India, and inside India.

The work that needed to be done in Europe included establishing a Free India Government, which would sign a treaty with the Axis powers to provide for India's liberation in the event of an Axis victory. The aim of the treaty was to convince Indians that the Axis powers were guaranteeing their freedom once victory had been achieved. The Axis countries, in return, would be given special privileges when a free government had been formed in India. The Free India Government would also set up legations in all the friendly countries in Europe and start propaganda, especially through the radio, exhorting Indians to rise up in revolt against the British. Arrangements would be made to send necessary materials to India to help the rebellion, via Afghanistan. The broadcasts would be made in the name of Radio Free India.

A headquarters would be set up in Kabul to maintain communications between Europe and India, and provided with the necessary equipment. Subhas claimed that his agents were already at work in the independent tribal zone. Their activity needed to be coordinated for large-scale attacks on British bases, for which experts needed to be dispatched from Europe.

Isolated anti-British elements like the Faqir of Ipi also needed to be integrated into the overall plan. The area needed to be developed into a powerful centre of propaganda, with fully equipped printing shops and radio transmitters. Agents from the independent zone would select scouts from the NWFP.

Broadcasts to India needed to be made in a 'grand style', from a European station initially, followed by other transmitters in the independent zone. His agents and party members would be instructed to obstruct the British administration by inducing people, through propaganda, to not join the army, not pay taxes and refuse to obey the British laws. Indian units in the army were to be approached to rise up in rebellion and strikes were to be coordinated in those factories that supported the British war effort. Materials required for supporting acts of sabotage (an idea that he imbibed from the Italian minister in Kabul, Pietro Quaroni) against strategic railway lines, bridges and factories would also be supplied. Insurrection would be organized among the civilian population in various parts of the country, 'which could then be used as a springboard for the revolution of the masses'.

Subhas also repeated his argument that in the event of an uprising by the Indian soldiers, a contingent of soldiers from the Axis powers, equipped with the most modern equipment would help to drive the British out of India. Significantly, he reduced the number of soldiers required from the initial 1,00,000 that he had mentioned to Woermann to 50,000.

Translating this plan into action needed funds. Subhas proposed that the expenses would have to be borne by the Axis powers, but it would be treated as a loan to the Free India Government, which would be repaid in full when an independent government took charge of free India.[8] According to N.G. Ganpuley, one of the key associates of Subhas in Germany, a personal allowance for Subhas was fixed at GBP 800 per month, and the monthly grant for the Free India Centre that came into being in November 1941 started with GBP 1200 but increased to GBP 3200 in 1944. In addition to these, there were expenses related to the Indian Legion.[9]

Ganpuley noticed Subhas's fastidiousness about matters relating to accounts. Although there was no obligation to submit any accounts to anyone, Subhas 'was very particular about the proper use of public funds'. The accounts were 'managed very ably without the least trouble, from its beginning in 1941 till the end in April 1945'.[10] This observation is in

absolute contrast to the controversy regarding the accusation of financial
irregularities in the BPCC during 1939–40.

Subhas's reading of Japan's possible role, in an explanatory note
attached to the memorandum, was prescient. The fall of Singapore was
still ten months away.

> The overthrow of British power in India can, in its last stages, be
> materially assisted by Japanese foreign policy in the Far East. If Japan
> decides on expansion southwards it will lead to an open clash with Great
> Britain. If war then breaks out, it appears more than certain that the
> East Indies and Far Eastern squadron of the British Navy will, under the
> present circumstances, be no match for the Japanese navy. And even if
> America comes to the rescue of the British Navy, a Japanese victory could
> still be hoped for. A defeat of the British Navy in the Far East including
> the smashing up of the Singapore base, will automatically weaken British
> military strength and prestige in India. India is therefore, intensely
> interested in the developments in the Far East. And since Japanese
> expansion southwards necessitate a prior agreement between the Soviet
> and Japan, India is greatly interested in a pact which will, on the one
> hand, expedite a settlement of the China Affair and will, on the other,
> enable Japan to move more freely and confidently towards the South.[11]

Woermann forwarded Subhas's memorandum to the foreign minister's
secretariat to be submitted to Ribbentrop 'at once', along with his own
views on the proposals. Woermann expressed his doubts about whether
it was time to officially announce the liberation of India as one of the war
aims of the Axis powers. He also questioned the wisdom of recognizing a
Free India government in Berlin and thereby 'elevating Bose as the chief
of an Indian government', and selecting a particular political group like
the Forward Bloc as the representative of India over the other parties,
particularly when there was the distinct possibility of such a move producing
an unfavourable political response in India. On the financial proposal,
Woermann recommended generous financial support to Subhas, but felt
that it was too early to discuss a German military expedition to India.[12]

It was in the city which he had made the centre of his activities in Europe
during his exile nearly a decade ago that Subhas had his first meeting with
Ribbentrop on 29 April, at the Hotel Imperial in Vienna. This was his first
meeting with someone of the top echelon of the Nazi Government, and

Subhas knew that to take his plan forward it was imperative to convince and impress Ribbentrop. He, of course, could not have known in which manner Ribbentrop had already been informed by Woermann's cautious opinion.

At the beginning of the conversation, Ribbentrop wanted to understand the Indian situation from Subhas's point of view. The British had been able to subdue Indians with their small army despite strong, anti-British sentiments, because Indians were entirely without weapons, Subhas explained. The defeat of France had sunk the morale of the British in India, and some rebellions in the army, albeit sporadic, had created the proper psychological moment for a mass movement. Many among the Indian officers in the army were nationalists and they listened to the Hindustani news broadcasts from Berlin. However, the morale of the British in India had also been somewhat raised by their recent victories in Africa.

'Gandhi did not wish to shut the door in the face of the English', Subhas told Ribbentrop, replying to his question on the attitude of Gandhi. He was a man of compromise, who spoke in terms of assistance to the British in his first rush of sentiment when the war broke out. Gandhi made the mistake of believing that the British would become more accommodative due to the pressure of the war, whereas in reality, British policy had turned more conservative and reactionary than before the war.

Speaking of himself, Subhas thought that in destroying England, the Führer was also working for India, and Indians therefore ought to hope for his victory.

What would happen if the British left India? Subhas argued that a nationalist government would be formed and it would be possible to eliminate the religious differences which had been artificially exaggerated by the British. The current Indian constitution, for example, did not allow a Muslim of the same political views to elect him simply because he belonged to a different religion. In free India, the Indian army would disintegrate and there would be some obvious difficulty until newly trained Indian officers could take the place held by the British officers.

At this juncture, Subhas brought up the idea of recruiting Indian prisoners of war (POWs) to help in the insurrection he had planned in India. These prisoners would undoubtedly be ready to fight against England, and if publicized, it would have a great impact on the rest of the British Indian army. Subhas well understood the repercussions of such a step on the British Government. The Government would lose much of their confidence in the Indian troops and would not be able to employ them as unconditionally as they did then, he explained. The idea of utilizing the POWs occurred to him, according to Ganpuley, when he saw that some POWs were employed by the Germans to translate Hindustani programmes broadcast over radio.[13]

After hearing Subhas's assessment of the situation and future plans, it was Ribbentrop's turn to tell his side of the story. He went into a long lecture, starting with the bluff that Germany's attitude had changed from being friendly towards England to a resolve to completely defeat it. Any American intervention was not going to make a difference: The American affair 'was the greatest bluff in the history of the world'.

The most important question, in Ribbentrop's view, on Subhas's proposals was 'to choose the proper time for the actions which might be undertaken'. Being hasty and choosing the wrong moment would produce the exact opposite result of what was desired, and hence, it was important to proceed step by step. He made it clear to Subhas that in order to avoid opposition from within India, it would be imperative to take Gandhi into account before implementing his plans. Nothing should be done that would give the British a chance to project Gandhi against Subhas.

Ribbentrop suggested that in order to keep Subhas's presence in Germany a secret, he would arrange for suitable quarters outside Berlin. Subhas was confident that the British were still unaware that he was in Germany.

The meeting ended with Ribbentrop promising another round of discussion in the near future, after further examination of the issues involved in Subhas's proposal. In the meantime, Woermann was to keep in touch with him to take the discussions further. There was no assurance yet about a declaration of independence from the Axis powers, and the next meeting between the two would happen only after five months.[14]

While Subhas was negotiating his plan of action with the Germans, a separate plan for India had also been prepared in April by the Italian Foreign Ministry. The key components of the plan were similar to what Subhas had formulated, and included radio broadcasts, setting up a revolutionary committee in Italy, supplying arms and ammunition to the frontier tribes, dropping of propaganda pamphlets in Indian languages amongst British Indian troops, recruiting suitable candidates for technical, military and political training from amongst Indian POWs in North Africa and thereafter transporting them to work as political agents in India's north-west frontier. The possibility of raising an army from amongst the POWs was also under consideration. The Italian Ministry of Popular Culture too planned setting up a propaganda centre in Afghanistan in the guise of an archaeological mission.[15]

Subhas met Woermann again on 3 and 4 May, handing over a supplementary memorandum. Setting up a Free India government seemed unlikely, but Subhas never let up the pressure for an immediate declaration on India's independence. Citing the recent German victories in North Africa, Yugoslavia and Greece he argued that with the British prestige shattered, a psychological moment had emerged when the Axis powers 'can capture the imagination of the entire Orient by an open declaration of policy with regard to the Orient and, in particular, with regard to India and the Arab countries'. Knowing that the Axis countries were viewed in India as predatory powers with ambition of global domination, the importance of such a declaration would been clear to him. It was critical to send the right message across.

In addition to a declaration, he suggested the commencement of organizing revolts against the British in India and in the Arab countries at the earliest, as well as to concentrate on attacking the British rule in India. To facilitate the offensive on India, Subhas suggested bringing down the pro-British government in Afghanistan. In listing out the advantages for the Axis powers in taking these steps, Subhas again demonstrated his ability to think a few steps ahead and integrate future possibilities into his plan. In this case, he did not rule out the possibility of a conflict between Germany and the Soviet Union. If his suggestions were implemented, Subhas emphasized, then even in the case of such a conflict Germany would have the sympathy of all the Oriental countries. However, if the conflict broke out before the implementation of these measures, he warned, Germany would lose the sympathy of the Oriental countries which it had gained because of its fight against British imperialism. Had he sensed that something like operation Barbarossa would become a reality in just over a month? In any case, he made it a point to mention that the indirect help of Soviet Russia or of Turkey would be essential for opening up a channel of communication between Germany, Afghanistan and India.[16]

The German decision to assist in the coup on 1 April in Iraq, that installed Rashid Ali al-Gaylani as prime minister, by bringing down the pro-British government, provided a nudge to the foreign ministry's initiative towards India. Woermann noted on 10 May that Hitler had agreed to issue the Free India Declaration within eight to ten days, that Subhas was to be received by Ribbentrop again and intensive preparations had begun to be set in motion for the radio propaganda.[17]

The head of the Foreign Office Broadcasting Bureau submitted a detailed plan to Ribbentrop in early May for improving the existing system. He proposed that broadcasts should be made in other languages such as Bengali, Telugu and Tamil in addition to Hindustani, which had been going on since the end of 1939. The technical challenges were that only short-wave broadcasts from Europe could be received in India, whereas the stations in Asia which could be used for medium-wave broadcasts (such as Kabul, Saigon, Bangkok and Chungking) had a range of only about 310 miles during the day and 495 miles in the night. The plan estimated that out of 1,20,000 private radio receivers in India, only about 30,000 were equipped to received short-wave transmission, and among them, about 22,000 were owned by Indians. In response to Subhas's plan, the Bureau recommended setting up a powerful black transmitter at the Dutch broadcasting station at Huizen, which had been built to broadcast to the Dutch colony in Indonesia.[18]

Subhas submitted another plan on 20 May, this time to set up a Free India Centre (*Zentralstelle Freies Indien*), apart from reiterating the need for the declaration on India's right to independence. The FIC was to serve as the brain of the Indian revolution, direct global propaganda against British imperialism, publish an official organ in German, Italian, French and Spanish for distribution in different countries, organize and send practical help to Indians for the revolution, organize a Free Indian Legion for fighting against England on the side of the Axis powers and to conduct propaganda among the Indian troops fighting for England in the different war fronts. Subhas asked the Foreign Office to depute, on a full-time basis, some special officers to collaborate with the FIC.

The importance of Soviet Russia's involvement in his scheme was reiterated by Subhas in his proposal. 'A German–Soviet agreement on the question of India would be exceedingly desirable', to enable sending 'men and materials through Russia to Afghanistan and India', he emphasized.[19]

In the meantime, he worked with the Political Department in drafting the Free India Declaration. Among other things, Subhas's draft from the second half of May specified that Germany:

Recognises the inalienable right of the Indian people to have full and complete independence, to enjoy the fruits of their toil and have all the necessities of life, so that they may have full opportunities of growth. She assures the India people that the new order which she is out to establish in the world will mean for them a free and independent India . . .

. . . It will, of course, be for the Indian people to decide what form of Government they should have, when they are free . . . But it is only natural that Germany, in keeping with her own tradition, would like to see in India a united nation, in which every individual is guaranteed food, work, necessities of life and equal opportunities of growth, regardless of religion, class or any other consideration.

Germany conveys its sincerest good wishes to the Indian people in their struggle for freedom and declares that she is prepared to render them such assistance as lies in their power, so that the goal of liberty may be reached without delay. She now waits for the day when independent India will have her own national Government. Germany will gladly recognise that government and establish friendly relations with it.[20]

The failure of the Iraqi coup, however, had a negative impact on the German Government's intent to issue the declaration. Ribbentrop's office informed Subhas that the declaration was to be postponed for a short while, but that the foreign minister had agreed to begin preparations for the establishment of the FIC immediately.[21]

Germany had also started working on recruiting captured Indian soldiers almost immediately after Subhas made the suggestion to Ribbentrop. The OKW (*Oberkommando der Wehrmacht*, the armed forces high command) had already developed a plan in 1940 to send a commando troop to the Indian frontier. To discuss and take the plan forward, cavalry officer Walter Harbich met Subhas in April 1941. The Abwehr (German military intelligence service) was tasked with starting the process of putting together a small group from among the Indian POWs. Interrogations carried out at the end of April, among the first group of 1000 captured soldiers and 37 officers in the Italian POW camp at Derna in Cyrenaica, described their attitude as strongly anti-British. However, the Italians were not yet ready to hand over the POWs to Germany, and wanted to use them first.[22]

The Germans flew a small band of twenty-seven soldiers from amongst the 15,000 Indian troops captured in Libya by the Afrika Korps to Berlin on 18 May 1941. After extensive interviews, seven were retained in Berlin and the rest were sent to Annaburg. Four soldiers, however, were brought back within some time, and all of them lodged in the Schlieffenufer barracks in Berlin. Shedai met this group of POWs towards the end of July. Gurbachan Singh Mangat, one among the POWs in the barracks, came to know about Subhas's presence in Berlin from Shedai. Three soldiers from the barracks and a group of civilians under N.G. Ganpuley, who visited the Annaburg camp in August to assess the condition of the POWs, identified several shortcomings, including the supply of rations and also the attitude of one Indian civilian who made unfulfilled promises to the soldiers. The Annaburg camp by that time housed around 1400 Indian POWs.[23]

While Subhas was inching ahead with his negotiations, not quite satisfied with the pace of progress or with the cautious approach of the German Government, he was invited to Rome by the Italian Government towards the end of May. The fact that he would be met by Mussolini before he had met Hitler was a bit of a thorny issue for the Germans, but they agreed to the plan since there was going to be no publicity on the meeting.

The Italian Government was brought up to speed by the Germans on the discussions that had been held so far with Subhas, and were told that the German Government intended to work very closely with him on all matters related to India. The Germans were not too keen on Subhas spending much time in Italy; they wanted him back as soon as possible as 'extensive plans of large scope are being considered here regarding which the Italian Government has likewise been informed and which in certain circumstances are to be executed on short notice'. The German embassy in Rome was instructed not only to provide all assistance and necessary funds to Subhas, but to report regularly on his movements and his meetings.[24] Subhas reached Rome on 29 May, with Emilie accompanying him.

The month-and-a-half-long trip to Italy was disappointing for Subhas. There was no meeting with Mussolini, and the two meetings he had had with the Italian foreign minister and son-in-law of Mussolini, Count Gian Galeazzo Ciano, on 6 and 26 June, led nowhere. After their first meeting Ciano noted in his diary:

> I receive Bose, head of the Indian insurgent movement. He would like the Axis to make a declaration on the independence of India, but in Berlin his proposals have been received with a great deal of reserve. Nor must we be compromised, especially because the value of this youngster is not clear. Past experience has given rather modest results.[25]

Shortly thereafter, at a meeting in Venice on 15 June, Ribbentrop gave Ciano the inside view of the German Government about Subhas:

> While being of the opinion that Bose must be helped in his propaganda work by putting the necessary means at his disposal, Ribbentrop considers premature any public declaration on the part of the Axis on the subject of the future settlement in India. The Fuehrer did not receive Bose, precisely to avoid any definite commitment on the subject.[26]

Apart from the disheartening response from the Italian Government, Subhas found an irritant in Rome who, apprehensive of being turned into a subordinate to Subhas, made all efforts to scuttle his plans. This was a man called Muhammad Iqbal Shedai, originally from Sialkot in Punjab, who had left India for Europe, after the First World War, trying to do something against the British Raj. Living in Rome from 1940, he became influential with the Italian Government and started broadcasting to India over a station called Radio Himalaya. The Government of India had been monitoring the broadcasts, and in early March 1941, had been able to tentatively locate it to Italy, although confusion over its exact location continued as long as the station lasted. The Office of the Controller of Broadcasting reported on 4 March 1941:

> The pronunciation and delivery of the announcer are unmistakeably that of a Punjabi Muslim . . . since, barring the communists there are practically no political workers in the country for whom these broadcasts evince any sympathy, they are not likely to have much effect.[27]

He had also succeeded in making contacts with the Indian POWs captured by the Italians in North Africa.[28] Shedai and his close coterie claimed to represent the Ghadr and the Kirti Kisan Party, and the broadcasts over Radio Himalaya were claimed to have been made on behalf of the Indian Republican Party, with strong communist overtones.

The extent to which Shedai was keen to keep Subhas away is evident from the two reports he submitted to the Italian Government after their meeting on 1 and 3 June. In a meeting at Shedai's house that lasted for four hours, Subhas shared some of his thoughts with him and his two associates, Ajit Singh and Labh Singh. It is evident from Shedai's notes that none of them had any idea about Subhas's work or stature. After the first meeting, Shedai informed the Italian Foreign Office:

> After talking with Bose for four hours my friends, after deep thinking, have told me to inform my Italian friends that we absolutely refuse to cooperate with him as he has not gained our confidence . . . in our opinion he is not apt for any kind of revolutionary work. He has no following either in India or abroad.[29]

After the second meeting, he was more spiteful in his letter to Blasco Lanza d'Ajeta, the Italian diplomat, especially in his complaints regarding Emilie:

> He now wants to see the Duce and he thinks that he will impress him about his work which is nothing but imaginary . . . I have told you that all parties in India are against Mr Bose and especially the All India National Congress which expelled him from its ranks for three years. It is a pity that none has faith in him . . . If he can be of some use at present he must be used but I would request you to be very careful . . .
>
> I should also inform you that he has a German girl secretary to whom he tells everything. So please take full care in talking with him. He told me that the girl was his old friend and he had no secret from her. He also told me that I could talk with him in her presence quite free. But I had to be very cautious (sic).[30]

At the third meeting on 10 June, which too turned out to be unfruitful, Shedai's associates, according to the account that he provided to another Italian official, told Subhas that neither the Ghadr party nor the Kirti Kisan Party would cooperate with him.[31] Shedai, however, also claimed that at Subhas's insistence he had agreed to help him at a personal level, and that Subhas wanted him to carry on his radio propaganda from Germany. Shedai was clearly anxious to not lose out to Subhas whatever influence, in his own inflated opinion about himself, he had on the Italians and the Germans. He soon approached the Italian Government to depute an Italian official with him so that he could go to Berlin and 'see what was happening there as regards India and other Oriental countries'. He was, at the same time, very keen to impress the Italians by showing that despite several requests from the Germans to move to Berlin, he had refused, and if they ever received an official request to transfer him to Germany they should know that it was not due to his wish. His present request was 'only to know what work Mr Bose wants to do' and 'influence the Germans also that they should work on the proper line'.[32]

As Subhas went about his meetings emphasizing his main demand for a declaration of independence from the Axis powers, the Germany embassy noted that all those who had come in contact with him found him to be a 'first-rate personality' who greatly impressed the Italians. In view of his dogged perseverance with the declaration, the German embassy wondered whether it would not be useful to keep him in relative silence in one of the neutral countries until the time came when he would be needed. Woermann, however, disagreed with the idea.[33]

The biggest jolt that Subhas received while in Rome was the news of Germany's invasion of Russia on 22 June 1941. In fact, his reaction to the invasion was another reason why the Germans wanted to keep him aside for the moment. He wrote to Woermann that the 'public reaction in my country to the new situation in the East is unfavourable towards your Government'.[34]

On his return to Berlin from Rome, after spending a week in Vienna, Subhas minced no words at his meeting with Woermann and Secretary of State, Wilhelm Keppler, on 14 July. He told Woermann that 'sympathies of the Indian people were very clearly with Russia' because they 'felt definitely that Germany was the aggressor and was for India, therefore another dangerous imperialist power'. Subhas expected that the British Government was likely to exploit the situation by introducing new reforms, which would lend voice to 'that section of the public that is always in favour of compromise' to present any threat of a German attack on India 'not as one intended to liberate the Indian people but to substitute British rule by German rule'.[35]

Woermann received Subhas's clear-headed reading of the situation based on his direct knowledge of the Indian political situation from the typical German foreign policy perspective. His impression was that Subhas had been strongly influenced by Soviet propaganda as he was far away from Berlin. 'It will therefore be one of our first tasks to put him right in this respect', he wrote in his memorandum to Ribbentrop:

Here Mr Bose became very emphatic and asked that the Reich Foreign Minister be requested to issue this proclamation as speedily as possible. Each day that passed meant an advantage to England because of the reforms that she intended to introduce in India . . . he saw no reason to postpone this proclamation.[36]

Subhas's patience was growing thin. It had been over four months and there was still no concrete progress to talk about. Yet, there was little that he could do at the moment other than pressing the foreign office and Ribbentrop himself to do something soon. He wrote to Ribbentrop on 15 August, explaining the grave impact of the time that had been lost. At the time he had arrived, Subhas wrote, the 'situation in my country was then exceedingly favourable for the success of my proposals', but the situation was much worse at that point. He was 'alarmed to see how effective' the 'Soviet–British–American propaganda machine' was in presenting Germany as an aggressor out for dominating the world, particularly the Orient. This had led to a situation where even those who had spent their lives in fighting the British Raj had started thinking that if there was no hope of attaining independence with the help of the Axis powers, 'it is better to make peace with the British on the best terms available'. If the Axis powers did not declare their policy regarding India immediately, most Indians would be on the side of the Allied powers.

The situation was further complicated by India being turned into the central military base of the British Empire, which meant that even if Germany occupied England, the British would carry on their war using India as their base. America too had started playing an active role in Asia, and if they succeeded in bringing a compromise between Gandhi and the British, as they had done with Chiang Kai-Shek and the Chinese Communist Party, then the position of those standing for independence and revolution would be considerably weakened. Lastly:

> . . . if there is no declaration regarding Indian Independence, the nearer the German armies move towards India, the more hostile will the Indian people become towards Germany. The march of the German troops towards the East will be regarded as the approach, not of a friend, but of an enemy.[37]

In forwarding Subhas's letter to Ribbentrop, Woermann was sympathetic but patronizing in his views. He thought that Subhas's urgency stemmed from his concern that his influence in Indian politics would 'vanish if he remains inactive here any longer', but 'this should not be held against him'.

Although he agreed that looking at the issue solely from India's point of view, 'it would be urgently desirable to have the declaration regarding a free India issued soon', but the problem was that it could not 'be viewed from this standpoint alone'. Taking off from Subhas's prediction that the Anglo–Soviet guarantee to Turkey indicated that a British attack on Iran was imminent, Woermann suggested the entry of British troops into Iran 'would perhaps be an event that would offer a plausible occasion for an Indian declaration, which could then be placed in the even larger context of the British rape of the eastern nations'.[38]

Subhas's reference was to Churchill's announcement of promising all economic and technical assistance to the Soviet Union immediately after the latter had been invaded by Germany. His argument was that the road to Afghanistan would be cut off after the attack on Iran, which would make it difficult to execute their plans. The Soviet and British forces invaded neutral Iran on 25 August.

The point of utilizing the invasion of Iran in issuing the declaration was emphasized by the Secretary of State, Ernst von Weizsaker, too, on the very same day that the invasion was taking place. 'This appears to be an especially opportune moment. A fitting occasion like this will be hard to come by again,' he wrote to Ribbentrop, who chose to remain silent on this point.[39]

No amount of sympathy from the German Foreign Office mattered unless it had been endorsed by Hitler. When Subhas's plan was presented to Hitler in early September, he agreed to it but decided to postpone the execution to avoid a British invasion of Afghanistan triggered by issuing the declaration at that moment.[40] Subhas was informed that Ribbentrop would meet him soon to discuss the matter. It is hard to find Hitler's reasoning convincing, as although German and Italian non-official residents were made to leave the country under pressure from the British and Soviet Governments, the British were especially wary of any conflagration in Afghanistan. Several factors, including the Russian occupation of northern Afghanistan and the negative reaction among Sunni Muslims in India made the British take all precautions to avoid a war in the region.[41]

In the meantime, Shedai was doing his best to queer the pitch for Subhas, complaining to the Italians that Subhas was working against their interests, as he sensed that the Germans were going to put him under Subhas. After his visit to Berlin in mid-August, Shedai wrote a bitter letter to the Italian Foreign Office, accusing Subhas of 'playing a dangerous game simply for his personal and selfish ends', and of trying to 'create bad blood between Italy and Germany'. He had thought, Shedai wrote, that he 'could co-operate with him [Subhas] but now I think it is very unwise and rather dangerous to help him to achieve his selfish and wicked ends'. Shedai reserved special ire for Adam von Trott zu Solz of the German Foreign Office who had been asked to attend on Subhas on the recommendation of Woermann. 'Von Trott is with Bose and it is he who has made him Excellency and the future Viceroy of India, probably with the consent of Keppler', he wrote. After visiting the POW camp at Annaburg, he reported that the 1300 Indian soldiers at the camp were very unhappy with the German treatment and that they preferred to be in Italy. Moreover, they had started believing that Germany wanted to occupy India. Shedai claimed to have told Subhas, whom he considered 'unfit' for the task of raising a revolutionary army, that he had 'committed the greatest crime by bringing them over to Germany, but he does not care a bit for these poor devils as he wants to be the head of the Indian Legion as the C-in-C'.[42]

Quite irrespective of his scheming against Subhas, Shedai also made some valid points on his visit to the Annaburg camp. In his letter of 21 September 1941, to the Counsellor at the German Embassy in Rome, Shedai pointed out that putting Indian officers, who were loyal to the British, with other soldiers was a mistake as it gave the opportunity to the officers to convince the soldiers that Germany was going to occupy India. The Red Cross packets received by the soldiers from England led them to believe that the British Government was taking care of them. Moreover, the Indians involved in the recruitment process made some big promises to the soldiers, on behalf of the German Government, which could not be kept. This led to further disillusionment among them.[43] These points, however, are the same as the observations of the three soldiers from the Schlieffenufer camp who, along with Ganpuley, had gone for an inspection of the Annaburg camp.

Shedai also argued that Subhas belonged neither to the same provinces as the soldiers, nor the same class and, therefore, did not have the understanding of their mentality that was required to win them over for the planned Indian Legion. In fact, Gurbachan Singh Mangat, who could have been privy to Shedai's letter to the Italian Foreign Office, recounted his racist outburst against Subhas in a very crude language. *'Yeh dhoti topi wale Bengali mulk ki azadi ke lie kya karenge? Desh ko azad to Panjab ke bahadur saput hi karenge'*, Shedai told Mangat. (What can the dhoti-topi-wearing Bengalis do in the fight for the freedom of the country? It is the brave sons of the Panjab who would free the country).[44]

There was reason for Shedai to be worried about Subhas's influence among the Germans. As Trott noted, Shedai was the 'moving figure in the whole of the Indian, and part of the eastern activities of the Italian Foreign Ministry', and he had 'the absolute confidence of those in the competent departments and is also known in Berlin'.[45]

It was no surprise then that the Italians moved quickly in early October to put Shedai in charge of *Centro India*, a special office under their Foreign Ministry to direct all India-related activities, resulting in much gloating by Shedai.[46] The Italian move probably nudged Ribbentrop in mid-October to ask Keppler and Ritter to examine the possibility of using Indian POWs for propaganda purposes. The Indian question had been put under the charge of Wilhelm Keppler, a *Schutzstaffel* (SS) General and a friend of Himmler, who was attached to the Foreign Office as Secretary of State for 'special duties'. The Foreign Office had transformed the working group on India (*Arbeitskreis Indien*) in its information department to a special Indian bureau (*Sonderreferat Indien* or SRI) in the summer of 1941, which reported to Keppler.[47] While Adam von Trott zu Solz was put in charge of the SRI, among its members were Ludwig Alsdorf, a former professor of Indology at the Münster University, and Franz-Josef Furtwängler, a former trade union leader who had written books on India. The Foreign Office also appointed journalist and author Giselher Wirsing as Subhas's German language instructor.[48]

Thus, while Weizsäcker remained in charge of the political approach towards India, the responsibility of propaganda activities remained with Keppler. The SRI now had administrative control over the one million Reichsmark which was granted by Ribbentrop for India-related activities.[49]

Unhappy with the delay on all counts, Subhas first travelled to Brussels and Paris, accompanied by Emilie, to explore the possibility of recruiting capable Indians for the planned Free India Centre, as Berlin had only about forty Indians at that time, and then to Badgastein to attend to his health.[50] In Paris, Subhas met A.C.N. Nambiar who was then living in Foix, and asked him to join the Free India Centre. In view of his personal experience of German persecution and, as he would later add, partly due to his problem with pork, Nambiar was unwilling to join.

Sensing Subhas's dissatisfaction, Woermann sent Trott to Badgastein to convey Ribbentrop's message of postponing the declaration and personally explain the situation to him.[51]

On his return to Berlin, Subhas was allotted a spacious house at 6–7 Sophienstrasse, Berlin–Charlottenburg, as his private residence, where he moved in with Emilie. The villa, recalled Alexander Werth, a close friend of von Trott in the Foreign Office, 'soon became the centre of all Indian activities in Berlin'.

Although the declaration of independence was being constantly postponed, the work on setting up the Free India Centre (*Zentralstelle Freies Indien*) or the Azad Hind Sangh made progress. The FIC was inaugurated on 30 October, and the first meeting at its office, on 10 Lichtensteinallee, was held on 2 November 1941.[52] The Centre was to function as the focal point for the activities of Indian nationalists abroad, as an administrative nucleus for an independent India (for which a planning committee was set up within FIC in December) and was to concentrate on broadcasting propaganda under the new Azad Hind Radio, which commenced almost immediately. The propaganda material produced by the FIC was to be sent to India through Afghanistan, to be distributed among the frontier tribes and Indian soldiers.[53]

Meeting with the representatives of the Foreign Office, Home Office and the Ministry of Propaganda to prepare the organizational plan for the FIC, Subhas demanded for it the status of a legation of a free county with financial independence and complete freedom in radio propaganda. When the German officials refused his demand, Bose issued a stern warning:

> I have not come to Europe to live an idle, luxurious exile. I know your secret service is efficient. But so is the British CID in India, and I have risked my life to escape them. I shall not mind trying to go elsewhere if my mission requires it.[54]

Through Keppler's intervention, the FIC was accorded the status of an independent establishment with financial autonomy, diplomatic immunity and complete freedom over radio transmissions.[55]

The disparate group of Indians who gathered around Subhas in the early phase of the FIC was rather small, as his presence in Germany remained unknown to even local Indians for the first six months.[56] The first person to join Subhas almost immediately after his arrival in Berlin was the medical practitioner Dr K.R. Dhawan, who was the Foreign Office's confidante on Indian issues. Emilie Schenkl and M.R. Vyas too, who had known Subhas from the days of his exile in Europe, joined soon after. Subhas wrote to Emilie the day after he reached Berlin, asking her if she could join him as his secretary. The Foreign Office too sent her a telegram asking her to confirm whether she could join Subhas.[57] They were followed by N.G. Ganpuley. Abid Hasan (or Zainal Abedin Hassain, as mentioned in British intelligence files) and N.G. Swami joined in August 1941, and A.C.N. Nambiar and Girija Kanta Mookerjee joined in January 1942. Among the other Indians in Germany who joined Subhas were K.A. Bhatta, D.R. Keni, Ambika Charan Majumdar, Khurshed B. Mama, Ali Mohammed Sultan, Braja Lal Mukherji, Lekh Raj Ahuja, Saidudin Swallhay, and P.B. Sarma.[58]

In the first meeting of the FIC, Subhas outlined his ideas about the nature of work at the Centre, and the staff swore allegiance to him as their leader for attaining India's freedom. Apart from framing the objectives, rules and regulations of the FIC, the first meeting decided on a few core issues that would define the Indian movement in Europe. 'Jai Hind' was adopted as the war cry, Subhas was given the honorific of 'Netaji', Tagore's 'Jana Gana Mana', which invoked the destiny of India in the name of the various provinces and religions of India, was decided upon as the national anthem and Hindustani, as had been advocated by Subhas in his speech at the Haripura Congress, was chosen as the national language. The Congress flag with the charkha in the centre was replaced by a springing tiger, and that was adopted as the national flag.[59]

Radio broadcasting was at the heart of Subhas's propaganda plan. At the time of his arrival in Berlin, a German shortwave transmitter was broadcasting a half-hour news programme in Hindi.[60] Subhas insisted on the Azad Hind Radio having an independent wavelength, and was under no circumstances mixed up with German broadcasting. Barring the German technicians, the radio department had only Indians—all of them in their twenties and thirties—who would listen to the news from different parts of the world, with the focus being on the All-India Radio and the BBC, writing the daily newsreel for India, which would be translated to different languages and then read out. According to Ganpuley, no censorship was exercised by the German authorities, and copies of daily programmes were submitted to the Foreign Office after they had been broadcast. The success of the broadcasting programmes led the Germans to increase the allotted time from forty-five minutes daily to three hours. At the very beginning, the radio talks were written by Subhas himself, and was then translated into Hindustani, Bengali and other Indian languages by rotation. However, with the increase in the allocation of broadcasting time, the number of languages in which programmes were aired every day also increased, going on to include English, Hindi, Persian, Pushtu, Tamil and Telugu. Gujarati and Marathi languages were also included in the rotation.[61]

Ribbentrop met Subhas in Berlin for the second time on 29 November. By that time, the Indian and the British Governments had already announced that he had gone over to the enemy. He showed Ribbentrop the newspaper clippings from the *Times*, *Daily Mail* and *Daily Express* which branded him as a traitor and pressed hard on the need to make a reply so that his followers did not start defecting. Subhas also brought up the matter of objectionable passages in *Mein Kampf* relating to Indians, seeking broadcasts clarifying Germany's real thoughts behind those.

After boasting about how the German army was going to destroy the British Empire, Ribbentrop explained that Germany would not need any more colonies after colonizing Russia. In his scheme of division of global power, Ribbentrop speculated that the US would become heir to the British possessions in the western hemisphere, the Axis powers would dominate Europe, the Grand Mufti of Jerusalem would lead in creating a new Arab world and Japan would get its justified claims in the Far East.

The new line of argument, on the declaration of independence on India that came from Ribbentrop in that meeting, was simply a new excuse for delaying the declaration. 'The Axis could speak only when the military had a firm basis in the Near East, for otherwise any propaganda effect would come to nought', Ribbentrop told Subhas. 'It was a guiding principle of German policy', Ribbentrop elucidated, 'not to promise anything that could not be carried out later'. He tried to substantiate his argument with the example of Iraq's failed coup, where Rashid Ali al-Gaylani's Government was thrown out and, as a result, both he and the Grand Mufti had had to take asylum in Germany. Therefore, Germany would proceed only when success was in view, for example, when the German troops had crossed the Caucasus. He tried to assure Subhas that the time was not far off.[62]

What really was going on in his mind, however, is clear from Ribbentrop's mid-November brief for Hitler, more than two weeks before his meeting with Subhas. More than the position of the German troops, issuing the declaration hinged on British attitude towards Germany. Among other things, Ribbentrop wrote:

> . . . The point of departure for our policy with regard to India, similarly to that toward the Arab question, must be the publication of a declaration by the Axis Powers concerning a free India. We know that Bose has been insistently urging since the spring that such a declaration be issued by the Axis Powers as early as possible. The moment for such a declaration, however, will come only when it is clearly discernible that England does not manifest any willingness to make peace even after the final collapse of Russia . . .
>
> As may be seen from the enclosed copy of State Secretary Keppler's memorandum of November 13, an English counterpropaganda action has recently begun which is intended to discredit Bose with the Indian population as having gone over to the Axis Powers and to promote his antagonist, Pandit Nehru, as in accordance with England's intent . . . Our decision to defer for the time being a declaration of the Axis Powers concerning a free India will not have to be altered by us despite the reports circulated by the English. On the contrary, they confirm that the English camp is already beginning to show anxiety as a consequence of Bose's presence in Germany.[63]

Ribbentrop was clearly more concerned about his reading of the British mind rather than the impact of British propaganda on the Indian mind.

Woermann had reiterated in his November memorandum to Ribbentrop that a solely propaganda focused movement could not expect much success without a concomitant declaration of India's independence.[64] Yet, for both Ribbentrop and Hitler, the question of going full blast with a declaration, accompanied by publicity, was pegged on England's attitude towards Germany and not on the requirements of the Indian situation. The Indian question was little more than a point to pressurize the British to adopt a conciliatory approach towards Germany. All activity was only preparatory in nature to achieve that goal. In fact, the British rule in India provided a role model to Hitler for the German colonization of Russia.

Disappointing as the meeting with Ribbentrop was, there was some progress in the next few days when the Italians and Germans met on 8 and 9 December to coordinate their activities with regard to India. Subhas attended the meeting on the second day, although Shedai was there for both the days. The meeting was able to reach some concrete decisions.

It was decided that the formation of the Indian Legion would be in German hands. Both Germany and Italy took an anti-Muslim League stand, agreeing that the Pakistan movement was being exploited by the British to increase divisions among Indians. With Shedai's known Islamic and pro-Pakistan views, this decision was certainly a blow to his position. Although the Italian officials acknowledged the German argument about the Indian independence declaration being timed to an appropriate military situation, they argued that in view of the Japanese willingness to issue such a declaration, which had been conveyed to them in early December, the question needed reconsideration. The Germans informed that they were making preparations for a clandestine radio station from where Subhas would speak, so that it would become clear to the world that he was speaking from Germany and not an Indian station, and thereby increase the value of the broadcast.

The second day of the meeting, which Subhas attended, focused more on the Indian Legion, work on which was to start immediately. The overall political control was to remain with the Foreign Office but recruitment for the Legion was to be done together by the Foreign Office, Subhas and his associates at the Free India Centre, in cooperation with the German officers in charge of the POWs at the Annaburg camp. The Legion would be raised as a German infantry battalion equipped with anti-aircraft guns and light field artillery. Although Indian officers would be given leadership positions later on, the Legion would be trained exclusively under German officers during the first three months.

The idea of raising a corresponding unit for the Libyan front was dropped because of Subhas's objection. A strong Axis publicity for Indian independence was to start at the earliest in view of the developments in East Asia and Jawaharlal's anti-Axis public reaction.[65]

In aiming to set up the Indian Legion, which he imagined as the nucleus of a patriotic army in independent India, Subhas had set himself the task of converting mercenaries into nationalist soldiers. There had been a number of efforts to infiltrate units of the Indian army and gain their sympathy in preparation of rebellion, but there was no precedence of carving out a battle-ready and well-equipped nationalist army at a large scale.

Accompanied by Abid Hasan and N.G. Swami, Subhas visited the Schlieffenufer camp, which at that time had twenty-four Indian POWs on

11 December. The meeting was an emotional experience for Subhas as well as for the soldiers. They greeted each other in silence, with tears flowing from their eyes for the first few minutes. Subhas told the soldiers that the Axis powers would give them training, supplies and arms, but the blood that needed to be shed to attain freedom had to be of Indians. The Indian Legion was going to form the nucleus of Free India's army and they would have to keep high the image of Indians in Europe by their behaviour. An additional responsibility for them was clearing the communal and sectarian atmosphere in India. Subhas's speech was very well received by the group, with their representative's address to him beginning with '*Mere Pujya Netaji*'.[66]

Subhas's first visit to the Annaburg POW camp was marked by hostility from the non-commissioned officers of the British Indian Army.[67] The training of the Legion started in February 1942 under Walter Harbich, an Abwehr officer who had been interacting with Subhas since the time he had arrived.

While these developments were taking place in Berlin and Rome, the situation in East Asia was set to change completely over the next four months. After the attack on Pearl Harbour on 7 December, the Japanese forces took Bangkok on 8 December, Hong Kong on 25 December, Borneo on 31 December, Manila on 3 January 1942, Singapore on 15 February, Rangoon on 7 March, Java on 8 March and Sumatra by 28 March.[68]

Things had been shaping up in East and Southeast Asia rather differently.

Just over a couple of weeks before the Free India Centre had been inaugurated in Berlin, two strangers came face to face in a clandestine meeting in Bangkok on 12 October 1941, at the quarters of the Japanese military attaché, Colonel Tamura. Major Fujiwara Iwaichi, sent to Bangkok by the Chief of the Imperial Japanese Army General Staff Field Marshal, Hajime Sugiyama, was meeting Giani Pritam Singh. The brief given to Fujiwara, a staff officer of the 8th Section of the 2nd Bureau of the Imperial General Headquarters (IGHQ), was to foster close cooperation between Japan and the Indian nationalist movement, especially in the context of the concept of the co-prosperity sphere, and the impending Japanese offensive in Southeast Asia. Singh, a Sikh priest from Lyallpur in Punjab, who had had a brush with the nationalist movement in India resulting in imprisonment, had arrived in Bangkok in 1933, and formed the Independence League of India (later renamed Indian Independence

League), with his network including former members of the Ghadr party and their sympathizers. Singh soon introduced to Fujiwara another revolutionary—the elderly Baba Amar Singh, who had spent ten years in prison in the Andaman Islands and also in Rangoon, along with Subhas in 1927, before reaching Thailand.[69]

Fujiwara and Pritam Singh got along very well and developed plans to influence Indian officers and men in the British Indian army, and to better organize the League. Singh also asked Fujiwara to put his organization in touch with Subhas in Berlin. Accordingly, an agreement was drawn up on 1 December, between the League and the Japanese military authorities. While the Japanese pledged all possible help to the Indian nationalists and assured them that Japan had no ambitions in India, whether political or economic, they also promised to honour the lives, property and freedom of Indians in the region. In turn, the League agreed that its members would advance with the Japanese army into Southern Siam and Malaya carrying out anti-British campaigns, and promote cooperation between the Indian residents and the Japanese army in the zones of military operation. It was another clause in the agreement, however, that would lead to the raising of an army of liberation. According to this clause, an army was to be formed from among the POWs of the British Indian army and Indian civilians. Signed by Tamura and Amar Singh, the agreement was sent to the IGHQ, as well as to the headquarters of the 25th Army to which Fujiwara was directly reporting.[70]

As the Japanese forces landed in Thailand on 8 December, Fujiwara and his team, which had been named Fujiwara Kikan by then, moved along with the League members and followed the victorious Japanese army, setting up local League branches in the cities of Thailand as the army moved southwards. Small groups of the League, along with members of F Kikan, started visiting the battle fronts. After Fujiwara and Singh reached Alor Star on 14 December, they were contacted by Major Mohan Singh of the 1/14 Punjab Regiment that had been completely overrun by the Japanese forces.[71]

Mohan Singh was bitter with his British superiors, but he was not ready to trust the Japanese until he had met with Fujiwara's boss, General Yamashita, the commander of the 25th Army, who handed over the control of the Indian POWs to Singh. Mohan Singh also asked the Japanese to help in getting Subhas to the Southeast Asian front, so that he could take over the leadership of the planned movement. Towards the end of December,

Singh informed Fujiwara about his readiness to cooperate with the Japanese in raising a volunteer army from the Indian POWs if they agreed to certain conditions, including according an allied army status to the Indian army and handing over the control of all Indian POWs, whether they agreed to join the army or not, to him. The army, Singh proposed, should be named the Indian National Army. By that time, thousands of Indian civilians had come forward to join the League and contribute towards the welfare of the Indian POWs.[72]

A committee of the POWs, men who were, until a few days before, in the British Indian army, formed to deliberate on the agreement with the Japanese, as Fujiwara informed:

> We consider it a point of great honour for us to accept the kind, valuable and venerable leadership of Mr SC Bose. We all know that he is an extremist who believes in revolutions and radical changes. People in India are most anxiously waiting for any movement started by Mr. Bose. . . . He is a leader whose name will stir up a great revolution amongst the Indian masses, which would have a strong reaction in the Indian Army. It will cause a split in the Indian National Congress circles and the majority of the Congress will join Mr Bose. We, the members of the Indian National Army, are prepared to shed every drop of our blood for SC Bose. His very name puts new life into us . . . The day Mr SC Bose's name comes before us we promise that if it suits our purpose we will openly condemn the Indian National Congress.[73]

The Indian Association in Thailand, an organization of Indian businessmen, had, in the meantime, met in December and chosen Swami Satyananda Puri as the representative of the Indian community. Puri, born as Profulla Kumar Sen, was a former Anushilan Samiti revolutionary, who later taught at the Calcutta University and set up the Thai–Bharat Cultural Lodge in Bangkok in 1940.[74]

Subhas met Oshima, the Japanese ambassador in Berlin, on 17 December and Woermann the next day, trying to speed up a joint declaration of independence by the Axis powers. Oshima assured Subhas that he would speak personally to Ribbentrop shortly to reach an agreement.[75] The opportunity arising out of the Japanese advance towards India was clearly visible to Subhas. He was impatient to move to the south-eastern theatre where he felt he would be more effective, being closer to home. Subhas

asked Oshima to get the Japanese Government to agree to his transfer
to Southeast Asia where he would organize the Indian independence
movement with their help.[76] On 18 December, the German ambassador
to Thailand informed the Foreign Ministry about the move afoot to raise
an Indian army from the imprisoned Indian troops and volunteers, and
that a committee of Indian nationalists headed by Swami Satyanand Puri
and Deb Nath Das wanted Subhas to be brought in from Europe.[77] When
Ribbentrop himself raised the matter of transferring Subhas to the Far East,
in his meeting with Oshima on 2 January 1942, the latter agreed to the idea.
Hitler, however, maintained silence on the declaration of independence for
India when the issue was raised by Oshima on the next day.[78]

His next interaction with the Japanese, where he met the military
attaché Bin Yamamoto on 28 January, was positive in intent and spirit, but
ended without any definite commitment on the Japanese side. In the event
of an air attack on Calcutta, Indians should be sufficiently prepared with
prior information from the Japanese, or else it would be exploited by the
British Government to build public opinion against them, Subhas warned.
Yamamoto assured Subhas that the Japanese would inform the public of
Calcutta that only British military installations were Japanese targets and
not the civilian population. He also agreed to Subhas's suggestion that
the Japanese should aim to overrun the British power in India in the
immediate aftermath of their Burmese occupation, taking advantage of the
panic or shock effect it was bound to produce, similar to that after the
fall of Dunkirk. However, there was no commitment from Yamamoto on
the joint Axis declaration.[79] Subhas had presented similar arguments in a
meeting of Abwehr, where he had been invited to speak the previous day,
and where Yamamoto too had been present. He made another presentation
to the same group in the first week of February.[80] The Japanese embassy in
Rome also suggested that in Tokyo's view, the right time for the declaration
would be when the Japanese troops were closer to the Indian border.[81]

With the fall of Singapore on 15 February 1942, Japanese premier Hideki
Tojo referred to India in his speech to the House of Peers the very next day,
arguing that the fall of Singapore was 'an excellent opportunity for India . . .
to break off from Britain's callous domination and to join in the establishment
of the Greater East Asia Co-Prosperity Sphere'. He continued:

The Japanese Empire wishes India to be an Indians' India, and she is
anxious to see that she is restored to past greatness. In this, Japan will

offer her all help and assistance. If India abandons her tradition and history and forgets her missions under the spell of Britain's power and propaganda, and continues to follow her, then I shall feel very sorry for the Indian people for wasting this God-sent opportunity.[82]

Until then, Subhas had refused to shed his disguise as Orlando Mazzotta, or to speak over the radio without an accompanying declaration of independence for India from the Germans and Italians. In view of the enormous implications of the capture of Singapore, which he had highlighted months before to the Germans, he then changed his plans.

Subhas sent a letter to Woermann on 16 February, indicating that he was ready to make a broadcast over radio and, at the same time, warning him about the possible British reaction to Tojo's statement. 'Knowing the methods of British diplomacy', he wrote, they would work to arouse an anti-Japanese feeling in India and try to demonstrate that India was anti-Japanese. Moreover, to achieve these goals, he suspected, the British Government would 'manoeuvre to get prominent Indians like Nehru to issue anti-Japanese statements'. It was, therefore, critically important 'for freedom-loving Indians to immediately declare before the whole world that they will fight England till the last and will heartily cooperate with all those who will help India to attain her independence'.[83]

That Subhas's reading of the British mind was on point was demonstrated when Chiang Kai-Shek and his wife arrived in India on 9 February as the Viceroy's guest. Apart from their discussions with the Viceroy and the commander-in-chief of the army, the couple met those who mattered in India's politics, spoke at meetings organized by the All-India Women's Conference and All-India Students Federation, and travelled to Peshawar and Bengal. The focus of their interactions was of course to generate public opinion for solidarity with China, and to stress on the horrors of Japanese aggression. The visiting couple met with the Congress president, Azad, in Delhi, and on 18 February, had a meeting of more than four hours with Gandhi and Jawaharlal at Birla Park in Calcutta where Gandhi had been staying.[84]

The *Amrita Bazar Patrika*'s editorial captured the prevalent mood:

It would have been a great disappointment to Calcutta had the city been denied the opportunity of offering a cordial welcome to Madame Chiang Kai-Shek and the Marshal . . . In common with the rest of our countrymen and Englishmen we are full of admiration for the great Chinese soldier and patriot under whose leadership our comrades in China have been defending their country and their freedom against a relentless foe . . . Equally tenacious has been the struggle of the Russians whom also we may claim as an Asiatic people. Mr Churchill in a previous speech, frankly admitted that if India and the countries of the Middle East have been saved so far from the tide of German invasion, the credit should go first and foremost to the Russians. . . . The Marshal's visit will draw even closer our country and China . . .[85]

Speaking to a crowd of 50,000 on 20 February, at a public meeting chaired by Kiran Shankar Roy in Calcutta's Shraddhananda Park, Jawaharlal warned against the danger of seeking help from outside: 'If any Indian thought that way, it would not be a sign of courage, but a sign of cowardice and weakness':

Some people imagined that because some countries like Japan and Germany or any other country happened to be fighting against the Britishers to-day, they might deserve the sympathy of the Indians. Long before the war started, the National Congress had been repeating its policy in regard to Fascism, in regard to aggression and in regard to many things that Japan had done and Germany had done . . . Did anybody think that they would change the opinion because the Fascist powers were to-day at war with England? . . . Japan and Germany represented the very worst type of imperialism.[86]

Addressing the Congress workers at the BPCC office the next day, Jawaharlal announced that 'he would resist Hitler and Japan with all his might', because 'he disliked all that Hitler stood for with his hideous gospel'.[87]

Another platform that was gaining much support and sympathy at this time was the Friends of Soviet, comprising left-leaning leaders. A conference of the organization in Lucknow, towards the end of February, was attended by Jawaharlal, Sarjojini Naidu, Purushottam Das Tandon, Sampurnanand and Hasrat Mohani, among others. The conference passed resolutions stating that the destruction of the Soviet Union would be harmful to humanity, as it represented certain values which were important to the progress and development of humanity, and decided to send a delegation of representative Indians to strengthen the ties of friendship.[88] Similar platforms like the Anti-Fascist Convention were also mobilizing public opinion against the Axis powers.[89]

In Berlin, two days after he had written to Woermann, Subhas submitted a draft of his public statement to the Foreign Office. The Italians were already keen on him making public broadcasts, and Ribbentrop found that the Japanese too were ready to rebroadcast Subhas's speech.[90] Subhas spoke over the Azad Hind Radio in late February.[91]

'For about a year I have waited in silence and patience for the march of events and now that the hour has struck, I come forward to speak', he announced. In his brief speech, Subhas limited himself to presenting the broad outlines of the global scenario and clarifying his stand regarding the struggle for India's freedom. Notably, Subhas neither disclosed his location, nor said anything that could confirm his presence in Germany:

The fall of Singapore means the collapse of the British Empire . . . The Indian people who have long suffered from the humiliation of a foreign yoke . . . must now offer their humble thanks to the Almighty for the auspicious event which bears for India the promise of life and freedom.

British Imperialism has in modern history been the most diabolical enemy of freedom and the most formidable obstacle to progress . . . the enemies of British Imperialism are the natural allies of India—just as the allies of British Imperialism are today our natural enemies.

. . . we find in India those who openly support British Imperialism. There are others who, whether intentionally or unintentionally, help the British cause while often camouflaging their real motives by talking of cooperation with China, Russia and other Allies of England. There is, however, the vast majority of the Indian people who will have no compromise with the British Imperialism but will fight on till full independence is achieved.

. . . The hour of India's salvation is at hand. India will now rise and break the chains of servitude that have bound her so long. Through India's liberation will Asia and the world move forward towards the larger goal of human emancipation.[92]

Subhas's broadcast was repeated many times through Axis radio stations in Europe and in Asia, and most of the top German newspapers gave it front page coverage. Goebbels noted in his diary on 2 March that 'Bose's appeal has made a deep impression on world public opinion', and again on 4 March that in London, 'there is boundless wrath about the appeal of Bose, whose present abode is fortunately not known'. Some insight into the German thinking is also reflected in his noting that 'We are doing everything possible to pour oil on the fires without being caught at it.'[93]

On the radio, Subhas delivered five speeches each in the months of March and April. The British Government, of course, was monitoring his broadcasts. The Viceroy noted that 'Bose's broadcasts have excited more curiosity than interest in India and except in Bengal have had not much effect'.[94] The reports from the provinces in India to the Home Department, however, provide more information, and clearly bring out the impact of Subhas's broadcast in the two major eastern states, particularly in the context of the Japanese advance towards India. The Bihar Government reported:

> There is now a very great danger of the people getting demoralised and the broadcasts from Germany and. Japan help to aggravate the panic. People of the Subhas Bose group and the Forward Bloc are looking forward to creating chaos in the country. This inference is drawn from the prominence which has been given by the German Radio to the speech of Mr. Subhas Bose recently broadcast from some unknown station that as soon as the Japanese land in India an Independent Indian Government (Azad Hindustan) will be declared by the Subhas Bose group . . . From conversations with the groups connected with the Forward Bloc it appears that they are looking forward to para-troops from Japan dropping arms to the people who would go over to the Bose group.

The Bengal Government reported:

> Among the educated population, perhaps for the first time and in the most marked degree, those whose genuine sympathies are with Government and who are fundamentally loyal have been severely shaken . . . there is widespread belief . . . that Subhas Bose is with the enemy . . . that, should the Japanese set foot in India, there would be organised efforts on the part of the Forward Bloc and possibly other groups to create diversions with the definite intention of assisting the invaders.
>
>   . . . in the Dacca Division pro-fascist or pro-enemy activities are reported on the part of the Jugantar party, the Anushilan Samiti and

the Forward Bloc. The Forward, which is the organ of the Jugantar party, very recently published an article affirming that nothing must be permitted to distract members from their primary object which is the defeat of British Imperialism and that, even if pursuit of this object involves falling under another alien domination, this possibility must be 'courageously' accepted.[95]

Although the German Government had made it clear that they were not yet ready to issue the declaration on India's independence, the SRI continued to push ahead with its plans and programmes. Trott submitted a plan of action to Keppler, which laid out the details for publicity culminating into the declaration, although no date had been specified. Notably, Trott's note recommended that the Axis powers should avoid interfering in India's domestic affairs as well as not criticize Gandhi and Jawaharlal. Sensitive to Indian realities, Trott suggested that Axis propaganda should heavily emphasize on India's self-determination and their non-interference in India's internal affairs.[96]

Subhas presented a modified plan to be executed as the Japanese forces marched through Burma, in a meeting between the Japanese military representatives and the Abwehr on 26 February. He recommended that a Free Burmese Government should be announced as soon as the Japanese drove out the British forces from Burma and Rangoon, and that it should be set up as the headquarters of Indian nationalists with an Axis radio station. He wanted to be in Rangoon as soon as possible, and suggested that to pre-empt any compromise between the British Government and Jawaharlal, the Japanese army should march into India accompanied by Indian nationalists. The Forward Bloc, he claimed, would prepare the ground to start a revolution the moment Japanese forces landed in India. This would, he said, coincide with the landing of special commando forces in the tribal territories and the NWFP so that a two-pronged offensive could have maximum impact.[97]

As Subhas continued to press his plan and progressed with the FIC and the Indian Legion, the situation in India and East Asia was developing rapidly.

After the fall of Singapore, Major Fujiwara formally received the surrender of the British Indian troops in a meeting held at Farrer Park, and announced that the 45,000 Indian POWs would be handed over to Mohan Singh, who had around 55,000 Indian POWs under him after that. It was here that Singh formally announced the plan to raise an army. The announcement was received with enthusiasm from the rank and file, but the officers were cautious. The Prisoners of War headquarters was set up at Neesoon in Singapore under Lt Col N.S. Gill, with Lt Col J.K. Bhonsle as the Adjutant and Quarter Master General, and Lt Col A.C. Chatterji as the Director of Medical Services.[98]

Japan's entry into the Southeast Asian theatre had also set into motion efforts by the Indian nationalist groups in Japan to consolidate themselves and explore the possibilities of exploiting the situation to further India's goals. Representatives of the Indian community in Japan, including Rash Behari Bose and Anand Mohan Sahay, met immediately after the Malayan offensive, and decided to cooperate with the Japanese for attaining India's freedom, but only after ascertaining that the Japanese did not have any territorial ambitions on India. A subsequent meeting on 26 December urged Japan to help India achieve its goal of complete independence, and pledged to support the Japanese forces in Southeast Asia. While Rash Behari was entrusted with the task of negotiating with the Japanese Government, Sahay was asked to organize the Indian community and open branches of the Indian Independence League all over Japan.[99]

Following Singapore's fall and Tojo's 'India for Indians' speech on 16 February 1942, Rash Behari convened a conference of leaders of the Indian communities in Japan and Southeast Asia from 28 to 30 March, to be held at the Sanno Hotel in Tokyo. The scepticism about this move, emanating from the distrust of the Japanese among the Indians in Southeast Asia, led them to hold a meeting among themselves to decide upon the strategy to be adopted at the Tokyo conference. Meeting in Singapore on 9 and 10 March, the nationalist leaders of the Indian communities in Malaya, Singapore and Thailand were keen to have the approval of the Indian National Congress for such a movement. Agreeing, however, that Japan's support was necessary for the attainment of India's independence, the meeting resolved that Subhas should be requested to take charge of the independence movement in East Asia. Not yet ready to commit to anything definite, the meeting decided to send delegates to Tokyo as a goodwill mission.[100]

In a terrible mishap, the plane carrying four Indian delegates to Tokyo—Satyananda Puri, Pritam Singh, K.A.N. Aiyer and Captain Mohammad Akram—crashed after taking off from Saigon on 13 March as it approached Tokyo, killing all the passengers.

A twist in the reportage of the plane crash caused a sensation in India. Subhas 'has been killed in an air crash off the coast of Japan according to Lyons radio', reported *The Observer*. Although the news report added that no mention of Subhas had been made in a Bangkok despatch to the German News Agency, the first part was too sensational to be moderated by it.[101] A follow-up report by the Associated Press was spread out in newspapers across the world. 'The whole nation mourns with you the death of your and her brave son. May God give you courage to bear the unexpected loss', Gandhi wired to Prabhabati on 29 March. 'By the death of Bose we have lost one of the most vivid, vital and romantic personalities of India. He had the courage of his convictions and death came to him as a brave man', Bhulabhai Desai said in a statement. Although Lucknow observed a hartal, Chandra Bhan Gupta expressed his doubts at the authenticity of the news while speaking at a public meeting.[102] The truth was out quickly, however, and Gandhi and Azad wired to Subhas's family the next day, 'Thank God, what purported to be authentic has proved to be wrong. We congratulate you and the nation'.[103]

'This is Subhas Chandra Bose, who is still alive, speaking to you over the Azad Hind radio,' Subhas broadcast, as the rumour of his death spread wide and fast. 'The latest report about my death is perhaps an instance of wishful thinking', he said. He continued, 'I can imagine that the British Government would, at this critical hour in India's history, like to see me dead since they are now trying their level best to win India over to their side for the purpose of their imperialistic war.'[104]

An air of suspicion and mutual distrust hung around the Tokyo conference. While Rash Behari was projected as the leader of the independence movement in East Asia by the Indians in Japan as well as the Japanese authorities, his proximity to the Japanese was not received well with the representatives from Southeast Asia, many of whom were meeting him for the first time. Leaders such as S.C. Goho, N. Raghavan and K.P.K. Menon suspected that the Japanese would push their own agenda through a compliant Rash Behari. In fact, Mohan Singh later described Rash Behari as a well-known Japanese puppet.[105] Having broken away with Rash Behari, Anand Mohan Sahay was absent from the conference. Another person who had kept away was Raja Mahendra Pratap, who had, by then, come to regard Rash Behari as a Japanese puppet.[106]

In his message to the conference, Tojo announced:

The Japanese Government cannot remain indifferent to the fact that Britain is going to make India the base of its Eastern defence. In view of this fact, the Japanese Government sincerely expects that the Indians would throw away the British Yoke by themselves and create an independent India.[107]

The Conference decided that all the nationalist organizations would merge into the Indian Independence League and set up new branches. The supreme executive body of the IIL would be the Council of Action—an elected body of representatives from the civilian Indian communities and the proposed INA, with Rash Behari elected the president. The council was to be aided by a larger and more broad-based body, the Committee of Representatives.

'Unity, Faith and Sacrifice' was adopted as the motto of the independence movement in greater East Asia. As a safeguard against Japanese domination and interference, the conference bound the Council of Action to the approval of the Committee of Representatives before taking any military action against India that would be contrary to the wishes of the Indian National Congress. Moreover, any such military action could be taken only by the Indian National Army under the command of Indians.[108]

On 11 March, Winston Churchill announced in the House of Commons that Stafford Cripps, the Lord Privy Seal and the Leader of the House, would proceed to India to present proposals from the British Government which represented a 'just and final solution' of the Indian problem. After arriving in Delhi on 23 March, Cripps made it clear that there was no time for long discussions and that only small adjustments arising out of his consultations with the various parties would be made in the proposals finalized by the British Cabinet.

The objective of the proposed Cabinet decisions was to accord the full status of Dominion to India, for which a constitution-making body would be set up immediately at the end of the war. However, if any province was not prepared to accept the constitution, it could frame its own constitution and would be accorded the same status as the Indian Union. The princely states would also have the freedom to decide whether they wanted to join the Indian Union or not. The constitution-making body would sign a treaty with the British Government regarding complete transfer of power from British to Indian hands, which would make provisions for protection of racial and religious minorities, but would not impose any restriction on the Indian Union regarding its relation with other members of the British Commonwealth. Until the constitution was in force, the British Government would retain control of the defence of India, but the resources of India required for the war would be organized by the Government of India in cooperation with the peoples of India.[109]

The initial euphoria emerging out of expectations from his visit soon gave way to disappointment. The Congress working committee passed a resolution on 2 April, rejecting the Cripps proposals, arguing that they belonged to an uncertain future and that some of the provisions were in negation of both democracy and self-determination. Moreover, the principle of non-accession for a province was a blow to the conception of the unity of India. Retention of the defence portfolio under British control too was not an acceptable proposition, and this became the bone of contention over which the negotiations broke down. The Congress logic was that any proposal 'concerning the future of India must demand attention and scrutiny, but in today's grave crisis, it is the present that counts, and even proposals for the future are important in so far as they affect the present'.[110]

The rejection was followed by a lengthy correspondence between Azad and Cripps, which eventually reached a deadlock by 11 April. Azad wrote to Cripps that although the Congress had not accepted the proposals:

> we are yet prepared to assume responsibility provided a truly national government is formed. We are prepared to put aside for the present all questions about the future, though as we have indicated, we hold definite views about it . . . the National Government must be a cabinet with full power and must not merely be continuation of the Viceroy's Executive Council.

Cripps, on his part, argued that only a change in the existing constitution could install a representative national government, which was not possible under the existing circumstances.[111] The Muslim League and the Hindu Mahasabha too announced their rejection of the proposals. Although Cripps met a number of political parties and other organizations, he refused to meet representatives of the Forward Bloc. He was also informed by J.C. Gupta about the 'necessity for mobilising all elements' to counteract the influence that Subhas still had in Bengal, including a section of the extremists 'who, owing to their communist sympathies, were anxious to take a full part in the defence of India at the present time'.[112] The Government declared the Forward Bloc an unlawful organization on 22 June 1942.[113]

Subhas commenced a series of broadcasts as the Cripps Mission was announced by Churchill. 'There is no end to British intrigues. Now they are uselessly making a lot of fuss over a possible enemy invasion of India', Subhas said in his broadcast on 19 March. Whether governed by Conservative or Labour leaders like Churchill and Cripps, Subhas said, the British Government had been causing starvation in India and 'want the Indians to work like serfs and ceaselessly toil and fret for them'. Cripps's visit proved that all party differences in Britain disappeared when it came to India. India would never have been a party to the war if the Government had not arbitrarily dragged India into it. Just as in September 1939, when they were responsible for bringing India into the war, they were responsible at that point for bringing the war into India. Subhas said that 'Every Indian who works to strengthen British hands, betrays the cause of his motherland. Such a man is a traitor to India'.

No sane Indian could be pleased with the Cripps proposals, Subhas argued, nor be prepared to trust empty British promises. He added that 'Only one who lives in a fool's paradise could imagine that India still cares for Dominion Status'. The proposals were another attempt at the age-long British policy of divide and rule. Regarding Cripps's argument that the existing constitution could not be changed during the war, Subhas reminded that in October 1939, he had suggested that a provisional government commanding the confidence of the majority of Indians be set up and be made responsible to the central Legislative Assembly, a suggestion that received support from the Congress too.

By retaining full military control of India, the British Government on the one hand wanted to exploit India's resources, and thereby to force 'the enemies of Britain to attack Britain's military base in India, so that the Indian people may be provoked into voluntarily entering the war as Britain's ally'.

Subhas took a more direct and personal approach by broadcasting an open letter to Cripps from the Azad Hind Radio on 31 March, exposing the hypocrisy of the entire affair. Among other things, he said:

> It is understandable that the present Prime Minister and the Cabinet should make use of you for this purpose. But it passes one's comprehension that you, Sir Stafford, should accept such a job. You are well aware of the

reactionary character of the present Cabinet. The presence of Labourites in it does not alter its real character . . .

In the days when you fought with the British Labour Party in vindication of your own principles and convictions, you commanded the admiration of many people including myself . . . That fundamental position of yours has altered so radically that you accepted a portfolio under Mr Winston Churchill, than whom a more anti-Indian Englishman it is difficult to find in the whole of Britain . . . One can easily understand Mr Churchill . . . Even the British Labour Party's attitude we can perhaps understand. British Labour leaders are in reality as Imperialistic as the Conservatives are, though they may talk in a more polite and seductive manner. We have faced the Labour Party's administration in 1924 and again from 1929 to 1931.

On both these occasions we had to spend our time in British prisons, sometimes without any trial whatsoever. India will never forget that between 1929 and 1931 a Labour Cabinet was responsible for putting about 100,000 men and women into prison, for ordering large-scale lathi charges on men and women all over the country, for shooting down of defenceless crowds as in Peshawar, and for burning houses and dishonouring women as in the villages of Bengal. You were one of the sharpest critics of the Labour party when in London in January 1938, I had the pleasure of making your acquaintance. But today you appear to be quite a difference man.

. . . knowing as you do that the Indian National Congress stands for undiluted independence is it not an insult to India that a man of your position and reputation should go out there with such an offer in his pocket? . . .

. . . British politicians and the British propaganda machine have been continually reminding us since 1939 that the Axis Powers are a menace to India and now we are being told that India is in danger of an attack by the enemy. But is not this sheer hypocrisy? India has no enemies outside her own frontiers. Her one enemy is British imperialism and the only adversary that India has to get rid of is the perpetual aggression of British Imperialism . . . I am convinced that if India does not participate in Britain's war there is not the least possibility of India being attacked by any of the Axis Powers.[114]

On 6 April, Subhas thanked Tojo for his declaration of 'India for Indians', stating that the 'present war which the Tripartite Powers are waging against

Britain and America, is of vital interest to India, and the Indian people are, therefore, following with joy and satisfaction the continued defeats of the Anglo-American forces'.[115]

Noticeably, although Subhas kept speaking on what Congress in general stood for, in none of his speeches he commented on the Congress leadership. It was in his broadcast of 10 April that he launched a bitter attack on the Congress leaders, without naming anyone other than M.N. Roy, who he thought were ready to compromise with the British Government:

> ... some of our liberal friends have endeavoured to facilitate a compromise by suggesting that the Governments of the Allied Powers and of the British Dominions should guarantee to India that Britain's promises will be redeemed when the war is over. But what value is there in such guarantees when we have no power to enforce their fulfilment? Have we forgotten what happened to President Wilson's 14 points? ... I am sure that even if some people are still blind the vast majority of our countrymen realise that the United States of America are playing a role of father to the insane and they regard themselves as the heirs of the British Empire that has gone into compulsory liquidation. It is comical to see men who have been and still are slaves of the British suddenly developing megalomania in the company of men like Sir Stafford Cripps and Louis Johnson and then appointing themselves saviours of the British Empire ... It is no less comical that the Indian saviours of British Imperialism are the men who regard themselves as international democrats ... Simply because they are humoured and lionised by the wily British ... they talk of lining up with the progressive forces of the world. They do not talk frankly of co-operating with Britain but camouflage their real motives by asking the Indian people to co-operate with China or Russia or America ... I consider it my duty to warn my countrymen that in the present crisis which faces India compromise-hunting is like war-mongering ... To make a compromise with England now, on the basis of co-operation in Britain's war effort, is converting India into an enemy of the Tripartite Powers and forcing these powers to attack not only Britain's military base in India but all those Indians who co-operate in Britain's war effort ... And when the British flee the country on the eve of their defeat, just as General MacArthur and General Wavell have done elsewhere, they will burn and destroy everything in accordance with their new-fangled scorched-earth policy ... The British have at long last realised that they

do not enjoy any moral prestige in India. That is why they commandeered the services of Marshal Chiang Kai-shek and this why Mr Louis Johnson have been rushed to India, carrying letters from the White House in his pocket.[116]

Concluding the speech, Subhas urged that Indians 'should without any delay renew the national struggle for independence and on a more intensified scale'. It was on India to fight for its own freedom.

Subhas's speeches were broadcast in several languages by twelve Axis radio stations, including those in Bangkok, Tokyo and Shanghai. According to the German legation in Bangkok, the All-India Radio commented almost daily on Subhas's speeches without mentioning his name. Although missing in the Indian press, the speeches received a fair amount of coverage in British and American reportage.[117]

Soon after the breakdown in talks with Cripps, Jawaharlal stopped over at Calcutta on his way to Assam, reiterating his anti-Axis views to the Congress workers and journalists. By this time, despite his broadcasts being listened to by many Indians, Subhas had become the man-not-to-be-named in press reports. At a meeting of about 100 Congress workers in the house of Bijoy Singh Nahar on 18 April, Azad 'exhorted Congress workers to make it clear to themselves as well as to the people that it would be dangerous to take even a passive attitude towards any aggressor, whether it was Japan or Germany'. The Congress considered the forces represented by Hitler and Japan as dark forces, which, if victorious, would lead to the permanent slavery of India, as Jawaharlal told the gathering. 'The attitude of the Congress', he explained, 'in this war was that of non-belligerency and not exactly of neutrality'.[118] Gandhi expressed similar views: 'It is folly to suppose that aggressors can ever be benefactors. The Japanese may free India from the British yoke, but only to put in their own instead'.[119]

Speaking at a public meeting in Howrah the next day, Jawaharlal said that the Forward Bloc was set up as an anti-Congress organization, and although he did not question the sincerity of its motive, there was no question of cooperation between the Bloc and the Congress. He explained that non-cooperation with Britain in the existing circumstances meant an open invitation to Japan:

If we had wanted, we could have completely broken the war effort in India. But the Congress deliberately did not want to do so in spite of its antipathy to the British Government for the larger cause. So while we went to prison we did not become definitely hostile and obstruct the war effort. Today, when invasion threatens us any action of deliberate obstruction like Satyagraha that we might take, it will have the effect of helping another power which we do not want today.[120]

This attitude was set to undergo a complete change in just over three months.

Lauding the words of Azad and Jawaharlal, the *Amrita Bazar Patrika* cautioned against the 'deceptive language of aggressors and conquerors' with special reference to Japan's 'Asia for Asiatics' slogan. Without naming Subhas, the newspaper's editorial commented:

In ordinary circumstances this kind of propaganda would be taken for what it is worth, but the alleged broadcasts from the Axis stations by some well-known Indians who in the past worked and suffered for the emancipation of the motherland have unfortunately introduced an element of complexity into the situation.[121]

Jawaharlal's most outspoken statement, however, was reserved for a meeting at the Congress House in Gauhati:

Hitler and Japan must go to hell. I shall fight them to the end and this is my policy. I shall also fight Mr Subhas Bose and his party along with Japan if he comes to India. Mr Bose acted very wrongly though in good faith.[122]

If the Japanese army invaded Assam, people should follow a policy of 'no surrender and no submission', put obstacles and difficulties in their way, and get shot down if necessary.

Taking a different view of matters, Rajagopalachari announced in Madras that if the Japanese 'made the mistake of invading India, they would find their entire strength swallowed up, they would meet with certain defeat and that would be their end'.[123]

Propelled by the intensification of developments in the wake of the Cripps Mission, the Japanese Government decided to come out with a joint declaration for India's independence, the draft for which they presented at the Tripartite Liaison Conference on 11 April, promising 'India for Indians' and 'Arabia for the Arabs'. Although both Mussolini and Ciano welcomed the Japanese initiative, the Germans were not entirely satisfied with the draft. They, therefore, produced another German draft. Ribbentrop submitted both the drafts to Hitler along with his memorandum on 16 April, arguing strongly in favour issuing the declaration. Hitler, however, was not in a mood to oblige just because the Japanese wanted it. The upside of his response was that he gave his consent to the idea of transferring Subhas to East Asia. At the same time, the Liaison Conference in Tokyo decided to invite Subhas to Japan.[124]

Mussolini soon changed his views when he met Hitler at Salzburg on 29 April, where Hitler argued against issuing the declaration at that point of time on the grounds of an uncertain response in India to the declaration, or even a possible clamp down by the Indian Government on all opposition, thus making it powerless and in consequence making the British Government even stronger. He asked Japan to be informed that Italy and Germany would issue the declaration when the position of the Axis powers was strong enough in the Indian Ocean and the Near East to lead to an uprising in India and the Arab countries that could be supported militarily. Subhas, however, was able to change Mussolini and Ciano's minds again by his persistent arguments when he met them at Rome on 4 May. Hitler remained the only obstacle, as another memorandum by Ribbentrop on 14 May too failed to sway him.[125]

Frustrated by the dilly-dallying of Italy and Hitler's obstinate refusal to issue the joint declaration, Subhas wrote to Ribbentrop on 22 May that although he had done 'some useful and enduring work for India' in Germany, it was now 'absolutely essential' that he should be in the east. Due to the rapid advance of the Japanese forces on India's frontier, the conditions in India were now ripe for a revolution.[126] Obviously he was not aware that Hitler had already agreed, in principle, to his transfer to East Asia, but he was encouraged by Mussolini's recent offer to provide air transport for him.

Amidst disagreements within the SRI about the justification of transferring Subhas to East Asia, Woermann wrote to Ribbentrop, arguing that Hitler must receive Subhas before he left Germany. Ribbentrop submitted another memorandum to Hitler urging him to issue an immediate declaration on India, but as usual, it was stonewalled.

Finally, more than a year after he had reached Germany, Subhas was flown to Hitler's headquarters on the morning of 27 May. According to

Walter Schellenberg, a close confidante of Himmler, who was with the Foreign Intelligence Service (AMT VI) of the Reich Security Main Office (RSHA), the meeting was organized by the SS.[127] First he met Ribbentrop, who promised all help to transfer him to East Asia, but also discouraged him not to fly by an Italian plane as that would be too risky. Subhas was then received by Hitler in the afternoon, in the presence of Ribbentrop, Keppler and Walter Hewel.

Calling him an 'old revolutionary' Subhas opened by thanking Hitler for the German Government's hospitality and support. He emphasized that the time had come for military cooperation with the Japanese forces, but India attached great value in maintaining close contacts with Germany and Italy and did not wish to depend solely on Japan. He then made his case for his transfer to somewhere in East Asia, as close as possible to India. Breaking into a long lecture on global politics, Hitler thereafter clarified that it would make no sense to issue the declaration of independence if the enemy was not defeated once and for all. India was too far away, he said, and could be reached only through a defeated Russia. He would have asked Subhas to continue to stay in Germany if the German forces were at the frontiers of India so that he could kindle the revolution there. But since it might take one to two years to reach there, he advised Subhas to go to East Asia to carry on the revolutionary struggle. The British hegemony could only be broken if there was an Indian uprising destroying lines of communication, obstructing supply lines and troop transports at the time of an attack from outside. He was, however, not aware if the Japanese really wanted to exert such a pressure. Hitler also advised Subhas to avoid undertaking a journey by air and offered to put a submarine at his disposal to take him to Bangkok. When Subhas asked him to issue a clarification over certain insulting passages in *Mein Kampf* which were exploited by enemy propaganda, Hitler could only offer a lame and racist excuse—that those passages were directed against certain tendencies among the suppressed peoples to form a united front against their oppressors, particularly because some groups within Germany also wanted to build a resistance along Indian lines.[128]

The only assurance of help that thus came out of an extremely disappointing meeting was that of providing a submarine. Ribbentrop and Oshima reached an agreement in June on the urgent necessity to transfer Subhas to East Asia. Japan's approval for his transfer by an Italian aeroplane arrived in mid-August.[129]

Subhas also met Heinrich Himmler and Hermann Göring. While Göring promised Subhas air force training, Himmler talked about the Upanishads and Kalidasa's *Shakuntala*.[130]

In the meantime, the raising of the Indian Legion had made definite progress. As in every other sphere of activity in Germany, Subhas negotiated hard to ensure the independence of the Legion. He demanded from the German Government that the Legion would be provided the same training by German instructors as received by recruits in the German army, be maintained as self-reliant, independent units within the German army, and ensured parity with corresponding German units in terms of arms, uniform, pay and supplies. He also put the condition that the Legion would only fight against the British forces on the way to India or within India. The German officers who trained the Indian soldiers would be replaced later on by suitable Indian officers.[131]

Subhas visited the POWs at the Annaburg camp on 21 December 1941 to begin the recruitment process. But it was not only about recruiting soldiers for the Indian Legion. Subhas was engaging with a new constituency, and as rightly pointed out by Ganpuley, the visit was 'to feel the pulse those who were there, to see with his own eyes the kind of material which was available and, only after that, to form his own opinion as to how far they would respond to his call and what chances he had in making his great project a success'.[132]

The initial experience was not a happy one. The first meeting with the non-commissioned officers (NCOs)—elderly men with ten to fifteen years of service—was 'rather reserved and cold'.[133] The officers reacted to Subhas's speech with distrust and scepticism, coughing loudly and shuffling their boots to overpower his words.[134]

The behaviour of the officers has been attributed to their perception of Subhas's speech as a call for betrayal, and also to their fear of consequences such as losing jobs and pensions. Ganpuley believed that had Subhas walked in without any prior announcement, the reception would have been more favourable. The arrangements for Subhas's security measures gave them the time to reflect and prepare.[135]

The reception by the other POWs on the second day was, however, completely different. Subhas was received amidst great enthusiasm with cheers and garlands, made of paper and whatever other material they could arrange for. 'They seemed very little cowed down by the NCO's threats. They broke out in loud cheers of joy, forgetting the consequences, forgetting the prison surroundings, when they saw amongst them their national leader,' Ganpuley reminisced.[136]

Subhas selected fifteen men, from amongst the Indian students living in Berlin and the POWs, as the first batch of the Legion to receive training. The group of fifteen were given a send-off on 25 December at the office of the FIC, where all the Indian residents of Berlin converged. The first group was given a farewell on 26 and 27 December at the Anhalt railway station by the Indian residents amidst cries of 'Azad Hind Zindabad', 'Inqilab Zindabad' and 'Netaji Zindabad'. While a large share of the recruits was sent to Frankenberg, near Chemnitz, a smaller group was sent to the Regenwurm camp near Meseritz for training.[137]

A further 300 were recruited in the next four months, and another 300 in the next six. With the increase in the number of recruits, the training camp was shifted from Frankenberg to Königsbrück, near Dresden. A deputation comprising the Legion Commander, his aide-de-camp, one representative of the FIC, an officer from the Foreign Office and two legionaries from the first batch was sent to Rome in July 1942 to negotiate with the Italian Government and bring to Germany about 700 Indian POWs held in a camp near Rome. Shedai had raised a military unit out of the POWs in Italy called Centro Militare India in April 1942, but the unit was disbanded in November 1942 on account of a mutiny among the troops. By Ganpuley's estimate, the strength of the Indian Legion had grown to 3500 by December 1942.[138] The special unit which was trained in Meseritz also moved to Königsbrück.

The swearing-in ceremony of the Legion, now with the official name Infanterie-Regiment 950 (Indische), took place in September 1942. The Indian soldiers took the oath in German and Hindustani:

> I swear by God this sacred oath that I will give unconditional obedience to the Fuhrer of the German nation and people Adolf Hitler as supreme commander of the Wehrmacht in the liberation struggle of India under the leadership of our leader Subhas Chandra Bose. I will any time be prepared as a brave soldier to lay down my life for this oath.

After the oath was read out, Subhas added, 'I shall lead the army to India when we march together.'[139]

The legionnaires wore German uniforms with the national insignia of the German Reich. They also wore an Indian tricolour badge on the right upper arm with a springing tiger and 'Freies Indien' written above. The Legion became the first army with Hindustani as the command language.

On 12 June 1942, Subhas appeared for his first press conference in Berlin, where he spoke about his journey from India and the objective of his stay in Europe. He said that Hitler, Mussolini and Tojo were the best friends that Indians had outside India in their fight against British Imperialism, whose end was 'not only inevitable but is near at hand'. In contrast to his earlier outburst against the Indians who he felt were eager to compromise with the British Government, his message at the press conference was more nuanced and a definite statement of his views:

> Among the Indian nationalists, though there are sometimes differences in speed and also in method, all are united on the question of Independence. I do not regard any Indian nationalist as a political opponent, though I regard myself as the vanguard of the national army . . . In this struggle, some nationalists may fight only with the weapon of civil disobedience or passive resistance, but those who stand with me, will not hesitate to draw the sword when the time comes.[140]

In Southeast Asia, yet another conference was organized, for the decisions of the Tokyo conference to be ratified by a larger body of Indian representatives, in Bangkok from 15–23 June. The different organizations in East Asia were merged into a single Indian Independence League (IIL). This conference, attended by delegates from the Indian communities in Japan, Manchukuo, Shanghai, Hong Kong, the Philippines, Borneo, Java, Celebes, Sumatra, Thailand, Malaya, Burma and the Indian POWs received goodwill messages from the prime minister and foreign minister of Japan, the prime minister of Thailand, and was attended by representatives of the German and Italian Governments. The Axis powers issued a joint declaration that they had no territorial interest in India.[141]

~

As, according to the Congress working committee, the failure of the Cripps Mission 'showed in the clearest possible manner that there was no change in the British Government's attitude towards India and that the British hold on India was in no way to be relaxed', the committee passed a resolution on 14 July in its meeting at Wardha, demanding an immediate withdrawal of British rule from India. Apart from its standard claim of immediate freedom strengthening the anti-Fascist war efforts, the working committee curiously found it necessary to impress that the Cripps Mission's failure:

> . . . has resulted in a rapid and widespread increase in ill-will against Britain and a growing satisfaction at the success of Japanese arms. The Working Committee view this development with grave apprehension as this, unless checked, will lead to a passive acceptance of aggression. The Committee hold that all aggression must be resisted, for any submission to it must mean the degradation of the Indian people and the continuation of their subjection . . . The Congress would change the present ill-will against Britain into good-will and make India a willing partner in a joint enterprise of securing freedom for the nations and peoples of the world and in the trials and tribulations which accompany it.[142]

If this demand was ignored, the working committee declared, the Congress would then be compelled to launch a non-violent movement under Gandhi to attain the country's liberty. In view of the magnitude of implications of the resolution, it was referred to the All India Congress Committee (AICC) for a final decision.

Explaining the resolution at the AICC meeting held at the Gowalia Tank Maidan in Bombay on 7 August, Azad said:

> What this resolution says is this: Let us not depend on promises. Let us have a declaration of Indian Independence forthwith and we, on our part, shall immediately enter in a Treaty of Alliance with the United Nations for the sole purpose of fighting and winning this war.[143]

The resolution, calling for 'a mass struggle on non-violent lines on the widest possible scale', was passed by an overwhelming majority on 8 August. 'I have pledged the Congress and the Congress will do or die,' Gandhi declared on the passing of the resolution.[144]

The Government was prepared and immediately clamped down, arresting Gandhi and the members of the working committee before dawn on the next day. Within the week, almost all Congress leaders who mattered were in jail.

Just before the AICC met in Bombay to ratify the Quit India resolution, Subhas gave his detailed assessment of the political dynamics of the ensuing movement in an article published in *Azad Hind*. While supporting Gandhi's demand for withdrawal of the British Government from India, he warned about the possibility of compromise at some stage:

> One should not suffer from any fond illusion that the Congress resolution shuts the door on a compromise and means war to the bitter end. On the contrary, prominent followers of the Mahatma have made transparently clear statements after the resolution was passed on the 14th July, pointing out that the Congress was offering cooperation in the Allied war-effort and was appealing to the United Nations to intervene in the Indian question . . . That no compromise between the Congress and the British Government has taken place is not because the former [Gandhi wing] is opposed to it, but because the latter [left wing/Forward Bloc] is not prepared to grant the minimum that is needed for making a compromise possible . . . But from my experience of the big campaigns of 1921 and 1930–32, I must say that there is always the danger of the situation being mishandled by Gandhi at a later stage.

It was, therefore, necessary to be careful while giving full support to Gandhi. Subhas outlined the Forward Bloc's strategy, which included giving strong support to Gandhi, campaign against any compromise and against stationing Allied armies in India, and build up opinion in favour of armed struggle if passive resistance failed. According to him, India should not offer cooperation in the war as the price of independence and, at the most, should remain neutral if India's independence was recognized.[145]

With his speeches gaining wide publicity, Subhas suggested more measures that would strengthen the Indian movement not only in Europe, but also which could have significant impact within India. He asked for two more secret radio stations (National Congress Radio and Waziristan Radio), dropping leaflets over Indian towns by Axis aircraft, sending Axis agents and paratroopers to the NWFP, to send him to Egypt to convert the maximum number of Indian POWs and to open branches of FIC in other European countries.[146] Despite the support and encouragement Subhas received from the SRI, the German Government was not likely to move forward with these plans, the focus then being on transferring Subhas to

East Asia—and, as expected, they did not. The two radio stations, however, were brought into operation.[147]

Subhas spoke again on 17 and 31 August, trying to guide the movement which had largely gone underground by then, and providing points of action. In his speech on 17 August, Subhas laid out fifteen points of action, which ranged from gradually expanding the movement in phases, converting the movement into a guerrilla war targeting Britain's war production and paralysing the administration, boycott of British goods, occupying government institutions like law courts and secretariat buildings, stopping payment of taxes, organizing strikes in factories, destroying visible symbols of British imperialism and disrupting communication and transportation infrastructure.[148]

On 11 September, Subhas laid the foundation of a new Indo–German Society (*Deutsch–Indische Gessellschaft*) in Hamburg. 'Jana Gana Mana', the national anthem, was played here for the first time with full orchestra accompaniment, and the performance was published in the form of a gramophone record.[149]

Having arranged his flight to East Asia with the Italians, Subhas handed over the responsibilities of the FIC to Nambiar. This handover didn't go down well with everyone. Girija Mookerjee, for instance, recollected:

His [Nambiar's] function was never defined but as he was the oldest of us all, one took it for granted that he should have a special position in it. But in spite of his remarkable competence, he [Nambiar] fell so far short of Subhas's mental and intellectual stature that it did not seem possible for many of us to accept him as Subhas's substitute.[150]

The FIC staff, at that point of time, included twenty-five Indians and ten Germans. On 14 October, Subhas was given a farewell by the Foreign Office in the presence of Ribbentrop. The flight was, however, delayed due to increased risks, lack of secrecy among Italians, problems on the Japanese side, and finally cancelled in the second week of November. During this time, Subhas travelled to Czechoslovakia, France and Belgium, and returned to Berlin via Vienna in mid-November.[151]

An agreement was reached between Berlin and Tokyo in mid-January 1943, on the arrangements for Subhas's journey. As the Japanese refused to send a submarine to Europe, it was agreed that a German U-180 submarine would carry Subhas halfway to Madagascar, where he would move to a Japanese U-boat I-29. Subhas finally left from the Kiel harbour on 8 February 1943, accompanied by Abid Hassan.[152]

Frustrated by the lack of progress in Europe, Subhas was becoming restless to reach Southeast Asia, but the developments there were not looking bright either. The first setback was the replacement of Major Fujiwara by Colonel Hideo Iwakuro, under whom the liaison agency, then named Iwakuro Kikan, was expanded, but lacked the sensitive and sympathetic touch of Fujiwara. The growing tensions along multiple strands among Mohan Singh, the Council of Action and the IIL, Iwakuro and the Japanese Government prevented the progress of the INA and the IIL, thus resulting in several missed opportunities, and thereby demotivating the entire movement.

While Singh wanted 30,000 armed troops for the INA, he was allowed to raise only one division comprising about 17,000 armed troops. The formation of the INA was formally proclaimed on 1 September 1942. M.Z. Kiani, the Chief of General Staff, set up the INA headquarters, organized three guerrilla brigades—Gandhi, Nehru and Azad—special groups for sabotage, intelligence, propaganda, medical services, reinforcements, a base hospital and an Officers' Training School under Lt Col Shah Nawaz Khan. The Gandhi, Nehru and Azad brigades were commanded by Major I.J. Kiani, Aziz Ahmed and Prakash Chand, and the Field Force Regiment was commanded by Lt Col J.K. Bhonsle. The special services groups were formed in small sections, to be attached to the advancing Japanese columns.

Although Singh wanted the remaining POWs to be trained as reserve units, the Japanese wanted them to be used as labour units, which aggravated the atmosphere of distrust towards the Japanese. In October, a new department set up in the Iwakuro Kikan took over the control of not only all Indian POWs who refused to join the INA, but also all the surplus INA volunteers who were waiting to be absorbed into the INA in future.[153]

Negotiations between the Council of Action and the Japanese Government also broke down by the end of November, over a lack of response from the Government on the resolutions adopted at the Bangkok conference, recognition of the Council as the 'Supreme Executive of the Indian Independence Movement in East Asia', a categorical declaration on India's independence and a formal recognition of the INA. As a result, the council called off the plan for troop movement to Burma.[154]

Trouble was also brewing over Mohan Singh's decision-making on the deployment of the INA, which the Council of Action complained was done unilaterally, without consulting it. The thorny issue of deciding on the civilian or military control of the INA was precipitated by individual distrust and rivalry among the leadership, leading to a showdown between Singh and Rash Behari, which resulted in the dismissal of Singh as the commander of the INA and his arrest on 29 December. The story of the first phase of the INA came to an end within four months of its formation.

On 4 February 1943, Tojo reiterated in the House of Representatives that far from having any territorial ambitions on India, Japan would provide all assistance to see India free.

Through his dogged efforts, Rash Behari was able to reorganize the INA by mid-February 1943, which was now clearly put under the control of the IIL. Only about 8000 troops rejoined the reorganized INA with Lt Col J.K. Bhonsle as the Director of the Military Bureau, Lt Col Shah Nawaz Khan as the Chief of General Staff, Major P.K. Sahgal as Military Secretary, Major Habibur Rahman as the Commandant of the Officers' Training School and Lt Col M.Z. Kiani as the commander of the army. The IIL was also reorganized with many of its former leaders either moving away or being relegated to the background. Col. Iwakuro, in the meantime, clarified that although the Japanese Government agreed with the Bangkok conference resolutions, there would be no formal declaration since the IIL was a political organization and not a state. Moreover, the POWs who had not joined the INA would remain under Japanese control.[155]

A number of officers refused to work with Rash Behari, although they expressed their keenness to remain with the INA if Subhas took charge. The Japanese were, however, wary of a potential personality conflict if Subhas was brought over from Germany to take charge of the independence movement in East Asia. Rash Behari's health was already breaking down. 'Mr Bose was exhausted in mind and body, having fallen ill with a fit of his chronic disease—consumption', as Iwakura recalled. However, Iwakuro was surprised by Rash Behari's reaction when he took the proposal to the latter:

Mr Rash Behari Bose agreed at once and told me to welcome him from the bottom of his heart . . . I can hardly believe that there is a man like Mr Rash Behari Bose who built up a great work despite many difficulties and transferred unconditionally his work and position to another person,' he recalled later.[156]

Lt Gen. Seizo Arisue, the newly appointed chief of the Second Bureau of the IGH, also had the same experience when he met Rash Behari in Singapore in February 1943:

> Mr Rashbehari (sic) called me to a special room and while partaking Indian rice-curry, requested me to make a speedy arrangement to bring Mr Subhas Chandra Bose. Myself and my colleagues had no objection to comply with it, but we were much worried as to the seniority positions between the two Boses . . . He assured me that we should have no worry on this point, and that he would subordinate himself to Mr Chandra Bose . . . Immediately on my return to Tokyo, I hurriedly negotiated with the German authorities to bring Netaji Subhas Chandra Bose to the Far East and to receive him in Japan.[157]

A similar sentiment was shared by Subhas too, although he had never met Rash Behari in person. Syn Higuti, the attaché to ambassador Oshima in Berlin, recalled what Subhas had told him about Rash Behari:

> I don't know him. But the fact that he is fighting for the independence of India in Tokyo for so many years is very encouraging. I shall be happy if I can fight as a soldier under Mr Rash Behari Bose, as it is good for the independence of India.[158]

~

A day before the leaders of the ILL and the INA were to meet at a joint conference, from 27 to 30 April in Singapore, to decide upon a new constitution for the IIL, a Japanese I-29 submarine that had been waiting at the southern tip of Africa, south-east of Madagascar, made contact with the German submarine carrying Subhas and Abid Hasan.

The rough weather making their transfer impossible, both the submarines moved further north-east to find calmer waters, but in vain. After many hours of joint efforts, the two men were finally transferred to the Japanese submarine, in a rubber boat connected to both submarines by a rope, when the shark-infested waters became a little calmer on the morning of 28 April 1943.

Although the Japanese I-29 had sailed from Penang, it returned to Sabang Island, off the north coast of Sumatra on 6 May, completing probably the only instance in the world's history of transfer by submarine of a national leader from one continent to another. Present in Sabang to welcome Subhas was his old acquaintance, Colonel Yamamoto, the former military attaché at the Japanese embassy in Berlin. By the time Subhas arrived, Yamamoto had replaced Iwakuro as the head of the liaison agency, now called Hikari (meaning light and glory) Kikan.

Subhas left Sabang on the morning of 11 May, in a plane sent by the IGHQ, and he reached Tokyo on 16 May. He spent a night each at Penang, Saigon, Manila, Taiwan and Hamamatsu on his way.[159] Now that he had finally reached Japan, a year and a half later than what he had wanted, there was very little time to lose. The immediate task before him was to revive the flailing movement in the Far East and reorganizing the INA into a fighting force, but he knew that without a full-blooded support from the Japanese Government the efforts would not reach the last mile— the entry of the INA into the Indian territory. It was, therefore, imperative to start at the top, to convince Tojo of the Indian perspective and obtain his firm commitment.

Yamamoto succeeded in arranging meetings with Field Marshal Sugiyama, foreign minister Mamoru Shigemitsu, the navy minister and key officials of the army, navy and the foreign ministry, but Tojo was reluctant to meet. Apart from his preoccupation with the Pacific War, the unpleasant experience with the ILL and the INA in the past few months, the lack of direct relevance of the INA in terms of military operations and his own lack of a proper estimate of Subhas prevented him from granting a quick meeting. The scepticism was reinforced by a group of officers in the army who had a rather bleak view about the Indian movement. The more Yamamoto tried to keep Subhas busy by taking him around for the next ten days to visit factories, schools and hospitals, the more his impatience grew.[160]

A reluctant Tojo, persuaded by Sugiyama and Shigemitsu, who were deeply impressed by Subhas, agreed at last to meet him on 10 June. The impact was immediate. A charmed Tojo offered to have a more detailed meeting four days later. The meeting on 14 June was held with Shigemitsu and other officials in attendance. While Tojo explained the concept of the Greater East Asia Co-Prosperity Sphere, Subhas bluntly asked whether Japan was ready to give unconditional help to the Indian independence movement. An enthralled Tojo agreed instantaneously. Subhas pushed for discussing the possibility of a military thrust into India, but the topic involved operational details for which Tojo was not prepared to commit anything without proper consultation with his colleagues. By the end of the meeting, Subhas had won a friend in Tojo.[161]

The impact of the meeting Subhas became manifest on 16 June, when Tojo spoke at the 82nd extraordinary session of the Diet. With Subhas present as a special invitee, the Japanese prime minister looked towards him and declared:

> We are indignant about the fact that India is still under the relentless suppression of Britain and are in full sympathy with her desperate struggle for independence. We are determined to extend every possible assistance for the cause of India's independence.[162]

A couple of days before the second meeting with Tojo, Rash Behari came to the Imperial Hotel where Subhas was staying to meet him. When asked about the purpose of his visit to Tokyo, at a dinner party he hosted for the officers of the INA the night before he flew from Singapore, Rash Behari told them that he was going to bring back a present for them. The first meeting between the representatives of two generations of India's revolutionaries was an emotional one. As Yamamoto ushered Rash Behari into Subhas's room, they shook hands and then embraced. Choked with emotion, it took a while for both to find their voices back. There was much to talk about and they did so in Bengali. 'I have never seen him so happy,' Yamamoto recalled, talking about Rash Behari's state of mind as he took Subhas's leave for the day.[163]

Subhas made his presence in Japan public on 19 June when he held his first press conference. In a broad sweep, he issued a clear call to arms and reiterated the fivefold charges against British imperialism that had been framed by Gandhi during the civil disobedience movement: British domination meant for India moral degradation, cultural ruin, economic impoverishment and political servitude. It was now time to develop the civil disobedience movement into an armed struggle, which alone could 'bring about the freedom of India'. Subhas also said that only when 'the Indian people receive the baptism of fire on a large scale will they qualify for their freedom'.[164]

The speech broadcast two days later by radio NHK Tokyo was a more detailed and punchier one, in which Subhas gave his analysis of the present war situation and ridiculed the British army for their setbacks. The 'Anglo-

American propagandists . . . had been rending the skies with their boasting and bragging' about a few small successes in the western theatre, which made it clear 'that they badly need some success however insignificant to bolster up the sinking morale of their people'. The fate of the war, he said, 'depends on the situation in Europe, in Asia and in the high seas' and as far as India was concerned, no amount of Allied propaganda could conceal the fact that the Japanese army stood on the frontiers of the country. Taking a dig at India's commander-in-chief (elevated to the position of Viceroy by the end of the month) Field Marshall Wavell's 'feverish attempts to put up fortifications on the eastern frontier of India', he asked, 'If it took twenty years to build Singapore, and only one week to lose it, how long will it take the ever-retreating British Commander-in-Chief or his successor to withdraw from his eastern fortifications?' What face could the commander-in-chief show when, after advertising 'all over the world that the campaign for the reconquest of Burma had begun . . . his troops had to run back to India, leaving all their bag and baggage behind as soon as the powerful Japanese Army began its counter-offensive?'

Subhas followed it up with a scathing attack on the strategy adopted by the Congress leaders. Referring to the Congress policy of keeping the door for a negotiated settlement open in the hope that the British Government would respond, Subhas held that 'it is not midsummer madness that British politicians refuse to recognise India's independence, though they are in a terrible plight. It is midsummer madness that we should expect the Englishman to voluntarily give up his empire, simply because he has fallen on evil days.' In the current situation, he said, paraphrasing Ribbentrop, the 'British Empire has been losing one part of its territory to its enemies, and another part of it to its friends'. The only hope, therefore, for the British to 'make up for this colossal loss is to exploit India more ruthlessly when the war is over'.

Subhas continued, 'The worse England's position becomes during the war, the more difficult will it be to retain a firm grip over India'. Yet, 'British Imperialism will ultimately break, but it will never bend,' as that is how 'empires have always behaved in the history of mankind'. He issued a strong word of caution against efforts at a compromise as 'in attempting a compromise, British politicians will never recognise India's independence but will only try to bluff the Indian people, and through protracted negotiations will only try to sidetrack the issue of independence'.[165]

The next day, Tokyo radio broadcast his second speech in which he thanked the Germans for their help and expressed his conviction about the victory of the Axis powers.

Recording another speech for broadcast and presenting his plan to the Japanese Government for establishing a provisional government, Subhas left Tokyo on 27 June to arrive in Singapore on 2 July. Before leaving Tokyo, he received a telegram from the Burmese head of state, Ba Maw: 'Burma hereby pledges to fight on your side', he wrote.[166]

Senior officers of the INA and the IIL, Japanese embassy and military staff and leading Indian civilians stood waiting at the airport with great expectations, as Subhas's plane touched down at the airport around mid-day. Dressed in a light brown civilian suit and wearing a Gandhi cap, Subhas stepped out of the plane followed by Rash Behari, Abid Hasan, Yamamoto and another officer of the Hikari Kikan. A select group of INA men were ready with a guard of honour. Rash Behari introduced him to the leaders of the IIL and the officers of the INA. As the news of Subhas's arrival became known, 'a sea of humanity—Indians, Chinese, Malayans and Japanese—jostled and got themselves crushed' for a look at him. 'Like Caesar, it was a case of Veni, Vidi, Vici for him.'[167]

At the same time, there was no scope for rest or relaxation. As M. Sivaram, a journalist and the then spokesman of the IIL reminisced:

From the day of his arrival, Subhas Bose's residence was besieged with callers—Japanese officers of the Hikari Kikan, German officers of the submarine station in Singapore, Indian officers of the National Army, civilian officials of the League, prominent Indian residents, and hundreds of others who came only for a 'darshan' of the great leader. The spacious waiting room on the ground floor of Subhas Bose's residence was always full, even at midnight.[168]

'Friends and comrades in arms! You might ask me what I did in Tokyo? What present have I brought for you?'—Rash Behari Bose threw this question at the audience in the Cathay Hall on 4 July for a meeting of the IIL's committee of representatives who had gathered from all territories. He said, 'Well, I have brought for you this present.' The audience broke into a wild cheer as the senior Bose pointed to Subhas seated next to him. Subhas appeared to be in deep thought, while the auditorium reverberated with shouts of joy for a long time. The leadership of the IIL and the command of the INA were then formally handed over to him, with Rash Behari becoming the supreme adviser. Subhas's impassioned speech in Hindustani kept being interrupted frequently, with loud cheers after every few sentences by an audience barely able to control its excitement.[169]

It was important to allay the fears about Japanese attitude towards the movement, and Subhas addressed the issue squarely. Seeking outside help for a country's liberation might be new to India, but it was an age-old practice in the western world, which he elaborated with examples. He asked the Indians to trust him; 'I shall be loyal to India alone.' The goal was set clearly: there would be hunger, thirst, privation and forced marches on the road to Delhi. It was not known how many would live to see India free. What was more important was that India should be free and the march to freedom would culminate with the victory parade of the Azad Hind Fauj in Delhi's Red Fort. He was going to organize a provisional government to prepare the Indian people and lead the Indian revolution to its conclusion.[170]

The next day Subhas, dressed in a khaki tunic, breeches, knee-high boots and wearing a khaki cap, reviewed the INA, which was renamed the Azad Hind Fauj by him, at the municipal square by the sea. The reorganized army paraded under the command of Lt Col M.Z. Kiani in its full strength of over 15,000 officers and men. He formally announced to the world that India now had its national army. It was the proudest day of his life.

> Throughout my public career, I have always felt that though India is otherwise ripe for independence in every way, she has lacked one thing, namely, an army of liberation. George Washington of America could fight and win freedom, because he had his army. Garibaldi could liberate Italy, because he had his armed volunteers behind him.

The Fauj had a twofold task in front of them, as Subhas explained: 'With the force of arms and at the cost of your blood, you will have to win liberty', and when India becomes free, 'you will have to organise the permanent army of Free India whose task it will be to preserve our liberty for all time'. India's national defence should be built up on such an unshakable foundation that never again in its history would it lose its freedom. His promise to the soldiers was 'I shall be with you in darkness and in sunshine, in sorrow and in joy, in suffering and in victory.'

Subhas gave the Azad Hind Fauj their battle cry, 'Chalo Delhi! To Delhi!'[171]

The seriousness of intent among Japan's top brass was evident when Tojo, who had flown from Manila, took the salute of the Fauj the following day. Standing beside Subhas, Tojo reiterated that Japan had no territorial, military or economic ambitions in India, and that his government would provide all possible help to attain India's liberation from the British rule.[172] He also conveyed the Japanese Government's support to Subhas's plan for establishing the provisional government, and recognized the Fauj's status of an allied army, something that had been held back from the first INA.[173]

Giving a call for total mobilization on 9 July, Subhas outlined the way he envisaged the impact of the Azad Hind Fauj:

> Indians in East Asia are going to organise a fighting force which will be powerful enough to attack the British Army in India. When we do so, a revolution will break out, not only among the civil population at home, but also between the Indian Army . . . Let the slogan of the three million Indians in East Asia be—'Total Mobilisation for a Total War.' Out of this total mobilisation, I expect at least three hundred thousand soldiers and . . . thirty million dollars.

He also gave a call for 'a unit of brave Indian women to form a "Death-defying Regiment" who will wield the sword, which the brave Rani of Jhansi wielded in India's First War of Independence in 1857'.[174] Subhas then elaborated on his vision when he addressed the women's section of the IIL on 12 July. About 600 women from the audience promptly volunteered to join the regiment.[175]

The first step towards the formation of the provisional government was to reorganize and expand the IIL, which Subhas completed in less than two weeks after his arrival in Singapore. This was a difficult task, especially with the personality clashes and differences in opinion among the leaders of the Indian communities that slowed down the movement before Subhas's arrival.

In the new scheme of things announced on 13 July, the IIL was organized into twelve departments, of which eight were new. The new ones were the departments of recruitment (responsible for recruitment in the Azad Hind Fauj), training (to train all recruits until they were taken over by the army), supplies, health and social welfare, overseas, women, reconstruction (to prepare plans for future administration of India and to train people for that purpose), and education and culture. The publicity department under S.A. Ayer was renamed as the department for publicity, press and propaganda. Apart from these, there were the military bureau and the general secretary's department, which was to liaise with the Hikari Kikan and coordinate the activities of the different departments. Lt Col A.C. Chatterji was appointed the first secretary general of the league's headquarters.[176]

The reorganization of the IIL had a visible impact. 'The way he [Chatterji] went about the business gave everybody the impression that the League Headquarters had already settled down as a vast official establishment, just awaiting transfer to New Delhi', recalled Sivaram. For the first time, 'Indians in East Asia began thinking of the League as a regular Government of India in the making'.[177]

While the organizational consolidation was going on, Abid Hasan pitched for popularizing the salutation for Subhas that had gained currency at the Free India Centre in Germany. Fearing some resistance on account of the term's resonance with 'Fuehrer', Sivaram introduced the prefix 'Netaji' in a 'quiet and subtle way' in the news and comments in the League's newspapers which were published in English, Hindustani, Tamil and Malayalam.

> Very soon, 'Netaji' became extremely popular among Indians throughout
> East Asia, and equally well understood by the Chinese, Japanese, Thais,
> Burmese and other races in the region.[178]

Subhas himself had already introduced and recommended the use of 'Jai Hind' at a luncheon reception by the Indian community held at the Singapore Cricket Club in early July.[179]

On 29 July, Subhas arrived at Rangoon to attend the inauguration ceremony of the independent Burmese Government to be held on 1 August, as the special guest of Ba Maw, whom he had met in Singapore in the first week of July. In Rangoon, Subhas reviewed a parade of the Azad Hind Fauj troops, addressed large rallies and visited the tomb of the last Mughal emperor, Bahadur Shah Zafar. From Rangoon, he went to Bangkok, where he was received by the Thai prime minister. Subhas returned to Singapore on 14 September to address a massive public meeting at Farrer Park, commemorating the first anniversary of the Quit India movement, which was on the next day.[180]

Receiving the news of the raging famine in Bengal that resulted in thousands of deaths, Subhas made an unconditional offer of 1,00,000 tons of rice, which he said was stored at a harbour close to India at that time. The moment the British Government accepted his offer, he would reveal the name of the harbour and arrange for safe conduct of ships to collect the rice. More rice would be sent in a similar fashion subsequently.[181] The British were, however, in no mood to oblige.

If the organizational challenges were being met literally on a war footing, the negotiations with the Japanese army regarding the operation of the Fauj were not going along expected lines despite a strong backing from Tojo and his colleagues in the Cabinet. Soon after his arrival in Singapore, Subhas met Field Marshal Count Hisaichi Terauchi, the commander-in-chief of the Southern Expeditionary Forces, to discuss the role to be played by the Azad Hind Fauj. Having a very poor opinion of the Fauj's soldiers, who he believed would find the temptation to cross over to the British side difficult to resist, Terauchi was reluctant to have the Fauj in the battlefield along with the Japanese forces, except for roles limited to gathering information, infiltration and propaganda among the British forces. For him, the Fauj was composed of soldiers who were once mercenaries and had been demoralized by the defeat inflicted upon them by the Japanese. He, therefore, argued for the Japanese forces doing all the fighting and liberating India. All he wanted was the personal cooperation of Subhas to ensure the goodwill and sympathy of the Indians.

Terauchi's terms were naturally humiliating for Subhas and he would not accept them under any circumstances. 'Any liberation of India secured through Japanese sacrifices is to me worse than slavery', he bluntly told Terauchi. For the soldiers of the Azad Hind Fauj to stay behind the Japanese Army, in what essentially was a battle for India's independence, was against national honour. Quite contrary to what Terauchi thought, the purpose of Japanese help should have been mainly to supplement the Fauj's effort. The maximum sacrifices should come from Indians themselves. Terauchi had to give in to Subhas's passionate and forceful arguments. He proposed that one regiment of the Fauj would be deployed in the ensuing Imphal campaign as a test case, and if their performance could meet the Japanese standard, the rest of the Fauj would be deployed too.[182]

Back from meeting Terauchi, Subhas convened a meeting of the top brass of the Azad Hind Fauj. Among those present were J.K. Bhonsle, M.Z. Kiani, Aziz Ahmed, Shah Nawaz Khan, I.J. Kiani, Gulzara Singh,

Habibur Rahman and P.K. Sahgal. After much consultation, it was decided that a new regiment, the No. 1 Guerrilla Regiment, would be raised by selecting the best soldiers from the three existing regiments, with Shah Nawaz Khan as its commander, Colonel Thakur Singh as the second-in-command and Colonel Mahboob Ahmad as the regimental adjutant. The three battalions that constituted the regiment were commanded by Major P.S. Raturi, Major Ran Singh and Major Padam Singh. The regiment was raised at Taiping in September and the soldiers themselves named it Subhas Brigade. Repeated instructions from Subhas not to name the regiment after him fell on deaf ears.[183]

'In the interest of the Indian Independence Movement and of the Azad Hind Fauj, I have taken over the direct command of our army from this day', read the Special Order of the Day issued on 25 August 1943. 'I regard myself as the servant of 38 crores of my countrymen', the new Supreme Commander or the Sipah-Salar of the Fauj declared in the Order. He was determined to discharge his duties 'in such a manner that the interests of these 38 crores may be safe in my hands and that every single Indian will have reason to put complete trust in me'.[184]

The post of the Supreme Commander, however, remained a civil one and Subhas wore his military uniform without any insignia of rank.[185]

Subhas reorganized the Azad Hind Fauj completely. Lt Col J.K. Bhonsle was appointed the Chief of Staff. The Supreme Headquarters of the Fauj consisted of the Supreme Commander, the Chief of Staff and heads of the different branches. Pocket allowances and rations were increased for the troops.[186]

With Subhas taking over command of the Fauj and restructuring it, the focus turned to the expansion of the army. 2000 more POWs had joined the army after Subhas's arrival, but its strength was nowhere close to what Subhas had envisaged. The response from civilians, however, was overwhelming. The capacity of the volunteer training camps, a number of which were opened in Singapore and in different parts of Malaya, had to be expanded as the offers for enlistment exceeded the existing capacity. Senior officers of the army were sent to Bangkok, Hong Kong and Shanghai to facilitate civilian recruitment and training. Some of the civilian training centres in Burma, which had been under Japanese control, were gradually brought under the League after Subhas's arrival. A short training course of ten weeks was put in place to meet the demand for commissioned and non-commissioned officers (NCO) in the expanding army. The Azad School in Singapore, which was set up to train instructors, started training NCOs instead.[187]

The volunteer recruits were given not only physical and military training to develop them into good soldiers, but also spiritual training through lectures and plays to inculcate the culture and heritage of India in them. This was supplemented by literacy campaigns carried out in Hindustani, in view of the high rate of illiteracy and also to ease the problems of communication between Indians belonging to different linguistic groups. Simple Hindustani was adopted as the common language, with suitably modified Roman alphabet as the script. Printing of two newspapers for the troops—*Voice of India* in English and the Hindustani *Awaz-i-Hind* printed in Roman script—was initiated.[188]

Although the point of disagreement with Terauchi had been resolved, a major difference persisted with the Hikari Kikan over the strength of the army. Subhas aimed to raise an army of 30,00,000 through his plan of total mobilization, but his immediate goal was to expand the army to three divisions made up of 30,000 regulars and another unit of 20,000 mainly from civilian volunteers. To implement this plan, he insisted that the Hikari Kikan should bring back and hand over the Indian POWs, whom they had moved out of Singapore in 1942 to use as labour force, to him. The Hikari Kikan refused to give in, insisting that they had the right of control over the POWs who had not joined the INA. Moreover, since they could provide arms for only 30,000 troops, the Kikan wanted to restrict the total strength of the Fauj to that number, including civilian recruits.[189]

While Subhas kept up with a tight schedule of travel and public meetings, he was acutely aware of making an impact on the local Indian population, to rouse their spirit. If they were to be mobilized, they had to be imbued with an unprecedented level of enthusiasm, to be made to feel special as Indians. The way he carried himself, 'his triumphant tours', recalled Sivaram, 'swelled the average Indian heart with pride'. When travelling, he would be escorted by two Japanese military trucks with mounted machine guns, armed motorcycle corps and a fleet of cars carrying members of his personal staff, all flying the Indian tricolour. 'He travelled by the fastest Japanese bomber when he went to Thailand and Burma and insisted on taking with him at least half a dozen of people, including an army staff officer, a couple of ADCs, a personal physician, a publicity man, a valet and an orderly', in addition to the 'usual retinue of interpreters and secretarial staff'.

> In political showmanship and the tactics of mass appeal, Subhas
> Chandra Bose was a regal genius and an accomplished expert. Driving
> up to address mammoth meetings, standing upright in a huge open car,
> smilingly acknowledging the cheers of jubilant crowds lined up along the
> streets—Subhas was leadership personified.[190]

The freshly appointed Supreme Allied Commander of the Southeast
Asia Command, Louis Mountbatten, received a blistering welcome
from Subhas. Speaking at Kuala Lumpur on 5 September, he called
Mountbatten an 'amphibious monster' ridiculing his alleged mastery in
land and sea operations. Pointing to his appointment as the Supreme
Allied Commander following his role in the disaster of the Dieppe raid,
Subhas asked sarcastically, 'I challenge you to show me one country in the
world today where promotions are made not for success, not for victories,
but for defeats'. Then he issued a direct challenge: 'I can assure Lord Louis
Mountbatten that a much bigger and greater Dieppe is waiting for him in
East Asia.'[191]

The work towards the formation of the provisional government was
going on, but the lower ranks of the Japanese army in Singapore and a
group of officers in the Hikari Kikan were not favourable towards the plan,
fearing a loss of authority over the Indians. On 9 October, however, the
IGHQ and the Japanese Government took the formal decision to recognize
the provisional government if Subhas was able to form it.[192]

The Provisional Government of Free India was set up with its seat in
Singapore, within two weeks of this decision, at a conference of the IIL
attended by delegates from all parts of East Asia and thousands of Indians
from all over Malaya. The beginning was modest. As the Head of State,
prime minister, and minister of war and foreign affairs, Subhas appointed
Anand Mohan Sahay as secretary with ministerial rank and three ministers
in his Cabinet: Capt. Lakshmi in charge of women's organizations, S.A.
Ayer in charge of publicity and propaganda and Lt Col A.C. Chatterji in
charge of finance. In addition, there were eight representatives of the armed
forces (Lt Col Aziz Ahmed, Lt Col N.S. Bhagat, Lt Col J.K. Bhonsle, Lt
Col Gulzara Singh, Lt Col M.Z. Kiani, Lt Col A.D. Loganadan, Lt Col
Ehsan Qadir and Lt Col Shah Nawaz Khan) and eight civilian advisers
(Karim Gani, Debnath Das, D.M. Khan, A. Yellappa, J. Thivy, Sardar
Ishar Singh, and A.N. Sarkar as legal adviser) representing the Indian
community in East Asia. Rash Behari remained the supreme adviser.

Subhas was visibly moved while taking the oath of allegiance. After reading a few words, it seemed that he would break down. 'He was so moved that at one stage minutes passed but his voice could not triumph over the emotion which struggled in his throat', reminisced Shah Nawaz Khan, one of the military advisers.

> Each one of us had been mentally repeating each word of oath. We were all leaning forward, physically trying to reach the granite figure of Netaji. The whole audience was merged with him. Pin-drop silence. With lips tightly closed and eyes glued, body tense, we waited for him to overcome the struggle over emotion.[193]

Subhas stopped to wipe his tears with a handkerchief, and then read the oath:

> In the name of God, I take this sacred oath that to liberate India and the thirty eight crores of my countrymen I, Subhas Chandra Bose, will continue this sacred war of freedom till the last breath of my life.
>
> I shall remain always a servant of India and to look after the welfare of thirty eight crores of my Indian brothers and sisters shall be for me my highest duty.
>
> Even after winning freedom, I will always be prepared to shed even the last drop of my blood for the preservation of India's freedom.

The members of the Government thereafter took their oath:

> In the name of God, I take this holy oath that to liberate India and the thirty eight crores of my countrymen, I ____ will be absolutely faithful to my Leader Subhas Chandra Bose and shall be always prepared to sacrifice my life and all I have for fulfilling this pledge.

The provisional government was planning not only towards an armed struggle, but was keenly studying the problem of post-war reconstruction too, Subhas explained in his speech. 'We can visualise the conditions that we shall find at home when the Anglo-Americans and their allies are expelled from our country', and, therefore, people were being 'trained for work of rapid reconstruction within India simultaneously with the progress of military operations'.[194]

Opening the training camp for the Rani of Jhansi Regiment at Singapore the next day, where 156 volunteers were going to be trained to start with, Subhas hoped that very soon the numbers would reach to 1000 volunteers. Apart from the central camp at Singapore, he announced, more camps in Thailand and Burma would start training women volunteers.[195]

The provisional government received recognition from the Japanese Government on 23 October:

> In connection with the formation of the Provisional Government of Free India headed by Mr. Subhas Chandra Bose, the Japanese Government, in the belief that this is a big step forward towards the fulfilment of Indian independence, about which the Indian people have long dreamed, hereby recognises the Provisional Government of Free India and pledges every possible assistance and cooperation to help its ultimate objective.[196]

Declarations of recognition followed from the governments of Burma, Germany, Philippines, Thailand, Italy, Croatia, Nanking and Manchuria.[197] A message of personal congratulations arrived from Eamon de Valera.

Five minutes past midnight, in the early morning of 24 October, the provisional government declared war on Britain and the United States, and immediately notified the Japanese Government of its decision. Responding to the declaration, the Japanese Southern Army command under Field Marshal Terauchi issued a statement of support, reiterating that Japan had no territorial or economic ambition in India.[198] The Japanese were aware of the scepticism among Indians in East Asia, and were leaving no opportunity to remind them time and again about their pledge of unconditional support given by Tojo to Subhas.

Subhas announced the decision to go to war with Britain and the United States at a massive rally attended by over 50,000 people in Singapore. Asking all those gathered to listen to him to ratify the decision, Subhas told them, 'If you too are ready from this moment onward to sacrifice everything, all you have in this world and your lives to translate this declaration into action, if you mean to lay down your lives in the coming fight for India's freedom, then stand up and raise your hands.'[199]

As soon as Subhas read the declaration, 'shouts and slogans rent the skies and volley after volley of frenzied cheering greeted the news' and the audience was uncontrollable, breaking the cordon at several places in their effort to reach the platform, and 'It seemed as if the whole congregation had become hypnotised and was gradually being pulled towards him'. When Subhas asked them to stand and raise their hands, 'a forest of hands went up', while 'the Fauj soldiers lifted their rifles and placed them on their shoulders, giving their consent by a forest of bayonets'.[200]

The promise that followed the declaration of war was certain to lift the spirit of the Indians present to an astronomical height. Subhas had already made this promise on 15 August, but its repetition on this occasion carried a different weight. He declared that he would set his foot 'on the holy soil of India before the end of the year'.[201]

Both Sivaram and S.A. Ayer recounted the wild cheer that emanated from the Indians in the audience as well as the consternation the promise caused among the Japanese. The Japanese officers attached to Subhas's staff 'seemed to have gone mad', running around looking for Japanese newspaper correspondents to suppress his statement. The Japanese censors in the broadcasting station took out their ire on Sivaram and Ayer, telling them that the speech could not be broadcast unless the statement promising to stand on Indian soil before the end of the year was deleted. To get around the problem, the two rang up Subhas and asked whether he could broadcast the speech himself. Subhas readily agreed, increasing the hassles of the Japanese censors, who had no idea how to stop Subhas from repeating the statement. After running between Hikari Kikan, the Southern Command headquarters and other authorities, they decided that Subhas was free to speak on radio as he wished, but Japanese broadcasts would not make any reference to that particular statement.[202]

As it later turned out, Subhas had made the promise out of a pure impulse, and without any assurance from the Japanese authorities. He made sure through his negotiation skills that the promise was kept.

The opportunity to negotiate came soon enough when he travelled to Tokyo to attend the Greater East Asia Conference that opened on 5 November. Subhas arrived at the Haneda airport in Tokyo on 31 October, accompanied by A.C. Chatterji, J.K. Bhonsle, S.A. Ayer, Anand Mohan Sahay, D.I. Raju and Abid Hassan. On 2 November, the foreign minister, Mamoru Shigemitsu, hosted a dinner reception at his residence for Subhas. The conference brought together the governments supported by the Japanese in East and Southeast Asia. While Wang Ching-wei and Chou Fu-hai of the Nanking Government, Premier Chang Ching-hui of Manchukuo, President José Laurel of the Philippine Republic, prime minister Ba Maw of Burma and Prince Wan Waithayakon (representing

Premier Pibulsonggram) of Thailand attended as participating delegates in the conference, Subhas took the seat of an observer. Neither was India a part of the Greater East Asia Co-Prosperity Sphere planned by the Japanese, nor was Subhas ready to commit the provisional government or the people of India to any decision of the conference.[203]

A resolution moved by Ba Maw that 'no emancipation of Asia was possible without liberation of India' and therefore all the participating governments should 'extend full sympathy and support to the Indian struggle for freedom' was adopted unanimously. Attending the conference on the second day, Subhas expressed his gratitude for the pledge of support extended to the Indian movement. Highlighting the difference of the conference with the many international conferences and congresses held during the past hundred years, he remarked, 'this is not a conference for dividing the spoils among the conquerors', or 'for hatching a conspiracy to victimise a weak power'. He added that 'This is an assembly of liberated nations, an assembly that is out to create a new order in this part of the world, on the basis of the sacred principles of justice, national sovereignty, reciprocity in international relations and mutual aid and assistance.'[204]

As soon as he reached Tokyo, Subhas set out to clear the hurdles he was facing in his dealings with the Hikari Kikan and the Japanese army in Southeast Asia. There were several issues, such as the strength of the Azad Hind Fauj, financial help from the Japanese Government, planning the military campaign in India and transfer of Indian territory already under Japanese occupation to the provisional government.

Meeting Subhas on 1 November, Tojo agreed to hand over the administration of evacuee Indian property in Burma to the provisional government. But his response was tentative when Subhas placed the request to transfer the Andaman and Nicobar Islands, which had been occupied by the Japanese in March 1942, to the provisional government. The transfer of the islands would give the provisional government a foothold over Indian territory and enhance its prestige. Moreover, it had a symbolic significance of being the place where the most dangerous among India's revolutionaries were imprisoned under the most inhuman conditions. No less important were the facts that the transfer would presage the liberation of the whole of India and establish Japan's sincerity. At a later meeting, Subhas told the Chief of the Military Affairs section of the Imperial Navy that he would like to appoint a governor to the islands and visit them personally.

There were, however, strong arguments in favour of Japan's reluctance. Objections from the Japanese navy were expected as the islands were strategically critical for Japan during the Pacific War. Moreover, without a navy, the provisional government did not have the capability to defend the islands.

Despite these limitations, the Japanese Government and the IGHQ accepted Subhas's wishes, but with restrictions so that their own war interests were not compromised. Accordingly, Tojo made a formal declaration immediately after Subhas's speech at the Greater East Asia Conference on 6 November: 'I would like to announce here and now that Japan is ready to transfer the Andaman and Nicobar Islands to the Provisional Government of Free India in the near future.'[205]

At the Greater East Asia National Rally the next day, at Tokyo's Hibiya Park, Subhas said, 'Part by part, Indian territory will be liberated, but it is always the first piece of territory that has the most significance.' He continued by saying that 'We have renamed the Andamans as "Shaheed", in memory of the martyrs, and the Nicobars as "Swaraj".' The Japanese prime minister's announcement showed the sincerity of Japan in honouring its commitments.

A liaison conference between the IGHQ and the Japanese Government on 10 November decided that while the date of actual transfer of the islands to the provisional government would be decided separately at a future date, its staff would be allowed to stay in the islands and participate in its administration as long as that did not come in the way of Japan's war operations. The scope of the provisional government's participation in the administration of the islands would also be increased gradually until they were handed over to them. The Imperial Navy communicated to Subhas that it would organize his visit to the islands and that the appointment of a governor would have to wait until the complete transfer. Until then, the provisional government could appoint a Chief Commissioner to oversee the administration.

The Japanese Government and the IGHQ, however, agreed that even at this stage, Subhas could tell the world that the transfer had already taken place.

In further meetings with Tojo and Sugiyama, Subhas succeeded in clearing some of the obstacles that were placed before him by the liaison agency and the Japanese army in the south-east. It was agreed that in the Imphal campaign, the Azad Hind Fauj would have the status of an allied army under Japanese operational command. Its actual role would be decided by the commander-in-chief of the Burma Area Army. Subhas extracted an agreement from the Japanese for raising the second division and planning for the third division of the Fauj, and also to train cadets for the Fauj in Japan. As far as financing the Fauj was concerned, while the expenditure related to the ex-POWs would be borne by the Japanese, the civilian recruits would have to be paid for by the provisional government.[206]

On the completion of the Tokyo trip, Subhas flew to Nanking on 17 November. The Nanking Government held a national rally in his honour, and invited him to inspect the Military Academy. Ernst Woermann, his key point of contact at the Germany foreign ministry, had recently been posted as the German Ambassador to China. Apart from attending a number of receptions and parties thrown in his honour, Subhas broadcast two speeches over radio, aimed at the Chunking Government of Chiang Kai-shek.[207]

According to Japanese sources, Subhas made the broadcasts at his own initiative, without being asked either by the Japanese or by Weng. It was probably an attempt to wean Chiang away from the Allied camp and to bring together the two nationalist governments, in the context of recent steps taken by the Japanese Government providing greater administrative control to the Wang regime: a goal that he must have known to be near impossible.

When India's army of liberation reached India's frontier, they would have to fight the British army and probably the Chinese troops too. 'I do not understand why Chinese should fight for the British in India', to help a foreign power to continue its domination in that country, he asked. He reminded the Chunking Government that out of India's sympathy towards Chinese people, the Congress had sent a medical mission when he was the party's president. Subhas wanted to impress upon his listeners that the situation in East Asia had changed completely and Japan had adopted a new policy, which was demonstrated by the declaration of independence of Burma and the Philippines, and the establishment of the Provisional Government of Free India. As far as China was concerned, Japan had declared its intention of withdrawing troops from China once peace was restored. China's only problem then was achieving unity, and there was no reason why they should wait till the end of the war. It was possible by means of an honourable peace between China and Japan to start the national reconstruction and economic recovery of China.[208]

Subhas arrived at Shanghai on 21 November from Nanking, and travelled to Manila the next day, where he met President Laurel and attended a rally of local Indians. His whirlwind tours continued to recruit more volunteers, raise funds and garner support for the movement. After returning briefly to Singapore, meeting Terauchi in his headquarters at Saigon on the way, he flew to Djakarta on 10 December and then to Surabaya, Borneo and Sumatra.[209]

Accompanied by D.S. Raju, Anand Mohan Sahay, Ehsan Qadir, Shamsher Singh and a couple of Japanese army officers, Subhas arrived in the Andaman Islands on 29 December. Received by Rear Admiral S. Ishikawa, the Japanese commander in charge of the islands, Subhas was taken from the airport to Ross Island, where he was put up in the official residence of the former British governor. At a conference in the evening to discuss the gradual transfer of the civil administration of the islands, the Japanese promised to transfer as many departments as possible, starting with the education department. The transfer of the police department remained a point of contention, as the Japanese were not ready to hand it over to the provisional government, insisting that maintaining law and order in the islands must remain with the Japanese army for the present.

On the morning of 30 December, Subhas attended a huge rally at the Gymkhana Maidan in Port Blair, hoisting the national tricolour to the accompaniment of the national anthem. A guard of honour was presented by the IIL volunteers, Japanese armed forces and senior students. 'These islands in the near future will become Indian territory', he told the audience. Thanking Japan for its support, he pointed out that 'Entry into Delhi at the cost of our blood or to fight our way to death in the present struggle for independence are the only two ways to repay Nippon's sincerity and friendship towards us'. Thereafter, he visited the Cellular Jail.

On the next day, Subhas heard a detailed report on the administrative activities in the islands at a meeting in the headquarters of the Japanese military administration, and discussed the working arrangements for the Chief Commissioner and other provisional government staff that he would send to the islands shortly.[210]

As the war preparations reached the final stages, Subhas constantly worked to lift the spirits of the soldiers and reinforce the dream that he had presented to them. In a statement, he said:

They say in Europe—'All roads lead to Rome.' Here in East Asia all the above-mentioned roads lead to India's metropolis—and to the ancient

Red Fortress that lies in its bosom. Delhi is our destination and to Delhi we shall travel by many roads . . . But it will be a long and weary march from here to the Viceroy's house and to the Red Fortress in India's capital. So let us lose no time. Let us gird up our loins and commence the march as soon as we can. The roads to Delhi are the roads to freedom.[211]

While inspiring the troops, Subhas was not painting a rosy picture. Rather, his warning was for a grim situation. On 26 January, he reminded them:

The Indian campaign will not be a 'Blitzkrieg' like the Malayan campaign. The enemy has had time to utilise the lessons of his disastrous defeats in East Asia. He has also had time to bring reinforcements to India from remotest parts of the world. Moreover, on the soil of India, Britain will fight her last battle and before she goes down, she will certainly fight desperately. . . . Consequently, we must launch the last struggle after we are fully prepared for a long and bitter fight.[212]

The Subhas Regiment of the 1st Division, although under-equipped due to its deployment at a short notice, left Taiping in November 1943, arriving in Rangoon in early 1944, with arrangements being made for the onward despatch of the remainder of supplies to Burma. The enthusiasm among the soldiers had reached a fever pitch, so that those who were sick or were found medically unfit threw themselves on the railway tracks to stop the train from carrying the troops, refusing to be left behind.[213] Considering Burma as the springboard for the offensive towards India, Subhas moved the headquarters of the Supreme Command of the Azad Hind Fauj to Burma on 25 January 1944. He himself had arrived in Rangoon on 7 January, and brought forward the headquarters of the provisional government too.[214]

The Hikari Kikan did the same, but with a change in its leadership. Colonel Yamamoto, promoted to Major General, was replaced by Lt Gen Isoda Saburo on the same day. During his last trip to Tokyo, Subhas had made known his displeasure about Yamamoto to the Japanese Government. The stubbornness with which the chief of the liaison agency had refused to yield on the question of expansion of the Azad Hind Fauj became a major obstacle to Subhas's plans. He, therefore, got consent directly from the Government, proving the point about his direct access to the decision-makers in Tokyo. Replacing Yamamoto with a higher ranking officer was also a step to placate Subhas.[215] Isoda arrived in Rangoon from China, where he was commanding the 22nd Division of the Japanese army, on 10 February, and met Subhas after his arrival.[216]

Two days after arriving in Rangoon, Subhas announced that he had appointed Lt Col A.G. Loganadan as the Chief Commissioner of the Andaman and Nicobar Islands. Loganadan, who was in Bangkok at that time first travelled to Singapore to select the staff for the provisional government's administration in the Andamans. Accompanied by Major Mansoor Ali Alvi, Lt Mohammad Iqbal, Lt Suba Singh and civilian stenotypist Srinivasan, he arrived at Port Blair on 18 February, taking charge of the administration over a month later on 21 March.[217]

The campaign was about to begin, but several inadequacies beleaguered the troops. The regiment had only five lorries to transport rations, ammunitions, battle casualties and that too without a proper workshop or spare parts. The lack of even pack animals meant that men had to carry reserve ammunitions, machine guns and medicines. Although it was known that winter in the areas where the regiment was going into action was severe, the men were provided with only one thin cotton blanket and one warm shirt. Mosquito nets too were missing despite the areas being infamous for malaria. In the absence of emergency rations, Subhas himself took keen interest in having *shakarpara* biscuits prepared for all soldiers.[218]

The arms provided to the Fauj too were deficient. When the forces reached Burma, they had neither artillery nor mortars of their own. Their machine guns were of medium size and lacked spare parts. The guerrilla regiments had no wireless equipment or telephones. Many men had to march barefooted because of a shortage of boots.[219]

Before the campaign started, Subhas, accompanied by Shah Nawaz Khan, met Lt Gen. Masakazu Kawabe, the Commander-in-Chief of the Burma Area Army that had been formed in March 1943 to defend Burma against the British forces, to discuss the modalities of cooperation between the Azad Hind Fauj and the Japanese army. Subhas disagreed with Kawabe—to split the Subhas Regiment into small groups which would be attached to the larger Japanese formations—and instead insisted that it should not be split into formations smaller than a battalion. Moreover, the command of all the Fauj units had to remain entirely with Indian officers and the Fauj had to be allotted an independent sector in the front. Subhas insisted that all liberated Indian territory was to be handed over to the Fauj for administration, for which purpose A.C. Chatterji had been appointed the governor-designate of liberated territories. All captured dumps of arms, ammunitions and machinery were also to be handed over to the provisional government. Kawabe agreed with the points raised by Subhas.

Since the Fauj had the status of an allied army, it was also agreed that junior officers of either army would salute the senior officer of the other. Turning down Kawabe's suggestion that in the case of two officers of equal rank, the Indian officer should salute the Japanese officer first, Subhas pointed out that it would mean accepting an inferior position as an army and a nation. Kawabe agreed to Subhas's suggestion that both officers should salute at the same time. However, when Subhas refused the suggestion that the Fauj was to be governed by Japanese military law, which meant that the Japanese military police could arrest any Fauj soldier without referring the case to Subhas, and insisted that they would be governed by its own Army Act, Kawabe referred the matter to Tokyo. On this point too, Subhas had his way as the Japanese Government accepted his argument.

Finally, Subhas told Kawabe that he had ordered his soldiers to shoot any Indian or Japanese who was found looting or raping on Indian soil.[220]

When Lt Gen Tadashi Katakura, Chief of the General Staff to Kawabe, informed Subhas that the Japanese army had decided to launch an air attack on Calcutta, he strongly objected to the plan. Apart from causing panic and suffering, the attack would lead to a loss of confidence in him. The Japanese dropped the plan.[221]

Shah Nawaz received his final orders for proceeding to the front from Kawabe on 27 January 1944. The Japanese commander-in-chief made it clear to him that the 3000-strong Subhas Regiment, that had been given independent sectors to operate, would be keenly watched and judged for its fighting qualities. According to the plan presented by Kawabe, the No. 1 Battalion of the regiment under Major P.S. Raturi was to proceed to the Kaladan valley, where the British had deployed their West African Division. No. 2 Battalion, under Major Ran Singh, and No. 3 Battalion, under Major Padam Singh, was to proceed to the Chin Hill area of Haka and Falam. These two battalions would be under the command of Shah Nawaz. Some Japanese officers and NCOs were attached to each battalion to act as liaison officers between the Fauj and the Japanese headquarters.[222]

Subhas bade farewell to the 1st Guerrilla Regiment on 3 February through a rousing speech. 'It was one of the most inspired and moving speeches that he has ever delivered in East Asia,' recalled Shah Nawaz. The advance parties of the three battalions moved out by train the next day: that of the No. 1 Battalion to Prome, and No. 2 and No. 3 Battalions to Mandalay.[223]

A unit of the Bahadur group, under Major L.S. Misra, about 200 strong, attached to the 55 Division of the Japanese army, had already been deployed in the Arakan campaign. The 55 Division launched its attack on 4 February, cutting off the 7 British–Indian Division from the 5 Division, and disconnecting the line of communication of the 15 Corps of the British–Indian army. The reconnaissance and subversive activities of the Bahadur and the Intelligence groups had a significant role in this quick success.[224] The British forces, however, neither surrendered nor retreated and held their ground, as the Allied air superiority made it possible to provide them with supplies and reinforcements, and later airlifted them to the Imphal theatre.[225]

On 10 February, Shah Nawaz, commanding the No. 2 and No. 3 Battalions of the Subhas Regiment, received orders from Lt Gen Renya Mutaguchi, the commanding officer of the Japanese 15th Army, to prevent the British forces from advancing to Kalewa and thereby threatening the main supply lines of the Japanese forces, and to carry out offensive operations on the Haka Falam front. Shah Nawaz established his regimental base at Myitha Haka on 24 February 1944, and took over the charge of defence of Falam on the next day and of Haka on 3 April. In March, the 3rd Battalion was called upon from Kalewa to take part in action against Tiddim. In May, a part of the 2nd Battalion raided the British patrol-base at Klang, about 20 miles west of Haka.

The No. 1 Battalion of the Subhas Regiment established its base at Kyauktaw in mid-March. The battalion pushed northward by taking Kaladan, Paletwa, Daletme and eventually Mowdok, a place on the Indian side of the Indo–Burma border. A part of the battalion continued to be at Mowdok up to September 1944.

The Japanese 15th Army crossed the Chindwin River and started moving towards India in the middle of March, with three divisions (the 33rd Division, the 15th Division and the 31st Division) carrying out the main Japanese operation against Imphal and Kohima. According to the Japanese plan, the 33rd Japanese Division was to cut off the British 17th Division and advance up to Imphal. The Japanese Division succeeded in cutting off large parts of the British Division, but was not able to destroy it, and was confronted by another British Division as it proceeded towards Imphal, thus being held up at Bishenpur (in Manipur), south of Imphal.[226]

Subhas persuaded Kawabe to allow the 2nd and 3rd Regiments of the Azad Hind Fauj's 1st Division to join the 15th Army. The regiments led by the Divisional Commander, M.Z. Kiani, moved out of Rangoon in mid-March to Shweygin and Kalewa, the base camps of the Japanese army on both the banks of the Chindwin River. From the base camps, the two regiments moved up to Tamu, near the Indo–Burma border. The 2nd Regiment, under the command of Lt Col I.J. Kiani, joined the Yamamoto unit which planned to capture the Palel airfield on 1 May. Taking the Palel airfield would not only ease the approach to Imphal but also make more supplies available. A task force of the regiment mounted an attack on Palel from the south, while the Yamamoto unit attacked it from the west. The task force and the remaining regiment, however, suffered serious setbacks, and the operation came to a halt with the onset of the monsoon in mid-May. The 3rd Regiment, under Lt Col Gulzara Singh, was delayed due to the lack of transport, having to trek about 230 miles to reach its forward position at Min Thar in the third week of May when the monsoon had already commenced. The 3rd Regiment occupied the villages of Lamyang, Keiplam and Khoset and was heavily engaged around the village of Bongli at the end of June and early July. With the monsoon setting in, the 4th Regiment was unable to proceed beyond Mandalay.[227]

In early June, the main force of the 2nd and the 3rd Battalions under Shah Nawaz was called up to Kohima to reinforce the Japanese garrisons which were under counterattack of the British forces. The battalions, however, could not get there due to the incessant rains before the withdrawal from the Imphal plain had begun. They were allowed to join the 1st Division at the Palel front in July, after Subhas put pressure on the Japanese, but it was too late as the division soon began to retreat towards Kalewa.[228]

The Southern Army headquarters instructed Lt Gen. Kawabe on 3 July to fall back to Manipur. An upset Kawabe refused to meet Subhas when the latter called upon him on the same day. On 5 July, the Regional Army issued orders cancelling the Imphal operations completely. Accordingly, the Japanese 15th Army and the Azad Hind Fauj began their retreat.[229]

Between February and May 1944, the Azad Hind Fauj had crossed into Indian soil in the Arakan sector and Bishenpur in the Imphal sector. The initial success in the Arakan sector caused much enthusiasm, and Subhas hailed their success through a Special Order of the Day issued on 9 February and another statement issued on 21 February. On 21 March, he issued a proclamation urging Indians to cooperate with the Azad Hind Fauj and its allied forces, and about a week later, made citations and gave awards to thirteen members of the army who had fought in the Arakan sector. The week of 6–13 April was celebrated as the National Liberation Week. Lt Gen. Mutaguchi urged on 1 March that the preparations for taking over the civilian administration of the liberated areas should proceed, and on 22 March, prime minister Tojo declared in the Japanese Diet that the liberated areas in India would be placed completely under the administration of the provisional government.[230]

At that time, the Japanese Government gifted Subhas an aeroplane. On 5 April, he moved the site of the headquarters of the Japanese 15th Army to Maymyo, taking along part of the provisional government along with him. However, he returned to Rangoon after some time, leaving behind some members of the government at Maymyo.

After inspecting the forward positions of the Japanese and Fauj troops on the front in May, Kawabe had little doubt that the Imphal campaign had failed. On his return from the front, he called on Subhas and discussed in general the difficult conditions under which the Japanese and the Fauj soldiers were fighting. Subhas immediately offered to meet the pressing needs of the front line by sending the remaining forces, including the Jhansi regiment. Being cut off from the front from May, Subhas had little information about the impending setback. Kawabe too did not tell him the bitter truth. Subhas absorbed himself with planning for the enlarged activities of his government, which would follow the end of the first phase of the campaign for freedom with the fall of Imphal.[231]

M.Z. Kiani pointed out a key strategic blunder in the Japanese plan for capturing Imphal. The Japanese 15th Army under Mutaguchi progressed rapidly after crossing the Chindwin River and laid a siege on Kohima. As fierce fighting continued at Imphal and Kohima, the Japanese forces chose not to bypass Kohima and capture Dimapur, which was the nearest rail-head and supply base in Eastern Assam. While some Japanese commanders advocated proceeding to Dimapur, others preferred waiting till Imphal fell. If the Japanese-INA forces had been able to capture Dimapur, the supply link of the British forces would have been cut off, putting the forces in Imphal and Kohima in a dangerous situation. The Japanese decision of not attacking Dimapur gave the time and opportunity to the British 2nd Division which was in reserve, to reinforce the forces in Kohima and contain the Japanese forces.[232] With the onset of monsoon and closure of the supply routes, the depleted Japanese forces were compelled to retreat, thus opening up Burma to the Allied forces' offensive.

Subhas came to realize the extent of the Imphal disaster in September, when he inspected the wounded soldiers who had been returning from the front. The Japanese had to take a large share of the blame for the failure, and both he and his commanders were bitter about the inability of the liaison agency to keep the Fauj supplied with minimum war materials and rations. The relations with the liaison agency deteriorated beyond repairs. Realizing the downside of wholly depending on the Japanese for supplies, he decided to organize a War Council to look into the requirements of the future military campaign. He was convinced that instead of serving any useful purpose, the liaison agency only stood between him and the Japanese Government.[233]

Speaking at a rally of Indians in Rangoon on 4 July 1944, Subhas expressed satisfaction at the response he received from the Indian community in East and Southeast Asia, both in terms of men and money. There were sufficient recruits and the problem was in making necessary arrangements to train them quickly. The Azad Hind Government had also received much more than the target of Rs 3 crore. He expected a steady flow of money. The National Bank of Azad Hind Limited established in April was a success too, with some branches that had already been opened and more set to open soon. One area that he marked out for improvement was supplies. Although the Department of Supplies did good work, it was not adequate. More specifically, he emphasized the need to develop transport capabilities so that the Government was no longer dependent on the Japanese.[234]

As the Imphal campaign faced a rout, the All-India Radio 'launched a vigorous propaganda offensive against Subhas' and the INA. Letters written by the INA officers about their poor conditions were read out and soldiers who had deserted the INA were made to speak over the radio.[235]

To hold up the fighting spirit of the Indians, the Azad Hind Government issued orders to celebrate Netaji Week from 4 to 10 July and large-scale celebrations were held everywhere, with mass meetings and demonstrations.

Another setback came in the form of the resignation by the Tojo Government in July. Kuniaki Koiso became the new prime minister of Japan. Subhas sent him a message reiterating that 'we will fight side by side with Japanese and other friendly powers until we win independence by crushing our common enemy'. Koiso reciprocated by promising to extend all possible assistance to the Indian independence movement. Towards the end of October, Subhas received word from Tokyo that the Japanese Government would confer the highest decoration on him. To the surprise of the Japanese Government, he politely turned it down, saying, 'I would like to accept it together with my men when we have won independence'. On 1 November, he flew to Tokyo to hold consultations with the new government.[236] This was to be his third visit to Japan.

Subhas signed an Indo–Japanese Loan Agreement with the Japanese Government. The past practice had been to write an IOU every time the provisional government borrowed money from the Japanese. Subhas wanted a more formal arrangement so that he could prevent Japan from putting India under any obligation after India became a sovereign state. The Japanese Government accepted his proposal, and the agreement was initially concluded on a tentative basis. Subhas also extracted a promise for the establishment of a diplomatic mission.[237]

Subhas was told by the Japanese in mid-April 1945 that the Imphal campaign was over and that they could not defend Burma any more. From Pyinmana, Subhas moved down with his team first to Rangoon and from there to Bangkok. It required much persuasion by his senior officers, as he refused to move out of Rangoon, preferring to stay back to be with the retreating INA soldiers. He keenly monitored the retreating soldiers to ensure that they received proper medical attention, and at the same time, planned for the next phase of the campaign to liberate India. By 15 August, when Japan surrendered, it was clear to him that he had to shift his base of operation. Once again, due to the circumstances, Subhas started his journey towards the unknown.

10

The Quagmire of Isms

'Who was Subhas Chandra Bose?' asked the headline of a November 2019 story in *Newsweek*. The one-line answer read 'Bose was an Indian nationalist leader who worked with the Nazis and the Japanese Empire to rid the subcontinent of the British during World War Two.'

The incident that triggered the question and elicited the insightful answer was a controversy that erupted in the United States because an Indian who held a prominent political post chose to wear a T-shirt that had an image of Subhas on it, seventy-three years after he disappeared. In December 2018, Saikat Chakrabarti, the chief of staff to US Congresswoman Alexandria Ocasio-Cortez, had appeared on a *Now This News* video, speaking about working with Ocasio-Cortez.[1]

Associate Dean and Director of the Global Social Action Agenda at the Simon Wiesenthal Center, Rabbi Abraham Cooper, asked Chakrabarti to apologize 'for wearing a t-shirt of a Nazi collaborator'. Cooper told the *Jewish Journal*, which claims to be the largest Jewish weekly newspaper in the US measured by print and digital readership, that while Bose may be considered a folk hero to some in India, it was still inappropriate to wear such a shirt. To Cooper, Subhas was 'a person who not only sat with Adolf Hitler, but who worked to keep World War II going—aiding and abetting both the Nazis and Imperial Japan'.[2]

No less illuminating were the views attributed in the *Newsweek* story to an associate professor in Indian history at the University of Cambridge, who opined that Chakrabarti deserved some of the controversy. 'Born, educated and made in India', the academic echoed the Rabbi's view that wearing such a T-shirt outside India is highly controversial, since one 'can't whitewash the fact' that Subhas did 'take help from the Nazis', and it is difficult to say for sure if 'he was free of the kind of ideologies that led to

454

such human catastrophes'. The associate professor was quoted to have said that Subhas remains present in India, like a 'zombie', 'undead' or 'ghostly figure.[3]

Apart from everything else, the most remarkable thread common to these views, which actually represent two very different contexts, is that it is alright to admire Subhas within India, but not outside of it.

The line demarcating the understanding and treatment of Subhas within and outside India, though, is not a clear one. The unthinking and symbolic depiction that characterizes a large part of western media and academia has influenced their Indian counterparts too. By this formula, Gandhi represents truth and non-violence that won India its freedom, Jawaharlal represents democracy that kept the freedom alive, and Subhas was an Axis collaborator who would have been a dangerous proposition had he succeeded. There are, in fact, very few exceptions who have taken a deeper, broader and balanced view.

A key difference between India and the West on this point is Subhas's relevance in current politics. While he faintly features as a representative Indian political figure in the international discourse (for that matter anyone except Gandhi and Jawaharlal do), apart from in some limited regions, Subhas has remained an immensely popular figure in India. His popularity has been sustained despite a strong undercurrent of indifference and the deep-seated disdain of the officialdom even after seven and a half decades of independence. The contest among political parties to appropriate his image, albeit with some reservations, therefore, is still an ongoing process.

Yet, at the core, the problem with Subhas is the same. The way he defied stereotypes, broke the acceptable boundaries of different ideologies and schools of thought, challenged established norms, powers and icons that came to dominate politics in India and the world made him extremely inconvenient to deal with. He became more than an irritant, someone who was sought to be eliminated both by the prime minister of England and the Viceroy of India. His absence in India after the war was undoubtedly a relief, not only to the British but to many national leaders as well. However, the unexpected mass upsurge that resulted from the INA trials and the consequent mutinies in the armed forces aggravated this irritation. As Philip Mason, Joint Secretary, War Department, in the dying days of the Raj observed, 'Congress leaders were secretly as much perturbed as the British' in the face of that 'storm of public feeling'.[4]

The challenge thrown to the Empire's hold on India by Subhas and the Indian National Army (INA) was noted by Eric Hobsbawm:

> The test of the British Raj in India was not the major rebellion organised by Congress in 1942 under the slogan 'Quit India', for they suppressed it without serious difficulty. It was that, for the first time, up to fifty-five thousand Indian soldiers defected to the enemy to form and 'Indian National Army' under a Left-wing Congress leader, Subhas Chandra Bose, who had decided to seek Japanese support for Indian independence.[5]

Not only losing hold over the Indian army, which was the bulwark of the Raj, but being compelled to desist from giving them exemplary punishment were festering sores that could never be forgotten by the champions and the loyal labourers of the Raj.

Mason was being honest in his foreword to Hugh Toye's biography of Subhas when he acknowledged that:

> There are elements in Bose's character which are repellent to an English reader—his arrogance and refusal to compromise, the assurance with which a man who . . . proposed that India should pay 'a blood sacrifice' to get liberation the way he chose . . .

There was grudging admiration as well—'no one can doubt the stature of the man, his intellectual scope and the passion with which he held his convictions'. That Mason found it difficult to appreciate Toye's words of admiration for Subhas was clear from the comparison he drew:

> . . . it is perhaps not too fanciful to suppose that he first acquired that kind of intellectual involvement with his prey that Sleeman, more than a hundred years before, had felt with the Thugs.[6]

If Mason's way of expressing his views on Subhas was a bit polished, his contemporary, Francis Tuker, the chief of India's Eastern Command at that time, had no need for it. He introduced Subhas as 'a plump Bengali Brahman of overweening personal ambition', in his memoirs. In Tuker's estimate,

> Subhas Chandra Bose and his INA captains had done as evil and efficient a job as did Goebbels and his propaganda men in Germany . . . A Military

Dictator, he permeated the core of the INA body with a rigid, utterly intolerant, tightly-closed and diseased mentality.[7]

All these were in the public domain. Yet, in the secrecy of the bureaucracy there was a different strand of thought too. When the top bureaucrats in British Indian Government were racking their brains to find the best way to deal with the INA soldiers, additional secretary in the Home Department, R Tottenham, the man who had compiled the charges against Gandhi for the 1942 disturbances, proposed an entirely new course of action to the home member R.F. Mudie. After giving his views on the possible alternatives, Tottenham wrote to Mudie on 17 September that there was another course of action

> . . . which I have not mentioned, but which I do not think should he summarily dismissed. This is that we should make friends with Subhas Bose, as they have done with Aung San in Burma. To make rebels your allies is often the wisest course, if they are worth having as allies. Whether Subhas would he worth having is another question. All that can be said is that he would probably be much better than Gandhi, Nehru or any of that crowd; and if he could be used to displace their leadership, we should I believe be doing India a good turn.[8]

Mudie gave a wry response a day later: 'There is a good deal in the idea of making friends with Bose (except that I hope he's dead!).'

The idea was dead as soon as it was born. The remarkable thing about it is that such a thought could even cross the mind of a top bureaucrat, amongst the main current of abhorrence towards Subhas.

Mason was not alone in his abhorrence for Subhas. P.J. Griffiths, while reviewing *The Springing Tiger* for the London-based Royal Institute of International Affairs in 1959, was as explicit as possible:

> This is a very sympathetic study of a character whom most English people find singularly unattractive . . . Bose was a natural fanatic and a supreme egoist, who said frankly that after independence India must have a firm undemocratic government for at least twenty years, and, of course, he visualised himself as the dictator. It is fortunate for India that her destinies lay in the hands of saner spirits such as Gandhi and Vallabhbhai Patel . . .[9]

What is significant is the continuity of this attitude towards Subhas. Thirty years after *The Springing Tiger*, the journal of the American Historical Association, 'the largest professional organisation serving historians in all fields and all professions',[10] published a review of the next major biography of Subhas by a western scholar. The professor of history at the University of Minnesota, who reviewed *Brothers Against the Raj* by Leonard Gordon, found it 'disturbing' that the book lacked any 'historiographical discussion of Subhas Bose's much-publicised authoritarian personality, militarism, and fascist proclivities'. He believed that the book's facts left one with 'no doubt that Bose was as pathetic and tragic as the Bengal whose heritage and culture he could not escape'.[11]

Similar to this was Günter Grass's discomfort in the mid-1980s, which turned into annoyance when, amidst the terrible poverty of Bengal and Bangladesh, the ghost of Subhas Bose kept haunting him, most often in the form of statues and photographs and occasionally through discussions with people: 'during our brief trip to Bangladesh, the mere mention of the Bengali Führer will unleash almost fanatical hymns of allegiance', he found. He was also annoyed with how the Calcutta wing in the Victoria Memorial Museum, 'though not totally suppressing Gandhi's importance, it banishes him to its outer fringe'. Putting up Subhas's photo at the same place was nothing but 'mutton-headed hero worship—for nowhere in this commodious museum is it made clear that there was a conflict between Bose and Gandhi, that Bose openly avowed dictatorship, that he admired Mussolini and Hitler'.[12]

The pattern of distinguishing Subhas as the bad boy among the Indian nationalist leaders started soon after the news of his presence in Germany became publicly known. Described as 'Among the slick, satisfied top handful of Congress politicians . . . Bose stands out', in the *Time* magazine in 1938,[13] and admired in the British press during his short visit to England in January 1938, Subhas gradually became the villain.

Early in 1942, Subhas had still not earned the epithets that went on to be popularly associated with his name from later that year. News reports were still describing him as 'left wing Indian political leader long regarded as an Axis sympathiser', 'Axis-sponsored Indian nationalist', and even as an 'Indian opposition leader'.[14] The news agency, the Associated Press (AP), noted that the publicity given to Subhas's speeches by the German radio news service rivalled that given to Hitler's speeches.[15] On 7 March 1942, *The Boston Daily Globe* and the *Los Angeles Times* carried a news report by the AP highlighting Jawaharlal's demand for the immediate formation of a provisional national government. It quoted the critics of the British Government in London worrying that if it was not done, 'a decisive number of the native masses are bound to regard Axis-sponsored Subhas Chandra Bose, outlawed former Mayor of Calcutta, as their deliverer'. The story elaborated:

> Britons well informed of the Indian problem said today that Nehru's remarks reflect his own and Mohandas K Gandhi's views that the persuasion of Bose is so great that only swift execution of British freedom promises will counter it . . . The London sources said there was real danger of a Bose-inspired revolt flaring behind the backs of the British now fighting in Burma.
>
> Bose's supporters were said to have a majority where India's most martial peoples are concentrated. These are on the north-west frontier, in the Punjab and Maharatta (sic). Moreover, he is said to still control Bengal—next door to Burma—as tightly as Tammany ever bossed New York, even though he is reported somewhere in Axis European territory. Daily recordings of Bose's voice, expounding the theory of revolution, are flooding India from the Bangkok radio.[16]

In a story published on top of its masthead on 5 August 1943, the *San Francisco Examiner* quoted the US Office of War Information claiming that Subhas, who according to them was 'one of the five most influential men in all India', was 'as dangerous to the United Nations' cause "as a match in a powder house"'.[17]

Until 1942, Subhas was still described as 'a left-wing leader'[18] or an 'extreme Indian Nationalist leader'.[19] By the middle of 1942, the British press had started calling Subhas 'the Indian Quisling.'[20] *The Observer* labelled Subhas as the 'star Radio Quisling of the Indian firmament'.[21] The use of the Axis-related pejoratives was noticeably more frequent in the British press in comparison to its American counterpart. Thus, 'Axis puppet Bose arrives in Japan',[22] and the 'Indian Traitor's "First Act"'[23] after forming the Azad Hind Government was to declare war on Britain and America, and 'Indian Quisling Declared War'.[24] At the Greater East Asia Conference, they wrote 'Asiatic Puppets Confer'[25] and 'Tojo Gives "Pep" Talk to East Asian Quislings'.[26] When Subhas was received by the Japanese emperor, one of the headlines was 'Bose sees his boss'.[27] An American newspaper ran a daily knowledge test for its readers asking for which country the 'forty-six-year-old Chandra Bose heads the puppet government proclaimed by Japan',—Burma, India, Siam, or Philippines.[28] While an American newspaper informed its readers that the INA was 'commanded by traitor and puppet' Subhas[29] Australian newspapers declared that it was the 'evil genius of Bose' that was behind the army.[30] When the Imphal campaign ended, 'India's Renegade Army Fails in Revolt', readers were told.[31] After his reported death in a plane crash in August 1945, readers in Australia were reminded that he was 'The Man who Promised India to Hitler'.[32] *The New York Times* was more forthright: 'Indian puppet is reported killed.'[33]

Putting up a strong defence in *The New York Times* against the allegations that Gandhi was pro-Japanese, his famous biographer Louis Fischer too labelled Subhas as a 'Japanese puppet'. 'The British whom I saw in India know how very pro-British Gandhi is and how much his non-violent approach has helped them during the last twenty years,' Fischer argued.[34]

Influential Indian voices abroad were also contributing to the development of the western world's attitude towards Subhas. *Warning to the West*, a book written by the US-based Gujarati writer, Krishnalal Shridharani, received wide publicity in the American press. After complaining that British bureaucrats were trying to tarnish Gandhi's image as a pro-Japanese fifth columnist with the aim of turning American opinion against him, Shridharani delved into the question of 'The Choice: Nehru or Bose?'

Shridharani imagined Asia's disillusionment with the West as a stepladder at the bottom of which was Madame Chiang Kai-shek, with the 'least cause for grievance'. On the middle rung of the ladder stood Jawaharlal, 'a spiritual child of both East and West' who 'has espoused institutions of democracy' despite being 'an avowed enemy of British imperialism'. Jawaharlal held 'the key to the West's future in the East—but that key has to be used by Anglo-American hands'.

On the topmost rung of the disillusionment ladder was Subhas, who would 'join up with anyone who fights the British', and believed that 'India and Asia can never meet the West on equal terms save through a thorough defeat of the Saxon launched by a Japanese spearhead':

> Bose is more dangerous than the Americans and the British realise. For
> he has never been known to be a fascist and he is not regarded as a fifth

columnist by most Indians; in fact, he had communistic leanings. He is simply anti-British, and anti-Saxon beyond hope . . .

Bose can never be brought back to the democratic camp. But the growth of his following in Asia, and especially in India, can be checked. Bose's only strength, apart from his Japanese support, arises from British stubbornness and failure to yield. They can prick Bose's bubble reputation by recognising Asia's equality. If Nehru had something like the freedom of India to offer to the masses, even Bengal would refuse to listen to Bose and would fight for the United Nations . . . It is Nehru or Bose.

. . . The manifest choice between Nehru and Bose proves that the battle of Asia is as much psychological as military. The final outcome will not depend entirely upon military might and soldierly prowess; it will greatly depend on preventing Nehrus from becoming Boses.[35]

A reviewer of the book observed: 'His statement of Japan's propaganda aims is the best part of his book, and there is one specific warning of importance. It is against the collaborative activities in India of Subhash [sic] Chandra Bose.'[36]

Sirdar J.J. Singh, president of the India League of America and former AICC member complained in December 1944 to the INS Staff Correspondent, Alfred Tyrnauer, that in order to exploit the famine of Bengal, Subhas, the '"chief propagandist" of the Japanese, was appealing daily over the radio to Bengalese [sic] followers to revolt against the British'. Singh expressed concerns over the 'effect of this propaganda on the distressed Indians, many of whom have been fanatical followers of Bose'. Only the release of Gandhi and Jawaharlal from prison 'could prevent a deterioration of the political situation', Singh argued.[37]

The *Manchester Evening News* reported on 19 April 1944 a warning from the Indian League in London that 'the political war waged by Japan through the medium of Subhas Bose can only be effectively met by a complete change in policy towards India'.[38]

With this outlook, it was but natural for the western press to note time and again when they felt the resurgence of Subhas in the Indian polity in the later years. As early as in 1957, *The New York Times* noted that the memory of Subhas, who in their opinion was 'condemned as a war criminal', was strong as ever. The newspaper stated, 'Even leaders of Mr Nehru's Congress Party say that if Mr Bose were to return he would sweep Bengal and pose a real threat to Mr Nehru's leadership throughout the country.'[39] The Western press was again surprised to find during the Chinese war of 1962 that India had adopted Subhas's spirit over Gandhi's.

The Sunday issue of the *Chicago Tribune* ran the amusing headline 'War Reveals Indians' Violent Side', on December 1962. The *Tribune* and many other newspapers that day carried an AP story which informed the world that:

> On the whitewashed walls of many Indian homes is the picture of a man little known outside this country and representing a side of the Indian character that is also little known. The picture is of Subhas Chandra Bose, who presumably died in 1945 in a plane crash on Formosa. He was a rival of Jawaharlal Nehru for leadership of the political movement that expelled the British from India . . .
>
> The man known to the world as the symbol of the independence movement was Mohandas K Gandhi, an apostle of non-violence. Bose represented another tradition—that of violent battle . . . This second tradition is now coming to the front as India faces China. It is in ready response to the call for national defense sounded by Nehru, the man of peace turned war leader at the age of 73.[40]

Two-and-a-half decades later, when on the occasion of Subhas's birth centenary and the fiftieth year of India's Independence, *The New York Times* reported that 'India Rehabilitates Wartime Leader Who Fought For Japan', the fact that did not escape its notice was that the 'adulation heaped on Mr Bose today involved doctrinal gymnastics by several of India's leading political parties that had previously condemned Mr Bose's wartime role'. If adulation was there, criticism was not far away. There were Indians who questioned whether Subhas deserved the honours. *The Statesman* of Calcutta asked in an editorial that although Subhas was not a fascist himself,

> . . . can it be assumed that he was ignorant of what National Socialism was about? Could he have been blind to the real nature of Japanese imperialism in Asia, its atrocities and cruelties? How did he hope to reconcile all this with his own vision of independent India?[41]

The original strand of the western assessment was not lost at any time, however. Reviewing Gerard H. Corr's book, *The War of the Springing*

Tigers, in 1978, Milan Hauner, whose seminal research on Subhas's relations with the Axis powers still remains the singular point of reference for researchers, described Subhas as 'a former leading Congressman and a Bengali nationalist with strong authoritarian ambitions'. Hauner upheld Corr's assessment of Subhas's personality:

> . . . Corr rightly says that Bose, as an extremist himself, created extreme reactions, 'people were either for him to the point of idolatry or they were totally opposed.' India today is still poorly equipped to resist the temptation of a charismatic dictator.[42]

The opinions of politicians and their parties within India, although a little different, were no less conflicted. The mass upheaval of support for the INA soldiers and adulation of Subhas compelled many leaders to change their wartime attitudes, at least publicly. Thus, Jawaharlal, who led the Congress's diatribe against Subhas, proclaiming once that he would fight Subhas if he came with the Japanese army, mentioned him specially during his independence speech in 1947.[43] 'Jai Hind' was adopted as the national salutation, and Tagore's 'Jana Gana Mana', which was selected by Subhas as India's national anthem, received Jawaharlal's approval. Subhas became 'Netaji' for all leaders, including Gandhi and Jawaharlal.

It was easy to misrepresent, lampoon and reduce Subhas to the image of a Nazi sympathizer with authoritarian ambitions by the Western press, but that was not the case in India. The formulation adopted by the Congress very early on was that of a brave but misguided patriot who fell from the high pedestal of the Gandhian soul of modern India. Thus, in deference to his popularity, important occasions were celebrated and commemorative postal stamps were issued, but always calibrated with the caution that he would not take the centre stage or deflect the continued spotlight on the Nehru–Gandhi family. Subhas's associates and family members continued to be spied upon by the Central and the state governments until the 1970s, a fact that came to be known in the second decade of the new millennium because of the transparency campaign of the author and his friends. The official files on the INA were declassified only on Subhas's birth centenary, and there were over 300 files from 2015 onwards. The intelligence files, many of which deal with the search for a 'dead' Subhas, however, are yet to be made public.

This being the attitude of the Congress party, the opposition parties have tried to represent Subhas as their mascot, with varying degrees of success, but more often than not accompanied with controversy, as they had to inevitably make some departure from their past ideological positions.

This ideological adjustment was probably the most challenging for the two major communist parties of India, which emerged from the undivided Communist Party of India (CPI), which berated Subhas incessantly from 1940 to 1945. Like the other political parties, the communist attitude started changing in the face of the INA-inspired mass upheaval from the end of 1945.

The CPI faithfully followed the British propaganda line, leading the most virulent attacks on Subhas and the Forward Bloc during the war. The party's mouthpiece, *People's War*, published a cartoon on 19 July 1942, showing a Japanese soldier riding a donkey that had Subhas's face. The Forward Bloc was heaped with epithets such as fifth columnists, gangsters, unscrupulous disruptors, black crew, and Jap agents.

Subhas 'was a patriot once', declared the *People's War*, who had turned into 'the contemptible and miserable position of a marionette in Axis hands', comparable to 'a hangman at the head of a life-saving mission', 'And now this puppet has the temerity to insult our patriotism and intelligence by attempting to persuade us from the Berlin radio!' The 'Forward Blocists' were the anti-national adherents of the 'traitor Bose', 'the henchman of Japanese imperialism'. He had become 'the running dog of Jap Fascism' and was 'the future dictator by the grace of Tojo and Co'.

In the wake of the uprising in August 1942, the *People's War* explained:

> The actual programme of this upsurge, sabotage of nation's defences, has brought out of their wretched holes the entire Forward Blocist gang. From Berlin their master Bose gives the call. Everywhere, when this movement is widespread, we find the Forward Blocist traitors in the lead, to do the dirty job of their foreign masters.[44]

P.C. Joshi, the general secretary of the CPI, predicted that 'When Desh Gaurav Subhas comes with the Japanese army, Jayaprakash and other Congress Socialists will emerge from their hideouts to meet him. Thereafter they will together form a Japanese-sponsored provisional government'.[45]

It is indeed interesting that Joshi would link Jayaprakash Narayan with Subhas in the background of the former's public dissociation from the latter after the Tripuri Congress. Later, however, Jayaprakash completely changed his outlook towards Subhas's policy and programme. In an undated and unsigned letter to Subhas, which was received when Subhas was in the midst of his preparations to leave India, Jayaprakash admitted that Subhas was right all along:

> I am writing this letter not without considerable anxiety. Anxiety, because I am not sure how you will receive it. I did not know if you will take me seriously when I say that at no time did I bear any personal ill-will against you. There were political differences, which I did not try to hide. But anything more than that there never was. On the other hand, I have always admired your courage and steadfastness. And now, when it has been driven home to me, I admire your prescience and foresight.
>
> Here I have been turning things in my mind. Recent events have led me to reorient my entire thinking. I admit that the Anti-Compromise Conference and the stand that you and Swamiji [Sahajananda Saraswati] took have been completely vindicated. I shall say so publicly at the first opportunity I get.[46]

The invectives and the cartoons depicting Subhas in the lowest possible light continued as long as the war lasted.

The Government was happy with Joshi's serial tirade against Subhas, but these also created some new problems. R. Tottenham, additional secretary in the Home Department, wrote to H.V.R. Iengar on 22 November 1943:

> The military authorities here are considerably perturbed by an article by P.C. Joshi [in] the issue of the 'People's War' dated November 21st which quotes extensively from Japanese broadcasts (in contravention of the Defence of India Rules on the subject) relating to Subhas Chandra Bose, and, in particular, the activities of the Indian National Army. We recognize that Joshi's intentions may have been laudable, but, apart from the contravention of the law which the article involves, we are most anxious, for obvious reasons, that, as little publicity as possible should be given to the activities of Bose and the Indian National Army.[47]

On 19 November, the Department of Information and Broadcasting had issued a directive that laid down clear guidelines for dealing with Subhas and the INA:

Very careful consideration has been given to the likely influence of the Bose propaganda on public opinion. It has been decided that to indulge in extensive mentions of Bose's activities in order to counter his propaganda officially, would only have the effect of giving extra publicity to the Indian National Army Movement. The ban on any mention of Bose and the INA—except by oral propagandists in reply to hecklers - therefore stands. Material is, however, being collected and plans laid for effective counter-propaganda measures should these seem advisable at a later stage.

Non-official anti-Bose propaganda will be given encouragement . . . as it tends further to undermine Bose's prestige as a politician and as a man, but will be discouraged when it tends merely to publicise the INA. Special publicity should be given to any anti-Bose statements which may from time-to-time be made by prominent Indian politicians.[48]

The Home Department and the director of public relations further suggested that instead of using the term Indian National Army in official correspondence, 'all concerned should get into the habit of calling this organisation "Bose's Army" or "Bose's Puppet Force" or something equally derogatory, so as by no chance to heighten the prestige of the INA'.[49]

Iengar met Joshi on 25 November and reported back to Tottenham the discussion that was 'conducted in a friendly spirit':

I had a long talk with P.C. Joshi . . . His arguments were as follows . . . The Government of India seem to think that to tell people, particularly in Eastern Bengal where there is famine, that Bose is coming with an Indian army and with plenty of rice, will demoralize them, and make them welcome Subhas Bose. The Government of India also seem to think that the article is giving a great deal of publicity to enemy broadcasts which otherwise would not be widely known. Joshi considers both these arguments completely invalid. It is common talk in Eastern Bengal, both in towns and in villages, that Bose has promised to come, and they are so sick of the famine that they are prepared to welcome him or anyone else who can bring them rice. In other words, the mischief which the Government of India ascribe to the article is already there. (Joshi sarcastically remarked that only the Government seem to be ignorant of what is being talked about in Eastern Bengal). The Communist Party considers that the people are so demoralized and consequently so ready to welcome Bose that it is essential to tell them of the great danger inherent in their present attitude, and this can only be done by articles of the sort now in question.[50]

The scale and intensity of the attack from the Indian communists was at its peak, but this was not the first time he was under fire from them. In the early 1970s, Gautam Chattopadhyay, son of Subhas's close friend, Kshitish Prasad Chattopadhyay, and who had joined the CPI in the early 1940s, traced the relation between Subhas and the Indian communists from 1921.

In line with the policy enunciated by Lenin of forming a united front against imperialism, of communists and nationalists, the Communist International (Comintern) invited Subhas and Chiraranjan in 1922 as delegates to the next Congress of the Comintern. Although the visit did not materialize, Subhas, according to Chattopadhyay, was friendly and helpful towards the communists. In particular, he helped in providing shelter to Abani Mukherjee and Nalini Gupta—two communists from abroad. The communists also stood in support of both Subhas and Jawaharlal in the Congress sessions of 1927, when the resolution setting complete independence was passed for the first time and 1928, when the two youth leaders opposed Gandhi's resolution. The Comintern overturned Lenin's united front strategy in 1928, suggesting a break with 'bourgeois nationalism'. Gandhi, Jawaharlal and Subhas were labelled as 'representatives of the capitalist class working against the fundamental interests of the toiling masses'.[51]

Although Chattopadhyay claimed that Subhas was elected the president of the All-India Trade Union Congress (AITUC) with the help of communists and left nationalists, the Intelligence Bureau (IB) noted that it was in fact M.N. Roy's group and not the CPI which obtained Subhas's support, leading to the walkout by the hard-line communist leaders S.V. Deshpande and B.T. Ranadive who formed a separate trade union. The IB categorized the communists at the beginning of the 1930s into four broad groups: (1) The CPI, (2) M.N. Roy's party and the emerging Congress Socialist Party, (3) converted terrorists, and (4) the Ghadr Party.[52]

Subhas's 1933 speech at the Indian Political Conference in London drew sharp criticism from *The International Press Correspondence*, the international press service of the Comintern, which held that Subhas's new programme would only lead to further enslavement of toiling masses. According to the newspaper, Subhas's difference from Gandhi was just a matter of degree, and both discouraged 'revolutionary violence' in the same manner. The key objection of the communists with Subhas's programme of Samyavadi Sangha was that at a time when the communist movement was just beginning to consolidate, they feared that such a programme would 'hinder the revolutionary intellectuals and the workers from joining the ranks of the Communist Party', and 'the formation of the CP of India'.[53]

The CPI had similar apprehensions when it broke off from the Forward Bloc in December 1939. According to Hirendra Nath Mukerjee, while Jawaharlal was trapped in Gandhi's web of magic, Subhas's programme, although bold, was bound to fail because it was devoid of true revolutionary socialism.[54] In an article issued in March 1940, criticizing Subhas for not launching a struggle for civil liberties, Joshi explained:

> Workers, peasants, students have already adopted the proletarian technique of struggle—mass action. They have already come under the influence of Socialism. The effort of the Forward Bloc to win over these movements for its satyagraha or political policy has to be resisted as the infiltration of bourgeois influence over the masses.[55]

A more detailed and theoretical elucidation came in March 1946, when Joshi responded to the accusation by the AICC that the CPI had acted against the Congress policy and programme from June 1942 onwards. Joshi grasped that the crux of the allegation was that 'you accuse us of betraying our own country for the sake of the Soviet Union', for changing the party's slogan of 'Imperialist War' to 'People's War' as soon as Germany invaded the Soviet Union. The CPI had been following the Congress line, Joshi argued back.[56]

Joshi explained that viewing the war as an opportunity for Indians to revolt was an outdated line of thought, which, if followed, would turn them into 'national chauvinists who seek allies wherever they may be, even including reactionary fascists'. There was, of course, no elucidation of the party's views on Stalin's pact with Hitler.[57]

'We resisted Subhas Bose's move for a rival Congress as disruptive of national unity though it needed some courage to stand up to Bose in Bengal', Joshi wrote in his report. 'Throughout Bengal ran the whisper campaign that Subhas Bose's invasion would bring in its wake lakhs of bags of rice for our starving people', but the CPI understood that 'Bose had placed himself under Japanese protection and it was common sense that his army of liberation could come to India only in the footsteps of the far stronger Japanese'.[58]

Claiming 'Subhas Chandra Bose ultimately chose the Axis powers as his allies', Chattopadhyay has pointed out that the 'differences between Bose and the CPI were too profound and basic to patch up this time'.

Both the CPI and the Government of India at times faced tricky situations. One such situation arose when *People's War* published an article on 15 August 1943, eulogizing veteran Ghadr leader Gurmukh Singh, and demanding his release from prison. The Intelligence Bureau, however, found out through its sources that Singh had stopped believing in the 'people's war' line and argued that Subhas should not be called a traitor 'because his alliance with the Japanese was on a par with Lenin's dealing with the Germans in 1917'.[59]

Yet, there were reasons for the Government to be satisfied with lifting the ban on the CPI in 1942. As F.C. Bourne, the Chief Secretary to the Government of Punjab noted in his letter to the Secretary, Home Department, Government of India:

The Party is genuinely opposed to Subhas Chandra Bose and his fifth columnists, the Forward Bloc and the Congress Socialist Party, and has given practical proof of its readiness to cooperate in intelligence plans to expose and arrest them.[60]

The mass upsurge during the INA trials led the CPI to revise its position vis-à-vis Subhas, just like the other parties. The new position, succinctly expressed by E.M.S. Namboodiripad, was 'the Communist Party or even prominent Congress leaders like Jawaharlal Nehru had no sympathy to the decision of Subhas Bose to help the advance of Japan by forming the INA. But none of them questioned the sense of patriotism of Bose'. Thus, the reassessment of Subhas had two components. First, Subhas was a patriot, and second, that 'his historical perspective was basically wrong during the second world war, because he failed to assess the axis powers as the potential aspirants for domination over the whole world'.[61]

There have occasionally been admissions by some members of the communist parties in India about their error in assessing Subhas. Those admission, however, is restricted to their earlier assessments of Subhas 'being a kind of quisling of the axis powers'. Depending on the occasion, one of these two strands gets more attention than the other.

The ideological difference remains at a more subterranean level, and although it guides the overall leftist outlook towards Subhas, it is not often articulated openly. The ideological dimension has been expressed perceptively by Hiren Mukerjee in his short biography of Subhas. Mukerjee admitted the endurance of Subhas's popularity in the face of so much political opposition when he wrote that Subhas's 'appeal to Indian patriotic sentiment was, of course, more powerful than that of those who had begun to think and speak in terms of . . . scientific socialism'. Yet, it bothered him, and probably other communists, that the Soviet Union to Subhas 'was no more than one among other likely allies, in certain circumstances and for opportunist reasons, of the Indian struggle for freedom' and not an ideological fountainhead. Subhas 'perhaps never cared to study and ponder over Leni's class work on imperialism' and his fascist inclinations were even more dangerous:

> The publication in 1934 of Subhas Chandra Bose's *The Indian Struggle* proposing a synthesis of communism and fascism, to be dubbed Samyavada, was a misfortune, since it repelled the communists who though Bose's concept not only wrong but also very dangerous. It was so unlike the stand of Jawaharlal who had stated categorically that between fascism and communism there was 'no middle road' and that between the two 'I choose the communist ideal'. . . It will be untruthful not to say that in the communist estimation, Jawaharlal Nehru, for all his vacillations in practice, was a fundamentally more clear-sighted and therefore in the long run reliable friend . . . than was Subhas Chandra Bose with his predominantly nationalist ardour and a susceptibility towards meretricious would trends that fascism had highlighted . . . With his total nationalist concentration he mobilised enormous strength in himself no doubt, but at the same time he suffered on account of a lack of rapport with the revolutionary role of Marxism-Leninism in the present historical approach.[62]

In a similar strain, Harkishen Singh Surjeet complained that in his struggle for India's freedom, Subhas was equally ready to build an alliance with socialists and fascists, without making any distinction between fascism and socialism. He was influenced by the autocratic tendencies of the fascist regimes, Surjeet claimed.[63]

Jyoti Basu, the then chief minister of West Bengal, raised a more hypothetical question. He argued that even if the Azad Hind Fauj won

The Quagmire of Isms 471

with the help of the Axis powers, Subhas would not be in a position to keep Germany and Japan in check. He gave the examples of Japanese atrocities in the Andaman and Nicobar Islands and the death penalty issued by the Germans to those soldiers of the Indian Legion who refused to fight against anyone but the British.[64]

The deep distrust about Subhas is also evident from Muzaffar Ahmad's writing. Unable to bear with Subhas's criticism of Marxism, which he felt was intolerable, Ahmad challenged Subhas to a debate in a meeting of the BPCC. He took Subhas's ignoring of his challenge as a show of contempt and vanity.[65] Ahmad was shocked when he heard that Akbar Shah of the North-West Frontier Province (NWFP) had joined the Forward Bloc. He wrote in his memoirs:

When in 1939, we found Akbar Shah join Subhaschandra Basu's Forward Bloc, we were astounded. To resume active politics after such a long time and that too the politics of Subhaschandra Basu—this was something which it is difficult for a Communist to conceive of [sic].[66]

The communist critique touched upon Subhas's spiritual side too. According to another communist leader, it was Subhas's spiritual outlook that prevented him from being able to understand the fundamental difference between communism and fascism. He failed to grasp the capitalist manoeuvres due to his spiritual inclinations.[67] Although he did not mention Subhas specifically, it would not be irrelevant to mention Ahmad's strong dislike for the show of religious inclinations inside prison. The fact that Bengal revolutionaries drew inspiration from the communal hatred-spewing *Anandamath* of Bankim Chandra Chattopadhyay became a key obstacle to his joining the revolutionary societies, as Ahmad came to believe that one of the goals of the revolutionary movement was establishing the Hindu Raj. According to him, this mentality started changing in the 1920s, and it was only in the 1930s that a large number from these societies converted to Marxism–Leninism.[68]

A slew of protests arose from the left and left-of-centre scholars, journalists and politicians accusing the Bharatiya Janata Party (BJP)-led Government and prime minister Narendra Modi of appropriating Subhas's legacy when he announced the declassification of files, renamed the Ross Island as Netaji Subhas Chandra Bose Dweep, the Neil Island as Shaheed Dweep and the Havelock Island as Swaraj Dweep, and hoisted the national flag at the Red Fort on the seventy-fifth anniversary of the formation of the Azad Hind Government.

'Lacking icons of their own, India's ruling party and government have attempted to appropriate leaders of the freedom struggle other than Jawaharlal Nehru. However, it is not as easy to lay false claim to the political legacy of Subhas Chandra Bose as it is to that of Vallabhbhai Patel', wrote Sugata Bose, a Harvard professor and a grandnephew of Subhas.[69] Congress spokesperson Abhishek Manu Singhvi accused the BJP and Modi of a conspiratorial attempt to appropriate the legacy of Subhas.[70] Calling Subhas a 'secular leftist', Subhashini Ali, daughter of Lakshmi and P.K. Sehgal, pointed out that 'To appropriate Netaji with BJP's Hindutva ideology is an unsuccessful attempt to assume the mantle of patriotism'.[71] A news portal associated with the Congress party accused Savarkar of betraying Subhas and the INA by supporting the British war effort and exhorting Hindus to join the British Indian army.[72] Historian and author S. Irfan Habib claimed that the Rashtriya Swayamsevak Sangh (RSS) was appropriating national icons like Vallabhbhai, Bhagat Singh, and Subhas as it did not have any of its own to whom the people of India could connect.[73]

The Hindutva camp's critique of Subhas is not as cogent as that of the leftists. Other than the Hindu Mahasabha campaign against him in 1940 over his alliance with the Muslim League, criticism from the Hindu nationalists has remained scattered and sporadic. More than at Subhas, the main thrust of the Mahasabha's criticism was directed at the Congress which 'lamentably betrayed the interests of the Hindus'.[74] In fact, it would not be an exaggeration to say that there is no officially sponsored body of criticism from the Hindu right camp as far as Subhas is concerned. While the overall tone of the sporadic critiques has been eulogistic, instances of harsh criticism are present too. The most obvious difference between the critiques by the left and the right is that while the former is focused more on ideological deliberations, the latter focuses more on the personality of Subhas.

Despite his bitter confrontation with Subhas during 1940, Syama Prasad Mookerjee always held Subhas in high esteem. Regarding the Gandhian high command's treatment of Subhas during the 1939 presidential elections, Mookerjee noted in his diary, 'This is not Democracy but a low type of Fascism'. Mookerjee noted in his diary on 21 October 1944, more than a year before the INA trials were to spark the mass unrest:

We [Hindu Mahasabha], specially I, had no personal grudge against Subhas. Indeed I had for him admiration and affection, and genuinely believed that there was no other person who could come near him in the political field of India, specially Bengal. His trouble however was too much of first person singular . . . He was so much exposed to public criticism and ridicule due to his unholy alliance with the League that he soon came down from the high pedestal on which his countrymen had placed him.

. . . In any case, his name is today associated with unique romantic adventure—a man, a patriot who so hated foreign rule and so eager to see his country free, that he risked all, and completely identified himself with the enemy . . . If England wins—as she is likely to—and continues to hold her sway over India, it is doubtful if he will ever be permitted to return to India.[75]

Although Subhas had been critical of Savarkar in the second volume of *The Indian Struggle* for being 'oblivious of the international situation and was only thinking how Hindus could secure military training by entering Britain's army in India',[76] the *Forward Bloc* took a nuanced view on the Hindu Mahasabha leader in 1939 and 1940. In its 30 December 1939 issue, the *Forward Bloc* severely criticized Savarkar's presidential address at the Hindu Mahasabha session in Calcutta:

Mr Savarkar's Presidential address at the Calcutta session of the Hindu Mahasabha has in it a considerable element of tub-thumping. We are constrained to remark that its outline is seriously disturbed at places by ill-laid emphasis. His attack on the Congress is one of his weak spots. Its accuracy arid justice are both questionable. The Congress is not infallible and it has made many mistakes in the past, but its general policy is informed by a spirit of service to all India. While the Muslim League has been rancorously mean and the Mahasabha raucously outrageous, from its intermediate balanced position the Congress has all along tried to deal justly with both and has alone attempted an equitable settlement of the communal question which the other two have rendered more and more insoluble . . . But the Hindu Mahasabha has been doing incalculable harm to the idea of Indian nationhood by underlining the communal differences—by lumping all the Muslims together. Mr. Jinnah and his confederates constitute only a speck in the vast mass of Indian Muslims and that vast mass is gradually awaking to a sense of

responsible nationhood. We cannot oblige Mr Savarkar by ignoring the
contributions of the nationalist Muslims to the cause of India.

In the same issue, however, Subhas's party mouthpiece carried a longer
article on Savarkar by S. Krishna Iyer, that mourned the loss of Savarkar to a
sectarian ideology. The opening paragraphs of the article were remarkable:

> Mr. Savarkar is one of the most romantic figures that the Swadeshi
> movement of the first decade of the century threw upon the Indian scene.
> Cast in the mould in which true heroes are made, the whole career of this
> brave son of Maharastra (sic) is one long thrilling tale of daring dreams
> and adventures with their inevitable concomitant in life-long sufferings.
> All eyes in the country turned on him when he came out to breathe free
> air after continuous confinement for the incredible period of twenty-
> five years. A lesser man would have been thoroughly squeezed out by
> this repression, but Mr. Savarkar stood the test well and brought back
> absolutely unimpaired the originally rich dower of Nature to him—a keen
> intellect and a singularly dynamic character. What a startling amount of
> steel he has in his mental make-up! But alas! instead of consecrating his
> splendid gifts to the Nationalist cause represented by the Congress, he
> has chosen to hover round the banner of the Hindu Mahasabha and sing
> a communal hymn. I can quite anticipate the familiar retort with which
> Mr. Savarkar will seek to meet this remark; he will readily say that in
> Hindusthan Hinduism forms the sole base of nationalism and all other
> influences must either be subordinate to it, swell it, or get wiped out of
> the picture. Hero most of his countrymen will differ from him, retaining
> at the same time the highest regard for his personal character.[77]

Claiming that the swadeshi movement 'owed its origin to a reaction
against the swamping influence of Western culture that set in with
the first introduction of English education in the country', Iyer argued
that 'All reactions carry a large dose of excess along with them and the
Swadeshi movement fell back on the ancient culture of the land, typified by
Hinduism, with a jealous, almost pathological fervour'. Savarkar, he wrote,
was a product of this movement:

> Mr. Savarkar has evidently been embittered by the sinister growth of
> Muslim communalism in the country. It is undoubtedly a most sickening

and dangerous phenomenon in Indian politics to-day. But his panacea for the grave evil is undoubtedly of a desperate nature. It is neither practicable nor prudent to divide the country in two warring camps and thus prepare it for a future bloodbath. Rather the call should be for communal unity for the sake of fighting the common evil—foreign domination. It has escaped Mr. Savarkar that Muslim communalism is an artificially bolstered up thing, devised and engendered by a few men at the top with an eye on the loaves and fishes of office and bigger slices of official patronage. When the-better mind of the nation will be roused, it will disappear like fog-screen before the rising sun.[78]

Subhas was critical of Savarkar's politics, but the publication of such an article clearly demonstrates a healthy respect towards the individual. Had his attitude been completely inimical towards Savarkar and the Hindu Mahasabha, there would not have been any alliance with the latter for the Calcutta Corporation elections in the next year.

The background to the alliance was explained by Subhas in a signed editorial in the *Forward Bloc*. Before the elections, Subhas explained, he had issued an appeal to all the parties, particularly to the Hindu Mahasabha and the Muslim League, 'asking for their cooperation in the domain of civic affairs, in spite of any differences that might exist on other questions'. The Hindu Mahasabha happened to respond first. While Subhas credited the 'pro-nationalist elements in the Hindu Mahasabha' for striking the alliance with him, he blamed 'the die-hard communal elements . . . who were throughout opposed to any understanding with the Congress' for wrecking it. The basis of the understanding was 'a sound one' which would have ensured the 'triumph of nationalism and not communalism in due course'. Indians needed to come together to resist the domination of the Corporation by the British. It was 'a basis on which similar understanding could be arrived at with any other organisation'. The editorial was written before he reached an understanding with the Muslim League, and made it clear that the Forward Bloc was looking for a new alliance. Notable was Subhas's assessment of the Hindu Mahasabha, following the break-up:

The above action of the Hindu Mahasabha is the beginning of a new phase in its history. It has come forward to play a political role and to make a bid for the political leadership of Bengal, or at least of the Hindus of Bengal who have been the backbone of Nationalism in this country.

With a real Hindu Mahasabha, we have no quarrel and no conflict. But with a political Hindu Mahasabha that seeks to replace the Congress in the public life of Bengal and for that purpose has already taken the offensive against us, a fight is inevitable. This fight has just begun.[79]

Savarkar too showed admiration and appreciation for Subhas wherever he referred to him publicly. About a month after Subhas left India, Savarkar sent a message to the organizers of the All-India Subhas day, observed on 23 February 1941, expressing anxiety for his safety: 'May the gratitude, sympathy and good wishes of the nation be the source of never-failing solace and inspiration to him wherever he happens to be'.[80]

Again, in one of his last interviews given in 1965 to the RSS mouthpiece, the *Organiser*, out of the four key factors listed by Savarkar that led to India's independence, three were directly or indirectly linked to Subhas. According to Savarkar:

There are many factors, which contributed to the freedom of Bharat. It is wrong to imagine that Congress alone won Independence for Hindusthan. It is equally absurd to think that non-cooperation, Charkha and the 1942 'Quit India Movement were sorely responsible for the withdrawal of the British power from our country. There were other dynamic and compelling forces, which finally determined the issue of freedom. *First*, Indian politics was carried to the Army, on whom the British depended entirely to hold down Hindusthan; *second*, there was a revolt of the Royal Indian Navy and a threat by the Air Force; *third*, the valiant role of Netaji Subhas Bose and the INA; *four*, the War of Independence in 1857, which shook the British; *five*, the terrific sacrifices made by thousands of revolutionaries and patriots in the ranks of the Congress, other groups and parties.[81]

There is, however, a small but extreme and shrill section amongst the present generation of the Hindu right wing which perceives Subhas as a devout Hindu who failed to understand Islam. The various strands of this school of thought are articulated in a blog that is popular among the adherents of this line of thinking. The central thesis of this school of thought is that as opposed to leaders such as Lajpat Rai, Bipin Chandra Pal and Sarat Chandra Chattopadhyay, Chittaranjan Das and Subhas were victims of 'Islamophile secularism'. It argues:

. . . when it came to understanding Islam and its objectives, as a thinker
and as a leader, it must be said that Bose was not very different from the
other Marxist-Secularists. Bose is really an uncomforting case in point,
that even deeply religious Hindus, of excellent intellectual gifts, untiring
patriotism and great leadership acumen, can remain utterly gullible to the
Islamic propaganda and keep causing self-injury to the nation.[82]

The list of specific charges against Subhas according to this point of view
is long, but the main ones include: his in-principle support to the Khilafat
movement; his support to the Bengal Pact; ending his speeches with
'Inquilab Zindabad' rather than with 'Vande Mataram' or 'Bharat Mata Ki
Jai'; his championing of Urdu and Farsi over Hindi; substitution of 'Vande
Mataram' as the national anthem by a 'de-sanskritized' 'Jana Gana Mana';
his belief that there were nationalist Muslims who were, in reality, soft
jihadists; naming the INA regiment after Abul Kalam Azad and not after
Chandra Shekhar Azad, Ashfaqullah or Azeem Ullah; his alliance with
the Muslim League after its Pakistan declaration; starting the Holwell
movement to appease Muslims; and finally, that many Muslim soldiers of
the British Indian army joined the INA to serve their communal interests.[83]

The perceptions and political projection of Subhas's image, coming
from different ideological camps, can therefore be summed up as follows:

- A fascist collaborator and sympathizer, and an authoritarian with
  dictatorial ambitions
- A communist
- An appeaser of Muslims

~

The idea of 'misguided patriot' was most eloquently articulated by Gandhi
over the years after Subhas left India. Although, remarkably, the personal
warmth remained unchanged between Gandhi and Subhas, the ideological
and policy differences only deepened 1939 onwards.

In the course of a conversation on 15 May 1942, Gandhi told B.G.
Kher, the former premier of Bombay,

I believe that Subhas Bose will have to be resisted by us. I have no proof,
but I have an idea that the Forward Bloc has a tremendous organization

in India. Well, Subhas has risked much for us; but if he means to set up a Government in India, under the Japanese, he will be resisted by us.[84]

When Louis Fischer, while interviewing Gandhi on 4 June, expressed shock that he had expressed condolence at the news of Subhas's death (which subsequently proved to be false), Gandhi explained:

I did it because I regard Bose as a patriot of patriots. He may be misguided. I think he is misguided. I have often opposed Bose. Twice I kept him from becoming president of Congress. Finally he did become president, although my views often differed from his. But suppose he had gone to Russia or to America to ask aid for India. Would that have made it better?

Fischer argued back, 'Bose is a young man with a propensity for dramatic action, and were he to succumb in Germany to the lure of Fascism and return to India and make India free but Fascist, I think you would be worse off than under British rule.' Gandhi avoided a direct response, but what he said what Subhas's view that he had shared with his Jewish friend Kitty Kurti during his exile in Europe: 'There are powerful elements of Fascism in British rule, and in India these are the elements which we see and feel every day.'[85]

While talking to foreign correspondents in July, Gandhi's tone was much more sympathetic. He told the journalists, 'You know the case of Shri Subhas Bose, a man of great self-sacrifice who might have had a distinguished career in the Indian Civil Service, but who is now an exile because he cannot possibly tolerate this helpless condition and feels that he must seek the help of Germany and Japan.'[86]

On receiving the news of Subhas's death again in 1945, he wrote to Amrit Kaur on 24 August, 'Subhas Bose has died well. He was undoubtedly a patriot though misguided.'[87]

Asked by the United Press of India in the context of Subhas's address to him as the Father of the Nation whether Subhas enjoyed the same esteem and affection from him, Gandhi responded

I have not read what Subhas Babu is reported to have said about me. But I am not surprised at what you tell me. My relations with him were always of the purest and best. I always knew his capacity for sacrifice.

But a full knowledge of his resourcefulness, soldiership and organizing ability came to me only after his escape from India. The difference of outlook between him and me as to the means is too well known for comment.[88]

On 24 February 1946, Gandhi explained again both his admiration and differences with Subhas in the *Harijan*:

The hypnotism of the Indian National Army has cast its spell upon us. Netaji's name is one to conjure with us. His patriotism is second to none. (I use the present tense intentionally). His bravery shines through all his actions. He aimed high but failed. Who has not failed? Ours is to aim high and to aim well. It is given to everyone to command success. My praise and admiration can go no further. For I knew that his action was doomed to failure, and that I would have said so even if he had brought his INA victorious to India, because the masses would not have come into their own in this manner. The lesson that Netaji and his army brings to us is one of self-sacrifice, unity irrespective of class and community, and discipline. If our adoration will be wise and discriminating, we will rigidly copy this trinity of virtues, but we will as rigidly abjure violence. I would not have the INA man think, or say, that he and his can ever deliver the masses of India from bondage by force of arm. But, if he is true to Netaji and still more so to the country, he will spend himself in teaching the masses, men, women and children to be brave, self-sacrificing and united.[89]

Gandhi's acknowledgement of the impact Subhas and the INA had on the Indian armed forces came out during his discussion with the army men at the Uruli Kanchan camp in Maharashtra, in March. There was a time when soldiers in the Indian army were not allowed to read civil newspapers, but now they could tell their officers that they were going to meet Gandhi without the fear of being stopped.

I know, there is a new ferment and a new awakening among all the army ranks today. Not a little of the credit for this happy change belongs to Netaji Bose. I disapprove of his method, but he had rendered a signal service to India by giving the Indian soldier a new vision and a new ideal.[90]

Yet, when the INA soldiers started receiving massive adulation across the country, Gandhi felt the need to reiterate his differences with them and their leader. At a prayer meeting in Delhi on 5 April 1946, he clarified

> India has accorded to the released INA men a right royal welcome. They have been acclaimed as national heroes. Everybody seems to have been swept off his feel before the rising tide of popular sentiment. I must, however, frankly confess to you that I do not share this indiscriminate hero worship. I admire the ability, sacrifice and patriotism of the I. N. A. and Netaji Bose. But I cannot subscribe to the method which they adopted and which is incompatible with the one followed by the Congress for the last twenty-five years for the attainment of independence.[91]

Subhas's attitude towards Gandhi was not substantially different from the one Gandhi had shown towards him. He never lost the genuine respect and warmth towards the Mahatma. At the same time, as he had often said, he would not give up his political principles in deference to him.

Subhas outlined Gandhi's contribution to the Indian freedom struggle in a speech broadcast from Bangkok on 2 October 1943.

> For twenty years and more Mahatma Gandhi has worked for India's salvation, and with him, the Indian people too have worked. It is not exaggeration to say that if, in 1920, he had not come forward with his new weapon of struggle, India today would perhaps have been still prostrate. His services to the cause of India's freedom are unique and unparalleled. No single man could have achieved more in one single lifetime under similar circumstances.[92]

Two of Gandhi's greatest contributions were about 'the indispensable preconditions for the attainment of independence'—national self-respect and self-confidence, and 'a country-wide organization, which reaches the remotest villages of India'. Significantly, he thought that the closest parallel to Gandhi as a leader was Mustapha Kemal 'who saved Turkey after her defeat in the last World War and who was then acclaimed by the Turks as the *Gazi*.'[93] This comparison presents an interesting contrast to the words of Vallabhbhai Patel at a meeting of the Gandhi Seva Sangh in May 1939. 'Gandhi is the world's best Hitler', Vallabhbhai said, explaining that he kept everyone under control by his love and patience.[94]

Subhas made the phrase 'Father of our Nation' immortal in his broadcast of 6 July 1944, when he addressed Gandhi after his release from prison. It was a justification for the course of action he had chosen:

There is no Indian, whether at home or abroad, who would not be happy if India's freedom could be won through the method that you have advocated all your life and without shedding human blood. But things being what they are, I am convinced that if we do desire freedom we must be prepared to wade through blood.

. . . It was the easiest thing for me to remain at home and go on working as I had worked so long. It was also an easy thing for me to remain in an Indian prison while the war lasted. Personally, I had nothing to lose by doing so . . . By going abroad on a perilous quest I was risking not only my life and my whole future career, but also what was more, the future of my party. If I had the slightest hope that without action from abroad we could win freedom, I would never have left India during a crisis.

. . . I know the propaganda that our enemy has been carrying on against me . . . Not even my worst enemy can ever dare to say that I am capable of selling national honour and self-respect. And not even my worst enemy can dare to assert that I was nobody in my own country and that I needed foreign help to secure a position for myself.

. . . Father of our nation: In this holy war for India's liberation, we ask for your blessings and good wishes.[95]

Speeches such as these reflected Subhas's genuine admiration for Gandhi, but also had an element of political strategy. He had to negotiate his position in the midst of the two conflicting factors: individual admiration and complete political separation. It was also not unknown to him that Indian masses across the world looked up to Gandhi for guidance and treated him as a mystic politician.

The political differences were articulated more freely by Subhas in his private correspondence and discussions. From the Presidency Jail he wrote to elder brother Sarat on 24 October 1940 about Gandhi's plan for individual civil disobedience:

But is not this any eyewash? It is neither cooperation nor mass struggle. It pleases nobody and will lead us nowhere. And this campaign has nothing to do with Swaraj. It can only bluff a certain section of our countrymen who are gullible into thinking that something effective is being done by Gandhiji.

. . . This latest phase of Gandhism with its sanctimonious hypocrisy . . . is sickening to a degree. One is forced to wonder which is a greater menace to India's political future—the British bureaucracy or the Gandhian hierarchy. Idealism that is devoid of Realism and whose only content is a frothy sentimentalism of a sanctimonious character can never be fruitful of results.[96]

Subhas's desperation at the politics of the Congress leadership grew as he was helplessly confined to the prison. A week later, he again wrote to Sarat:

The more I think of Congress politics, the more convinced I feel that in future we should devote more energy and time to fighting the High Command. If power goes into the hands of such mean, vindictive and unscrupulous persons when Swaraj is won, what will happen to the country! If we don't fight them now, we shall not be able to prevent power passing into their hands. Another reason why we should fight them now is that they have no idea of national reconstruction. Gandhism will land free India in a ditch—if free India is sought to be rebuilt on Gandhian, non-violent principles. India will then be offering a standing invitation to all predatory powers.[97]

After a telephone conversation with Rash Behari Bose from Berlin, Subhas sent him a letter dated 11 July 1942, explaining the intricacies of the parties and personalities in the freedom struggle.

Regarding Mahatma Gandhi, I am sorry to say I cannot agree with you. Gandhi's epoch in India's history came to an end in 1939. He has imparted political consciousness to the Indian masses and he built up an All-India organization. But he stands pledged to non-violence and passive resistance. With such methods you can never expel the British from India and can never win independence. Therefore, Gandhi, while talking of independence, always keeps the door open for a compromise with the British. Since Gandhi wants a compromise with England, he will never become pro-Axis . . .

. . . Consequently, there is no room for cooperation with Gandhi. Every show of strength and defiance that Gandhi puts up, is always followed by an attempt at a compromise . . . It would be a fatal mistake now to lionise Gandhi or praise him too much. This will strengthen Gandhi's position and show that we lack self-confidence . . . To expect that Gandhi will come over to our point of view is only an idle dream. Consequently, to strengthen Gandhi's position by praising him too much, amounts to weakening our own following and committing political suicide. You may occasionally pay a compliment to Gandhi as a political manouvre [sic], but you should always remember that Gandhi will never come over to your side.[98]

As far as the attitude of the two chief lieutenants of Gandhi were concerned, they were quite at variance from each other. Vallabhbhai Patel's attitude hadn't undergone much change since 1931, when he had made his displeasure known to Morarji Desai for his plan to invite Subhas for a youth conference. Soon after Desai had become the secretary of the Gujarat Provincial Congress Committee (GPCC), he was approached by the youth workers in the province to invite Subhas to preside over a youth conference. Desai suggested that Jawaharlal should be invited instead of Subhas because 'Subhash [sic] Babu differed in his methods and manner of work from Gandhiji'. Desai approached Vallabhbhai to write to Jawaharlal, but being unhappy about not being consulted prior to making the plans, Vallabhbhai refused. He was also unhappy about Desai's talk of the possibility of inviting Subhas if Jawaharlal refused the invitation. As it happened, Jawaharlal turned down the invitation and Subhas agreed to preside over the conference. 'When the Sardar learnt about this he told me [Desai] that what had happened would create difficulties.' As the date for Gandhi's return from the Round Table Conference was close, Vallabhbhai advised Desai to drop the idea of the conference. 'He felt that this was the best way of avoiding Subhash [sic] Babu's proposed visit to Gujarat and told me so plainly,' Desai recollected in his memoirs.[99]

In 1950, Vallabhbhai shared his views with Taya Zinkin, a journalist and the wife of a British Indian civil servant, 'that he had been very careful indeed not to reinstate any of the officers who had gone over to Subhash [sic] Bose's INA. Vallabhbhai told her that he 'also saw to it that they did not thrive in politics'.[100]

Speaking to Zinkin around 1959–60, Jawaharlal probably made the most explicit admission about his relation with Subhas, when he told her,

It is true, I did let Subhash down. I did it because I had realised that, at that
stage, whatever one's views might be about the way India should develop,
Gandhi was India. Anything which weakened Gandhi, weakened India.
So I subordinated myself to Gandhi, although I was in agreement with
what Subhas was trying to do. I suppose it is right to say that I let him
down. India had to come before either of us.[101]

~

Subhas's first recorded reference to fascism appears in his first speech as
the mayor of the Calcutta Corporation on 24 September 1930. Presenting
his plan and recollecting the programme adopted by Chittaranjan Das,
he said, 'we have here in this policy and programme a synthesis of what
modern Europe calls Socialism and Fascism'. Then, he explained what he
implied by the usage of these two terms—'We have here the justice, the
equality, the love, which is the basis of Socialism, and combined with that
we have the efficiency and discipline of Fascism as it stands in Europe
today'.[102]

Those who are susceptible to translate this statement as Subhas's early
conversion to fascism should be directed to the opinion expressed by the
British Chancellor of the Exchequer in January 1927. The Chancellor
declared, 'If I had been an Italian I am sure I would have been wholeheartedly
from start to finish with Fascismo's triumphant struggle against the
bestial appetites and passions of Leninism'. About Mussolini, who was
once recruited by Samuel Hoare as a British agent at a weekly payment of
GBP 100, he added, 'I could not help being charmed, as so many other
people have been, by his gentle, simple bearing and his calm, detached
poise, despite so many burdens and dangers.'[103] The man who appeared
to be a deep admirer of Mussolini and fascism was Winston Churchill. It
has been argued by some scholars that until Italy attacked Abyssinia (now
Ethiopia) in 1935, Mussolini and his politics was widely admired. Among
the Indians who would find Mussolini worthy of appreciation were Suniti
Chatterjee, Syama Prasad Mookerjee, Binoy Kumar Sircar, and no less,
Tagore and Gandhi as well.[104] George Bernard Shaw, to whom Jawaharlal
Nehru wrote in 1948, 'I suppose a part of myself, such as I am today, has
been moulded by that reading [of your books]', proclaimed in a public
speech in December 1933 about Mussolini's political programme of
creating a corporate state, 'I say "Hear, hear! More power to your elbow."

That is precisely what the Fabian Society wants to have done, because it is clearly a necessary part of socialism.'[105]

These were days when one could say a few good things about fascism without being branded a fascist. And clearly, Subhas, instead of being an ideologue, was trying to pick elements from different systems that he believed would be good for the country. This idea of synthesis stands in stark contrast to the bloody conflict between the communists and the fascists. His idea of a synthesis would generate a controversy nearly eight years later, and he would clarify his ideas further then.

Subhas had his direct exposure to fascism and National Socialism (Nazism) about three years later when he was exiled from India.

The central theme of all his activities in Europe during his stay there, from March 1933 to March 1936, was to generate support for India's independence movement. His approach was eclectic, without any ideological inclination, which included efforts at improving trade and cultural ties with the countries that he visited, learning more about the resistance movements and governance (especially municipal governance), and disseminating information about India. He approached the Polish embassy in Vienna with a business proposal for establishing commercial ties. He had a list of products that could find demand in the Indian market and was keen to explore the possibility of exporting Indian products to Poland. The embassy issued letters of recommendation to the State Export Institute, Chamber of Commerce and Industry, and to the Central Union of Polish Industry. After the formation of the Indian-Central European Society in May 1934, Subhas had Otto Faltis set up a branch at Warsaw. The Polish Government was receptive, but the proposals made no progress since Subhas was not able to visit again.[106]

If he was interested in the Heimwehr in Austria, he was, at the same time, keen to learn more about the Czech youth movement (Sokol) and the history of the Czechoslovakia Legion created during the First World War with British and Russian help to fight for the country's liberation from outside.[107]

Subhas's trip to Germany in July 1933, immediately after his visit to Warsaw, was organized by Lothar Frank, a member of the Nazi Party, on behalf of the Indo-German Society. Frank saw to it that every courtesy was extended to Subhas on behalf of the Government, including arranging his stay at the state guest house, Harnack-Haus. Subhas, however, would not be tied down to Government hospitality and moved out to a hotel at his own expense. His attempts to meet Hitler, with the objective of having the offensive passages in *Mein Kampf* retracted, failed. Frank mentioned that he arranged a number of interviews with the dissident leaders in the Nazi Party, from whom Subhas tried to learn about the methods of operating such secret groups.[108]

His attempts at obtaining some sort of support in Germany for India's freedom movement, however, showed no signs of any effort to please the Government. As has been correctly summarised by one of his biographers, 'Bose protested the anti-Indian actions, criticized Nazi racism directed against Indians whenever he could, and worked for positive connection between India and Germany.'[109]

Nephew Asoke Nath Bose's accounts show how Subhas engaged with the Indian students in Europe in making known his objections to the racist points of view and observations of the Nazis. On being approached by the students in Berlin and Munich, he took up the matter of insulting references to Indians in a pamphlet written by Alfred Rosenberg with the German authorities, but with no success. He guided the students in Munich to protest against the hate campaign against Indians by drafting for them a 'lengthy and strongly-worded memorandum' to the German foreign minister. This action was followed by the students in Berlin, Dresden and in other places.[110] He also issued a protest against Hermann Goering's remark that Gandhi was an anti-British Bolshevik agent. According to Lothar Frank, Subhas's efforts somewhat reduced anti-Indian reporting in the German press.[111]

Subhas himself wrote a memorandum on 5 April 1934 to Foreign Office councillor Dyckhoff, sharply critical of the German attitude towards Indians. He forcefully argued that relations between Germany and India would improve only once the attacks on Indians stopped and racial legislation, which was being considered then, withdrawn.[112]

Franz Thierfelder, the director of the German Academy in Munich, was one of the persons with whom Subhas developed a friendly relationship. Two of his letters to Thierfelder clearly demonstrate Subhas's attitude to Nazi Germany. On 7 November 1935, Subhas wrote:

> As you know, since my first visit to Germany in 1933, I have tried to improve relations between Germany and nationalist India. Unfortunately, certain situations arose which affected this friendship in an adverse manner. In fact, the new regime . . . contributed to a certain extent to the

worsening of ties that had existed earlier between India and Germany . . .
The reasons are:

1) The present pro-British attitude of the German government.
2) The race-propaganda, which among the unintelligent people in Germany, promotes a general scorn against the coloured races.
3) A disdainful attitude towards contemporary India among the highest German leaders which is evident in their writings and reports.
4) The blocking or censor of pro-Indian articles and the wilful promotion of anti-Indian articles in the German media.

In making demands to amend the situation, Subhas was a realist. In a battle of propaganda, he was careful not to create obstacles out of high morals. He was not preaching to the Germans: their political ideology was not his concern. His only concern was how they treated Indians and India:

> I consciously avoid demanding anything which might be difficult to implement. For example, if a pro-British policy brings advantages to Germany, I have no reason to demand an anti-British policy, though as Indians we would welcome any such German attitude or policy. Similarly, I do not demand that you give up your race theory, no matter how many scientific reasons we might offer against it. We only want it to be modified so that it wittingly or unwittingly, does not provoke any bad opinion about Indians. Moreover, we also do not wish for once that you write in favour of Indians in the German press if you do not want to—we only ask that you do not write against India . . . We, nationalists, will do as much for Germany as Germans do for India.[113]

Just before embarking on his journey back to India in March 1936, Subhas again wrote to Thierfelder. This time, he was as blunt as possible:

> . . . I regret that I have to return to India with the conviction that the new nationalism of Germany is not only narrow and selfish but arrogant . . . Apart from this new racial philosophy and selfish nationalism there is another factor which affects us even more. Germany in her desire to curry favour with Great Britain finds it convenient to attack India and the Indian people . . . I am still prepared to work for an understanding

between Germany and India. This understanding must be consistent with our national self-respect.[114]

In the number of articles that Subhas wrote while in Europe, his political outlook is discernible. The first political piece that he wrote on the power struggle in Austria in February 1934, between the ruling combine of Christian Socials and Heimwehr, and the socialists and Nazis—'The Austrian Riddle'—was published in the April 1934 issue of *The Modern Review*. It was an objective analysis, but Subhas found the suppression of the socialists to be 'a tragedy of history'. He found an article that argued for a rapprochement between the Catholic Church and socialism in Austria to be exceedingly well-written. As a 'student of history' he forecast that 'the German-speaking peoples of Germany and Austria should ultimately be drawn into one political unit.'[115]

While being in prison in 1935, Jawaharlal must have been reading some of Subhas's pieces published in the Indian press. His prison diary's entry on 19 March 1935 indicates that he did not like what he had read. Since 'The Austrian Riddle' was the only major political article written by Subhas before that date, Jawaharlal in all likelihood referred to that article. He was also probably the first leader of a natural stature to insinuate that Subhas was a fascist: 'Subhas seems to be writing a deal of nonsense. He can only think in terms of being himself a Mussolini.'[116]

Soon after Italy's invasion of Ethiopia in October 1935, Subhas wrote another article, 'The Secret of Abyssinia and its Lessons', which was published in *The Modern Review* in November 1935. The invasion followed the imperialist logic of the West, he argued. The lesson to be drawn from the attack was that 'in the 20th century a nation can hope to be free only if it is strong, from a physical and military point of view, and able to acquire all the knowledge which modern science can impart'. He was clear that Italy was doing wrong to Ethiopia and found it strange that yet the country was criticizing 'other imperialist powers hoping thereby to secure mitigation of the wrong that she is doing to Abyssinia'. Later, he would term the Italian aggression as 'rape of Abyssinia'.[117] Explaining in minute details the equations of power play between the western forces, Subhas raised the question of why the Indian troops were sent by the British Government to Ethiopia. It was done, he explained, 'with the idea of committing Indian support to British policy in Abyssinia and on the other hand, to remind Italy that the vast resources of India are behind Great Britain'.[118]

Subhas kept writing analytical pieces until the end of 1937, around the time of his European tour, before taking up the Congress president's post.

In August 1937, while recuperating at Dalhousie, he wrote his assessment of the past, present and future politics of Europe. Partly goaded by the rise of Germany under Hitler, the Soviet Union was focusing on building up socialism within its boundaries, moving away from its attempts to stir up revolutions in other countries. The League of Nations had failed in its objectives with Japan, Germany and the United States having decided to stay out of it. The rise of Nazi Germany changed the power equations in Europe, leading to the Laval–Mussolini Pact due to which Italy gave up its territorial ambitions in Europe, and the Franco–Soviet Pact aiming to envelope Nazi Germany in order to reduce the threat from its rising military power and ambition. Although Britain at first challenged Italy over Abyssinia, it had to beat 'a quick retreat before the bluff and swagger of Mussolini'. Thus humiliated, Britain had 'set about strengthening her naval and aerial bases in the Mediterranean', with Italy replying by intervening in the Spanish civil war. Germany was wary of getting into a war with Britain and would take all measures to avoid it. Subhas believed that 'One thing is certain. If war comes, it will come as the result of a German challenge to the status quo in Central and Eastern Europe'. But would a war happen? Subhas thought that it depended on Britain. War would break out if Germany was sure that Britain and France would remain neutral. Although, Subhas was more or less certain some time before that war was going to break out in Europe in the next two to three years, he seemed to be less certain then.[119]

He wrote that Germany under Hitler, 'an incalculable factor', 'has been dreaming dreams which can be fulfilled only through the arbitrament of war'. 'Drang Nach Osten' (Drive to the East) was the one phrase that summed up the political doctrine of Nazi Germany, a doctrine which postulated that 'Germany should give up the idea of being a naval or colonial power', and instead focus on expansion on the continent towards the East, to become a continental power. Germany's new social philosophy, Subhas explained, was 'the purification and strengthening of the German race through the elimination of Jewish influence and a return to the soil'. In practical politics, he predicted, this meant annexation of Austria, Memel, Danzig, the German-speaking part of Czechoslovakia, the Polish corridor and the Silesian coalfields, Ukraine and possibly also of the German-speaking parts of Switzerland, Italian Tyrol and other adjoining countries.

Soon thereafter, Subhas wrote his analysis of the war between China and Japan, which was published in October 1937. About a year and a half before, while addressing a meeting in Paris, he had observed that 'It is necessary for us to think of the means of preventing the growth of Japanese imperialism in Asia'. He had argued for the need of a strong and unified China and India to act as a counterbalance to Japanese imperialism.[120] Now, tracing the history of conflict between Japan and other Asian countries, the economic imperatives of Japan and her relation with the western powers vis-à-vis their strategic interests, Subhas concluded:

> . . . with all our admiration for Japan, where such admiration is due, our whole heart goes to China in her hour of trial. China must still live—for her own sake and for humanity. Out of the ashes of this conflict she will once again rise phoenix-like as she has so often done in the past.[121]

The striking feature of all these articles is a clear-headed analysis from a seasoned observer of international politics. The critique of British imperialism is of course there, but equally discernible is the clear stand taken by Subhas against the expansionist positions of Italy, Germany and Japan. There is not the slightest hint of any affinity towards these three powers, although all of them were aligning against England. More stress is laid on the objective analysis of international developments than on moral judgements on the internal issues of these countries.

~

Was Subhas anti-Semitic?

As seen at the beginning of the chapter, there have been insinuations that Subhas harboured anti-Semitism. It is often pointed out that before he joined the Axis, Subhas had opposed Jawaharlal's idea that the European Jews could be given sanctuary in India. The fact of the matter is that Jawaharlal's resolution was turned down by the working committee of Congress on which occasion, Subhas, by Jawaharlal's own admission, 'didn't express himself definitely'. Subhas wrote that he was 'astounded' that Jawaharlal moved such a resolution and explained his attitude:

> Foreign policy is a realistic affair to be determined largely from the point of view of a nation's self-interest. . . . Frothy sentiments and pious

platitudes do not make foreign policy. It is no use championing lost causes all the time and it is no use condemning countries like Germany and Italy on the one hand and on the other, giving a certificate of good conduct to British and French imperialism.[122]

Jawaharlal's own thinking came to light from his correspondence with Subhas later in the aftermath of the Tripuri controversy. In his letter dated 3 April 1939, Jawaharlal clarified that 'It was not from the point of view of helping Jews that I considered this question, though such help was desirable where possible without detriment to our country, but from the point of view of helping ourselves by getting first-rate men for our science, industry, etc. on very moderate payment. . . . Their coming here on low salaries would have helped us also to bring down other salaries'.[123]

On a personal level, Subhas was as humane and enlightened as any other Cambridge alumni like him. Between 1933 and 1939, for example, he had for friends Kitty and Alex, a sensitive, newly married Jewish couple in Berlin. After being advised by Subhas, the couple went to the US, and from her Massachusetts home in 1965, Kitty Kurti wrote her tribute for 'Netaji'—a book titled *Subhas Chandra Subhas as I Knew Him*. In it, she wrote that Subhas 'did not attempt to hide' from her his deep contempt for the Nazis. In the same vein, he cited India's exploitation by British imperialism and explained why he had to do business with the Nazis. 'It is dreadful but it must be done. India must gain her independence, cost what it may,'[124] he told the couple after a meeting with Hermann Göring. Of Jews, Subhas said, 'they are an old and fine race' gifted with 'depth and insight' and felt that they had been 'miserably persecuted'[125] across the centuries.

~

As far as reaching out to Germany and Italy for help is concerned, certain facts are conveniently ignored or forgotten before levelling the allegation that he went over to the enemy.

Firstly, as seen in the earlier chapters, from the conception of his plan to go out of India, Subhas had settled the question of his destination—it was the Soviet Union, and Germany or Japan were not even under consideration. Even Lala Shankarlal's trip to Japan was with the aim of getting in touch with the Soviet embassy in Tokyo. Subhas had ended up in Berlin and Rome only because the German and Italian legations in Kabul had opened their doors to him when the Russians were reluctant. As Pietro Quaroni, the Italian ambassador in Afghanistan told Louis Fischer:

> Bose waited for more than a month in Kabul for his Soviet Visa. The Russians could not make up their minds to admit him. Finally the German minister in Kabul asked Berlin to intercede in Moscow. The Russians did not want him in Russia.[126]

It is difficult to answer if Subhas would have chosen Germany as his destination in view of the ideological outpourings against the atrocities committed by the Nazi regime in the Indian press by the Indian intelligentsia and politicians. Newspapers were full of stories about the inhuman treatment by the Nazis of Jews and Indians, alongside people from other vanquished countries. Even his own journal, the *Forward Bloc*, had run commentaries on the imperialist and authoritarian regimes of Germany and Japan.

Secondly, the constant principle that Subhas followed was that of national interest above everything else, including internal politics of other countries. In his presidential address at Haripura, Subhas stated clearly:

> In connection with our foreign policy, the first suggestion that I have to make is that we should not be influenced by the internal politics of any country or the form of its state. We shall find in every country men and women who will sympathise with Indian, freedom, no matter what their own political views may be. In this matter we should take a leaf out of Soviet diplomacy. Though Soviet Russia is a communist state, her diplomats have not hesitated to make alliances with non-socialist states and have not declined sympathy or support coming from any quarter.[127]

The only reason that he could not include the examples of Russia's non-aggression pact with Germany and the division of spoils in Poland and its subsequent alliance with Churchill's England was that they were to happen in the future. It was England's interest that spurred Churchill to hold Stalin's hand. The estimated 1–1.1 crore deaths (revised in recent times from the earlier estimates of 2–3 crore) did not stir his conscience or that of those who wax eloquent about his strategy. 17 lakh people were arrested in the Soviet Union in 1937–38 alone, of whom 8,18,000 were supposed to have been shot.[128]

Subhas repeated his argument during a broadcast over the Azad Hind Radio on 31 August 1942:

> Do not be carried away by ideological considerations; do not bother about the internal politics of other countries, which is no concern of ours. Believe me when I say that the enemies of British imperialism are our friends and allies. It is to their interest to see the British Empire broken up, and India is once again free.[129]

Subhas's reaching out to Nazi Germany was in continuation of existing contacts between Germany and Indian patriots in the national interests of their respective countries. Girija Mookerjee, who was with Bose in Germany in between 1941–43, explained that 'even Imperial Germany during the World War I had taken up the cause of Indian independence and the German Foreign Office had, therefore, a precedent to go by':

> Men who weighed this question at the German Foreign Office were men of career, who were neither National Socialists nor did they belong to the inner coteries of Hitler. They were German civil servants who performed their duties as good German citizens during the war. These men, guided by the desire to advance German national interests in India, thought it advisable for political reasons to support the movement sponsored by Netaji in Germany.[130]

In his first radio broadcast from Berlin on 1 May 1942, Subhas stated that 'my concern is, however, with India, and if I may add further, with India alone'. When he raised with Hitler, at their meeting on 27 May 1942, the issue of his disparaging comment about Indians in *Mein Kampf*, Hitler answered that his words were 'directed at certain tendencies among the suppressed peoples to form a united front against their oppressors'.[131] Churchill, on the other hand, was never asked for an explanation of his disparaging comments on Indians, by those who opposed Subhas, so he never had to offer any explanation.

Subhas was naturally grateful to the Italians, Germans and the Japanese for all their help, but remained clear-headed about the leaders, their power equations and their own political posturing. Focused on extracting the help required for India's liberation from a reluctant Hitler, Subhas had to play along the game of propaganda and do what was required to win a battle of perception. While it was imperative for him to portray the Axis bloc as a valuable and trusted ally, it was equally important for them to show the British that he had been won over.

Yet, the reality was that he was there seeking help, not as an armchair critic. His purpose was to obtain as much help as possible without compromising on self-respect or India's interest. There is little doubt that he achieved whatever little was possible under those conditions admirably. 'He wanted to keep his own liberty of action and he did not want to be branded as pro-Nazi,' recalled Girija Mookerjee.[132] And when it was required, he did not mince words. During his meeting with Hitler, for instance, irritated by the dictator's patronizing attitude, he shot back, asking Adam von Trott zu Solz to 'Please tell His Excellency that I have been in politics all my life and that I do not need advice from anyone.'[133] Bose's personal assessment of Hitler was that he 'was a German version of the Fakir of Ipi'.[134]

It would not be an exaggeration to state that Gandhi and Jawaharlal were far closer to the British in mind and spirit (despite being on opposite sides) than Subhas was ever with the Axis leaders despite being dependent on their help.

There is considerable data by way of the statements of those who mattered, official records and sworn testimonies to prove that all such assumptions about Subhas and the Japanese are not correct.

In 1972, Bose's military secretary, Colonel Mahboob Ahmed, then a senior Ministry of External Affairs (MEA) official, in his deposition before the Khosla Commission stated:

> There was a great deal of respect for Netaji for his personality, for his person, amongst the Japanese that we came across, and his relation with the Japanese government was that of the two interests at that stage coinciding. That is to get the British out of India.

On his part, Subhas was never a fair-weather friend. At the close of the war, a Japanese Government communication to him in June 1945 referred to their 'spiritual' ties and said:

> Nippon Government pays deep respect with its whole heart to Your Excellency's cooperation with Nippon on the moral strength to the

utmost in order to attain Indian independence without resorting in the
least to the opportunism of following in the wake of the powerful in spite
of the present unfavourable world situation to Nippon.[135]

The National Archive in Melbourne, Australia, has a file on Subhas
made up of formerly secret German–Japanese diplomatic communication
intercepted by the Australian Navy. On 30 July 1943, Japanese Ambassador
Hiroshi Oshima sent this account of his conversation with Hitler about
Subhas:

> Speaking of Bose, I said: 'It was good of you to think of sending Bose to
> East Asia. We thank you very much . . . He is working hard on plans to
> bring India into line. The Japanese government too has absolute faith in
> him and is giving him carte blanche where India is concerned.'
>
> Hitler answered: 'Yes, I am very satisfied with what Bose is doing.'[136]

What it meant was explained in a report titled 'INA's role in Imphal
battle', filed in *The Hindu* on 10 December 1945. During the Red Fort
trials, General Tadasu Katakura, Chief of the Japanese staff of Burma Area
Army, testified that 'though INA troops had come [to be under] overall
Japanese command, they . . . had their own operational assignment'.

At the Red Fort trial, the defence counsel called five Japanese witnesses
who had been closely involved with the INA. Ohta Saburo of the Japanese
Foreign Ministry produced documentary evidence that Japan recognized
the free and independent status of the Azad Hind Government. Mastumoto
Shunichi, Vice-Minister of Foreign Affairs and chief of the Treaty Bureau
during the war, testified that the Japanese Government had helped Subhas
and the INA for two reasons: to promote Japan's own war aims and also
to help India achieve independence, which was one of Japan's war aims.
Lieutenant General Tadasu Katakura testified that that the Japanese Army
never used the INA soldiers as labourers.[137]

Those keen on passing a moral judgement on Subhas's pact with the
devil would do well to apply the holier-than-thou outlook on free India's
conduct and come up with a similar snap judgement.

In 1980, Indira Gandhi said of Subhas Bose that while he was a
patriot, 'because of our strong feelings against fascism and Nazism, we
could not approve of any alliance with Hitler's Germany or Japan'.[138] But,
since 1947, New Delhi has extended a friendly hand to all sorts of leaders

reviled, especially in the Western world, as the worst dictators and tyrants of our times. The list includes Libyan leader Muammar Gaddafi, Nicolae Ceausescu of Romania and Robert Mugabe of Zimbabwe, the last ranked No. 1 in the Forbes' list of world's ten worst dictators in 2011.[139] Mugabe was once compared to Adolf Hitler by Britain. He took it as a compliment, proclaiming 'Let me be Hitler tenfold'.[140] India continues to enjoy friendly relations with Kim Jong-un's regime in North Korea. According to an official note put up on the website of the Indian embassy in Pyongyang, the relations between both the nations are 'generally characterised by friendship, cooperation and understanding'. It further tells us that India and North Korea have a 'commonality of views' on many issues such as disarmament.[141] This is notwithstanding the fact that North Korea has been more supportive of Pakistan on the issue of Jammu and Kashmir, and is widely believed to have defence ties with India's sworn enemy in the fields of ballistic missiles and nuclear technology. 'India reaches out, wants to upgrade ties with North Korea', read a story in *The Hindu* on 16 September, 2015.[142] The Americans were not very pleased about the India–North Korea friendship, but then we had our national interest to think of first, not America's.

It is not Aung San Suu Kyi, the winner of the Nobel Peace Prize and the Jawaharlal Nehru Award, but the Burmese junta which received the most support from the land of Gandhi when they were in charge. Cut to our times—India has virtually turned a blind eye to the allegations that the Burmese under Suu Kyi's leadership engaged in 'ethnic cleansing' of the Rohingyas. All we are hearing from our Government is that we have our own security concerns first.

In fact, it has been argued that 'Mahatma Gandhi was "accommodative" of violence of the Arab Palestinians, even as he advised the Jewish people to counter Germany's ruler Adolf Hitler through non-violence', in a 2017 book *Squaring the Circle: Mahatma Gandhi and the Jewish National Home* by P.R. Kumaraswamy of the Jawaharlal Nehru University's School of International Studies. According to a report in *The Hindu*, Kumaraswamy contends that 'some of the writings of the Mahatma on Israel were not brought to the public by his secretary Pyarelal'. He further told the paper that Mahatma 'had imbibed Islam and Christianity's "anti-Jewish prejudices".'[143] This might be disputed, but there is no running away from the fact that so long as Nehru and his family ruled India, Israel was not allowed to open its embassy in New Delhi. Why? On 16 February 2005,

The Guardian (London) carried an article by Israeli historian Benny Morris on the recently discovered correspondence between Albert Einstein and Jawaharlal Nehru on the necessity of India's support for the birth of a Jewish state. Giving moral and historical arguments in his four-page letter of 13 June 1947, the great scientist appealed to Nehru as a 'consistent champion of the forces of political and economic enlightenment' to rule in favour of 'the rights of an ancient people whose roots are in the East'. Nehru's July 11 answer was that national leaders, 'unfortunately', had to pursue 'policies. . . [that were] essentially selfish policies':

> Each country thinks of its own interest first . . . If it so happens that some international policy fits in with the national policy of the country, then that nation uses brave language about international betterment. But as soon as that international policy seems to run counter to national interests or selfishness, then a host of reasons are found not to follow that international policy.[144]
>
> On 29 November, India voted at the United Nations General Assembly with 12 Islamic countries against the partition of Palestine, and against the formation of a Jewish State. Noted activist Balraj Puri, who received honours such as the Padma Bhushan and the Indira Gandhi Award for National Integration, testified that Nehru too placed national interest above everything else. In his book *Kashmir: Towards Insurgency*, which was praised by former prime minister Dr Manmohan Singh, Puri recalled Nehru telling him in a private conversation in 1953 that India had 'gambled on the international stage on Kashmir' and consequently, 'till things improve, democracy and morality can wait. National interest is more important than democracy . . .'[145]

The standard Indian version of Bose's interaction with Nazi Germany, as articulated by most intellectuals and thinkers, does not take the idea of 'national interest first' into consideration. Senior journalist Sumit Mitra, writing in *The Telegraph* (Kolkata) of 17 April 2005, harangued that Bose was sitting 'in the lap of Hitler when the air of Auschwitz was acrid with the smell of the gas chamber'. The fact is that when Bose arrived in Berlin, the gas chambers had not yet started operating. The Holocaust began much later and there is nothing to show that Bose or anyone in his team had any clue about it. The world discovered the horrors of the Holocaust only after the war ended, by which time Bose was in Southeast Asia, planning his future course of action, and looking at the endgame. After visiting Auschwitz (former Nazi death camp in Poland), prime minister Benjamin Netanyahu remarked the following on 13 June 2013, according to the leading Israeli daily *Haaretz*: 'The Allied leaders knew about the Holocaust as it was happening. They understood perfectly what was taking place in the death camps. They were asked to act, they could have acted, and they did not.'[146] Bearing him out was this revelation in *The Independent* (London) of 17 April 2017:

> Newly accessed material from the United Nations—not seen for around 70 years—shows that as early as December 1942, the US, UK and Soviet governments were aware that at least two million Jews had been murdered and a further five million were at risk of being killed, and were preparing charges. Despite this, the Allied Powers did very little to try and rescue or provide sanctuary to those in mortal danger.[147]

~

Then there is the 'what if' scenario of Germany or Japan occupying India after driving out the British. The Japanese atrocities in the Andaman and Nicobar Islands are presented as evidence of what could have happened in mainland India had they stepped in.

According to the archival documents-based study of historian T.R. Sareen[148] the British and Indian officials evacuated the islands by the end of February 1942, taking along with them about 180 military convicts belonging to the Central India Horse, who were found to be pro-Japanese. A scorched earth policy ensured that vital infrastructural facilities were destroyed so as not to fall into Japanese hands. Over 6000 convicts were left behind, about 4500 of whom had been living under supervision—about 606 in the Cellular Jail while the rest were free. After the Japanese naval forces occupied the islands, the responsibility of their administration was left to a civilian governor. The administration was supported by committees set up with the inhabitants as members—for instance, the Peace Preservation Committee. The new administration, headed and manned by Indians, aimed to utilize the old government system as much as possible and retained some key officials such as the superintendent of police.

A branch of the Indian Independence League (IIL) was established within a fortnight of the Japanese occupation. Due to the lack of interest among government officials (many of whom were worried that payments to their families in India would stop if the British Government came to know of their anti-British activities) and absence of nationalist sentiment amongst the criminal convicts who formed the bulk of the islands' population, the IIL had a very slow start.

Problems started with the bombing by the Allied air force of the islands and the Japanese supply ships, compelling the Japanese and Indian administrators to round up many inhabitants on the suspicion of pro-British attitude and of supplying information to the British secretly. The administrative charge soon passed from the civilian governor to the Japanese naval commander, Rear Admiral S. Ishikawa. Persecution of the inhabitants intensified with the increasing Allied air raids of even secret Japanese targets, and the inability of the civil administration to expose the suspected spy network. As noted by Sareen, 'by the beginning of 1943, the British intelligence was remarkably well-informed about the state of affairs in the Andamans'. Apart from air reconnaissance and the network of loyal agents left behind, the Allied forces landed small reconnaissance patrols by submarines. Intrigues among the Indian subordinate staff, aimed at gaining favours from the Japanese, exacerbated the situation. A large number of people were arrested, tortured and even hanged and shot by firing squad.

When Subhas visited the islands, the extent of atrocities had declined and there was no reason for him to suspect any foul play. According to his personal physician Dr Raju, who had accompanied him, the Japanese did bring to his notice that the islands were full of British spies. After A.D. Loganadan took charge as the Chief Commissioner in March 1944 and served in that capacity for nearly seven months, he too apprised Subhas of the problem of spies, making all efforts to secure the handling of the spy cases by the Azad Hind Government. His intervention went on to save a number of lives and improved the overall situation. Unhappy with the speed of handover of administrative departments to the Azad Hind Government, Subhas called back Loganadan, who had left the Andamans in October 1944, leaving Major A.A. Alvi to act as officiating Chief Commissioner. The situation continued to improve and in February 1945, the Japanese Governor announced that no more unfounded spy cases would be taken up and that these would be decided in cooperation with the Azad Hind Government.

Right after independence, the question of how to remember this episode came up amongst India's politicians and policymakers. While a number of parliamentarians kept raising the issue of renaming the islands as Shahid and Swaraj in the fashion of Subhas, the ruling dispensation did not give any indication that that issue even mattered to them. In fact, in response to H.V. Kamath's question in 1951, the then home minister, C. Rajagopalachari, went to the extent of saying that his Government had no information that the Provisional Government of Free India under Subhas had ever renamed the islands.[149]

Moving a resolution in the Lok Sabha on 11 March 1960 to rename the islands as Shahid and Swaraj, Subiman Ghose of the Forward Bloc said, 'I am offering an opportunity to the Government to liquidate a fraction of the huge debt that the country owes to Azad Hind Fauj and its supreme commander'. The minister of state for home affairs, B.N. Datar requested Ghose to withdraw his resolution on the grounds that 'there have been many martyrs in different parts of India, and there have been many places associated with the martyrdom of a number of great martyrs, whose services have brought Swaraj to India', and, therefore, 'whenever any memorial has to be raised, then it ought not to be in respect of a far-flung island, but it should be on the mainland itself'. 'I thought that the Tripuri episode had been forgotten but I think up till now that has not been forgotten', Ghose quipped.[150]

In 1969, in response to points raised by Samar Guha, the then home minister, Y.B. Chavan, informed that the people of the islands, represented by the ministry's consultative committee, were not keen to change the name. What he conveniently omitted was that the members of the committee were nominated by his Government and, therefore, would only follow the Government's line. When Guha introduced a private member's Bill in Lok Sabha in 1978 for renaming the islands, home minister Charan Singh coaxed him to withdraw it, with the assurance that Guha would get a chance to present his case to the consultative committee, which had been transformed by the Janata Government into an elected body. The Member of Parliament from Andaman and Nicobar at that point suggested a referendum among the people of the island. With the fall of the Government before long, nothing was achieved.[151]

The demand has persisted since then, but no Government appeared to have given it serious thought until the current NDA Government took the decision to commemorate the achievements of Subhas and his INA on the platinum jubilee of the setting up of the Provisional Government of Free India.

Did the Japanese really want to conquer India? The most definitive answer on this comes from an investigation carried out by the British Government after the war was over. An inquiry was conducted by the British Government in May 1948 to find an answer to the question whether the Japanese ever seriously contemplated an invasion of India. Lt Col J.G. Figges, the assistant military adviser to the United Kingdom Liaison Mission in Japan interrogated six senior officers of the Japanese navy and eight senior officers of the Japanese army. Following the interrogation of the navy officers, Figges came to the conclusion that 'neither the Japanese Government nor the High Command ever seriously considered invading India by sea'.

Colonel Takashi Katakura, the wartime Senior Staff Officer (Operations) of the Burma Area Army told Figges the inside story of the Japanese Arakan and Imphal campaigns. Figges reported about Katakura's statement that:

> . . . the orders as received by his Army from the higher formation called only for an attack against the British Army with limited objectives. The object, he stated, was to clear Burma of the British and to establish a series of defensive strong points from which to repel any subsequent British attempts to enter Burma . . . General [Tateki] AYABE, commanding Burma Area Army, went to Tokyo to urge a reconsideration of the plan. He was particularly worried by the inadequacy of the supply and transport resources for such a deep advance (280 km) and also by the fact that the attack would have to be made almost entirely without air support in face of growing British air strength . . . But in Tokyo, General AYABE's pleas fell on deaf ears and he was told to carry on with the operation. One cannot help feeling that in this almost brutal rejection of a reasoned argument by a respected Commander in the field, the higher authorities in Tokyo must have been influenced by arguments from some outside source. The explanation would seem to be Subhas Chandra Bose's colourful one-man propaganda.

Major General Momoyo Kunomura, Chief of Staff of the Japanese 15th Army, explained to Figges that the Japanese army had clear orders against the deep penetration of India. The plan of the campaigns was that the Japanese 33rd Division would defeat the main British forces in a frontal attack and subsequently draw off other British forces in reserve. At a later stage, the 31st and the 15th Divisions would cross the Chindwin River, thus encircling the British forces. This would give the opportunity to the INA to march across the frontier without opposition. Figges reported that 'according to several Japanese officers who were engaged in these operations, they did not, even up to the last, entirely abandon hope that Subhas Chandra Bose would in fact be able to turn their defeat into victory'. Based on the interrogations, Figges concluded that:

> . . . the Japanese Higher Command did not seriously contemplate an invasion of India by land in 1944. They did, however, hope to inflict such a serious defeat on the British Indian forces that Subhas Chandra Bose would be able to lead his Indian National Army unopposed into India and thus achieve virtually a bloodless conquest.[152]

It is doubtful as to how many people who raise the objection on the basis of this 'what if' scenario realize that it was the creation of a shrewd British mind, and no less than that of Winston Churchill. On 30 April 1937, Churchill wrote to Ghanshyamdas Birla:

> You should seriously consider the present state of the world. If Great Britain were persuaded or forced for any cause, Indian or European, to withdraw her protection from India, it would continuously become the prey of Fascist dictator nations, Italy, Germany or Japan and then indeed with the modern facilities there would be a severity of government even worse than any experienced in bygone ages. The duty of the Indian electorate and of Congress is to take up the great task which has been offered them, and show that they can make India a happier country; and at the same time do everything they can to win the confidence of Great Britain, and offer to her gratitude and loyalty for being the guardian of Parliamentary government and Indian peace.[153]

~

There is little doubt about Subhas's overall socialist outlook, his emphasis on the State's critical and primary role in the removal of industrial backwardness, poverty and social evils. Time and again he declared himself to be a socialist and after Congress presidential elections, the pivot of his politics was leftism. What then was his brand of leftism?

Subhas's interest in workers' and peasants' issues manifested early in his political career, when he planned to form a political outfit called the Young Bengal Party in 1923, with the aim of attaining complete independence.[154] The party programme included advocacy of pro-labour issues such as stopping the exploitation of workers, fixing minimum wage, no cut in wages during periods of illness, accident compensation and pension. The rights of the peasants would include stoppage of unjust collection, maximum rate of interests for loans, full freedom to fell trees, dig wells and tanks and the construction of buildings, freedom to transfer land rights, and landownership rights.

By the time Subhas entered politics, the Bolshevik revolution had made a deep impact on the Bengal revolutionary circles, among which many were his close friends. Many of the leading revolutionaries, though not yet converts, were trying to grasp the import of the events and the terminologies. The name of Lenin had permeated into the countryside and in Calcutta, 'references to Lenin and the Russian revolution became more and more frequent' in newspapers and journals such as *Sankha*, *Bijolee*, *Atmashakti*, *Bengalee*, *Dainik Basumati* and *The Modern Review*. Upendranath Banerjee's articles were leaning towards socialism, Sachindranath Sanyal was writing a biography of Lenin, Hemanta Sarkar was advocating 'Karl Marx's socialism and Lenin's Bolshevist concept', Atul Sen of Dacca wrote a book on the revolutionary transformation of Russia, with a preface by Chittaranjan Das, Nazrul Islam wrote a short story in which a character crosses over to communist Russia, Khitish Prasad Chattopadhyay met M.N. Roy, Virendranath Chattopadhyay and Abani Mukherjee in Berlin and revolutionaries like Satis Pakrasi and Bhupendra Kumar Datta were voraciously reading up on the new ideology.[155]

Intelligence agencies were being fed with information and often plain rumours by informers about Subhas's links with communism. It was reported that he wrote to Ramananda Chatterjee's son in Cambridge, requesting him 'to find out the best method of introducing communism into India' as it was the only method of India's salvation. In August 1922, Subhas and Chiraranjan were invited by M.N. Roy to attend the fourth Congress of the Communist International to be held in Moscow in December that year. However, the police informer also noted that Subhas was unwilling to accept the invitation. In February 1923, a letter from the Communist International, addressed to Subhas as the editor of *Banglar Katha*, was intercepted by the police. It also came to the notice of the intelligence officers that Subhas had received another letter from M.N. Roy, in which he discussed cooperation with the Swarajya party and asked Subhas to go to Germany along with some 'brilliant boys' to obtain training in communist revolutionary methods.[156]

There cannot be any doubt about Subhas's increasing exposure to the gradually consolidating communist movement, and that few of his friends in the revolutionary groups were strongly attracted towards communism. However, most of the information provided by informers to the intelligence departments was hardly more than market gossip. His writings from that period, later published as the book *Taruner Swapno*, show no leaning towards the international or Indian communist movement. Rather, his reaction to the Bengal Government's offer in April 1927, to free him if he agreed to go to Europe and not return to India before the expiration of the Bengal Ordinance in 1930, provides a clear insight into his view on the Indian communist movement and its international linkages. Subhas was apprehensive that he would be falsely implicated by Government agents abroad if he accepted the offer. 'I am almost sure that however cautious, and even timid, I may be during my stay in Europe', Subhas wrote to Sarat:

> All my caution and even timidity will be put down as shrewdness and cunning and all sorts of sinister activities, of which I shall be the author, will be imagined where there are none . . . It is thus possible that by the time 1929 draws near, I shall have been painted as a Bolshevik agent (for in Europe there is only one nightmare today viz. the Bolshevik nightmare) of the darkest dye . . .
>
> If I had the remotest intention of becoming a Bolshevik agent, I would have jumped at the offer made and taken the first available boat to Europe. If I succeeded in recouping my health, I could then have joined the gay band who trot about from Paris to Leningrad talking of world revolution and emitting blood and thunder in their utterances. But I have no such ambition or desire.[157]

Once out of jail, Subhas started taking part in labour movements. When 14,000 workers in the East India Railway workshops in Lilooah went on a strike in March 1928, Subhas issued a public appeal for financial aid to the striking workers. Responding to a reception by the Bengal Nagpur Railway Indian Labour Union at Kharagpur, he asked them too to come forward to help the striking labourers and stressed on the need to achieve unity amongst their ranks. He also intervened in the strikes by workers in the jute mills in Howrah and Rishra.[158]

His initiation into the role of a political leader representing labour interests took place when he was sought both by the striking workers and the management to find a resolution to a labour strike at the Tata Iron and Steel Company (TISCO) at Jamshedpur, in August 1928. As the newly elected president of the Jamshedpur Labour Association (JLA), Subhas worked out a settlement between the striking workers, who were showing signs of exhaustion, and a stubborn TISCO management opposed to conciliation, which he believed to be the best possible solution under the circumstances, but which nonetheless left a section of workers dissatisfied.[159] A local lawyer, Manek Homi, who led the striking workers before Subhas's arrival and had a role in inviting him to Jamshedpur, opposed the settlement and formed a rival union called Jamshedpur Labour Federation (JLF). While Homi was stationed in Jamshedpur, Subhas, with his increasing role in provincial and national politics, could spare only a limited amount of time to the labour association's work.

The next year, his involvement in labour activities continued through a strike at the Golmuri Tinplate factory, owned by the Burmah Oil Company (BOC, with two-thirds stake) and TISCO (one-third). A dispute arose over payment of wages and suspension and lock-out of workers at the beginning of the year. Homi, who led the Golmuri Tinplate Workers' Union (GTWU) then, arrived at a settlement with the management. However, a strike by the workers began in early April, which was opposed by Homi, who saw the hands of the Bengali workers behind it, complicated by the Congress's attempts to capture the labour movement. The striking workers contacted Jawaharlal, V.V. Giri, N.M. Joshi and asked Subhas to intervene. Jawaharlal addressed the workers in May and Subhas arrived in June, convincing more workers to join the strike and arranging financial aid for the strikers. Subhas also mobilized workers at the Budge Budge mills of the BOC, who went on a strike in August. Jawaharlal, Subhas, Giri and Nilkantha Das again arrived at Jamshedpur. Subhas called for a boycott of BOC products and wrote to legislators in Bengal and the Central Assembly for withdrawing tariff privileges given to the Tinplate company and BOC. The workers' strike, however, fizzled out by the end of November.[160]

At the same time, Subhas took up the cause of the jute cultivators, who, he pointed out, were facing the problems of overproduction, fall in demand and unremunerative prices. As the president of the Bengal Provincial Congress Committee, he argued for restricting the production of jute by reducing jute acreage. He also argued for focusing on producing jute goods through cottage industry to reduce jute workers' dependence on large mills and extended his support to the striking jute mill workers.[161] In the Bengal Legislative Assembly, he spoke in support of an adjournment motion moved by B.C. Roy. If the modest demands of the workers for 'decent living wages' were not met, Subhas warned, 'a time would come when they would not be satisfied with the present demand'.[162]

Subhas continued to intervene in labour disputes and address workers and their unions through the subsequent years, but it was never really possible for him to take on the role of a trade union leader. Notwithstanding his interventions, he remained an outsider. Although he headed a number of unions at this time of the great depression, his focus remained on the broader picture. As a nationalist political leader, he aimed to find a common ground between Indian entrepreneurs and labour interests as much as his involvements were curtailed by frequent imprisonments. His stated goal was to have the labour force strengthen the Congress movement. As Subhas himself pointed out in his presidential address at the annual meeting of the Calcutta Corporation Employees' Association in December 1928, his position was 'anomalous'. He was at one time 'connected with the executive administration', was a councillor, connected to a political party, and also involved with the labour movement: 'You will understand that it is not very easy for one person to play so many roles at one and the same time.'[163]

Even before he got involved in the Jamshedpur disputes, Subhas made a crucial point regarding the labour movements in India. Speaking at the All-Bengal Youngmen's Conference at Basirhat in April 1928, he argued that it was critical for workers to find leaders from amongst their ranks. 'Until they could find out leaders from the labourers the movement could not be said to have a sound basis', he pointed out and warned about workers falling prey to dishonest leaders.[164]

In December 1929, Subhas succeeded Jawaharlal as the president of the All-India Trade Union Congress (AITUC), in the midst of a clash between the moderate section of the trade union leaders and the communist groups. Amidst his futile attempts to reconcile the warring factions, Subhas spoke in favour of the rising left wing in the trade union movement and about the crucial role socialism was to play in building a new India. In his presidential address at the Calcutta session of the AITUC on 4 July 1931, Subhas highlighted the problems of employment and retrenchment. Since 'Labour today wants the right to work', it became 'the duty of the state to provide employment to the citizens and where the state fails to perform this duty it should accept the responsibility of maintaining them'. He further argued for the sharing of profits by employers to ensure decent wages for and the upliftment of the living standards of the workers.[165]

Soon after the Calcutta session, however, Subhas launched a scalding attack on the 'Moscow communists and their Bengal followers', who 'followed blindly the dictates of Moscow in the matter of their ideals, methods and tactics' for disrupting the AITUC and opposing the Congress. Notably, he characterized the members of AITUC who did not subscribe to either right or the communist factions as a socialist group and probably placed himself there. The socialists, Subhas claimed, were 'prepared to work in cooperation with every other party in the country but they are not going to be dominated by any of them much less by the Moscow Communists'.[166]

'I want a socialist republic in India', he declared in 1931, although it was not possible for him at that moment to lay out the contours of such a state:

> With regard to the methods, and tactics employed by the Bolsheviks in Russia, I may say that they will not necessarily suit Indian conditions. As a proof of this, I may say that in spite of the universal and human appeal of communism, communism has not been able to make much headway in India, chiefly because the method and tactics generally employed by its protagonists are such as tend to alienate rather than win over possible friends and allies.[167]

Despite his outspokenness against India's communist party, the chief complaint against which was that they followed Moscow's line, Subhas wanted to reach out to the Soviet leadership. The Comintern had, however, already taken a critical stance against him in view of his utterances in Europe.

Before it became convenient to paint Subhas as a Nazi collaborator, the British Government tried their best to show him as a communist. In June 1935, the IPI reported that Charles Tegart, the former commissioner of police in Calcutta, had received information that if Subhas could be 'tarred with the Communist brush', plans for his reception by the mayor of Dublin and awarding a degree by the National University of Ireland could be prevented. A note was prepared in response which, despite its laborious efforts, could hardly show Subhas as a communist:

> There is little doubt that Bose's political philosophy is to some extent tinged with Communism. This is probably due to the influence of M.N. Roy, the exceptionally able ex-member of the Executive Committee of the Communist International, with whom Bose had frequent secret dealings in India in 1931 . . . Bose, indeed, relied very largely on the support of his (Roy's) powerful following which had gained control of the All India Trades Union Congress. In 1931 Bose was elected President of the Nau Jawan Bharat Sabha, virtually a Communist concern. During the earlier part of his stay in Europe (1933) Bose made several attempts to effect a rapprochement with Moscow. His chief lieutenant on the Continent was and still is an Indian Communist who was deported from Germany by the Nazis on account of his Communist intrigues. Bose was actually interviewed by a representative sent from Moscow for the purpose, but the negotiations failed to achieve the desired result. It may have been that the Communist International formed the opinion either that Bose was reluctant entirely to sever his relations with Gandhi or that he leant too much towards the particular brand of Communism practised by M.N. Roy, with whom the Communist International were not on good terms. Whatever the reason, the Communist International's press organs did not hesitate to criticise Bose somewhat severely.[168]

Subhas, on the other hand, was quite aware of the game that was being played. He would later write in the second volume of *The Indian Struggle:*

> During his stay in Europe, the writer was everywhere watched and followed by the agents of the British Government who tried their best to prevent his making contacts with different governments and with important personalities in different countries. In Fascist or pro-Fascist countries, the British agents tried to paint him as a Communist. In Socialist or democratic countries, on the other hand, they tried to describe him as a Fascist.[169]

In Haripura, Subhas responded warmly to the message from the British Communist Party acclaiming the session as a new phase in the struggle for freedom. The British intelligence claimed that Subhas had had a secret meeting with B.F. Bradley, Harry Pollitt and Rajani Palme Dutt during his England visit.[170] 'I am greatly encouraged by the attitude of the leaders of the British Communist Party whose general policy with regard to India seems to me to be in keeping with that of the Indian National Congress', Subhas said in his presidential address.

In 1939, Subhas again reached out to the Soviet Union. Through his nephew, Amiya Bose, he sent a secret letter to Russian agents in London, the whole clandestine operation being facilitated by Soli Batliwala and the Communist Party of Great Britain (CPGB), which was then the conduit for communication between the CPI and the Comintern. According to Amiya, Subhas proposed that if the Soviet Government attacked India from the North-West frontier, Subhas would organize a mass insurrection within the country.[171] The relation between the CPI and Subhas, as noted earlier, went downhill from early 1940. From Germany and Japan, Subhas criticized the CPI for the party's collaboration with the Government. His criticism, however, was not made in the same rabid manner as the CPI's was for him. In a broadcast from Berlin Radio on 28 June 1943, Subhas said:

> Soviet Communists lost a great many followers in India, because on the outbreak of the present Soviet-German War, the Indian Communist Party derided to work in close concert with British oppressors of India.[172]

In fact, in *The Indian Struggle*, Subhas had outlined the reasons why he foresaw that communism would never be adopted in India. Firstly, he wrote, communism had no sympathy with nationalism, whereas the freedom movement was a national movement. Lenin's thesis on the relation between nationalism and communism had been sidestepped after the failure of the Chinese revolution. The second reason was Russia's disinterest in sparking a world revolution, with its focus on internal affairs and a decline in its prestige due to its pacts with capitalist countries and joining of the League of Nations. Thirdly, the anti-religious and atheistic character of Russian communism would not fit into the Indian environment, where 'a national awakening is in most cases heralded by a religious reformation and a cultural renaissance'. The fifth reason, he felt, was that although communist theory had made 'certain remarkable contributions in the domain of economics' such as state planning, it was weak in other aspects such as monetary problem.[173] Later, however, he retracted his argument about the conflict between nationalism and communism at an interview with Rajani Palme Dutt in January 1938, where he said:

> I should point out also that Communism as it appeared to be demonstrated by many of those who were supposed to stand for it in India seemed to me anti-national, and this impression was further strengthened in view of the hostile attitude which several among them exhibited towards the Indian National Congress. It is clear, however, that the position today has fundamentally altered. I should add that I have always understood and am quite satisfied that Communism, as it has been expressed in the writings of Marx and Lenin and in the official statements of policy of the Communist International, gives full support to the struggle for national independence and recognises this as an integral part of its world outlook.[174]

His later utterances, however, indicate that this statement was more a tactical retreat than a change in belief.

Subhas had urged Jawaharlal to preside over the All-Bengal Students' Conference in Calcutta, held on 22 September 1928. Like Subhas, Jawaharlal too sang paeans to the youth, and had similar things to say about empowering different disadvantaged groups in the society, but the thrust of his message was very different. His was a message of socialism in contrast to nationalism. 'I have placed before you the ideals of internationalism and socialism as the only ideals worthy of the fine temper of the youth', he told them. As far as his attitude to communism was concerned, he said that:

> . . . though personally I do not agree with many of the methods of the communists and I am by no means sure to what extent communism can suit the present conditions in India, I do believe communism as an ideal of society. For essentially it is socialism, and socialism I think is the only way if the world is to escape disaster.[175]

Speaking at the same conference, Subhas outlined where he differed with Jawaharlal in the sphere of ideas. He too believed in internationalism, but not in the form which obliterated distinctive characteristics of different nations.[176] The expression of nationalism by Chittaranjan, a humanist, poet, essayist, thinker and a politician fiercely proud about his Bengali

heritage rolled into one, was in stark contrast to the critique of nationalism
by Tagore. In their quarrel, Subhas was completely on his political mentor's
side. From Mandalay Jail, he had criticized the 'shallow internationalism
in life and literature of Tagore and his school which did not realize the
fundamental truth in nationalism'.[177] He would touch upon the topic now
and then, but his speeches and writings lacked the lyrical exuberance of his
guru.

While speaking at the Maharashtra Provincial Conference, Subhas
responded to the charge of nationalism being 'narrow, selfish and aggressive'
from the perspective of 'cultural internationalism':[178] his response was more
in the nature of a political project that he envisioned rather than at an
abstract, conceptual level. He pointed out that Indian nationalism, far
from being any of these, was 'inspired by the highest ideals of the human
race, viz., Satyam (the true), Shivam (the good), Sundaram (the beautiful)':

> Nationalism in India has instilled into us truthfulness, honesty, manliness
> and the spirit of service and sacrifice. What is more, it has roused the
> creative faculties which for centuries had been lying dormant in our
> people and, as a result, we are experiences a renaissance in the domain of
> Indian art.[179]

In fact, he would return to the philosophical aspects of the independence
movement repeatedly in his speeches around this time. Organizing the
movement was the immediate problem, but equally important was to
impart a character to it. Subhas was not yet advocating a particular form of
political and social organization for independent India. Rather, he focused
on defining the components which would make up the whole, and wished to
lay the ground for post-independence reconstruction. He was preoccupied
with questions such as: What was the most desirable political system for
India's development? What were the roles of the students and the youth?
How should India balance between nationalism and internationalism?

The ideal of the youth was to break the shackles of all oppression,
injustices, and malpractices to create a new nation, he told a youth conference
at Pabna. Creation of a new order had to follow the destruction of status
quo. Subhas invoked Krishna's stern castigation of Arjun in the battlefield
of Kurukshetra—'*Klaivyam masma gamah Partha*'—as the message which
contained the essence of immortal youth. The youth movement, just like
the national movement, was not merely a political movement. It had

to weave together varying strands of art, literature, philosophy, science, commerce, and sports for the development of a national life.

He refused to stand behind any particular 'ism' at this point. No 'ism' (he referred to anarchism, socialism, communism, Bolshevism, syndicalism, republicanism, constitutional monarchy, and fascism) was adequate to lift humanity out of misery unless individual characters were strengthened. Indians, he said, had every quality except tenacity of purpose—what was needed, therefore, was the ability to sacrifice everything for the sake of an idea. As Vivekananda had pointed out, the basis of nation formation as well as of establishing an effective 'ism' was to create good human beings first. Whatever 'ism' India chose for itself, it had to be moulded in accordance with its traditions and had to answer well to the requirements of present conditions. It was equally important to pay attention to the nationalist aspect of the movement as to the internationalist aspect. The latter was required to be the foundation of lasting global peace based on common understanding, development and exchange of knowledge, and the emphasis on the latter was critical to be able to create a nation based on new ideals. The responsibility for this regeneration was on the shoulders of the youth.

The national awakening would not take place unless the foundations of Indian society were shaken up. For most people, as he pointed out, social oppression was a greater reality than political oppression.[180] The never-changing aim was complete freedom—social, economic and political. Most people could relate more immediately to social oppression than to state-led oppression, and it was futile to expect the oppressed sections to join in the political movement.[181] He said that the 'hypocrisy that is going on in the name of society, religion and state must be crushed ruthlessly'.[182] Therefore, 'Privileges based on birth, caste or creed should go, and equal opportunities should be thrown open to all irrespective of caste, creed or religion.'[183]

If it was important to break out of the restrictive traditions of the past, it was equally important to remain connected with the achievements of the past and be proud of one's heritage. The politics of nation-making did not take away anything from his consciousness of being a Bengali. In his presidential address the 1929 Bengal Provincial Conference at Rangpur in North Bengal (now in Bangladesh),[184] Subhas took his audience through the history of the province, stressing on its tradition of rebelliousness, the unique identity the region maintained in ancient times, the vivacity of the Bengalis leading to experimentations with social and political forms and their achievements in spreading ideas in other countries, the syncretic culture during the Muslim rule, the reform movements, and lastly the emergence of the nationalist movement. Aware of the increasing influence of Marxist thought, especially amongst the revolutionary groups, he reiterated his conception of India's traditional forms of socialism. Vivekananda and Deshbandhu were the icons of his variant of socialism, who struggled throughout their lives to uplift the downtrodden. Again, he voiced his opposition to accepting any 'ism' as a package. Every 'ism' had elements of truth—what was good in socialism should be accepted; but accepting tenets of socialism did not mean that the discipline, organization and obedience of fascism were to be disregarded. He referred to how the Soviet Union had to implement the New Economic Policy in contravention to the orthodox communist philosophy to suit its unique needs. He argued that if an 'ism' is imposed on a country by disregarding its history and its present conditions, it would either lead to a revolution or give rise to a contrary ideology like fascism. Most important, however, was the development of personality. No 'ism' could succeed without good human beings.

He was only too aware of the barriers to building up that mass movement in the form of caste and religious divisions, the position of women in the society and the tentative links between the Congress and the industrial labour and peasants. Throughout this period, these themes kept resonating in his speeches as the basis of attaining social, economic and political freedom.[185]

Subhas explained the philosophical basis of the volunteer movement that he was trying hard to organize. It also had something to do with his wish to end Bengal's intra-party conflict, which he had repeatedly bemoaned. Drawing a comparison with other countries, he said that groups there were formed on the basis of different programmes and ideologies, and not centring on individuals, which was the case in Bengal. The number and influence of old and new dadas (elder brothers or the more experienced seniors) were ever increasing. In the tradition of Bengal's politics, more dadas meant more localized organizations, and consequently, more fractious politics. The youth, therefore, had to break free from their influence.[186] The reason he offered was that for many centuries India had focused only on the development of the individual self at the cost of the ability to create a strong society with all-round development. This traditional emphasis on the individual and lack of

societal consciousness had resulted in the inability to work together: one
felt slighted if they had to work under the leadership of another person.
An all-encompassing jealousy for the other had led to a peculiar situation
where each person seemed to be saying, 'If the country has to be freed,
it must be freed by me or not at all.' Only strict discipline could remove
this drawback of the character, and that, Subhas said, was his motive to
propagate the volunteer movement.[187]

Subhas was already an icon to the students and the youth. His
messages to the student community touched upon various issues. 'You
might be hating the British, might be cursing them, but I will ask you
learn from them how to honour women', he told a student meeting. If
India was to make any progress, the practice of child marriage must be
abolished, women must have the freedom to remain unmarried and practice
brahmacharya (celibacy), they must be given access to education, especially
vocational training, physical training must be made available, and widows
must be allowed to be remarried. He hit out at the concept of the 'good
boy' who was 'at the mercy of elders at home, subjected to strictures in
school, treated as immature by the society and looked at with suspicion by
the police and the Government'.[188] He went ahead to advocate inter-caste
(asabarna) marriage, which he claimed would increase the vitality of the
society.[189] Infusing a sense of discipline was, for him, a key remedy for the
ills such as jealousy and infighting within the several groups. He stressed
on the need for a volunteer movement.[190]

Subhas found the source of his beliefs and convictions in the
spirituality and the historical tradition of India. It is only too well known
that Subhas had been spiritually inclined since his childhood, and that the
Ramakrishna–Vivekananda tradition had had a tremendous impact on his
adolescent mind. The goal of his life—*Atmano Mokshartham Jagaddhitaya
cha* ('for your own salvation and for the service of humanity')—had been
settled early.[191] Even as his spiritual quest intensified with time, the two
elements of personal salvation and service of humanity remained deeply
intertwined. Meditation, study of scriptures, a vow of *brahmacharya* went
hand in hand with intense service, without care for personal welfare.
His leaving home in search of a guru is too well known to be repeated.
These two ideals, which came to be informed by his systematic study of
Western Philosophy, formed the bedrock of his politics. Subhas stood at
the intersection of several traditions—the individual, the collective, the
esoteric and rationality.

There were certain issues that we find occurring repeatedly in his speeches. For instance, he was extremely sensitive, intolerant even at times, in the matter of Indians collaborating with the British system. His simple point was that the day all Indians refused to cooperate and collaborate, the Empire would collapse. But there were occasional outbursts which were quite strong in nature. For instance, one of his speeches in a North Calcutta public meeting invited criticism from *The Modern Review*. He had said:

> Our fight for freedom is not simply against British Imperialism but also against those individuals or groups in our country which function as so many allies of imperialistic power. We must spot out such blacklegs from amongst our kith and kin and at first try to persuade them to join the fighting ranks for national emancipation. Should these endeavours not meet with the desired result, we should not hesitate to take drastic steps to amputate such diseased limbs from our body politic without being deterred by any form of sickly sentimentalism. For traitors, in the garb of friends, deserve to be dealt with more ruthlessly than open and avowed enemies.[192]

He went on to say that for an act of indiscipline as seen in the case of B.N. Khare, the offender should have been blown off from the mouth of a canon. Noting that 'Mahatma Gandhi also said that in Germany Dr Khare would have been shot', the magazine's editorial piece observed, 'Such words may lead people to suspect that in India what stands in the way of political opponents being shot is not ahimsa or non-violence, but lack of the political power to shoot'. It advised that instead of Germany, Gandhi and Subhas should have spoken about what would have happened to Khare in USA, Britain or France.[193]

~

Where, then, does Subhas's idea about a synthesis of communism and fascism fit in?

Subhas expanded this idea of the synthesis in *The Indian Struggle* while discussing his thoughts on the emergence of a new party that he had described in detail in his speech at the Indian Political Conference in 1933. In that speech, Subhas had pointed to England's contribution to global history in the seventeenth century in the form of its ideas of 'constitutional and democratic Government', France's contribution in the eighteenth century through its ideas of liberty, equality and fraternity, Germany's contribution in the nineteenth century through Marxist philosophy, and Russia's contribution in the twentieth century through its achievement in 'proletarian revolution, proletarian Government and proletarian culture'. In that context, he argued that the 'next remarkable contribution to the culture and civilisation of the world, India will be called upon to make'. He did not elucidate what that contribution would be. In fact, his speech was marked by the absence of any ideological overtone, focusing solely on the struggle to free India from British rule.[194]

This 'remarkable contribution' of India, Subhas explained in *The Indian Struggle*, would be *Samyavada*, a 'doctrine of synthesis or equality' that would emerge out of a synthesis of the common traits between communism and fascism. He differed from Jawaharlal's stated position that one had to choose between some form of communism and some form of fascism as he found it to be 'fundamentally wrong'. 'Unless we are at the end of the process of evolution or unless we deny evolution altogether, there is no reason to hold that our choice is restricted to two alternatives,' Subhas argued. His considered view was that 'the next phase in world-history will produce a synthesis between Communism and Fascism', and it would not be a surprise if that synthesis was produced in India.

There existed several common traits between the two schools of political thought, despite their antithetical positions. These common traits, which included supremacy of the state over the individual, denouncement of parliamentary democracy, dictatorship of the party that ruthlessly suppressed all dissenting minorities, and a belief in industrial planning would form the basis of the synthesis. The party that would bring in this synthesis would not stand for 'a democracy in the Mid-Victorian sense of the term, but will believe in government by a strong party bound together by military discipline, as the only means of holding India together and preventing a chaos, when Indians are free and are thrown entirely on their own resources'. It would not only introduce 'state-planning for the re-organisation of the agricultural and industrial life of the country', but also 'seek to build up a new social structure on the basis of the village communities of the past, that were ruled by the village "Panch"' and would 'strive to break down the existing social barriers like caste'. It would establish a new monetary and credit system and abolish landlordism, introducing a uniform land tenure system for the whole of India.[195]

In response to the ruckus created by these views which, by any standards, were authoritarian in nature, Subhas clarified his position in an interview to Rajani Palme Dutt. It was a weak clarification and did not explain his views on dictatorship of the party or suppression of dissent. Subhas told Dutt:

> What I really meant was that we in India wanted our national freedom, and having won it, we wanted to move in the direction of Socialism. This is what I meant when I referred to 'a synthesis between Communism and Fascism'. Perhaps the expression I used was not a happy one. But I should like to point out that when I was writing the book, Fascism had not started on its imperialist expedition, and it appeared to me merely an aggressive form of nationalism.[196]

Further clarification came in his speech at the Haripura Congress, where he argued in favour of the Congress taking over power after India became free:

> I know that it will be argued that the continuance of a party in such circumstances, standing behind the state, will convert that state into a totalitarian one; but I cannot admit the charge. The state will possibly become a totalitarian one, if there be only one party as in countries like Russia, Germany and Italy. But there is no reason why other parties should be banned. Moreover, the party itself will have a democratic basis, unlike, for instance, the Nazi Party which is based on the 'leader principle'. The existence of more than one party and the democratic basis of the Congress Party will prevent the future Indian state becoming a totalitarian one. Further, the democratic basis of the party will ensure that leaders are not thrust upon the people from above, but are elected from below.[197]

'I have no doubt in my mind that our chief national problems relating to the eradication of poverty, illiteracy and disease and to scientific production and distribution can be effectively tackled only along socialistic lines', he declared.

Subhas, however, never really gave up the idea of the synthesis between political ideologies, although it shifted somewhat from communism–

fascism to socialism–nationalism. He returned to the theme of synthesis in one of his last major speeches, where he laid out before the faculty and students of the Tokyo Imperial University the past, present and future of India in November 1944. Referring to his proposition in *The Indian Struggle*, Subhas said, 'it would be our task in India to evolve a system that would be a synthesis of the systems in vogue in different parts of the world'. Then he went on to compare national socialism and communism. Both were anti-democratic, authoritarian and anti-capitalistic. Whereas national socialism had been able to 'create national unity and solidarity and to improve the condition of the masses', it had not 'been able to radically reform the prevailing economic system which was built up on a capitalistic basis'. The great achievement of the Soviet experiment, on the other hand, was planned economy, but it was deficient in that it did not 'appreciate the value of national sentiment':

> What we in India would like to have is a progressive system which will fulfil the social needs of the whole people and will be based on national sentiment. In other words, it will be a synthesis of Nationalism and Socialism.[198]

The free Indian state, of necessity, would have to be authoritarian:

> If we are to have an economic structure of a socialistic character, then it follows that the political system must be such as to be able to carry out that economic programme in the best possible way. You cannot have a so-called democratic system, if that system has to put through economic reforms on a socialistic basis . . . with a democratic system we cannot solve the problems of Free India. Therefore, modern progressive though in India is in favour of a State of an authoritarian character, which will work as an organ, or as the servant of the masses, and not of a clique or of few rich individuals.[199]

These have to be studied in the context of his political views that Subhas expressed over a decade and a half ago. At the Maharashtra Provincial Conference, he was emphatic: 'If we want to make India really great we must build up a political democracy on the pedestal of a democratic society.'[200]

Does this really prove that Subhas went on to become an authoritarian, wannabe dictator from a democrat? That would be too simplistic a presumption. Clearly, Subhas here was talking about his own political views which evolved over a period of time with his increased exposure to global political systems, what he believed to be the most effective form of Government for a free India to get rid of its myriad ills. To appear to be a certified democrat was not his prerogative. His other utterances of this time help put these views in context. At the press conference of 12 June 1942, he said:

> I regard myself as a servant of the Indian nation and my present task is to lead the fight for India's independence. But as soon as India is free, it will be the duty of the Indian people to decide what form of Government they desire and who should guide the future Indian state. I certainly have my own ideas regarding post war reconstruction in Free India, but it will be for Free India to decide upon them. So long as I remain outside my country, I shall not do anything which will not meet with the widest approval of nationalist circles in India.[201]

If Subhas had any dictatorial streak in his personality, its manifestation would have been the easiest in Germany and Japan, where he had absolute authority over the organizations that he led. All available accounts from his Indian colleagues and Japanese friends, none of whom had any reason to be a sycophant, invariably paints the picture of a person who had democratic values embedded within himself.

~

As time went by, the synthesis of tradition and modernity and the welfare of the collective became Subhas's public face, overshadowing the esoteric which he began to guard under an intense sheath of privacy. This, perhaps, was inevitable in a sense, as politics became his mainstay; a distance developed with the groups with which he had become associated during this student days in Calcutta. Even Hemanta Sarkar, his closest friend from 1912, moved away from him for political differences. The continued personal connect notwithstanding, their ideological difference was too wide to bridge. The one person who continued to have the privilege of discussing with Subhas his deeper spiritual thoughts was Dilip Kumar Roy, son of the famous poet, composer and playwright Dwijendra Lal Roy, who had been his friend from his college days at Cambridge. Although Dilip might not have known every detail of his friend's spiritual practice, he was perhaps the best informed among his friends, as Subhas would reveal to him his deeper spiritual self. He was also the most sensitive to Subhas's sustained inner conflict between the mystic and the worldly.

Writing the preface to his reminiscences of Subhas in 1966, Dilip summed up his impression: 'Subhas was a mystic par excellence and not a politician.'[202]

Yet, the question of religion in the public space was something that he could not avoid. There were several instances where he had to negotiate the interface between the private and the public aspects of religion. These instances help in understanding Subhas's views on Hinduism as an organized religion and his position on the treatment of religion by the state.

Two of the earliest instances of the intersection between religion and politics, which Subhas experienced, took place under Chittaranjan's leadership. While in one of them, the Tarakeshwar Satyagraha, Subhas had practically no role other than being a spectator, he took up the other one—the Bengal Pact—with enthusiasm.

Chittaranjan intervened in the affairs of the Shiva temple in Tarakeshwar, a few miles north-west of Calcutta, on receiving complaints regarding immorality and financial extortion by the mahant (the head priest). He launched a campaign in April 1924, according to Subhas, 'for taking peaceful possession of the temple and the attached property, with a view to placing them under the administration of a public committee'. The mahant received support from the Government and posted Gurkha guards to protect the temple, leading to clashes between the Swarajist satyagrahis and the police. The mahant eventually resigned, with one of his disciples taking up the post. A settlement was reached by which the income from the endowments and contributions from the pilgrims would be spent on the pilgrims and in nation-building activities. The agreement could not be executed as a civil suit was filed by the local Brahman Sabha.[203]

Chittaranjan's Bengal Pact hit at the bases of the communal strife in Bengal: it aimed to dispel the fear of Hindu domination which was being played upon by the Muslim communalists, and at the same time, addressed the economic grievances, which both Chittaranjan and Subhas believed, if properly addressed, could remove the communal division. The outlook demonstrated their confidence as far as their own religious standing was concerned, and the distance they were ready to go to carry forward the work of the 'nation in the making'. A similar confidence, utterly devoid of the persecution complex of 'Hinduism in danger' is visible from the stand he took regarding cow slaughter and playing music in front of mosques.

Bringing the different religious communities together did not mean giving up the attachment with his own religion. Subhas's prison notebooks, containing random notes written during his stay in the Mandalay jail, show a lesser-known side of his thinking on Hinduism. Since it was not directly relevant to his politics or his individual spiritual practice, it has not received much attention. The notes show that he was reflecting upon the expansion of the Hindu religion in other continents. Noting that only Christianity and Islam are preached in Africa, he asked 'Why should Hinduism not be preached there?' He remembered the efforts of Swami Vivekananda in taking Hinduism to the Western world. That was a good thing insofar as influencing Western society and philosophy, but the Europeans and Americans were not going to adopt Hinduism, he argued. There was a better chance of Africans adopting Hinduism. The resultant benefits will be threefold, he wrote:

> Firstly, what is gained by preaching the truth is always there. Secondly, Africans not yet civilised or only half-civilised will be fully civilised in the light of Hinduism and civilisation. Thirdly, by being aggressive Hinduism will acquire further strength and as a result of being preached in a different country will be compelled to shed many of its prejudices and dogmatism . . . If two hundred lakhs of Africans embrace Hinduism then undoubtedly the influence of the Hindus and of India will be quite powerful in Africa. If India wants to be a world power then the preaching of Hinduism will facilitate the process.[204]

The conflict with the jail authorities in Burma as well as in Calcutta, over the Hindu prisoners' religious freedom, also establish that he was least worried about being seen as a religious person and would not shy away from asserting his religious rights.

Another controversy that pitched Subhas against Rabindranath erupted in early 1928, around organizing Saraswati Puja in a hostel of the City College in Calcutta. The college being an institution of the Sadharan Brahmo Samaj, which did not believe in idol worship, the authorities allowed the students to organize the puja outside the hostel campus but not within. The students, however, disregarded the warning by the college authorities and held the puja inside the campus of the Ram Mohan Roy Hostel, as a consequence of which disciplinary action was taken against about six of them, the hostel was shut down and an early summer vacation declared. A number of students transferred to other colleges. In the ensuing confrontation between the students and the authorities, Subhas came out in support of the students.[205]

Rabindranath expressed his views in an article in *The Modern Review*. Had the students not insisted on organizing the puja in a Brahmo hostel, the 'religion of the Hindus' would not have 'in any way been hurt', and 'it is Religion which is hurt by needlessly hurting the feelings of any religious community'. He had taken up the pen, Rabindranath wrote, because the incident was not a matter of local clash, but involved a higher principle. In spite of its rules against image worship, the college had been accepted by students of various religions. 'If now some group of men should, by propaganda of cajolery or intimidation, succeed in putting it into difficulties, that would be sowing the seed of rankling thorns in the mind of one of the communities of our countrymen', he argued. The logical question that followed was if such behaviour would 'amount to a cultivation of the spirit of Swaraj which is to give legitimate freedom of self-expression to all natural differences in the communities that come under it'.

Rabindranath presented several analogies to explain his arguments. 'Would it be right to restrain Mahomedan students,' he asked, 'if in accordance with their own religion they wanted to sacrifice a cow in the grounds of a hostel occupied by them but managed by the Hindus?' If cow slaughter is a sin for the Hindus, 'the Musalmans have proclaimed in their history, in letters of blood, that it is a sin beyond all other sins to worship any created thing as God'. Rabindranath dared those 'who are so loud in their assertion that their religion demands the performance of their own sectarian worship even on ground occupied by a different sect,' to demonstrate their belief 'on Musalman and Christian territory'. Thereafter, he went on to praise the Christian rulers of India:

> Those who are the rulers of India are Christians. As to power, they have more than is possessed by any other religion in India. As for contempt and hatred, they are wanting in neither for the Hindu rites and practices And yet they have not taken to thrusting the Christian form of worship into our homes, our schools, our temples. Had they done so, they would doubtless have had showers of benedictions on such crusade from the

pious pundits of their own church. Nevertheless, they have preferred to do without such benediction, rather than propagate their religion by force in the fields sacred to non-Christian religions.[206]

C.F. Andrews joined in the chorus, asserting that 'the students' attempt to coerce the college authorities into allowing public image worship to be performed in the Ram Mohun Roy Hostel is contrary to the spirit of mutual toleration and forbearance which was introduced by the Unity Conference and confirmed by the Madras Congress Resolution, in December 1927'.[207] Announcing his support for the Hindu students at a students' meeting in the Albert Hall on 1 March 1928, Subhas claimed that the resolution of the dispute was simple, although efforts were afoot to make a mountain out of a molehill. The Hindus were an extremely tolerant community and he was unwilling to impose his own religious beliefs on anyone else. At the same time, it was beyond his comprehension 'how the enlightened and progressive Brahmo leaders could stoop so low to force their belief on Hindu students'.[208] On 18 May, he issued another statement urging the college authorities to allow religious freedom to students of both the communities. 'The relationship between Brahmo Samaj and the Hindu community is not the same as those between Hindus and Muslims or Hindus and Christians', he emphasized. For Subhas, the Brahmos were part of the Hindu community: it had become a tradition for the Brahmos to introduce themselves as Brahmo-Hindus, and many leaders of their community had been playing an active role in the Hindu Mahasabha. He appealed to the authorities for a little more tact and less vengefulness in dealing with the students.[209]

After the publication of Rabindranath's essay in *The Modern Review*, Subhas responded to the points raised by the poet at another meeting in the Albert Hall on 19 June:

I am very sorry to see Rabi babu and Mr Andrews get involved in this matter . . . When sometime back we had requested Rabindranath to join our political movement, he had refused. I fail to understand why then he has been summoned now and why he has agreed to join the issue. He has raised the question of Hindu–Muslim relationship in his essay. At the risk of being sounding arrogant I say this comparison is wrong. The City College affair is really a domestic affair like a conflict between Shaktas and Vaishnavas. He has also asked why organising the Puja is being

forced now when for so many years there had been no such demand.
Should we then continue to remain an enslaved nation just because we
have remained so for a hundred and fifty years?

Whenever religions have been in conflict in our country, a synthesis
has been found. Images of Hari–Hara, Kali–Shiva, Hara–Gauri and
Kali–Krishna, etc., are examples of that synthesis . . . We establish the
divine spirit within idols and worship the infinite within the finite. There
is no need for any conflict. Worship of idols by Hindus does not demean
the religious beliefs of the Brahmos.

The question of religious tolerance has also come up. Toleration
of others' beliefs does not mean giving up one's own belief. Toleration
is true when every individual is allowed to observe his own religion. In
my opinion, the Brahmo leaders have shown greater intolerance by not
allowing the students to do the puja.

Being a civic festival, Saraswati Puja has a societal value too . . . It
is not right to deprive the society from the pure and unmixed joy on the
occasion of the puja. It also has a value from the perspective of art and
culture. If symbols are necessary in the world of art, what can be the
objection to symbols in religion?

There is no substance in the allegation that disrespect has been shown
to Raja Ram Mohan Roy by organising the puja. Certainly, he had his
differences with idol worship, but it was he who aggressively defended
the Hindus against the Christian missionaries when they campaigned
against idol worship.[210]

The Bengali satire magazine, *Shanibarer Chithi*, led by its editor Sajanikanta
Das, too defended the college authorities, the primary target of its satire
being 'Subu Bose'. Sajanikanta was convinced that the students were in
the wrong and the dispute became protracted only because of Subhas's
involvement. Although his Brahmo colleagues in the magazine were
hesitant to hit out in strong language, Sajanikanta claimed that being a
Hindu himself, he was not restricted by such hesitation in attacking the
Hindu religionists. He wrote satirical articles and poems attacking Subhas
in quite a tasteless manner, calling him '*Khoka Bhagawan*' (baby God),
ridiculing his illness in Mandalay Jail and his bachelor status. Mocking
Subhas's religiosity, Sajanikanta wrote that it had become a fashion to
grow a tuft of hair (like Brahmins) in Cambridge. Sajanikanta admitted
later in his memoirs that Subhas's role in the City College affair angered

him so much that the magazine continued to lampoon him for a long time for all his other activities, especially for his role as the General Officer Commanding (GOC) of the volunteer corps during the Calcutta Congress held in December that year. So intense was his dislike for Subhas that Sajanikanta abstained from participating in the Calcutta Congress.

A repentant Sajanikanta apologized in his memoirs:

> Later Gok Subhas [named so for his role of GOC] turned the table on us by truly becoming Netaji Subhaschandra, rejecting our satire and making it an object of ridicule. Today all of us are proud of him and our unadulterated respect for him has put a cover on our earlier shame.[211]

No less striking was the change in the attitude of Sajanikanta's one-time colleague, Nirad C. Chaudhuri, who, as long as he wrote for an English readership, could barely find anything appreciable in Subhas other than his indifference towards money and women. Later, he came to include Subhas as one of the six greatest Bengalis of all time. Referring to a character in Bankim Chandra Chattopadhyay's novel, *Krishnakanter Will*, in an essay written a few years before his death, Chaudhuri claimed that if he had the means, he would have built a temple and established a golden idol of Subhas. If he could find anyone equal to Subhas he would gift that idol to him, Chaudhuri declared.[212]

The City College controversy was settled around July, but as a fallout, Subhas was barred from entering the college, a ban that was removed a decade later when he became the Rashtrapati.[213]

Subhas was drawn into the controversy that erupted in 1937 over the alleged communal overtone of 'Bande Mataram'. Objections were raised by a section of the Muslims and by the British bureaucracy too. On being informed by Lord Brabourne, the governor of Bombay at that time, Henry Craik, the home member in the Viceroy's Council, complained to Lord Baden-Powell that the song was included in the second edition of *Scouting for Boys in India*. 'It actually originated as a hymn of hate against Muslims', Craik wrote on 30 March 1937. Baden-Powell assured him that the song would be taken out of the book in the next edition.[214] The Muslim League took the position that the song was 'positively anti-Islamic, idolatrous in its inspiration and ideas and definitely subversive of the growth of genuine nationalism in India'.[215]

While staying in Kurseong after his return from Dalhousie, Subhas wrote to Rabindranath asking for his views. Although he had composed the music for the song, Rabindranath's growing internationalism had drawn him away from the inherent essence of the song. The poet wrote to Subhas:

> There can be no argument about the fact that at the heart of Bande Mataram is the worship of Durga. Bankim has shown Bengal in the form of Durga in the song, but the worship of this form can never be accepted by any Muslim . . . The song is appropriate for *Ananda Math* which is a novel, but it cannot be universally accepted by the National Congress, which is place for meeting of all religions of India. The unreasonable stubbornness of some fanatic Muslims of Bengal is intolerable, but when we imitate them in being obstinate over an unfair demand it become shameful.[216]

Subhas asked Jawaharlal too to consult the poet on this matter. His letter of 17 October to Jawaharlal clearly demonstrates his perspective on the issue of communal politics:

> I have always agreed with you that on the question of Hindu–Muslim unity economic questions are of paramount importance. Communal Muslims are in the habit of raising bogeys from time to time—sometimes it is music before mosques, sometimes inadequate jobs for Muslims and at present it is 'Bande Mataram'. 'Bande Mataram' has suddenly sprung into importance probably because it was sung in Legislatures thereby demonstrating Congress victory. While I would gladly try to meet all doubts and difficulties raised by nationalist Muslims, I do not feel inclined to attach much importance to what the communalists say. If you give them the fullest satisfaction on the question of 'Bande Mataram' today, they will not be long in bringing up other questions tomorrow, simply in order to pander to communal feeling and embarrass the Congress.[217]

The Congress working committee which met in Calcutta adopted a resolution that only the first two stanzas would be sung at national gatherings. Although the song had never been adopted by the Congress as the national anthem of India, its long association with the sufferings made the first two stanzas 'a living and inseparable part of our national movement'. There was nothing in the stanzas, the working committee felt, to which anyone can take exception. However, organizers had the freedom to sing 'any other song of unobjectionable character, in addition to, or in the place of, the Bande Mataram song'.[218]

While Subhas engaged with the political manifestation of religion, the fear of losing himself completely to the spiritual quest never left him. This is apparent from a conversation which Dilip had with him in 1938, and reported many years later:

> I want you [Subhas] to fulfil your life following your *swadharma*, to wit, the deepest call of your nature. Why waste it? Come along with me to Pondicherry. One who has the capacity to become a nation-builder should not fritter away his precious energy in building a futile party which cannot achieve anything worthwhile even in the best of time. 'I know Dilip,' he retorted. 'But I can't turn to Yoga branded 'defeated' by life.' His lips quivered and sparks flew from his eyes. 'Can't you at least come away with me for a few months, if only to see your way clearer?' 'But no, Dilip. Even that is impossible. Because if I go with you into even a temporary seclusion, I am afraid I may not be able to come out again into the open with the fire of the fighter in me.' He did not care to win peace not even a truer vision, because he loved the cause of his country too dearly.[219]

The conflict deeply influenced Dilip, making him recall that:

> . . . the more I admired Subhash [sic] the more I prayed that he might be rescued from the perfidious tentacles of political adventurers. I reminded him again and again years later, when I saw him fighting with his back to the wall, that politics was not his native line, *swadharma*; but alas, he was born with an obstinate streak of rational madness.[220]

The mystical streak in him not only drove Subhas to build his political life on the foundation of the spiritual, but he also attempted to pass it on to the next generation. In a letter written to his nephew Amiya in February 1934, Subhas outlined the fundamentals of a moral life, prominently featuring *sanyas*, or renunciation.[221] *Sanyas*, wrote Subhas, manifested itself in different forms in different ages. The form required for the current age was *karma sanyas*, which implied completely dedicating one's life to a great ideal and in the process sacrificing narrow self-interest. In other words, it implied 'selfless work'.

It is remarkable that Subhas would feel it necessary to even broach the topic of *sanyas* in a general letter of guidance to a young nephew in his early twenties. Understandably, he did not bring up the deeper aspects of sadhana leading to that *sanyas*, although he did touch upon the subject of *brahmacharya*, for this was not a letter on spiritual guidance, but only a moral one. There is no known record of what exactly his spiritual practices were, but undoubtedly Subhas was going deeper with his sadhana. In a letter to Dilip written on 5 March 1933, he gave some insight: He was 'torn' between the symbols of divinity—Shiva, Kali and Krishna. He had to choose one of these according to his 'prevalent mood'. He wrote that 'Of these three again, the struggle is between Shiva and Shakti'. While Shiva, the ideal Yogi fascinated him, the appeal of Kali the Mother was no less. He had also moved on from the 'ordinary rationalistic view' that mantras were like symbols, being no more than aids to concentration. Now, he admitted that:

> . . . my study of Tantra philosophy gradually convinced me that certain Mantras had an inherent Shakti—and that each mental constitution was fitted for a particular Mantra. Since then, I have tried my best to find out what my mental constitution is like and which Mantra I would be suited for. But so far I have failed to find that out because my moods vary and I am sometimes a Shaiva, sometimes a Shakta and sometimes a Vaishnava. I think it is here that the Guru becomes useful—because the real Guru knows more about ourselves than we do—and he could at once tell us what Mantra we should take up and which method of worship we should follow.[222]

Subhas never spoke about it in public but that he was channelizing his quest for spiritual realization through an intense and systematic sadhana is indicated by the meetings he had in 1938 and 1939 with those who were considered to be spiritual adepts. He did not keep any record of these meetings, nor did he ever share their details with anyone. Whatever fragmented information is available is from the disciples of these gurus. The three names that have emerged from these sources are Anandamayee Ma, Barada Charan Majumdar, and Tara Khepa of Tara Pith. Although what transpired between them is not known, these were clearly not social calls. Each of these gurus were experts in *tantrasadhana* and it would not be a stretch to link Subhas's visits to that.

The worsening crisis over his re-election as the Congress president appeared to tilt the balance in the tussle between the spiritual and the political in favour of his 'first love of life—the eternal call of the Himalayas', albeit for a limited time. The Tripuri experience compelled him to articulate the struggle in public, and also led to his reluctant acceptance of the occult. It also showed glimpses of how he would react to the kind of politics he was subjected to:

> Owing to the morally sickening atmosphere of Tripuri, I left that place with such a loathing and disgust for Politics as I have never felt before during the last nineteen years. As I tossed in my bed at Jamadoba, by day and by night, I began to ask myself again and again what would become of our public life when there was so much of pettiness and vindictiveness even in the highest circles. My thoughts naturally turned towards what was my first love in life—the eternal call of the Himalayas. If such was the consummation of our Politics—I asked myself—why did I stray from what Aurobindo Ghose would describe as 'the life divine'. Had the time now come for me to tear the veil of Maya and go back to the fountain-head of all love? I spent days and nights of moral doubt and uncertainty. At times the call of the Himalayas became insistent.[223]

The realization that a much larger section of the country, beyond the small coterie of Congress schemers, stood solidly behind him helped him sail through the bitterness, but only for the time being.

As amulets, *prasadi* flowers, leaves and ashes (purportedly bestowed with special divine powers) piled up, being sent by numerous astrologers and sadhus, Subhas treated them with due respect but with an 'exceedingly rationalistic frame of mind'. Yet, when a professor of Calcutta University, 'an erudite scholar in Sanskrit Literature and a man of exemplary character' conveyed to him the conclusion of a 'number of Pundits and astrologers' who had met to discuss his illness that 'somebody in some part of the country had been practising what is known in the Tantra-Shastra as *Marana-Kriya*—that is, attempt to kill by tantric process or will power', he could not ignore it. Subhas took a middle ground on the phenomenon, expressing an unwillingness to believe it and yet showing a reluctance to ignore the source—leaving it open to the interpretation that it was a momentary weakness induced by the crisis. Afterwards, he claimed to have relieved himself of the amulets and rings which he had temporarily worn by suppressing his 'innate rationalism'.[224]

His public attitude towards amulets and *prasadi* flowers notwithstanding, his private sadhana continued. As his jail mate from July 1940 till the time he was released for home internment in January 1941, and his close political follower, Narendra Narayan Chakravarti observed, Subhas continued his Kali worship in a room in the Presidency jail. The effect of the Kali worship in the dark of the night, when everyone else had gone to sleep, startled Chakravarti, leaving him wondering which one of Subhas's identities was more representative of the man: revolutionary or that of a *sadhaka*?[225] In keeping with his strict privacy on the matter, the sessions of meditation and worship would typically take place in the middle of the night. Chakravarti also noticed that Subhas carried with him a pocket-sized version of *Chandi* and the Gita—incidentally, in 1940 too, when Subhas organized Durga puja in the jail, though not entirely with the happy cooperation of the Government.

His regular puja and sadhana, to the extent possible, continued during the War, as has been recorded by S.A. Ayer. This continued focus on the practice of spiritualism with personal realization as the goal, as opposed to mere theorizing, even while running a government in exile and leading an army, is an indicator of the intensifying call of the spiritual realm. Ayer recalled:

> Whenever he [Subhas] was not actually doing some work or talking to somebody, he would withdraw within himself in a trice and would be in communion with God . . . Sanyasi was writ large on his forehead even when the Supreme Commander's cap rested majestically on his head at an alluring angle over his right brow.
>
> Many a night, after dinner, while in Singapore, he used to send his car to the Ramakrishna Mission to fetch the Swami in charge or his fellow-missionary, Brahmachari Kailasam, and spend a good two hours or so in spiritual communion before retiring into his study sometime after midnight, to go through official papers. Or, late at night, he used to drive incognito to the Mission, there change into a priestly silk dhoti, shut himself up in the prayer room, rosary in hand, and spend a couple of hours in meditation . . .

. . . The only external symbol of his godliness was the tiny little leather bag—the tiniest article of his personal luggage, holding the two-and-a-half by two-inches Gita, the small rosary of beads (*tulsi mala*) and his spare reading glasses.[226]

What Subhas told Ba Maw, the head of the Burmese Government at the time, according to whom 'the dream element in Subhas . . . constituted the deepest part of him', therefore, assumes a great significance in this context:

'I often have moments,' he once told me, 'when I would like to give up everything and spend my days in prayer and contemplation. But I must wait till India is liberated.'[227]

Yet, this intensely spiritual man was the one who was trusted by Muslims who were affected by the environment of religious strife. M.Z. Kiani, with whom Subhas left the responsibility of representing the Azad Hind Government at the time he left Singapore in August 1945, was one such person who was keenly aware of the politics of religion. Kiani described the attitude of the Muslim soldiers as one of dilemma: on the one hand they were apprehensive of being dominated by the Hindus (they 'believed that talk of having a secular state in India was only a camouflage') and on the other hand they were reluctant to stand aside when an army of liberation was being raised. 'In India there was at least the humaneness of Mahatma Gandhi and the liberalism of Pandit Nehru to allay somewhat the apprehensions of the Muslims; but in the Far East, there was at the time only the stark dictatorship of Mohan Singh', he reminisced. It was in this scenario that the likelihood of Subhas taking up the leadership of the movement helped them reach the decision to join the INA:

However, there being the likelihood of Subhas Chandra Bose later coming to lead the movement, a decision in the matter became easier. Bose was known to be an upright man and had a solid politic standing in India. At a secret meeting, therefore, it was decided to join the movement.[228]

From faraway East Asia, Subhas had the same impact within India too. Sheikh Mujibur Rahman, the first president of Bangladesh, who was at that time an emerging leader in the Muslim League, recorded his dilemma of those days in his memoir:

When we listened to Subhas Bose addressing us on the radio from Singapore we used to get excited. It seemed to us then that if he managed to land his troops in Bengal it would be easy for us to oust the English. But then again it occurred to us that having him in Bengal would not bring us any nearer to Pakistan. And what would happen to the millions of Muslims of the country then? But then again I thought that someone who could leave everything in his country to spearhead a movement for its independence could never be parochial in his outlook. In my mind, my respect for Subhas Bose continued to grow.[229]

Subhas kept addressing the communal issue in India from Germany and East Asia. In incessant criticism of Jinnah and the Muslim League, he always made the distinction between communal and nationalist Muslims. Over the Azad Hind Radio, he said on 25 March 1942:

British propaganda has tried to create the impression that the Muslim League is almost as influential a body as the Congress, and that it represents the majority of India's Muslims. This, however, is far from the truth. In reality there are several influential and important Muslim organisations which are thoroughly nationalist. Moreover out of the 11 provinces in British India out of which only 4 have a majority of Muslims, only one, the Punjab, has a cabinet which may be regarded as a Muslim League cabinet. But even the Punjab Premier is strongly opposed to the main programme of the Muslim League, namely the division of India. Consequently, it seems that the Muslim League only commands a majority in a single province of India. But even then it is said that the majority of the Muslims will not stand for Indian independence.[230]

On the Wavell Plan too, he saw an understanding between the Viceroy and the Muslim League. In his broadcast to Indians from Singapore on 19 June 1945, he said:

You are now violently condemning the Viceroy and you are criticising him for giving an equal number of seats in the Executive Council to caste Hindus and to Muslims. But why don't you go deeper into the question and find out the idea behind it? So far not one single Indian leader has done so, judging from the reports that are now before me. I regret that the members of the Hindu Mahasabha have taken what appears to be their own peculiar line. Our objection should not be to Muslims getting a majority of seats on the Executive Council. The moot question is what type of Muslims will come into the Executive Council? If we have Muslims of the type of Maulana Abul Kalam Azad, Asaf Ali and Rafi Ahmed Kidwai, the destiny of India will be safe. And I personally believe that it is only right to give all the freedom to such patriots. There is no difference between a patriotic Muslim and a patriotic Hindu . . . I have no doubt in my mind that in the offer of Lord Wavell there is a secret understanding, either explicit or implicit, between the Muslim League and the British Government . . . I, therefore, ask you, nay, I implore you, to ponder deeply over the matter and reject this shameless and sinister plan of Lord Wavell . . . I want to say that though I do not agree with the line of approach of the members of the Hindu Mahasabha and of the anti-Pakistan front, I feel very strongly that they have done a great service to India by giving an outspoken expression of their opposition to Lord Wavell's plan.[231]

When Subhas had met Jinnah in June 1940, he had offered him to become the first prime minister of free India, but found him to be besotted only with the idea of Pakistan.[232] Regarding Jinnah, Subhas was clear in his broadcast from Bangkok on 18 July 1943. 'I believe', he said, 'that Mr Jinnah is doing great harm to the National cause by advocating Pakistan':

The Muslim League is a pro-British body and is supported mainly by 'yes-men' and traitors. That is why the Viceroy frequently calls Mr Jinnah and consults him on important matters. It is the British who are the creators of the Muslim League, which is supported by the millionaires and landlords . . . He (Jinnah) is misleading the simple-minded Muslims by lending charm to Pakistan and playing upon their religious fanaticism. We all know that India will be plunged into a welter of chaos and confusion if the Pakistan scheme comes to fruition.

He presented the example of the INA which 'is mainly composed of Muslim soldiers' who worked in 'perfect harmony' with their Hindu comrades, to prove the hollowness of Hindu–Muslim divide which he claimed was a British creation.[233]

Although the leaders of free India presented the communal harmony in the INA as India's ideal, the forces of communal hatred that were unleashed proved to be too strong, especially in the absence of Subhas.

11

Marriage

Like so many other aspects of his life, there is a controversy about whether Subhas Bose ever got married. Although officially accepted by the Indian Government and Subhas's family, not an insignificant number of people, especially in Bengal, are sceptical about the fact of his marriage. It might be convenient to dismiss these people as fringe groups, but there are genuine questions here that need to be addressed separately, more so when a section of Subhas's own family and some of his close associates had refused to accept that he had married.[1]

Surprisingly, very little authentic documentation was available regarding the issue of Subhas's marriage, until government files were declassified in 2014 and 2015 by the Government of West Bengal and the Central Government respectively. The story that had been constructed till then was largely based on personal recollections of various people, including Emilie Schenkl herself, Subhas's former associates in Europe and a section of his family.

Just how sensitive these files were considered to be until very recently can be judged from the response of the Prime Minister's Office (PMO) in 2013 and again in 2015 to the author's request for obtaining copies of three files related to Emilie. The PMO informed that the files were exempt from disclosure under section 8 (1)(a) read with section 8 (2) of the Right to Information Act. Section 8 (1)(a) of the Act stipulated that the Government could refuse 'information, disclosure of which would prejudicially affect the sovereignty and integrity of India, the security, strategic, scientific or economic interests of the State, relation with foreign State or lead to incitement of an offence', whereas Section 8 (2) allowed the Government to release even such information which was otherwise legally protected if public interest outweighed 'harm to protected interests'.[2] In other words, the Indian Government felt until 2015 that hell would break lose if the documents pertaining to the alleged marriage of Subhas Chandra Bose were disclosed.

Declassification of these three files, alongside other files, now allow a nearly complete reconstruction of how the news that Subhas had married an Austrian lady reached India and the initial reaction it elicited, which, in turn, throws new light on the existing story of Subhas's relationship with Emilie. A significant amount of information was also available from unclassified files at the National Archives, but strangely, they seem to have evaded the attention of earlier biographers of Subhas.

The first person in India to hear that Subhas had left behind a widow and a daughter in Vienna was not Sarat, as would be expected, but Jawaharlal. Dr Abdul Hafiz Akmat and his wife had met Emilie through Subhas in 1940 and had grown close to her. After the war was over, he got in touch with Jawaharlal to inform him that Subhas and Emilie were married. Jawaharlal passed on the information to Vallabhbhai Patel while asking Akmat for more details. Akmat sent more information to Jawaharlal on 22 June 1947, through a note which stated, among others things:

I have been able to get the following information, which is quite reliable.

1. The late Mr SC Bose has left his testament with the mother of the child and it now appears that she was married to him. She has this testament with her and probably a copy of it can be had, but of course it is not quite easy to get it through the post.
2. The child is now 4 ½ years old. About the parentage of the child there is no doubt on account of the great resemblance which the child bears to the father, the testament and the confirmation of the mother of the child. . . .
5. At present she is living with her family in a very pitiable state. Her father is already dead. The grandmother and the mother of the child are sacrificing everything in order to keep the child alive and healthy, but in spite of it the position of the mother and the child is precarious. They need immediate help.

The memory of the late Mr SC Bose can only be honoured if India helps without delay his wife and his only child. It should not be forgotten that she was his most trusted friend, companion and co-worker during the most trying periods of his life.

According to the latest information I have received just now, it seems that some months ago Mrs SC Bose sent a copy of this testament together with a letter to Mr Sarat Chandra Bose, but as she has received no answer, it seems very likely that these have not reached their destination. The whole affair is so tragic and I cannot help adding and asking whether it is the fault of the poor faithful girl to have faithfully worked with the late Mr Bose for India for which she has now got into this tragic state. I am quite sure that you will take immediate steps to help this deserving soul.[3]

Jawaharlal forwarded the note to Patel on 7 August, asking him to depute Nathalal Parikh 'who is in Antwerp and ask him to inquire into the matter and arrange help if necessary'.[4] Patel wrote to Parikh on the same day, asking him to find out if the information was correct, and if it was, to make arrangements to help Emilie and Anita. Nathalal visited Emilie and later wrote about what he had heard from her: '. . . in the beginning of 1942 he proposed and got married to her at a quiet ceremony in Vienna. It was a Gandharva Vivaha because they could not be married under the then existing German marriage law.'[5]

On receiving the initial information from Dr Akmat, Jawaharlal had also gotten in touch with A.C.N. Nambiar to find out more. Nambiar confirmed the facts to Jawaharlal through his letter dated 12 August 1947. 'I am able to affirm that B[ose] was very deeply and seriously attached to S[chenkl] and in Europe no other woman entered his life the same way. S was to my knowledge intensely devoted to B,' Nambiar informed Jawaharlal. He also wrote that 'B, it would appear, has given a note to S, prior to his departure from Europe, affirming a sort [sic] of Hindu marriage with S useful for an eventual legitimation of fatherhood'. He pointed out that Subhas did not want any publicity about his marriage and fatherhood at the time of his secret departure from Europe, constrained by the prevailing German laws and also due to 'other considerations, both of a family character and political nature'. Nambiar also told Jawaharlal that he had 'hinted about the matter and a responsibility in regard to the child to one of Subhas's nephews'.[6] Recently released documents in the British archives indicate that this nephew was Sarat Bose's son Amiya Bose, to whom he wrote three letters 'hinting' about Emilie and Anita but claimed to have not got any response.[7]

Unknown to Jawaharlal, Nambiar and Amiya, all this correspondence was intercepted by India's Intelligence Bureau (IB) and shared with the Indian Political Intelligence (IPI) in the UK. Post-Independence, IB passed on this intelligence to MI5.

During his protracted interrogation, which lasted about five weeks after his arrest in June 1945, Nambiar told his interrogator, Captain Naurang Singh Bains of the Combined Services Detailed Interrogation Centre (CSDIC), that Subhas had decided to keep the fact that he had had a child with Emilie without marriage a strict secret. According to Nambiar, Subhas accepted the 'inevitable consequence of retirement from politics' when the story of his relationship with Emilie would become known to his followers in Europe and India, and Emilie hoped that 'with the success of his mission he would regularise their relationship'. Subhas, according to Nambiar, had decided to marry her, against the advice of his associate Otto Faltis. Nambiar told Bains, 'I believe that with the failure of all his plans Bose will now give up political activity in order to be able to rejoin Frl Schenkl and his child'.[8]

Nambiar, however, divulged none of this to Leonard Gordon, the American biographer of the Bose brothers (Sarat and Subhas), when he wrote to Gordon decades later that 'I cannot state anything definite of the marriage of Bose referred to by you, since I came to know of it only a good while after the end of the last world war'.[9]

The CSDIC described the relationship between Subhas and Emilie in the most demeaning manner in a note appended to Nambiar's interrogation report:

> She first came into contact with Bose in 1933 in Vienna where she worked as Bose's typist. Bose fell in love with her and kept her as a mistress. She accompanied Bose on most of his tours. After Bose's departure to India in 1937, she remained in touch with him through correspondence. When Bose arrived in Vienna in 1941 . . . (Emilie) stayed throughout in his house as his wife.[10]

Vallabhbhai wrote to Sarat on 7 August 1947, the same day that he had also written to Nathalal Parikh, informing him about Subhas's marriage, enclosing the note received by Jawaharlal from Dr Akmat. Patel's letter was also intercepted by the West Bengal Special Branch. Sarat's response was one of indignation and disbelief. Referring to the report on Emilie and Subhas's marriage, he wrote a week later:

I have read the enclosure to your letter very carefully. I cannot accept the report contained therein as true. I wish you had referred the matter to me before writing to Nathalal. I do not think Nathalal has the training necessary to make enquiries of this nature and he may do more harm than good. After all, if Subhas left a family (which I do not believe) it is up to me and not to Nathalal to assist the family.[11]

On 29 August, Sarat wrote to Patel again, informing him that 'I am making enquiries and if I feel satisfied about the truth of the report, I shall certainly do the needful'. Around the same time, Jawaharlal also forwarded Nambiar's note to Sarat, and in November, Parikh sent him a photocopy of Subhas's 'testament' mentioned by Dr Akmat, which in reality was a letter from Subhas to Sarat, written on the eve of his voyage to Southeast Asia, informing him that he had married Emilie and that he had a daughter.[12] The letter from Subhas, which appears to have been written in a hurry in Bengali on 8 February 1943, read:

Today once again I am embarking on the path of danger. But this time towards home. I may not see the end of the road. If I meet with any such danger, I will not be able to send you any further news in this life. That is why today I am leaving my news here—it will reach you in due time. I have married here and I have a daughter. In my absence- please show my wife and daughter the love that you have given me throughout your life. May my wife and daughter complete and successfully fulfill my unfinished tasks—that is my ultimate prayer.[13]

Sarat finally wrote to Emilie on 10 April 1948, eight months after he first received the information from Vallabhbhai. Unknown to Sarat, Emilie had already written to him with all details nearly over two years ago. Not receiving a response to her letter dated 12 March 1946, she sent the same letter two more times—on 15 April and again on 1 August 1946. None of the letters reached Sarat. Emilie, in her letter to Sarat, had written that she and Subhas had married according to Hindu custom in January 1942:

You will be surprised to get a letter from a person unknown to you. I had for a long time hesitated till I decided to write to you in a matter regarding your family as well as mine . . .

I started working with your late brother, Sjt Subhas Chandra Bose, in 1934, when he wrote his book 'The Indian Struggle', as his secretary. You might perhaps have known that when ever he was in Europe, I have worked with him.

Your brother has come to Europe again in 1941 and asked me, if I could come and join him in Berlin to work with him. I agreed and joined him in April 1941 and we worked together till Autumn 1942.

Your brother asked me, when I was in Berlin, if I would accept his proposal to marry him. Knowing him since years as a man of good character and since there was a mutual understanding and we were fond of each other, I agreed. The only difficulty was to get the necessary marriage permission from the German Government. Though Austrian by birth, I had at that time been [a] German subject and therefore, [had] to obey German laws. And it was very difficult for a German to get the permission to marry a foreigner. And since we both did not want to beg for a favour and wanted also to avoid making an affair of the whole matter, we decided to settle it between ourselves and got, therefore, married according to Hindu fashion in January 1942. The whole thing was kept a secret, only two friends knowing about it.

On November 1942, a daughter was born to us. I had returned to Vienna in September already, in order to avoid unnecessary talking and difficulties with the German authorities. I have kept my maiden name and nationality therefore.

Our daughter's name is ANITA-BRIGITTE. She should actually bear the name of AMITA, but the German authorities would have certainly objected to such an unusual name so we chose the name Anita which is almost sounding like Amita. Brigitte was chosen by me because its short form in German in Gita.

Your brother had unfortunately only once seen your daughter when she was four weeks old . . . The day before left for the East he wrote a letter to you which he asked me to have photocopied and sent to you in case anything should happen to him. This letter is written in Bengali and he informed you about his marriage and birth of his daughter.[14]

Sarat smelled political conspiracy in the way the matter was unfolding. After recounting how he got to know of her, Sarat wrote to 'Madame Schenkl' in his letter of 10 April 1948:

It is difficult these days to trust many people here. Most of the eminent Congress leaders were political enemies of my brother and tried their best to run him down. Their attitude does not seem to have changed much, even after all that has happened since 1941.[15]

Again, on 8 July 1948, he wrote:

My wife and I went to Bombay last month and returned to Calcutta on the 4th of this month. The propaganda that is being carried on in Bombay is subtle. The suggestion is that my brother had committed a sin and had left you stranded. It is also being circulated in Bombay that Sardar Patel came to your rescue and that he has paid you Rs 18,000. I know that it is altogether false propaganda . . . Of course I did not expect anything better from eminent Congress leaders who were political enemies of my brother, or from Nathalal Parikh who joined them in September, 1945.[16]

Sarat must have gotten more detailed information by then from Nambiar who was living in his house at the time of writing this letter.

Emilie wrote to Patel, thanking him for sending Parikh to find out how they were doing. As a gesture of thanks, she sent with Parikh a photograph of Vithalbhai Patel, Sardar Patel's elder brother, which had been in her custody. Emilie also shared with Patel the letter she had written to Sarat and a note containing some additional information about her and Subhas. The note cleared the legal position on their marriage:

According to law I am not married to [be] Mrs Subhas Chandra Bose. I am therefore still bearing maiden name. It is only the custom here that a woman having a child is entitled to call herself Mrs instead of Miss, whether she is married or not [sic].[17]

She also made it clear to Patel that, 'We are living under somewhat poor conditions, but this is only due to the fact that the situation in Austria is desperate and we are not worse off than all the other people of Austria'. Thus, 'I have never asked for any financial help.'[18]

Vallabhbhai at this time proposed that Emilie and Anita could be provided financial help out of the INA relief funds. Jawaharlal appeared to be perplexed at Sarat's reaction ('Sarat Bose has refused to have anything to do with her') and approved 'the idea of a sum being set aside in trust for assistance to the daughter of Subhas Bose'.[19]

Following his initial scepticism and correspondence with Emilie for some time, Sarat travelled to Europe towards the end of 1948 to meet her (accompanied by his wife and their three children), and welcomed her into the family. Henceforth, Sarat was Emilie's *Mejdada* too, as her letters to him show. Sarat's children too started writing letters to their 'Aunty'. As far as Anita was concerned, Emilie wrote to Chitra (Sarat's daughter) in June 1949, 'It still seems funny to her that all of a sudden she has got so many sisters and brothers'.[20] Sarat called Emilie and Anita to spend time with him again in Switzerland when he went there to recuperate in mid-1949.

Two days after Sarat and his family left Vienna, Emilie wrote to Nathalal on 9 December about her experience: 'Sarat Babu is a real brother to me and her wife a real sister. All of them were charmed about Anita and Anita loves them dearly. I am really sorry we had not met before.'[21]

Yet, quite strangely, even after clearing up his own doubts and accepting Emilie and Anita into the family, Sarat never spoke publicly about Subhas's marriage although the news, mostly in distorted forms, had started making appearances across the country. This is all the more perplexing because he was not unaware of these rumours—people known to him brought them to his attention. Some of these letters were intercepted by the state intelligence departments and it cannot be ascertained whether all of them reached Sarat, but some certainly did.

Therefore, maintaining secrecy over the marriage could not have been the reason. The Government and the people already knew and they were talking, often in uncharitable ways. The best way to stop that would have been to provide the complete picture. It was not a family matter either. Subhas was a major public figure and an attempt to draw an artificial line claiming his marriage to be a family matter was unreasonable.

~

On 21 April 1949, M.R. Vyas who worked under Subhas at the Free India Centre in Germany, informed Sarat about a story published in a Gujarati biweekly of Ahmedabad, called *Hindu Samaj*, which reported that Subhas had a nine-year old son by his (civil) marriage to a 'German lady' and that she would be visiting India soon. Vyas wrote that this was not an isolated case of reporting as one of his friends had seen a similar report in a British newspaper.[22] Around the same time, Abid Hasan, Subhas's close aide in both Germany as well as Southeast Asia, sent Amiya Nath Bose a paper cutting of an Urdu weekly published from Pune, called *The Sadaji Vijai*, that also reported the existence of an eight-year-old son of Subhas.[23]

When Ramgati Ganguly, general secretary of the United Provinces Forward Bloc, asked Sarat in April 1949 about the authenticity of a news article published in the Hindi daily, *Sanmarg*, which reported Sarat's meeting with Emilie and also the existence of an eight-year-old son, Sarat's response was cryptic and puzzling. 'You should completely ignore such articles', Sarat replied, without providing any further insight.[24]

The controversy started as soon as the news of Subhas's marriage was made public in 1951, which, according to one family member, was done in a 'rather clumsy and ungracious manner'.[25] Over a year after Sarat's death, Suresh Chandra Bose's son, Arabinda, released some photographs of Emilie and Anita to the press on 4 May 1951, claiming that he was the first member of the family to have met Emilie after the war in September 1947. Arabinda explained that the news of Subhas's family was not made public earlier to ensure their safety 'because Austria was then under the occupation of the Allied Powers', oblivious of the fact that the British intelligence was aware of their existence way back in 1945. He also claimed that the family was not surprised to learn about the marriage as they were aware of their closeness from 1934, knew about the letters she used to write to him and some even used to joke about their relationship.[26]

Strangely, while Sarat had been doubting the truth of the information given to him by Vallabhbhai, Arabinda had already visited Emilie but did not share that information with him. Probably getting to know about this from Emilie, Sarat complained in his letter of 8 July 1948 that Arabinda 'has not yet handed over to me copies of the snaps he took when he was there, though I was told in Bombay last month that he had shown them to some people there'.[27]

General Mohan Singh, who was then the chairperson of the Forward Bloc (Marxist), reacted sharply to the news. Speaking at a public meeting in Calcutta's Shraddhananda Park, he questioned the timing of the publicity just before the first general elections in the country, calling it a well-planned conspiracy to defame Subhas and to prove that he was dead.[28]

Needless to say, one public statement from Sarat Bose would have been enough to clear all confusion and conspiracy theories regarding the marriage of Subhas. The question, therefore, is why he maintained the silence. It has been argued on behalf of some family members that Sarat wanted to bring Emilie back to India and then announce it publicly, but was stopped by his sudden death on 20 February 1950. There was also his increasingly intense political confrontation with the Congress leadership, which kept him completely occupied, even with his declining health and his perception that they were hitting him below the belt in spreading rumours about Subhas and Emilie.

But Sarat would have been acutely aware of another eventuality, especially keeping in mind his own initial reaction to the news: that of a strongly negative public reaction. Knowing Bengal's society intimately and being conscious of Subhas's image among people, it would not have been difficult for him to sense the kind of reaction he was going to face if he went public. This can be gauged from the reaction of some people who knew Subhas closely.

Nirad C. Chaudhuri was not a fan of Subhas Chandra Bose's politics or what he thought to be Subhas's understanding of politics. He considered his own understanding of geopolitics and military matters to be superior to that of Subhas. Yet, as an individual, his respect or admiration for Subhas seems to have grown with age, so much so that he considered him to be one of the six greatest Bengalis of all time.

Chaudhuri wrote about his initial reaction on hearing the news of Subhas's marriage in his memoirs *Thy Hand, Great Anarch!*, and in greater detail in an article published in the 'Subhas' centenary issue of the Bengali *Desh* magazine. There, he wrote:

> I clearly remember that the news of Subhas leaving behind a widow and a daughter in Germany came as a terrible blow to me. Being nearly fifty years of age at that time, I couldn't be emotional like an immature person, yet I was shocked. Therefore, I completely disbelieved the report at first.
>
> . . . To me the question of having a wife or a paramour was irrelevant. Because of my impression of Subhas—the impression which almost everyone would have had during our times—this surrender of a man like him to an ordinary woman could not have but appeared to be a fall.
>
> The reason for this was a mindset inculcated among my contemporaries from our childhood. We strongly believed that those dedicated to the service of the country had no right to be interested in a woman. This belief came from Bankim Chandra's Anandamath . . .

... Therefore, I kept wondering how could it be possible for him to deviate.

The question troubled me even more because of my knowledge about his character after I came to know him personally. I was introduced to him in October 1937. Since I worked as Sarat Babu's secretary until 1940, I got to know him very closely. I used to say at that time that of all Bengali political leaders I could trust only two with money and women— Sarat and Subhas . . . I had no doubt about them in my mind.

Let me narrate a story to illustrate how strongly his friends believed that a woman's love could never make Subhas stray from his path. Once, during a discussion on Subhas, a common friend that we had remarked that the only way Subhas could be cured of his madness was if a saucy beauty of Calcutta ravishes him. Then he would feel compelled to marry the woman from his sense of righteousness . . .

... It was natural for me to disbelieve that such a man could fall for an ordinary affair.[29]

One might very well disagree with Chaudhuri's opinion but his reaction reflected the response that the news of Subhas' marriage would have elicited from a cross section of the society.

It was not Chaudhuri alone who thought along those lines. Someone like Nathalal Parikh, who came to know Subhas in Europe when he was tending to the terminally ill Vithalbhai Patel, found that the 'news of Subhas's marriage in Germany came quite as a surprise to everyone in India'. The reason for the surprise, as is clear from Parikh's reminiscences, was not that Subhas married an Austrian woman unknown to all, but because he was known as someone who had taken the vow of being a celibate. The image of an ascetic was so strongly associated with Subhas that Parikh found an analogy of his journey to East Asia and leaving his wife and child behind with that of Buddha and Mahavira.[30]

Subhas's resolution to remain a celibate in order to surrender his life to the service of the motherland is well known from the accounts of his childhood friend Hemanta Kumar Sarkar. 'I might not be worth being called a Sannyasi any more, but I feel just as proud as in earlier days if you call me by that name', he wrote to Hemanta.[31] Throughout his life, the inner conflict between the divergent urges to devote his life to gain knowledge, to plunge into action for national liberation, and to return to a life of quiet meditation would remain his characteristic feature.[32] By his own admission he was not to marry[33] and in his single-minded quest there was no place for a romantic or sexual relation. 'I did not have any worldly ambition to start with and I . . . resolved to live a life of celibacy', a twenty-four-year-old Subhas wrote to Sarat from Cambridge.[34] The concept of *brahmacharya* (celibacy) was central to his worldview.[35] The struggle, then, was to reconcile his personal values with social mores, which often drove him to be stiff and awkward in his interaction with women.

When, in 1946, Hemanta published a compilation of letters that he had exchanged with Subhas, he reminisced:

> In the matters of money and women, Subhas was a disciple of Ramakrishna in his youth . . . Although his mother found many excellent matches for him, he refused. I knew of some women who were extremely keen to marry him. One of them even came to me for advice on how to marry him. I told her that I can make Subhas agree to marry her, but she must be prepared for the eventuality when on the first night he would ask her with folded hands, 'Why did you do this to me, mother?'[36]

The most remarkable, however, are the writings of the other childhood friend of Subhas, Dilip Kumar Roy, who maintained his close friendship as long as Subhas remained in India. The only reference among his copious reminiscences to Subhas's romantic relationship was a vague explanation in the passing, almost as if he was not quite convinced of it. Referring to Subhas's suffering at the hand of the Gandhian leadership, Dilip wrote:

> His utter loneliness amounting to a sense of dereliction haunted me and I did implore him to leave this futile gamble with the dice loaded heavily against him, a gamble that had baulked him cruelly of his victory when it seemed almost within his reach after having been re-elected as the President of the Congress . . . An inescapable consequence of this was that Subhash [*sic*] felt a growing disharmony and restlessness because life, at every turn, insisted on giving him the opposite of what he had tapped for, till it became so intolerable that he sought some solace through a romantic-cum-emotional release: but there too he failed . . .[37]

Other than this fleeting reference, all of Dilip's writings describe the ascetic and mystic nature of Subhas. He summed up Subhas in his memoirs as follows:

From the very beginning I had known Subhas as a valiant practitioner of austerities and by nature a celibate . . . Every now and then he used to say that one who has heard the call of the motherland will stray from his duty (*swadharma*) if he pays attention to call of the domestic or the family life. He was extremely fond of the last poem of Rabindra Nath's *Balaka* (A Flight of Swans)

> The sacred conch shell of the home is not for you
> Neither is the lamp lit in the evening
> Nor are the wet eyes of the beloved
> The blessings of the summer storm await you on every road

As do the thunderbolts of the rainy nights.[38]

It is worth recalling that Subhas extracted three promises from Dilip—never to have alcoholic drinks, never to visit night clubs, and never to dance with a woman. Dilip kept these promises throughout his life.[39] 'Subhas never found it easy to abdicate his reserve in any give-and-take with the fair sex. He was unaccountably stiff with them,' wrote Dilip. He advised constant guard against 'the two formidable temptations of this so-called European culture—wine and women'. There were more important tasks to be accomplished—did the Indian students come all the way to England to get involved in relationships with landladies' daughters and waste the country's money, or to acquire skills to serve the country?[40]

We find Subhas, then thirty-seven years of age, advising his young nephew, Amiya Nath Bose, in February 1934: 'Whether you practise *brahmacharya* after marriage or not, you must do it now.'[41] He then went on to explain the types of *brahmacharya* and the ways to undertake the practice based on his own experience.

Subhas himself had written, in great detail, in *An Indian Pilgrim* about the importance he accorded to the control of sexual impulses in his spiritual quest. As he was writing the book at the age of forty years, he was still struggling with the sexual instinct, but at the same time, he started questioning the method and the model he had been following:

Perhaps the most bitter struggle I had with myself was in the domain of sex-instinct. It required practically no effort on my part to decide that I should not adopt a career of self-preferment, but should devote my life to some noble cause . . . But it required an unceasing effort, which continues till today, to suppress or sublimate the sex-instinct . . .

It is now a moot question whether we should spend so much of our time and energy in trying to eradicate or sublimate an instinct which is as inherent in human nature as in animal life . . . Firstly, is complete conquest of sex, that is, a complete transcending or sublimation of the sex-instinct, indispensable to spiritual advancement? Secondly, even if it is, what is the relative importance of sex-control in a life which is devoted not so much to spiritual development as to social service—the greatest good of the greatest number[42]

Then, he noted cryptically, 'As I have gradually turned from a purely spiritual ideal to a life of social service, my views on sex have undergone transformation'. Even if this meant a transition from the model of *Anandamath*, there was no discussion about it.

The public perception about Subhas's outlook towards women was also shaped by his visible efforts to encourage and engage more women in the political arena. The volunteer force of 2000 that Subhas recruited during the 1928 Calcutta Congress consisted of 250 women, led by Latika Ghose, a niece of Aurobindo.[43] One of his closest political associates was Leela Nag (Roy), a pioneer in India's women's rights movement. In his speeches from Southeast Asia, Subhas would refer to the inspirational work of the revolutionary sisters Bina Das and Kalyani Das (Bhattacharya).

Speaking at a public meeting on crime against women, at the Albert Hall in Calcutta on 19 August 1938, Subhas made a few strong comments. He observed that the people of India had in their midst a larger number of men with a greater degree of bestiality in their character than in any other country. He expressed surprise at the fact that Indians still claimed to be spiritual people. Reserving seats for women on public transport would be quite unnecessary 'if we were a people who really respected womanhood'. 'He exhorted our young men to see to it that all women could move about freely and to teach a lesson on the spot to anyone who dared to annoy or molest any woman by look, word or deed', reported *The Modern Review*. Subhas strongly recommended opening gymnasiums in all villages and towns to teach girls and women the art of self-defence.[44]

He was opposed to whipping as a punishment, but he would have offenders against women soundly flogged in addition to other punishments.

To women, his advice was to reform their dress, shorten their veils and walk boldly with firm steps.

With people's perception of Subhas being such, they needed some time to prepare the ground for breaking the news, and this was precisely the time that Sarat was denied by his intensely busy schedule and ill health during the last two years of his life, which was terminated only by a sudden death.

While Sarat's silence is one of the reasons for the controversy and confusion, another reason is the way the issue has been handled by the family, including Emilie herself, especially regarding their claims about the date of marriage.

Writing in the 20 August 1972 issue of the *Illustrated Weekly of India*, Krishna Bose (Sarat's daughter-in-law and Sisir's wife) implied that the marriage had taken place in early 1941.[45] *A Beacon Across Asia*, a biography of Subhas edited by Sisir and published by the Netaji Research Bureau in 1973, claimed that 'in February 1942 Subhas Bose married her [Emilie] according to Indian rites'.[46] Five years later, Sisir himself claimed in an affidavit filed at the Calcutta High Court that Subhas married Emilie in 1942. He went further to claim that the marriage was valid under German and Indian laws.[47] Sisir, however, avoided giving any details regarding the marriage in his memoirs published in Bengali, named *Bosu Bari*, in 1985. Sisir's elder brother Asoke's memoirs, *My Uncle Netaji*, published in 1977, also did not contain any specifics about the marriage. Even *India in Axis Strategy*, Milan Hauner's excruciatingly detailed study, based on German archival documents and published in 1981, had no information on the marriage other than referring to Emilie as Subhas's common law wife, that is, a relation not recognized by law.

A very different public stand was taken by two members of the family. Just before Anita arrived in India for the first time in December 1960, Suresh Chandra Bose sent a telegram to Emilie, advising her to call off the visit as there was a controversy regarding Anita's parentage. He also sent a statement to the Calcutta newspapers, stating that he did not believe in the story of Subhas's marriage. The story was suppressed by the efforts of the Bose family and apparently Suresh Bose later reconciled himself to accept Anita as Subhas's daughter.[48]

Gopal Das Khosla, a retired chief justice of the Punjab High Court who was in charge of the second official inquiry on Subhas's mysterious disappearance, published a book titled *Last Days of Netaji*, based on his experience of conducting the inquiry from 1970 to 1974. Dwijendra Nath Bose, son of Subhas's eldest brother Satish Chandra Bose, filed a defamation suit against Khosla, for writing that Subhas had married Emilie, and Aroon Purie for publishing the book:

> That your petitioner's uncle Netaji Subhas Chandra Bose has all along been strictly a celibate with his life dedicated to the cause of the liberation of his Motherland and Welfare of the common people and universally known as such to all his countrymen and yet the said author of the impugned publication, GD Khosla, Accused No. 1 falsely and maliciously seeks to defame him with the following vile, hurtful and false imputations: 'Bose had left a widow and daughter in Austria.' This is wholly false, fabricated and defamatory designed to please Netaji's political enemies.[49]

Dwijen highlighted other objectionable parts of the book too. According to the order passed by the court, both Khosla and Purie had to read out an unqualified apology in the open court. Among the witnesses who deposed in favour of Dwijen were Suhrid Mullick Chowdhury, Member of Parliament, and Satya Ranjan Bakshi, confidante of Subhas and Sarat.

The whole thing was given an entirely new shape by Emilie herself in November 1971, when she told B.R. Nanda, director of the Delhi-based Jawaharlal Nehru Memorial Museum & Library (NMML), that that she had in fact gotten married to Subhas in December 1937. Very strangely she also requested Nanda, who was interviewing her for the oral history project, not to include her answer in the transcript. Seven years later, in October 1978, she repeated the same information to historian Leonard Gordon when he interviewed her for the biography that he was writing of Sarat and Subhas.[50] This change of date and the way it was done raises many questions. It is incomprehensible as to why Emilie would give a false date of marriage to Sarat, Jawaharlal, Vallabhbhai, the bureaucrats of Indian Foreign Service who regularly met her and to her friends, and then change it suddenly twenty-five years later, that too with great secrecy, only to divulge it to two persons who were not family members. Most puzzling is that while Emilie gave a new date of marriage to B.R. Nanda, she held it back from Sisir and Krishna who had visited her around the same time, although Krishna claimed to have pestered her for her suggestions on a paper she had been writing at that time on women in Subhas's life.[51]

Incidentally, the time when Emilie claims that she and Subhas got married, was also the time that Subhas was writing his unfinished autobiography. Although he mentioned in a footnote that his views on sex had undergone a change, he wrote in the main text of the book that he was still continuing with his 'unceasing effort' to 'suppress or sublimate the sex-instinct'.[52]

A curious anecdote is available from a letter by Jawaharlal to Padmaja Naidu, with whom he was romantically linked, about an incident that must have taken place soon after Subhas's return from Europe in early 1938. No details about the incident are available, but Jawaharlal's comments are intriguing. He wrote to Naidu:

> Nan has read to me a part of your letter to her relating to Subhas. I think it is disgraceful how you turn people's heads. Do you propose to collect the scalps of Congress Presidents? But no. Be kind to him and loving. Soften him and make him more human. I like him very much and I think that most people judge him harshly because of certain mannerisms and affectations.[53]

Subhas himself cannot be absolved of his share of responsibility for creating this mystery. Public reaction has been influenced to a great extent not only by his silence, but by his direct public denial of marriage on many instances. When he landed in Karachi in January 1938, someone asked him whether he was thinking of getting married. 'I have no time to think of that,' was his response.[54] If Emilie's revised version is to be believed, he was already married. Ba Maw recalled that when someone asked Subhas in Southeast Asia about when he intended to marry, he laughed back and said, 'When India is free.'[55]

His behaviour in this matter, however, is understandable and perhaps justifiable. From 1938 onwards, he was on the national scene as never before. Following his split from the Congress and going on, virtually, a warpath with the colonial Government, any talk about his personal life would have been a massive distraction. It would not only have provided an opportunity to his detractors for spreading salacious rumours, given the unusualness of his relationship, but would have spelt danger for Emilie and her family. What is inexplicable, if Emilie's amended version of their marriage is true, is Subhas not sharing such an important development in his life with at least Sarat. If it had to be kept a secret, Sarat was one person who could have managed to do it. That Subhas did not doubt this is evident from his sharing his escape plan in 1941 with his elder brother.

However, there is at least one instance where one of his close associates has claimed that he confided in her about his anxiety over the issue of marriage. 'I have done something that I don't know whether people in India will be able to understand,' Subhas told Lakshmi Sahgal in a post-dinner conversation. 'Do you think people in India will understand?' he asked her again.[56]

Yet, when all accounts are put together, Subhas's relationship with Emilie does strike a deviant note in the context of his whole life. There have been attempts at trivializing the dominant spiritual theme in his life, as in the instance of a claim by some of his family members that 'popular misconceptions of Subhas Chandra Bose's asceticism stem from an overemphasis on values and attitudes he may have held very early in his youth'.[57] As we have seen earlier, notwithstanding his attempt to segregate a life of social service from a life seeking a spiritual goal, Subhas's deep spiritual sadhana continued. It is doubtful if he could separate the two in practice. An additional point of reference here would be Ba Maw's testimony:

> 'I often have moments,' he once told me, 'when I would like to give up everything and spend my days in prayer and contemplation. But I must wait till India is liberated.'[58]

Leonard Gordon has tried to link Subhas's discussion of the theme of love in the context of his philosophical faith in *An Indian Pilgrim* to his ongoing relationship with Emilie.[59] However, the voluminous reminiscences of Dilip Kumar Roy show that love was a very central theme in Subhas's philosophical outlook in a much wider context.

12

The Covert Operative

Thousands of people, who had gathered from near and far in the open grounds near the iconic Shankar Math in Barisal, heard him with rapt attention as Subhas spoke with his characteristic passion about the need to organize and launch a mass movement for complete independence. He was delivering the presidential address at the district political conference in July 1929. When his speech was over, the poet Sabitri Prasanna Chattopadhyay, who had accompanied Subhas from Calcutta, noticed that he was missing from the podium. Suddenly, the chief organizer of the conference appeared by his side and signalled to follow him. 'Where?' Sabitri Prasanna asked. 'Just come. Subhas babu has asked for you,' came the response.

Sabitri Prasanna was led up to the door of the Shankar Math, which he found closed. As he waited, wondering what was going on, the door of the Math opened, and one by one came out the leading revolutionaries of Bengal: Arun Chandra Guha, Surendra Mohan Ghose, Trailokyanath Chakraborty and a few more. Subhas came out at the end, with another man, who was not too tall, was dark-complexioned, and had a receding hairline. 'Meet Master da,' Subhas smiled and said to a surprised Sabitri Prasanna, and hurried back to the conference. It was the first time Sabitri Prasanna met Surjya Sen, the man who was set to become a revolutionary icon in the country in about nine months as the leader of the Chittagong armoury raid.

A band of revolutionaries from different districts thus met with Subhas in utmost secrecy, in the midst of a very public event. No one knew about what had been discussed, but Sabitri Prasanna surmised later on that it had something to do with the events of April 1930.[1]

The close association that Subhas had with the revolutionary groups during his student days introduced him to the techniques of covert operations that was at the core of these groups. On his way back from England, Subhas smuggled in a copy of the proscribed *Memoirs of a Revolutionist* by Peter Kropotkin for one of his friends, Bhupendra Kumar Datta, who was associated with the Jugantar group.[2] It soon became a recurring theme, one of the characteristic strands of his entire political career that has not yet received adequate attention from researchers and biographers. The officers of the British and Indian intelligence services were probably the only ones who could be said to have adequately grasped this less-discussed side of Subhas. He was constantly followed, informers often remained close to him and more often than not, Subhas was aware of it. In this game of cat and mouse, Subhas succeeded phenomenally in hoodwinking them time and again even with fewer resources at his disposal.

The first occasion when Subhas faced the consequences of being tailed by a network of informers was in 1924. Still a greenhorn in politics, he had been appointed the Chief Executive Officer of the Calcutta Corporation. He was to be imprisoned in October, but a secret Bengal Government report shows the extent of surveillance he was under from the time that he had joined the national movement, on the basis of which the case against him was built. In fact, the information also throws some light on the infiltration of the revolutionary groups by the police and intelligence agencies. As the Government report noted:

> The story against him is derived from 10 different informers of 4 different police offices; from 5 intercepted letters; from information received from two districts in Bengal; from information given by the Director of the Intelligence Bureau at Simla . . .[3]

An 'extremely reliable agent' named K.G.S., and two more identified as A.S.P. and X.Y. consistently supplied information on Subhas, which would have been impossible without remaining close to him and his associates in the revolutionary groups. Ironically, another informer was successful in extracting information from Hari Kumar Chakravarti and others, that the political prisoners in the Midnapore Jail had written to Subhas and Anil Baran Roy warning them about police informers.

It appears likely that one of the reasons behind the fallout between Subhas and his childhood friend Hemanta was the former's suspicion that the latter could be a spy, when Gopinath Saha assassinated Ernest Day mistaking him to be Police Commissioner Charles Tegart. K.G.S. reported that Subhas had made arrangements for watching Hemanta's movements until he found out the truth.[4]

Subhas and his associates in the revolutionary groups also succeeded in creating networks amongst Government servants, information regarding most of which would have remained unknown because of the secretive nature of the work. One such case was that of Amulya Mukherji, an assistant jailor, who was dismissed from his job in 1927 because of his involvement in serious accounts irregularities. After Mukherji was dismissed, it was discovered that he acted as the contact person between revolutionaries inside jail and those outside. Mukherji joined Subhas as his secretary in 1939.[5]

Numerous police reports, now available in various archives, testify to the fact that this pattern of surveillance continued throughout Subhas's political career.

Not only was he followed in the ship in which he travelled to Europe in 1933, but all his movements and communications were recorded and reported by officers of the Indian Political Intelligence (IPI) to the concerned authorities. Declassified in 1997, the IPI files show the magnitude of surveillance on Subhas, along with Gandhi, Jawaharlal and Vallabhbhai.

Subhas had signed the contract for publishing his *The Indian Struggle* with Wishart by June 1934, but thanks to the IPI, it can be seen that he was contemplating writing the book and had a synopsis ready many months before. The structure of the book laid out in the synopsis, which the IPI managed to get their hands on in September 1933, was very different from the final form in which the book was published. Subhas planned to write the book in sixteen chapters: on the geography and natural resources of India, the problems of race, caste, languages and religion, the culture of India, Indian women, social changes across generations, India's political traditions and princes, economics, unemployment and education, India's place in world politics, and finally, on the relationship between England and India, including the evolution of the freedom struggle. Only the last section itself was planned in eighteen sections.[6]

Had Subhas succeeded in completing the book the way he had planned, it would have been a massive and invaluable compendium of his thoughts on India's development. It clearly demonstrates that Subhas was not consumed solely by the thought of liberating India at the cost of

100

612

8.3.34.

It is satisfactory that Bose is not having success in finding a publication for his autobiography or his other book.

My dear Clauson,

——— Please refer to my 2654 dated 29.9.33., with which was enclosed a synopsis of a book which Subhas BOSE contemplated writing entitled "The Indian Problem".

I now enclose for your information, a copy of the synopsis of an autobiography which he purposes writing. Although neither of these works has as yet gone beyond the synopsis stage, he has been endeavouring to secure advance contracts for them, with, however, little success. I propose to devote a paragraph to his literary efforts in a Note which is in process of preparation.

Yours sincerely,

DVW.

Synopses of the books planned by Subhas promptly reached the British sleuths.
India Office Records: L/P&J/12/214. British Library.

thinking of an independent India's reconstruction and development, as has been alleged by many authors.

It appears that Subhas changed his mind about the contents of the book and prepared a new synopsis for one that was more autobiographical. Although different again from the final form in which it was published, this synopsis was closer to *The Indian Struggle* than the previous one. Clearly, he must have decided to take a large part out of this book to include in his actual autobiography, which he started writing only in 1937, and focused more on his commentary on Indian politics from 1920. This synopsis too reached the IPI in March 1934, about three months before Subhas signed his book contract.

The question that has remained unanswered is critical. How did the synopsis, something that only a few people close to him in Europe could have access to, reach the IPI?

The surveillance not only continued but was most likely strengthened when Subhas became the *Rashtrapati*. It has been suggested that at the heart of his conflict with Gandhi and the Congress high command was certain findings about his activities by the intelligence agencies. It was, however, not only the British who were involved in the surveillance and its consequences, but also the Congress chief minister of Bombay, K.M. Munshi, a staunch follower of Gandhi's non-violence creed, who was embroiled in the controversy.[7]

A flutter was created in the official circles by two articles published in the *Bombay Sentinel* in July 1938, titled 'Clear Up Nazi Cob-Web In India' and 'Challenge To Come Out In The Open', accusing Dr Oswald Urchs, a member of the National Socialist party, of spying and propaganda activities in India under the pretext of commercial activities. Questions were raised in the Legislative Assembly, on the basis of these articles, by Congress members Mohan Lal Saxena and S. Satyamurti in August and in September 1938. The intelligence agencies were monitoring the activities of Urchs and his organization, but the Government wanted to give an impression that it was not too interested in the matter, lest the Nazi agents in India were alerted.[8]

When Subhas met Urchs on 22 December 1938, in the presence of N.G. Ganguly, it would have been noted by the intelligence agencies. Pratul Chandra Ganguly, a revolutionary associate of Subhas in Calcutta and a member of the Bengal Legislative Assembly, recounted to A.K. Mazumdar how Subhas used to clandestinely meet the German officials in Bombay:

. . . during 1938, Netaji, who was then President of the Congress, spent some time in Bombay where he was in active contact with the German Consul. Netaji took great precaution while meeting the Consul; for example, he would go to a friend's house for lunch, after which he would retire for rest, and all the guests would naturally depart. He would then change his dress, and put on sufficient disguise to hide his identity and go out to meet the Consul in the house of another friend, changing his taxi on his way.[9]

Although there might be some element of truth in such stories, and it certainly has good ingredients for a spy thriller, there is clearly much embellishment in these accounts, which came to create an enigmatic aura around Subhas.

However, it was not all just imagination. K.M. Munshi, the then chief minister of Bombay, wrote to Mazumdar that when Subhas was in Bombay:

. . . .there were stories current that he met people and even went out to see people in disguise. The Government of India knew my relations with Gandhiji and Sardar, and often saw to it that confidential information reached Gandhiji through me. On one such occasion, I was shown certain secret service reports that Netaji had contacted the German Consul in Calcutta and had come to some arrangement with him, which would enable Germany to rely upon him in case there was a war. I conveyed the information to Gandhiji, who naturally felt surprised. . . . Later, after 1942, I think, Lata Shankerlal and another . . . who knew me well, consulted me about some strange documents. In the course of the consultation, T was shown the draft of a treaty which Netaji had entered into with Japan through Shankerlal.[10]

It is more than likely that such clandestine affairs and linkages with German officials would have played a role in turning Gandhi away from the possibility of re-electing Subhas as the Congress president. Never an admirer of the clandestine methods of the revolutionary societies, Gandhi articulated his position with utmost clarity at the time of withdrawing the civil disobedience movement in 1933. Regarding secret operations, he said:

There is nothing inherently wrong in them. I fully admit the purity of purpose and the great cleverness of the workers in conducting the campaign by secret methods, devised to meet the situation created by repressive measures of the Government. But secrecy is repugnant to satyagraha and hampers its progress. It has undoubtedly contributed in a great measure to the present demoralization of the people. I know that a ban on secrecy will stop some of the activities which appeared to keep the Congress before the public eye. But this doubtful benefit will be outweighed by the certain elimination of a method which is foreign to the spirit of satyagraha and which interferes with its efficacy.[11]

The contrary point of view was articulated by a revolutionary of yesteryears, Rash Behari Bose. In a January 1938 letter to Subhas, he wrote,

In a subject country no constitutional and legal organisation can ever secure freedom . . . Only unconstitutional or illegal organisations from the British point of view can lead the country to independence. The Congress became an unconstitutional body at the time of the civil disobedience movement and hence it could do immense work.[12]

This was thus another fundamental difference in matters of principle between Gandhi and Subhas and those who had been associated with revolutionary societies. Whether making use of secret intelligence supplied secretly by the Government to Gandhi violated his principle is a moot point, but it is difficult to ignore the fact whatever impact the next big mass movement—the Quit India movement—had, was because it operated with some success by going underground. Gandhi, of course, went on to disown the movement, but it didn't prevent the party he led to take credit for it.

That, however, was not the end of the matter. On 18 July, at the height of his confrontation with the Bombay Government and the Congress high command, Subhas accused Munshi of setting a spy on him. Munshi did not refute the allegation, and only said that Subhas was being treated in the same manner as other Congress leaders.[13] A question was again raised in October in the Bombay Legislative Assembly, regarding Subhas being followed by Government agents during his Karnataka tour. Munshi clarified that one sub-inspector was present as a stenographer at all the public meetings of Subhas, and only in Belgaum there were two of them. The Government had made this arrangement only to be aware of the opinions of important leaders on key issues, Munshi explained.[14]

The one incident in Subhas's life that has achieved legendary status is his escape from British surveillance to leave India in 1941. There are strong views on both sides about whether it was a wise decision, but that does not take away from the execution of a meticulously laid plan. Multiple accounts by people associated with the event, often exaggerating their own role, lack of access to intelligence files and Subhas's own reticence about the journey had kept a veil of mystery over the planning and execution of such a daring and risky initiative. With much more information now at the disposal of researchers, the incident can be fairly reconstructed.

According to one account, while Subhas was exploring the possibility and the pros and cons of going out of India, he was at the same time secretly trying to reactivate the old revolutionary network of the First World War to help him create a mass upheaval that would eventually take the form of an armed revolution. In this task, he chose 'Maharaj' Trailokyanath Chakraborty. Maharaj went around, meeting a number of people, including Pandit Paramanand of the Lahore conspiracy case fame in Hamirpur, former Anushilan Samiti member and founder of the Rashtriya Swayamsevak Samiti, Keshav Baliram Hedgewar in Nagpur, and Ganesh Damodar Savarkar in Banaras. Having spent many years in the Cellular Jail in the Andamans, Maharaj knew both Pandit Paramanand and Ganesh Savarkar very well. The response, however, was not quite enthusiastic. Thereafter, Maharaj went out to survey the port and the hilly tracts in Chittagong. A few revolutionaries were also given the responsibility to collect or buy arms. Although much of these activities were successfully carried out in a clandestine matter, Maharaj was, before long, arrested on other charges. With Subhas too being imprisoned, the plan had to be aborted.[15]

Intelligence agencies also discovered to their horror that some of the soldiers of the 1/15 Punjab Regiment met Subhas a number of times in 1939, with the help of Niranjan Singh Talib. Four of them were discharged from the regiment and arrested.[16] Subhas advised Naik Indar Singh, the key contact in the regiment, to induce others to take steps like raising the national flag on Fort William, and to refuse to be sent to overseas posting. The plan fizzled out as a difference of opinion emerged between two others who were part of the talks—Rabi Sen of the Anushilan Samiti and Satya Ranjan Bakshi—after Subhas had to leave Calcutta for travelling to other provinces. While Bakshi pressed for immediate action, Sen advised caution until more regiments were contacted. At a secret meeting at the

unoccupied house of the Nepalese prime minister in Calcutta, they decided
to wait till the time was more conducive. However, the regiment was soon
moved out of Calcutta to Ambala and the plan remained unimplemented.
The deputy director of the Intelligence Bureau found the influence of this
contact on the desertion of a whole platoon of the regiment to the Japanese
in the Arakan front.[17]

A diverse set of people, ranging from Nirad C. Chaudhuri to V.D.
Savarkar, have been credited or have claimed credit for giving Subhas the
idea of going out of India. Close colleague and follower, Narendra Narayan
Chakravarti, has recounted Subhas giving hints of his plan to go out of
India, in his memoirs.

Savarkar's secretary, Balarao, has claimed that when Subhas met
Savarkar in Bombay on 22 June 1940, the latter advised Subhas to drop
his activities for achieving Hindu–Muslim unity and starting a mass
movement, and instead seek help from Britain's enemies. He specifically
suggested that Subhas should go to either Japan or Germany and raise an
army with the Indian soldiers captured by them to attack India via the Bay
of Bengal.[18] Balarao also wrote to the publisher of a biography of Subhas
and Rash Behari in a similar strain:

> . . . it was at a private and personal meeting between Netaji Subhas
> Babu and Savarkarji . . . that a definite suggestion was made to Subhas
> Babu by Savarkarji that he should try to leave India and undertake the
> risk of going over to Germany to organise the Indian forces there fallen
> in German hands as captives and then with the German help should
> proceed to Japan to join hands with Sri Rash Behari Bose. To impress
> this point Savarkarji showed to Subhas Babu a letter from Sri Bose to
> Savarkarji written just on the eve of Japanese declaration of war.[19]

Although Subhas, who was to be thrown into jail within the next two
weeks, wrote later about his meeting with Savarkar, he was bitter about the
latter's attitude. 'Mr Savarkar seemed to be oblivious of the international
situation and was only thinking how Hindus could secure military training
by entering Britain's army in India,' Subhas wrote.[20] It is quite possible
that the two discussed the possibility of Subhas seeking help from Britain's
opponents to lead an armed offensive on India, based on the abortive
attempt made during the First War, but it also appears that Balarao's
memory played truant, which led him to add more specifics than could

have been actually suggested by Savarkar. In particular, the idea of going to Japan from Germany (without any thought on how the armed force raised in Germany could be transported to Japan) and mixing it up with the Japanese declaration of war, which was still a year and a half away, indicates post facto embellishment.

In September 1972, Niharendu Dutta Majumdar told the G.D. Khosla Commission, which was at that time investigating Subhas's mysterious disappearance, that he had suggested to Subhas about going out of the country towards the end of 1939. According to Dutta Majumdar, Subhas was ready with his plan after the Ramgarh anti-compromise conference, but somehow it leaked out due to the carelessness of Baldev Singh, who was privy to the plan, and thus, Subhas started the Holwell monument removal movement to cover up his intention to leave the country.[21]

Dutta Majumdar did not give many details about how the plan was to be executed, but his timeline matches with that of a key player in the entire episode. Bhagat Ram Talwar, who played the role of the anchor in managing Subhas's journey from Peshawar till the Russian border, was approached to make arrangements for the trip in May 1940.[22]

Sometime after the conclusion of the Anti-Compromise Conference at Ramgarh in late March 1940, the Criminal Investigation Department (CID) of Delhi discovered that Lala Shankar Lal, member of the Forward Bloc working committee and president of the Tropical Insurance Company Limited, had handed over the responsibility of the company's affairs to another person and was missing. They also found that a passport, valid for China and Japan, had been issued by the Bombay Government in April 1940 in the name of Shankarlal Hiralal Gupta. On further investigation, the Intelligence Bureau found out that Shankarlal had secretly sailed from Calcutta on 9 April and travelled to Japan, purportedly to buy equipment for mining cobalt in Nepal. Shankarlal returned to India in July and managed to evade arrest. A case was, in the meantime, filed against him and his accomplice, but both were out on bail. Shankarlal was arrested on 9 November 1941 under the Defence of India Rules.[23]

During his subsequent interrogation, Shankarlal gave out the story of how the plan for Subhas's leaving India developed. His version was in line with Dutta Majumdar's, to the extent that the idea was first discussed towards the end of November 1939. According to Shankarlal, during the meeting of the Left Consolidation Committee at Lucknow in November 1939, Subhas had a private meeting with the representatives of the Kirti

Party, who insisted on seeking Russia's help for the revolutionary movement in India. Subhas was allegedly in agreement with the idea of joining hands with the Bolsheviks, 'even if this meant establishing a Soviet Republic in India'. During this discussion, Subhas told Shankarlal that he would go to Russia himself.[24]

At Ramgarh, Subhas told Shankarlal that his only way of going to Russia was through China, and accordingly he had applied for a passport. The Central Government, however, had refused to issue him the passport. Shankarlal proposed that since he was planning to go to Japan for business purposes, he could try to meet the Soviet ambassador in Tokyo. When Shankarlal arrived in Calcutta before his departure to Japan, Subhas briefed him in detail. Subhas asked him to meet Rash Behari Bose and gave a letter of introduction for the Soviet ambassador. In Japan, Shankarlal, unable to meet the Soviet ambassador, had long talks with a consul at the embassy and also with Rash Behari Bose. He returned to Calcutta without much success, other than vague assurances of help and Rash Behari's advice to work closely with Japan. Subhas was already in prison by the time he reached Calcutta on 9 July and, therefore, Shankarlal met Sarat Bose. Soon, he was arrested due to the forged passport case, but released on bail.

In December 1940, Shankarlal received a letter from Dwijen Bose asking him to come to Calcutta and meet Subhas. Although he briefed Subhas about his Japan trip, nothing of consequence came out of it. Subhas told Shankarlal that he had been considering ways and means of getting to Russia, for which four routes were open to him. One was to fly from Calcutta to Siam, the second being going to China via Burma. The third route was via Quetta and Iran, but he had no contacts to help him in Quetta. The fourth route was via Peshawar and Kabul. Of all these possible routes, Subhas told him, he was inclined to choose the route through Kabul. Shankarlal noted that a few days later, a meeting at Subhas's house took place with Mukand Lal Sarkar, Dwijen Bose, Mian Akbar Shah and a member of the Anushilan Samiti. Two members of the Anushilan Samiti had apparently already visited the North-West Frontier Province to assess the organizational strength of the Forward Bloc.

When Shankarlal visited Calcutta again during Christmas, he found Subhas evasive about his plan, and advised him to stay away to focus on his passport case, as he was under the limelight because of his visit to Japan. Shankarlal heard further details only after Subhas had left India, from Mian Akbar Shah.

It was not only Dutta Majumdar or Shankarlal, as Subhas was also sounding out a few other close comrades about going out of India. One of them was Nirajan Singh Talib, the editor of *Desh Darpan* in Calcutta and one of Subhas's staunch supporters. Talib later told his British interrogator that Subhas first broached the topic with him in March 1940, when he asked Talib whether he would agree to go to Russia to ensure the most suitable route before he himself went there. Talib demurred, giving the excuse of his family situation. According to Talib, Achar Singh Cheena (spelt variously as Chhina or Chena) of the Kirti Party arrived in Calcutta in June 1940, and stayed with him. Talib took Cheena to meet Subhas, who inquired if Cheena could take him to Russia. When Cheena agreed, Subhas suggested that he should go there first and make the necessary arrangements with the help of Akbar Shah. Subhas gave him some money for the purpose, but Cheena wanted more. Subhas, therefore, asked Talib to collect the necessary funds from Baldev Singh, who was later a defence minister of India.[25]

Baldev Singh, however, could not maintain secrecy. While meeting with B.N. Dey, chief engineer at the Calcutta Corporation, over drinks, Singh blurted out that Subhas could be in Moscow very soon. Dey turned up at Subhas's house the next day to find out whether the information was correct. Alarmed by the leakage of the information, Subhas instructed Talib to cancel all arrangements at once and planned to start the Holwell monument removal campaign from 3 July. He was arrested a day before that. Talib had, in the meantime, travelled to Amritsar to convey the message to Cheena. There, he met the Akali leaders, Master Tara Singh and Partap Singh Kairon, who would go on to become the third chief minister of Punjab, and shared some of the details with them.

When Tara Singh and Udham Singh Nagoke (later a member of the Rajya Sabha) came to Calcutta on the occasion of Guru Gobind Singh's birth anniversary celebrations, they informed Talib that Sardul Singh Caveeshar had asked them to meet Subhas. Accordingly, Talib took them to meet Subhas, who asked them what their attitude would be if Russia invaded India. He also inquired about the strength of their organization. Informing Subhas that the Akali Dal had about 50,000 members, half of whom were capable of handling firearms, Tara Singh said that if Russia invaded India, the Sikhs would rise in rebellion against the British and liberate Punjab as a price for their cooperation with the Russians.

Talib gave the impression to his interrogators that he had no more knowledge about Subhas's escape plan. He claimed that he was informed by Dwijen on 26 January that Subhas had gone over to Russia with the help of Akbar Shah.

From Lahore Central Jail, where he was later lodged, Talib wrote to the Home Department on 18 February 1944 that, 'I not only disapprove, but am deadly against of all his activities and plans which are prejudicial to the Defence of India, more specially since he has left this country (sic)'. Again, on 11 November 1944, a very ill Talib wrote to the Home Member:

> I am sincerely and fully convinced and solemnly believe that India's betterment lies only in bitterly opposing, by every Indian and through all means, the bloody Japan's aggression particularly and all kinds of fascist designs generally. Whosoever, is in any way siding with or looking upon Japaneses (sic), however even big or small personality, he may be, he is surely an enemy of India.

The Government, however, would not have any of it. The deputy director of the Intelligence Bureau noted on 11 March 1944 that:

> Niranjan Singh Talib's reply is sheer nonsense and it is difficult to imagine that he can think for a moment that the Government which passed the order detaining him can be so ignorant of the case against him as to be able to accept for a moment the protestations he has made. There is not the slightest doubt of the grave extent of Talib's implication in Bose's prejudicial activities and plans. The summary of his statement . . . shows this convincingly and there is other material equally incriminating.

Not only Talib, but Sardul Singh Caveeshar too changed his statements after a period of imprisonment. 'After Mr Bose left India, knowing it to be dangerous and against law to have any contact with him, I made up my mind not to have anything to do with him,' he told his interrogators. It was, however, a poor attempt at creating a diversion, and the Government called his bluff by comparing, note by note, his previous statements to the police and their own information collected from other sources. The Intelligence Bureau noted that Caveeshar 'was a party to Bose's plans: to his get away and to the camouflage which attended his departure (sic)'.[26]

Subhas, however, had started his preparations long before his vanishing act. Around June 1939, on his insistence, arrangements were made by Satya Ranjan Bakshi to have the voluminous dossier maintained by the Special Branch of Calcutta Police brought over. According to this arrangement, the dossier would be brought to him around midnight and returned to its place before dawn. Subhas and nephew Amiya went through the pages and identified the possible sources who supplied information on Subhas to the police. This helped him plan the escape in a manner which caught the police completely off their guard.[27]

On the morning of 27 January 1941, Bengal leaders Kiran Shankar Roy, Syama Prasad Mookerjee, Rajen Deb, Hemanta Bose and many others descended on Subhas's Elgin Road house as the news of his disappearance spread across the city. Also present were officers of the local police and central intelligence. The apparent anxiety of those present, coupled with varying statements by family members, friends and political associates, created a confusing situation from where it was difficult to find an answer to the question troubling everyone: Where was Subhas?

Speculation was rife. While some claimed that since he was ill, he suffered from memory loss, others claimed that he was disgusted by political bickering and decided to become an ascetic. Family members largely tended to agree with the latter possibility. The last time some friends and a few family members met him was on 16 January, when Subhas was reported to have said that he was meeting them for the last time. He closeted himself in his room, with black curtains on all doors and windows. Only his nephew Arabinda was allowed to enter the room, but only after midnight, when all the lights in the room were switched off. In his room, Subhas meditated while sitting on a tiger skin, chanted mantras with the help of a *rudraksh* garland and started tantric sadhana. Various tantric symbols were found drawn on the floor of the room. Sometimes, members of the family could hear him reciting the *Chandi*. Members of the family claimed that he had cut his hair, but had started growing a beard and a moustache. On the night of 25 January, Arabinda was not summoned by Subhas, and the light in his room remained switched on till past midnight. The next day, when it was noticed that the food that had been given to him the previous day was still lying untouched outside his room, the search for him began. It was found that he had left home only in his dhoti, leaving behind his copy of *Chandi*, the *rudraksh* garland, his shawl, the slippers that he had been wearing for some time, and all other personal belongings.[28]

Two inspectors of the Special Branch of the Calcutta Police, accompanied by the local police, searched the house for three hours and interrogated everyone who lived in the house. In the meantime, a telegram from Aurobindo's ashram in Pondicherry, in response to a query sent by Sarat, confirmed that they had no information on Subhas's whereabouts.[29]

The thoroughly confused intelligence reports clearly demonstrate that Subhas had learnt the tricks to misdirect the probing police agents and beat them at their own game. The Central Intelligence Office in Calcutta reported to the Bengal Governor's office, just seven days before he was to be found missing, that they had obtained secret information to show that Subhas was 'toying with the idea of making some open demonstrations himself . . . before going back to jail'.[30]

After they had been caught on the wrong foot, the Central Intelligence Office speculated that:

> . . . (i) he may have become subject to one of his aberrations during which he fancies himself as a sannyasi as it appears that it is recorded in his horoscope that he is to become a sannyasi in his 46th year and he has just entered his 45th year having celebrated his 44th birthday on 23rd January, or (ii) his disappearance may be a planned action, the object of which is at present obscure.[31]

The police could very soon make out that the stories given by the family were not adding up. J.V.B. Janvrin, the Deputy Commissioner of Police, Special Branch, Calcutta pointed out at least two instances which did not fit into the general picture of Subhas becoming an ascetic. A senior journalist of the Associated Press told Janvrin that he had a long discussion on current politics with Subhas about twelve days before, and having known him for many years, he did not see the slightest hint of Subhas taking the path of renunciation.[32]

The giveaway, however, was a letter from Arabinda to a student leader in Lucknow, in response to an invitation to preside over a students' conference there, which had been intercepted. Among other things, Arabinda wrote:

> I must thank you and your comrades most sincerely for kindly inviting me to preside over your conference. But, of very late, unforeseen circumstances have cropped up in my life, which prevent me from being

in your midst to take my due share in our common struggle. You must excuse me, in spite of my not giving any positive reason for absenting myself from your conference. I am not giving you any explanation for sundry weighty reasons. I hope you will know them very soon—say within the 27th. In the meantime, I must keep my mouth shut.[33]

This needless bragging was sufficient to make clear that Subhas's disappearance was a planned act, and that at least some members of the family were involved.

Unconfirmed reports came in that Subhas had been arrested in Bihar, but on inquiry, the news was found to be false.

By 28 January, the sleuths were certain that Subhas had left Calcutta on 17 January, but remained uncertain about the destination. The way in which Subhas's close associate and the financial pillar of the Forward Bloc, Shankarlal Basal (fondly called Lala Shankarlal) had hoodwinked the British intelligence in May 1940 to travel to Japan and return undetected, led them to believe that Subhas might have taken the same route. Based on input from the Special Branch in Calcutta, the Intelligence Bureau sent out telegrams to Shanghai and Hong Kong on 30 January:

Subhas Chandra Bose ex-President Indian National Congress and Bengal Congress leader believed to have left Calcutta for Japan or Russia by s.s.'Thaisang' on 17th January stop Normally clean shaven but possibly now bearded and with a forged passport stop warrant for his arrest issued in India stop Please wire information if Bose identified or destination and purpose of journey discovered enroute stop Shall be glad to have all possible information regarding his activities in far East in due course.[34]

This theory, however, was not acceptable within the Government itself, and it was quickly pointed out by the Director, Intelligence Bureau that since S.S. Thaisang was a Hong Kong-bound British boat with stops at Penang and Singapore, it was 'doubtful whether Bose would have sailed on a British boat calling only at British ports'.

The Viceroy was annoyed. He felt that the fact that Subhas 'should have got away constitutes a reflection on the police force responsible for keeping a watch on him . . . He hopes to discuss with His Excellency the Governor during his visit there.'[35]

Subhas kept the details of the planning and execution of the whole affair so close to his chest that no one, neither in Germany nor in East Asia, ever got to know anything more than some sketchy information. In fact, on one occasion, Subhas explained that it was not yet the time to divulge the full secret, because he might need to utilize the same route in order to enter India after the War.

The first public account of Subhas's days in Afghanistan, before he crossed over to the Soviet Union, came from the man who had given shelter to Subhas in Kabul in 1941, Uttam Chand Malhotra, who published a series of articles in the *Hindustan Times* in 1946. The details from the members of Subhas's family, who claimed to have been involved, started to come out only in the 1970s. The first one to come was from Sarat's son, Dr Sisir Bose, when he presented a paper at an international seminar organized by the Netaji Research Bureau in Calcutta. Although Subhas's eldest brother, Satish's son Dwijendra Nath Bose, confirmed in 1956 that the only members of the family to be involved were he, Sisir, and their two other cousins Arabinda and Ila, he refused to give out further details, claiming Subhas had put them under an oath of secrecy. 'We were asked not to divulge the matter of his disappearance to anybody even if we were hanged by the British', Dwijendra emphasized.[36] Dwijen, however, had shared the details with Subhas's childhood friend, Hemanta Kumar Sarkar, when they were lodged in the same jail in the early 1940s.[37] Arabinda agreed with the claim on the oath of secrecy, and did not share any details. Dwijendra held on to his oath until he published his version of the events in 1974, in the Bengali magazine *Amrita*. This was followed by the account published by Sisir's eldest brother, Asoke Nath Bose, in 1977, in his memoirs, *My Uncle Netaji*.

Bhagat Ram Talwar too gave his side of the story in the same international seminar in 1973, where Sisir presented his paper. The official interrogation reports of the others, where more information was available, remained locked up for many decades after independence.

Uttam Chand recalled Subhas telling him that although he was to be smuggled out of India two months before (that is, in November 1940), he was unable to do so because of some urgent work in the Calcutta Corporation, and also because he had not been able to grow a beard. After settling the business in the Corporation, Subhas stopped leaving his house under the pretext of being advised complete rest by his physicians. People were not allowed to meet him and he could be contacted only by telephone.

In the meantime, he sent word to those who were to organize his escape to decide upon a date. At 8 p.m. on 15 January, he set out of the house, in the disguise of a Maulvi, and travelled by car to a railway station 40 miles from Calcutta. Uttam Chand could not remember the name of the station from where Subhas boarded a train to Peshawar. He had a second-class ticket for the train, and arrived at Peshawar on 17 January at 9 p.m.[38]

The versions available from the family members are in agreement with each other on the broad points, although there are minor variations.

When Dwijendra was informed by Lala Shankarlal, who had just returned from his secret trip to Japan, that the Japanese Government was ready to provide any required support to Subhas, Dwijendra conveyed the message to the latter in jail. But nothing could be done if Subhas remained imprisoned. Shankarlal, therefore, devised a plan to have Subhas released, in accordance with which Sardul Singh Caveeshar met the then Punjab Governor, Sir Henry Craik, who purportedly had some influence on the Viceroy, Lord Linlithgow, with a proposal that the Forward Bloc was ready to join the Viceroy's council and would cooperate in the Government's war efforts. This, however, would be possible only if Subhas was released. On behalf of Subhas, Caveeshar asked for the departments of Home, Finance and Defence to be given to the Forward Bloc nominees. As expected, Craik refused to believe that Caveeshar's proposal was at all genuine, and asked him to take the proposal to Sir Ramaswamy Mudaliar, a member of the Viceroy's council.

Unsure of whether this approach was going to yield any result, Subhas started his fast unto death. In the meantime, Dwijendra and Caveeshar met Mudaliar in Delhi, who assured him that he would take the necessary steps when the Viceroy visited Calcutta during the Christmas holidays. By the time the Viceroy reached Calcutta, Subhas had already been allowed to shift to his home. Therefore, when the call came, asking Subhas to meet the Viceroy, he avoided it on the grounds of his poor health.

Back in his Elgin Road house, Subhas had Akbar Shah, the president of the Forward Bloc in the North-West Frontier Province, come over. Subhas asked Shah to make the final arrangements for Subhas to leave India through Afghanistan. Shah returned after some time to brief Subhas on the details of the arrangements that he had made.

Once the decision was made that Subhas would leave his house in disguise, in Sarat's Wanderer car, he asked Sisir to prepare to drive him till Gomoh station. Neither Dwijen nor Arabinda were given the responsibility, as being actively associated in politics with Subhas, there was the risk of their movements being monitored. Some funds were arranged from a few friends, including the physician Debesh Mukherjee, who had been a part of the medical mission sent to China by the Congress under Subhas's presidency. Dwijen claimed that Subhas had given him a letter to be secretly carried and delivered to Mao Tse Tung.

Sisir arrived at the Elgin Road house, from Sarat's house at Woodburn Park, on the evening on 16 January, driving the Wanderer. He had been following the same routine for the past few days so that the watchers of the Special Branch did not suspect anything to be out of order. While Ila and Arabinda helped in packing, Dwijen kept an eye on the agents of the Special Branch posted to watch the house, and found that they had dozed off in the wintry night. At half-past midnight, Subhas went down with Sisir and sat in the car. Arabinda put the luggage, a suitcase and a holdall, into the car. Slowly, Sisir drove the car out of the house and then towards Dhanbad.[39]

Asoke, Sarat's eldest son, who was living in Bararee near Dhanbad at that point, was summoned by his mother on some urgent family matter. When he reached on 21 December, Asoke was asked to see Subhas immediately. Asoke noted 'almost an entire regiment' of policemen posted outside the house—he could count at least twenty-five at any time of the day. About eight or ten watchers were posted near the junction of Elgin Road and Woodburn Road, and an equal number at a little distance away on Elgin Road. Subhas confided in Asoke his plan to 'undertake a secret journey to north-west India' and that he was thinking of 'making a short halt somewhere near Dhanbad'. The date was not yet certain, but as a matter of precaution, he asked Asoke to discharge or send home on long leave any of his servants who might have seen Subhas before. Asoke returned home on 25 December.

On the night of 16 January, Subhas boarded the Wanderer car in the guise of a Pathan, complete with a beard that covered a scar resulting from the removal of a mole that was his identification mark, and in clothes appropriate for a Pathan, which was driven away by Sisir.

At 7 am on 17 January, Sisir drove into Asoke's bungalow, just as Asoke and his wife were sitting down for breakfast. Sisir had dropped off Subhas at a distance so that he would walk up to Asoke's house to avoid being seen to be travelling with Sisir. In some time, one of Asoke's servants handed over to him a visiting card that announced the name of Mohd.

Ziauddin, Travelling Inspector, Empire of India Life Assurance Co. Ltd. With all pretentions, precautions and secrecy maintained, Subhas was driven to the Gomoh station by Asoke, his wife and Sisir, where Subhas took the Delhi–Kalka mail at midnight. Before leaving, he informed them that he was travelling to Peshawar. His plan was to get down at a wayside station before reaching Delhi and take the Frontier Mail to Peshawar.[40]

Bhagat Ram Talwar of the Kirti Party was approached by two of his comrades, Ramkishan and Achar Singh Cheena, in May 1940 in his village at Ghalla Dher to discuss the arrangements that needed to be made to help a 'very important person' to cross over to the Soviet Union. The three travelled to Peshawar to meet Abad Khan, who had been in the transport business and who had been a key link for the revolutionaries between India and Kabul. After a week's reconnaissance, the four comrades decided upon a route and Cheena was asked to convey the information to the very important person.[41]

In early July, Ramkishan was sent to Kabul with the plan to moving forward to the Soviet Union to make fresh contacts. Since Ramkishan was not able to achieve much in Kabul, Cheena too was sent up to assist him. Both having failed to establish contact with the Soviet Union through their embassy, they decided to cross the border and enter Soviet Union. On reaching the border, while Cheena successfully crossed the Amu River, Ramkishan was swept away by the current and lost his life.

When Subhas was released from the prison, Cheena was still in the Soviet Union. Subhas, therefore, convened a meeting of the Forward Bloc, whereby Mian Akbar Shah arrived in Calcutta. Akbar Shah himself had the experience of crossing over to the Soviet Union, where he studied at the 'University of the Toilers of the East'. On his return from Calcutta, Shah contacted Bhagat Ram seeking his help, to be told that they were already on the case. After meeting Abad Khan in Peshawar, along with Bhagat Ram, Shah sent word to Subhas. Bhagat Ram was informed that Subhas would be arriving by the Frontier Mail on 19 January 1941.

According to Bhagat Ram, Subhas got off the train at Peshawar and went to the Taj Mahal Hotel, clandestinely followed by Akbar Shah. Subhas was moved to another house, arranged by Bhagat Ram and his comrades, on the next morning. Bhagat Ram met Subhas for the first time on the evening of 21 January 1941. For the next phase of the journey, he was to continue with the same name, but had to act to be deaf-mute. He wore a Malaysia cloth salwar, kameez, leather jacket, khaki *kulla* (a conical cap or turban), lungi as headgear and Peshawari chappals. Bhagat Ram assumed a new name—Rahmat Khan.

After two months of struggle and suffering and playing a cat and mouse game with the local police and inquisitive people, while keeping up the undercover garb, Subhas was seen off by Bhagat Ram as he crossed over the border into the Soviet Union. This time, he assumed another identity—that of an Italian named Orlando Mazzota.

The same manner of misdirection is evident in the last leg of Subhas's journey in Southeast Asia, where his companions were found to be in disagreement with each other regarding the destination. To have a proper understanding of this phase, it is critical to have in mind some of his characteristic traits.

The first trait was that of meticulous planning. Subhas was bold but rarely impulsive, and never without a plan of action in any situation. The best example of this trait is his planning for escape in 1941, hoodwinking the formidable British police and spy network, leaving them clueless. By the time he was able to meet the Italian ambassador in Kabul, Pietro Quaroni, in February 1941, just over a month after he had left home, he was ready with a plan to set up a Free India Government in Europe.

The second trait that is intricately linked with the first is his capability to adapt, modify and innovate in response to changing circumstances. Many a time in his life, he faced circumstances which seemed to have a dead end. However, he invariably utilized the crises to innovate and emerge stronger. Some examples of such dead ends include:

a. When he was rusticated from Presidency, the future looked absolutely bleak.
b. He prepared for a career in education, but on his return from England, he was turned into an administrator by Deshbandhu C.R. Das when he was appointed the CEO of the Calcutta Corporation.
c. Hardly six months into that job, Subhas was thrown into jail in faraway Mandalay for nearly three years, without any charges or a trial. He utilized the time to prepare himself. Once he returned, he took to politics like a natural.
d. Again, within five years, he was exiled and had to stay abroad for nearly the next four years. He utilized this time to work for India

in Europe and to build his network. On his return, he was selected to be the *Rashtrapati*.

e. Faced with the opposition from the Congress's old guard, and eventually banned from the Congress, he formed his own party to pursue his radical brand of politics.

f. In the face of opposition from the leftists, the Hindu Mahasabha, the Congress and the Muslim League Government, he had his back against the wall. Following that, he was imprisoned. He chalked out a new course of action and reached Berlin.

It is in light of these traits that the final three months of Subhas in Southeast Asia need to be analysed. When things did not move according to his expectations in Germany, he shifted his base to Southeast Asia. As the war approached its end and everything seemed lost, he was again ready with a plan for the next phase.

Thus, he was not only planning, but constantly reinventing himself. August 1945 was another such crossroads, when it was time to do exactly that. He was not a person who would give up, at least not until India was free.

The third trait that is absolutely critical to understand what happened in August 1945 is Subhas's ability to maintain secrecy—a trait he had picked up from the revolutionary societies he was associated with. Information was shared with people only on a need-to-know basis, and even then, no one had the full picture of what was going on in his mind.

The critical phase started when Subhas was told by the Japanese, in mid-April 1945, that the Imphal campaign was over and that they could not defend Burma any more. From Pyinmana, Subhas and his team move down first to Rangoon and from there to Bangkok. The wealth of information available from the scores of witness accounts given to the Shah Nawaz Committee and the G.D. Khosla Commission, investigating the disappearance of Subhas in August 1945, provide an excellent basis for assessing his secret planning during this period.

Subhas refused to leave Rangoon, because he wanted to wait for the retreating soldiers. He was even ready to give up his life if required. After much persuasion by his senior officers, he reluctantly agreed and left the town three days after the Japanese had evacuated. Rangoon was captured by the British forces just four days later, on 29 April.[42] The objective was to continue the struggle from Malaya, where some of the forces were still available. His overwhelming concern at that stage was the successful evacuation of the Rani of Jhansi regiment, and as many soldiers as possible.[43] Among others, accompanying Subhas in the journey from Rangoon to Bangkok were the chief of Hikari Kikan, Saburo Isoda, and the Japanese Minister designate for the Azad Hind Government, Teruo Hachiya.[44]

On reaching Bangkok on 14 May, Subhas was received by a group of staff officers of the Southern Army Headquarters, who had been sent there by Field Marshal Terauchi to receive him. Among them was Admiral Nakado, who had suggested to Subhas that he should establish contact with Russia.[45] What did they discuss? We do not know. According to historian Joyce Lebra, Terauchi wanted Subhas to shift his HQ to Saigon, but Subhas wanted to move it with the INA units to China, and ultimately to the Soviet Union. As a preparatory step, he ordered the strengthening of the IIL and INA in Shanghai.[46]

Subhas had been trying to establish contact with the Soviet Government for quite some time. When he visited Tokyo for the last time in September–October 1944, he tried to contact the Soviet ambassador, Jacob Malik, without success. Therefore, he asked Kiani to deliver a letter to the Soviet embassy, who said that 'Since they would not receive any communication at the gate, I had to ride a bicycle up to the gate and just throw the envelope near the sentry post'.[47] On his way back from Tokyo, when Subhas met A.M. Sahay, who had lived in Japan for a long time, he asked Sahay to meet Malik. Sahay went, but was discouraged from meeting him by Foreign Minister Shigemitsu and Home Minister Uzawa. When he returned to Singapore and informed Subhas about the matter, Subhas told him that if the struggle was to go on, then the efforts to contact Soviet Union must continue.[48] In fact, the British intelligence officers later found that there were rumours that Subhas had visited the Soviet Union during the same trip. Subhas's elder brother Suresh Chandra Bose, a member of the Netaji Inquiry Committee led by Shah Nawaz Khan in 1956, who submitted a dissentient report, documented this claim in his report.

In Bangkok, Subhas held frequent meetings with his ministers to discuss the developing situation in the world, and to ponder over the question of what to do next. Mussolini and Hitler were dead. Germany had surrendered on 7 May. The questions he asked at that point were: How long could Japan hold out? What should the INA do? Should Subhas try to contact Russia again? Would Russia be encouraging the next time or refuse to deal with him?

The consensus of opinion in the Cabinet was that Subhas should press the Japanese very hard to put him in touch with somebody or the other who held a prominent position in the Moscow hierarchy, and find out how his overtures would be received. Meanwhile Subhas, with less than a handful of his most trusted lieutenants, would be ready, at short notice, to fly out of Thailand to Indo-China, China, Japan, or some other place that was nearest to the Russian territory, to avoid falling into the hands of the Anglo-Americans, when he could not keep up the fight any more.[49]

According to Isoda, Subhas proposed to move his HQ to Saigon, with branches in Shanghai and Peking (or any other place in North China). The reason for selecting Peking was that it would place Subhas close to the Russian territory, from where he would be in a better position to contact the Russians. The Japanese Government approved this plan in mid-May 1945, after some initial reluctance.[50]

While staying in Bangkok, Subhas sent S.A. Ayer and A.C. Chatterji to Saigon, to strengthen the propaganda through press and radio broadcasts, and to prepare the place as the next base of the Azad Hind Government.[51] The IIL was strengthened and the collection of funds intensified. Chatterji got in touch with the Japanese Southern Army HQ to explore the option of Subhas moving to Northern China, with at least a brigade of the INA, as the last resort. Anand Mohan Sahay was sent from Bangkok to Saigon, from where he went on to Hanoi to better organize the IIL in North Indo-China.[52] According to Kunizuka, the intelligence officer attached with Hikari Kikan, Subhas knew that the days of Japanese resistance were numbered, and sooner or later, Malaya, Siam and French Indo-China would fall to the Allied forces. Therefore, he was contemplating moving his HQ to North China, near the Mongolian border. He anticipated that his next allies were going to be the Russians.[53]

Sometime in June, Morio Takakura, Staff Officer at the IGHQ, landed in Bangkok for consultations with Subhas, Terauchi and Isoda. Takakura told the Khosla Commission two things. Firstly, that the Allied Forces had decided to arrest Subhas if he was found in Tokyo. Secondly, that the Japanese military circles had decided that it would be better for Subhas to go to an area where he could have some freedom of action rather than coming to Japan—for instance, the Soviet–Manchuria border. Subhas took his actions on the basis of these decisions. That is why he went with

Lt Gen. Shidei, and the IGHQ was aware that Subhas was moving to Manchuria with Shidei.

Thus, Subhas's plan of going to Russia was known in the Japanese Government and military circles, and efforts were being made to facilitate it.

After staying at Bangkok for a few weeks, Subhas moved the HQ to Singapore on 16 June. Isoda stayed back at Bangkok. According to Zaman Kiani, the two main tasks at Singapore were to keep the morale of the people high and to augment the 3rd INA Division for a possible defensive role. Subhas again formally asked the Japanese Government to contact the Russian authorities on his behalf in June 1945, just before moving to Singapore. The Japanese Government responded by refusing to make the effort.[54]

Although a meeting of his council of ministers on 16 June resolved to continue the fight,[55] according to one biographer of Subhas:

> Bose understood by June 1945 that the Japanese could offer him no further help. Behind the scenes Foreign Minister Togo and several advisers close to the Japanese emperor were trying to conclude the war with a surrender that protected the imperial institution. The Japanese, too, were seductively reaching out to the Russians, unaware that the latter had already committed themselves to enter the war against Japan.[56]

There is a substantial gap in information for the period between mid-June to the end of July—other than the public events, administrative activities and broadcasts, we do not have a clear idea on what exactly he was doing. It is difficult to believe that Subhas was not using this time to plan his post-war activities and to take concrete steps to implement that plan. He was not the kind of a person to just plan, sit back and wait for things to materialize on their own. He was also not the type to wait for the circumstances to decide for him what to do next.

Things started moving rapidly from August. Hiroshima (6 August) and Nagasaki (9 August) were bombed. On 11 August, in the early morning, Subhas received the news of Russia's invasion of Japan. According to Ayer, on the morning of the 12th, he was informed of Japan's surrender by Lakshmayya, General Secretary of the IIL Singapore headquarters, and Mr Ganapathy, acting Secretary of the Publicity Department of the IIL. However, T. Negishi, interpreter at the Malayan branch of the Hikari Kikan, claimed that he travelled from Singapore to Seremban to personally deliver a letter from the Japanese ambassador in Thailand to Subhas on the morning of 12 August regarding Japan's surrender. Surprisingly, no one seems to have noticed the presence of Negishi—neither Ayer nor Habib mentioned him in their accounts. In fact, Habib claimed that the news of Japan's surrender was received by Subhas after he had reached Singapore in the afternoon on that day. Negishi claimed that when he delivered the letter to Subhas, nobody was around. If this was true, it demonstrates the secrecy maintained by Subhas when he so desired.

Soon, it was time to put his plans into action.

Subhas was at Seremban during this period. With him on that morning, on 12 August, were Major General Alagappan, Colonel G.R. Nagar, Colonel Habibur Rahman and S.A. Ayer. They were joined by Dr Lakshmayya and Mr Ganapathy. Subhas asked Raghavan and Swami from Penang and Thivy from Ipoh to join him at Singapore, where he moved to on the same morning. Major General Kiani and Habibur Rahman had also been sent for.

In the evening, they attended a meeting which continued till 3 a.m., to discuss organizational and administrative measures to be taken. Other meetings continued till the afternoon of 14August. Habibur Rahman said that when A.N. Sarkar and some others suggested that 'Subhas should leave Singapore and go away to some other safer place as the Allies would adopt a very vindictive attitude towards him', Subhas refused; but, 'ultimately it was decided that he would stay there. The consensus of opinion was that Subhas should stay there because at that stage he could not look for protection or help from any country.'[57]

The Cabinet met again at 10 p.m. on 15 August and continued talks till 3 a.m.[58] Subhas kept in touch with the Japanese commander-in-chief, to keep abreast of the rapidly developing war situation in East and Southeast Asia. According to Kiani, Subhas wanted some of the INA units to go to the jungles and continue to fight under Kiani even after the British had reoccupied Malaya. However, he gave up the idea when Kiani explained the negative effects of it and 'it was unanimously agreed that we should also lay down our arms but continue the struggle in other ways after being repatriated to India'.[59]

According to Ayer, during these meetings, it was more or less decided that Subhas would stay on in Singapore with all the ministers and face the British when they eventually landed on the island. Despite opposition from his Cabinet, Subhas himself favoured the option of staying back in

Singapore. However, Ayer wrote, Subhas was inclined to reconsider the decision after having a talk with A.N. Sarkar.[60] Habib recalled, 'It was decided that Subhas should not stay there and explore possibility if he could secure asylum so as to continue the struggle. It was decided that Subhas should visit Tokyo and try to obtain a decision regarding separate surrender by INA and the Azad Hind Government'.[61]

Kiani's version is very different. According to him, Subhas wished to go away from Singapore and outside of the countries which were likely to be occupied by the Allied forces so that he did not fall into their hands. His intention was to reach Manchuria, and knowing or just anticipating that the Russian forces would occupy that province, he wanted to be captured by them with the possibility of ultimately being taken to Moscow. He wanted to take some officers with him, including Kiani. Kiani opposed his idea of going to Russia and favoured staying back in Singapore. Subhas was unambiguous about his determination to never again fall into British or American hands—he was sure that the British would try to humiliate him. This he would never accept.[62]

On the contrary, Ayer claimed that Subhas had to be persuaded to leave Singapore: 'It did not take us long to persuade Subhas finally that he must get out of Singapore'. The next question was about the destination: 'Out of Malaya definitely, to some Russian territory certainly, to Russia itself, if possible' was the final decision. There would be no reason to go to Japan after Japan's surrender, which is what Subhas and his Cabinet concluded as well.[63]

Subhas selected six people to accompany him—Habibur Rahman, Colonel Pritam Singh, Major Abid Hassan, Debnath Das, Major Swami, and S.A. Ayer.

Pritam Singh told the Shah Nawaz Khan Committee that he had had a conversation with Subhas after the meeting on the 13th or 14th, when Subhas told him that he had contacted Russia through the Japanese Foreign Minister Shigemitsu, but did not divulge his plan. This was another example of Subhas sharing information selectively, only on a need-to-know basis.

On 15 August, Major General Alagappan gave Subhas a map of the land route from Hanoi to Harbin in Manchuria, up to the point of crossing the River Amur.[64]

At 9.30 a.m. on 16 August, Subhas boarded the flight to Bangkok along with Habib, Ayer, Pritam Singh and interpreter Negishi, and reached at around 3 p.m. According to Ayer, no one in Bangkok had been informed about Subhas's arrival, and Major General Bhonsle arrived with transport two hours later only after he had been informed by the Japanese. Subhas received a stream of visitors till the morning of 17 August, as news of his presence soon spread.[65] However, Bhonsle told the Shah Nawaz Khan Committee that he had had prior intimation of Subhas's arrival: 'I received a personal telegram from Subhas saying that he was arriving in Bangkok on the 16th of August and leaving for Tokyo on the 17th'. Lt Gen Isoda told the SNK Committee that Subhas was received at the airport by him, Mr Hachya, Lt Col Takagi, Col Kagawa, Lt Nyui (Isoda's adjutant) and General Bhonsle.[66]

A different version comes from Kunizuka, who was in Bangkok. He told the SNK Committee that as soon as Subhas reached Bangkok, he went to the residence of General Isoda for a discussion on the next course of action. The following alternatives were discussed:

1. That Subhas should fly to Tokyo and seek shelter in Japan like Dr Ba Maw of the Burmese Government—this was considered undesirable as Japan was a small country and he was sure to be found out by the occupation forces.
2. That he should surrender with his forces in Bangkok to Lord Mountbatten—this idea was detested by Subhas as he hated the thought of surrendering to the British.
3. That he should fly to Manila and surrender to General MacArthur— this was considered to be little better than the second course of action, but was not favoured by Subhas.
4. That he should proceed to Manchuria to join the Russians who had already occupied Manchuria—this was considered the best option by Subhas, for which he had prepared himself for a long time, and he asked General Isoda to make the necessary arrangements for his transport.

Isoda corroborated Kunizuka's account in his statement to the Shah Nawaz Khan Committee. Isoda recalled that three to four INA officers were accompanying Subhas, but he could not remember who they were. According to him, Subhas needed funds and he wanted to go to Russia. But eventually, the plan that they settled on was that Subhas would first go to Tokyo, thank the Japanese Government for their assistance, secure more financial aid if necessary and then proceed to Russia via Manchuria.[67] Kinji Watanabe (civilian interpreter attached to the military branch of the Hikari Kikan) reached late for the meeting at Isoda's house in Bangkok. He was called to interpret a conversation between Lt Gen. Isoda and Col Kagawa on the one hand, and Subhas, Maj. Gen. Bhonsle and Lt Col Habibur Rahman on the other. By the time Watanabe reached Isoda's house, the conversation was almost over, and Isoda was speaking without any interpreter. They were discussing how to get Subhas to his destination. It was generally understood that he was to get to the Russians, probably to Manchuria. There were some doubts as to whether the Southern Command in Saigon had any planes to offer to Subhas. With regard to Subhas's going to Russia, both the embassy and the Hikari Kikan generally understood that he was going to hand himself up to the Russians in Manchuria.[68] To the Shah Nawaz Khan Committee, Watanabe said that 'It was the first time I heard Subhas making a mention of his desire to go to Russia. The plan that was discussed was that the Japanese side would assist him to go to Manchuria via Saigon, Formosa, Japan and Manchuria.'[69]

Realizing the importance of this meeting, the Combined Services Detailed Interrogation Centre (CSDIC) reinterrogated Habibur Rahman. Completely changing the thrust of the discussion, Habib told the CSDIC that the main subject under discussion was the separate surrender of the Azad Hind Government and INA. It was only when one of the senior Japanese officials present asked what Subhas himself intended to do that they discussed the possibility of his transfer to Russia. However, they thought that in view of the strained Russo–Japanese relations, the Japanese Government or Army were not in a position to negotiate with Russia, and so Subhas, according to Habib, apparently told the Japanese that he had actually decided to remain in Singapore and surrender with the rest of the Azad Hind Government and the INA. Habib claimed that he was not aware of any other talks by Subhas or members of the Government or staff regarding his transfer to Russia. Rahman claimed that Subhas had confided in him insofar as matters relating to the Armed Forces were concerned, but did not discuss his political plans with him. The CSDIC concluded that 'It is considered that even if B1269 [code name for Rahman] was in the know of Bose's plans, he would not disclose them. His manner is not very convincing. He talks in a secretive way even if no one is about.'[70] Does that not sound suspicious? While the Japanese had no doubt that they were discussing how to help Subhas reach Russia, Habib had no recollection of such a critical decision!

Hachiya told the Shah Nawaz Khan Committee that at the time of leaving Bangkok he was under the impression that Subhas was to proceed to Manchuria either directly or via Japan: 'I think he was first going to Japan. My impression was that he wanted to go to Japan to discuss his future plans and make necessary arrangements with the authorities in Japan.'[71]

It was decided that on the next day, Subhas would fly to Saigon. It was after this meeting that Subhas returned to his HQ for further consultation with his ministers. Subhas handed over a list of about ten persons whom he wanted to accompany him to the Japanese.

Despite holding such an important post in the Azad Hind Government and being so vocal about his role, Ayer seems to have had no clue about this meeting. Neither did Negishi, but he too had no doubt about Subhas's objective. Negishi told Shah Nawaz:

> As far as I could make out, Subhas's intention was to go to Manchuria. He wished to contact Russians because he was convinced that Russia was the only country which would later on fight against the British. The idea of Subhas in coming to Saigon was that he would contact FM Terauchi, discuss further plans and also obtain transport.[72]

By dawn, Subhas was ready to leave. Gulzara Singh, who had replaced N.G. Swami in Subhas's team since Swami could not reach Singapore in time, told the SNK Committee that 'We knew we were going in the direction of Japan, but I had an idea that we were heading for Russia.' In the meeting on 16 August, as Gulzara Singh recounts, Subhas had said 'there was no other country where we could go . . . but we have got no contact with them and we do not know what is going to be their treatment towards us. He also said that a Japanese officer who had long been in Manchuria would probably guide us. He did not give the name of the Japanese officer.'[73] It is, therefore, clear that Subhas knew that a Manchuria-specialist Japanese soldier would be in the same plane as him in Saigon. The presence of Lt Gen. Shidei was not a surprise to him. There is no evidence to show that anyone else in his team was aware of this. This is independently verified by Negishi:

The army HQ suggested to Subhas that a plane was proceeding to Manchuria with General Shidei on board. General Shidei was supposed to be an expert on Russian affairs in the Japanese army and was considered to be a key man for negotiations with Russia. It was suggested that Subhas should accompany him to Manchuria.[74]

Subhas gave an affectionate embrace to those who were there to see him off, with tears flowing down his cheeks—Permanand, Isher Singh, Pandit Raghunath Sastri, P.N. Pillai, Bhaskaran, Captain Rizvi and one Sunil.

The flight took off from Bangkok at 8 a.m. on 17 August, and reached Saigon at 10 a.m. According to Ayer, they flew in two planes. While Subhas was with Habib, Pritam Singh, Ayer and Kiano (a Japanese liaison officer) in one plane, the other one carried Lt Gen. Isoda, Mr Hachiya, Col Gulzara Singh, Major Abid Hassan and Debnath Das.[75] Ayer forgot to mention that Negishi and Col Kagawa were also part of the team travelling to Saigon.

Kunizuka cabled the Japanese authorities in Saigon about Subhas's departure. He also informed Subhas that the plane from Bangkok would only take him till Saigon. The Japanese Expeditionary Forces in Saigon would make arrangements for his journey to Manchuria.[76] When the team reached Saigon, they still had no idea about where they were going. Kunizuka offered a contrasting account, by stating that it was already decided beforehand that Subhas was going to Manchuria.

According to Isoda, they were received at the aerodrome by Col Tada of the Southern Army, who told them that there was only one seat available. It was then decided that Isoda would fly to Dalat—the HQ of Terauchi—and try to negotiate for more seats. Curiously, in his accounts, Ayer made it seem that Isoda and the other Japanese went along without any plans. In another lapse, he completely wiped out the critically important presence of Col Tada. Ayer's account of approaching Terauchi sounds more like a fishing expedition than to consolidate Subhas's escape plan.

While the Japanese were away, Subhas and his team went to rest at the house of Naraindas, the secretary of the housing department of the IIL, in the outskirts of Saigon. Ayer wrote that only one Indian—Chandra Mal—appeared to have known about Subhas's arrival and stay in Saigon. He was there at the aerodrome. Officers of the IIL had dispersed and no one else was present. Ayer, however, does not explain how Chandra Mal got to know about Subhas's presence in Saigon.

As they waited, a Japanese officer, Kiano, arrived to inform them that one plane was ready to leave, and that only one seat was available; however, he had no idea about where the plane was going. Subhas refused to entertain the idea of leaving on that plane unless he was informed about the destination of the flight.[77]

At Dalat, Terauchi's office told Isoda that he had agreed to make two or three seats available, apart from the one for Subhas. However, on returning to Saigon, Isoda was informed by Tada that only one additional seat could be spared.[78]

According to Ayer, when Isoda returned to inform Subhas, he was taken into a room where Habib was the only additional person allowed. Although Habib confirmed the occurrence of such a meeting, neither Isoda nor Hachiya mentioned a meeting with only Habib and Subhas.

Subhas insisted on taking the full team with him, and finally agreed, after consultation with them, to go with only one more person, only on the condition that the rest of his party would follow him the next day.

At that very moment, Subhas removed any remaining vestige of confusion about his destination. Isoda told the Shah Nawaz Khan Committee:

> Subhas told me at Saigon in his house that he would like to go to Russia via Dairen. After reaching Dairen he would try and contact the Government in Tokyo by flying direct from Dairen to Tokyo. If circumstances did not permit this, then he would proceed direct to Russia from Dairen. . . It was expected that all the passengers on board would get off the plane at Dairen and then if the circumstances were favourable, Subhas would undertake the journey to Tokyo and return to Dairen. In case the circumstances for his going to Tokyo were not favourable, he would enter Manchuria independently and try and contact the Russian forces there.[79]

According to Ayer, Subhas gathered Habib, Abid, Debnath, Ayer, Pritam and Gulzara into his room, and informed them that the plane was ready, and that the Japanese had offered only one seat to him. Although he was negotiating for an additional seat, there was no guarantee that it would be made available. Subhas and Habib went back to the meeting with the Japanese. A few minutes later, he came back to inform them that he would get one more seat and that Habib would accompany him. Turning to Ayer and Gulzara, he asked them to be ready too, just in case more seats were available.[80] This elaborate description by Ayer appears quite odd. Isoda had already ascertained that there was at least one more seat available for the flight from Saigon. So why would Subhas mention that only one seat had been offered and then renegotiate, as if Isoda was the deciding authority?

Regarding the destination of the flight, Ayer wrote: 'We did not ask him and he did not tell us. But we knew and he knew that we knew. The plane was bound for Manchuria.' Habib said:

> During our discussions with the Japanese, it was known that the plane would go to Tokyo via Formosa and some of the passengers were destined for Manchuria. I cannot say exactly whether the same plane was to take some passengers to Tokyo and from there to Manchuria or there was transhipment of one party or the other on the way.[81]

As Subhas's chosen companion, Habib's ignorance seems quite intriguing. Was it indeed ignorance, or a feeble attempt at a cover-up to confuse the others?

The information, that Subhas was heading to Manchuria, was not limited only to those around him. When A.M. Sahay was informed, between 18 and 20 August, that Subhas had left for Tokyo, he tried to travel to Manchuria:

> Although I was told that Subhas's destination was Tokyo, I was confident he was acting according to his original plan and was proceeding ultimately to Manchuria. I hoped either to rejoin him in Manchuria or to reach there earlier to make arrangements for his reception.[82]

An enduring mystery was created by divulging selective information, withholding information and by deliberate misleading and misdirecting. It should of course be added that Subhas had willing and committed partners in this game of creating a diversion. These, combined with political intrigues and a changing global order, increases the complexity of this mystery to an unbelievable level—so much so that it took decades to get to the bottom of the truth regarding his fate. Yet, so intricate was the plot that many questions remain unanswered till date.

13

The INA and Independence

By early July 1944, the Azad Hind Fauj troops holding Kohima had retreated to Tamu, and the forces attacking Imphal from Bishenpore in the west fell back to Tiddim. The Gandhi Brigade (No. 2 Guerrilla Regiment) which was defending the Tamu–Palel area, for which they received valuable help from the Naga tribes, eventually retreated towards Kalewa. The Azad Brigade (No. 3 Guerrilla Regiment) retreated from the vicinity of Mintha to Kalewa. The No. 2 Motor Transport Company, with 20 lorries, evacuated about 7000 men traversing 100 miles of road with knee-deep mud and overflowing streams. By the end of September 1944, the headquarters of the No. 1 Division had withdrawn to Mandalay and its No. 1, No. 2 and No.3 regiments were located at Budalin, Mandalay and Choungou respectively. According to Shah Nawaz Khan's estimate, the Imphal campaign cost the Azad Hind Fauj the lives of about 4000 men.[1]

Apart from the strategic error of not capturing Dimapur, the other factor that weakened the Japanese–Azad Hind Fauj offensive was moving the Japanese air force to the pacific theatre. Besieged at Imphal with the options of fighting on or surrendering, the British forces continued to hold ground with the help of 'Box defence' and reinforcements from the Arakan sector. According to Shah Nawaz, although the British forces in Imphal tried evacuating to Dimapur, it was rendered impossible by the blockade of the Kohima Road by the Japanese forces and Azad Hind Fauj.[2]

G.S. Dhillon, however, claimed that after deciding to surrender, the British forces in Imphal changed their mind. In his memoirs, *From My Bones*, Dhillon wrote:

Our forces cut off Kohima road and threatened Silchar and Dimapur. Col. Gulzara Singh marched 250 miles, outflanked the enemy with his

Azad Brigade. We were virtually knocking at the very gates of the fortress of Imphal. The 14th Army of the enemy was at the verge of surrender. Actually, they had decided to surrender. It was at this crucial stage that two of our important officers, Major Prabhu Dayal and Major JBS Grewal (sic), not being able to endure thirst and hunger any longer, went over to the enemy . . . It was from these two deserters that the enemy learnt that the INA and the Japanese were in a poor state in respect of food and ammunition . . . At such a crucial juncture, orders went to the 14th British Indian Army to postpone their surrender. The 5th Division was dropped into Imphal to reinforce the fortress from the air.[3]

Garewal was the second-in-command of the No. 2 Guerrilla Regiment, and his 'defection was quite serious as he knew of his Regiment's disposition and of the position of various Headquarters', according to M.Z. Kiani.[4]

In September, Subhas was stationed at Ye-U where he met with the retreating forces, and from there proceeded to Mandalay, about 100 miles to the south. After conferring with the Divisional and Brigade commanders, he went to Maymyo in early October to visit the base hospital, which had around 2000 patients. A detachment of the Rani of Jhansi Regiment took care of the patients at the hospital. In the middle of October, Subhas arrived in Rangoon to assess the current situation and plan for the future with his Cabinet. The key decisions taken at the Cabinet meeting were to continue fighting the British forces, intensify resource mobilization, setting up a war council and to ask the Japanese Government to abolish the Hikari Kikan and appoint an ambassador representing the Government. The total strength of the Azad Hind Fauj increased to 50,000 in some time, because of the fresh mobilization efforts.[5] The No. 4 Guerrilla Regiment (Nehru Brigade) also moved to Myingyan, about 65 miles south east of Mandalay in October, where the command of the regiment was taken over by G.S. Dhillon. The objective of the regiment was to prevent the British forces from crossing the Irrawaddy.

The evacuation of the No. 1 Division continued and by the end of January 1945, the new divisional headquarters were set up at Pyinmana, approximately 180 miles south of Mandalay. On 14 February, the British forces crossed the Irrawaddy, forcing Dhillon's forces to withdraw to Mount Popa and Kyaukpadaung, where they continued to fight valiantly and hold ground, sometimes pushing back the enemy forces to retreat despite being underequipped.

On 18 February 1945, Subhas arrived at Pyinmana to inspect the troops of the No. 1 Division as well as the troops of the No. 2 Division which had been brought forward to Mount Popa and Kyaukpadaung. Subhas moved up to Meiktila even as Mandalay, just about 85 miles north, had been taken by the British forces, which continued to move down through the Mandalay–Meiktila–Rangoon road. Meiktila was 'the nerve centre of the Japanese rail and road communication', and once captured, 'the entire Japanese force in Burma would be paralysed'. 'At that critical hour when it was absolutely clear even to a lay man that the fight for Burma was over and the defeat of the Axis powers was only a matter of days,' Shah Nawaz recalled, 'Netaji was supremely confident of our victory.' He wanted the Azad Hind Fauj to fight till the last man and 'leave behind such a legend and tradition of heroism that future generations of Indians would be proud of them'.[6] On 18 February, the No. 2 Infantry Regiment of the No. 2 Division under the command of P.K. Sehgal also reached Mount Popa.

Subhas had planned to visit his troops at Popa, 70 miles west of Meiktila, and insisted on going even when informed by the Japanese that the British forces were just 40 miles north-west of Meiktila. Despite pleading by Shah Nawaz, Mahboob Ahamad and others, he refused to move to a safer place. Instead, Subhas smiled at Shah Nawaz and said, 'You do not have to worry about my safety, as I know England has not yet produced the bomb that can kill Subhas Chandra Bose'. 'Netaji seemed to live a charmed life', Shah Nawaz stated, from his experiences with him. Somehow tricked into not going to Popa, Subhas returned to Pyinmana and from there to Rangoon, under the risk of being attacked by enemy forces, on receiving urgent messages from M.Z. Kiani and the Japanese. The stores and men of the Azad Hind Fauj were moved to Pyinmana too.[7]

Having occupied Meiktila in early March, the British forces pushed southwards. The Japanese forces mounted an offensive to recapture Meiktila in view of its strategic importance. To help the Japanese forces attacking Meiktila, it was decided that the Azad Hind Fauj and Japanese units would launch an attack at Pyinbin to destroy the British forces there. Despite fierce fighting and strong resistance put up by various units of the Azad Hind Fauj, they were no match for the British forces with their superior firepower, air force backup and troop strength. The units at Popa were ordered to withdraw on 10 April. The troops under P.K. Sehgal surrendered on 28 April. The troops under Shah Nawaz Khan, including G.S. Dhillon, surrendered on 18 May.[8]

M.Z. Kiani was informed by the Japanese around mid-April 1945 that they could not defend Burma any more. This, Kiani felt, was a shock to Subhas as it brought the curtains down on his dream of entering India at the end of the year. From Pyinmana, Subhas moved south to Rangoon with his team. With the British forces advancing, the Japanese evacuated Rangoon on 21 April. Subhas insisted that others could move to Thailand if they so wished, but he would stay back, regardless of the consequences. It was after much argument and persuasion that he agreed to leave Rangoon, but only after ensuring the withdrawal of as many soldiers as possible, especially the Rani of Jhansi Regiment. One batch of the regiment had already been sent home in March. He refused to take up the Japanese offer of flying out in a special plane placed at his disposal. A 'Janbaz' force of about 300 volunteers, specially selected from the remaining soldiers of the No. 1 Division, was created to escort the Ranis.[9] Before leaving Rangoon on 24 April, Subhas promoted all the officers left in Burma by one rank, except those officers who already had a General's rank.[10]

Since it was impossible to evacuate all troops from Rangoon due to the lack of transport and food supplies en route, A.D. Loganadan was given the responsibility to stay back in charge of about 6000 soldiers.[11] The authority of the Government of Burma having collapsed with Burmese Premier Ba Maw and his ministers leaving the city on the night of 23 April for safe haven in Japan, and the rebellion of the Burma Independence Army under Aung San, the soldiers of the Azad Hind Fauj stepped in to maintain law and order in the area until the British forces took over.[12]

Subhas started out from Rangoon on the night of 24 April, his convoy comprising four cars and twelve lorries, three of which were provided exclusively for the Ranis who numbered about a hundred. In the absence of ferrying facility, the group crossed the Sittang River, forced to abandon the vehicles. The Japanese set a number of vehicles on fire. Ayer saw Subhas standing on the bank of the river at 3 a.m. 'It was an awe-inspiring scene, Netaji standing there and fires raging round him and lorries scattered all over the place', he remembered. Although Subhas's car was made available, he refused to travel in it when everyone else was forced to walk. Eight days of forced march continued.

Netaji was in his top-boots. Few people can do forced marches in top-boots. He never slackened the pace of his walk. He never fell back even once. There he was at the head of the column doing a steady three to four miles an hour . . . Netaji sad down on the ground under a tree and got his top-boot removed and for the first time we all knew that he was having a number of blisters on both his feet.[13]

When the party took a break,

> The Head of the State, Premier and Foreign Minister of the Provisional Government of Azad Hind, Netaji Subhas Chandra Bose, on the historic retreat from Rangoon to Bangkok, sat under a tree on a blanket that was spread on the ground full of dust and dead leaves . . . Thoroughly tired, dishevelled, very hungry, with his feet aching, every limb paining, unshaven, thirsting for a cup of tea and of course for a morsel of food sat Netaji Subhas Chandra Bose on the ground under the tree . . . It was obvious that his thoughts were now as ever, for the safety and comfort of each and every one of his comrades on the trek.[14]

Twenty-one days after leaving Rangoon, Subhas and his party reached Bangkok on 14 May, vehicles and a train being made available for the last leg of the journey.

The adviser to the Azad Hind Government, A.N. Sarkar, waited for Subhas and his team on the bank of the Chao Phraya River to receive and escort them to a hotel nearby:

> I was extremely pained to see Netaji's appearance when her arrived in Bangkok—tanned and sunburnt with stubble beard, but bright eyes and sombre face. His uniform was dirty, torn at places and some buttons missing. Yet, his gait was straight and simple. Sipping tea from the cup, he looked silently at everyone around him. Breaking the silence all of a sudden, he asked me, 'Is everything alright?' I noted the familiar faint smile and inquisitive eyes.[15]

As Japan's surrender was announced on 15 August, it was finally time for Subhas to leave Singapore for an 'adventure into the unknown'. He had been conducting meetings with senior officers and ministers almost non-stop since the news of Japan's surrender reached him on the 12th at Seremban. The meetings continued as he rushed back to Singapore and called in the other trusted members of the Azad Hind Government who were, at that moment, in other towns. Decisions were taken and instructions were issued one after the other on matters relating to the surrender of the INA, the tasks for the different branches of the Indian Independence League (IIL), making provision for adequate supplies, disbanding the Rani of Jhansi Regiment camp in Singapore and sending home the five hundred girls who were still in the camp, payments to the soldiers, etc. On the afternoon of 14 April, Subhas had a tooth extraction. In the evening, he arrived at the open-air theatre where the Ranis were performing a drama on the life of Rani Lakshmibai of Jhansi, written by P.N. Oak, the aide-de-camp to J.K. Bhonsle, at the end of which the 3000 soldiers sang the national anthem, 'Subh Sukh Chain', together. A.N. Sarkar arrived from Bangkok to convey an urgent message to Subhas only to be told to join him for dinner.

The next morning, Subhas sifted through half a dozen models and rolls of paper containing designs prepared by Cyril Stracey for a memorial to the fallen soldiers of the Azad Hind Fauj. Subhas had already laid the foundation of the memorial on 8 July, in the presence of Isoda Saburo, chief of the Hikari Kikan, and the senior officers and members of the Cabinet and leaders of the Indian community.[16] 'I want this memorial to rise on the sea face of Singapore before the British forces make a landing here', Subhas told Stracey.[17]

M.Z. Kiani and J.K. Bhonsle were given the charge of the Azad Hind Fauj troops in Singapore and Bangkok respectively. In his last order issued on 16 August, Subhas appointed Kiani as the head of the Azad Hind Government. Aware of the fact that British propaganda had been painting the Fauj as a puppet army of the Japanese, Kiani asked the Japanese to state clearly during their surrender that they had no direct control over the Fauj, which had to be treated as an independent army. If the British passed any order through the Japanese, the Fauj would defy it, as Kiani himself made. On the other hand, if the British negotiated with him directly, Kiani was prepared to surrender unconditionally.

Kiani was summoned by the General Officer Commanding of the Fifth Indian Division that had taken over Singapore, and given written instructions on behalf of the Supreme Commander, South East Asia Command (SEAC) for surrender.[18]

The memorial for the fallen heroes of the Azad Hind Fauj was ready, but had a very short life. It was blown away by dynamite soon after disarming the soldiers of the Fauj. Even someone as mild-mannered as Ayer could not control his rage thinking about it:

I wonder why they did it. Honouring the dead, even when they belonged to the enemy is a tradition accepted in the code of all civilised nations. It was not expected of the British that in the hour of their victory they would let the baser part of themselves to dominate them. as long as even a single soldier of the INA lives, this crime of the British, this vandalism will never be forgotten or forgiven.[19]

~

Ravaged by the monsoon, destroyed by diseases due to a lack of food, medicine, clothing and transport, and defeated by vastly better armed and supplied Allied armies, the Azad Hind Fauj remained an unknown entity to the ordinary Indian. Let alone the story of their bravery in the face of terrible adversity, their existence itself was also a secret. Although the press around the world were publishing stories about them, mostly to mock and ridicule them, the press and the Government in India adopted a policy of silence. 'When we were in Ahmednagar Prison', Jawaharlal recalled, 'we had heard vaguely about the formation of an Indian National Army in Malaya', but 'knew very little about it'.

More information reached Jawaharlal (and presumably other Congress leaders too) in June 1945, when the Government of India released the members of the Congress working committee who had been thrown into jail at the onset of the Quit India movement in August 1942. However, he decided to maintain silence about it because 'the Japanese war was going on then and did not think it proper to say anything in public about what I heard'.[20] Thus, he spoke once the war was over.

It was on 10 May 1945 that the existence of the Azad Hind Fauj, or the Indian National Army (INA), was officially announced, with some details about it. Strikingly, the line of propaganda adopted in the press statement, which was drafted in a way so as to paint a pathetic picture of the army in the larger context of the failure of the Axis bloc through selective information and misinformation, remained the predominant way of looking at the INA in the circles of Indian officials and largely continues to remain so in the western world.

Within months of the Pacific War coming to an end, the scene was to change drastically.

Disclosing that a number of Indian POWs had been recruited by the Germans and the Japanese to fight on their side, the statement said:

These Indian soldiers have in the vast majority of cases seized the first chance of escaping from their Axis masters. Axis propagandists, with the help of Subhas Chandra Bose, paid particular attention to Indians. Every effort was made to persuade them that by joining Bose's so-called Indian National Army they would be fighting for the freedom of their countrymen. A few believed him to be a sincere patriot. Others, after Pearl Harbour, the fall of Malaya and Singapore and the invasion of Burma, felt the Allies were losing the war in the Far East and that they had better come in on the winning side. But many stood fast.

In Italy, an Indian Axis-formed unit mutinied when it learned that it was to fight against the Allies, and had to be disbanded. In France, a number of prisoners of war discarded their German uniforms and joined the Marquis, against whom they had previously enlisted to fight.

Indians landed from the Japanese submarine on the Indian coast, promptly reported to the nearest officer of the Indian Army and revealed their orders to him. At Bose's earnest request a defensive position in Burma was entrusted to his army in February of this year. His troops took the first opportunity of coming over to our lines.

Disappointed at the results they were getting, both the Germans and the Japanese tried bribery and coercion . . . Some, driven by hunger and brutality, pretended to change their allegiance. Many thousands who would not cooperate were sent by the Japanese to labour camps in the Southwest Pacific and later were found by advancing Allied forces living in conditions of indescribable filth and suffering.

These Indian prisoners of war had stood up to barbarous treatment with the same spirit which has carried the Indian Army to victory in every theatre of war and earned the praise of every Allied commander.[21]

It was claimed that approximately 3000 Indians had surrendered within the previous two weeks in the area of Meiktila, and were found to be well-equipped with the best of the British arms captured at Singapore and elsewhere.

Highlighting the 'evil genius of Bose', the war correspondent of the *Sydney Morning Herald* reported from Calcutta that it was 'not yet permissible to give the full details of the Indian National Army'. The INA story 'has been one of the most closely censored episodes of the war', commented the *Amrita Bazar Patrika*, and added that 'Subhas Chandra Bose's name was rarely allowed to be mentioned in the Indian press but his broadcasts were known to have been listened to by many Indians'. The Government authorities felt that disclosing that Indians were fighting on the side of the Japanese would dishearten Indian soldiers fighting on the Allied side because of their fear that they would be shooting at their own people. It was also argued, explained the *Patrika* report, that it would create a bad global impression to disclose that Indians had taken up arms against the Empire.

Although a few days before, the *Patrika* had published a 'totally unverified rumour' on the front page that Subhas, 'the Number One puppet of the Japanese military' had recently died in Moulmein[22] the news report on the INA was tucked in an inside page without any editorial comment. Another news item, which found a place on the front page a couple of days later, quoted an Indian connected with the Indian Independence League in Rangoon about Subhas's retreat from Rangoon to Bangkok. The Azad Hind Government would further retreat to Singapore if it was compelled to move by the advancing Allied forces. 'There is always (the) sea to jump into', the Indian was reported to have said when asked 'And from there?' by the special war correspondent of the Associated Press of India (API).[23]

The story of the INA was now out in public domain, but there was not yet any reaction from the Indian political parties. In contrast, the working committee of the Hindu Mahasabha adopted a resolution on 14 May, appealing to the Allied powers to demonstrate to the world that the blood and sacrifice of the Indians led to the liberation of their motherland and marked the end of exploitation and subjugation of India.[24] A public statement from Jawaharlal would appear in the press only on 17 August.

On 16 May, there was more news of surrender of a 600-strong battalion of the INA, 'the organisation formed under pressure by the Japanese', to units of the 14th Army at Magwe, on the east bank of Irrawaddy. The API correspondent, reporting from the advance headquarters of the Allied army, alleged that with the defeat of its 'protector' Japanese forces and large number of its own soldiers surrendering, the INA had changed its purpose to safeguard the lives of millions of Indians in the Japanese-occupied territories.[25]

The convenient narrative of the INA being an army formed under coercion, from which soldiers were deserting in large numbers, soon received a jolt. Inconvenient questions regarding the army's status soon came to the fore. The API war correspondent reported from Rangoon, 'while it is true that majority of the army is composed of POWs, most of whom probably joined under some form of duress or coercion, there is a considerable number who apparently joined quite freely'. It was estimated that about 40 per cent of the army was made up of Indian civilians. 'The Major General commanding the INA force in Rangoon claims that he and his troops should be treated as prisoners of war', since his Government had declared war on Britain. The Azad Hind Government was 'not an irridentist (sic) movement in exile', but a Government with territory recognized by eight governments, as the Major General pointed out.[26]

The top brass of the Indian Army remained derisive of the INA. An assessment from 1946 presented opinions such as 'the INA was 95% "ballyhoo" and 5% "serious business"'. It was 'still an embryo organisation' when it went to war; a 'purely guerilla force . . . with no aircraft, no artillery, no heavy mortars, no tanks or AFVs', a 'David against Goliath but a David without a sling'. 'It was never a cause of real trouble or annoyance to the Allies',[27] the report concluded. What the report conveniently ignored in its hurried assessment, no doubt spurred by an intense dislike of the very idea of the INA, was that it takes decades to build a formidable army, whereas Subhas had less than a year before the INA plunged into the Arakan, Imphal and Kohima campaigns.

The fundamental problem, however, was a trickier one of conflicting principles. It was a direct confrontation between the points of view of the British, who saw the Fauj soldiers as traitors, and the Indians, for whom these men were patriots. 'The Indian National Army (INA) had broken their oath of loyalty and had taken part in savage acts against their fellow prisoners of war who refused to fight for the Japanese', which was a point of view that Louis Mountbatten held on to even as late as 1968 while delivering the Second Nehru Memorial Lecture.[28]

When Jawaharlal arrived in Singapore on 18 March 1946 during the Burma and Malaya tour, Mountbatten deputed Brigadier J.N. Chaudhuri, later India's army chief, to ensure that Jawaharlal's visit went smoothly. Jawaharlal was received at the airport by the top officials of the former Indian Independence League (IIL), who had closely worked with Subhas, including N. Raghavan and S.C. Goho. Thousands gathered to give him a rapturous welcome[29]

When he came I told him he could go where he liked and could do what he liked but asked him to refuse the invitation of local Indians to lay a wreath on the memorial of the Indian National Army . . . I pointed out that when India became independent she would need to rely on men who did not break their oath and that soldiers should be loyal to the Government they had undertaken to serve. He saw the point and agreed not to lay their wreath.[30]

Mountbatten, for whatever reason, recounted only half the story. The *Amrita Bazar Patrika* reported that on 19 March:

> Scheduled to lay a wreath at the spot where the INA Memorial stood during the Japanese occupation, Pandit Jawaharlal Nehru disappointed thousands of his countrymen assembled at a small wooden plinth for the occasion. For some unexplained reason Pandit Nehru did not turn up but instead went direct to Singapore's 'Jalan Besar' stadium to address a mass rally of Indians.[31]

Jawaharlal went to the INA memorial and placed wreaths on it the next day, on 20 March.[32]

The extent of detestation that the British military establishment had towards the INA manifested itself in the memoirs of Francis Tuker, commander of the IV Corps that fought the Japanese at the Battle of Sittang Bend towards the end of the war, and General Officer Commanding, Eastern Command, India from January 1946. Vitriol oozed from almost every line he wrote. After his first brush with a dozen deserters from the INA in a jail in Pegu, he reflected:

> . . . they seem, after betraying their loyal brethren, to expect others to accept them at their own estimation, to hope in a dull, sneaking way that others will disregard the fact that they joined a Japanese Army to fight against their comrades. Let us hope that since they wanted to be Japanese they will just be sent packing off to make what way they can back to Japan, their spiritual home. We don't want them in India as a political tool to be used against the Indian Army.[33]

According to him, the Japanese POWs stunk, 'but at least were neither traitors to us nor to their own people', and 'showed themselves the superiors of the cowards and weaklings of the Indian Army we have just seen'. The INA was 'feeble, sordid and impotent'.[34]

The opinions of the Government were more nuanced, as they had to take a much broader view, taking the question of political repercussion into consideration. The Government of India moved fast on formulating a policy on the treatment of the INA soldiers. On 11 August 1945, the War Department sent a proposal to Frederick William Pethick-Lawrence, the Secretary of State for India, that members of the INA and the Indian Legion (950 Regiment), who had been given the epithets JIFs (Japanese-inspired fifth column) and HIF (Hitler-inspired fifth column), were to be classified into three categories and treated accordingly.

While those who were to be tried for criminal offence or whose release would be considered dangerous were termed 'Blacks', those who were members of 'an enemy organisation' and affected by enemy propaganda but not 'fundamentally or incurably disloyal' were termed 'Greys', and those whose loyalty was beyond question were labelled 'Whites'. Although evidence against 2000 soldiers was available for a trial, only 600 could be tried due to practical difficulties, as Wavell informed. Sufficient evidence did not exist against 5600 more Blacks. These 7000 would be detained as they posed a danger to security. The punishment for those who were to tried would either be death or transportation for life, and their pay would be automatically forfeited. Wavell estimated that the death sentence would be awarded in approximately fifty cases.

Those belonging to the Grey category were to be discharged from the army and their pay forfeited for the period spent as POWs, although as an act of grace, they would still retain the family allotments made during that period and allowed ordinary pension excluding the time spent as POWs. In addition, they would be given leave with pay for forty-two days before being discharged. The Whites would continue to serve in the army.

The Government also proposed to issue a public statement, emphasizing that it was going to 'treat with mercy and generosity the rank and file of those soldiers who yielded to pressure and who were so misguided as to join the forces raised by the enemy'.[35] The Government communiqué was issued on 27 August.[36] Strongly disagreeing with the idea of detaining such a large number of soldiers without any trial, Pethick-Lawrence asked whether a way could be found to bring them to trial and sought an elucidation on the difficulties for doing so. He also asked for a modification of the proposal in view of Japan's surrender, wondering whether that had not reduced the danger to security.[37]

At a meeting of the India and Burma Committee of the British Cabinet, observing that the 'general issue of principle was a serious one', Attlee held that 'if we were about to establish self-government in India', then nothing could be worse than letting the impression grow that 'rebellion was an easy thing that need not be taken seriously'. Attlee added that the difficulties to bring the offenders to trial also need not be overestimated. At the same time, he agreed with the general principle of either bringing the soldiers of the INA to trial or releasing them. The same meeting also agreed to hold elections in India, in the Centre as well as in the provinces, 'designed primarily to provide an electoral college for framing the new constitution'.[38]

Wavell provided a prescient estimate of the situation to Pethick-Lawrence in his telegram of 20 August. His anxiety was palpable. Having to deal with Subhas appeared to be such a thorny problem that he went to extent of suggesting that Subhas be eliminated instead of being allowed to return to India.

> . . . whatever policy we adopt, there may be serious trouble in the districts. This is the first occasion on which an anti-British politician has acquired a hold over a substantial number of men in the Indian Army, and the consequences are quite incalculable. Many of the INA men obviously have a great regard for Bose and he may yet become a national hero. The Cabinet should consider very carefully what to do about him. If he could be disposed of without being sent back to India, I am sure it would be a good thing.[39]

The Government of India also responded to Pethick-Lawrence's queries the next day. The difficulty in bringing to trial all the 2000 Blacks against whom there was evidence was primarily about the shortage of manpower. 250 officers of the Army would have to sit in the courts martial as a full-time commitment to close the cases within one year. In addition, officers with legal experience would need to be appointed as prosecutors and the Commander-in-Chief would need to deal with forty cases on a weekly basis. The end of the war with Japan did not alter the fact that the 7000 Blacks were 'all ardent supporters of Bose and believe in violent means for the overthrow of the existing Government of India'. Neither the Central nor the provincial governments were ready to 'face with equanimity the immediate and especially the simultaneous release' of the Blacks, and some provinces were even apprehensive about releasing the Greys.

The most worried of the lot was the Government of Bengal. 'Bengal in particular stated that their Terrorists were eagerly awaiting the return of these determined persons trained in the use of arms, and methods of violence', Pethick-Lawrence was told. The Government was worried about the impact of the INA men on the army: '. . . there is the obvious threat to the reliability of the Army and its recruiting areas'.

Amnesty could be considered only after 'a really satisfactory political settlement in India', but until then 'the authorities throughout India . . . must be allowed to use powers provided in war time to deal with a problem of unparalleled difficulty.'

The matter had already started becoming political, the Government noted. Moreover, it noticed that 'Indian political leaders, and in particular both Gandhi and Jawaharlal Nehru are taking keen interest in this matter.' It was, therefore, critically important to forestall any criticism by the early publication of the statement of policy regarding the INA soldiers.[40]

Even while agreeing with the difficulties mentioned by the Government of India, Pethick-Lawrence still would not agree to the indefinite detention of the INA soldiers. As a way out, however, he agreed to have them in military custody, while further investigations were conducted to determine the possibility of bringing them under trial by court martial.[41]

Even as the discussions were going on, nine INA men out of the thirty that had been captured had already been executed before the end of the war.[42] The political troubles were just beginning to take shape.

The impact of the INA trials cannot be fully appreciated on a stand-alone basis by delinking it from the country's political situation at the end of the war. In particular, the manoeuvres of political parties had a strong linkage with the aftermath of the Quit India movement.

In August 1942, Gandhi launched the Quit India movement. The Congress leaders who had hounded and ridiculed Subhas, for a proposal to give to the British Government an ultimatum of six months, now came together to demand immediate freedom in the middle of a war which England was fighting with its back against the wall. 'Let us have a declaration of Indian independence forthwith and we, on our part, shall immediately enter into a Treaty of Alliance with the United Nations for the sole purpose of fighting and winning this war,' declared Maulana Azad while opening the AICC meeting on 7 August 1942. The demand for freedom only meant that the reins of the Government should be in Indian hands and did not imply that the Allied forces would have to leave Indian soil, he clarified. A free India would mean more help to the Allied war effort.[43] Gandhi had allowed foreign forces to remain on Indian soil to prevent the Japanese from invading India, Jawaharlal explained. India could have no trust on Japanese declarations, Vallabhbhai said. 'Let me emphasise that there should be no underground activity. There should be no secret movement. It is a sin', Gandhi warned on 8 August.[44]

The call to the British to quit India was given, but Gandhi clarified:

... the actual struggle does not commence this moment. You have only placed all your powers in my hands. I will now wait upon the Viceroy and plead with him for the acceptance of the Congress demand. That process is likely to take two or three weeks. What would you do in the mean while? What is the programme, for the interval, in which all can participate? As you know, the spinning-wheel is the first thing that occurs to me ... Every one of you should, from this moment onwards, consider yourself a free man or woman, and act as if you are free and are no longer under the heel of this imperialism.[45]

Until the actual programme was finalized and launched, journalists were to give up writing under restrictions, newspapers to refuse to publish government notes, princes were to renounce their property and accept sovereignty of the people, government servants were to declare their allegiance to the Congress, soldiers were to refuse to fire on their own people, and students were to give up their studies only if they could continue till independence.[46] It was to be an 'open rebellion of a non-violent character'.[47]

'Congress offer of cooperation on condition of independence', ran a headline in the *Amrita Bazar Patrika* the next day.[48] 'Statement by Government: Challenge Accepted', wrote *The Observer*. The Government announced that it was going to take preventive action.[49] By the early morning of 9 August, the Government swooped down, arresting all the top leaders of the Congress.

Speaking from Germany, Subhas urged his followers to provide all support to Gandhi: 'There is not the slightest doubt that he has been influenced by the objective military situation and also by the propaganda of the Forward Bloc'. Maulana Azad would later write that Gandhi's 'admiration for Subhas Bose unconsciously coloured his view about the whole war situation'.[50] At the same time, Subhas vehemently opposed the

Congress plans to appeal to the United Nations (which 'mean in reality Britain and America—the other nations being mere puppets') and to allow the continued stationing of Allied forces on Indian soil ('which would mean, in practice, that the British Government—or the Allied Powers—could, with the consent of the Congress, prolong their occupation of India').[51]

Going much beyond the programme suggested by Gandhi on 8 August, Subhas drew up a fifteen-point action plan in his broadcast from Germany on 17 August. He called for converting the open non-violent rebellion of Gandhi into a 'guerrilla war without arms' aimed at destroying Britain's war production and paralysing the British administration in India. The action points included the boycott of British goods, holding public meetings defying official bans, organizing marches to the houses of high-ranking government officials, occupying law courts and secretariat buildings, non-payment of taxes, erecting barricades on streets, punishing British police and prison officers who showed special zeal in oppressing Indians, organizing strikes or slowing down production in war factories, organization of guerrilla bands by students, slowing down work in Government offices, stopping business with English firms, and destroying all visible symbols of British imperialism such as stamps, monuments and British flags, etc. Efforts were to be made to interrupt telegraph, telephone and postal services as well as transport services.[52]

Subhas was far away from India physically, but in certain ways, he was influencing the movement that was taking shape. The Central Intelligence Officer at Lucknow reported on 6 August that when Bal Krishna Keskar of the foreign department of the AICC visited Professor Raja Ram Shastri of the Kashi Vidyapith at Benares, he 'expressed the opinion that Japan would not attack India in the event of British withdrawal and would possibly bring Subhas Bose to influence Mr Gandhi, and through him others of the Congress, to enter into a treaty with her and other powers including Britain and adopt a neutral attitude'. In spite of Gandhi's explicit forbidding of secret activities, he planned to go underground after the AICC meeting.[53]

The Government of Assam reported to R. Tottenham, additional secretary in the Home Department, Government of India, that 'one group of the local Congress were acting on behalf of the Forward Bloc, sincerely believing that Subhas Bose was definitely landing in India with the Japanese troops by the end of August'.[54]

The arrests of the Congress leaders produced an instantaneous and spontaneous mass upsurge throughout the country, marked by mass meetings and clashes with the authorities and even setting up parallel Governments in some places:

> Huge crowds attacked police stations, post office, law courts, railway stations and other symbols of Government authority. National flags were forcibly hoisted on public buildings in defiance of the police . . . Crowds of villagers . . . physically removed railway tracks, and cut telephone and telegraph wires. Elsewhere, small groups of individuals blew up bridges . . . Students went on strike in schools and colleges all over the country and busied themselves taking out processions, writing and distributing illegal news-sheets . . . They also became couriers for the emerging underground networks. Workers too struck work: in Ahmedabad . . . Bombay . . . Jamshedpur . . . Ahmednagar and Poona . . . By the end of 1942, over 60,000 persons had been arrested. Twenty-six thousand people were convicted and 18,000 detained under the Defence of India Rules.[55]

The Deputy Inspector General of Bihar reported on 7 September, and thereafter throughout September, in a similar vein:

> The Congress insurrection has continued to monopolise public attention and the only aspect of war which has aroused any interest is the prospect of an early Japanese invasion which, according to several reports, is now the insurgents' main hope. Axis broadcasts are freely listened to everywhere, and with their stories of bombardment of Assam, aeroplanes over Calcutta and national armies waiting on the Frontier under the leadership of Subhas Bose have played an appreciable part in fomenting unrest and prolonging resistance.[56]

The Secretary of State for India informed the British War Cabinet by a memorandum on 14 October that 'Axis broadcasts may well have played some part, though its extent cannot be estimated, in stimulating subversive activities, particularly in areas such as Bengal, where the influence of Subhas Chandra Bose persists'.[57]

An all-out, brutally repressive response from the Government succeeded in bringing an end to the first phase of the movement within a span of six to seven weeks, after which the mass movement transformed into an underground one.[58] This too fizzled out in some time.

Yet, if two characteristics of 1942 stood out, they were, firstly, that the movement was closer to the conception of Subhas than of Gandhi, and secondly, although the Congress leaders decried the Government repression unleashed on the people, they could not claim credit or associate the party with the movement in the way it shaped up.

Accused of starting the movement knowing that it was going to be a violent one, Gandhi laid all the blame at the door of the Government and decided to commence a fast for twenty-one days from 9 February 1943.[59] Violence was never a part of the August resolution, he argued.[60] In February 1943, the Government of India published a booklet compiling various documents and publications that purportedly showed Gandhi's awareness of the impending violence.[61]

The author-journalist Khushwant Singh put it bluntly, when he wrote that the movement, contrary to the impression the people of India have been given since 1947 through officially sanctioned propaganda, was 'crushed within three weeks'.[62] Khushwant Singh was far from being an admirer of Bose. 'It was during this period, when the Congress leaders were ineffective, that Subhas Chandra Bose was exerting himself for India's independence,' Singh wrote.

According to a noted historian, 'By the end of 1942, the British had definitely come out victorious in their immediate total confrontation with Indian nationalism, and the remaining two and a half years of the war passed without any serious political challenge from within the country.'[63]

The failure of the Cripps Mission and the subsequent August movement had alienated the friends of the Congress in the Labour Party.[64] Arguing on the grounds that the future of the British Commonwealth depended on its relation with India, the newly appointed Viceroy, Field Marshal Archibald Wavell, recommended the reconstruction of the Viceroy's Council to be represented by the major political parties in India. The talks that commenced at Simla between the parties from 25 June, however, failed due to Mohammad Ali Jinnah's insistence that all Muslim members of the Council must be nominated by the Muslim League.

The state of mind of the leaders at this time was described by Gandhi to a journalist. It was unfortunate, he said, 'that most of his colleagues had come out of jail tired and dispirited and without the heart to carry on the struggle. They wanted a settlement with Britain and what is more, hungered for power.'[65]

With the Labour Government coming to power in July 1945, Viceroy Wavell conveyed to the Secretary of State, Pethick-Lawrence, the near-unanimous decision of the provincial governors for holding elections to the provincial and central legislatures. The meeting of the India Committee of the British Cabinet decided on 17 August that the aim of the elections should be to put in place something like a constitution-making body. Wavell arrived in London on 26 August to discuss matters further. At subsequent meetings of the India Committee, while Wavell argued for holding discussions with Indian leaders after the elections to reach an agreement over the procedure for constitution-making, Cripps and Attlee felt that the only hope for making any progress was to hold the parties against a definite plan of action that would compel them to come to an agreement in the face of the realities. After much deliberation, the British Government decided to go with Wavell's plan of holding discussions with the elected representatives after the elections to ascertain whether a modified Cripps scheme or some other formula was acceptable to them.[66]

All the background discussions, of course, were a secret when Wavell announced the elections on 19 September. The failure of 1942 was such a shattering blow that the All-India Congress Committee (AICC), which met in late September 1945 in Bombay, saw little hope for independence at that time. Vallabhbhai Patel moved a resolution on 23 September, reading:

> Neither the end of the War nor the change of Government in Britain appears to have resulted in any real change in British policy towards India, which seems to be based on delaying every advance and in attempting to create new problems and fresh complications. It is significant that there is no mention in these [British] broadcasts of the Independence of India.[67]

This was the backdrop against which the Congress party geared up to go to the general elections in the winter of 1945–46, as announced by the new Labour Government, as a precursor to reaching an agreement about the question of India's freedom. The British were insisting on a substantial agreement between the Congress and the Muslim League, before granting independence. The war had affected the British capacity to rule India further. The Congress election manifesto would go on to articulate that 'in these elections, petty issues do not count nor do individual or sectarian cries—only one thing counts: the freedom and independence of our motherland'.[68] The 'sectarian' jibe was aimed at the Muslim League, bent on partitioning India along religious lines. The Congress was all for secularism, in contradiction to the League's claim that it alone had the right to represent the Muslims of India. At this crucial juncture, the Red Fort trials commenced against the INA soldiers.

It made all the sense for the Congress party to make the best of this opportunity.

Jawaharlal first expressed his opinion on the INA on 16 August 1945 while speaking at a meeting of Sikhs at Srinagar. The INA presented a dilemma similar to the 1942 movement. It went against the Congress's creed of non-violence, and yet, with public opinion turning in its favour, the developments could not be ignored. At the first meeting of the AICC in September after the release of the Congress leaders, he defended the 1942 uprising as:

> Leaderless and without guidance from the quarters to which they were used to look for help, the people took the initiative into their own hands. How could you and me, sitting here now, pass judgment on their action?[69]

Therefore, he took the line of argument that the soldiers were misguided but their patriotism was unquestionable. He firmly said, 'I have always considered them misguided people, but have never doubted their patriotism'.[70] This was the line that was adopted by the Congress too.

Even while giving the best compliment to Subhas on 23 January 1946 that 'perhaps I might have done the same thing if I were in his position', he qualified the praise by saying, 'But I have always believed, and I still cling

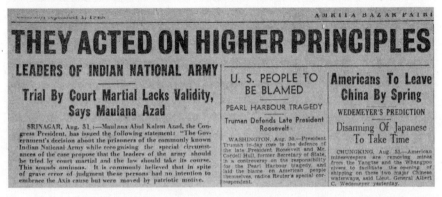

Statement of Congress president Maulana Abul Kalam Azad on the INA trials. *Amrita Bazar Patrika*, Vol. 76, Issue 6 (1 September 1945), British Library, EAP262-1-1-5191.

to this belief, that it is dangerous to take the help of another country for gaining freedom'.[71] It is difficult to reconcile the two sentences and make sense of them.

Sometime in September, Jawaharlal wrote to V.K. Krishna Menon that the soldiers of the INA, 'are the pick of the Indian army, a splendid lot, and it is worth remembering that not only is there widespread interest in them and in their fate among all classes of Indian civilians, but their old comrades of the Indian army are also intensely interested'.[72]

At the September 1945 AICC meeting, the Congress paid a backhanded compliment to the INA soldiers. The INA resolution moved by Jawaharlal Nehru said:

> The AICC is, however, strongly of the opinion that . . . it would be a tragedy if these officers, men and women were punished for the offence of having laboured, however mistakenly, for the freedom of India. They can be of the greatest service in the heavy work of building up a new and free India.

An amendment to the resolution was moved by Shrish Chandra Chatterjee, who argued that the INA under Subhas was the first organized army that fought the imperialist forces which was subjugated, and it was not desirable for the AICC to call their methods mistaken. The amendment was rejected.[73]

In other words, the Congress positioned itself as a magnanimous organization which would support patriots who were 'mistaken' in not following the creed of non-violence. Come independence, however, the INA soldiers were dropped like hot potatoes despite the exalted resolutions of the AICC.

The AICC formed a INA Defence Committee comprising Tej Bahadur Sapru, Bhulabhai Desai, K.N. Katju, Jawaharlal Nehru, Raghunandan Saran and Asaf Ali (convenor).

Patel was more forthcoming in his assessment. Writing to Biswanath Das, later to be the chief minister of Orissa, in January 1946, he noted that the benefits accruing to the Congress on account of the INA trials did not mean that the party would yield ground to Subhas Bose or his men. All that was happening was tactical.

> Naturally, our efforts have resulted in raising the strength of the Congress. The Forward Blocists may also try to derive strength and reorganise their

forces in these circumstances. But their efforts are bound to fail if they do not see things in their proper perspective. The Congress recognises the sacrifice and bravery of the INA people. That does not mean that the stand their leader took or the policy that the Forward Bloc followed in this country was right. The Congress has never accepted that position nor is there any reason to do so in the future. However, we must, for the time being, be a little more tolerant of their mistaken belief, if any, regarding the so-called justification of their attitude.[74]

Thanks to records declassified by the UK Government, it is now possible to have a more extensive insight into why Congress leaders came around to backing Bose's INA, even though violence had no place in their worldview.[75] In fact, the Director of Intelligence at the headquarters of the India Command recorded that 'Gandhi strongly disapproves of the "unthinking" glorification of the INA and its implied approval of violence.'[76]

On 23 October 1945, Brigadier T.W. Boyce of Military Intelligence (MI) sent a damning secret report to the Secretary of State for India in London. To understand the Congress game plan, the MI had used a mole of theirs. Capt. Hari Badhwar had first joined the INA, then switched sides and finally gave evidence against the INA men during the Red Fort trials.

Sourcing his information to Asaf Ali, a leading Congress working committee member, Capt. Badhwar reported that before taking a stand on the INA issue, the Congress high command had sent Ali out on a recce mission to gauge public feeling. He travelled across India and discovered that people were overwhelmingly in support of the INA. 'This inflamed feeling forced Congress to take the line it did,' Badhwar told Boyce. In his freewheeling talks with Badhwar, Asaf Ali, free India's first ambassador to the United States, offered the information that 'Congress leaders had realised that those who joined the INA were far from innocent', and that was why Jawaharlal always made it a point to refer to them as 'misguided men', even in his public speeches. Ali was positive that as and when the Congress came to power, they 'would have no hesitation in removing all INA (men) from the Services and even in putting some of them on trial'. Badhwar asked Ali why could the Congress not 'repudiate their championship of the INA' when they knew 'the true facts?'—Asaf Ali replied that 'they dare not take this line as they would lose much ground in the country'. Boyce's comment at the end of his note was: 'In other words, the present policy [to back the INA] is one of political expediency.'[77]

Much has been made about Jawaharlal donning the lawyer's gown to defend the INA. Dwijendra Nath Bose, Subhas's nephew, who had been tortured in jail during the freedom movement, was also not impressed with the argument that Nehru had set aside all past acrimony to defend the INA soldiers during the Red Fort trials:

> Do you understand the word *namavali*, which means the words 'Hare Krishna Hare Rama' are printed on clothing worn by Brahmins? So, Panditji thought it proper to wear that *namavali* of INA to cross the river of election.[78]

According to K.K. Ghosh, who was the first to write an authoritative and comprehensive account of the INA in 1960s, the Congress 'had no political programme ready at hand to rejuvenate' the dull political atmosphere. As a 'ready-made issue' the cause of the INA officers offered the Congress 'an opportunity to organise an all-India nationalist front against the British'.[79] Several records in the *Transfer of Power* series, released in the 1970s by the British Government, show that the Congress leadership's defence of the INA was motivated by a desire to excel in the elections of 1946. The Commander-in-Chief of British–Indian armed forces, General Claude Auchinleck, wrote to Field Marshal Viscount Wavell on 24 November 1945 that 'the present INA trials are agitating all sections of Indian public opinion deeply and have also provided the Congress with an excellent election cry'.[80] Similarly, Wavell was informed by Sir M. Hallett of the United Provinces (UP) on 19 November 1945 that 'the publicity on this subject (INA trials) has been a useful gift to political parties, especially the Congress, in their electioneering campaign'.[81] The then Governor of UP wrote to the Viceroy in the same month that those hitting the streets were actually suggesting that 'Bose is rapidly usurping the place held by Gandhi in popular esteem'.[82]

Another report from the Director of Intelligence at the India Command headquarters noted that the Congress's general secretary, J.B. Kripilani, said that the Congress sponsoring of the INA was intended for election purposes, and that after the elections, the Congress would drop the matter.[83]

The perceptive politician that he was, Jawaharlal was very much aware of the charges being levelled against the Congress. When he came across the issue initially, he wrote to Claude Auchinleck on 4 May 1946 that there was no thought of exploiting it for political purposes. The reactions in the country then surpassed his imagination and things started changing:

> It is sometimes said that we have exploited this INA situation for political purposes. Almost everything in India fits in somewhere into the political picture because the fact of India's subjection dominates life here. But I can say with some confidence that there was no desire or even thought of exploiting the INA issue for political purposes when this matter first came before the public. . . . The sole thought before me was that thousands of my countrymen, whom I believed to be patriotic, were in grave danger. . . . It did not strike me at all at the time that political advantage could be taken of this affair. Then a strange and surprising thing happened, not strange in itself but very surprising because of its depth and extent. Though I had sensed the mood of the Indian people, I had not fully realised how far it went in this direction. Within a few weeks, the story of the INA had percolated to the remotest villages in India and everywhere there was admiration for them and apprehension as to their possible fate. No political organisation, however strong and efficient, could have produced this enormous reaction in India. It was one of those rare things which just fit into the mood of the people, reflect, as it were, and provide an opportunity for the public to give expression to that mood. . . . The widespread popular enthusiasm was surprising enough, but even more surprising was a similar reaction of a very large number of regular Indian army officers and men. Something had touched them deeply. This kind of thing is not done and cannot be done by politicians or agitators or the like. It is this fundamental aspect of the INA question that has to be borne in mind. All other aspects, however important, are secondary.[84]

On 15 October, Bhulabhai Desai and Asaf Ali wrote to Wavell suggesting that all decisions on bringing the INA soldiers to trial be postponed until the new legislatures and the Viceroy's Council were constituted.[85] Auchinleck advised Wavell to reject the suggestion, and the trials began as announced.[86]

The Viceroy was perturbed by the Congress taking up the INA issue so vigorously, but was at a loss about what could be done. He complained to the Secretary of State a couple of weeks before the first trials commenced:

The Congress leaders evidently intend to use the story of Subhas Chandra Bose's provision Indian Government of the INA for all they are worth . . . The Congress case is built up on a misrepresentation of the status of Subhas Chandra Bose's provisional Government of India and of the character and efficiency of the INA. They will compare Bose's Government to the Government of the Occupied European countries in the UK during the war, and the INA to de Gaulle's Free French . . . I hope we may at the trials be able to bring out the true character of the INA, who with a few exceptions were not patriots, but the cowards and weaklings who could not stand up to pressure as did their stouter fellow prisoners.[87]

Soon after the first trial at the Red Fort started on 5 November, Jawaharlal wrote to Abul Kalam Azad on 16 November that the 'Indian situation is developing very rapidly, perhaps too rapidly, and the temperature of the country is rising'.[88] He informed Vallabhbhai Patel that he had asked the three heroes of the INA trials, Shah Nawaz Khan, P.K. Sehgal and G.S. Dhillon whether they would agree to contest the forthcoming elections on the Congress ticket. All three agreed.[89]

Desai's powerful oratory and legal arguments kept the country absorbed with the proceedings. When he met an Indian officer at the Chelmsford Club on 15 November, Desai told him that the trials had given the INA their best weapon for propaganda, and the way things were going, it might lead to an armed revolution.[90]

In the face of public anger and much more in their own interest, the colonial rulers had to backtrack. India was sitting on a tinderbox. Viceroy Wavell received a letter from the UP in November 1945. It read that 'handwritten leaflets are said to have been found in a hotel that if any INA soldiers were killed, Britishers would be murdered. These may be rather petty matters, but they do show which way the wind is blowing'.[91]

No one knew India's internal situation better in those days than the Director of the Intelligence Bureau. Sir Norman Smith noted in a secret report of November 1945:

The situation in respect of the Indian National Army is one which warrants disquiet. There has seldom been a matter which has attracted so much Indian public interest and, it is safe to say, sympathy . . . the threat to the security of the Indian Army is one which it would be unwise to ignore.

On 14 November 1945, William Christie, the Chief Commissioner of Delhi, wrote to the Home Secretary, A.E. Porter:

> I am very worried about the effect that all this propaganda by the Congress and in the nationalist press extolling the virtues of the INA, without any counter propaganda, is having on the people generally and on the Government servants and the loyal element of the army in particular. I am particularly worried about the effect it must be having on the police, especially the lower ranks, and it is on their loyalty that we shall have to depend in the event of trouble—and in my opinion there is certainly going to be trouble within the next few months if the present unbridled latitude to the Congress and the Press continues.[92]

A report of the Director of Intelligence at the India Command quoted wives of officers having stated that according to their husbands, things would be worse than the mutiny of 1857. 'Americans also share this fear of serious trouble . . . most local non-official civilians seem to be in a very jumpy condition in anticipation of a serious rising,' the report pointed out.[93]

Meetings and processions were organized to observe Azad Hind Day throughout the country after the trials commenced. An INA Defence Committee set up in London commenced a Subhas Memorial Fund to help the INA soldiers. Students belonging to the Muslim League joined the students of the university and other educational institutions in Lucknow to protest against police assault on the students when they observed Azad Hind Fauj Day on 12 November. Section 144, prohibiting gathering of people, was imposed in the city for a month. Prominent citizens and students who took out processions in support of the INA soldiers in Cambellpur and Rawalpindi were arrested.[94] The released INA men returned to their home provinces amidst rousing welcomes. Their accounts, for instance when five released Oriya soldiers told reporters that about 2000 Oriyas had served in the INA, led to the provinces building a tie of pride with the national army.[95] Holding a mass rally and meeting in Calcutta to celebrate the anniversary Russian revolution, the Communist Party of India (CPI) demanded the release of all INA prisoners. Recently released from prison, Sarat Chandra Bose announced that at least Rs 1 crore would be necessary to provide adequate financial aid to the members of the INA and their families. At a rally organized by the All-Assam Students' Union, Subhas's portrait was auctioned for Rs 1200.[96] The INA Relief Fund Committee in Bengal announced observance of Azad Hind Fauj Day from 8 December. The *Amrita Bazar Patrika* set up a fund for providing aid to the INA soldiers on 21 November. The Hindu Mahasabha and the Congress jointly organized a general strike in Poona on 20 November.[97]

Exaggerated stories also kept appearing in the newspapers. The Amrita Bazar Patrika published a story on 19 November that the total strength of the INA was about 1,50,000, of which only 20,000 had been brought into India.[98]

Between 21 and 24 November, serious rioting broke out in Calcutta, followed by riots in Bombay, Karachi, Patna, Allahabad, Banaras, Rawalpindi and other places.[99] Clashes between demonstrators and the police took place in Lucknow, Madurai and Lahore too. Violence erupted in Calcutta when students, after holding a meeting to observe the Azad Hind Fauj Day, took out a procession. In the ensuing clash with the police, three were killed and fifty-eight were injured. Kiran Sankar Roy, Syama Prasad Mookerjee, Radha Binode Pal (vice chancellor of the Calcutta University and soon to be appointed a judge at the war crimes tribunal for the Far East), B.C. Roy and other leaders rushed to the location to bring the situation under control. The students, however, refused to move from the streets till the time they were allowed to take their procession through the prohibited zone, which the police had stopped them from entering. The Governor of Bengal too failed to convince the students.[100]

The situation worsened the next day when the agitation spread from the students to all sections in the city, and thirteen more were killed and 131 had to be admitted to hospitals.[101] The protests spilled on to the third day with a complete stoppage of all activities in the city. More clashes resulted in five deaths and fifty-six people were injured. The city returned to some normality after the Congress leaders went around pacifying the agitators.[102] As calm returned to Calcutta, reports started arriving on police firing on demonstrators in Bombay.

A soldier of the INA, who had been released from the Nijgunj detention camp, about 20 miles from Calcutta, told the press that nine INA men were killed and nine others injured by the indiscriminate firing of the officer in charge of the camp.[103]

Widespread rioting took place in Calcutta in November 1945 in protest against the trial of the INA soldiers. *Amrita Bazar Patrika*, Allahabad, Vol. 77, Issues 324 and 326 (22 and 24 November 1945), British Library, EAP262-1-1-5256.

Auchinleck was told by some of his advisers that the Indian Army had no sympathy towards the INA, but he believed otherwise. On 26 November, he wrote to Wavell:

> I know from my long experience of Indian troops how hard it is even for the best and most sympathetic British officer to gauge the inner feelings of the Indian soldier, and history supports me in tills view. I do not think any senior British officer today knows what is the real feeling among the Indian ranks regarding the INA. I myself feel, from my own instinct largely, but also from the information I have had from various sources, that there is a growing feeling of sympathy for the INA and an increasing tendency to disregard the brutalities committed by some of its members as well as the forswearing by all of them of their original allegiance.[104]

The trial of Shah Nawaz, Sehgal and Dhillon came to an end on 31 December. Sehgal and Dhillon, found guilty of waging war against the King, were awarded the sentences of transportation for life, cashiering and forfeiture of pay and allowances while with the Japanese. The court found Shah Nawaz Khan guilty not only of waging war against the King, but also of abetment of the murder of Muhammed Hussain, and awarded him the same sentence as Sehgal and Dhillon. Auchinleck observed:

> I am not in doubt myself that a great number of them, especially the leaders, believed that Subhas Chandra Bose was a genuine patriot and that they themselves were right to follow his lead. There is no doubt at all from the mass of evidence we have that Subhas Chandra Bose acquired a tremendous influence over them and that his personality must have been an exceedingly strong one . . .

I believe that to confirm the sentence of transportation on these two officers would have the effect of making them into martyrs and of intensifying the political campaign of bitterness and racial antipathy now being waged by Congress in connexion with the 'I.N.A trials. I think too that to commute the sentence to a lesser term of imprisonment would have the same effect and that there is no compromise between confirmation of the full sentence and complete remission of it. I think we must also bear in mind the fact that if the sentences of imprisonment are confirmed they are almost certain to be remitted should an Indian National Government come into power. A reformed Executive Council even would, I think, be bound to press for a revision of sentence . . .

I propose, therefore, in all three cases to confirm the finding of the Court and to remit the sentences of transportation for life while confirming the sentences of cashiering and forfeiture of pay and allowances.[105]

P.K. Sehgal, G.S. Dhillon and Shah Nawaz Khan released.
Amrita Bazar Patrika, Vol. 78, Issue 4 (4 January 1946), British Library, EAP262-1-1-5531.

Illustration by Piciel (Pratul Chandra Lahiri), depicting the release of
Sehgal, Dhillon and Shah Nawaz.
Amrita Bazar Patrika, Vol. 78, Issue 4 (4 January 1946), British Library, EAP262-1-1-5531.

Shah Nawaz Khan bursts into tears on meeting Sarat Bose at Lahore, while P.K. Sehgal,
G.S. Dhillon look on.
Amrita Bazar Patrika, Vol. 78, Issue 10 (10 January 1946), British Library, EAP262-1-1-5537.

Shah Nawaz Khan and G.S. Dhillon speaking at a public meeting in Lahore in January 1946.
Amrita Bazar Patrika, Vol. 78, Issue 9 (9 January 1946), British Library, EAP262-1-1-5536.

Lakhs gathered at the Lahore railway station to catch a glimpse of Sehgal, Dhillon and
Shah Nawaz, January 1946.
Amrita Bazar Patrika, Vol. 78, Issue 17 (17 January 1946), British Library, EAP262-1-1-5544.

Subhas Bose's niece Bela Mitra applying tilak on Shah Nawaz Khan's forehead with her blood. *Amrita Bazar Patrika*, Vol. 78, Issue 25 (25 January 1946), British Library, EAP262-1-1-5552.

Shah Nawaz Khan rebuffing Jinnah's offer of help from the Muslim League: cartoon in the *Dawn* newspaper.
Amrita Bazar Patrika, Vol. 78, Issue 7 (7 January 1946), British Library, EAP262-1-1-5534.

A fresh round of rioting took place in Bombay during Subhas's birth anniversary celebrations on 23 January 1946. A procession organized by the Subhas Chandra Bose Birthday Celebration Committee started from Chaupati and made its way towards Bhendy Bazar, a predominantly Muslim area. Disturbances started when the police commissioner, who had issued an order the previous day, banning the procession from entering Bhendy Bazar and other Muslim-dominated areas, stopped the procession and asked it to take another route. Stopped by the police, the people in the procession squatted on the road with a large portrait of Subhas, refusing to move until they were allowed to proceed. The police, in response, fired tear gas to disperse the crowd. As people ran helter-skelter, stones were hurled at the police from adjoining buildings and lanes, prompting them to take recourse to a lathi charge. Amidst this confusion, about thirty women continued to sit on the road with Subhas's portrait. Bucketfuls of water were poured on them by the residents in the adjacent buildings to help them overcome the effects of the tear gas. Unofficial estimates put the number of people killed at ten, and those injured at 450.[106]

The clashes continued the next day, with the police again taking recourse to tear gas firing, lathi charges and firing, killing two and injuring sixty. Nearly sixty policemen also received injuries. The incidents of these two days led to widespread condemnation and criticism.[107]

By this time, Auchinleck had received many disturbing reports. On 29 December 1945, Sir Bertrand Glancy, the Governor of Punjab, wrote that 'enquiries made in the Punjab seem to suggest the existence of a very considerable degree of sympathy in the Indian Army for the INA'.[108] The Punjab Governor reported to Wavell on 16 January 1946 the massive response in Lahore to the visit of the Red Fort trio, observing that 'One disturbing feature is the attendance of Indian Army personnel in uniform at meetings held in honour of the INA accused.'[109] Himatsinhji (the first Lieutenant-Governor of Himachal Pradesh) again wrote to him on 17 February 1946 that 'the entire country is in a very hostile mood towards the British Government' and that 'the vast majority of Indians regarded the INA as, potentially, an army of liberation, and that this is the only issue upon which there is agreement between the Congress and the Muslim League'.[110] Consequently, Auchinleck was compelled to explain to his top military commanders on 12 February 1946, through a 'Strictly Personal and Secret' letter, about the reasons why the military had to let the INA 'war criminals' and 'traitors' get off the hook:

Having considered all the evidence and appreciated to the best of my ability the general trend of Indian public opinion, and of the feeling in the Indian Army, I have no doubt at all that to have confirmed the sentence of imprisonment solely on the charge of 'waging war against the King' would have had disastrous results, in that it would have probably precipitated a violent outbreak throughout the country, and have created active and widespread disaffection in the Army, especially amongst the Indian officers and the more highly educated rank and file.[111]

The nationalist fervour in the country had reached such levels by that time that it erased the differences between the Hindus and the Muslims. Violence had broken out in many states. *The New York Times* reported on 17 February 1946:

In spite of the uncompromising struggle between the two factions, last week for the first time since 1921, Moslems and Hindus together staged street protests and riot against the British in Calcutta, Bombay and New Delhi. The catalytic agent in this case was the Indian National Army, organised by a Japanese collaborator named Subhas Chandra Bose . . .

An editorial in *The Times of India* further elaborated on this on 26 February, that as a result of the Red Fort trials in Delhi, 'there was released throughout India a flood of comment which had inevitable sequel in mutinies and alarming outbreaks of civil violence in Calcutta, Bombay, Delhi and elsewhere'. At the same time, in London, a number of British MPs met Attlee on 13 February 1946 to give their frank reading of the situation. Among the observations and suggestions by the MPs were:

There are two alternative ways of meeting this common desire (a) that we should arrange to get out, (b) that we should wait to be driven out. In regard to (b), the loyalty of the Indian Army is open to question; the INA have become national heroes under the boosting of the Congress; the possibility cannot be excluded that Congress could form an 'Independent Indian Army' . . .

The effect of the INA trials have been very severe but markedly different among different elements in the Army. The old long service class, such as the VCOs, are deeply offended that the INA have not been treated with the full rigour of the law, but the younger generation are impressed by the political aspect. Nevertheless on the whole the Army could be relied on to do its duty except in the event of civil war in which case its loyalty would inevitably be divided among the combatants.

The INA trials had had a bad effect on the Army but it was reliable still for dealing with riots but not for anything more serious.[112]

After fifteen more INA men were court-martialled, the Government decided to discontinue the trials at the end of April 1946.

The most perceptive assessment of the country's situation towards the end of 1945 came from the man who was in one of the best positions to combine both a broad as well as a detailed view. It showed how unsettling the INA affair had been for the Government. In his assessment of the internal situation in India, Auchinleck made the following observations:

> It is possible that the Congress may excite popular feeling over some issue such as that of the INA to such an extent that they may lose control. On the other hand, their most recent utterances might be held to show that they realise this danger . . .
>
> . . . There are now large quantities of unlicensed arms throughout India and there will be may ex-INA men to use them, if they feel so inclined. There will also be a considerable number of ordinary demobilized soldiers in town and villages, many of whom may be persuaded to support Congress. All these men are train in the use of weapons, and members of the INA have some training in the technique of anti-British leadership. . . .
>
> . . . It can be concluded, therefore, that if and when trouble comes it may be on a greater scale than in August 1942 . . . Also there will be more arms and more men trained in their use at the disposal of the forces of disorder, and the disruption of communications is likely to be designed to isolate and gain control of large tracts . . .
>
> The Congress INA campaign has undoubtedly taken a strong hold of the country as a whole and must have an unsettling effect on the Armed Forces generally and make them receptive to Congress doctrine . . .
>
> As is to be expected, most Indian officers are Nationalists and may, therefore, be over persuaded by Congress propaganda . . .
>
> The release into recruiting areas of large numbers of potentially disaffected men from the INA with its possible contaminating effect on

individual service men through their families, and on the armed forces as
a whole through new recruits, or men returning from leave.[113]

The British Cabinet, however, was not fully satisfied with Auchinleck's
report, which failed to address a long-term question troubling their mind:
'consequences of the policy adopted for the trials on the Indian Army
of the future in its relationship to the Government of a self-governing
India'.[114]

The British Government was moving fast to execute its assurances on
the transfer of power. On 14 January 1946, a meeting of the India and
Burma Committee chaired by Attlee decided to send a mission of three
cabinet ministers to India towards the end of March, when the results of
the elections would be fully known. Wavell's idea of holding discussions
with the elected representatives and other leaders on the next course of
constitutional development was retained, but instead of Wavell, the
discussions were to be held by the three cabinet ministers. The decision
was taken primarily because Attlee did not have faith in Wavell's skills to
deal with such a situation.[115] The Cabinet Mission, comprising Pethick-
Lawrence, Cripps and A.V. Alexander, was formally announced in the
House of Commons and the House of Lords on 19 February 1946.

Fresh trouble had started just the day before when the ratings of the
Royal Indian Navy (RIN) in Bombay rose in revolt, starting with a strike
in the HMIS Talwar. The immediate triggers were bad rations, poor
quality food, differential pay and abusive behaviour of the commander
of the ship. The ratings declined to report for duty and refused meals
on the ship. When the negotiations started with the Flag Officer in
Bombay, fourteen representatives presented their demands for better
quality food, payments at par with the Royal Navy, penal action against
the commander, speedy demobilization, etc. To this, they added three
demands which were completely unrelated to their immediate cause of
grievance: release of the INA prisoners, immediate and impartial inquiry
into cases of firing on Indians across the country, and the immediate
withdrawal of Indian troops from Indonesia and the Middle East. A large
crowd of the ratings gathered in the harbour area, the Union Jack was
pulled down from the mast heads of all the ships and substituted with
Congress and Muslim League flags, meetings were held in the city and
the sailors marched in procession through the city raising anti-British
slogans.[116]

'About three thousand strikers . . . from the Royal Indian Navy in the Bombay harbour today demonstrated wildly and sometimes violently', the press reported on 20 February.[117] All the ships joined the strike by 20 February, and sympathy strikes were organized at Karachi, Vishakhapatnam, Madras, Cochin, Jamnagar and Bahrein. In Calcutta, 150 ratings went on a hunger strike. The mutiny lasted for seven days in Calcutta and six days in Bombay, two days in Karachi and one day in Madras.[118]

'Indian Navy strike develops into veritable mutiny', reported the front-page headline of the *Amrita Bazar Patrika* on 22 February 1946. Regular warfare between the mutineers and British soldiers took place for six hours inside the Castle barracks in Bombay, reported Vice Admiral Godfrey, the Flag Officer Commanding.[119] Thirty were killed and 500 injured in police and military firings, nearly thirty military lorries were burnt, and five to six banks were attacked and looted the next day. British troops opened fire using machine guns, army tanks paraded in the disturbed areas, and bombers flew over the city.[120] By the end of the month, civilian casualties amounted to 228 killed and 1046 injured, with 3 constables killed. Nine banks, thirty shops, ten post offices, ten police stations and sixty-four grain shops were looted and destroyed.[121]

'When at a tender age of 22 years the young sailor, B.C. Dutt was writing Indian National Army, INA, slogans on the wall of HMIS Talwar in Bombay he would have hardly imagined he would be acclaimed an icon who lit the spark for a "Potemkin" moment', wrote Admiral Vishnu Bhagwat, the former Chief of Naval Staff of India, in 2015.[122] The mutiny's genesis, according to its leader Dutt, could be traced back to the impact of what Subhas Bose did in Southeast Asia. In 1970, Dutt stated during an interview with the University of Cambridge that the sailors (ratings) who caused the RIN mutiny 'were unaffected by the "Quit India" ultimatum of the Indian National Congress in 1942'. But 'there was a tremendous upsurge in the country when the men of Subhas Chandra Bose's Indian National Army were brought to India in 1945'. Dutt stated that the news of the impending trial of the Azad Hind soldiers made naval ratings 'restless'. He explained what stirred his conscience:

One day a friend of mine, S.M. Shyam, returned from Malaya with strange tales of the Indian National Army. . . . He brought letters from

some member of the former Azad Hind Government addressed to
Jawaharlal Nehru and Sarat Chandra Bose, the elder brother of Subhas
Chandra Bose. He also brought relevant literature and photographs. In
the RIN this was considered high treason. In the course of clandestine
efforts at getting those photos and literature to the destination, I got
involved in the activities, which committed me to a cause officially illegal
but, to a man in my state of mind, ennobling. In the ensuing weeks, my
life changed. . . .I began to ask myself questions. What right had the
British to rule over my country?[123]

Dutt then found like-minded people on the signal training ship *HMIS
Talwar* at Bombay's dockyards. 'We called ourselves *Azad Hindis* (free
Indians)'. When the ratings sought Vallabhbhai Patel's advice, he said, 'In
the present unfortunate circumstances that have developed, the advice of
the Congress to the RIN ratings is to lay down arms and to go through
the formality of surrender which has been asked for.' He assured them
that the Congress would do its level best to ensure that there would be
no victimization, and that the legitimate demands of the ratings were to
be accepted as soon as possible.[124] To the Governor of Bombay, he sent a
message offering 'to do anything which he could to prevent bloodshed'.[125]
In contrast to Vallabhbhai, Jawaharlal came out strongly in support of the
ratings' mutiny after he arrived in Bombay a few days later, but deprecated
the violence they had unleashed. He also criticized Vallabhbhai and Azad
for assuring the ratings that their just demands would be accepted because,
as he pointed out, neither Vallabhbhai nor Azad had the power to do so.[126]

Auchinleck's prognostication in November 1945 was to the point,
when he wrote in his assessment report that:

> . . . anti-Government disorder on a large scale is unlikely until after the
> elections, that is before April, since this would not be in the interests of
> the Congress. Moreover, most of the political leaders and big business
> men seem at present to be opposed to violent methods.[127]

Speaking from the Red Fort on 16 August 1947, Jawaharlal declared that
India 'has achieved freedom under the brilliant leadership and guidance of
Mahatma Gandhi'.[128] Despite the colossal greatness of the Mahatma, the
statement was inaccurate and an oversimplification as amply demonstrated
by the flow of events described in this chapter. Yet, the myth that was

created seventy-five years ago remains the official version of events in India to this day.

The fact is that the only Gandhian movement nearly a decade after the Civil Disobedience movement was snuffed out at the planning stage, and thereafter there was no Gandhian movement. If anything troubled the British Government, it was the impact of the INA trials. The Labour Government moved rapidly, almost impatient to hand over power to the Indian leaders immediately after the elections of 1946. The main impediment to that pace was the impossibility of finding a common ground between Jinnah and the Congress. Independence was not the question on the top any more; it was to find a solution to the communal tangle. To get around the stalemate that evolved after the discussions on the Cabinet Mission, Attlee announced on 20 February 1947 the replacement of Wavell by Mountbatten, and fixed a date for the transfer of power by June 1948. Mountbatten advanced the deadline to August 1947.

In his autobiography, Attlee noted down the overarching factors that drove his decision-making:

> Although Indian leaders had no sympathy with Japanese imperialism, there were men who would see in the Japanese advance the opportunity of throwing off what they considered to be the imperial yoke from the neck of India. Indeed, Subhas Bose of Bengal was busily engaged in forming, from some of the Indian prisoners taken by the Japanese, an Indian National Army. Just as the defeat of Russia by Japan at the beginning of the century had intensified Asiatic nationalism, so it was clear to me that immediately the war ended Britain would be met by a very strong demand for equality on the part of Asians, who saw domination of Asia by Europeans in decline.
>
> Successive British Governments had declared their intention of giving India full self-government. The end of the war would certainly bring a demand for these promises to be implemented. Furthermore, our allies the American people had very strong views, shared by the Administration, of the evils of imperialism. Much of the criticism of British rule was very ill-informed but its strength could not be denied.[129]

Attlee later repeated similar arguments in his interview with journalist Francis Williams, which was first telecast by the BBC in 1959, and later turned into a book. He told Williams:

Then came the war and the Chamberlain Government declared India to be at war without asking any advice or opinion, or seeking support anywhere. That was a grave mistake. It promoted the general feeling that it wasn't India's war, so that when Japan came in there was a good deal of Asianism and a certain amount of wanting to go in with the Japs. It didn't extend very far, but it went some distance.[130]

Many luminaries who watched the events unfold agreed that the INA played a pivotal role in making India free. In a no holds barred interview in February 1955, with BBC's Francis Watson, Dr Bhimrao Ambedkar wondered, 'I don't know how Mr Attlee suddenly agreed to give India independence. That is a secret that he will disclose in his autobiography. None expected that he would do that.' Ambedkar told the *BBC* that from his 'own analysis', he had concluded what convinced the Labour party to take the decision to free India:

The national army that was raised by Subhas Chandra Bose. The British had been ruling the country in the firm belief that whatever may happen in the country or whatever the politicians did, they could never be able to change the loyalty of soldiers. That was one prop on which they were carrying on the administration. And that was completely dashed to pieces.

In October 1956, two months before Ambedkar passed away, Clement Attlee himself disclosed that very secret in a private talk. It would take two decades before Phani Bhusan Chakravartti, Chief Justice of Calcutta High Court and acting Governor of West Bengal, mustered the courage to make public what the former British PM had told him in the Governor's mansion in Kolkata in 1956:

The INA activities of Subhas Chandra Bose, which weakened the very foundation of the British Empire in India, and the RIN mutiny which made the British realise that the Indian armed forces could no longer be trusted to prop up the British.

Justice Chakravartti, the first Indian to become permanent Chief Justice of India's oldest court, also asked Attlee about the extent of Gandhi's influence upon the British decision to quit India. In Chakravartti words: 'Hearing this question, Attlee's lips became twisted in a sarcastic smile as he slowly chewed out the word, "m-i-n-i-m-a-l"!'[131]

In 1960, in Nuffield College, Oxford, Attlee reiterated his position to historian Barun De.[132] In 1967, at a New Delhi seminar to mark the 20th anniversary of Independence, the then British High Commissioner and famous broadcaster John Freeman opined that 'independence became certain after the 1946 revolt of the Royal Indian Navy'. Among those who had heard Freeman speak was would-be columnist Swaminathan Aiyar, brother of the Congress leader, Mani Shankar Aiyar. Swaminathan wrote in *The Economic Times* on 15 August 2007 that Freeman's admission 'astonished many youngsters in the audience, including me' for they 'had never been taught about the naval revolt'.

Some thirty years after independence, Lt Gen. S.K. Sinha came out with another inside account in an op-ed article titled 'The Army and Indian Independence' (*The Statesman*, 1 March 1976). The would-be Assam and Jammu and Kashmir Governor, as a young captain, along with fellow Lt Col Sam Manekshaw and Major Yahya Khan, were the only natives posted to the hitherto exclusively British Directorate of Military Operations in 1946. 'The real impact of the INA was felt more after the war than during the war', Sinha agreed, adding that 'There was considerable sympathy for the INA within the Army. . . . I am convinced that well over 90 per cent of officers at that time felt along those lines'. Finally, he stated:

> In 1946, I accidentally came across a very interesting document . . . prepared by the Director of Military Intelligence. It was a classified document marked 'Top Secret. Not for Indian Eyes.' . . . The paper referred to the INA, the mutinies at Bombay and Jabalpur and also to the 'adverse' effect on the Indian officers and men of the humiliating defeats inflicted by the Japanese on the white nations in the early days of the war. The conclusion reached was that the Indian Army could no longer be relied upon to remain a loyal instrument for maintaining British rule over India.

Attlee also explained why he set a specific time limit, till June 1948, for the transfer of power. He told Williams:

> I'd come to the conclusion from my own experience of Indians that there was a great deal of happiness for them in asking for everything, and putting down everything that was wrong in India to British rule,

and then sitting pretty. I thought that most of them were not really keen
on responsibility. They would talk and talk and talk, and as long as they
could put the responsibility on us they would continue to quarrel among
themselves. Therefore I concluded the thing to do was to bring them
right up against it and make them see they'd got to face the situation
themselves. I decided that the only thing to do was to set a time-limit and
say: 'Whatever happens, our rule is ending on that date.' It was of course,
a somewhat dangerous venture. But one had also to remember that
inevitably the machine of administration in India was running down.[133]

The assessment reports of the country's situation at the end of 1945 and
early 1946 by the Viceroy and the Commander-in-Chief provide a clear
insight on why the Attlee Government was in a rush.

Auchinleck's report on 24 November 1945, on the internal situation
in India, clearly stated, 'It is a reasonable assumption, therefore, that
widespread trouble either communal or anti-government or both is to
be expected in the late Spring'. As shown above, he expected the scale
of disturbances to be much greater than what was seen in 1942. He
pointed out the uncertainties around the army in such an eventuality—
uncertainties that were largely triggered by the INA: 'I consider that there
must be doubt as to the continued loyalty of the Armed Forces unless
Government produce a strong and unequivocal statement of policy
comprehensible by the rank and file.' The Government must have declared
that 'any armed insurrection will be put down, by force if necessary and
the leaders punished'. Auchinleck went to the extent of asking the British
Government to be prepared with plans for sending British reinforcement
troops to India for its reconquest:

If the Indian Forces as a whole cease to be reliable, the British Armed
Forces now available are not likely to be able to control the internal
situation or to protect essential communications, nor would any
piecemeal reinforcements of these forces be of much avail. To regain
control of the situation and to restore essential communications within
the country, nothing short of an organised campaign for the reconquest
of India is likely to suffice . . . The situation in India is, therefore,
extremely delicate . . . I request, therefore, that plans may be prepared
for the despatch to India of such British Formations as could be made
available.[134]

Auchinleck sent a similar assessment report to the British Chiefs of Staff about a month later.[135]

Wavell presented his assessment to the Secretary of State through a letter dated 27 December 1945. He noted that:

> The present Congress policy seems to be to avoid conflict at any rate until after the elections are over; while taking full advantage of the licence they are being allowed during the elections, to increase their influence and prestige, to stir up racial hatred against the British and communal feeling against the Muslim League, and to complete their organization for a mass movement, unless their demands are satisfied after the elections . . .
>
> After the elections, which will undoubtedly show overwhelming success for Congress, they will, unless we take the initiative, present their demands in some form or another, with the threat of a mass movement if not fulfilled . . .
>
> It would certainly not be wise to try the Indian Army too highly in the suppression of their own people. As time goes on, the loyalty of Indian officials, the Indian Army and the police might become problematical.[136]

As the national demand was overshadowed gradually by the communal issues, there too, the Government of India saw critical problems regarding the armed forces. On 18 January 1946, Wavell wrote to the Chiefs of Staff asking for three Brigade Groups to be sent to India with the 'object of providing steadying effect during Provincial elections and in period immediately after them'.[137] The Chief of the Imperial General Staff, Field Marshal Viscount Alanbrooke, informed Auchinleck on 4 February of the difficulties of meeting that demand, as British troops worldwide had reached an 'irreducible minimum' due to 'acute UK manpower situation'.[138] On 14 February 1946, Auchinleck explained the need for more British troops in India to Alanbrooke:

> . . . no one can forecast with any certainty the extent or degree of the hostile action with which we may have to deal. Such action may vary from complete rebellion aided by the whole or great majority of the Indian Armed Forces . . . to isolated civil disturbances . . .
>
> In addition to the above possibilities of anti-Government action there is the equally if not more serious possibility of a religious war on a large scale . . . it is more than likely that it will be impossible to rely on either

the Police or the Indian Armed Forces to take action for the restoration of law and order if this means firing on their own co-religionists. This means that British troops alone would be available to restore the situation and the use of British troops in such circumstances would almost certainly result in turning communal strife into anti-Government action by both parties. In this event we would again be faced by the risk of the Indian Armed Forces throw in their lot with the insurgent elements . . .[139]

The Commander-in-Chief had lost faith in his forces.

As Ba Maw incisively wrote in his autobiography, 'one man sowed and others reaped after him'.[140]

Illustration by Piciel (Pratul Chandra Lahiri), depicting the impact of the INA trials. *Amrita Bazar Patrika*, Vol. 78, Issue 27 (27 January 1946), British Library, EAP262-1-1-5554.

14

What If Subhas Returned?

The hypothetical scenario of Subhas Bose's return to India in 1945 or thereafter and its implications have been discussed by eminent thinkers. 'The implications of a defiant Netaji using the court to posit an uncompromising Indian nationalism would have been far-reaching', wrote columnist and lawmaker Swapan Dasgupta in 2004, referring to the possible impact of Netaji's presence at the Red Fort trials. Acknowledging that 'the absence of Bose foreclosed a monumental challenge which would have reshaped post-Independence politics', Dasgupta went on to postulate that Bose would not have been able to stop the partition of the country. Being disallowed in the Congress party, he 'would have attracted the socialists, a few who had gravitated to the Communist Party of India (CPI) and a section of the disaffected middle-classes', leading to a three-way political reorientation in the 1950s—the conservative Gandhians in Congress (led by Vallabhbhai Patel) teaming up with the Hindu Mahasabha, Jawaharlal allying with the communists (who 'hated Bose passionately'), and 'the populist Bose'. In visualizing the alternative reality, Dasgupta had no doubt that the 'primary casualty of Bose's re-emergence would have been the Congress and, particularly, Gandhi's anointed leader, Jawaharlal Nehru'. This, in Dasgupta's view, meant that 'Had he [Subhas] played his cards well, displayed organisational rigour and ideological flexibility, he may well have become the prime minister of India's first non-Congress government.'[1]

Historian Ramachandra Guha too argued in his piece written five years later that the presence of Subhas would not have stopped the partition of the country. According to Guha, even if Netaji rejoined Congress as a result of a truce manoeuvred by Gandhi, he would not stay in the party for long because he 'was too proud and independent-minded to have conceded the top spot to Jawaharlal Nehru'. Thereafter, he might have gone ahead with his own party or would have 'joined with other former Congressmen in nurturing a left-wing alternative to the ruling party', akin to the Praja Socialist Party experiment of Acharya Kripalani, Jayaprakash Narayan, and Ram Manohar Lohia, which in reality 'could not make a dent in the Congress hegemony'. Given Subhas's countrywide appeal, however, a socialist party led by him would have 'mounted a serious challenge to Nehru and his colleagues' and 'might, by 1957, and definitely by 1962, have given the Congress a real run for its money'.[2]

Writing in *The Times of India*, a grand-nephew of Abid Hassan—Subhas's private secretary in Germany and his companion in the three-month-long submarine journey from Germany to Southeast Asia—postulated three possible scenarios which could have materialized had Bose been present in independent India. First, Subhas would have split the Congress, leading a more leftist segment and thus squeezing out the CPI. Over time, his party would have squeezed out Jawaharlal's Congress and joined the Soviet Bloc. The second scenario envisaged was that of India being taken through the road of a 'quasi-fascist' regime of 'Ataturkism' by Subhas, driven by his 'strong streak of authoritarianism'. 'He would, as Ataturk did in Turkey, tower of [*sic*] the nation like a colossus' becoming 'an architect of the nation in every detail, shaping it according to his own benevolent dictatorial vision.' In the third scenario visualized by the author, in a variant of the authoritarian scenario, Subhas could have become a Mao Tse Tung, a Kim Il-sung or a Fidel Castro, taking India 'down the battered leftist socialist road to ruination'.[3]

It is also pertinent to recall Ram Manohar Lohia's views on the impact of a possible return of Bose. Like many Indians of his time, Lohia too had accepted the story of Bose's death in 1945, but that did not stop him from visualizing a 'what if' scenario:

[If] Netaji Subhas were ever to have returned home after his great and peerless adventure for freedom, he would have given six months of acute trouble to Mr Nehru but no more. If Mr Nehru had been able physically to survive the return of Mr Bose, he would have been on top again after six months, so that Subhas Bose, would either have to go in opposition or to become the second in command. Mr Bose did not possess Mr Nehru's cunning and refinement. He might indeed have tried to be clever on certain occasions, and I believe that he did. But he did not possess the sure touch of a master at such jobs and he made some big mistakes. . . . Whenever I remember my last exchanges with him, I am . . . sad that Mr Bose did not find some way to adjust in whatever loose manner with Gandhiji.

I wish often to give to Subhas Babu after his death what I withheld from him in his life. Netaji Subhas was the embodiment of the Haldighati spirit. His aim was clear, he accepted neither defeat nor the withdrawal of lassitude, and he tried to act in all situations. But one wishes that the Haldighati spirit was somewhat clever that it often is.[4]

The details may vary, but there is a broad agreement on two main points—that Subhas would have taken the centre stage leading to the marginalization of Jawaharlal, and that India's development story would have looked very different. If such an eventuality can be grasped by historians and authors, there is no reason to believe that the ruling dispensation, especially the agents in the Intelligence Bureau, did not consider the possibility. It may be an academic exercise now, but in the post-Independence years, when the spectre of Subhas's return hung in the corridors of power, it must have been looked at with a sense of urgency. That sense of urgency or desperation alone is reason enough for the elaborate surveillance that had been mounted for decades. It is clear that the ruling establishment either wanted to prevent Bose's showing up or at least be prepared for it.

These hypotheses, while interesting and valid to some extent, are also oversimplifications of reality that partly arise from misconceptions about Subhas. As a result, these scenarios missed out on a few important points that make the reconstruction of a 'what if' scenario much more complex and that much more fascinating. Much complexity can be inserted by a simple intervention—the time of Subhas's return. What would have happened if he returned in 1945, vis-à-vis say, 1950?

Nirad C. Chaudhuri, who believed Subhas died in the alleged plane crash at Taihoku in 1945, drew up his own scenario, assuming Subhas's return in 1945:

For the Gandhian Congress, too, Subhas Bose provided a windfall by his death. Had he lived and come back to India he would have swept public opinion in the whole of the country to his side, and for the Congress not to have identified itself with him would have been suicide. But going over to him would hardly have been much better. He would have left

only a minor role to play for the Gandhi–Nehru leadership and could
have dictated his terms, which the Gandhian Congress would have had
to accept. In this way Bose could have taken revenge for his expulsion in
1939.[5]

Firstly, finding a solution to the problem of dealing with the soldiers
of the Azad Hind Fauj was not an easy one. Neither Jawaharlal nor
Vallabhbhai were ready to reinstate the Fauj soldiers into the Indian Army,
and recommended various other options for them. That solution, which
became easy to implement with Subhas not being around, would have been
unthinkable in his presence. On more than one occasion, he had declared
that he wanted the Azad Hind Fauj to be at the core of the national army
in independent India. In that case, a confrontation with Jawaharlal and
Vallabhbhai would have been inevitable, making a simple continuation
of the British Indian army organization without any change virtually
impossible. Moreover, Subhas would not have accepted its continuation
with the British chiefs' presence in the army, navy and air force.

The two biggest issues that could have been potentially altered by the
presence of Subhas at the time of transfer of power was that of partition of
India and the country joining the British Commonwealth after accepting
the status of a British Dominion.

By the end of 1945, the general opinion among Congress leaders had
not yet veered towards accepting the idea of some sort of partition, and
the British Cabinet decision of sending a Cabinet Mission was yet to be
finalized. Under those circumstances, Subhas's presence would have made
a sea of difference. In fact, the Congress leaders, including Gandhi and
Jawaharlal, were championing the absence of communal feelings in the
INA. A letter from journalist Shiva Rao, which was shared with the British
Cabinet by the president of the Board of Trade on 28 November 1945, is
revealing. Rao wrote in his letter, dated 20 November, about the treatment
of religious difference in the INA:

> The men undergoing or awaiting trial are utterly indifferent to their
> own fate. There is not the slightest feeling among them of Hindu and
> Moslem. They told us yesterday that in their army they had abolished all
> such distinctions. Hindus and Moslems had to eat the same food cooked
> by the same people and no questions were asked. The fact is receiving
> wide publicity. A majority of the men now awaiting trial in the Red Fort

is Moslem. Some of these men are bitter that Mr. Jinnah is keeping alive a controversy over Pakistan.[6]

The sentiment would have undoubtedly strengthened infinitely in Subhas's presence. Jinnah, who was rebuffed by Shah Nawaz Khan in his efforts to draw the INA hero into the fold of the Muslim League, perhaps would have sensed a change of wind or a weakened position. The ease with which Mountbatten could secure Jawaharlal's agreement, and consequently the ease with which the Congress leadership acquiesced to Jawaharlal's point of view, would not have been possible in the presence of Subhas. In fact, it would have been extremely difficult for Mountbatten, if not impossible, to convert the entire negotiation on transfer of power into a competition between Jawaharlal and Jinnah.

On this, Subhas would have received full support from Gandhi, who was disheartened with his trusted and favoured disciples deserting him at this stage of negotiations. As Durga Das recorded his conversation with Gandhi in March 1947:

Devadas [Gandhi] and I called on Gandhi twice, and he told us that his followers had let him down badly. Now that power was within their grasp, they seemed to have no further use for him. As neither Nehru nor Jinnah would consent to take second place in a government at the Centre, both had agreed to partition the country, he said. Patel was directing all his energies towards saving India for the Hindus, and Azad was equally obsessed with the plight of the Muslims. Subhas Bose, Gandhi observed, had proved a true patriot by organising the INA and showing how Hindus and Muslims could work together in harmony. Gandhi said he would rather have a bloodbath in a united India after the British quit than agree to partition on a communal basis and give birth to two armed camps, perpetually in conflict.[7]

Of course, there would have been differences with Gandhi too. With his focus on securing the defence of the country, Subhas would have wanted to ensure a better-equipped and modernized armed forces, instead of the Commander-in-Chief asking for the disbanding of the army to follow the Gandhian ideal, as Rajendra Prasad later did. With a strong army and his keen sense of India having a mission and a message to the world, he would have probably striven harder to secure a better bargain at the United

Nations. With his emphasis on having a strong army, and maintaining the integrity of the nation, both the Kashmir problem and the China war would probably have taken a different course.

It is inconceivable that Subhas would have let India join the British Commonwealth as a Dominion without putting up all the opposition that he could muster. In such a scenario, India was more likely to see a clean break from the Empire, which leads to further hypothetical questions as to whether these western democracies would have pulled some strings to see a more favourable Jawaharlal at the helm. Subhas's association with the Axis Bloc, and the perception created about his being a potential authoritarian ruler, would certainly have been a major cause of headache to them. It is not inconceivable that a move towards branding him as a war criminal would have been initiated, creating another potential source of confrontation between a newly independent India, too sensitive about self-respect in the global platform, and the Western powers. That would not have been a pretty scenario.

Notes

Chapter 1: The Early Years (1909–19)

1. Charu Chandra Ganguly, 'Sahapathir Smritikatha', in *Smarane Manane Subhas Chandra*, edited by Rathindra Nath Bhattacharya, Vivekananda Pathagar, 1970, p. 28.
2. Subhas Chandra Bose, *Netaji's Life and Writings, Part One, An Indian Pilgrim*, Thacker, Spink & Co. (1933) Ltd, 1948, pp. 36–7.
3. Ganguly, 'Sahapathir Smritikatha', p. 28.
4. Bose, *An Indian Pilgrim*, p. 39.
5. Bose, *An Indian Pilgrim*, p. 41.
6. Bose, *An Indian Pilgrim*, p. 43.
7. Bose, *An Indian Pilgrim*, p. 42.
8. Bose, *An Indian Pilgrim*, p. 45.
9. Hemanta Kumar Sarkar, *Subhaser Songe Baro Bochhor*, 1946, p. 7. All direct quotes from this original Bengali publication are translations by the author.
10. Sarkar, *Subhaser Songe Baro Bochhor*, p. 3.
11. Suresh Chandra Banerjee, *Jiban Prabaha*, p. 62.
12. Banerjee, *Jiban Prabaha*, pp. 77–8.
13. Bose, *An Indian Pilgrim*, p. 53.
14. Banerjee, *Jiban Prabaha*, p. 80.
15. Sarkar, *Subhaser Songe Baro Bochhor*, p. 9.
16. Sarkar, *Subhaser Songe Baro Bochhor*, p. 10.
17. Sarkar, *Subhaser Songe Baro Bochhor*, pp. 4–5.
18. Bose, *An Indian Pilgrim*, p. 59.
19. Bose, *An Indian Pilgrim*, p. 60.
20. Later renamed Lajpat Rai Sarani. Asoke Nath Bose, *My Uncle Netaji*, Bharatiya Vidya Bhavan, 1989, p. 2.
21. Renamed Surjya Sen Street.
22. Banerjee, *Jiban Prabaha*, p. 82.

23. Bhupendra Kumar Dutta, 'Chhatra Jibone Subhas Chandra', in *Jayasree Netaji Subhas Chandra Bosu Janma Shatabarshiki Grantha*, edited by Bijoy Kumar Nag, Jayasree Patrika Trust, 1999, pp. 23–30.

24. Bose, *An Indian Pilgrim*, p. 77.

25. Sarkar, *Subhaser Songe Baro Bochhor*, pp. 10–2.

26. Sarkar, *Subhaser Songe Baro Bochhor*, p. 16.

27. Dilip Kumar Roy, *Smriticharan*, Ananda Publishers Pvt. Ltd, 2011, p. 197.

28. Dilip Kumar Roy, *Netaji, the Man: Reminiscences*, Bharatiya Vidya Bhavan, 2009, pp. 1–3.

29. *Centenary Volume*, Presidency College, Calcutta, 1955, p. 186.

30. Government of Bengal, Education Department, *Presidency College Register*, 1927, p. 313.

31. Hemendranath Dasgupta, *Subhas Chandra*, Jyoti Prokasalaya, 1946, p. 13.

32. Bose, *An Indian Pilgrim*, p. 76.

33. Bose, *An Indian Pilgrim*, pp. 77–8.

34. Bose, *An Indian Pilgrim*, p. 76.

35. Bose, *An Indian Pilgrim*, pp. 76–7; Sarkar, *Subhaser Songe Baro Bochhor*, pp. 16–7.

36. Jadugopal Mukherjee, *Biplabi Jibaner Smriti*, Indian Associated Publishing Co Pvt. Ltd, 1956, p. 49. Jadugopal described Banerjee's mess as 'Chheledhorar adda (a den for recruiting boys for the revolutionary societies)'.

37. Sarkar, *Subhaser Songe Baro Bochhor*, p. 19.

38. Dasgupta, *Subhas Chandra*, pp. 11–2.

39. Bose, *An Indian Pilgrim*, p. 84.

40. Bose, *An Indian Pilgrim*, p. 79; Sarkar, *Subhaser Songe Baro Bochhor*, pp. 21–4; Hemanta wrote that both of them became the sannyasi's disciples, whereas according to Subhas, they were only frequent and admiring visitors, and the urge to find the right guru became stronger after meeting him.

41. Subhas wrote in *An Indian Pilgrim* that he left with his friend H.P.C. (who, being a Brahmin, helped on some occasions) and was joined by another friend at Haridwar; thereafter they journeyed together. However, Hemanta's account does not mention any third person.

42. Sarkar, *Subhaser Songe Baro Bochhor*, p. 24.

43. Sarkar, *Subhaser Songe Baro Bochhor*, pp. 28–36.

44. Sarkar, *Subhaser Songe Baro Bochhor*, pp. 37–9.

45. Sarkar, *Subhaser Songe Baro Bochhor*, p. 40.

46. Sarkar, *Subhaser Songe Baro Bochhor*, pp. 42–8.

47. Bose, *An Indian Pilgrim*, p. 87.

48. Bose, *An Indian Pilgrim*, p. 87.

49. Letters to Hemanta during February–April 1915; *Netaji Subhaschandra Bosur Aprakashita Patrabali*, edied by Abul Ahsan Chowdhury, Shobha Prakash, 2007, pp. 109–29.

50. Bose, *An Indian Pilgrim*, pp. 86–87.
51. Letter to Hemanta, 27 March 1915; Chowdhury, *Aprakashita Patrabali*, p. 125.
52. Letters to Hemanta during February–April 1915; Chowdhury, *Aprakashita Patrabali*, pp. 109–29.
53. Letter to Hemanta, 25 July 1915; Chowdhury, *Aprakashita Patrabali*, p. 158.
54. *Centenary Volume*, Presidency College, Calcutta, 1955, p. 167.
55. Letter to Hemanta, 31 August 1915; Sarkar, *Subhaser Songe Baro Bochhor*, pp. 61–2 (translated by author from the original bilingual letter, with the original English parts shown in italics).
56. Bose, *An Indian Pilgrim*, p. 90.
57. Bose, *An Indian Pilgrim*, p. 90.
58. *Centenary Volume*, Presidency College, Calcutta, 1955, p. 167.
59. Bose, *An Indian Pilgrim*, p. 91.
60. Translated from letter to Hemanta in Bengali, dated 29 February 1916. Sarkar, *Subhaser Songe Baro Bochhor*, pp. 64–5.
61. Sarkar, *Subhaser Songe Baro Bochhor*, pp. 65–6.
62. Roy, *Netaji the Man*, pp. 24–5.
63. Sarkar, *Subhaser Songe Baro Bochhor*, pp. 65–6.
64. Suniti Kumar Chatterji, 'Subhas Chandra Bose: Personal Reminiscences', in *Netaji: His Life and Work*, edited by Shri Ram Sharma, Shiva Lal Agarwala & Co Ltd, 1948, p. 126.
65. Bose, *An Indian Pilgrim*, p. 92.
66. Narendra Narayan Chakraborty, *Netaji Songo o Prosongo*, Granthaprakash, 1967, p. 52.
67. E.F. Oaten, 'The Bengal Student as I knew Him,' in *Netaji and India's Freedom: Proceedings of the International Netaji Seminar 1973*, edited by Sisir K Bose, Netaji Research Bureau, 1975, p. 33.
68. Ananga Mohan Dam, 'Subhas Smriti', in *Smarane Manane Subhas Chandra*, edited by Rathindra Nath Bhattacharya, p. 31.
69. Bose, *An Indian Pilgrim*, p. 98.
70. Bose, *An Indian Pilgrim*, p. 100.
71. Ashok Nath, 'A Bengali Infantry Regiment in the Great War', in *Peace and Security Review*, Vol. 4, No. 7, 2011, pp. 34–7.
72. Bose, *An Indian Pilgrim*, p. 106; Letter to Hemanta; Sarkar, *Subhaser Songe Baro Bochhor*, pp. 69–70.
73. Bose, *An Indian Pilgrim*, p. 106.
74. Letter to Hemanta; Sarkar, *Subhaser Songe Baro Bochhor*, p. 66.
75. Bose, *An Indian Pilgrim*, p. 108.
76. Sarkar, *Subhaser Songe Baro Bochhor*, p. 72.
77. Bose, *An Indian Pilgrim*, pp. 108–9.

78. Bose, *My Uncle Netaji*, pp. 3–4.

79. Letter to Hemanta; Sarkar, *Subhaser Songe Baro Bochhor,* pp. 72–3;

80. Bose, *My Uncle Netaji*, pp. 3–4.

Chapter 2: The World Opens Its Doors

1. Roy, *Netaji the Man: Reminiscences*, p. 33.

2. Roy, *Netaji the Man*, p. 34.

3. Bose, *An Indian Pilgrim*, 1948, p. 114.

4. Bose, *An Indian Pilgrim*, pp. 115–7.

5. Letter to Hemanta, 12 November 1919; Hemanta Kumar Sarkar, *Subhaser Songe Baro Bochhor*, p. 76.

6. Letter to Charu Chandra Ganguly, 23 March 1920; *Subhas Chandra Bose, Netaji: Collected Works, edited by S.K. Bose and S. Bose*, Vol. 1, Oxford University Press, 1997, p. 205.

7. Letter to Hemanta, 2 March 1920; Sarkar, *Subhaser Songe Baro Bochhor*, p. 79.

8. Bose, *An Indian Pilgrim*, pp. 114–8.

9. Bose, *An Indian Pilgrim*, p. 85.

10. Bose, *An Indian Pilgrim*, pp. 85–6.

11. Letter to Hemanta, 12 November 1919; Sarkar, *Subhaser Songe Baro Bochhor*, pp. 76–77.

12. Roy, *Netaji the Man*, p. 30. Not an original assessment by Dilip, who obtained the idea from some other students who were probably reading too much into Subhas's fastidiousness regarding etiquette and public conduct, a behavioural trait driven by his overly sensitive nature of belonging to an occupied country. As a result of that, he demanded impeccable manners out of almost everyone around him; he was absorbed with the idea that the British should not be able to spot any flaw in the character and conduct of Indian students ('We must prove it home to them that we can more than hold our own against them. We must beard the lion in his own den.') Dilip, to be fair, also mentioned that he never thought of looking at this behavior as an 'inferiority complex' while they were students, and that Subhas 'overcame' the 'complex' afterwards.

13. Sarkar, *Subhaser Songe Baro Bochhor*, pp. 75–6.

14. Bose, *An Indian Pilgrim*, p. 119.

15. Roy, *Netaji the Man*, pp. 28–30.

16. Roy, *Netaji the Man*, p. 42.

17. Dilip Kumar Roy, *Smriticharan*, pp. 231–2. Kropotkin's (who Subhas called 'a giant among men') *Memoirs of a Revolutionist* was one of his favourite books (p. 242).

18. Bose, *An Indian Pilgrim*, p. 122.
19. Bose, *An Indian Pilgrim*, p. 123.
20. Roy, *Smriticharan*, p. 227.
21. Roy, *Netaji the Man*, p. 36. In spite of his feelings, it appears that Subhas was unable to fully let go of himself during this visit, and wrote a long letter to Mrs Bates on his way back to India. In this letter, which she showed to Dilip, 'with tears in her lovely eyes', Subhas apologized for not being able to 'express all he had felt' and requested her not to take it as his insensitiveness (p. 41).
22. Roy, *Smriticharan*, pp. 233–9.
23. Letter to Hemanta, 2 March 1920; Sarkar, *Subhaser Songe Baro Bochhor*, pp. 79–80.
24. Bose, *An Indian Pilgrim*, p. 124.
25. Letter to Charu Chandra Ganguly, 23 March 1920; *Netaji: Collected Works*, Vol. 1, p. 206.
26. Bose, *An Indian Pilgrim*, pp. 125–7.
27. Bose, *An Indian Pilgrim*, p. 129.
28. M.C. Chagla, *Roses in December*, Bharatiya Vidya Bhavan, 1975, p. 42.
29. G.D. Khosla, *Last Days of Netaji*, Thomson Press (India) Ltd, 1974, p. 3.
30. Letter to C.R. Das, dated 16 February 1921; *Netaji: Collected Works*, Vol. 1, p. 212.
31. Bose, *An Indian Pilgrim*, p. 130.
32. Letter to Sarat Chandra Bose, 6 April 1921; *Netaji: Collected Works*, Vol. 1, pp. 224–5.
33. Roy, *Smriticharan*, pp. 223.
34. Letter to Sarat Chandra Bose, 23 April 1921; *Netaji: Collected Works*, Vol. 1, p. 234.
35. Letter to Sarat Chandra Bose, 23 April 1921; *Netaji: Collected Works*, Vol. 1, p. 232.
36. Letter to Sarat Chandra Bose, 23 April 1921; *Netaji: Collected Works*, Vol. 1, pp. 232–3.
37. Letter to Sarat Chandra Bose, 20 April 1921; *Netaji: Collected Works*, Vol. 1, p. 228. According to Dilip, Indian students in London, Oxford and Cambridge sent Subhas a framed congratulatory message. One student even proposed a procession with Subhas in front of the Buckingham Palace. Subhas was furious at the proposal (*Smriticharan*, p. 222).
38. Letter to Sarat Chandra Bose, 23 April 1921; *Netaji: Collected Works*, Vol. 1, p. 235.
39. Bengal Provincial Congress, 1917. Ironically, this bonhomie would last just over a year. In a public meeting at Chittagong, in June 1918, Chittaranjan Das would go on to attack the *Bengalee*, and its editor, Surendranath

Banerjee, whom he called an imposter, infuriated by the sharp criticism by the paper. He also suspected behind-the-scenes machinations of Banerjee over the Montford reforms (C.R. Das, *India for Indians*, Ganesh & Co., 1921, pp. 124–142).

40. In 1892, Das gave up on his first attempt to give the Civil Service examination halfway through, feeling that he had not done well; in his second attempt next year, he was confident of success, but only 42 candidates were selected that year, instead of the earlier announced 50; Das ranked 43rd (Hemendranath Dasgupta, *Deshbandhu Chittaranjan Das*, Publications Division, 1977, p. 5). He joined the Middle Temple and was called to the bar in the same year (Prithwis Chandra Ray, *Life and Times of CR Das*, Oxford University Press, 1927, pp. 23–4).

41. Ray, *Life and Times of CR Das*, pp. 22–3.

42. Dasgupta, *Deshbandhu Chittaranjan Das*, p. 28.

43. Ray, Life and Times of C.R. Das, p. 55.

44. Dasgupta, *Deshbandhu Chittaranjan Das*, pp. 28–30.

45. Dasgupta, *Deshbandhu Chittaranjan Das*, p. 30.

46. Ray, *Life and Times of CR Das*, p. 57.

47. *Deshabandhu Chitta Ranjan, Brief Survey of Life and Work, Provincial Conference Speeches, Congress Speeches*, Published by Rajen Sen and B.K. Sen, 1926, p. xiv.

48. M.R. Jayakar, *The Story of My Life*, Vol. 1, Asia Publishing House, 1958, p. 185.

49. Chittaranjan Das, *India for Indians*, speech at a public meeting in Mymensingh, October 1917, p. 21.

50. Dasgupta, *Deshbandhu Chittaranjan Das*, p. 34.

51. Das, *India for Indians*, pp. 113–4; Jayakar, *The Story of My Life*, Vol. 1, p. 199.

52. 'I say the Hindus and Mahomedans of Bengal, living together side by side for so many generations, imbibing each other's culture, surrounded by the same atmosphere, the same climate, influenced by the same culture, the two together form the real Bengalee nation. Although we should not lose our own individuality, the spirit of isolation is not the best thing in national life and philosophy' (Das, *India for Indians*, pp. 63, 65–6).

53. Das, *India for Indians*, pp. 93–4. On the foreign links of the revolutionaries— 'I know these people—I have defended their cases—there is not one among the revolutionaries who wants to bring a foreign power in this country—be that foreign power Germany or Japan. I am prepared to prove it, if there is an enquiry . . .', p. 108.

54. *The History and Culture of the Indian People*, edited by R.C. Majumdar, Vol. 11, Bharatiya Vidya Bhavan, 2003, pp. 276–7; Judith Brown, *Gandhi's Rise to Power*, Cambridge University Press, 2007, pp. 132–3.

55. R.C. Majumdar, *History of the Freedom Movement in India*, Vol. 2, Firma K.L. Mukhopadhyay, 1963, pp. 505–6.

56. *The History and Culture of the Indian People*, Vol. 11, edited by Majumdar, pp. 281–2.

57. Das, *Deshabandhu Chitta Ranjan*, pp. 95–103.

58. L.F. Rushbrook Williams, *India in the Years 1917–18*, 1919, p. 66.

59. Das, *Deshabandhu Chitta Ranjan*, pp. 104–7.

60. Subhas Chandra Bose, Netaji's Life and Writings, Part Two, *The Indian Struggle*, Thacker, Spink & Co. (1933) Ltd, 1948, p. 88.

61. Bose, *The Indian Struggle*, pp. 80–1.

62. Srilata Chatterjee, *Congress Politics in Bengal*, Anthem Press, 2002, p. 103; J.H. Broomfield, *Elite Conflict*, University of California Press, 1968, p. 219; Rajat Kanta Ray, *Social Conflict and Political Unrest in Bengal*, 1875-1927, Oxford University Press, 1984, pp. 265–6.

63. Sabitri Prasanna Chattopadhyay, *Subhas Chandra O Netaji Subhas Chandra*, Jayasree Prakashan, 1986, pp. 19–20; 'Chhatra Jibone Subhas Chandra', Bhupendra Kumar Dutta in *Jayasree Netaji Subhaschandra Bosu Janma Shatabarshiki Grantha*, Jayasree Patrika Trust, 1999, p. 31; Bose, *The Indian Struggle*, p. 83.

64. Mahatma Gandhi, *The Collected Works of Mahatma Gandhi*, Vol. 22, Publications Division, Government of India, 1999, pp. 305–6. All volumes of the Collected Works of Mahatma Gandhi referred to in this book are the electronic versions published by the Publications Division, Government of India in 1999 and available at https://www.gandhiashramsevagram.org/gandhi-literature/collected-works-of-mahatma-gandhi-volume-1-to-98.php.

65. Later renamed Raja Subodh Mallik Square.

66. Chattopadhyay, *Subhas Chandra O Netaji Subhas Chandra*, pp. 20–4.

67. Chattopadhyay, *Subhas Chandra O Netaji Subhas Chandra*, pp. 24–5; Upendra Nath Banerjee, *Basumati*, Magh 1352, p. 410.

68. Hemendranath Dasgupta, *Subhas Chandra*, pp. 36–8.

69. *The Indian National Congress: 1920–23*, pp. 63–6.

70. Gandhi, *Collected Works*, Vol. 24, pp. 35–6.

71. Dasgupta, *Subhas Chandra*, p. 39.

72. Bose, *The Indian Struggle*.

73. Brown, *Gandhi's Rise to Power*, p. 314. Some of the traders broke the pledge by early October, according to Judith Brown, citing intelligence reports. Also see *Social Conflict and Political Unrest in Bengal*, pp. 286–7.

74. Bose, *The Indian Struggle*, p. 95.

75. Chatterjee, *Congress Politics in Bengal*, p. 52.

76. Dasgupta, *Subhas Chandra*, p. 40.

77. Sarkar, *Subhaser Songe Baro Bochhor*, pp. 136–8. Hemanta mentions Subhas's presence at a BPCC meeting in Barisal and at the Dacca District Conference in Manikganj.

78. Bose, *The Indian Struggle*, p. 94.

79. Dasgupta, *Subhas Chandra*, p. 42.

80. Chattopadhyay, *Subhas Chandra O Netaji Subhas Chandra*, pp. 33–5; Birendranath Sasmal, *Sroter Trina*, 1922, p. 29. The Bengali pamphlets were published at Sabitri Prasanna's Upasana press. In what reflected the meticulous care he took in planning a clandestine activity, Subhas instructed him to destroy all evidence of the work done in the press.

81. Dasgupta, *Subhas Chandra*, p. 43.

82. Dasgupta, *Subhas Chandra*, p. 43; Bose, *The Indian Struggle*, p. 95; Dasgupta, *Deshbandhu Chittaranjan Das*, p. 66.

83. Dasgupta, *Subhas Chandra*, pp. 45–6; Sarkar, *Subhaser Songe Baro Bachhar*; Dasgupta, *Deshbandhu Chittaranjan Das*, p. 68; Bose, *The Indian Struggle*, p. 98.

84. *Indian Annual Register 1921*, p. 320 (g–h).

85. *IAR 1921*, p. 320 (i).

86. Sasmal, *Sroter Trina*, pp. 55–72; Dasgupta, *Subhas Chandra*, p. 47.

87. *IAR 1921*, p. 320 (j).

88. Student participation ebbed after the arrest of leaders on the 10th, and the movement carried on 'by the enlistment of mill-hands and low class Muslims who were sometimes paid for courting arrest' (Ray, *Social Conflict and Political Unrest in Bengal*, p. 295).

89. Bose, *The Indian Struggle*, p. 98; The total number of convictions in Bengal during 1921 till mid-1922 was 9,163 with the United Province being at a distant second place with 2,772 arrests, showing the impact of the volunteer movement in Bengal (Note from Deputy Secretary to Government of India to Under-Secretary of State for India, cited in Brown, *Gandhi's Rise to Power*, p. 318).

90. Jayakar, *The Story of My Life*, Vol. 1, pp. 504–5; Viceroy's telegram of 18 December 1921; Annexe I of Appendix II of Cabinet 93 (21), Records of the Cabinet Office, CAB/23/27; The National Archives, UK.

91. Jayakar, *The Story of My Life*, Vol. 1, pp. 506–8; Bose, *The Indian Struggle*, p. 100.

92. Viceroy's telegram of 18 December 1921; Annexe II of Appendix II of Cabinet 93 (21), Records of the Cabinet Office, CAB/23/27; The National Archives, UK; *IAR 1921*, pp. 332–6; Sasmal, *Sroter Trina*, pp. 109–110; Bose, *The Indian Struggle*, p. 101. Looking back at this phase almost a decade and a half later, Subhas was scathing in his criticism. He felt that 'the promise of Swaraj' within one year was not only unwise but childish. It

made the Congress appear foolish before all reasonable men: 'No doubt the Mahatma's disciples have tried subsequently to explain away the point by saying that the country did not fulfill the conditions and so Swaraj could not be won within one year. The explanation is as unsatisfactory as the original promise was unwise' (Bose, *The Indian Struggle*, pp. 104–5).

93. Hemanta Kumar Sarkar, *Bandir Diary*, Indian Book Club, 1922, passim; Sasmal, *Sroter Trina*, pp. 98, 100–1, 135; Sarkar, *Subhaser Songe Baro Bachhar*, pp. 131–2.

94. Gandhi's letter to viceroy, 1 February 1922; Gandhi, *Collected Works*, Vol. 26, p. 60.

95. Gandhi's letter to members of Working Committee, 8 February 1922; Gandhi, *Collected Works*, Vol. 26, pp. 110–1.

96. Working Committee resolutions; Gandhi, *Collected Works*, Vol. 26, pp. 138–42.

97. Rajmohan Gandhi, *Patel: A Life*, Navajivan Publishing House, 2011, pp. 103–4.

98. Pattabhi Sitaramayya, *The History of the Indian National Congress*, Vol. 1, Working Committee of the Indian National Congress, 1935, p. 400.

99. Bose, *The Indian Struggle*, p. 108.

100. Bose, *The Indian Struggle*, pp. 115–6. Also see Dasgupta, *Deshbandhu Chittaranjan Das*, pp. 77–80.

101. Bose, *The Indian Struggle*, pp. 116–7. Also see Dasgupta, *Deshbandhu Chittaranjan Das*, p. 80; Sarkar, *Subhaser Songe Baro Bachhar*, p. 134. Sarat Chandra Bose made his formal entry into politics at this time as he accompanied Basanti Devi to the conference. Bose, *My Uncle Netaji*, p. 9.

102. Sarkar, *Subhaser Songe Baro Bachhar*, p. 135.

103. Dasgupta, *Subhas Chandra*, pp. 52–3; *Congress Politics in Bengal*, pp. 122–5; Subhas Chandra Bose, *Subhas Rachanabali*, edited by Sunil Das, Vol. 1, Jayasree Prakashan, 1997, p. 3.

104. Dasgupta, *Subhas Chandra*, p. 55.

105. Dasgupta, *Subhas Chandra*, pp. 53–4; Chattopadhyay, *Subhas Chandra O Netaji Subhas Chandra*, p. 38.

106. Chattopadhyay, *Subhas Chandra O Netaji Subhas Chandra*, pp. 41–2.

107. Chattopadhyay, *Subhas Chandra O Netaji Subhas Chandra*, pp. 43–5.

108. *Report of the Civil Disobedience Enquiry Committee*; *The Indian National Congress: 1920–23*, pp. 205, 219–24.

109. Dasgupta, *Subhas Chandra*, p. 58.

110. *IAR*, pp. 813–72 (n).

111. *IAR*, pp. 813–72 (n).

112. *IAR*, pp. 813–72 (n); Bose, *The Indian Struggle*, pp. 122–3.

113. Jadugopal Mukhopadhyay, *Biplabi Jibaner Smriti*, Indian Associated Publishing Co Pvt. Ltd, 1956, p. 50.

114. Mukhopadhyay, *Biplabi Jibaner Smriti*, p. 467.
115. Mukhopadhyay, *Biplabi Jibaner Smriti*, p. 49.
116. Mukhopadhyay, *Biplabi Jibaner Smriti*, p. 49.
117. Bhupendra Kumar Dutta, *Biplaber Padachinha*, Saraswati Library, 1953, p. 217; Mukhopadhyay, *Biplabi Jibaner Smriti*, p. 483.
118. Mukhopadhyay, *Biplabi Jibaner Smriti*, p. 49.
119. Dutta, *Biplaber Padachina*, p. 216.
120. Mukhopadhyay, *Biplabi Jibaner Smriti*, p. 479. However, the Government used agent provocateurs to provoke terrorist acts (pp. 479–80).
121. *IAR 1923*, pp. 143–63; *The Indian National Congress: 1920–23*, p. 240; Bose, *The Indian Struggle*, pp. 123–4. To set dominion status as the immediate goal was a compromise to settle the difference of opinion of the older generation of politicians with the younger ones who wanted complete independence.
122. *IAR 1923*, pp. 143–63.
123. *IAR 1923*, p. 169. The refusal of the provincial committees appeared obvious to another Gandhian and chronicler of the Congress, Sitaramayya, *History of the Indian National Congress*, p. 431.
124. *IAR 1923*, pp. 173–82.
125. *IAR 1923*, p. 187.
126. Dasgupta, *Subhas Chandra*, pp. 61–3; Bose, *The Indian Struggle*, p. 124–5.
127. *IAR 1923*, pp. 195–205; Ali later explained that the message from the Mahatma was conveyed to him by Devdas Gandhi, *IAR*, Vol.1., No. 1, 1924, pp. 37–40. The Bengal Gandhians revolted against the compromise resolution, with Shyam Sundar Chakravarti's *Servant* calling it fatuous (*Social Conflict and Political Unrest in Bengal*, p. 314).
128. *IAR 1923*, pp. 218–9.
129. *IAR 1923*, pp. 222–4.
130. Dasgupta, *Subhas Chandra*, p. 64.
131. *Social Conflict and Political Unrest in Bengal*, p. 315.
132. *Social Conflict and Political Unrest in Bengal*, p.317. That Das's strategy made an impact on the Government was confirmed by the Viceroy when he wrote to the Secretary of State in March 1924, 'With the members of His Majesty's Government, I have been impressed by the large number of members returned to the Indian Legislatures, Central and Provincial, with the professed object of seeking an immediate constitutional advance of a far-reaching character in India.' Viceroy's telegram to the Secretary of State, 21 March 1924, Cabinet Records, CAB/24/166/0003.
133. *Netaji: His Life and Work*, edited by Sharma, p. 57.
134. Roy, *Netaji the Man*, pp. 13–4.
135. Victor Alexander George Robert Bulwer-Lytton, *Pundits and Elephants*, London: Peter Davis, 1942, p. 44.

136. *Indian Statutory Commission*, Volume VIII, pp. 155–6.

137. J.H. Broomfield, *Elite Conflict in a Plural Society*, University of California Press, 1968, p. 245.

138. *IAR 1923*, Volume II Supplement, pp. 127–8.

139. *IAR 1923*, Volume II Supplement, pp. 121–7, 134–45.

140. *IAR 1923* Volume II Supplement, pp. 113–21, 129–33.

141. Memorandum by the Governor of Bengal, 31 August 1924, Cabinet Records, CAB/24/168/0060; The National Archives, UK.

142. Dasgupta, *Subhas Chandra*, pp. 65–6.

143. Broomfield, *Elite Conflict in a Plural Society*, pp. 330–1; Dasgupta, *Subhas Chandra*, pp. 68–9; Pramatha Nath Pal, *Deshapran Sasmal*, pp. 106–13.

144. Bose, *The Indian Struggle*, p. 136.

145. Dasgupta, *Deshbandhu Chittaranjan Das*, pp. 96–7.

146. Bose, *The Indian Struggle*, p. 137.

147. Bose, *The Indian Struggle*, pp. 136–7.

148. Sarkar, *Subhaser Songe Baro Bochhor*, pp. 140–1.

149. Gandhi, *Collected Works*, Vol. 28, pp. 14–17, 497–500.

150. Bose, *The Indian Struggle*, pp. 145-6; Gandhi, *Collected Works*, Vol. 28, p. 141.

151. Gandhi, *Collected Works*, Vol. 28, pp. 244–5, 248.

152. Viceroy's telegram to the Secretary of State, 4 February 1924, Cabinet Records, CAB/24/164/0064; The National Archives, UK.

153. *IAR 1924*, Vol. 2, pp. 132(d)–140; Broomfield, *Elite Conflict in a Plural Society*, pp. 251–7.

154. Lytton's address to the Bengal Legislative Assembly on 23 January 1924; *The Bengal Legislative Council Proceedings*, 1924, Volume XIV, No. 1, pp. 6–7.

155. Letter from Lytton to the Viceroy, 26 June 1924, Cabinet Records, CAB/24/168/0025; The National Archives, UK. Lytton's letter revealed to what extent the police had infiltrated the revolutionary organizations, when he explained that the Government could not afford to arrest Surendra Mohan Ghose, whom he thought to be the mastermind behind assassination attempts on Tegart, because then 'the identity of our only source of information of the workings of the inner circle and leaders of the revolutionary movement would at once be revealed'.

156. Viceroy's letter to the Secretary of State, 9 July 1924, Cabinet Records, CAB/24/168/0025.The National Archives, UK.

157. Minutes of Cabinet Meeting, 30 July 1924, Cabinet Records, CAB/23/48/0020; Telegram of Secretary of State to Viceroy, 8 August 1924, Cabinet Records, CAB/24/168/0048; The National Archives, UK.

158. Letter from the Chief Secretary to the Government of Bengal to the Government of India, 10 July 1924; Dispatch No. 2 of 1924 from Government of India to India Office, 9 August 1924, Cabinet Records, CAB/24/168/0048; The National Archives, UK.

159. Communication exchanged between the Viceroy, the Secretary of State and the Government of Bengal between 31 July and 11 September 1924, Records of the Cabinet Office, CAB/24/168/0048; Viceroy's telegram to Secretary of State, 30 September 1924, Cabinet Records, CAB/24/168/0062.

160. C.R. Das's statement as reported in the Daily Telegraph, dated 2 September 1924, Records of the Cabinet Office, CAB/24/168/0048.

161. Telegram from Viceroy to the Secretary of State, 22 October 1924, Records of the Cabinet Office, CAB/24/168/0079.

162. Bose, *The Indian Struggle*, p. 151.

163. *The Manchester Guardian*, 27 October 1924.

164. Bose, *The Indian Struggle*, p. 153; Dasgupta, *Subhas Chandra*, p. 74.

165. Dasgupta, *Subhas Chandra*, p. 75.

166. *IAR 1924*, Vol. 2, pp. 176, 180–1.

167. Statement on Bengal Ordinance, 30 October 1924; *Selected Works of Motilal Nehru (SWMN)*, Vol. 4, Vikas Publishing House Pvt. Ltd, 1986, pp. 296–9.

168. Message to UP Political Conference, Gorakhpur, 30 October 1924; Gandhi, *Collected Works*, Vol. 29, pp. 283–4.

169. Letter to Motilal Nehru, 30 October; Gandhi, *Collected Works*, Vol. 29, pp. 284–5.

170. 'Conflict of Interests', *Young India*, 31 October 1924; Gandhi, *Collected Works*, Vol. 29, pp. 289–91.

171. 'My Dissatisfaction', *Young India*, 2 November 1924; Gandhi, *Collected Works*, Vol. 29, pp. 297–8.

172. Speech in Reply to Corporation Address; Gandhi, *Collected Works*, Vol. 29, pp. 307–8. Gandhi was in Calcutta in the first week of November, where he issued a joint statement with Das and Motilal, recommending that the Congress should suspend the non-cooperation programme, and focus on the spread of hand spinning, removal of untouchability, and building communal unity. The Swaraj party was to represent the Congress in provincial and central legislatures and have its own funds.

173. *Bharatbarsha*, November–December 1924, p. 958; *Prabasi*, November–December 1924, pp. 240–1, 263–5.

174. Bose, *The Indian Struggle*, pp. 181–2; *The Calcutta Municipal Gazette*, p. 23; Bose, *My Uncle Netaji*, p. 16.

175. Letters to and from Sarat Chandra Bose, various dates; Subhas Chandra Bose, *In Burmese Prisons*, pp. 21–39.

176. Bose, *The Indian Struggle*, pp. 183–4.

Chapter 3: Reorganizing the Inner World (1924–27)

1. Letter to Sarat Chandra Bose, 10 July 1925; *Netaji: Collected Works*, Vol. 3, Permanent Black, 2009, p. 94.
2. Letter to Sarat Chandra Bose, 13 March 1926; *Netaji: Collected Works*, Vol. 3, p. 246.
3. Letter to Sarat Chandra Bose, 14 March 1925; *Netaji: Collected Works*, Vol. 3, pp. 46–8.
4. Expressing initial reluctance to contest elections to the Bengal Council in 1926, he wrote to Sarat, 'If I have to choose between civic work and politics—I am not sure that I shall feel inclined to give up a less humble but more tangible programme in favour of a more wordy one.' Letter to Sarat Chandra Bose, 17 March 1926; *Netaji: Collected Works*, Vol. 3, p. 259. Persuaded by Sarat, he agreed only in September 1926.
5. Letter to Sarat Chandra Bose, 24 January 1925; *Netaji: Collected Works*, Vol. 3, p. 37.
6. Letter to Sarat Chandra Bose, 22 May1925; *Netaji: Collected Works*, Vol.3, p 64–6. Letter to Sarat Chandra Bose, 6 June 1925; *Netaji: Collected Works*, Vol. 3, pp. 69–70.
7. Letter to Sarat Chandra Bose, 18 August 1925; *Netaji: Collected Works*, Vol. 3, pp. 105–6.
8. Letter to Santosh Kumar Basu, 26 April 1926; *Netaji: Collected Works*, Vol. 3, pp. 279–83.
9. Letter to Sarat Chandra Bose, 2 July 1925; *Netaji: Collected Works*, Vol. 3, pp. 72–3.
10. Letter to A.C. Ukil, June 1926; *Netaji: Collected Works*, Vol. 3, p. 305.
11. Letter to Dr A.C. Ukil, June 1926; *Netaji: Collected Works*, Vol. 3, pp. 302–5.
12. Letter to Gopa Bandhu Das, 7 April 1926; *Netaji: Collected Works*, Vol. 3, pp. 273–4.
13. Letter to Sarat Chandra Bose, 30 June 1926; *Netaji: Collected Works*, Vol. 3, p. 311.
14. Bulwer-Lytton, *Pundits and Elephants*, 1942, p. 69.
15. Bulwer-Lytton, *Pundits and Elephants*, p. 67.
16. Dasgupta, *Deshbandhu Chittaranjan Das*, p. 116; *The Indian Quarterly Register(IQR)*, Vol. 1, January–June 1925, p. 133.
17. *IQR*, Vol. 1, January–June 1925, p. 134.
18. 'Long Live Deshbandhu', Mahatma Gandhi, *The Collected Works of Mahatma Gandhi*, Vol. 32, p. 19.
19. Jawaharlal Nehru, An *Autobiography*, Penguin Books, 2004, p. 141.
20. Letter to Sarat Bose, 19 June 1925; *Netaji: Collected Works*, Vol. 3, pp. 71–2.
21. Dasgupta, *Subhas Chandra*, p. 82.

22. Letter to Basanti Devi, 6 July 1925; *Netaji: Collected Works,* Vol. 3, pp. 76–8.

23. Letter to Basanti Devi, 10 July 1925; *Netaji: Collected Works,* Vol. 3, pp. 94–5.

24. Letter to Sarat Chandra Chattopadhyay, 12 August 1925; *Netaji: Collected Works,* Vol. 3, pp. 107–11. An interesting contrast to this reminiscence is the assessment of a Bolshevik paper. *The Masses of India* wrote (cited in Rajat Kanta Ray, *Social Conflict and Political Unrest in Bengal,* pp. 345):

> In the brief and inglorious career of C.R. Das as the Swarajist leader, we have had the spectacle of a would-be Indian Menshevik who failed even to rise to the level of a Kerensky, having miserably 'bungled and mismanaged' an unquestionably revolutionary situation and having even forgotten to depose the English Tsar in India in his haste to pose as the premature champion of the interests of the liberal bourgeoisie.

25. Letter to Sarat Chandra Bose, 1 August 1925; *Netaji: Collected Works,* Vol. 3, pp. 302–3.

26. 'On Chitta Ranjan Das', written on 20 February 1926 for Hemendranath Dasgupta; Bose, *Subhas Rachanabali,* Vol. 4, pp. 20–30.

27. Ray, *Social Conflict and Political Unrest,* p. 349; Chatterjee, *Congress Politics in Bengal,* p. 131.

28. Lytton's letter to Birkenhead, 25 August 1925, cited in Ray, *Social Conflict and Political Unrest,* p. 347.

29. Sarat Chandra Bose's letter, 15 July 1925; Subhas's letter to Sarat Chandra Bose, 22 July 1925; *Netaji: Collected Works,* Vol. 3, pp. 73–6, 96–7.

30. Letter to Dr A.C. Ukil, June 1926; *Netaji: Collected Works,* Vol. 3, pp. 302–5.

31. Letter to Bhupendra Nath Bandopadhyay, undated, 1926; *Netaji: Collected Works,* Vol. 3, pp. 133–5.

32. Letter to Hari Charan Bagchi, undated, 1926; *Netaji: Collected Works,* Vol. 4, Netaji Research Bureau, 1982, pp. 139.

33. Letters to Sarat Chandra Bose, 17 March, 7 August, 13 August, 1 September 1926; *Netaji: Collected Works,* Vols. 3 and 4; letters from Sarat Chandra Bose, 6 August, 21 August, 27 August, 11 September 1926; *Netaji: Collected Works,* Vols. 3 and 4.

34. Letter to Sarat Chandra Bose, 13 November, 1926; *Netaji: Collected Works,* Vol. 4, p. 89.

35. Letter to Sarat Chandra Bose, 22 November 1926; *Netaji: Collected Works,* Vol. 4, p. 97.

36. Letter to Dilip Kumar Roy, 11 September 1925; *Netaji: Collected Works,* Vol. 3, p. 86.

37. Letter to Anil Chandra Biswas, undated; *Netaji: Collected Works,* Vol. 4, pp. 178–83.

38. Letter to Haricharan Bagchi, undated, 1926; *Netaji: Collected Works*, Vol. 4, pp. 139–41.

39. Among the other books that he requisitioned were *Tantrasar, Prantoshini, Brihat Tantrasar, Shaktananda Tarangini, Shyama Rahasya, Tara Rahasya*, Bengali translations of the *Sama Veda, Yajur Veda* and *Atharva Veda*, a comparative study between the Vedas and the Avesta. A list of books which he requested a friend to send to him also included *Haratatta Didhiti, Harivakti Bilas, Shuddhitattam, Shraddhatattam, Atri Samhita, Vishnu Samhita, Harit Samhita, Yajnyabalka Samhita, Usana Samhita, Ajnira Samhita, Yama Samhita, Upastamba Samhita, Sambarta Samhita, Kyattayan Samhita, Brihaspati Samhita, Parasar Samhita, Vyas Samhita, Sankhya Samhita, Likhita Samhita, Daksha Samhita, Goutam Samhita, Shatatap Samhita, Vashistha Samhita*, and *Baudhayan Samhita*.

40. Letter to Sarat Chandra Bose, 23 February 1921; Bose, *An Indian Pilgrim*, p. 222.

41. See Peter Heehs, *The Lives of Sri Aurobindo*, Columbia University Press, 2008, Kindle Edition, pp. 334–6.

42. Letter to Dilip Kumar Roy, 9 October 1925; *Netaji: Collected Works*, Vol. 3, p. 132.

43. Letter to Dilip Kumar Roy, 9 October 1925; *Netaji: Collected Works*, Vol. 3, pp. 130–1. Dilip shared this letter with Rabindranath: 'The letter from Subhas is wonderful. I am delighted to learn about the qualities of his head and heart which the letter reflects. What he has written about art cannot be contradicted', was Rabindranath's response (Dilip Kumar Roy, *Anami*, 1933, pp. 354–5).

44. Letter to Anath Bandhu Dutta, December 1925 (the year mentioned in the volume is 1926, but several references to just over a year of imprisonment makes it more likely to have been written in 1925); *Netaji: Collected Works*, Vol. 4, pp. 131–2.

45. Letter from Rajendra Dev, 9 November 1926; *Netaji: Collected Works*, Vol. 4, p. 94.

46. Letter to the Chief Secretary of Burma, 16 February 1926; *Netaji: Collected Works*, Vol. 3, pp. 221–6. The seven other signatories to the letter were: Jibanlal Chatterjee, Satyendra Chandra Mitra, Trailokyanath Chakraborty, Bipin Behari Ganguly, Surendra Mohan Ghose and Madan Mohan Bhowmick.

47. Bose, *The Indian Struggle*, p. 195; Letters to Sarat Chandra Bose, 1 March, 13 March, 26 March, 23 April 1926; *Netaji: Collected Works*, Vol. 3, pp. 315–6, 247, 271; Letter to Janakinath Bose, 8 March 1926; *Netaji: Collected Works*, Vol. 3, p. 246.

48. Letter from Janakinath Bose, 15 August 1926; *Netaji: Collected Works*, Vol. 4, pp. 48–9; Letters to Sarat Chandra Bose, 17 March, 30 April, 17 June

1926; *Netaji: Collected Works*, Vol. 3, pp. 258, 265, 307, 309; Letter from Tarubala Roy, 9 January 1926; *Netaji: Collected Works*, Vol 4, p. 313.

49. Letters to Bivabati Bose, 11 September and 16 December 1925, 12 February, 9 April, 27 July, 28 July 1926; *Netaji: Collected Works*, Vol. 3, pp. 118–23, 168–74, 216–9, 275–6, 342–4. For the Bengali versions, see Subhaschandra Bosu *Samagra Rachanabali*, Vol. 1, edited by Sisir K. Bose, Ananda Publishers Pvt. Ltd, 2012.

50. See Sarkar, *Subhaser Songe Baro Bochhor*, and Sasmal, *Sroter Trina*.

51. Letter to Hari Charan Bagchi, 6 February 1926; *Netaji: Collected Works*, Vol. 3, p. 208.

52. Letter to Basanti Devi, 20 December 1926; *Netaji: Collected Works*, Vol. 4, p. 119.

53. Letters from Sarat Chandra Bose, 8 October 1925 and 20 March 1926; *Netaji: Collected Works*, Vol. 3, pp. 141, 255; Letter from Dilip Kumar Roy, 21 November 1925, with a postscript dated 28 December 1925; *Netaji: Collected Works*, Vol. 3, pp. 137–8.

54. Letter to Bivabati Bose, 7 February 1927; *Netaji: Collected Works*, Vol. 4, p. 163.

55. House of Commons Debate, 29 March 1926, Vol. 193, Column 1624, accessed online at http://hansard.millbanksystems.com/commons/1926/mar/29/calcutta-corporation-mr-s-c-bose#S5CV0193P0_19260329_HOC_35.

56. House of Commons Debate, 14 March 1927, Vol. 203, Column 1616. Accessed online at http://hansard.millbanksystems.com/commons/1927/mar/14/mr-s-c-bose.

57. Bose, *The Indian Struggle*, p. 197.

58. House of Commons Debate, 21 February 1927, Vol. 202, Colum 1364. Accessed online at http://hansard.millbanksystems.com/commons/1927/feb/21/bengal-criminal-ordinance-act-detinues#S5CV0202P0_19270221_HOC_29.

59. *BLCP*, Vol. 25, No. 3, 21 March 1927, pp. 341–2.

60. Letter to Satyendra Chandra Mitra, 25 June 1927; *Netaji: Collected Works*, Vol. 4, p. 229.

61. Letter to Sarat Chandra Bose, 4 April 1927; *Netaji: Collected Works*, Vol. 4, pp. 196–203. The letter gives a glimpse of how Subhas viewed the Communists in Europe:

> If I had the remotest intention of becoming a Bolshevik agent, I would have jumped at the offer made and taken the first available boat to Europe. If I succeeded in recouping my health, I could then have joined the gay band who trot about from Paris to Leningrad talking of world revolution and emitting blood and thunder in their utterances. But I have no such ambition or desire.

62. Letter to the Inspector General of Prisons, Burma, 11 April 1927; *Netaji: Collected Works*, Vol. 4, pp. 213–5.

63. Letter from Sarat Chandra Bose, 16 April 1927; *Netaji: Collected Works*, Vol. 4, pp. 209–12.

64. House of Commons Debate, 9 May 1927, Vol. 206, Column 3. Accessed online at http://hansard.millbanksystems.com/commons/1927/may/09/mr-s-bose#S5CV0206P0_19270509_HOC_11.

65. Bose, *The Indian Struggle*, pp. 198–9.

66. House of Commons Debate, 23 May 1927, Vol. 206, Columns 1629-30. Accessed online at http://hansard.millbanksystems.com/commons/1927/may/23/mr-s-bose-release#S5CV0206P0_19270523_HOC_48.

67. Mahatma Gandhi to Sarat Chandra Bose, 9 April 1926; Gandhi, *Collected Works*, Vol. 35, p. 43.

68. 'Highly Unsatisfactory', published in *Young India*, 26 May 1927; Gandhi, *Collected Works*, Vol. 38, pp. 434–5.

69. Mahatma Gandhi to Satcowripati Ray, 12 June 1927; Gandhi, *Collected Works*, Vol. 39, p. 46. Most probably the telegram got misplaced.

70. Bose, *My Uncle Netaji*, p. 28.

71. Statement issued to Associated Press, 17 May 1927; *Rachanabali*, Vol. 1, p. 21.

72. Statement issued on 3 June 1927; *Rachanabali*, Vol. 1, pp. 21–2.

73. House of Commons Debate, 2 June 1927, Vol. 207, Columns 602-622. Accessed online at http://hansard.millbanksystems.com/commons/1927/jun/02/india#S5CV0207P0_19270602_HOC_307. Giving the current situation of detention, Winterton stated that 57 people were in prison and 99 were under restraint in villages or in their homes.

74. House of Commons Debate, 15 June 1927, Vol. 207, Column 1007. Accessed online at http://hansard.millbanksystems.com/commons/1927/jun/15/mr-subhas-bose#S5CV0207P0_19270615_HOC_223. Two days later Lansbury read out in the House parts of Subhas's letter and apologized for mistakenly assuming from Winterton's earlier statements that Subhas had been provided a trial by the Judges.

75. Gita Biswas, *Smritir Aloy*, Jayasree Prakashan, 1999, pp. 10–2. Sisir Bose; *Bosu Bari*, Anada Publishers Pvt. Ltd, 2013, pp. 32–4. Letter to Bivabati Bose, undated, 1927; *Netaji: Collected Works*, Vol. 4, p. 254.

76. From his letters written to Sarat from Mandalay, it can be seen that Subhas was as serious about learning the ropes of council politics as he was in any other work he took up. From Shillong, he advised Sarat, who had been elected from the Calcutta University constituency, that in each session he should do something to nurse his constituency. It was not possible, he knew, to do anything substantial, 'but one has to make a show—by means of

questions and resolutions'. Letter to Sarat Chandra Bose, 11 August 1927; *Netaji: Collected Works*, Vol. 4, pp. 250–1.

77. Letters to Satyendra Chandra Mitra, 25 June 1927 and 25 July 1927; *Netaji: Collected Works*, Vol. 4, pp. 230, 236.

78. Bengal Legislative Council Proceedings. Subhas did not participate in the debates on any of the three major legislations introduced in the council during these two sessions, but wrote a detailed critique of one of the bills— the Borstal School Bill on prison reforms for adolescent offenders.

79. Letter to Basanti Devi, 17 July 1927; *Netaji: Collected Works*, Vol. 4, p. 232.

80. Letters to Satyendra Chandra Mitra, 26 September 1927 and 1 October 1927; *Netaji: Collected Works*, Vol. 4, pp. 258–60. Statement issued from Shillong, 16 September 1927, *Rachanabali*, Vol.1, pp. 29–30.

81. Letter to Basanti Devi, 17 July 1927; *Netaji: Collected Works*, Vol. 4, p. 232.

82. Letter to Basanti Devi, 30 July 1927; *Netaji: Collected Works*, Vol. 4, p. 239.

83. Letter to Basanti Devi, 15 October 1927; *Netaji: Collected Works*, Vol. 4, p. 262.

84. Letter to Basanti Devi, 30 July 1927; *Netaji: Collected Works*, Vol. 4, p. 239.

85. Letter to Basanti Devi, 15 October 1927; *Netaji: Collected Works*, Vol. 4, p. 262.

86. The resolution was carried in the Unity Conference of Hindu and Muslim leaders held in Calcutta a day before.

87. *IQR* 1927, July–December, pp. 28–30, Bose, *Subhas Rachanabali*, Vol. 1, pp. 31–3.

88. Speech at a public meeting at Shraddhananda Park, Calcutta, 12 November 1927; Bose, *Subhas Rachanabali*, Vol. 1, pp. 34–6.

89. Dasgupta, *Subhas Chandra*, p. 94.

90. Appeal to Congress organizations in Bengal, 22 November 1927; *Netaji: Collected Works*, Vol. 5, pp. 214–5.

Chapter 4: Alap (1928–29)

1. Bose, *The Indian Struggle*, p. 252.
2. *Bengal Provincial Conference, 1928*, compiled by Yatindra Kumar Ghosh, Firma K.L. Mukhopadhyay, 1972, p. 13.
3. *Bengal Provincial Conference, 1928*, pp. 39–41.
4. Sitaramayya, *History of the Congress*, p. 541.
5. Interview to 'Indian Daily Mail'; Mahatma Gandhi, *The Collected Works of Mahatma Gandhi*, Vol. 41, pp. 71–2.
6. 'The National Congress', 5 January 1928, and 'Independence vs Swaraj', 12 January 1928, *Young India*, Gandhi, *Collected Works*, Vol. 41, pp. 84–5, 104.
7. Statement to the Press, 12 January 1928, Jawaharlal Nehru, *Selected Works of Jawaharlal Nehru (SWJN)*, Vol. 3, B.R. Publishing Corporation, 1988, pp. 16–7.

8. Nehru, *An Autobiography*, p. 79.

9. Michael Brecher, *Nehru: A Political Biography*, Oxford University Press, 2005, pp. 75–6.

10. *SWJN*, Vol. 2, p. 207.

11. Nehru, *Autobiography*, pp. 132–3.

12. Brecher, *Nehru*, p. 109; S. Gopal, the adulatory biographer of Jawaharlal, termed it as 'a turning point in Jawaharlal's mental development', S. Gopal, *Jawaharlal Nehru: A Biography*, Vol. 1, Oxford University Press, 1976, p. 100.

13. Gopal, *Nehru*, p. 101.

14. Brecher, *Nehru*, p. 110.

15. Letter to Jawaharlal Nehru, 17 January 1928; Gandhi, *Collected Works*, Vol. 41, pp. 120–2.

16. Letter to Mahatma Gandhi, 23 January 1928, *SWJN*, Vol. 3, pp. 18–9.

17. Statement on the Independence Resolution, published in *The Tribune*, 27 January 1928, cited in *SWJN*, Vol. 3, p. 21.

18. Letter to Satcowripati Roy, 12 June 1927; Gandhi, *Collected Works*, p. 46.

19. *Bengal Provincial Congress, 1928*, p. 39–40.

20. Dasgupta, *Subhas Chandra*, p. 95.

21. Nirad C. Chaudhuri, *Autobiography of an Unknown Indian*, Part II, p. 379.

22. 'Why I Voted for Mr Subhas Bose', *The Calcutta Municipal Gazette*, 14 April 1928, *The Calcutta Municipal Gazette: Subhas Chandra Bose Birth Centenary Number*, edited by Arun Kumar Roy, The Calcutta Municipal Corporation, 1997, p. 59.

23. Bose, *Subhas Rachanabali*, Vol. 1, pp. 166–7.

24. Dasgupta, *Subhas Chandra*, p. 96; Leonard A. Gordon, *Brothers Against the Raj*, Viking, 1990, p. 165.

25. *The Indian Quarterly Register 1928*, Vol. 1, p. 6.

26. 'Independent Mayor of Calcutta: A Swarajist Defeat', *The Times*, 3 April 1928.

27. *Calcutta Municipal Gazette*, 31 March 1928, p. 50.

28. Bose, *Subhas Rachanabali*, Vol. 1. p. 96.

29. *Calcutta Municipal Gazette*, 25 February 1928, p. 49.

30. *Calcutta Municipal Gazette*, 9 June 1928, p. 61.

31. Bose, *Rachanabali*, Vol. 1, p. 200.

32. Gandhi, *Collected Works*, Vol. 40, pp. 496–7.

33. Statement of S. Srinivasa Iyengar, *IQR 1927*, Vol. 2, pp. 99–102.

34. *House of Lords Debates*, 7 July 1925, Vol. 61, column 1086 (hansard. millbanksystems.com/lords/1925/jul/07/india) and November 24, 1927, Vol. 69, column 237 (hansard.millbanksystems.com/lords/1927/nov/24/ indian-statutory-commission).

35. *IQR 1927*, Vol. 2, p. 60.
36. Fortnightly Reports on the Political Situation in India, First Half of January 1928, File No. 1 January 1928; National Archives, New Delhi.
37. *IQR 1928*, Vol. 1, p. 1.
38. Fortnightly Reports, Second Half of January 1928.
39. Gopal Lal Sanyal, *Je Kathar Shesh Nei*, Jayasree Prakashan, 1985, pp. 85–7.
40. Speech at a public meeting in Howrah, 28 February 1928; Bose, *Subhas Rachanabali*, Vol. 1, pp. 74–6.
41. Letter to Subhas Chandra Bose, 15 March 1928; *SWJN*, Vol. 3, p. 161.
42. *IQR 1928*, Vol. 1, p. 6.
43. Chatterjee, *Congress Politics in Bengal*, p. 125. The name of the organization was changed in 1928 at the insistence of Subhas to All-Bengal Youth Association to accommodate women members (Tanika Sarkar, *Bengal 1928–34: The Politics of Protest*, p. 14).
44. Speech at a public meeting in Rajshahi, 13 April 1928; Bose, *Subhas Rachanabali*, Vol. 1, p. 118.
45. Reacting to the charge of a Missionary member of the Legislative Council that the students were good but were being exploited by political leaders, he said, 'I often wonder why the Indian students are advised against joining politics when the situation in England is absolutely the opposite.' Speech at Scottish Church College, 26 March 1928; Bose, *Subhas Rachanabali*, Vol. 1, pp. 93–4.
46. Speech at a meeting in Opera House, Bombay, 22 May 1928; Bose, *Subhas Rachanabali*, Vol. 1, pp. 177–9.
47. See discussion on the relationship between the nationalist movement and trade unions in Shiva Chandra Jha, *The Indian Trade Union Movement*, Firma K.L. Mukhopadhyay, 1970, pp. 116–20.
48. Clemens Dutt, 'Indian Politics: An Analysis', *Labour Monthly*, Vol. 7, July 1925, No. 7, pp. 399–409, https://www.marxists.org/archive/dutt-clemens/1925/07/x01.htm.
49. According to Gordon, 1928 recorded the maximum number of worker-hours lost until 1946–47. Gordon, *Brothers Against the Raj*, p. 171.
50. For Jamshedpur strike, see http://www.sacw.net/Labour/DSimeonLabourHist.html.
51. Presidential address at the Maharashtra Provincial Conference, Poona, 3 May 1928; published by the General Secretary, Reception Committee of Sixth Maharashtra Provincial Conference, Poona, 1928, reprinted in *Jayasree*, Poush 1414, pp. 380–98.
52. *Calcutta Municipal Gazette*, 19 May 1928, p. 60.
53. Bimal Prasad, *Pathways to India's Partition*, Vol. 2, Manohar, 2009, pp. 277–9.
54. Letter from Jawaharlal Nehru to Gandhi, 23 February 1928; *SWJN*, Vol. 3, p. 36.

55. According to the report, the committee was deliberately kept small with members representing specific points of view. Thus, Ali Imam and Shuaib Qureshi presented the Muslim point of view, M.R. Jayakar and M.S. Aney the views of the Hindu Mahasabha, G.R. Pradhan the non-Brahmin view, Sardar Mangal Singh represented the Sikh League, Tej Bahadur Sapru was the Liberal representative and N.M. Joshi the labour concerns. Although the report acknowledged the hard work of Jawaharlal in assisting the committee, it was silent on Subhas's role or what point of view he represented. *All Parties Conference: Report of the Committee Appointed by the Conference to determine the principles of the Constitution for India*, General Secretary AICC, Allahabad, 1928.
56. Letter from Motilal Nehru to Gandhi, 27 June 1928; Nehru, *SWMN*, Vol. 5, 1993, p. 325.
57. Letter from Motilal Nehru to Gandhi, 11 July 1928; *SWMN*, Vol. 5, p. 328. Some insight can be drawn from Subhas's temperament of reaching out to opponents from the suggestion that along with J.N. Basu (to whom he had lost in the mayoral elections recently), the hardline Islamist leader Abdur Rahim too should be invited from Bengal in the expanded final meeting of the committee in which Motilal wanted to invite non-members. The Nehrus agreed to invite Basu, but shot down the idea of inviting Rahim, fearing that his presence would further polarize the communal positions of the contending parties. It is possible that Subhas thought that by providing such a national platform to Rahim, his rabid communal position could be softened. Comparing Rahim to Mian Muhammad Shafi, the hardline leader of the Punjab faction of the Muslim League, Jawahar wrote to Subhas that 'I do not think that it is right for us to attach importance to people like Abdur Rahim', (Jawaharlal Nehru's letter to Subhas Chandra Bose, 27 June 1928, *SWJN*, Vol. 3, p. 46).
58. Fortnightly Reports, First Half of October 1928, File No. 1/1928-October.
59. *SWMN*, Vol. 6, 1995, p. 197.
60. *All Parties Conference: Report of the Committee Appointed by the Conference to determine the principles of the Constitution for India*, General Secretary AICC, Allahabad, 1928, p. 25.
61. Provisional Rules of the League, 31 August 1928, *The Tribune*, cited in *SWJN*, Vol. 3, 1988, p. 67.
62. Speech at the inaugural meeting of the Bengal Provincial Independence for India League, 2 October 1928, Bose, *Subhas Rachanabali*, Vol. 1, p. 257.
63. Nehru, *Autobiography*, p. 183.
64. Interview to the Press on 16 November 1928, *The Searchlight;* 21 November 1928, cited in *SWJN*, Vol. 3, p. 77.
65. Nirode K. Barooah, *Chatto: The Life and Times of an Indian Anti-Imperialist in Europe*, 2004, p. 248–9, footnote 20, p. 277. Living in the Soviet Union

since 1931, Chatto was arrested by the secret police in July 1937 and executed on 2 September. The information of his execution came to light for the first time through an article by Leonid Mitrokhin published in *Soviet Land* in April 1991.

66. Letter of Virendranath Chattopadhyay to Jawaharlal Nehru, 29 August 1928; *SWJN*, Vol. 3, p. 70, footnote 5.

67. Nehru, *Autobiography*, p. 162.

68. Nehru, *Autobiography*, p. 168.

69. Fortnightly Reports, First Half of October 1928; File No. 1/1928-October.

70. *IQR 1928*, Vol. 2, p. 21.

71. Gandhi's letter to Motilal Nehru, 19 June 1928; Gandhi, *Collected Works*, Vol. 42, p. 144.

72. Motilal Nehru's letter to Gandhi, 27 June 1928; *SWMN*, Vol. 5, p. 324.

73. Motilal Nehru's letter to Gandhi, 11 July 1928; *SWMN*, Vol. 5, p. 328.

74. Motilal Nehru's letter to J.M. Sengupta and Subhas Chandra Bose, 19 July 1928, Enclosure to Motilal Nehru's letter to Gandhi, 19 July 1928; *SWMN*, Vol. 5, p. 333.

75. Gandhi's letter to Motilal Nehru, 15 July 1928; Gandhi, *Collected Works*, Vol. 42, p. 251.

76. Mukhopadhyay, *Biplabi Jibaner Smriti*, p. 531.

77. Gandhi's telegrams to Motilal Nehru and Subhas Chandra Bose, 23 July 1928; Gandhi, *Collected Works*, Vol. 42, p. 279.

78. Motilal Nehru's telegrams to Gandhi, Subhas Chandra Bose and J.M. Sengupta, 24 July 1928; *SWMN*, Vol. 5, p. 339.

79. Gandhi's letter to J.M. Sengupta, 24 May 1928; Gandhi, *Collected Works*, Vol. 42, pp. 42–3.

80. Gandhi's letter to J.M. Sengupta, 21 June 1928; Gandhi, *Collected Works*, Vol. 42, p. 157.

81. Gandhi's letter to Subhas Chandra Bose, 14 August 1928; Gandhi, *Collected Works*, Vol. 42, p. 372.

82. Gandhi's letters to Motilal Nehru, 30 September and 18 October 1928; Gandhi, *Collected Works*, Vol. 43, pp. 65–6 and 120–1. Gandhi's letter to Satyananda Bose, 9 November 1928; Gandhi, *Collected Works*, Vol. 43, p. 205.

83. Dr B.C. Roy's letter to Gandhi, 28 October 1928; Gandhi, *Collected Works*, Vol. 43, pp. 523–4.

84. Gandhi's letter to Dr B.C. Roy, 3 November 1928; Gandhi, *Collected Works*, Vol. 43, pp. 176–8.

85. Telegram from Dr B.C. Roy to Gandhi, 28 November 1928, Gandhi, *Collected Works*, Vol. 43, p. 259.

86. Gandhi's letter to Dr B.C. Roy, 28 November 1928; Gandhi, *Collected Works*, Vol. 43, p. 273.

87. Gandhi's letter to Motilal Nehru, 28 November 1928; Gandhi, *Collected Works*, Vol. 43, pp. 274–5.

88. Telegram and letter of Gandhi to Dr B.C. Roy, 3 December 1928; Gandhi, *Collected Works*, Vol. 43, pp. 315–7.

89. Gandhi's letter to Satis Chandra Dasgupta, 3 December 1928; Gandhi, *Collected Works*, Vol. 43, p. 317.

90. Mohammad Ali, former President of the Congress and the Muslim League, burst forth with severe criticism of the Dominion Status clause, calling it a 'policy of a coward'; *IQR 1928*, Vol. 1, p. 104.

91. Proceedings of the All Parties Convention, 23 December 1928; *IQR 1928*, Vol. 1, pp. 102–3 and 113. As late as in October, Subhas was clearly in a dilemma. In a speech at the Tilak Vidyalaya in Nagpur on 4 October, he admitted that he was in a spot since, having signed the report, he could not criticize it. He explained that in spite of advocating complete independence at an individual level, he had agreed to the report's recommendation on Dominion Status for the sake of unity. Bose, *Subhas Rachanabali*, Vol. 2, p. 259.

92. Proceedings of the Subjects Committee meeting, 26 December 1928; *IQR 1928*, Vol. 2, pp. 28–32.

93. Proceedings of the Subjects Committee meeting, 27 December 1928; *IQR 1928*, Vol. 2, pp. 32–5.

94. Motilal Nehru, *SWMN*, Vol. 6, p. 449.

95. Jadugopal Mukherjee has given the insider's view that brought in this change. According to Mukherjee, after Jawaharlal's opposition to the Dominion Status resolution in the Subjects Committee, Gandhi convinced him, Iyengar and Subhas in a private meeting not to oppose the resolution, to which they agreed. Upon hearing this, the Bengal delegates and some revolutionaries (including Mukherjee, Trailokyanath Chakraborty, Satin Sen and others) met with Subhas and Sengupta. After much discussion, Subhas took the position that his assurance to Gandhi was in his personal capacity, but as the leader of BPCC it was his duty to reflect the dominant view of the province. Although Sengupta cautioned him that stepping back from his assurance to Gandhi at this point would stain his public image, Subhas had made up his mind to lead the opposition to the Dominion Status resolution (Mukhopadhyay, *Biplabi Jibaner Smriti*, pp. 533–4). According to another witness to the developments, novelist Sarat Chandra Chattopadhyay played an important role in convincing Subhas to speak against Gandhi's resolution. Sudhi Prodhan, *Subhaschandra, Bharat O Akkhashakti*, National Book Agency Pvt. Ltd, 2000, p. 29.

96. *IQR 1928*, Vol. 2, pp. 360–2.

97. *IQR 1928*, Vol. 2, pp. 366–8.

98. In an interview to *The Englishman*, Gandhi said that if the Congress demands were not met, 'on New Year's Day 1930, I shall wake up to find myself an Independencewallah'. Interview to the Press, 3 January 1929, Gandhi, *Collected Works*, Vol. 43, pp. 488–90.

99. *IQR 1928*, Vol. 2, p. 374.

100. Interview with Associated Press, 5 January 1929; Bose, *Rachanabali*, Vol. 2, p. 10.

101. Bose, *The Indian Struggle*, pp. 222–3.

102. *Report on the Administration of Bengal 1927–28*, Government of Bengal, pp. 14–6.

103. Fortnightly Reports, Second Half of December 1928; File No. 1-Poll.-1928.

104. 'The Congress', *Young India*, 10 January 1929; Gandhi, *Collected Works*, Vol. 43, p. 498.

105. File No. 233-1928, Home Department, Political; National Archives, New Delhi.

106. Telegram from Viceroy, Home Department, to Secretary of State for India, 19 January 1929; Cabinet Papers, File No. CAB/24/201; The National Archives, UK.

107. Different estimates on the number of workers have been provided by different sources. While Subhas stated a figure of 10,000, the Government of Bengal cited 20,000 (*Report on the Administration of Bengal, 1927–28*, p. 16) and Pattabhi Sitaramayya estimated the gathering to be 50,000 strong (Sitaramayya, *History of the Indian National Congress*, Vol. 1, p. 563).

108. *Report on the Administration of Bengal, 1927–28*, p. 16; Sumit Sarkar, *Modern India*, Macmillan India Ltd, 1996, p. 270; Sukumar Mitra, *Gandhiji, Subhaschandra O Banglar Biplabira*, Firma K.L. Mukhopadhyay Pvt. Ltd, 1998, p. 33.

109. 'The Congress', *Young India*, 10 January 1929; Gandhi, *Collected Works*, Vol. 43, p. 498.

110. 'Hindi in Bengal', *Young India*, 10 January 1929; Gandhi, *Collected Works*, Vol. 43, p. 500.

111. *IQR 1928*, Vol. 2.

112. Bose, *The Indian Struggle*, p. 224.

113. *Calcutta Municipal Gazette*, 17 November 1928, pp. 62–3.

114. *Calcutta Municipal Gazette*, 15 December 1928, pp. 67–9; Bose, *Rachanabali*, Vol. 1, pp. 289–91.

115. *IQR 1929*, Vol. 2, p. 59.

116. Fortnightly Reports, First Half of June 1929.

117. Speeches at Mysore Park, Calcutta, 16 January 1929 and at Hrishikesh Park, Calcutta, 18 January 1929; Bose, *Subhas Rachanabali*, Vol. 2, pp. 11–5.

118. 'The Congress', *Young India*, 10 January 1929; Gandhi, *Collected Works*, Vol. 43, p. 498.

119. 'Boycott', *Navajivan*, 3 March 1929; Gandhi, *Collected Works*, Vol. 45, pp. 153–4.

120. Resolution passed at New Delhi AICC meeting, 3 and 4 February 1929; *IQR 1929*, Vol. 1, p. 28.

121. Resolution passed at Calcutta AICC meeting, 3 January 1929; *IQR 1929*, Vol. 1, p. 26.

122. Calling the incident a 'test case', Gandhi later indicated that he would not have gone ahead with the burning of clothes if he was certain that such an act in a public place was indeed illegal. He was not yet ready for civil disobedience. However, he was happy that the 'high-handed action of the police gave the boycott movement an advertisement and an encouragement it would never have otherwise had'; 'That Test Case', *Young India*, 4 April 1929; Gandhi, *Collected Works*, Vol. 45, pp. 294–6.

123. Speech at a public meeting in Deshbandhu Park, Calcutta, 6 March 1929; Bose, *Subhas Rachanabali*, Vol. 2, p. 49.

124. Appeal published in newspapers, 16 March 1929; Bose, *Subhas Rachanabali*, Vol. 2, p. 55.

125. Speech at a public meeting in Rishikesh Park, Calcutta, 15 March 1929; Bose, *Subhas Rachanabali*, Vol. 2, p. 53.

126. Speech at a public meeting in Bhawanipur, Calcutta, 8 March 1929; Bose, *Subhas Rachanabali*, Vol. 2, p. 49.

127. Bose, *The Indian Struggle*, p. 222.

128. P.K. Ray, *Down Memory Lane*, Gian Publishing House, 1990, p. 78.

129. See Bose, *Subhas Rachanabali* and *Netaji: Collected Works* for speeches at Pabna (9 February), Malikanda Abhay Ashram (2 March), Sylhet (25 April), Jessore and Khulna (22 June), Hooghly (21 July), Rajshahi (17 and 20 August), Howrah (undated, but most likely September), and Midnapore (27 December).

130. Of the Binoy–Badal–Dinesh trio of the Writers' Building raid of 8 December 1930.

131. Ray, *Down Memory Lane*, pp. 88–9.

132. Fortnightly Reports, First Half of June 1929, File No. 17/29-Political.

133. Fortnightly Reports, First Half of July 1929, File No. 17/29-Political.

134. Fortnightly Reports, Second Half of July 1929, File No. 17/29-Political.

135. Ray, *Down Memory Lane*, p. 84.

136. See, for instance, his speech at the Mymensingh district conference, 21 April 1929; Bose, *Rachanabali*, Vol. 2, pp. 110–1; Speech at Howrah District Political Conference, 28 September 1929; Bose, *Rachanabali*, Vol. 2, p. 208.

137. Bose, *Subhas Rachanabali*, Vol. 2, pp. 197–204.

138. Presidential address at the Howrah Youth Conference, Date unknown, 1929; Bose, *Subhas Rachanabali*, Vol. 2, pp. 196–204.

139. Fortnightly Reports, First Half of October 1929, File No. 17/29-Political.

140. Fortnightly Reports, Second Half of October 1929, File No. 17/29-Political.

141. Presidential addresses at Punjab Students' Conference, Lahore, 19 October, pp. 42–53; First Central Provinces Youth Conference, Nagpur, 29 November, pp. 61–8; Central Provinces and Berar Students' Conference, 1 December 1929, *Netaji: Collected Works*, Vol. 6, pp. 80–7.

142. Presidential address at the Howrah District Conference, 28 September 1929; Bose, *Rachanabali*, Vol. 2, pp. 209–16 (translated by author from the original Bangla).

143. Irfan Habib, *To Make the Deaf Hear*, Three Essays Collective, 2010, p. 26.

144. Jogesh Chandra Chatterji, *In Search of Freedom*, Firma K.L. Mukhopadhyay, 1958, pp. 209, 211.

145. Dasgupta, *Subhas Chandra*, p. 107; Bose, *The Indian Struggle*, p. 228.

146. Ram Chandra, *History of the Naujawan Bharat Sabha*, Unistar Books Pvt. Ltd, 2007, pp. 17–8.

147. Habib, *To Make the Deaf Hear*, p. 35.

148. C.S. Venu, *Jatin Das*, p. 29.

149. Fortnightly Reports, First Half of April 1929, File 17/29-Political.

150. Fortnightly Reports, First Half of August 1929, File 17/29-Political

151. Kuldip Nayar, *Without Fear*, HarperCollins Publishers India, 2012, p. 95.

152. Dasgupta, *Subhas Chandra*, p. 107.

153. Fortnightly Reports, First Half of September 1929, File 17/29-Political.

154. Fortnightly Reports, Second Half of September 1929, File 17/29-Political; Second Half of October, November and December, File 17/29-Political.

155. Fortnightly Reports, Second Half of September 1929, File 17/29-Political.

156. The revolutionary landscape of Bengal can be quite confusing, with its numerous groups and subgroups, with their leaders and workers breaking away to join another group or form a new group. The intergroup and interpersonal relationships which were sometimes ideological but more often personal moulded the dynamics of Bengal's politics. Subhas aimed to organize the groups into a disciplined force without success, which would jeopardize his own political life over the next decade (see 'Report on the Dacca Sri Sangha up to 1929', in *Terrorism in Bengal*, compiled and edited by Amiya Kumar Samanta, Vol. 2, Government of West Bengal, 1995, pp. 988–90, for his efforts to unite the different groups in Dacca and how it fell through).

157. Bhola Chatterji, *Aspects of Bengal Politics in the Early Nineteen Thirties*, World Press, 1969, p. 2. Chatterji has speculated that the person responsible was Satya Ranjan Bakshi, although he has not cited any evidence for his claim.

158. Panchanan Chakraborti, 'Subhas Chandra Netaji Hoilen', in *Jayasree Netaji Subhas Chandra Bosu Janma Shatabarshiki Grantha*, edited by Bijoy Kumar Nag, Jayasree Patrika Trust, 1999, pp. 46–7.

159. Sanyal, *Je Kathar Shesh Nei*, pp. 217–8.

160. Bhupendra Kishore Rakshit Ray, *Sabar Alakkshye*, Bengal Publishers Pvt. Ltd, 1956, pp. 146–69.

161. 'Report on the Dacca Sri Sangha up to 1929', in *Terrorism in Bengal*, Vol. 2, pp. 991–3.

162. Bhupendra Kishore Rakshit Ray, *Bharate Sashastra Biplab*, Rabindra Library, 1960, pp. 241–8.

163. Padmini Sengupta, *Deshapriya Jatindra Mohan Sengupta*, Publications Division, Government of India, 1968, p. 107.

164. AICC file No. P-6/1929, Part II, cited in *Brothers Against the Raj*, p. 214.

165. Fortnightly Reports, First Half of August 1929, File 17/20-Political.

166. Fortnightly Reports, September 1929, File 17/29-Political.

167. *Netaji: Collected Works*, Vol. 6, edited by S.K. Bose and S. Bose, Netaji Research Bureau, 1987, pp. 36–40.

168. Subhas Chandra Bose, *Correspondence*, 1924–32, edited by Sisir Kumar Bose, p. 404.

169. Dasgupta, *Subhas Chandra*, p. 112.

170. In a demonstration of how fluid the support groups were and how quickly people moved from one camp to another, many of those who walked out of the BPCC meeting in protest became strong supporters of Subhas's later, including Jyotish Chandra Ghose, Hemanta Kumar Bose and Suresh Chandra Majumdar; Dasgupta, *Subhas Chandra*, p. 113. Kiran Shankar Roy, at this time a Subhas loyalist, would become an equally strong opponent in the next decade.

171. *Subhas Chandra Bose Correspondence*, 1924–32, p. 404.

172. Letter to J.M. Sarkar; Gandhi, *Collected Works*, Vol. 47, pp. 359–60.

173. *IQR 1929*, Vol. 2, pp. 284–6.

174. Subhas Chandra Bose's Letter to Motilal Nehru, 27 December 1929; *SWMN*, Vol. 6, Vikas Publishing House Pvt. Ltd, 1995, pp. 480–95; *IQR 1929*, Vol. 2, pp. 284–6.

175. Dasgupta, *Subhas Chandra*, p. 118.

176. Bazlur Rohman Khan, 'Some Aspects of Society and Politics in Bengal: 1927–36', Thesis submitted for the Degree of Doctor of Philosophy at the University of London, School of Oriental and African Studies, February 1979.

177. *IQR 1929*, Vol. 2, p. 22.

178. Statement published in newspapers on 11 December 1929; Bose, *Subhas Rachanabali*, Vol. 2, pp. 280–7.

179. Statement of Mr Crerar in the Central Legislative Assembly, 21 March 1929; *IQR*, Vol. 1, pp. 65–6.

180. *IQR 1929*, Vol. 1, p. 41.

181. Address at a protest meeting in Albert Hall, Calcutta, 22 March 1929; Bose, *Rachanabali*, Vol. 2, pp. 63–4.

182. Jawaharlal Nehru's letters to M.K. Basu (22 March), Motilal Nehru (24 April), and V. Chattopadhyay (20 June); *SWJN*, Vol. 2, pp. 331, 334–5.

183. Gordon, *Brothers Against the Raj*, p. 208.

184. Speech at the Bengal Provincial Conference at Rangpur, 30 March 1929, Bose, *Subhas Rachanabali*, Vol. 2, pp. 94–5.

185. *IQR 1929*, Vol. 1, p. 22; Fortnightly Reports, First Half of May 1929, File 17/29-Political.

186. Fortnightly Reports, First Half of April 1929, File 17/29-Political.

187. Gandhi, *Collected Works*, Vol. 46, p. 98.

188. Gandhi, *Collected Works*, Vol. 46, p. 113.

189. Statement to the representative of the Associated Press; *Netaji: Collected Works*, Vol. 6, pp. 8–9.

190. AICC proceedings, 27 September 1929; *IAR 1929*, Vol. 2, pp. 258–61.

191. AICC proceedings, 27 September 1929; *IAR 1929*, Vol. 2, pp. 258–61.

192. *IQR1929*, Vol. 2, p. 48.

193. *IQR 1929*, Vol. 2, p. 50.

194. *IQR 1929*, Vol. 2, pp. 50–1.

195. Nehru, *Autobiography*, p. 208.

196. Bose, *Correspondence*, p. 403.

197. Fortnightly Reports, Second Half of July 1929, File No. 17/29-Political.

198. Nehru, *Autobiography*, p. 206.

199. *IQR 1929*, Vol. 2, p. 300.

200. Bose, *The Indian Struggle*, p. 244; Nehru, *Autobiography*, p. 213.

201. *IQR1929*, Vol. 2, p. 306.

202. Gandhi, *Collected Works*, Vol. 48, pp. 167–8.

203. *IQR 1929*, Vol. 2, pp. 302–9.

204. Bose, *The Indian Struggle*, p. 244.

205. Nehru, *Autobiography*, p. 213.

206. Sitaramayya, *The History of the Congress*, p. 611.

Chapter 5: Crescendo (1930–32)

1. Mahatma Gandhi, *The Collected Works of Mahatma Gandhi*, Vol. 46, p. 431.

2. Gandhi, *Collected Works*, Vol. 48, p. 189.

3. Gandhi, *Collected Works*, Vol. 48, p. 216.

4. *The Indian Annual Register 1930*, Vol. 1, p. 334.

5. For a detailed discussion on the complex nature of hurdles Gandhi had to face before launching the civil disobedience movement, see Judith M. Brown, *Gandhi and Civil Disobedience*, Cambridge University Press, 2008, pp. 80–9.

6. Gandhi, *Collected Works*, Vol. 48, pp. 269–72.

7. Gandhi, *Collected Works*, Vol. 48, pp. 362–7.

8. Fortnightly Reports on the Political Situation in India, Second Half of January 1930, File No. 18-II-Political; National Archives, New Delhi.

9. Speech at Harish Park, 10 January 1930; Bose, *Netaji Collected Works*, Vol. 6, pp. 110–2.

10. Bose, *Subhas Rachanabali*, Vol. 3, pp. 13–4.

11. Fortnightly Reports, First Half of January 1930, File No. 18-II-Political.

12. In an indication of the fault lines within the movement, four of those arrested gave an undertaking in the High Court for the purpose of obtaining bail, to lead the life of a private citizen and not to participate in any meeting or procession until the disposal of their appeal against the Alipore Court verdict; Fortnightly Reports, Second Half of January 1929.

13. Gandhi, *Collected Works*, Vol. 48, p. 264.

14. Bose, *Rachanabali*, Vol. 3, p. 20.

15. Sengupta, *Deshapriya Jatindra Mohan*, pp. 111–36.

16. Fortnightly Report, First Half of February 1930, File No. 18/III/30.

17. Fortnightly Report, First Half of March 1930, File No. 18/IV/30.

18. Fortnightly Report, Second Half of April 1930, File No. 18/IV/1930; Leonard A. Gordon, *Brothers Against the Raj*, p. 226.

19. Dasgupta, *Subhas Chandra*, p. 126.

20. Fortnightly Report, Second Half of April 1930, File No. 18/IV/1930. Dasgupta, *Subhas Chandra*, pp. 127–8.

21. Dasgupta, *Subhas Chandra*, p. 129.

22. Manini Chatterjee, *Do and Die: The Chittagong Uprising 1930–34*, Picador, 2010, p. 88.

23. Ananta Singh, *Agnigarbha Chattagram*, Vol. 1, Vidyoday Library Pvt. Ltd, 1960, p. 262.

24. Chatterjee, *Do and Die*, p. 118.

25. Singh, *Agnigarbha Chattagram*, Vol. 1, pp. 261–2.

26. Singh, *Agnigarbha Chattagram*, Vol. 1, p. 253.

27. Gandhi, *Collected Works*, Vol. 49, p. 188.

28. Fortnightly Reports, Second Half of August 1930, File No. 18/IX/30-Political.

29. *The Calcutta Municipal Gazette: Subhas Chandra Bose Birth Centenary Number*, edited by Arun Roy, The Calcutta Municipal Corporation, 1997, pp. 85–6; Fortnightly Reports, First Half of August 1930, File No. 18/IX/30-Political.

30. *The Calcutta Municipal Gazette*, pp. 89–95.

31. Gandhi's letter to Subhas, 28 October 1930; *The Calcutta Municipal Gazette: Subhas Chandra Bose Birth Centenary Number*, p. 107.

32. Interaction with H.N. Brailsford, 20 November 1930; Bose, *Subhas Rachanabali*, Vol. 3, pp. 41–3.

33. Fortnightly Reports, Second Half of May 1930, File No. 18/6/30-Political.

34. Fortnightly Reports, First Half of August 1930, File No. 18/IX/30-Political.

35. Fortnightly Reports, First Half of December 1930, File No. 18/XIII/1930-Poll.

36. *The Calcutta Municipal Gazette*, pp. 114–6.

37. *The Calcutta Municipal Gazette*, pp. 117–8.

38. *The Calcutta Municipal Gazette*, pp. 121–2.

39. *The Calcutta Municipal Gazette*, p. 129.

40. Dasgupta, *Subhas Chandra*, p. 130.

41. Fortnightly Reports, First Half of January 1931, File No. 18/31-Political.

42. *The Calcutta Municipal Gazette*, pp. 132–5.

43. *The Calcutta Municipal Gazette*, pp. 130–43.

44. Jawaharlal Nehru, *Autobiography*, pp. 242, 639–41; Sitaramayya, *History of the Indian National Congress*, pp. 711–4.

45. *The History and Culture of the Indian People*, edited by R.C. Majumdar, Vol. 11, pp. 481–2.

46. *IAR 1931*, Vol. 1, p. 23.

47. Sitaramayya, *History of the Indian National Congress*, pp. 727–8.

48. *The Calcutta Municipal Gazette*, p. 143.

49. File No. 5/45/31 & KW (Unprinted), National Archives of India.

50. Bose, *The Indian Struggle*, p. 284.

51. Amales Tripathi, *Swadhinata Sangrame Bharater Jatiya Congress*, Ananda Publishers Pvt. Ltd, 1991, p. 164.

52. Gazette Notification dated 5 March 1931, File No. 5/45/31 & KW (Unprinted), National Archives of India.

53. Gandhi, *Collected Works*, Vol. 51, pp. 151, 155.

54. Bose, *The Indian Struggle*, p. 283. Subhas's allegation that a lot of money was spent in ensuring the presence of Gandhi's supporters at a remote place like Karachi finds support in a report of the Director of Intelligence Bureau: 'There is evidence of the fact that the expenses of the large majority of the Bengal delegates were paid by four prominent Bombay businessmen—all Mr Gandhi's proteges'; DIB's Weekly Reports, KW II to File 33/XI/31-Poll, National Archives of India.

55. Bose, *The Indian Struggle*, pp. 283–4, 288.

56. Fortnightly Reports, Second Half of March 1931, File No. 18/3/31-Poll.

57. Nehru, *Autobiography*, pp. 270–1.

58. *The Calcutta Municipal Gazette*, p. 151.

59. Bose, *The Indian Struggle*, p. 285.

60. Bose, *The Indian Struggle*, p. 286.

61. Statement on his arrival in Delhi; Bose, *Netaji Collected Works*, Vol. 6, edited by S.K. Bose and S. Bose, Netaji Research Bureau, 1987, pp. 145–7.

62. Nayar, *Without Fear*, p. 150.

63. A.G. Noorani, *The Trial of Bhagat Singh*, Oxford University Press, 2012, pp. 242–3.

64. Reports in *The Tribune*, cited in Noorani, *The Trial of Bhagat Singh*, pp. 102–3.

65. DIB's Weekly Reports, KW II to File 33/XI/31-Poll, National Archives of India.

66. 'The Gandhi Policy', *The Times*, 26 March 1931, p. 14.

67. DIB's Weekly Reports, KW II to File 33/XI/31-Poll, National Archives of India.

68. Nehru, *Autobiography*, p. 278.

69. 'The Gandhi Policy', *The Times*, 26 March 1931, p. 14.

70. *IAR 1931*, Vol. 1, pp. 385–6.

71. 'Congress and the Pact', *The Times*, 28 March 1931, p. 12.

72. Bose, *The Indian Struggle*, p. 289.

73. *IAR 1931*, Vol. 1, pp. 266–78.

74. DIB's Weekly Reports, KW II to File 33/XI/31-Poll, National Archives of India.

75. Bose, *The Indian Struggle*, p. 298.

76. DIB's Weekly Reports, KW II to File 33/XI/31-Poll, National Archives of India.

77. File 143, Home Department, Political, National Archives of India.

78. Statement to the press on 11 April 1931; *Netaji: Collected Works*, Vol. 6, pp. 162–3.

79. Statement issued on 13 April 1931; *Netaji: Collected Works*, Vol. 6, pp. 162–3.

80. Dasgupta, *Subhas Chandra*, pp. 134–5.

81. Fortnightly Reports, First Half of June 1931, File No. 18/6/1931-Poll.

82. *IAR 1931*, Vol. 1, p. 255.

83. Statement issued on 18 September 1931; *Netaji: Collected Works*, Vol. 6, pp. 212–5.

84. Statement issued on 18 September 1931; *Netaji: Collected Works*, Vol. 6, pp. 212–5.

85. Statement issued on 19 September 1931; *Netaji: Collected Works*, Vol. 6, p. 216.

86. Speech to Congressmen, 20 September 1931; *Netaji: Collected Works*, Vol. 6, pp. 217–9.

87. Gordon, *Brothers Against the Raj*, p. 2–51.
88. *Nehru, SWJN*, Vol. 5, p. 256.
89. *Nehru, SWJN*, Vol. 5, p. 256.
90. Vallabhbhai Patel, *Collected Works of Sardar Vallabhbhai Patel*, Vol. 3, edited by P.N. Chopra, Konark Publishers Pvt. Ltd, 1993, p. 234.
91. Letter to Jawaharlal Nehru, 7 October 1931; *CWSVP*, pp. 239–40.
92. Statement on 23 October 1931; *Netaji: Collected Works*, Vol. 6, pp. 231.
93. Statement on 17 December 1931; *Netaji: Collected Works*, Vol. 6, pp. 240.
94. *CWSVP*, Vol. 3, p. 244.
95. Statement on 14 October 1931; *Netaji: Collected Works*, Vol. 6, pp. 223–5.
96. Statement on 10 November 1931; *Netaji: Collected Works*, Vol. 6, pp. 232–6.
97. *The Calcutta Municipal Gazette*, p. 179.
98. Statement on 10 November 1931; *Netaji: Collected Works*, Vol. 6, p. 236.
99. Dasgupta, *Subhas Chandra*, p. 137.
100. *IAR 1931*, Vol. 2, pp. 28–9.
101. *IAR 1931*, Vol. 2, p. 273.
102. Fortnightly Reports, Second Half of December 1931.
103. Bose, *The Indian Struggle*, p. 331.
104. Fortnightly Reports, Second Half of December 1931, File No. 18/12/31-Poll; *The Manchester Guardian*, 29 December 1931; *IAR 1931*, Vol. 2 p. 31.
105. Bose, *The Indian Struggle*, pp. 298–302.
106. *IAR 1931*, Vol. 2, pp. 83–90.
107. *Netaji: Collected Works*, Vol. 6, p. 245.
108. *IAR 1932*, Vol. 1, pp. 1–11; Dasgupta, *Subhas Chandra*, p. 140.
109. Fortnightly Reports, First Half of January 1932, File No. 18/1/1932.
110. According to his weight chart, Subhas weighed 151 pounds (about 68.5 kg) at that time, against his 'physical equivalent' weight of 124 pounds (about 56 kg).
111. KW to File 30/93-1932, National Archives of India.
112. File 30/148/32-Poll, National Archives of India.
113. File 22/73/33-Poll, National Archives of India.
114. File 31/103/32-Poll, National Archives of India.
115. File 31/103/32-Poll, National Archives of India.
116. File 30/148/32-Poll, National Archives of India.
117. File 31/103/32-Poll, National Archives of India.
118. Fortnightly Report, Second Half of February 1933, File No. 18-2/1933-Poll.
119. File 22/73/33-Poll, National Archives of India.
120. Letter to a friend, 16 April 1932; *Netaji: Collected Works*, Vol. 6, pp. 245–7.
121. Letter to a friend, 22 April 1932; *Netaji: Collected Works*, Vol. 6, p. 249.
122. Parting message from S.S. Gange, 23 February 1933; *Netaji: Collected Works*, Vol. 6, pp. 262–3.

Chapter 6: The Unstoppable Outcast (1933–37)

1. Asoke Nath Bose, Preface in *Netaji's Letters to His Nephew, Arnold Publishers, 1992*; Bose, *My Uncle Netaji*, p. 70.

2. Letter to Kantilal Parekh, 7 March 1933; *Netaji: Collected Works*, Vol. 8, edited by S.K. Bose and S. Bose, Oxford University Press, 1994, p. 4. Kantilal Parekh was one of his contacts, on whom Subhas appears to have depended for funds. After asking him a few times whether he had been able to arrange funds for him and on probably not getting any response on that point, he wrote impatiently, 'What have you done about money? If you can collect some, please send by cable to American Express here. If you cannot send please let know finally without any hesitation or delicacy. You should have no delicacy in these matters. Please do not leave me in suspense—but let me know definitely if I can expect anything from you'; Letter to Kantilal Parekh, 7 March 1933, *Netaji: Collected Works*, Vol. 8, p. 7.

3. Subhas later made his annoyance known to the poet: 'When I was coming to Europe, you had kindly given me a letter of introduction to Mon. Romain Rolland, but that letter of introduction was written as if only to honour my request. I was therefore not able to make proper use of that letter and started correspondence with Mon. Rolland on my own'; Letter to Rabindranath Tagore, 3 August 1934; *Netaji: Collected Works*, Vol. 8, p. 77.

4. Gordon, *Brothers Against the Raj*, p. 273.

5. 'Indian Political Prisoners', *The Manchester Guardian*, 4 April 1933, p. 18.

6. 'Prisoners in India', *The Manchester Guardian*, 8 April 1933, p. 8; 'State Prisoners in India', *The Manchester Guardian*, 18 April 1933, p. 16.

7. Letters to Santosh Kumar Basu, 11 May and 23 May 1933; *Netaji: Collected Works*, Vol. 8, pp. 10–1, 13–4.

8. *The History and Culture of the Indian People, Vol. 10: Struggle for Freedom*, edited by R.C. Majumdar, pp. 520–1; *The Indian Annual Register 1932*, Vol. 2, pp. 7, 9.

9. Bose, *The Indian Struggle*, p. 347.

10. Nehru, *Autobiography*.

11. Gordhanbhai I. Patel, *Vithalbhai Patel: Life and Times*, Shree Laxmi Narayan Press, 1951, p. 1219.

12. Patel, *Vithalbhai Patel: Life and Times*, pp. 1217–8.

13. Letters to Satyendra Nath Majumdar, 19 October 1933 and 22 March 1934; *Netaji: Collected Works*, Vol. 8, pp. 35, 54–5.

14. Speech at the Third Indian Political Conference, 10–11 June 1933; *Netaji: Collected Works*, Vol. 8, pp. 241–63.

15. Letter to Satyendra Nath Majumdar, 28 April 1933; *Netaji: Collected Works*, Vol. 8, p. 9.

16. File 35/11/33-Poll, National Archives of India.
17. Letter to Satyendra Nath Majumdar, 22 March 1934; *Netaji: Collected Works*, Vol. 8, p. 55.
18. https://www.lexikon-provenienzforschung.org/faltis-otto.
19. Letter to Naomi C. Vetter, 9 December 1933; *Netaji: Collected Works*, Vol. 8, p. 43.
20. Herrn Kommerzialrat Otto Faltis, 'India and Austria', *The Modern Review*, February 1936, pp. 2005–7.
21. Letter to Naomi C. Vetter, 10 July 1933; *Netaji: Collected Works*, Vol. 8, p. 21.
22. Letter to Santosh Kumar Basu, 9 July 1933; *Netaji: Collected Works*, Vol. 8, p. 19.
23. Letter to Santosh Kumar Basu, 14 March 1934; *Netaji: Collected Works*, Vol. 8, pp. 58–9.
24. 'Reminiscences, Nathalal Parikh', in *Life and Work of Netaji Subhas Chandra Bose*, edited by P.D. Saggi, Overseas Publishing House, 1954, p. 38.
25. *Netaji: Collected Works*, Vol. 8, pp. 283–4.
26. Bose, *My Uncle Subhas*, pp. 98–9.
27. Letter to Naomi C. Vetter, 12 January 1934; *Netaji: Collected Works*, Vol. 8, p. 45.
28. Letter to Naomi C. Vetter, 12 January 1934; *Netaji: Collected Works*, Vol. 8, p. 45.
29. Bose, *My Uncle Netaji*, p. 90.
30. Letter to Santosh Kumar Basu, 7 April 1934; *Netaji: Collected Works*, Vol. 8, pp. 64–6.
31. Bose, *My Uncle Netaji*, p. 93.
32. Bose, *My Uncle Netaji*, p. 95.
33. *IAR 1934*, Vol. 1, p. 263.
34. *IAR 1934*, Vol. 1, p. 263.
35. *Struggle for Freedom*, edited by R.C. Majumdar, p. 541.
36. *IAR 1934*, Vol. 1, pp. 271–96.
37. *IAR 1932*, Vol. 2, pp. 233–7; Joya Chatterji, *Bengal Divided*, Cambridge University Press, 2002, pp. 20, 35.
38. Bose, *The Indian Struggle*, p. 373.
39. Chatterji, *Bengal Divided*, p. 22; Bidyut Chakrabarty, *The Partition of Bengal and Assam*, RoutledgeCurzon, 2004, p. 70.
40. Bose, *The Indian Struggle*, p. 408.
41. For a discussion on the realignment in the Bengal Congress, see Chatterji, *Bengal Divided*, pp. 44–50.
42. 'First Moslem Mayor of Calcutta', *The Times*, 11 April 1934, p. 13.
43. Letter to Satyendra Chandra Mitra, 18 October 1934; *Netaji: Collected Works*, Vol. 8, pp. 82–3.

44. Bose, *My Uncle Netaji*, p. 105.
45. The book received favourable reviews in the Berlin newspaper, *Berliner Tageblatt*, in March 1935.
46. 'Parliament', *The Times*, 5 February 1935, p. 7.
47. Letter from Romain Rolland, 22 February 1935; *Netaji: Collected Works*, Vol. 8, pp. 91–2.
48. Bose, *My Uncle Netaji*, p. 109.
49. 'What Romain Rolland Thinks', *The Modern Review*, September 1935, cited in *Netaji: Collected Works*, Vol. 8, pp. 302–9.
50. Bose, *My Uncle Netaji*, pp. 115–8.
51. Bose, *My Uncle Netaji*, pp. 118–9.
52. Bose, *My Uncle Netaji*, p. 121–2.
53. Bose, *My Uncle Netaji*, p. 123.
54. Letter to Naomi C. Vetter, 1 October 1935; *Netaji: Collected Works*, Vol. 8, pp. 106–7.
55. Bose, *My Uncle Netaji*, pp. 16–7.
56. Letter to Santosh Kumar Basu, 3 January 1936; *Netaji: Collected Works*, Vol. 8, pp. 129–30.
57. 'Indian Political Prisoners', *The Manchester Guardian*, 23 March 1936, p. 18.
58. *IAR 1936*, Vol. 1, p. 146.
59. *IAR 1934*, Vol. 2, pp. 260–7.
60. Chakrabarty, *The Partition of Bengal and Assam*, pp. 66–7.
61. *IAR 1934*, Vol. 1, pp. 340–4.
62. *IAR 1934*, Vol. 2, pp. 33, 37, 206.
63. *IAR 1935*, Vol. 2, p. 19.
64. Sarkar, *Modern India*, pp. 336–7.
65. Bose, *The Indian Struggle*, p. 366.
66. Letter to Jawaharlal Nehru, 4 March 1936; *Netaji: Collected Works*, Vol. 8, p. 144.
67. Letter to Jawaharlal Nehru, 13 March 1936; *Netaji: Collected Works*, Vol. 8, p. 156.
68. Letter to Subhas Chandra Bose, 23 March 1936; *SWJN*, Vol. 7, p. 407. Jawaharlal spoke about his advice in his presidential address in the Lucknow Congress too (*SWJN*, Vol. 7, p. 176):

   Recently, as you know, we have had a typical example of the way government functions in India in the warning issued to a dear and valued comrade of ours, Subhas Chandra Bose. We who know him also know how frivolous are the charges brought against him. But even if there was substance in them we could not tolerate willingly the treatment to which he has long been subjected. He did me the honour to ask me for advice and I was puzzled and perplexed, for

it is no easy thing to advise another in such a matter, when such advice might
mean prison. Subhas Bose has suffered enough at the cost of his health. Was
I justified in adding to this mental and physical agony? I hesitated and at first
suggested to him to postpone his departure. But this advice made me unhappy,
and I consulted other friends and then advised him differently. I suggested that
he should return to his homeland as soon as he could. But, it appears, that even
before my advice reached him, he had started on his journey back to India.

69. Statement to the Press in Geneva, March 1936; *Netaji: Collected Works*, Vol.
     8, pp. 345–6.
70. 'The Visit to Dublin'; *Netaji: Collected Works*, Vol. 8, p. 345.
71. Letter to Romain Rolland, 25 March 1936; *Netaji: Collected Works*, Vol. 8, p.
     163.
72. File 44/26/36-Poll-Part I, National Archives of India.
73. *IAR 1936*, Vol. 1, pp. 247, 251–2.
74. 'The Case of Mr Bose', The *Manchester Guardian*, 24 April 1936, p. 10.
75. The Fortnightly Reports from the provinces record widespread protest
     meetings and press coverage across the country. Curiously, the Reports
     also noted conspiracy theories claiming that 'the anti-Bengali feeling of
     Mr Gandhi and other non-Bengali leaders is in some measure responsible
     for the arrest, the motive alleged being a fear that if Mr Bose were present
     at Lucknow he would succeed in gaining influence over the Congress'.
     Pamphlets were found to being distributed in Nagpur asking Gandhi to
     explain who is responsible for Subhas's arrest. Fortnightly Reports, April
     1936, File 18/4/36-Poll, National Archives of India.
76. 'Subhas Day in Calcutta', *Amrita Bazar Patrika*, 11 May 1936, p. 7.
77. File 44/26/36-Poll-Part I, National Archives of India.
78. File 24/17/36-Poll, National Archives of India; Bose, *My Uncle Netaji*, pp.
     132–4.
79. Bose, *My Uncle Netaji*, pp. 137–8.
80. Letter to Anil Chandra Ganguly, 8 August 1937; *Netaji: Collected Works*,
     Vol. 8, p. 216.
81. Letter to Santosh Kumar Basu, 17 August 1937; *Netaji: Collected Works*, Vol.
     8, p. 220.
82. Letter to an employee of the Calcutta Corporation, 9 August 1937; *Netaji:
     Collected Works*, Vol. 8, pp. 218–20.
83. Mahatma Gandhi, *The Collected Works of Mahatma Gandhi*, Vol. 72, p. 265.
84. *IAR 1936*, Vol. 2, p. 190; *SWJN*, Vol. 7, pp. 553–4; Chatterji, *Bengal
     Divided*, pp. 51–3; Chakrabarty, *The Partition of Bengal and Assam*, pp. 74–7.
85. *IAR 1937*, Vol. 1, pp. 168 (a)–168 (n).
86. Chatterji, *Bengal Divided*, pp. 79–81.

87. Shila Sen, *Muslim Politics in Bengal 1937–47*, Impex India, 1976, p. 88.
88. Sen, *Muslim Politics in Bengal 1937–47*, pp. 90–5. Chatterji, *Bengal Divided*, p. 104. *IAR 1937*, Vol. 1, pp. 178–80. Humayun Kabir, then a KPP member, described the reason for the breakdown in *Muslim Politics 1906–1942* (p. 13):

> Congress indecision about acceptance of office not only indicated divisions of opinion within its ranks, but what is worse, it let slip the opportunity of capturing power in some of the provinces where through coalition with other groups, it might have formed the Government. In Bengal, Mr Fazlul Huq pleaded and pleaded in vain for active cooperation or even tacit support.
>
> Shila Sen has argued that providing external support, if accepting office was not feasible, would have saved the Congress from becoming a Hindu-only party in the legislature. Nirad C. Chaudhuri, who was then Sarat's private secretary, has claimed that at the early stages even Sarat was opposed to office acceptance (Nirad C. Chaudhuri, *Thy Hand Great Anarch*, p. 466).

89. *IAR 1937*, Vol. 2, p. 328.
90. Gandhi, *Collected Works*, Vol. 72, p. 380.
91. J.B. Kripalani, *My Times: An Autobiography*, Rupa & Co, 2004, pp. 322–3.
92. Letter to Mrs Woods, 9 September 1937; *Netaji: Collected Works*, Vol. 8, p. 225.
93. Bose, *My Uncle Netaji*, pp. 142–3.
94. Bose, *My Uncle Netaji*, pp. 142–3.
95. File 28/16/38-Political, National Archives of India. Subhas left the unfinished manuscript with Emilie, who handed it over to one of Subhas's nephews in 1947.
96. India Office Records L/PJ/12/217-1115/24.
97. 'Congress leader's visit to England', *The Manchester Guardian*, 7 January 1938, p. 8.
98. 'Mr Subhas Bose in London', *The Manchester Guardian*, 11 January 1938, p. 12.
99. *SWJN*, Vol. 9, p. 1.
100. India Office Records L/PJ/12/217-1115/24, British Library.
101. Bose, *My Uncle Netaji*, p. 150.
102. Gordon, *Brothers Against the Raj*, p. 348.
103. Gandhi, *Collected Works*, Vol. 72, p. 442.

Chapter 7: Rashtrapati (1938)

1. Letter to Basanti Devi, 6 February 1938; *Netaji: Collected Works*, Vol. 9, Permanent Black, 1995, p. 257.

2. *Jugantar*, 26 January 1938, p. 5.
3. Letter to V.K. Krishna Menon, 9 January 1938; Nehru, *SWJN*, Vol. 8, B.R. Publishing Corporation, 1976, p. 516.
4. *IAR 1938*, Vol. 2, pp. 396–401.
5. *Jugantar*, 12 February 1938; Bose, *My Uncle Netaji*, p. 153.
6. Letter to H.V. Kamath, 12 February 1938; *Netaji: Collected Works*, Vol. 9, p. 258.
7. Bose, *My Uncle Netaji*, p. 153; *Jugantar*, 15 February 1938.
8. Bose, *My Uncle Netaji*, p. 153.
9. Bose, *Subhas Rachanabali*, Vol. 4, pp. 71–3.
10. Gandhi, *The Collected Works of Mahatma Gandhi*, Vol. 72, p. 469.
11. *IAR 1938*, Vol. 2, pp. 334–5; *The Modern Review*, March 1938, pp. 354–5.
12. 'Indian Congress', *The Manchester Guardian*, 21 February 1938, p. 6; The reluctant acceptance of the validity of some of the points made by Subhas, followed by fussy and pedantic fault-finding while missing the overarching drift of his speech, which marked the review of the speech by *The Modern Review* (March 1938 issue), is a good demonstration of the intellectual snobbery of the nationalist English press of Calcutta with which he would soon run into a confrontation.
13. *IAR 1938*, Vol. 1, pp. 335–48.
14. Minoo Masani, the socialist leader, divulged the story behind the scenes nearly four decades later. According to his account, Jayaprakash Narayan informed Subhas that the CSP executive committee had decided to substitute one of the two socialist members of the working committee with Masani. However, to scuttle the move, Vallabhbhai fabricated a story against him which was soon found to be untrue. Although Subhas insisted on them joining the committee, the CSP refused to nominate any member in protest. Masani regretted the withdrawal decision and surmised that 'it may well have started a chain reaction which culminated in the resignation of Subhas Bose after his re-election'. Minoo Masani, *Bliss Was It in That Dawn*, Arnold-Heinemann, 1977, pp. 118–9.
15. *Jugantar*, 25 February 1938.
16. *Jugantar*, 6 March 1938.
17. *Jugantar*, 15 March 1938.
18. *Jugantar*, 20 March 1938.
19. *Jugantar*, 27 March 1938.
20. *IAR 1938*, Vol. 1, p. 314.
21. Bose, *Subhas Rachanabali*, Vol. 4, pp. 106–10.
22. Bose, *Subhas Rachanabali*, Vol. 4, pp. 110–5. The Principal of the Scottish Church College had initially refused to give permission for the reception, following which the Student Union launched an agitation culminating in

a strike in the college and the authorities closing it down indefinitely. The students also refused to sit for examinations. *Jugantar*, various issues of March and April.

23. Bose, *Subhas Rachanabali*, Vol. 4, pp. 116–20.

24. Fortnightly Reports, May 1938, File 18/5/38-Poll, National Archives of India.

25. *IAR 1938*, Vol. 1, p. 327.

26. Fortnightly Reports, May 1938, File 18/5/38-Poll, National Archives of India.

27. *Netaji: Collected Works*, Vol. 9, pp. 31–5.

28. *IAR 1938*, Vol. 1, p. 326.

29. *Jugantar*, 7 October 1938, p. 6.

30. Address delivered at the Industries Ministers' Conference, 2 October 1938; *Netaji: Collected Works*, Vol. 9, pp. 48–53.

31. Gandhi, *Collected Works*, Vol. 73, p. 321.

32. Interaction with Meghnad Saha at the third general meeting of the Indian Science News Association, 21 August 1938; *Netaji: Collected Works*, Vol. 9, pp. 43–8.

33. Inauguration speech at the first meeting of the National Planning Committee, 17 December 1938; *Netaji: Collected Works*, Vol. 9, pp. 62–4.

34. Bimal Prasad, *Pathway to India's Partition*, Vol. 2, Manohar, 2009, K.M. Ashraf, the Congress leader in charge of the programme in the AICC, complained to Jawaharlal in September 1938 that the 'Congress President has not even cared to visit us or given us any instruction whatever'. Jawaharlal himself did not show much effort to take the programme forward (p. 381).

35. Prasad, *Pathway to India's Partition*, Vol. 3, pp. 95–8.

36. Gandhi to Amrit Kaur, 16 May 1938; Gandhi, *Collected Works*, Vol. 73, p. 171.

37. Jinnah–Subhas correspondence; *Netaji: Collected Works*, Vol. 9, pp. 110–22.

38. *IAR 1938*, Vol. 2, pp. 269–71.

39. *IAR 1938*, Vol. 2, pp. 261–7.

40. N.B. Khare, *My Defence*, 1938, p. 7; Patel papers, File No. 17/1/381; National Archives of India.

41. N.B. Khare, *My Political Memoirs or Autobiography*, pp. 19, 613. Khare became a lifelong bitter critic of Gandhi. In 1943, he joined the Viceroy's executive council, which he claimed to have done on the basis of advice given to him by Subhas, whom he had met when Subhas was interned at home in January 1941.

42. *The CP Ministerial Crisis: Statement of Sjt Subhas Chandra Bose, President, All-India Congress Committee*, Patel papers, National Archives of India.

43. *IAR 1938*, Vol. 2, p. 281.

44. Birendra Kumar Bhattacharya, *Gopinath Bardoloi*, Publications Division, Government of India, 1986, p. 23.

45. *Netaji: Collected Works*, Vol. 9, p. 123.

46. Two Muslim ministers, Fakhruddin Ali Ahmed and Mahmud Ali, took oath as ministers on 13 October. *Jugantar*, 14 October 1938, p. 8.

47. *Jugantar*, various issues of September 1938; *IAR 1938*, Vol. 2, p. 292.

48. *Jugantar*, 9 July 1938.

49. *Netaji: Collected Works*, Vol. 9, pp. 39–40.

50. *Jugantar*, 12 and 13 July 1938.

51. Curiously, support for the federal scheme came from the firebrand revolutionary of the Swadesh era, Barindra Kumar Ghose, younger brother of Sri Aurobindo. *The Manchester Guardian* published a long letter from Ghose extolling the benefits of the scheme.

52. *Netaji: Collected Works*, Vol. 9, pp. 40–3.

53. *Jugantar*, 20 July 1938.

54. *IAR 1938*, Vol. 2, pp. 276–7.

55. *Jugantar*, 16 August 1938.

56. *Jugantar*, various issues of August and September 1938.

57. *Jugantar*, various issues of September 1938; *The Modern Review*, October 1938, p. 415.

58. Gandhi to Amrit Kaur, 25 June 1938; Gandhi, *Collected Works*, Vol. 73, p. 255.

59. *Jugantar*, 18 October 1938, p. 8.

60. *Jugantar*, 19 October 1938, p. 9.

61. *Jugantar*, 21 October 1938. The release of seventeen prisoners detained under Regulation III was completed in August 1938, with the release of the last three detenus. However, prisoners against whom litigation was instituted in the law courts were not released. *Jugantar*, 26 August 1938.

62. *Jugantar*, 9 November 1938.

63. *Jugantar*, 13 November 1938.

64. *Jugantar*, 15 and 16 November 1938. Responding to increasing pressure, the Bengal Government appointed an advisory committee towards the end of the year to look into the matter of convicted 'terrorist' prisoners under the chairmanship of former judge of the Calcutta High Court Rai Bahadur Surendra Nath Guha. The members of the committee were Sarat Chandra Bose, A.M.L. Rahman, Birat Chandra Mondal, Uday Chand Mahtab, Lalit Chandra Das, Curtis Miller and J.R. Blair. *Jugantar*, 6 January 1939.

65. *Jugantar*, 26 November 1938.

66. Fortnightly Reports, December 1938, National Archives of India.

67. *Jugantar*, 9 December 1938.

68. *Jugantar*, 16 December 1938.

69. *Jugantar*, 9 August 1938, p. 7; *The Modern Review*, September 1938, p. 286.

70. Yet, strangely, the Congress legislative party under Sarat's leadership chose to abstain from voting on a proposal by the Bengal Government for reservation of 60 per cent of government jobs for Muslims, 20 per cent for Scheduled Castes and 20 per cent for other communities. Although Narendra Narayan Chakrabarti, a member of the legislative assembly and close to the Bose brothers, tried to explain it away by claiming that government jobs were so few in number that the decision was inconsequential, the Congress stand drew widespread protest from the districts. The press questioned how Sarat, who had so stoutly opposed the Communal Award, could support such a blatantly communal policy.
71. Gandhi's letter to Subhas, undated, December 1938; Gandhi, *Collected Works*, Vol. 74, pp. 325–6.
72. Subhas Chandra Bose's letter to Gandhi, 21 December 1938; *Netaji: Collected Works*, Vol. 9, pp. 122–6.
73. *Jugantar*, 22 October 1938.
74. *Jugantar*, 23 October 1938.
75. *Jugantar*, 30 October 1938.
76. *Jugantar*, 4 November 1938.
77. *Jugantar*, 15 November 1938.
78. *Jugantar*, 8 November 1938.
79. *Jugantar*, 15 November 1938.
80. *IAR 1939*, Vol. 1, p. 467.
81. Kripalani, *My Times*, p. 329.
82. *Jugantar*, 15 December 1938.
83. Gandhi, *Collected Works*, Vol. 74, p. 335.
84. *Jugantar*, 22 December 1938.
85. Kripalani, *My Times*, p. 329.
86. Statement issued on 25 January 1939; *Netaji: Collected Works*, Vol. 9, p. 71.
87. *Netaji: Collected Works*, Vol. 9, pp. 65–6.
88. *Jugantar*, 17 January 1939.
89. Jugantar, 18 January 1939.
90. Statement issued on 21 January 1939; *Netaji: Collected Works*, Vol. 9, pp. 67–8.
91. *Jugantar*, 24 January 1939 (translated by the author).
92. *The Modern Review*, February 1939, p. 146; *Jugantar*, 27 January 1939 (translated by the author).
93. *Netaji: Collected Works*, Vol. 9, pp. 70–3.
94. *Netaji: Collected Works*, Vol. 9, pp. 70–3.
95. Statements issued by Subhas Chandra Bose, seven members of the working committee, Vallabhbhai Patel, Pattabhi Sitaramayya, Jawaharlal Nehru and Rajendra Prasad; *Netaji: Collected Works*, Vol. 9, pp. 67–87.

96. *Jugantar*, 27 and 28 January 1939.
97. *Jugantar*, 31 January 1939.

Chapter 8: Cul-de-sac (1939–40)

1. One of the most surprising developments, an indicator of the undercurrents of Bengal politics, that got covered up by the focus on the presidential election was the defeat of Sarat Bose in the elections for AICC delegates. Sarat received just one vote—his own. This was all the more surprising as Sarat was elected to preside over the year's Bengal Provincial Conference held in Jalpaiguri from 4 February. A councillor of the Calcutta Corporation who had been elected, offered to resign so that Sarat could become a nominated delegate. *Jugantar*, 4 February 1939, p. 9.
2. Mahatma Gandhi, *The Collected Works of Mahatma Gandhi*, Vol. 75, pp. 13–5.
3. *Masik Basumati*, Magh 1345, p. 711.
4. *Bharatbarsha*, Phalgun 1345, p. 473
5. Statement issued on 4 February 1939; *Netaji: Collected Works* Vol. 9, pp. 89–90.
6. *Jugantar*, 3 February 1939, p. 7.
7. *Indian Annual Register 1939*, Vol. 1, pp. 417–8.
8. *Jugantar*, 7, 8 and 9 February 1939.
9. *Jugantar*, 22 February 1939, p. 7.
10. *Jugantar*, 16 February 1939, p. 10.
11. *Jugantar*, 15 February 1939, p. 7.
12. Gandhi, *Collected Works*, Vol. 75, p. 40.
13. *Jugantar*, 18 February 1939, p. 7.
14. *Jugantar*, 21 February 1939, p. 9.
15. Kripalani, *My Times*, pp. 333–4.
16. 'My Strange Illness', *Netaji: Collected Works*, Vol. 9, pp. 97–8.
17. In his presidential address at the Tripuri Congress, Subhas argued that although the Haripura Congress stipulated that neither parliamentary work nor struggle against the Indian States should be carried on in the name of the Congress, it was now time to change that and let the Congress work more closely with the States' subjects.
18. Kripalani, *My Times*, pp. 354–60.
19. Kripalani, *My Times*, pp. 354–60.
20. Patel, *Vithalbhai Patel—Life and Times*, Vol. 2, p. 1251.
21. *Jugantar*, 22 February 1939, p. 9.
22. *Jugantar*, 28 February 1939, p. 7.
23. Pandit P.K. Malaviya's Statement, *National Herald*, 4 February 1939; *P.K. Malaviya Papers*, The National Archives of India.

24. *Jugantar*, 28 February 1939.
25. *Jugantar*, 4 March 1939.
26. Bipan Chandra *et al.*, *India's Struggle for Independence*, p. 364.
27. *IAR 1939*, Vol. 1, pp. 343–4.
28. *Jugantar*, 9 March 1939.
29. Rajmohan Gandhi, *Rajaji: A Life*, Penguin Books, 1997, p. 198.
30. *The Indian Review*, April 1939, p. 266.
31. *Jugantar*, 10 March 1939, pp. 9–10; *The Indian Review*, April 1939, p. 284.
32. *Jugantar*, 11 March 1939, p. 7.
33. *IAR 1939*, Vol. 1, pp. 322–5.
34. *IAR 1939*, Vol. 1, pp. 325–7.
35. *Jugantar*, 12 March, p. 9.
36. *Jugantar*, 13 March, p. 9.
37. *Jugantar*, 17 March, p. 10.
38. Masani, *Bliss Was It in That Dawn*, pp. 144–5.
39. *Jugantar*, 21 March 1939.
40. *Jugantar*, 11 March 1939; *The Indian Review*, April 1939, pp. 286–7.
41. *IAR 1939*, Vol. 1, p. 331.
42. Several issues of *Jugantar*, and *IAR 1939*, Vol. 1, pp. 327–43.
43. *Jugantar*, 15 March 1939.
44. Letter to Mahatma Gandhi, 25 March 1939; *Netaji: Collected Works*, Vol. 9, pp. 127–30. On 31 March, Subhas wrote to Gandhi (*Netaji: Collected Works*, Vol. 9, p. 140):

> When Pant's resolution was shown to me for the first time by Sardar Patel, I suggested to him (Rajen Babu and Maulana Azad were also there at the time) that if certain changes were made, the resolution in the amended form would be passed by the Congress unanimously. The amended form of the resolution was also sent to Sardar Patel, but there was no response from his side. Their attitude seemed to be—not a word, not a comma, should be changed . . . If the object of Pant's resolution was to reiterate faith in our principles and your leadership and guidance, that was provided in the amended resolution—but if the object was to avenge the result of the Presidential Election, then, of course, the amended resolution did not suffice.

45. Gandhi's letter to Sarat Bose, 23 March 1939; Gandhi, *Collected Works*, Vol. 75, p. 205.
46. Mahatma Gandhi's letter to Subhas, 30 March 1939; *Netaji: Collected Works*, Vol. 9, pp. 134–6.
47. Subhas–Gandhi correspondence, March 1939; *Netaji: Collected Works*, Vol. 9, pp. 127–81.

48. Letter to Gandhi, 29 March 1939; *Netaji: Collected Works*, Vol. 9, p. 133.
49. Letter to Jawaharlal Nehru, 19 October 1938; *Netaji: Collected Works*, Vol. 9, p. 183.
50. Letter to Amiya Nath Bose, 17 April 1939; *Netaji: Collected Works*, Vol. 9, p. 289.
51. Nehru, *SWJN*, pp. 711–2.
52. Subhas–Jawaharlal correspondence; *Netaji: Collected Works*, Vol. 9, pp. 182–236.
53. *Jugantar*, 18 March 1939.
54. *Jugantar*, 19 March 1939. A pro-Gandhi journal lamented that the way a large section of the Bengal Congress had been behaving, if they succeeded in forming the government then Gandhi and Jawaharlal would probably be banned from entering the province, Azad would be exiled, Prafulla Ghosh would be sent to the Andaman islands, Kiran Shankar Roy would be home interned and those who still had full faith in Gandhi would be hanged, article published in *Aarthik Jagat*, quoted in *Jugantar*, 4 April 1939.
55. *Jugantar*, 1 April 1939.
56. *Jugantar*, 6 April 1939.
57. *Jugantar*, 22 April 1939, p. 11.
58. *Jugantar*, 6 June 1939.
59. Rabindranath's letter of 29 March, and Gandhi's reply of 2 April 1939; Gandhi, *Collected Works*, Vol. 75, p. 226.
60. *Jugantar*, 30 March 1939.
61. *Jugantar*, 22–25 April 1939.
62. Gandhi's letter to Subhas, 29 April 1939; *Netaji: Collected Works*, Vol. 9, p. 181.
63. *Netaji: Collected Works*, Vol. 9, pp. 107–9.
64. *Jugantar*, 7 May 1939.
65. *IAR 1939*, Vol. 1, pp. 347–9; *Jugantar*, 31 April 1939. B.N. Khare wired his sympathies to Subhas for suffering a similar fate; *Jugantar*, 2 May 1939, p. 10.
66. *Jugantar*, 2 May 1939, p. 9.
67. *Jugantar*, 3 and 4 May 1939.
68. *Netaji: Collected Works*, Vol. 9, p. 109.
69. *Jugantar*, 4 May 1939, p. 9.
70. *Jugantar*, 6 May 1939, p. 10.
71. *Jugantar*, 9 May 1939, p. 10.
72. *Jugantar*, 9 May 1939, p. 9.
73. *Jugantar*, 16 May 1939, p. 10.
74. *Jugantar*, 21 May 1939, p. 4.
75. Speech at Kanpur, 21 May 1939; Nehru, *SWJN*, Vol. 9, p. 574.

76. *SWJN*, Vol. 9, pp. 575–80.

77. *Jugantar*, 30 May 1939, p. 11.

78. *Jugantar*, 10 and 13 May 1939.

79. *Jugantar*, 9 June 1939, p. 7.

80. *Jugantar*, 23 May 1939, p. 4.

81. *Jugantar*, 1 June 1939, p. 9.

82. *Jugantar*, 26 May 1939, p. 8.

83. *Jugantar*, 6, 7, 8 and 9 June 1939.

84. *Jugantar*, 16 May 1939.

85. *The Illustrated Weekly of India*, 18 September 1955, p. 19.

86. 'Mahatma Gandhi O Subhas Chandra Bosu', in Nirad C. Chaudhuri, *Amar Desh Amar Shatak*, translated by the author, p. 184.

87. *Jugantar*, 16 June 1939.

88. *Jugantar*, 22 June 1939.

89. *Jugantar*, 17–20 June 1939.

90. Masani, *Bliss Was It in That Dawn*, p. 147. *Jugantar*, 21 June 1939.

91. Masani, *Bliss Was It in That Dawn*, pp. 149–50.

92. *Jugantar*, 22 June 1939.

93. Jawaharlal Nehru's letter to H.V. Kamath dated 17 May, published in *Jugantar*, 4 July 1939.

94. *Jugantar*, 22 June 1939.

95. *Jugantar*, 23 June 1939.

96. *Jugantar*, 25 June 1939.

97. *Jugantar*, 5 July 1939.

98. *Jugantar*, 3–7 July 1939.

99. *Jugantar*, 8, 9 July 1939.

100. *Jugantar*, 11 July 1939.

101. *The Modern Review*, August 1939, p. 143.

102. Letter to Jawaharlal Nehru, 28 March 1939; *Netaji: Collected Works*, Vol. 9, p. 194.

103. Statement issued on 7 July 1939; *SWJN*, Vol. 9, pp. 582–3.

104. Statement issued on 13 July 1939; *SWJN*, Vol. 9, pp. 583–5.

105. Fortnightly Reports for the Month of July 1939, National Archives of India.

106. Statement published in Bombay Chronicle; Gandhi, *Collected Works*, Vol. 76, pp. 417–8.

107. Letter to Rajendra Prasad, 11 July 1939; Vallabhbhai Patel, *Collected Works of Sardar Vallabhbhai Patel*, Vol. 8, pp. 121–2.

108. Letter to Rajendra Prasad, 12 July 1939; *CWSVP*, Vol. 8, Konark Publishers Pvt. Ltd, 1996, pp. 122–3.

109. Statement to the Press, 13 July 1939; Gandhi, *Collected Works*, Vol. 76, pp. 121–3.

110. *Jugantar*, 15 July 1939.

111. *CWSVP*, Vol. 8, pp. 125–8.

112. Fortnightly Reports for the month of July 1939, National Archives of India.

113. Fortnightly Reports for the month of August 1939, National Archives of India.

114. *Jugantar*, 13 July 1939.

115. Fortnightly Reports for the month of July 1939, National Archives of India.

116. *Jugantar*, 19 July 1939.

117. Prafulla Ghosh's letter to Rajendra Prasad, 18 July 1939; *Dr Rajendra Prasad: Correspondence and Select Documents*, edited by Valmiki Choudhary, Allied Publishers Pvt. Ltd, 1993, Vol. 3, p. 185.

118. Fortnightly Reports for the month of July 1939, National Archives of India.

119. *Jugantar*, 13 July 1939.

120. Gandhi, *Collected Works*, Vol. 76, pp. 33–4, 413–6.

121. Statement to the Press, 15 July 1939; Gandhi, *Collected Works*, Vol. 76, pp. 133–4.

122. Vallabhbhai Patel's letter to Rajendra Prasad, 16 July 1939; *CWSVP*, Vol. 8, p. 15.

123. *Jugantar*, 8 July 1939.

124. *Jugantar*, 22 July 1939.

125. *Jugantar*, 29–30 July, and 1 August 1939.

126. Gandhi's statement to the press published in *The Hindu*, 2 August 1939; Gandhi, *Collected Works*, Vol. 76, pp. 195–6.

127. *Jugantar*, 4 August 1939. The agitation pressing the Government to release all political prisoners continued. At a public meeting at Shraddhananda Park, attended by around 40,000 people on 13 August, Subhas repeated his ultimatum to the Bengal Government; *Jugantar*, 15 August 1939. The Bengal Government announced on 13 November that the number of political prisoners had declined from 457 in 1937, when the Government had taken charge, to 87 on that date; *IAR 1939*, Vol. 2, p. 42.

128. Gandhi's statement to the press, 6 August 1939; Gandhi, *Collected Works*, Vol. 76, p. 214.

129. Congress working committee resolution, 9–12 August 1939; *IAR 1939*, Vol. 2, p. 215.

130. 'Hunger-strike', *Harijan*, 19 August 1939; Gandhi, *Collected Works*, Vol. 76, pp. 229–30.

131. *Jugantar*, 21 July 1939.

132. *Jugantar*, 26 July 1939.

133. *Jugantar*, 27 July 1939.

134. *Jugantar*, 1 August 1939.

135. *Jugantar*, 2 August 1939.

136. *Jugantar*, 10 August 1939.

137. *Jugantar*, 6 August 1939.

138. *IAR 1939*, Vol. 2, p. 14.

139. *Jugantar*, 12 August 1939; Sitaramayya, *The History of the Indian National Congress*, Vol. 2, p. 118.

140. *IAR 1939*, Vol. 2, pp. 21–3.

141. *Forward Bloc*, 19 August 1939, p. 9.

142. Statement to the Press, 23 August 1939; Gandhi, *Collected Works*, Vol. 76, p. 258.

143. *Forward Bloc*, 19 August 1939, pp. 10–1.

144. *Jugantar*, 18 August 1939.

145. *IAR 1939*, Vol. 2, p. 13; *Jugantar*, 24 August 1939.

146. *Jugantar*, 19 August 1939.

147. *Jugantar*, 20 August 1939.

148. *Forward Bloc*, 19 August 1939, p. 7.

149. *Jugantar*, 1 September 1939.

150. *Jugantar*, 26 August 1939.

151. *Jugantar*, 30 August 1939.

152. *Jugantar*, 30 and 31 August 1939.

153. *Jugantar*, 26 August 1939.

154. *Advance*, 1 September 1939.

155. *Jugantar*, 3 September 1939.

156. Subhas Chandra Bose, *The Indian Struggle*, Vol. 2, p. 28.

157. *Advance*, 5 September 1939; *Jugantar*, 5 September 1939.

158. *The Modern Review*, October 1939, pp. 376–7.

159. *The Modern Review*, October 1939, p. 377.

160. *Jugantar*, 21 September 1939.

161. *The Modern Review*, October 1939, p. 378.

162. First fortnightly report submitted by the Secretary of State for India to the War Cabinet, September 1939, WP (R)(39)(5), CAB 68/1/5, The National Archives, UK.

163. Statement to the Press, 5 September 1939; Gandhi, *Collected Works*, Vol. 76, pp. 311–2.

164. Nehru, *SWJN*, Vol. 10, p. 119.

165. *Advance*, 10 September 1939.

166. *IAR 1939*, Vol. 2, pp. 226–8.

167. Statement to the Press, 15 September 1939; Gandhi, *Collected Works*, Vol. 76, pp. 326–7.

168. Statement to the Press, 27 August 1939; Gandhi, *Collected Works*, Vol. 76, p. 273.

169. Editorial, *National Herald*, 23 September 1939; *SWJN*, Vol. 10, pp. 157–8.

170. *Jugantar*, 14 September 1939.

171. *IAR 1939*, Vol. 2, pp. 224–5.

172. *Jugantar*, 1 October 1939.

173. *Jugantar*, 28 September 1939.

174. *IAR 1938*, Vol. 1, p. 297; *Jugantar*, 18 September 1939.

175. *Jugantar*, 18 and 20 September 1939.

176. *Advance*, 24 September 1939.

177. *IAR 1938*, Vol. 1, p. 27.

178. *Advance*, 8, 9 and 10 September 1939; Fortnightly Reports, October 1939, National Archives of India.

179. Telegram from Viceroy dated 28 September 1939, CAB 67/1/24, The National Archives, UK.

180. *Jugantar*, 12 October 1939.

181. *IAR1939*, Vol. 2, pp. 384–9.

182. Statement to the Press, 18October 1939; Gandhi, *Collected Works*, Vol. 77, p. 12.

183. Congress Working Committee resolutions, 22–23 October 1939; *IAR 1939*, Vol. 2, pp. 236–7.

184. Cable to World Press, 23 October 1939; Gandhi, *Collected Works*, Vol. 77, p. 35.

185. 'Causes', article in *Harijan*, 28 October 1939; Gandhi, *Collected Works*, Vol. 77, pp. 37–9.

186. *Jugantar*, 14 October 1939.

187. *Jugantar*, 17 October 1939.

188. *Jugantar*, 18 October 1939.

189. *Jugantar*, 19 October 1939.

190. *Jugantar*, 24 October 1939.

191. Fortnightly Reports, October 1939; The National Archives of India.

192. *Jugantar*, 25 October 1939.

193. *Jugantar*, 31 October 1939.

194. 'The Next Step', *Harijan*, 4 November 1939; Gandhi, *Collected Works*, Vol. 77, pp. 62–3.

195. *IAR 1939*, Vol. 2, pp. 237–9.

196. *IAR 1939*, Vol. 2, pp. 239–41.

197. Syama Prasad Mookerjee, *Leaves from a Diary*, Oxford University Press, 1993, p. 16.

198. *IAR 1939*, Vol. 2, pp. 250–3.

199. *Amrita Bazar Patrika*, 5 January 1940, p. 10.

200. *Amrita Bazar Patrika*, 7 January 1940, p. 7.

201. *Amrita Bazar Patrika*, 20 January 1940, p. 7.

202. *Amrita Bazar Patrika*, 24 January 1940, p. 7.

203. *Amrita Bazar Patrika*, 2 January 1940, p. 6.

204. *Amrita Bazar Patrika*, 2 January 1940.

205. *Amrita Bazar Patrika*, 8 January 1940, p. 7.

206. *Amrita Bazar Patrika*, 31 January 1940, p. 7.

207. *Amrita Bazar Patrika*, 3 February 1940, p. 7.

208. *Amrita Bazar Patrika*, 4 February 1940, pp. 7, 11.

209. *Amrita Bazar Patrika*, 8 February 1940, p. 10.

210. *Amrita Bazar Patrika*, 10 January 1940, p. 8; *Amrita Bazar Patrika*, 11 January 1940, p. 8.

211. *IAR 1939*, Vol. 2, p. 250.

212. *Amrita Bazar Patrika*, 16 January 1940, p. 10.

213. *Amrita Bazar Patrika*, 26 January 1940, p. 7.

214. *Amrita Bazar Patrika*, 11 January 1940, p. 10.

215. *Amrita Bazar Patrika*, 13 January 1940, p. 10.

216. *Amrita Bazar Patrika*, 15 January 1940, p. 8.

217. *Amrita Bazar Patrika*, 16 January 1940, p. 10.

218. *Amrita Bazar Patrika*, 4 February 1940, p. 10.

219. *Amrita Bazar Patrika*, 17 January 1940, p. 10.

220. *Amrita Bazar Patrika*, 19 January 1940, p. 10.

221. 'The Dissentients', published in *Harijan*, 20 January 1940; Gandhi, *Collected Works*, Vol. 77, pp. 227–30.

222. *Amrita Bazar Patrika*, 6 March 1940, p. 10.

223. *Amrita Bazar Patrika*, 23 January 1940, p. 5.

224. *Amrita Bazar Patrika*, 30 January 1940, p. 9.

225. *Amrita Bazar Patrika*, 1 February 1940, p. 7.

226. *Amrita Bazar Patrika*, 12 February 1940, p. 9.

227. *Amrita Bazar Patrika*, 1 March 1940, p. 10.

228. *Amrita Bazar Patrika*, 5 March 1940, p. 8.

229. *Amrita Bazar Patrika*, 24 February 1940, p. 14.

230. *Amrita Bazar Patrika*, 19 February 1940, p. 5.

231. *Amrita Bazar Patrika*, 21 February 1940, p. 9.

232. *Amrita Bazar Patrika*, 29 February 1940, p. 9.

233. *Amrita Bazar Patrika*, 10 March 1940, p. 7.

234. *Amrita Bazar Patrika*, 21 February 1940, p. 7.

235. *Amrita Bazar Patrika*, 24 February 1940, p. 7.

236. *Amrita Bazar Patrika*, 24 February 1940, p. 8.

237. *Amrita Bazar Patrika*, 7 March 1940, p. 7.

238. *Amrita Bazar Patrika*, 8 March 1940, p. 8.

239. *Amrita Bazar Patrika*, 4 March 1940, p. 5.

240. *Amrita Bazar Patrika*, 9 March 1940, p. 8.

241. *Amrita Bazar Patrika*, 10 March 1940, p. 4.

242. *IAR 1940*, Vol. 1, pp. 235–6.

243. *Amrita Bazar Patrika*, 1 March 1940, p. 9

244. *Amrita Bazar Patrika*, 4 March 1940, p. 5

245. *Amrita Bazar Patrika*, 13 March 1940, p. 10.

246. *Amrita Bazar Patrika*, 17 March 1940, p. 7.

247. *Bengal Politics: Documents of the Raj, Vol. 2, 1940–43*, edited by E. Rahim *et al.*, The University Press Limited, 1999, p. 16.

248. Mookerjee, *Leaves from a Diary*, pp. 31–3.

249. *Amrita Bazar Patrika*, 8 March 1940, p. 7

250. Mookerjee, *Leaves from a Diary*, p. 33.

251. *Amrita Bazar Patrika*, 23 March 1940, p. 7.

252. *Amrita Bazar Patrika*, 17 March 1940, p. 8.

253. *Amrita Bazar Patrika*, 17 March 1940, p. 10.

254. Mookerjee, *Leaves from a Diary*, p. 34.

255. *Amrita Bazar Patrika*, 18 March 1940, p. 8.

256. *IAR 1940*, Vol. 1, pp. 228–9.

257. *IAR 1940*, Vol. 1, p. 230.

258. *IAR 1940*, Vol. 1, pp. 342–6.

259. *Amrita Bazar Patrika*, 25 March 1940, p. 7.

260. *Amrita Bazar Patrika*, 30 March 1940, p. 9.

261. *Amrita Bazar Patrika*, 19 April 1940, p. 7.

262. *Amrita Bazar Patrika*, 26 April 1940, p. 8.

263. *Amrita Bazar Patrika*, 28 April 1940, p. 7.

264. *Amrita Bazar Patrika*, 28 April 1940, p. 8.

265. *Amrita Bazar Patrika*, 5 May 1940, p. 7.

266. *Amrita Bazar Patrika*, 1 May 1940, p. 7.

267. *Amrita Bazar Patrika*, 3 May 1940, p. 7.

268. *Amrita Bazar Patrika*, 4 May 1940, p. 7.

269. *Amrita Bazar Patrika*, 9 May 1940, p. 8.

270. *Amrita Bazar Patrika*, 16 June 1940, p. 7.

271. *Amrita Bazar Patrika*, 8 May 1940, p. 7.

272. Letter to Satyendra Nath Majumdar, 28 April 1933; *Netaji: Collected Works*, Vol. 8, pp. 9–10.

273. Letter to Satyendra Nath Majumdar, 22 March 1934; *Netaji: Collected Works*, Vol. 8, p. 55.

274. *Amrita Bazar Patrika*, 3 June 1940, p. 5.

275. *Netaji: Collected Works*, Vol. 10, p. 128.

276. *Amrita Bazar Patrika*, 8 June 1940, p. 7.

277. *Netaji: Collected Works*, Vol. 10, pp. 115–26.

278. *Netaji: Collected Works*, Vol. 10, p. 128.

279. *IAR 1940*, Vol. 2, p. 175.

280. Rahim *et al.*, *Bengal Politics: Vol. 2*, pp. 22–31.
281. *Netaji: Collected Works*, Vol. 10, p. 128.
282. Sugata Bose, *His Majesty's Opponent*, The Belknap Press, 2011, p. 177.
283. *Weekly Amrita Bazar Patrika*, 4 July 1940, p. 1.
284. *Weekly Amrita Bazar Patrika*, 11 July 1940, p. 12.
285. *Weekly Amrita Bazar Patrika*, 18 July 1940, p. 7.
286. *Weekly Amrita Bazar Patrika*, 1 August 1940, p. 15.
287. Letter to the Superintendent of the Presidency Jail, 30 October 1940; *Netaji: Collected Works*, pp. 187–9.
288. *IAR 1940*, Vol. 2, p. 38.
289. Letter to the President, Indian Legislative Assembly, 1 November 1940; *Netaji: Collected Works*, pp. 189–90.
290. Letter to the Deputy President, Indian Legislative Assembly, 14 November 1940; *Netaji: Collected Works*, p. 190.
291. Letter to the Governor, Chief Minister and Council of Ministers, Government of Bengal, 26 November 1940; *Netaji: Collected Works*, Vol. 10, pp. 192–8.
292. Letter to Premier and Council of Ministers, Government of Bengal, 9 December 1940; *Netaji: Collected Works*, Vol. 10, p. 200.

Chapter 9: The Phoenix Rises

1. *Amrita Bazar Patrika*, 28 January 1941, p. 5.
2. Member of the Council of State from 1936 to 1947; later, a Jana Sangh member of the third Lok Sabha from the Shahabad constituency of Uttar Pradesh.
3. *Amrita Bazar Patrika*, 11 November 1941, p. 7.
4. Hansard, Volume 376, 27 November 1941, https://hansard.parliament.uk/Commons/1941-11-27.
5. Milan Hauner, *India in Axis Strategy*, Klett-Cotta, 1981, pp. 240–5.
6. Jan Kuhlmann, *Netaji in Europe*, p. 37.
7. *Documents on German Foreign Policy*, US Department of State, Series D, Vol. 12, pp. 442–3.
8. *Documents on German Foreign Policy*, US Department of State, Series D, Vol. 12, pp. 499–502.
9. N.G. Ganpuley, *Netaji in Germany: A Little-Known Chapter*, Bharatiya Vidya Bhavan, 1959, p. 38.
10. Ganpuley, *Netaji in Germany*, p. 47.
11. Hauner, *India in Axis Strategy*, p. 663.
12. *Documents on German Foreign Policy*, US Department of State, Series D, Vol. 12, pp. 527–8.

13.   Ganpuley, *Netaji in Germany*, p. 63.

14.   *Documents on German Foreign Policy*, US Department of State, Series D, Vol. 12, pp. 670–8.

15.   Kuhlmann, *Netaji in Europe*, pp. 46–7.

16.   Supplementary memorandum by Subhas Chandra Bose, 3 May 1941; T.R. Sareen, *Bose in Germany: A Documentary Study 1941–44*, Manjuli Prakashan, 2007, pp. 117–9.

17.   Hauner, *India in Axis Strategy*, pp. 249–50.

18.   Hauner, *India in Axis Strategy*, pp. 251–2.

19.   Detailed plan of work submitted by Bose to the German Foreign Office; Sareen, *Bose in Germany* pp. 125–7.

20.   Draft of Free India Declaration; Hauner, *India in Axis Strategy*, pp. 664–5.

21.   *Documents on German Foreign Policy*, US Department of State, Series D, Vol. 12, pp. 878–9.

22.   Hauner, *India in Axis Strategy*, p. 256.

23.   Gurbachan Singh Mangat, *The Tiger Strikes*, Gagan Publishers, 1986, pp. 36–54.

24.   *Documents on German Foreign Policy*, US Department of State, Series D, Vol. 12, pp. 902–3.

25.   Galeazzo Ciano, *The Ciano Diaries 1939–1943*, edited by Hugh Gibson, Simon Publications, 2001, p. 363. Most authors, following Malcolm Muggeridge, have translated the phrase 'questogiovanotto' as 'upstart'. Some others, as in the work cited, have followed the more literal 'youngster'. As Milan Hauner has pointed out, Ciano was not only younger than Subhas, but he could not match the latter's political experience.

26.   Galeazzo Ciano, *Ciano's Diplomatic Papers*, edited by Malcolm Muggeridge, Odhams Press Limited, 1948, pp. 446–7.

27.   File 7-x(P)/41(Secret), National Archives of India.

28.   Leonard A. Gordon, *Brothers Against the Raj*, pp. 449–50.

29.   Shedai's account of his meeting with Bose, 1 June 1941; Sareen, *Bose in Germany*, pp. 135–6.

30.   Shedai to Marchese B Lanza D'Ajeta, 4 June 1941; Sareen, *Bose in Germany*, pp. 137–8.

31.   Shedai to Don Prunas, 11 June 1941; T.R. Sareen, *Subhas Chandra Bose and Nazi Germany*, Mounto Publishing House, 1996, pp. 123–4.

32.   Shedai to Marchese B Lanza D'Ajeta, 18 July 1941; Sareen, *Subhas Chandra Bose and Nazi Germany*, pp. 130–2.

33.   Hauner, *India in Axis Strategy*, p. 258.

34.   Letter to Woermann, 5 July 1941; Sareen, *Bose in Germany*, p. 141.

35.   Memorandum by Woermann, 17 July 1941; Sareen, *Bose in Germany*, pp. 143–4.

36. Memorandum by Woermann, 17 July 1941; Sareen, *Bose in Germany*, pp. 143–4.

37. Memorandum by Woermann, 18 August 1941; Sareen, *Bose in Germany*, pp. 145–7.

38. Memorandum by Woermann, 18 August 1941; Sareen, *Bose in Germany*, pp. 145–7.

39. *Documents on German Foreign Policy*, US Department of State, Series D, Vol. 13, pp. 388–9. Hauner, *India in Axis Strategy*, p. 361.

40. Minute by Woermann, 6 September 1941; Sareen, *Subhas Chandra Bose and Nazi Germany*, p. 144.

41. Hauner, *India in Axis Strategy*, pp. 306–39.

42. Shedai to Dr Prunas, 4 September 1941; Sareen, *Subhas Chandra Bose and Nazi Germany*, pp. 138–43.

43. Shedai to Doertenback, 21 September 1941; Sareen, *Subhas Chandra Bose and Nazi Germany*, pp. 148–53.

44. Mangat, *The Tiger Strikes*, p. 71.

45. Rudolf Hartog, *The Sign of the Tiger: Subhas Chandra Bose and His Indian Legion in Germany, 1941–45*, Rupa & Co, 2001, p. 48.

46. Hans Georg Mackensen to Foreign Ministry, 4 October 1941; *Subhas Chandra Bose and Nazi Germany*, p. 155. Shedai wrote to Italian Foreign Ministry official A. Alessandrini on 4 October 1941 (Sareen, *Subhas Chandra Bose and Nazi Germany*, p. 157): 'Now they know what we can do. It is they who will need our cooperation and instructions and not we. They have not anybody who is able to work either on Radio or among the prisoners.' The Italian counterpart to the SRI was *Ufficio India*. Hauner, *India in Axis Strategy*, p. 367.

47. Hauner, *India in Axis Strategy*, p. 358.

48. Kuhlmann, *Netaji in Europe*, pp. 60–1.

49. Kuhlmann, *Netaji in Europe*, p. 63.

50. Hauner, *India in Axis Strategy*, p. 364.

51. Subhas to Woermann, 25 September 1941; Sareen, *Subhas Chandra Bose and Nazi Germany*, pp. 154, 178.

52. Gordon, *Brothers Against the Raj*, p. 454.

53. Hauner, *India in Axis Strategy*, p. 365.

54. M.R. Vyas, *Passage Through a Turbulent Era*, Indo-Foreign Publications & Publicity, 1982, p. 318.

55. Kuhlmann, *Netaji in Europe*, p. 68.

56. Girija K. Mookerjee, *Europe at War (1938–46)*, Meenakshi Prakashan, 1968, p. 207.

57. Bose, *Netaji: Collected Works*, Vol. 7, pp. 216–7.

58. Kuhlmann, *Netaji in Europe*, pp. 68–72.

59. Ganpuley, *Netaji in Germany*, p. 43.

60. Kuhlmann, *Netaji in Europe*, p. 43.

61. Ganpuley, *Netaji in Germany*, pp. 47–59.

62. Records of conversation between Ribbentrop and Bose, 29 November 1941; Sareen, *Subhas Chandra Bose and Nazi Germany*, pp. 163–7.

63. Brief for the Fuhrer, 13 November 1941; *Documents on German Foreign Policy*, US Department of State, Series D, Vol. 13, pp. 774–9.

64. Hauner, *India in Axis Strategy*, p. 372.

65. Minutes of meetings held on 8 and 9 December 1941; Sareen, *Subhas Chandra Bose and Nazi Germany*, pp. 170–4.

66. Mangat, *The Tiger Strikes*, pp. 64–9.

67. Hauner, *India in Axis Strategy*, p. 371.

68. Hauner, *India in Axis Strategy*, p. 391.

69. Joyce Lebra, *Jungle Alliance*, Asia Pacific Press, 1971, p. 4; K.S. Giani, *Indian Independence Movement in East Asia*, Singh Brothers, 1947, p. 18; T.R. Sareen, *Japan and the Indian National Army*, Agam Prakashan, 1986, p. 14.

70. Sareen, *Japan and the Indian National Army*, pp. 22–4. Historian Joyce Lebra, however, claimed that the agreement was signed by Fujiwara and Pritam Singh (*Jungle Alliance*, p. 10).

71. Sareen, *Japan and the Indian National Army*, p. 31; K.K. Ghosh, *The Indian National Army*, Meenakshi Prakashan, 1969, pp. 23–4.

72. Ghosh, *The Indian National Army*, p. 28; Sareen, *Japan and the Indian National Army*, pp. 38–9.

73. Ghosh, *The Indian National Army*, p. 31.

74. Ghosh, *The Indian National Army*, p. 41; *Who's Who of Indian Martyrs*, Vol. 2, edited by P.N. Chopra, Publications Division, Government of India, 2013, p. 290.

75. Memorandum by Woermann, 18 December 1941; Sareen, *Subhas Chandra Bose and Nazi Germany*, p. 177.

76. Hauner, *India in Axis Strategy*, p. 415.

77. Report of Herr Thomas, German ambassador in Thailand to Foreign Ministry, 18 December 1941; Sareen, *Subhas Chandra Bose and Nazi Germany*, pp. 175–6.

78. Hauner, *India in Axis Strategy*, p. 416.

79. Minutes of meeting between Bose and Yamamoto, 28 January 1942; Sareen, *Subhas Chandra Bose and Nazi Germany*, pp. 239–41.

80. Hauner, *India in Axis Strategy*, p. 421.

81. Hauner, *India in Axis Strategy*, p. 417.

82. *Testament of Subhas Bose*, edited by 'Arun' (pseud.), Rajkamal Publications, 1946, p. 250.

83. Bose to Woermann, 17 February 1942; Sareen, *Subhas Chandra Bose and Nazi Germany*, pp. 242–3.

84. *The Indian Annual Register 1942*, Vol. 1, pp. 195–212.

85. *Amrita Bazar Patrika*, 18 February 1942, p. 4. The following weeks saw the celebration of China Day on 7 March at the instance of the Viceroy, with much fanfare and news reports highlighting the 'bestial conduct' of the Japanese army in Southeast Asia.

86. *Amrita Bazar Patrika*, 21 February 1942, p. 6.

87. *Amrita Bazar Patrika*, 22 February 1942, p. 5.

88. *Amrita Bazar Patrika*, 24 February 1942, p. 5.

89. *Amrita Bazar Patrika*, 21 April 1942, p. 4.

90. Hauner, *India in Axis Strategy*, p. 427.

91. There is some disagreement over the date of broadcast. While according to Milan Hauner, Subhas's speech was broadcasted on 27 February after the Japanese gave their consent for re-broadcasting, according to archival documents compiled by T.R. Sareen, the date was 19 February.

92. First statement by Bose from Azad Hind Radio, 19 February 1942; Sareen, *Subhas Chandra Bose and Nazi Germany*, pp. 244–5.

93. Hauner, *India in Axis Strategy*, p. 428.

94. The Marquess of Linlithgow to Viscount Halifax, 27 March 1942; *The Transfer of Power*, edited by Nicholas Mansergh, Vol. 1, 1970, p. 504.

95. Fortnightly Reports for the Month of March 1942, File No. 18/3/42-Poll., National Archives of India.

96. Hauner, *India in Axis Strategy*, pp. 430–1.

97. Hauner, *India in Axis Strategy*, pp. 431–2.

98. Ghosh, *The Indian National Army*, pp. 35–6.

99. Sareen, *Japan and the Indian National Army*, pp. 56–7.

100. Sareen, *Japan and the Indian National Army*, pp. 57–8; Ghosh, *The Indian National Army*, pp. 35–6.

101. *The Observer*, 29 March 1942, p. 5.

102. *Amrita Bazar Patrika*, 30 March.

103. *Amrita Bazar Patrika*, 30 March.

104. Broadcast, 25 March 1942, *Netaji: Collected Works*, Vol. 11, p. 80.

105. Ghosh, *The Indian National Army*, pp. 48–9.

106. Lebra, *Jungle Alliance*, p. 47.

107. Giani, *Indian Independence Movement in East Asia*, p. 45.

108. File No. 1/3/42-Poll (I), National Archives of India.

109. *Amrita Bazar Patrika*, 24 March 1942, p. 5; *The History and Culture of the Indian People: Struggle for Freedom*, Vol. 11, edited by R.C. Majumdar, pp. 637–8.

110. *IAR 1942*, Vol. 1, pp. 224–5.

111. Azad–Cripps correspondence, *IAR 1942*, Vol. 1, pp. 226–36.
112. Interview with Mr J.C. Gupta, 1 April 1942; *The Transfer of Power*, Vol. 1, pp. 598–9.
113. *IAR 1942*, Vol. 1, p. 94.
114. Broadcasts on 13, 19, 25 and 31 March 1942; *Testament of Subhas Bose*, pp. 2–14.
115. Broadcast on 6 April 1942; *Testament of Subhas Bose*, p. 14.
116. Broadcast over Azad Hind Radio on 13 April 1942; *Netaji: Collected Works*, Vol. 11, pp. 89–93.
117. Hauner, *India in Axis Strategy*, p. 475.
118. *Amrita Bazar Patrika*, 19 April 1942, p. 6.
119. *IAR 1942*, Vol. 1, p. 77.
120. *Amrita Bazar Patrika*, 20 April 1942, pp. 3, 6.
121. *Amrita Bazar Patrika*, 20 April 1942, p. 4.
122. *Amrita Bazar Patrika*, 26 April 1942, p. 4.
123. *Amrita Bazar Patrika*, 24 April 1942, p. 4.
124. Hauner, *India in Axis Strategy*, p. 479.
125. Hauner, *India in Axis Strategy*, pp. 479–83.
126. Letter to Ribbentrop, 22 May 1942; *Netaji: Collected Works*, Vol. 11, pp. 100–1.
127. Walter Schellenberg, *Hitler's Secret Service*, Pyramid Books, 1971, p. 254.
128. Hartog, *The Sign of the Tiger*, pp. 22–8; Hauner, *India in Axis Strategy*, pp. 484–6.
129. Hauner, *India in Axis Strategy*, pp. 487–8. Based on some German documents, Milan Hauner has claimed that the Japanese were indecisive about having Subhas in Japan and were considering, especially in the build-up to the Quit India movement, whether it would be better to rely on Gandhi and Jawaharlal. According to Hauner, Japan decided in favour of Subhas as late as in January 1943. It, however, seems unlikely that these were the reasons for the indecision as both Gandhi and Jawaharlal had taken a very vocal and public stand against Japan.
130. Kuhlmann, *Netaji in Europe*, p. 117.
131. Kuhlmann, *Netaji in Europe*, p. 121.
132. Ganpuley, *Netaji in Germany*, p. 66.
133. Ganpuley, *Netaji in Germany*, p. 69.
134. Romain Hayes, *Bose in Nazi Germany*, p. 76.
135. Kuhlmann, *Netaji in Europe*, p. 122; Ganpuley, *Netaji in Germany*, p 69.
136. Ganpuley, *Netaji in Germany*, p. 69.
137. Ganpuley, *Netaji in Germany*, pp. 75–6; Kuhlmann, *Netaji in Europe*, p. 122.
138. Ganpuley, *Netaji in Germany*, pp. 81–96
139. Kuhlmann, *Netaji in Europe*, p. 166.

140. Press Conference on 12 June 1942; *Netaji: Collected Works*, Vol. 11, pp. 109–12.

141. Sareen, *Japan and the Indian National Army*, pp. 68–9; Ghosh, *The Indian National Army*, pp. 54–5.

142. Sitaramayya, *The History of the Indian National Congress*, Vol. 2, pp. 840–2.

143. *IAR 1942*, Vol. 2, p. 237.

144. *Amrita Bazar Patrika*, 9 August 1942, p. 6.

145. 'Full Support to Gandhi', early August 1942; *Netaji: Collected Works*, Vol. 11, pp. 122–31.

146. Hauner, *India in Axis Strategy*, p. 547. Ribbentrop explained to Subhas during this farewell that paratroopers could be sent to the NWFP only after the German forces crossed Transcaucasia (Hauner, *India in Axis Strategy*, p. 559).

147. Identifying Axis broadcasts as a challenge, British intelligence officer Laurence Brander admitted, 'At the moment we are not winning the radio war that rages every night'; *The History of Broadcasting in the United Kingdom*, Vol. 3, Oxford University Press, 1970, p. 512.

148. *Netaji: Collected Works*, Vol. 11, 132–47.

149. Ganpuley, *Netaji in Germany*, p. 44.

150. Mookerjee, *Europe at War: 1938–46*, p. 210.

151. Hauner, *India in Axis Strategy*, pp. 559–60; Gordon, *Brothers Against the Raj*, pp. 487–8.

152. Hauner, *India in Axis Strategy*, p. 561.

153. Lebra, *Jungle Alliance*, pp. 83–4; Ghosh, *The Indian National Army*, p. 97.

154. Ghosh, *The Indian National Army*, pp. 106–7.

155. Lebra, *Jungle Alliance*, pp. 98–100; Sareen, *Japan and the Indian National Army*, pp. 105–6; Ghosh, *The Indian National Army*, p. 125.

156. 'A Memory of the Late Rash Behari Bose, by Hideo Iwakura', in *Rash Behari Basu: His Struggle for India's Independence*, edited by Radhanath Rath, Biplabi Mahanayak Rash Behari Basu Smarak Samity, 1959, pp. 57–8.

157. 'My Memories of Late Mr Rash Behari Bose, by Seizo Arisue', in *Rash Behari Basu*, pp. 50–1.

158. 'Mr R.B. Bose and Subhas Chandra Bose, by Syn Higuti', in *Rash Behari Basu*, pp. 61–2.

159. Tatsuo Hayashida, *Netaji Subhas Chandra Bose: His Great Struggle and Martyrdom*, Allied Publishers, 1970, pp. 25–7.

160. Lebra, *Jungle Alliance*, pp. 114–5; Hayashida, *Netaji Subhas Chandra Bose*, p. 29.

161. Lebra, *Jungle Alliance*, pp. 115–6; Hayashida, *Netaji Subhas Chandra Bose*, pp. 29–30.

162. Hayashida, *Netaji Subhas Chandra Bose*, p. 30.

163. Shah Nawaz Khan, *My Memories of INA and Its Netaji*, Rajkamal Publications, 1946, p. 66; Hayashida, *Netaji Subhas Chandra Bose*, p. 28.

164. *Testament of Subhas Bose*, pp. 143–4; *Netaji: Collected Works*, Vol. 12, pp. 17–9.

165. Broadcast on 21 June 1943, *Testament of Subhas Bose*, pp. 54–8.

166. Hayashida, *Netaji Subhas Chandra Bose*, pp. 42–3.

167. Khan, *My Memories of INA and Its Netaji*, p. 270; M.Z. Kiani, *India's Freedom Struggle and the Great INA*, Reliance Publishing House, 1994, p. 75.

168. M. Sivaram, *The Road to Delhi*, Charles E. Tuttle Co, 1967, p. 121.

169. *The Flame Burns Bright*, Documentary film produced by the Films Division, Government of India, 1973.

170. *The Flame Burns Bright*, Films Division; Khan, *My Memories of INA and Its Netaji*, p. 272; *Testament of Subhas Bose*, p. 64.

171. *Netaji: Collected Works*, Vol. 12, pp. 45–8.

172. *Netaji: Collected Works*, Vol. 12, p. 49; Lebra, *Jungle Alliance*, p. 120.

173. Hayashida, *Netaji Subhas Chandra Bose*, p. 51; Sivaram, *The Road to Delhi*, p. 127.

174. *Netaji: Collected Works*, Vol. 12, pp. 51–4.

175. Khan, *My Memories of INA and Its Netaji*, p. 128.

176. *Netaji: Collected Works*, Vol. 12, pp. 60–3; Lebra, *Jungle Alliance*, p. 121.

177. Sivaram, *The Road to Delhi*, p. 129.

178. Sivaram, *The Road to Delhi*, pp. 133–4.

179. A.C. Chatterji, *India's Struggle for Freedom*, Chuckervertty, Chatterjee & Co. Ltd, 1947, p. 76.

180. Hayashida, Netaji Subhas Chandra Bose; Ba Maw, Breakthrough in Burma, Yale University Press, 1968, p. 326.

181. *Netaji: Collected Works*, Vol. 12, p. 79.

182. Ghosh, *The Indian National Army*, pp. 148–9; Khan, *My Memories of INA and Its Netaji*, p. 265.

183. Khan, *My Memories of INA and Its Netaji*, pp. 265–6.

184. *Netaji: Collected Works*, Vol. 12, pp. 80–1.

185. Kiani, *India's Freedom Struggle and the Great INA*, p. 76.

186. Chatterji, *India's Struggle for Freedom*, pp. 93–4.

187. Ghosh, *The Indian National Army*, pp. 152–3.

188. Chatterji, *India's Struggle for Freedom*, pp. 100–1.

189. Ghosh, *The Indian National Army*, pp. 151–2.

190. Sivaram, *The Road to Delhi*, pp. 139–40.

191. *Netaji: Collected Works*, Vol. 12, p. 93.

192. Ghosh, *The Indian National Army*, p. 154.

193. Khan, *My Memories of INA and Its Netaji*, p. 279.

194. *Netaji: Collected Works*, Vol. 12, pp. 108–17.

195. *Netaji: Collected Works*, Vol. 12, p. 127.
196. Hayashida, *Netaji Subhas Chandra Bose*, p. 64.
197. Ghosh, *The Indian National Army*, p. 155.
198. Hayashida, *Netaji Subhas Chandra Bose*, p. 65.
199. *Netaji: Collected Works*, Vol. 12, p. 129.
200. Khan, *My Memories of INA and Its Netaji*, pp. 282–3; Chatterji, *India's Struggle for Freedom*, pp. 141–2.
201. *Netaji: Collected Works*, Vol. 12, p. 131.
202. Sivaram, *The Road to Delhi*, pp. 140–1.
203. Lebra, *Jungle Alliance*, pp. 130–1; Hayashida, *Netaji Subhas Chandra Bose*, p. 66; Chatterji, *India's Struggle for Freedom*, p. 150.
204. Hayashida, *Netaji Subhas Chandra Bose*, p. 66; *Netaji: Collected Works*, Vol. 12, p. 149.
205. Hayashida, *Netaji Subhas Chandra Bose*, p. 69.
206. Ghosh, *The Indian National Army*, pp. 161–5; Lebra, *Jungle Alliance*, pp. 130–6; Hayashida, *Netaji Subhas Chandra Bose*, pp. 66–72; Sareen, *Japan and the Indian National Army*, pp. 121–3.
207. Hayashida, *Netaji Subhas Chandra Bose*, pp. 74–5.
208. *Netaji: Collected Works*, Vol. 12, pp. 161–2.
209. Hayashida, *Netaji Subhas Chandra Bose*, p. 76; Ghosh, *The Indian National Army*, p. 165.
210. T.R. Sareen, *Sharing the Blame*, S.S. Publishers, 2002, pp. 107–10.
211. *Netaji: Collected Works*, Vol. 12, p. 171.
212. *Netaji: Collected Works*, Vol. 12, pp. 180–1.
213. While according to Shah Nawaz Khan, the Subhas Regiment left Taiping for Rangoon in batches, between 9 and 24 November (Khan, *My Memories of INA and Its Netaji*, p. 70), M.Z. Kiani has written that they moved in September (Kiani, *India's Freedom Struggle and the Great INA*, p. 78); Chatterji, *India's Struggle for Freedom*, p. 158.
214. Ghosh, *The Indian National Army*, p. 170.
215. Lebra, *Jungle Alliance*, p. 136.
216. Deposition of Isoda Saburo at the Netaji Inquiry Committee, 1956, Annexure to File PS-56/NEC, Ministry of External Affairs, National Archives of India.
217. Sareen, *Sharing the Blame*, pp. 116–9.
218. Khan, *My Memories of INA and its Netaji*, pp. 71–2.
219. Chatterji, *India's Struggle for Freedom*, p. 164.
220. Khan, *My Memories of INA and Its Netaji*, pp. 73–5; Chatterji, *India's Struggle for Freedom*, p. 165.
221. Khan, *My Memories of INA and Its Netaji*, p. 76.
222. Khan, *My Memories of INA and Its Netaji*, p. 77.

223. Khan, *My Memories of INA and Its Netaji*, p. 78.

224. Ghosh, *The Indian National Army*, p. 174; Khan, *My Memories of INA and Its Netaji*, p. 79.

225. Kiani, *India's Freedom Struggle and the Great INA*, pp. 90–1, 97.

226. Ghosh, *The Indian National Army*, p. 174; Kiani, *India's Freedom Struggle and the Great INA*, pp. 97, 114–5.

227. Kiani, *India's Freedom Struggle and the Great INA*, pp. 99–101; Ghosh, *The Indian National Army*, pp. 176–7.

228. Kiani, *India's Freedom Struggle and the Great INA*, p. 115.

229. Hayashida, *Netaji Subhas Chandra Bose*, p. 90.

230. Ghosh, *The Indian National Army*, pp. 177–8.

231. Ghosh, *The Indian National Army*, pp. 179–80.

232. Kiani, *India's Freedom Struggle and the Great INA*, pp. 96–7, 120–1.

233. Ghosh, *The Indian National Army*, pp. 191–2.

234. *Netaji: Collected Works*, Vol. 12, p. 206,

235. Sivaram, *Road to Delhi*, p. 205.

236. Hayashida, *Netaji Subhas Chandra Bose*, pp. 94–6.

237. Hayashida, *Netaji Subhas Chandra Bose*, p. 97.

Chapter 10: The Quagmire of Isms

1.   David Brennan, 'Who Was Subhas Chandra Bose? Alexandria Ocasio-Cortez Senior Staffer Criticized for Sporting Image of Nazi Collaborator', 7 November 2019, *Newsweek*, https://www.newsweek.com/who-was-subhas-chandra-bose-alexandria-ocasio-cortez-senior-staffer-criticized-sporting-image-1448687.

2.   Aaron Bandler, 'Wiesenthal Center Calls on AOC's Chief of Staff to Apologize for Wearing Nazi Collaborator Shirt', 11 July 2019, *Jewish Journal*, https://jewishjournal.com/news/united-states/301444/wiesenthal-center-calls-on-aocs-chief-of-staff-to-apologize-for-wearing-nazi-collaborator-shirt/.

3.   Brennan, 'Who Was Subhas Chandra Bose?'.

4.   Philip Mason, foreword to *The Springing Tiger*, by Hugh Toye, Cassell, 1959, p. x.

5.   Eric Hobsbawm, *Age of Extremes: The Short Twentieth Century 1914–1991*, Viking, 1995, p. 216.

6.   Mason, foreword to *The Springing Tiger*, p. xii.

7.   Francis Tuker, *While Memory Serves*, Cassell, 1950, pp. 69–72.

8.   Policy towards civilian war traitors other than members of the INA etc., File No. V/4/45-M.S., Home Department, Government of India, National Archives, UK.

9.   *International Affairs*, Vol. 35, No. 4, October 1959, p. 491.

10. Website of the American Historical Association, https://www.historians. org/about-aha-and-membership.

11. *The American Historical Review*, Vol. 97, No. 1, February 1992, pp. 270–1.

12. Günter Grass, *Show Your Tongue*, Harcourt Brace Jovanovich, 1989, pp. 14, 41.

13. Chariot of Freedom, *Time*, 7 March 1938.

14. *Chicago Daily Tribune*, 2 and 14 March 1942; *Los Angeles Times*, 13 March 1942.

15. *Los Angeles Times*, 13 March 1942.

16. *The Boston Daily Globe*, 7 March 1942; *Los Angeles Times*, 7 March 1942.

17. *San Francisco Examiner*, 5 August 1943.

18. *Los Angeles Times*, 7 May 1942.

19. *Manchester Guardian*, 30 May 1942.

20. *Evening Standard*, 10 June 1942; *The Manchester Guardian*, 29 July 1942.

21. *The Observer*, 23 August 1942.

22. *The Boston Daily Globe*, 19 June 1943.

23. *Derby Evening Telegraph*, 20 October 1943.

24. *Gloucestershire Echo*, 25 October 1943.

25. *Nottingham Evening Post*, 5 November 1943.

26. *Leicester Evening Mail*, 5 November 1943.

27. *Evening Express*, 6 November 1944.

28. *The Charlotte Observer*, 11 December 1943.

29. *The New York Times*, 24 March 1944.

30. *The Sydney Morning Herald*, 11 May 1945; *The Age*, 12 May 1945.

31. *The Windsor Daily Star*, 4 June 1945.

32. *The Sydney Morning Herald*, 24 August 1945.

33. *The New York Times*, 24 August 1945.

34. *The New York Times*, 17 May 1944.

35. Sridharani, *Warning to the West*, International Book House Ltd, 1943, pp. 170–87.

36. *The Bakersfield Californian*, 24 December 1942.

37. *Waterloo Daily Courier*, 8 December 1943.

38. *Manchester Evening News*, 19 April 1944

39. *The New York Times*, 17 February 1957

40. *Chicago Sunday Tribune*, 2 December 1962.

41. *The New York Times*, 24 January 1997.

42. *Modern Asian Studies*, Vol. 12, No. 3, 1978, pp. 526–7.

43. Nehru, *SWJN*, Second series, Vol. 4, p. 2.

44. Sitaram Goel, *Netaji and the CPI*, Society for Defence of Freedom of Asia, 1955, pp. 9–16.

45. *Jana Juddha*, 21 July 1943; Translated from Bengali by the author.

46. *Netaji: Collected Works*, p. 163. Jayaprakash admitted that the letter was written by him during a visit to the Netaji Bhawan, Calcutta.

47. Policy Towards the Communist Organ People's War, File No. 7/15/43-Poll (I), National Archives, New Delhi.

48. Policy Towards the Communist Organ People's War, File No. 7/15/43-Poll (I), National Archives, New Delhi.

49. Policy Towards the Communist Organ People's War, File No. 7/15/43-Poll (I), National Archives, New Delhi.

50. Policy Towards the Communist Organ People's War, File No. 7/15/43-Poll (I), National Archives, New Delhi.

51. Gautam Chattopadhyay, *Subhas Chandra Bose and Indian Communist Movement*, People's Publishing House, 1973, pp. 1–8.

52. H. Williamson, *India and Communism*, Government of India Press, 1935, pp. 167, 181.

53. Chattopadhyay, *Subhas Chandra Bose and Indian Communist Movement*, pp. 10, 21–2.

54. Hirendra Nath Mukhopadhyay, *Taree Hote Teer*, Bangla Academy, Dhaka, 1971, p. 387.

55. Goel, *Netaji and the CPI*, pp. 12–3.

56. P.C. Joshi, *Communist Reply to Congress Working Committee's Charges*, Bengal Provincial Committee, Communist Party of India, 1946, pp. 1–3.

57. Joshi, *Communist Reply*, pp. 6–7.

58. Joshi, *Communist Reply*, pp. 14, 63.

59. 'Policy Towards Communists', File No. 7/5/44-Poll (I).

60. 'Policy Towards Communists', File No. 7/5/44-Poll (I).

61. E.M.S. Namboodiripad, *A History of Indian Freedom Struggle*, Social Scientist Press, 1986, p. 832.

62. Hiren Mukerjee, *Bow of Burning Gold*, People's Publishing House, 1977, pp. 107–9.

63. Harkishen Singh Surjeet, 'Mahan Deshpremik Subhas Chandra Bosu', in *Subhas Chandra O Amra*, edited by Anil Biswas, Ganashakti, 1997, pp. 7–12.

64. Jyoti Basu, 'Netaji O Amra', in *Subhas Chandra O Amra*, pp. 13–8.

65. Muzaffar Ahmad, *Myself and the Communist Party of India*, National Book Agency Pvt. Ltd, 1970, p. 498.

66. Ahmad, *Myself and the Communist Party of India*, p. 189.

67. Sudhi Pradhan, 'Swadhinata Andolan O Subhas Chandra Bosu', in *Subhas Chandra O Amra*, pp. 13–8.

68. Ahmad, *Myself and the Communist Party of India*, pp. 28–9.

69. Sugata Bose, 'Netaji, Now Appropriated by the Rightwing, Was Unflinching in His Commitment to Religious Harmony', *The Wire*, 23 January 2020, https://thewire.in/history/netaji-subhas-chandra-bose-religious-harmony.

70. 'BJP Desperate to Rewrite History, Appropriate Netaji's Legacy: Congress', *The Indian Express*, 21 October 2018, https://indianexpress.com/article/india/bjp-desperate-to-rewrite-history-appropriate-netajis-legacy-congress-5411662.

71. 'Savarkar Had Called Netaji a Hindu Jihadi: Subhashini Ali', Outlook, 25 January 2021, https://www.outlookindia.com/website/story/india-news-savarkar-had-called-netaji-a-hindu-jihadi-subhashini-ali/371803.

72. 'How the Hindutva Gang Backstabbed Netaji Subhash Chandra Bose', *National Herald*, 23 January 2018, https://www.nationalheraldindia.com/opinion/how-the-hindutva-gang-backstabbed-netaji-subhash-chandra-bose.

73. 'RSS Appropriates Icons as They Don't Have Their Own: Irfan Habib', *The Times of India*, 2 November 2019, https://timesofindia.indiatimes.com/india/rss-appropriates-icons-as-they-dont-have-their-own-irfan-habib/articleshow/71866350.cms.

74. Mookerjee, *Leaves from a Diary*, p. 28.

75. Mookerjee, *Leaves from a Diary*, pp. 34–6.

76. Bose, *The Indian Struggle: 1935–1942*, Vol. 2, p. 34.

77. *Forward Bloc*, Vol. 1, No. 21, 30 December 1939, p. 6.

78. S. Krishna Iyer, 'Mr Savarkar's Panacea', *Forward Bloc*, Vol. 1, No. 21, 30 December 1939, p. 8.

79. *Forward Bloc*, Vol. 1, No. 34, 30 March 1940, pp. 3–4.

80. *Amrita Bazar Patrika*, 23 February 1941, p. 7.

81. Vikram Sampath, *Savarkar: A Contested Legacy 1924–1966*, Viking, 2021, pp. 548–9.

82. Sarvesh K Tiwari, 'Subhas Chandra Bose—Another Look Part 1: The Seeds of Islamophile Secularism', https://bharatendu.com/2011/02/10/subhas-chandra-bose.

83. Tiwari, 'Subhas Chandra Bose', https://bharatendu.com/2011/02/10/subhas-chandra-bose.

84. Gandhi, *Collected Works of Mahatma Gandhi*, Vol. 82, p. 284.

85. Gandhi, *Collected Works of Mahatma Gandhi*, Vol. 82, pp. 408 9.

86. Gandhi, *Collected Works of Mahatma Gandhi*, Vol. 83, pp. 107–8.

87. Gandhi, *Collected Works of Mahatma Gandhi*, Vol. 87, pp. 398-9.

88. Gandhi, *Collected Works of Mahatma Gandhi*, Vol. 89, pp. 237-8.

89. Gandhi, *Collected Works of Mahatma Gandhi*, Vol. 89, p. 403.

90. Gandhi, *Collected Works of Mahatma Gandhi*, Vol. 90, p. 125.

91. Gandhi, *Collected Works of Mahatma Gandhi*, Vol. 90, p. 194.

92. Subhas Chandra Bose, *Netaji: Collected Works*, Vol. 12, edited by S.K. Bose and S. Bose, pp. 100–5.

93. *Netaji: Collected Works*, Vol. 12, pp. 100–5.

94. *Jugantar*, 9 May 1939, p. 12.

95. *Netaji: Collected Works*, Vol. 12, pp. 212-22.

96. Letter to Sarat Bose, 24 October 1940, *Netaji: Collected Works*, Vol. 10, p. 159.

97. Letter to Sarat Bose, 31 October 1940, *Netaji: Collected Works*, Vol. 10, pp.160-1.

98. T.R. Sareen, *Bose in Germany: A Documentary Study 1941-44*, 2007, pp. 279-81.

99. Morarji Desai, *The Story of My Life*, Vol. 1, S. Chand & Company Ltd, 1974, pp. 96-7.

100. Taya Zinkin, *Reporting India*, Chatto & Windus, 1962, p. 14.

101. Zinkin, *Reporting India*, p. 217.

102. *The Calcutta Municipal Gazette: Subhas Chandra Bose Birth Centenary Number*, edited by Arun Kumar Roy, 1997, p. 93.

103. *The New York Times*, 21 January 1927, p. 7.

104. Kayan Kundu, *Meeting with Mussolini: Tagore's Tours in Italy, 1924 and 1926*, Oxford University Press, 2015, pp. 206–12.

105. *The New York Times*, 10 December 1933, p. 167.

106. Marek Moroń, *Visit of Subhas Chandra Bose to Poland in July 1933: New Documents, New Conclusions*, 2015, pp. 3–15.

107. Lothar Frank, 'India's Ambassador Abroad', by in *A Beacon Across Asia*, edited by S.K. Bose, A. Werth and S.A. Ayer, Orient Longman, 1996, p. 40.

108. Frank, *A Beacon Across Asia*, pp. 42–3.

109. Gordon, *Brothers Against the Raj*, p. 276.

110. Bose, *My Uncle Netaji*, pp. 83–93.

111. Frank, *A Beacon Across Asia*, pp. 45–6.

112. Gordon, *Brothers Against the Raj*, pp. 281–2.

113. Letter to Dr Thierfelder, 7 November 1935; *Netaji: Collected Works*, Vol. 8, pp. 111–5.

114. Letter to Dr Thierfelder, 25 March 1936; *Netaji: Collected Works*, Vol. 8, pp. 165–8.

115. Subhas Chandra Bose, 'The Austrian Riddle', *The Modern Review*, April 1934, pp. 461–8.

116. Nehru, *SWJN*, Vol. 6, p. 332.

117. Subhas Chandra Bose, 'Europe—Today and Tomorrow', *The Modern Review*, September 1937, p. 318.

118. Subhas Chandra Bose, 'The Secret of Abyssinia and its Lessons', *The Modern Review*, November 1935, pp. 571–7.

119. Bose, 'Europe—Today and Tomorrow', *The Modern Review*, September 1937, pp. 317–23.

120. *Netaji: Collected Works*, Vol. 8, p. 349.

121. Subhas Chandra Bose, 'Japan's Role in the Far East', *The Modern Review*, October 1937, pp. 368–76.

122. Letter from Subhas Chandra Bose to Jawaharlal Nehru, 28 March 1939; Subhas Chandra Bose, *A Bunch of Old Letters: Written mostly to Jawaharlal Nehru and some written by him*, 1988, Asia Publishing House, 1960, p. 334.

123. Letter from Jawaharlal Nehru to Subhas Chandra Bose, 3 April 1939; Bose, *A Bunch of Old Letters*, p. 352.

124. Kitty Kurti, *Subhas Chandra Bose as I Knew Him*, Firma K.L. Mukhopadhyay, 1966, p. 11.

125. Kurti, *Subhas Chandra Bose as I Knew Him*, p. 39.

126. Notes of Louis Fischer for his interview with Pietro Quaroni, 15 November 1946, Seeley G. Mudd Manuscript Library, Princeton University Library.

127. *Netaji: Collected Works*, Vol. 9, p. 27.

128. Brown, *The Rise and Fall of Communism*, p. 76.

129. *Netaji: Collected Works*, Vol. 11, p. 141.

130. Mookerjee, *Subhas Chandra Bose*, pp. 75–6.

131. Hartog, *The Sign of the Tiger*, pp. 27–8.

132. Girija K. Mookerjee, *This Europe*, Saraswaty Library, 1950, p. 132.

133. Frank, *A Beacon Across Asia*, p. 117.

134. Hartog, *The Sign of the Tiger*, p. 28.

135. Netaji Inquiry Committee Report, Government of India, 1956, p. 65.

136. Item no 12, series B5555\O. Extract from communication intelligence, Top Secret 091927 August 1943, Berlin (Oshima) to Tokyo 30th July, National Archive of Australia, Melbourne Office.

137. Moti Ram, *Two Historic Trials in Red Fort*, 1946, pp. 120–5.

138. S.K. Dhawan, *Selected Thoughts of Indira Gandhi: A Book of Quotes*, 1985, p. 39.

139. Tim Ferguson, 'World's Worst Rulers: Scratch One Now?', *Forbes*, 22 August 2011, https://www.forbes.com/sites/timferguson/2011/08/22/worlds-worst-rulers-scratch-one-now/#46f727916190.

140. Andy Lines, 'Let Me Be Hitler Tenfold: How lion-meat loving Robert Mugabe built £8million personal fortune as country lurched into financial chaos', *Mirror*, 16 November 2017, https://www.mirror.co.uk/news/world-news/let-hitler-tenfold-how-lion-11529464.

141. 'India–DPR Korea Relations', Embassy of India, Pyongyang, https://mea.gov.in/Portal/ForeignRelation/India_DPRK_Bilatral_Brief_2019.pdf

142. Kallol Bhattacharjee, 'India Reaches Out, Wants to Upgrade Ties with North Korea', *The Hindu*, https://www.thehindu.com/todays-paper/india-reaches-out-wants-to-upgrade-ties-with-north-korea/article7656719.ece.

143. Kallol Bhattacherjee, 'Mahatma Gandhi Was "Accommodative" of Arab Violence, Claims Book', *The Hindu*, 19 October 2017, https://www.

thehindu.com/news/national/gandhi-was-accommodative-of-arab-violence-claims-book/article19883767.ece.

144. Benny Morris, 'Einstein's Other Theory', *The Guardian*, 16 February 2005, https://www.theguardian.com/world/2005/feb/16/israel.india.

145. Balraj Puri, *Kashmir, Towards Insurgency, Tracts for the Times*, 1993, p. 55.

146. Asher Izrael, 'No, the Allies Couldn't Have Stopped Auschwitz', *Haaretz*, https://www.haaretz.com/opinion/no-the-allies-couldn-t-have-stopped-auschwitz-1.5331661. Izrael argued, 'The Allies, who knew of the mass murder of Jews and kept silent about it, could have used other means—such as intelligence, propaganda, agents, a smuggling network to neutral countries, and statements from the Vatican and other diplomatic officials—to stop it. Perhaps such methods could have helped to combat it.'

147. Andrew Buncombe, 'Allied Forces Knew about Holocaust Two Years before Discovery of Concentration Camps, Secret Documents Reveal', *Independent*, 18 April 2017, https://www.independent.co.uk/news/world/world-history/holocaust-allied-forces-knew-before-concentration-camp-discovery-us-uk-soviets-secret-documents-a7688036.html.

148. T.R. Sareen, *Sharing the Blame: Subhas Chandra Bose and the Japanese Occupation of The Andamans 1942–45, 2002.*

149. Parliamentary Debates, Vol. 10, No. 1–13, Part I, 28 September 1951, Columns 1814–5, Parliament of India.

150. Lok Sabha Debates, Second Series, Vol. 40, Nos 25 and 35, 11 and 25 March 1960, Lok Sabha Secretariat, New Delhi.

151. Lok Sabha Debates, Fourth Series Vol. 32, No. 24, 22 August 1969, Columns 31–44, Lok Sabha Secretariat, New Delhi.

152. Cabinet Minute About Japanese Policy Towards India, 26 May 1948, *Select Documents on Indian National Army*, edited by T.R. Sareen, pp. 358–64.

153. G.D. Birla, *In the Shadow of the Mahatma: A Personal Memoir*, Orient Longmans Ltd, 1953, p. 254.

154. Hemanta Kumar Sarkar, *Subhaschandra*, D.M. Library, 1927, pp. 16–7. Sarkar has mentioned that 1913 was the year in which Subhas planned to form the party, but it appears to be a typographical error.

155. Gautam Chattopadhyay, *Communism and Bengal's Freedom Movement*, Vol. 1, People's Publishing House, 1970.

156. File No. L/P&J/12/214, British Library.

157. *Netaji: Collected Works*, Vol. 4, pp. 199–200.

158. Bose, *Subhas Rachanabali*, Vol. 1, pp. 126–7; Political Situation in India, March 1928, National Archives of India; Gordon, *Brothers Against the Raj*, pp. 172–3.

159. Dilip Simeon, *The Politics of Labour Under Late Colonialism*, Manohar, 1995, pp. 64–9.

160. Simeon, *The Politics of Labour Under Late Colonialism*, pp. 81–114; Gordon, *Brothers Against the Raj*, pp. 205–6.

161. Balai Mondal, *Subhas Chandra Bose: President, All-India Trade Union Congress*, 2011, pp. 132–3.

162. *Indian Quarterly Register 1929*, Vol. 2, p. 183.

163. *The Calcutta Municipal Gazette: Subhas Chandra Bose Birth Centenary Number*, edited by Arun Kumar Roy, pp. 67–9.

164. Mondal, *Subhas Chandra Bose: President, All-India Trade Union Congress*, pp. 124–5.

165. Statement issued on 6 December 1929 and Presidential Address at the All-India Trade Union Congress, 4 July 1931; *Netaji: Collected Works*, Vol. 6, pp. 68–73 and 190–6.

166. Statement issued on 11 July 1931; *Netaji: Collected Works*, Vol. 6, pp. 196–200.

167. Speech at Uttar Pradesh Naujawan Bharat Sabha, Mathura, 23 May 1931.

168. India Office Records, L/P&J/12/215

169. Bose, *The Indian Struggle*, Vol. 2, p. 13.

170. Communist Activities in India, India Office Records, L/P&J/12/431.

171. Amiya Nath Bose, 'Subhas Chandra Bose: Reminiscences', in *Jayasree: Netaji Subhas Chandra Basu Janmashatabarshiki Grantha*, edited by Samar Guha, 1999, pp. 375–7.

172. *Testament of Subhas Bose*, edited by Arun, p. 185.

173. Bose, *The Indian Struggle*, pp. 431–2.

174. 'R. Palme Dutt interviews Subhas Bose', *Daily Worker*, London, 24 January 1938.

175. Presidential address at the Bengal Students' Conference, 22 September 1928; *Indian Quarterly Register 1928*, Vol. 2, pp. 458–63

176. Speech at All-Bengal Students' Conference, 22 September 1928; Bose, *Rachanabali*, Vol. 1, pp. 249–51.

177. Letter to Sarat Chandra Bose, 1 August 1925; *Netaji: Collected Works*, Vol. 3, pp. 302–3.

178. Speech at the Bengal Provincial Conference at Rangpur, 30 March 1929; *Rachanabali*, Vol. 2, pp. 94–5.

179. *Netaji: Collected Works*, Vol. 5, pp. 244–5.

180. Presidential Address at Youth Conference, Pabna, 9 February 1929; Bose, *Rachanabali*, Vol. 2, pp 28–36.

181. Speech at Sabuj Sangha, 16 March 1929; Bose, *Rachanabali*, Vol. 2, pp. 56–9.

182. Presidential address at the Howrah Youth Conference, Date unknown, 1929; Bose, *Rachanabali*, Vol. 2, p. 202 (Translated from Bengali by the author).

183. *Netaji: Collected Works*, Vol. 5, p. 247.

184. The election was not unanimous. Subhas faced a contest from two other candidates—Jyotish Chandra Ghose and Nripendra Chandra Banerji. An arrangement was arrived at through the mediation of Bepin Behari Ganguly that Ghose would withdraw in favour of Banerji. This arrangement, however, broke down and Subhas won the triangular contest. Nripendra Chandra Banerji, *At the Cross-roads (1885–1946)*, p. 219.

185. See, for instance, his speeches at the Mymensingh District Conference, 21 April 1929 (Bose, *Rachanabali*, Vol. 2, pp. 109–22), Jessore District Conference, July 7 1929 (Bose, *Rachanabali*, Vol. 2, pp 147–54), Barisal District Conference, July 19 1929 (Bose, *Rachanabali*, Vol. 2, pp. 155–65).

186. Presidential address at the Howrah Youth Conference, Date unknown, 1929; Bose, *Rachanabali*, Vol. 2, pp 196–204.

187. Presidential address at the Howrah Youth Conference, Date unknown, 1929; Bose, *Rachanabali*, Vol. 2, p. 213.

188. Presidential address at the Srihatta District Students' Conference, April 25 1929; Bose, *Rachanabali*, Vol. 2, pp. 123–33.

189. Presidential address at the Hooghly District Students' Conference, July 21 1929; Bose, *Rachanabali*, Vol. 2, p. 173.

190. Presidential address at the Howrah District Conference, September 28 1929; Bose, *Rachanabali*, Vol. 2, pp. 213–5 (Translated from Bengali by the author).

191. Bose, *An Indian Pilgrim*, p. 42

192. *The Modern Review*, October 1938, p. 411.

193. *The Modern Review*, October 1938, p. 411.

194. *Netaji: Collected Works*, Vol. 8, p. 256.

195. Bose, *The Indian Struggle*, pp. 428–31.

196. 'R. Palme Dutt interviews Subhas Bose', *Daily Worker*, London, 24 January 1938.

197. *Netaji: Collected Works*, Vol. 9, pp. 13–4.

198. Bose, *The Indian Struggle*, pp. 119–20.

199. Bose, *The Indian Struggle*, pp. 116–7.

200. *Netaji: Collected Works*, Vol. 5, p. 247.

201. Hauner, *India in Axis Strategy*, p. 678.

202. Roy, *Reminiscences*, p. vii.

203. Bose, *The Indian Struggle*, p. 144; Broomfield, *Elite Conflict in a Plural Society*, pp. 160–1; Dasgupta, *Deshbandhu Chittaranjan Das*, pp. 104–5.

204. *Netaji: Collected Works*, Vol. 5, pp. 8–9.

205. Bazlur Rohman Khan, 'Some Aspects of Society and Politics in Bengal: 1927–36', Thesis submitted for the Degree of Doctor of Philosophy at the University of London, School of Oriental and African Studies, February 1979, pp. 204–5; *Bharatbarsha*, Year 15, Vol. 2, Issue 5, p. 798.

206. Rabindranath Tagore, 'The Saraswati Puja in the City College Hostel', *The Modern Review*, May 1928, pp. 594–7.
207. C.F. Andrews, 'The City College', *The Modern Review*, May 1928, p. 600.
208. Bose, *Rachanabali*, Vol. 1, edited by Sunil Das, pp. 77–8.
209. Bose, *Rachanabali*, Vol. 1, p. 176.
210. Bose, *Rachanabali*, Vol. 1, pp. 211–2.
211. Sajanikanta Das, *Atamsmriti*, pp. 244–53 (Loose translation by author).
212. Nirad C. Chaudhuri, 'Subhaschandra Basu Chhoyjon Shresthatomo Bangalir Ekjon', *Desh*, 13 January 1996, p. 100.
213. Bijoy Ratna Majumdar, 'Taruner Abhijan', *Subhas Smriti*, edited by Bishwanath De, 1970, pp. 193–6.
214. File No. 71/37-Poll, National Archives of India.
215. *Indian Annual Register 1937*, Vol. 2, p. 406.
216. Nepal Majumdar, *Rabindranath o Subhaschandra*, pp. 72–3 (Loose translation by author).
217. *Netaji: Collected Works*, Vol. 8, pp. 226–7.
218. *IAR 1937*, Vol. 2, pp. 327–8.
219. Roy, *Reminiscences*, p. 51.
220. Roy, *Reminiscences*, p. 55.
221. Letter to Amiya Nath Bose, 21 February 1934. Copy of the original in possession of the author.
222. Roy, *Reminiscences*, pp. 67–8.
223. Subhas Chandra Bose, 'My Strange Illness', *The Modern Review*, 1939.
224. Bose, 'My Strange Illness', *The Modern Review*, 1939.
225. Narendra Narayan Chakravarti, *Subhas Sanga O Prasanga*, Volume 2, 1967, pp. 77–8.
226. S.A. Ayer, *Unto Him a Witness: The Story of Subhas Chandra Bose in East Asia*, Thacker & Co. Ltd, 1951, pp. 268–9.
227. Maw, *Breakthrough in Burma*, p. 349.
228. Kiani, *India's Freedom Struggle and the Great INA*, p. 58.
229. Sheikh Mujibur Rahman, *The Unfinished Memoirs*. Kindle Edition.
230. *Netaji: Collected Works*, Vol. 11, p. 83.
231. *Testament of Subhas Bose*, pp. 87–95.
232. Bose, *The Indian Struggle*, p. 34.
233. *Testament of Subhas Bose*, pp. 189–90.

Chapter 11: Marriage

1. In a dipstick poll conducted by the author on Facebook, which elicited over 600 responses, the number of people who believed and disbelieved the story

of marriage was nearly the same, pointing towards the general level of lack of information on the topic.

2. Right to Information Act, 2005, *The Gazette of India Extraordinary*, Part II, Section I, No. 25.

3. Dr Abdul Hafiz Akmat to Jawaharlal Nehru, 22 June 1947; Correspondence re Mrs S. Bose, Sardar Patel papers, National Archives of India.

4. Jawaharlal Nehru to Vallabhbhai Patel, 7 August 1947; Correspondence re Mrs S. Bose, Sardar Patel papers, National Archives of India.

5. 'Reminiscences', Nathalal Parikh in *Life and Work of Netaji Subhas Chandra Bose*, edited by P.D. Saggi, 1954, p. 50.

6. A.C.N. Nambiar to Jawaharlal Nehru, 12 August 1947; Correspondence re Mrs S. Bose, Sardar Patel papers, National Archives of India.

7. File KV2/3904, the National Archives, Kew, UK.

8. Statement of A.C.N. Nambiar to CSDIC, File KV2/3904, pp. 72–3, the National Archives, UK.

9. Leonard A. Gordon, *Brothers Against the Raj*, 1990, p. 345.

10. Appendix B to Statement of A.C.N. Nambiar to CSDIC, File KV2/3904, the National Archives, UK.

11. Vallabbhai Patel to Sarat Chandra Bose, 7 August 1947; Sarat Chandra Bose to Vallabhbhai Patel, 14 August 1947; *Sardar Patel's Correspondence*, Vol. 5, edited by Durga Das, Navajivan Publishing House, 1973, pp 86–8.

12. Sarat Chandra Bose to Emilie Schenkl, 10 April 1948; Madhuri Bose, *Bose Brothers and Indian Independence: An Insider's Account*, Sage Publishing, 2015, p. 237.

13. *Netaji: Collected Works*, Vol. 11, p. 205.

14. Emilie's letter to Sarat Chandra Bose, 12 March 1946; Correspondence re Mrs S. Bose, Sardar Patel papers, National Archives of India.

15. Sarat Chandra Bose to Emilie Schenkl, 10 April 1948; Bose, *Bose Brothers and Indian Independence*, p. 237.

16. Sarat Chandra Bose to Emilie Schenkl, 8 July 1948; Bose, *Bose Brothers and Indian Independence*, p. 238.

17. Emilie's letter to Vallabhbhai Patel, undated; Correspondence re Mrs S. Bose, Sardar Patel papers, National Archives of India.

18. Note appended to Emilie Schenkl's letter to Vallabhbhai Patel, undated; Sardar Patel papers, National Archive of India.

19. Jawaharlal Nehru to Vallabhbhai Patel, 22 July 1948; Correspondence re Mrs S. Bose, Sardar Patel papers, National Archives of India.

20. Copy of intercepted letter from Emilie Schenkl to Chitra Bose, 23 June 1949; Special Branch File No TP502/49 IV.

21. Emilie's letter to Nathalal Parikh, 9 December 1948, File I-L-3-15, Sardar Patel papers, National Archives of India.

22. Intercepted letter of M.R. Vyas to Sarat Chandra Bose, 21 April 1949; File TP 502/49 II, Special Branch, West Bengal.

23. Copy of intercepted letter of Abid Hasan to Amiya Nath Bose, 18 April 1949; File TP 502/49 II, Special Branch, West Bengal.

24. Sarat Chandra Bose's letter to Ramgati Ganguly, dated 28 April 1949; Shiva Prosad Nag, *Liu Po-Cheng or Netaji?*, 1956, pp. 10–1.

25. Krishna Bose, *Emilie and Subhas: A True Love Story*, Niyogi Books, 2016, p. 76.

26. *Hindustan Standard*, 5 May 1951; *Jugantar*, 5 May 1951.

27. Sarat Chandra Bose to Emilie Schenkl, 8 July 1948; Bose, *Bose Brothers and Indian Independence*, p. 238.

28. *Jugantar*, 9 May 1951.

29. Loose translation of Chaudhuri, 'Subhas Chandra Bosu Chhoyjon Shreshthotomo Bangalir Ekjon', p. 106.

30. Parikh, *Reminiscences; Life and Work of Netaji Subhas Chandra Bose*, pp. 49–50.

31. Sarkar, *Subhaser Songe Baro Bochhor*, p. 81.

32. Roy, *Smriticharan*, p. 201.

33. Letter to Sarat Bose, 22 September 1920; *Netaji: Collected Works*, Vol. 1, p. 209.

34. *Netaji: Collected Works*, Vol. 1, p. 231.

35. Roy, *Smriticharan*, p. 227.*Netaji: Collected Works*, Vol. 1, p. 231.

36. Sarkar, *Subhaser Songe Baro Bochhor*, p.iii.

37. Roy, *Netaji—The Man: Reminiscences*, p. 156.

38. Translation by the author; Roy, *Smriticharan*, p. 241.

39. Roy, *Smriticharan*, p. 231.

40. Roy, *Netaji—The Man: Reminiscences*, p. 38.

41. A copy of the handwritten letter is in the possession of the author.

42. Bose, *An Indian Pilgrim*, 1948, pp. 64–5.

43. Vera Hildebrand, *Women at War: Subhas Chandra Bose and the Rani of Jhansi Regiment*, HarperCollins Publishers India, 2016, pp. 65, 91.

44. 'How to Stop Crimes Against Women', *The Modern Review*, September 1938, pp. 290–1; *Jugantar*, 20 August 1938, p. 10.

45. Gordon, *Brothers Against the Raj*, pp. 344–5.

46. *A Beacon Across Asia*, edited by S.K. Bose, A. Werth and S.A. Ayer, p. 47. Quite amusingly, the centenary edition of the book published in 1996, picked February 1942, even after the publication of *Brothers Against the Raj* and the publication of the collection of Subhas's letters to Emilie in 1994, in which the Netaji Research Bureau announced the revised date of marriage to be 26 December 1937.

47. Affidavit of Sisir Kumar Bose, 23 August 1977, Suit No 436 of 1977, in the High Court at Calcutta in the matter of Netaji Research Bureau & Anr Vs Jayashree Prakashan. Unpublished copy in possession of author.

48.   Bose, *A True Love Story*, p. 19.
49.   Case No C/63 of 1975 in the Court of the Chief Metropolitan Magistrate, Calcutta; Dwijendra Nath Bose Vs GD Khosla and two others. A copy of the affidavit and judgment is in the possession of author.
50.   Gordon, *Brothers Against the Raj*, pp. 344, 701.
51.   Bose, *A True Love Story*, pp. 24–8.
52.   Bose, *An Indian Pilgrim*, p. 63.
53.   Jawaharlal Nehru, *SWJN*, Vol. 13, pp. 695–6.
54.   Dasgupta, *Subhas Chandra*, p. 155.
55.   Maw, *Breakthrough in Burma*, p. 349.
56.   Peter Ward Fay, *The Forgotten Army: India's Armed Struggle for Independence 1942–45*, The University of Michigan Press, 1995, pp. 311–2.
57.   Editors' introduction by Sisir Kumar Bose and Sugata Bose to *Netaji: Collected Works*, Vol. 7, p. xviii.
58.   Maw, *Breakthrough in Burma*, p. 349.
59.   Gordon, *Brothers Against the Raj*, p. 344.

Chapter 12: The Covert Operative

1.   Sanyal, *Je Kathar Shesh Nei*, pp. 226–7.
2.   Datta, *Biplaber Padachinha*, p. 28.
3.   *IOR*: L/P&J/12/214, British Library.
4.   'History Sheet of Subhas Chandra Basu', 30 April 1924; *IOR*: L/P&J/12/214, British Library.
5.   File No. 44/22/44-Poll (I), National Archives of India.
6.   'The Indian Problem'; *IOR*: L/P&J/12/214, British Library.
7.   For the Munshi affair, see Bose, *His Majesty's Opponent*, p. 154.
8.   File No. 22/52/38-Political and 22/57/38-Political, Home Department, Political Section, National Archives, New Delhi.
9.   A.K. Majumdar, *Advent of Independence*, Bharatiya Vidya Bhavan, 1963, p. 155.
10.   Majumdar, *Advent of Independence*, p. 408–12.
11.   *The Indian Annual Register 1933*, Vol. 2, p. 333.
12.   Letter from Rash Behari Bose, 25 January 1938; *Netaji: Collected Works*, Vol. 9, edited by S.K. Bose and S. Bose, p. 254.
13.   *Jugantar*, 21 July 1939.
14.   *Jugantar*, 17 October 1939.
15.   Lalit Kumar Sanyal, *Biplab Tapas Maharaj Trailokya Nath*, pp. 254–7.
16.   File No. 44/22/44-Poll (I), National Archives of India.
17.   File No. 44/24/44-Poll (I), National Archives of India.
18.   *Hindu Mahasabha Parva*, p. 348, quoted in Sampath, *Savarkar*, p. 265.

19. Letter of Balarao Savarkar to K.C. Das, 2 June 1954; J.G. Ohsawa, *The Two Great Indians in Japan*, 1954, pp. 94–5.
20. Bose, *The Indian Struggle: 1935–1942*, p. 34.
21. Testimony of Niharendu Dutta Majumdar, Proceedings of the Netaji Inquiry Commission, Vol. 13, 22 September 1972, National Archives, New Delhi.
22. Bhagat Ram Talwar, *The Talwars of Pathan Land and Subhas Chandra's Great Escape*, People's Publishing House, 1976, pp. 56–7.
23. Detention of Lala Shankar Lal Basal Under the Defence of India Rules, File No. 94/23/41-Poll (I); Activities of Shankar Lal Basal, File No. 149/41-Political (I), National Archives of India.
24. The subsequent information on Shankarlal Basal sourced from File No. 44/12/44-Poll (I), National Archives of India.
25. The following information on Niranjan Singh Talib has been sourced from File No. 44/24/44-Poll (I), National Archives of India.
26. File No. 44/52/44-Poll (I), National Archives of India.
27. Bose, *My Uncle Netaji*, p. 183.
28. *Jugantar*, 28 January 1941.
29. *Amrita Bazar Patrika*, 28 January 1941.
30. File No. 241/41-Poll, Home Department, Political (Internal) Section, National Archives, New Delhi.
31. File No. 135, Home Department, Political (Internal) Section, National Archives, New Delhi.
32. File No. 135, Home Department, Political (Internal) Section, National Archives, New Delhi.
33. File No. 135, Home Department, Political (Internal) Section, National Archives, New Delhi.
34. File No. 135, Home Department, Political (Internal) Section, National Archives, New Delhi.
35. File No. 135, Home Department, Political (Internal) Section, National Archives, New Delhi.
36. Evidence of Sri Dwijendra Nath Bose, Report of the Shah Nawaz Committee, File No. PS-56/NEC, National Archives, New Delhi.
37. Sarkar, *Subhaser Songe Baro Bochhor*, p. 152.
38. 'When Subhas Bose was Ziauddin', *Hindustan Times*, 2 March 1946.
39. 'Netajir Antardhaner Akathito Kahini', *Amrita Bazar Patrika*, 11 and 18 October 1974.
40. Bose, *My Uncle Netaji*, pp. 197–208.
41. Talwar, *The Talwars of Pathan Land*, pp. 56–7.
42. Chatterji, *India's Struggle for Freedom*.
43. Kiani, *India's Freedom Struggle and the Great INA*.

44. Deposition of K. Kunizuka, intelligence officer attached with Hikari Kikan to the Netaji Enquiry Committee, 1956, Annexure to File No. PS/56/NEC.
45. Hayashida, *Netaji Subhas Chandra Bose.*
46. Lebra, *The Jungle Alliance.*
47. Kiani, *India's Freedom Struggle and the Great INA.*
48. Interrogation report of A.M. Sahay, T.R. Sareen, *Indian National Army: A Documentary Study*, Vol. 5.
49. Ayer, *Unto Him a Witness.*
50. Deposition of Isoda Saburo, to the Netaji Enquiry Committee, 1956, Annexure to File No. PS/56/NEC.
51. Ayer, *Unto Him a Witness.*
52. Chatterji, *India's Struggle for Freedom.*
53. Deposition of K. Kunizuka, intelligence officer attached with Hikari Kikan to the Netaji Enquiry Committee, 1956, Annexure to File No. PS/56/NEC.
54. Deposition of K. Kunizuka, intelligence officer attached with Hikari Kikan to the Netaji Enquiry Committee, 1956, Annexure to File No. PS/56/NEC.
55. Abid Hasan Safrani, *The Men From Imphal*; John A. Thivy, *The Struggle in East Asia, Netaji Research Bureau, 1971.*
56. Gordon, *Brothers Against the Raj*, p. 537.
57. Deposition of Habibur Rahman to the Netaji Enquiry Committee, 1956, Annexure to File No. PS/56/NEC.
58. Ayer, *Unto Him a Witness.*
59. Kiani, *India's Freedom Struggle and the Great INA.*
60. Ayer, *Unto Him a Witness.*
61. Deposition of Habibur Rahman to the Netaji Enquiry Committee, 1956, Annexure to File No. PS/56/NEC.
62. Kiani, *India's Freedom Struggle and the Great INA.*
63. Ayer, *Unto Him a Witness.*
64. Deposition of Alagappan to the One-Man Netaji Inquiry Commission: 1970–74.
65. Ayer, *Unto Him a Witness.*
66. Deposition of J.K. Bhonsle to the Netaji Enquiry Committee, 1956, Annexure to File No. PS/56/NEC.
67. Deposition of Isoda Saburo, to the Netaji Enquiry Committee, 1956, Annexure to File No. PS/56/NEC.
68. Report of E. Finney (Assistant Director, Intelligence Bureau), 12 November 1945.
69. Deposition of Kinji Watanabe to the Netaji Enquiry Committee, 1956, Annexure to File No. PS/56/NEC.
70. CSDIC report of 25 March 1946.
71. Deposition of Hachiya, to the Netaji Enquiry Committee, 1956, Annexure to File No. PS/56/NEC.

72. Deposition of T. Negishi to the Netaji Enquiry Committee, 1956, Annexure to File No. PS/56/NEC.
73. Deposition of Gulzara Singh, to the Netaji Enquiry Committee, 1956, Annexure to File No. PS/56/NEC.
74. Deposition of T. Negishi, to the Netaji Enquiry Committee, 1956, Annexure to File No. PS/56/NEC.
75. Ayer, *Unto Him a Witness*.
76. Deposition of K. Kunizuka, intelligence officer attached with Hikari Kikan to the Netaji Enquiry Committee, 1956, Annexure to File No. PS/56/NEC.
77. Ayer, *Unto Him a Witness*.
78. Deposition of Isoda Saburoto the Netaji Enquiry Committee, 1956, Annexure to File No. PS/56/NEC.
79. Deposition of Isoda Saburo to the Netaji Enquiry Committee, 1956, Annexure to File No. PS/56/NEC.
80. Ayer, *Unto Him a Witness*.
81. Deposition of Haibur Rahman to the Netaji Enquiry Committee, 1956, Annexure to File No. PS/56/NEC.
82. Deposition of A.M. Sahay to the Netaji Enquiry Committee, 1956, Annexure to File No. PS/56/NEC.

Chapter 13: The INA and Independence

1. Khan, *My Memories of INA and Its Netaji*, pp. 121–4.
2. Khan, *My Memories of INA and its Netaji*, pp. 124–5.
3. G.S. Dhillon, *From My Bones*, Aryan Books International, 1999, pp. 214–5.
4. Kiani, *India's Freedom Struggle and the Great INA*, p. 130.
5. Khan, *My Memories of INA and Its Netaji*, pp. 126–31.
6. Khan, *My Memories of INA and Its Netaji*, pp. 141–3.
7. Khan, *My Memories of INA and Its Netaji*, pp. 144–8.
8. Khan, *My Memories of INA and Its Netaji*, pp. 163–95; Dhillon, *From My Bones*, pp. 345–9.
9. Kiani, *India's Freedom Struggle and the Great INA*, p 153; Chatterji, *India's Struggle for Freedom*, p. 259.
10. Sareen, *Indian National Army: A Documentary Study*, Vol. 4, pp. 195–6.
11. Hildebrand, *Women at War*, pp. 181–2.
12. Kiani, *India's Freedom Struggle and the Great INA*, p. 154; Maw, *Breakthrough in Burma*, p. 393.
13. Ayer, *Unto Him a Witness*, pp. 19–29.
14. Ayer, *Unto Him a Witness*, p. 27.
15. A.N. Sarkar, 'Netajir Jiboer Ek Prishtha', in *Jayasree: Subarna Jayanti Grantha*, edited by Amalendu Basu and Sunil Das, 1983, p. 195.
16. File No. 380/INA-Part XIII, National Archives of India.
17. Ayer, *Unto Him a Witness*, pp. 51–60.
18. Kiani, *India's Freedom Struggle and the Great INA*, pp. 164–6.

710   Notes

19. Ayer, *Unto Him a Witness*, p. 61.
20. Foreword by Jawaharlal Nehru, in Khan, *My Memories of INA and Its Netaji*.
21. *The Sydney Morning Herald*, 11 May 1945; *Amrita Bazar Patrika*, 11 May 1945, p. 4.
22. *Amrita Bazar Patrika*, 8 May 1945, p. 1.
23. *Amrita Bazar Patrika*, 14 May 1945, p. 1.
24. *Amrita Bazar Patrika*, 15 May 1945, p. 3.
25. *Amrita Bazar Patrika*, 16 May 1945, p. 8.
26. *Amrita Bazar Patrika*, 19 May 1945, p. 5.
27. 'Part played by the INA in active operations against Allied forces', CSDIC (I), 12 May 1946, File No. INA 402, National Archives, New Delhi.
28. *Nehru Memorial Lectures: 1966–91*, edited by John Grigg, Oxford University Press, 1992, p. 20.
29. *Amrita Bazar Patrika*, 19 March 1946, p. 1.
30. *Nehru Memorial Lectures: 1966–91*, p. 20.
31. *Amrita Bazar Patrika*, 20 March 1946, p. 8.
32. *Amrita Bazar Patrika*, 22 March 1946, p. 8.
33. Tuker, *While Memory Serves*, p. 52.
34. Tuker, *While Memory Serves*, p. 54.
35. Telegram from Governor General (War Department) to Secretary of State, 11 August 1945; *Transfer of Power*, edited by Nicholas Mansergh, Vol. 6, pp. 49–52.
36. *The Manchester Guardian*, 28 August 1945, p. 6.
37. Telegram from Secretary of State to Governor General (War Department), 17 August 1945; *Transfer of Power*, Vol. 6, pp. 75–6.
38. 1st Meeting of the India and Burma Committee, 17 August 1945; *Transfer of Power*, Vol. 6, pp. 79–80.
39. Field Marshal Viscount Wavell to Lord Pethick-Lawrence, 20 August 1945; *Transfer of Power*, Vol. 6, p. 107.
40. Governor General (War Department) to Secretary of State, 21 August 1945; *Transfer of Power*, Vol. 6, pp. 110–1.
41. Secretary of State to Government of India (War Department), 23 August 1945; *Transfer of Power*, Vol. 6, pp. 142–3.
42. John Connell, *Auchinleck: A Biography of Field Marshal Sir Claude Auchinleck*, Cassell, 1959, p. 797.
43. *The Indian Annual Register 1942*, Vol. 2, p. 236.
44. *IAR 1942*, Vol. 2, pp. 237–54.
45. Gandhi's speech at the AICC, 8 August 1942; Gandhi, *Collected Works of Mahatma Gandhi*, Vol. 83, p. 196.
46. Gandhi's speech at the AICC, 8 August 1942; Gandhi, *Collected Works of Mahatma Gandhi*, Vol. 83, pp. 197–200.

47. Interview to the Press, 14 July 1942, Gandhi: *Collected Works of Mahatma Gandhi*, Vol. 83, p. 101.

48. *Amrita Bazar Patrika*, 9 August 1942, p. 5.

49. *The Observer*, 9 August 1942, p. 5.

50. Maulana Abul Kalam Azad, *India Wins Freedom*, Orient Blackswan, 2010, p. 40.

51. 'Full Support to Gandhi', in *Netaji: Collected Works*, Vol. 11, pp. 122–31.

52. *Netaji: Collected Works*, Vol. 11, pp. 132–9.

53. Congress Movement, 1942. File No. 3/31/42-Poll (I), National Archives of India.

54. Congress Movement, 1942. File No. 3/31/42-Poll (I), National Archives of India.

55. Bipan Chandra *et al.*, *India's Struggle for Independence*, pp. 461–3.

56. File No. 3/5/42, National Archives of India.

57. Connection of Enemy Agencies with the Recent Disturbances, 14 October 1942, War Cabinet, File No. CAB/66/29/47, National Archives, UK.

58. Chandra *et al.*, *India's Struggle for Independence*, p. 463.

59. Letter to Linlithgow, 29 January 1943; Gandhi, *Collected Works of Mahatma Gandhi*, Vol. 83, p. 281

60. Government of India, *Correspondence with Mr Gandhi: August 1942–April 1944*, 1944, p. 1.

61. Government of India, *Congress Responsibility for the Disturbances: 1942–43*, 1943.

62. Khushwant Singh, 'History of One's Own Making', *Hindustan Times*, 28 June 2003.

63. Sarkar, *Modern India*, p. 404.

64. R.J. Moore, *Escape from Empire: The Attlee Government and the Indian Problem*, Clarendon Press, 1983, pp. 12–3.

65. Durga Das, *India from Curzon to Nehru and After*, Rupa, 2012, p. 217.

66. Moore, *Escape from Empire*, pp. 33–8.

67. *IAR1945*, Vol. 2, p. 93.

68. *IAR1945*, Vol. 2, p. 112.

69. *IAR 1945*, Vol. 2, p. 85.

70. Jawaharlal Nehru, *SWJN*, Vol. 14, p. 66.

71. Nehru, *SWJN*, Vol. 14, p. 374.

72. Nehru, *SWJN*, Vol. 14, p. 98.

73. *IAR 1945*, Vol. 2, pp. 92–3.

74. Vallabhbhai Patel's letter to Biswanath Das, 5 January 1946; *Collected Works of Sardar Vallabhbhai Patel*, Vol. 10, pp. 165–6.

75. The Congress Working Committee resolution of 11 December 1942, drafted by Mahatma Gandhi himself, emphasized 'the need for Congress strictly to

adhere to the non-violent creed in their struggle for political freedom', *IAR 1945*, Vol. 2, edited by N.N. Mitra, p. 33.

76. HQ India Command/Director of Intelligence, No. 37 Daily Security Summary, 20 December 1945, National Archives.

77. *Transfer of Power*, Vol. 6, pp. 387–8.

78. Excerpted from the record of Dwijendra Nath Bose's examination before the Khosla Commission on 9 August 1972.

79. Ghosh, *The Indian National Army*, p. 208.

80. *Transfer of Power*, Vol. 6, p. 531.

81. *Transfer of Power*, Vol. 6, p. 506.

82. *Transfer of Power*, Vol. 6, p. 469.

83. HQ India Command/Director of Intelligence, No. 30 Daily Security Summary, 12 December 1945, National Archives.

84. Jawaharlal Nehru's letter to Claude Auchinleck, 4 May 1946; Nehru, *SWJN*, Vol. 15, pp. 90–1.

85. *Transfer of Power*, Vol. 6, pp. 341–4.

86. Connell, *Auchinleck*, pp. 801–2.

87. Field Marshal Viscount Wavell to Lord Pethick-Lawrence, 22 October 1942; *Transfer of Power*, Vol. 6, p 375.

88. Nehru, *SWJN*, Vol. 14, p. 118.

89. Nehru, *SWJN*, Vol. 14, p. 121.

90. Connell, *Auchinleck*, pp. 802–3.

91. *Transfer of Power*, Vol. 6, p. 507.

92. Government of India, Home Department, File No. 21/6/45, Policy as to publicity in relation to the Japanese-sponsored 'Indian National Army'.

93. HQ India Command/Director of Intelligence, No. 85 Daily Security Summary, 19 February 1946, National Archives.

94. *Amrita Bazar Patrika*, 15 November 1945, p. 5.

95. *Amrita Bazar Patrika*, 17 November 1945, p. 5.

96. *Amrita Bazar Patrika*, 18 November 1945, pp. 4–5.

97. *Amrita Bazar Patrika*, 22 November 1945, p. 5.

98. *Amrita Bazar Patrika*, 19 November 1945, p. 4.

99. Ghosh, *The Indian National Army*, p. 215.

100. *Amrita Bazar Patrika*, 22 November 1945, p. 1.

101. *Amrita Bazar Patrika*, 23 November 1945, p. 1.

102. *Amrita Bazar Patrika*, 24 November 1945, p. 1.

103. *Amrita Bazar Patrika*, 25 November 1945, p. 1.

104. Connell, *Auchinleck*, p. 806.

105. Connell, *Auchinleck*, pp. 807–9.

106. *Amrita Bazar Patrika*, 24 January 1946, p. 1, 5.

107. *Amrita Bazar Patrika*, 25 January 1946, p. 1, 5.

108. Margaret M. Wright, *The Military Papers, 1940–48, of Field Marshal Sir Claude Auchinleck: A Calendar and Index*, 1988, p. 305.
109. B. Glancy (Punjab) to Field Marshal Viscount Wavell, 16 January 1946, *Transfer of Power*, Vol. 6, p. 807.
110. Wright, *The Military Papers*, p. 309.
111. *Transfer of Power*, Vol. 6, p. 944.
112. *Transfer of Power*, Vol. 6, pp. 947–50.
113. Appreciation of Internal Situation in India, 24 November 1945; *Transfer of Power*, Vol. 6, pp. 576–8.
114. India and Burma Committee Meeting, 28 November 1945; *Transfer of Power*, Vol. 6, p. 559.
115. India and Burma Committee Meeting, 14 January 1946; *Transfer of Power*, Vol. 6, p. 786; Moore, *Escape from Empire*, p. 44.
116. G.D. Sharma, *Untold Story: 1946 Naval Mutiny; Last War of Independence*, Vij Books India Pvt. Ltd, 2015, pp. 76–80.
117. *Amrita Bazar Patrika*, 20 February 1946, p. 1.
118. Ghosh, *The Indian National Army*, p. 233.
119. *Amrita Bazar Patrika*, 22 February 1946, p. 1.
120. *Amrita Bazar Patrika*, 23 February 1946, p. 1.
121. J. Colville (Bombay) to Field Marshal Viscount Wavell, 27 February 1946; *Transfer of Power*, Vol. 6, p. 1083.
122. B.C. Dutt, *Mutiny of the Innocents*, Bhashya Prakashan, 2015, p. 10.
123. Arun Gandhi, Interview with B.C. Dutt, 26 January 1970, https://www.s-asian.cam.ac.uk/archive/audio/collection/b-c-dutt/.
124. *Amrita Bazar Patrika*, 23 February 1946, p. 1.
125. J. Colville (Bombay) to Field Marshal Viscount Wavell, 27 February 1946; *Transfer of Power*, Vol. 6, p. 1081.
126. Nehru, *SWJN*, Vol. 15, pp. 1–5.
127. Appreciation of Internal Situation in India, 24 November 1945; *Transfer of Power*, Vol. 6, p. 577.
128. Nehru, *SWJN*, Vol. 4, p. 2.
129. C.R. Attlee, *As It Happened*, The Viking Press, 1954, p. 180.
130. Francis Williams, *A Prime Minister Remembers*, Heinemann, 1961, p. 205.
131. Justice Phani Bhusan Chakravartti described his interaction with Attlee in a letter dated 30 March 1976, to Sureshchandra Das, publisher of historian Dr R.C. Majumdar. Subsequently, in 1978, a facsimile copy of Chakravartti's letter was published by Dr Majumdar in his autobiographical book in Bengali, *Jibaner Smritideepe, 1959*.
132. Barun De, 'Experiments with Truth in a Fractured Land', *The Telegraph*, 30 January 2007.
133. Williams, *A Prime Minister Remembers*, pp. 208–9.

134. Appreciation of Internal Situation in India, 24 November 1945; *Transfer of Power*, Vol. 6, pp. 577–83.

135. General Auchinleck to Chiefs of Staff, 22 December 1945; *Transfer of Power*, Vol. 6, pp. 675–7.

136. Field Marshal Viscount Wavell to Lord Pethick-Lawrence, 27 December 1945; *Transfer of Power*, Vol. 6, pp. 686–8.

137. General Auchinleck to Chiefs of Staff, 18 January 1946; *Transfer of Power*, Vol. 6, p. 813.

138. Field Marshal Viscount Alanbrooke to General Auchinleck, 4 February 1946, *Transfer of Power*, Vol. 6, p. 879.

139. General Auchinleck to Field Marshal Viscount Alanbrooke, 14 February 1946, *Transfer of Power*, Vol. 6, p. 975.

140. Maw, *Breakthrough in Burma*, p. 348.

Chapter 14: What If Subhas Returned?

1. Swapan Dasgupta, 'What If Netaji Came Back?', *Outlook*, 23 August 2004, https://www.outlookindia.com/magazine/story/what-if-netaji-came-back/224857.

2. Ramachandra Guha, 'Netaji versus Panditji—What If Subhas Chandra Bose Had Returned after the War?', *The Telegraph*, 10 October 2009.

3. Anvar Alikhan, 'What If Netaji Had Returned to India . . .', *The Times of India*, 19 April 2015.

4. Rammanohar Lohia, *Guilty Men of India's Partition*, B.R. Publishing Corporation, 2017, pp. 88–9. 'Spirit of Haldighati' is a reference to the heroic battled waged by Maharana Pratap against the Mughal forces in the battle of Haldighati (in Rajasthan) on 18 June 1576.

5. Nirad C. Chaudhuri, *Thy Hand Great Anarch*, Chatto & Windus, 1987, p. 799.

6. 'Situation in India', CAB/129/5, National Archives, UK.

7. Das, *India from Curzon to Nehru*, p. 239.

Index

715